Free Will

MANCHESTER
1824

Manchester University Press

Free Will

Art and power on Shakespeare's stage

Richard Wilson

Manchester University Press

Manchester and New York

distributed in the United States exclusively
by Palgrave Macmillan

Published by Manchester University Press
Oxford Road, Manchester M13 9NR, UK
and Room 400, 175 Fifth Avenue, New York, NY 10010, USA
www.manchesteruniversitypress.co.uk

Distributed in the United States exclusively by
Palgrave Macmillan, 175 Fifth Avenue, New York,
NY 10010, USA

Distributed in Canada exclusively by
UBC Press, University of British Columbia, 2029 West Mall,
Vancouver, BC, Canada V6T 1Z2

British Library Cataloguing-in-Publication Data
A catalogue record for this book is available from the British Library

Library of Congress Cataloging-in-Publication Data applied for

ISBN   978 0 7190 9178 0   hardback

ISBN   978 0 7190 9179 7   paperback

First published 2013

Typeset in 10/12 Sabon by
Servis Filmsetting Ltd, Stockport, Cheshire
Printed in Great Britain
by Bell & Bain Ltd, Glasgow

For François Laroque
The Good Companion

Contents

Acknowledgements

Part of Chapter 1 was originally published in *Shakespeare Studies*, 36 (2008); an earlier version of Chapter 2 in *Shakespeare and Wales*, edited by Willy Maley and Philip Schwyzer (Farnham: Ashgate, 2009); Chapter 6 in *Shakespeare Jahrbuch*, 143 (2007); a section of Chapter 8 in *Shakespeare, Satire, Academia: Eine festliche Schrift für Wolfgang Weiß* (Heidelberg: Universitätsverlag, 2012); and a portion of the Epilogue in *Volkommenheit: Ästhetische Perfektion in Antike, Mittelalter und Früher Neuzeit*, edited by Verena Lobsien, Claudia Olk and Katharina Münchberg (Berlin: de Gruyter, 2010).

Note on texts

All quotations from Shakespeare are from the Norton Edition, based on the Oxford text, edited by Stephen Greenblatt, Walter Cohen, Jean Howard and Katharine Eisaman Maus (New York: Norton, 2007).

Introduction

... thus was I not constrained, but did it
On my free will.

[Antony, 3,6,56–7]

Free Will is a book about art and power on Shakespeare's stage, and how the sovereignty of the playwright is complicated by his service as a player. Shakespeare's plays and poems are full of expressions of a will to 'liberty, freedom, and enfranchisement!' [*Julius*, 3,1,80], and a refrain that runs through them is that 'I breathe free breath' [*Love's*, 5,2,705]. Repeatedly, statements such as 'Thought is free' [*Twelfth*, 1,3,58; *Tempest*, 3,2,123], or 'A man is master of his liberty' [*Errors*, 2,1,7], connect these works not only to the liberal ideology that 'I was born free' [*Julius*, 1,2,97], but to an aesthetic emphasis on 'free speech' [*Measure*, 1,1,70] as the 'law of writ and liberty' [*Hamlet*, 2,2,383]. They belong, that is to say, to a political culture evolving from royal to popular sovereignty, in which 'the jolly Briton laughs from's free lungs' [*Cymbeline*, 1,1,68–9] as the signifier of emerging national identity. And if the sovereign subject is already being defined in Shakespeare's texts by such assertions as that 'the streets [are] as free for me as you' [*Shrew*, 1,2,231], a desire to 'speak our free hearts each to other' [*Macbeth*, 1,3,153] is also keyed in them to the writer's creative liberation, and to a confidence that 'The fated sky / Gives us free scope, only doth backward pull / Our slow designs when we ourselves are dull' [*All's Well*, 1,1,200–2]. So this author's drive to 'speak freely' [*Comedy*, 5,1,286] undoubtedly made him a precursor of modern aesthetic autonomy. For only a writer so conscious of 'giving reins and spur to my free speech' [*Richard II*, 1,1,55] could have had a poet utter the definitively modern idea that 'the author's drift' [*Troilus*,

3,3,108] is released from determination to soar into aesthetic space by its own airy disinterestedness:

> My free drift
> Halts not particularly, but moves itself
> In a wide sea of tax. No levelled malice
> Infects one comma in the course I hold,
> But flies an eagle flight, bold and forth on,
> Leaving no tract behind.

[*Timon, 1,1,45–50*]

'I must have liberty / Withal', asserts Shakespeare's near-namesake Jaques, 'as large a charter as the wind, / To blow on whom I please'; but his master the Duke seizes on this somatic metaphor to call him a 'libertine', who will breathe into 'the general world' (which we might consider the public space of the Globe) all the infections he 'with licence of free foot has caught' [*As You, 2,7,47–68*]. This edgy exchange about the body of the writer is thought to allude to a 1599 ban on satire; and so its 'backward pull' refers the will to 'free speech and fearless' [*Richard II, 1,1,123*] to an older sovereignty, and the embodied politics of patronage and personhood. As Aristotle thought the *telos* of tragedy was to purge its material circumstances, and Hegel considered the highest vocation of art was to dissolve itself and 'become a thing of the past', so Terry Eagleton reads such conflict between speech and body in these plays as 'an allegory of class struggle', and connects the irony that Shakespeare's self-transcendence is 'jeopardized by the very language in which it is articulated' to his bourgeois subject position.[1] But in *Free Will* I relate the embodiment of his language to his dual role as both player and playwright, and to the founding rupture outlined by Jürgen Habermas, Ernst Kantorowicz, Carl Schmitt and others, from a regime of meaning based on personal presence to one of symbolic representation. At the same time, I suggest, Shakespeare's human comedy 'bodies forth' [*Dream, 5,1,14*] all the twists of presence and representation traced by theorists such as Jacques Rancière. For while an author may rejoice that 'the free breath of a sacred king' [*John, 3,1,74*] has but 'a little scene, / To monarchize' [*Richard II, 3,2,160–1*], the actor fears the promise that 'thou shalt be free as mountain winds' [*Tempest, 1,2,499*] is one that only monarchs give. Shakespeare's poetic personality is wedded to individual freedom, writes Peter Holbrook, which is 'the signature of his art'.[2] Yet unlike Milton, whose keywords a generation later could be 'liberty', 'justice', 'right' and 'toleration' (but whose freedom, as Marx noted, meant that for *Paradise Lost* he earned a mere £5), he ends in a double-bind of willed dominance and willing submission, when his last sole-authored work resounds to cries of 'Freedom, high-day, freedom!' [2,2,177], as the slave Ariel is promised he will 'to the elements / Be free' by Prospero, a master who pleads to be 'set free' [5,1,321; Epi.20] himself.[3]

In *Free Will* I argue that Shakespeare's plays rehearse what political theorists like Claude Lefort describe as the 'dissolution of the markers of certainty' that made possible the advent of modern democracy, whereby the power embodied in the person of the prince, and tied to a transcendental authority, was eclipsed by new institutions in which power became 'an empty place'.[4] But before he pledges Ariel 'thou shalt have thy freedom' [5,1,98], and begs the audience for freedom for himself, Shakespeare's sorcerer also renounces his 'rough magic' in a speech that both enacts and effaces his 'so potent art' [5,1,50], and that critics therefore read as *his creator's own obviation*, or farewell to the stage. This valediction has been the focus of two of the most vital yet distinct conversations in recent Shakespeare studies, which *Free Will* attempts to bring together. One of these is about the sovereignty Prospero surrenders, which, as Stephen Greenblatt remarks in *Will in the World*, has a scope of which a 'Free and Absolute' monarch such as King James could only dream, but that, as the exception to every rule, the artist is now thought to possess: 'it is an excess of power, more than any mortal should have'.[5] This debate is therefore concerned with the extent to which these plays not only stage the endgames of sacred kingship, but inherit its political theology of presence, the incarnational doctrine that sovereignty borrows its form from God. The myth of Shakespeare as a devoted royalist may be in retreat; but one of the themes of *Free Will* is how stubbornly royalty persists; and in criticism it has merely mutated into a yet more alarming religiosity that opposes the plays to representative democracy, as idealizations of a 'high Christian royalism' said to be the heart of any 'Christian social order'.[6] In this way political theology connects these Renaissance texts to the messianic religious current in contemporary philosophy, and by extension, to American realpolitik. Deriving from Schmitt's infamous maxim that 'Sovereign is who decides on the exception', the importance of this latest spiritual turn for criticism has therefore been that it compels us to question how much Shakespeare's 'free foot' is itself simply another measure of sovereign exceptionality.[7] The other debate that has energized recent Shakespeare studies has taken place in blithe innocence of political theology, let alone its presidential implications, yet it raises many of the same issues, as it concerns Prospero's decision to 'drown [his] book' [57], and so is about the degree to which his creator participates as an authorial agent in the emerging regime of print. For even as the notion of Shakespeare as mystic monarchist wanes, critics are busy replacing it with a new version of the sovereign author. Thus, in *Shakespeare's Literary Authorship*, Patrick Cheney asserts that by juxtaposing printing and playing in the magus's grand renunciation, the dramatist highlights his own singularity as 'the consummate "man of the theatre" paradoxically engaged with the art of printing poetry'. For this branch of criticism, therefore, the fact that it is based on Shakespeare's favourite printed book, Golding's translation of Ovid's *Metamorphoses* makes Prospero's speech an affirmation, rather than abdication, of authorial sovereignty. So, when this artist-magician summons his theatrical 'demi-puppets' to dance upon the sand with the 'printless foot' [34–6] of his poetic metres, we should regard this, Cheney maintains, as an invocation of the disembodied 'counter-authorship' which Shakespeare constructed in reaction to the guileless self-presentation of contemporaries: a poetic 'omnipotence' that is all the more universal or 'occult' for being that of a *deus absconditus*.[8] What this return to the hidden authorship of Shakespeare has in common, therefore, with the taste for political theology is an unreflecting commitment to a poetry of sovereignty, and so to Hazlitt's Schmittian mystification that because 'the language of poetry naturally falls within the language of power', Shakespeare's 'poetry is right-royal', the exception of a 'lordly beast'.[9]

In contrast to the current *doxa* of Shakespeare as the exemplar of either sacred monarchy or monarchic selfhood, *Free Will* argues that his plays are systematically engaged in untying freedom from royalty by dismantling *sovereignty in all its forms*. They thereby confront the perennial problem that has been acutely analysed for our time by the philosopher Daniel Dennett, who writes that between free will and determinism human beings could have enough of what he calls the 'elbow room' to act *as if* they were free agents, were it not for 'the self-imposed bondage we create by the very exercise of our freedom'.[10] Just as Dennett's 'elbow room' is the human capacity to break the endless repetitive series that perpetuate behaviour in other species, so Shakespeare's 'elbow room', I propose, is that of the actor differentiating a given part, even as his default position or *bearing* is the alert but incumbent one of attentiveness involved in waiting for a prompt, as if on starter's orders, that he associates with a player's 'pause' [*Hamlet, 2,2,467*]. In *Free Will* his work is thus interpreted in terms of the primal scene of attendance on the other in which he situates his actor Bottom: 'When my cue comes, call me, and I will answer' [*Dream, 4,1,196*]. Instead of a 'subject position', Shakespeare seems, therefore, always to fall back to what might be better termed an *abject position*. For it is in this doubled and ironic act of *waiting* that his plays cheat determination, I conclude, with something close to Simone Weil's conviction in 'Human Personality', her meditation on *impersonality*, that 'The only way into truth is through one's own annihilation; through dwelling a long time in a state of extreme and total humiliation':[11]

> If it be now, 'tis not to come. If it be not to come, it will be now. If it be not now, yet it will come. The readiness is all. Since no man has aught of what he leaves, what is't to leave betimes? Let be.
> [*Hamlet, 5,2,158–61*]

Between a politics of presence and a poetics of representation, or the rival absolutisms of state and stage, the convolutions of dramatic creativity in Shakespearean culture are neatly illustrated by the fact that the first English play ever dedicated to a patron, one Lady Cheyney, in 1573, was Henry Cheeke's *Free Will*. That the sovereign and the creature remain mutually dependent and determining in the circularity of such creation is an idea made explicit in *The Tempest* itself, a work seemingly designed to show how the emancipation of the slave enacts only new forms of enslavement, as the age-old intimacy of liberty and bondage makes it 'impossible to envision freedom independent of constraint or personhood and autonomy separate from the sanctity of property or proprietal notions of the self'.[12] But the actor's promptitude for a service 'as willing / As bondage e'er of freedom' [*3,1,89*] shapes the notion of agency, I contend, throughout these works, where 'our bending author' [*Henry V, Epi.2*] returns again and again to the craven body language of a resistance that depends upon restraint. Thus, when the former galley-slave Othello demands to 'know thy thoughts', Iago counters that 'I am not bound to that all slaves are free to' [*Othello, 3,3,140;166*]. And in *The Tempest* itself, the music accompanying the seductive song 'Thought is free' turns out to be 'the tune of our catch, played by the picture of Nobody' [*3,2,118–22*]. No doubt the self-effacing 'Nobody' who created such scenes of *ressentiment* saw the joke that the great emancipating declaration 'Thought is free' was made in the first line of the first poem published by his own real royal master, James.[13]

'Others abide our question. Thou art free', Matthew Arnold poeticized; and it has always been tempting to account for Shakespeare's imperviousness to inquiry in terms of Isaiah Berlin's famous distinction between negative and positive liberty, as an artist engaged in a typically premodern reaction to absolutism, rather than the exercise of any positive freedom.[14] Yet this formula does not do justice to the airiness of this 'author's drift', nor the way he transcends the 'backward pull' of sovereignty with a creaturely subservience that leads so many to see him as a *supporter* of absolutism, whose deference to 'the strongest party' sees him always 'leaning to the arbitrary side of the question', as Hazlitt believed.[15] Ever the post-structuralist *avant la lettre*, Shakespeare knows well enough that the entry into the symbolic order is a form of castration. Thus this dramatist's giving over of the self to the other seems more like that of the Velázquez described by the Spanish philosopher Ortega y Gasset as an artist who finessed the Habsburg court he served, not by fighting for freedom but by reflecting his own insignificance with an 'exemplary understanding of non-existence'.[16] Early modern creative autonomy was the incidental by-product, in this analysis, of a carefully calibrated performance of *nonentity*. So when Shakespeare begins *A Midsummer Night's Dream* in impatience at 'how slow / This old moon wanes! [*1,1,3*]; or has the dotard king ask, 'Dost thou call me fool?' in *King Lear* [*1,4,129*], his impertinence might have sounded innocent. Yet that last insolence was still cut from his 1623 Folio. Scholars have taken to minimizing the repressiveness of Tudor and Stuart censorship. But the recent discovery beneath a portrait of Queen Elizabeth of a serpent over-painted by the Tudor rose hints at just how perilous the exercise of such 'free scope' could be.[17]

Contrary to the image propagated in films, TV series and popular biographies of a Shakespeare in love with the monarchy, in Sonnet 107, marking the eclipse of the 'mortal moon' Elizabeth, the Bard was quite capable of calling the Tudors a dynasty of 'tyrants'.[18] So, how did this poet have 'unearnèd luck ... to 'scape the serpent's tongue'? [*Dream, Epi.10*]. In *Free Will* I propose that the 'free drift' of his writing was generated in a negative dialectic with the wealth and power that summoned it into being, and that this allowed his text 'to hold a mirror up to nature, to show virtue her own feature, scorn her own image' [*Hamlet, 3,2,20–1*], far more critically than a mere Renaissance prince like Hamlet could have imagined. Thus I am interested here in applying Theodor Adorno's insight that 'the complete disgust for power in *Antony and Cleopatra*, as well as Prospero's gesture of resignation', is mediated by the 'form and pressure' [22] of these plays, for with Shakespeare 'The liberation of form ... holds enciphered within it above all the liberation of society'; hence the impossible project that seems to define his career, of art separated from sovereignty, 'sweet sounds' dissociated from 'treasons, stratagems, and spoils' [*Merchant, 5,1,83*]. Adorno's maxim that 'Art is negative knowledge of the actual world' meets Keats's about Shakespeare's 'negative capability' as a refusal of the factual in this approach.[19] But I am also guided by Pierre Bourdieu's perception that art is liberated to the extent that it critiques *itself*, 'a reflexivity that is one of the foremost manifestations of the autonomy of a field', and that what makes the greatest creators their own best critics is the capacity of their work not only to liberate itself from mimetic relations but to analyse that determination to resist determination as an enabling fiction. In Shakespeare's case, this means considering the critical thinking behind his abiding resistance to the mutation in the logic of sovereignty that institutionalized the new kingship of literary authorship itself.[20]

One of the surprises of our era is how, after an age of self-service, we are reverting to a state of affairs like that in sixteenth-century Europe, where, as Greenblatt writes, 'the hallmark of power and wealth was to be waited on'.[21] At a time when globalization is universalizing a neo-feudal service economy, and with it the per-formance of skivvying servility; or when, as Wayne Koestenbaum relates in his hymn to abjection, *Humiliation*, YouTube and reality TV have given us unprecedented scenarios of self-degradation and defilement; Shakespeare's dramatization of the strange interde-pendency of servitude and sovereignty has never appeared more relevant.[22] Thus, 'Power through service is your motto', explains Head Chef to his scullions in *The Cook*, Wayne Macauley's

Lucianic *Timon*-like satire on the decadent *grand bouffe* of late
capitalism, 'By subjugating ourselves we become strong'; and in his
plays and poems the Renaissance writer seems to fully anticipate
this postmodern twist in the master–slave dialectic.[23] Celebrated in
his own time as 'mellifluous and honey-tongued Shakespeare', this
courtly 'Melicert', 'Our pleasant Willy', had internalized, that is to
say, those counter-intuitive rites of self-abjection by which strength
is supposed to issue out of sweetness, and the powerful are conse-
crated by the abasement to which they submit.[24] So, 'I have sounded
the very base-string of humility' [*1Henry IV, 2,5,5*], reports his most
winning king. Yet in staging his own 'abject position' as a 'waiter'
upon orders and servitor to sovereigns, the dramatist seems also
to anticipate Michel Foucault's sceptical self-analysis of what the
philosopher termed the Ubu-esque strategies of such an inverted
sovereignty, and to be on his guard against this Uriah Heep posture
of false modesty, 'this grotesque cog in the mechanism of power', as
though 'our humble author' [*2Henry IV, Epi, 23*] was wary of all
the cunning ruses of his own paramountcy:

> Ethnologists have identified the phenomenon in which the person to
> whom power is given is at the same time ridiculed or made abject
> or shown in an unfavourable light, through a number of rites and
> ceremonies. Is this a case of a ritual for limiting the effects of power
> in archaic or primitive societies? Perhaps. However, I do not think
> that showing power to be abject, despicable, Ubu-esque or simply
> ridiculous is a way of limiting its effects and of magically dethroning
> the person to whom one gives the crown. Rather, it seems to me to be
> a way of giving a striking form of expression to the unavoidability,
> the inevitability of power, which can function in its full vigour and
> at the extreme point of its rationality even when in the hands of
> someone who is effectively discredited. This problem of the infamy
> of sovereignty, of the discredited sovereign, is, after all, Shakespeare's
> problem.[25]

For Foucault, in the Collège de France lectures where he surpris-
ingly returned to the speaking subject, it was because Shakespeare
obstinately refused to sing 'power's ode', dreaming instead of 'the
freedom to roam', and of 'free genesis, self-accomplishment ... a
freedom against the world', that his dramas rank among the foundations of modern critical thought.[26] In *Free Will*, however, I argue
that Shakespeare's will to freedom took a less romantic or self-
expressive form, when he did sing power's ode, but *back to itself*.

Jacques Derrida has reminded us with his notion of 'iterabilité' how 'every repetition both iterates and alters'.[27] And as Foucault himself saw, the dramatist lived and wrote in a literary culture of chiasmus that found liberation in the 'tireless dialectic' and 'endless variations and repetitions' of a 'sea of words', where poets like Sir Philip Sidney 'played very prettily' to serious purpose with the near-miss of *paronomasia* (when words 'mock one another by their much resemblance', as rhetorician George Puttenham explained), and a space for the modern writer was opened by the cruel *non-reciprocity* of the sovereign and her creature.[28] Puns have been called 'the foundation of letters'.[29] But Shakespeare's contrarian anti-authorship has the chiasmic iterability, I infer, of repetition in Kierkegaard's rueful account of theatre-going, where he recounts how whenever he went back to the theatre anticipating an exact repeat performance, 'the only thing that repeated itself was that no repetition was possible'. The philosopher then tells an anecdote reminiscent of the television comedy *Yes, Minister*, about a Jeeves-like dignitary who, after the queen had addressed some assembly, rose to speak and attempted to repeat exactly the same words: 'Question: what view did he have of the meaning of his repetition?'[30] This is the question also addressed by *Free Will*.

What view did Shakespeare have of the meaning of his repetition of the queen's speech, his recomposition of 'power's ode to itself'? The answer, I propose, can be inferred by recourse to the psychoanalytic concept of foreclosure: that the subject is formed in subordination; and Judith Butler's performative thesis that it is precisely by repeating, internalizing and thereby turning back upon itself the social order that the subject becomes an agent: 'recasting the power that constitutes me as the power I oppose'.[31] In a previous work, *Secret Shakespeare*, I deduced that these texts create a drama out of silence by defying the order to perform. But here I concede that their creator was, in fact, an obsessive, perhaps even involuntary, mimic in performing 'as you like it', and found in the *topos* of 'this great stage of fools' [*Lear, 4,6,177*] a template for the dialectic of determinism and free will. So if the Shakespearean phenomenon marks a tipping-point in the epochal transfer of sovereignty from prince to poet that, according to Kantorowicz, commenced with Dante, I argue that such self-abnegation can indeed be likened to those masochistic rites of humiliation by which kings were traditionally degraded prior to their coronation, Ubu-esque states of 'induced weakness in a future ruler (defeat, illness, beatings, maltreatment, murder)', intended to affirm not merely the 'power of weakness' but also the *weakness of power* itself.[32] *Free Will* is thus a book about the creaturely echo-effect with which Shakespeare strove to minimize the sovereignty of his own writing, and generated a world of difference that exceeds the context of its enunciation not by contradicting, but by answering power back in its own words. The Shakespeare I imagine here causes the same angelic devastation, in fact, as J. Hillis Miller attributes to Derrrida himself, as a *répétiteur* who protests he always remained faithful to the rules: 'I have repeated exactly and micrologically, and look what happened! The "system" disarticulated itself, deconstructed before my eyes'.[33]

Derrida is a constant provocateur in *Free Will* because this thinker who wished he had studied to be a 'Shakespeare expert', since 'everything is in Shakespeare', remains our most productive theorist of those questions about sovereignty, in both the self and state, that these plays and poems pose.[34] Out of his own narcissism and charisma, Derrida generated the most thorough deconstruction we yet possess of the theme that constitutes the focus of this study: the artist's paradoxical desire for powerful powerlessness, 'a design on mastery, and a renunciation of mastery on a scale infinitely more powerful than can be found elsewhere ... an adventure of power and unpower, a play of potence and impotence ... out of proportion to other types of discourse, and sometimes even with all the rules of art'.[35] The theorist identified the *folie de grandeur* of this masterful unmastering with the writer's obligation of attendance on 'a call (or an order, desire, or demand)' of the other, a notion that has obvious affinity with the Shakespearean patience that 'the readiness is all'.[36] Conceived in reaction to the historical determinism of Foucault and Bourdieu, this Derridean stress on the spectral futurity or *readiness* of writing works to reaffirm the sign over its referent, and so seems peculiarly apt for a poet-playwright who scorned the sovereignty of Edmund Spenser's *The Faerie Queene*, for its overdetermined referentiality 'In praise of ladies dead and lovely knights', as 'the chronicle of wasted time' [Sonnet 106]. In *Will Power: Essays on Shakespearean Authority* I defined my methodology, in contrast to the 'old historicist' and biographical criticism that effaces the *literary* signifier in its scavenging after facts, as a dialogue between such 'high theory and low archives'; and in *Free Will* this approach meets its exemplary analogue in Shakespeare's struggle to escape his own historicity, and throw off 'the weight of this sad time' [*King Lear*, *5,3,122*].[37]

After *Will Power* had excavated the real material conditions of Shakespearean authority, *Secret Shakespeare* explored the connections between the recalcitrance of the plays and the negative theology of 'God Almighty's fools'. Now *Free Will* extends this immanent critique of Shakespearean fooling to consider these works as experiments in the radical passivity that Judith Halberstam describes in *The Queer Art of Failure* as subverting paramountcy with the ethos of *not* winning: the wisdom that there is something powerful in nullity, and that 'to fall short, to take a detour, to find a limit, to lose our way, to forget, to avoid mastery', might be enough 'to bring the winner down'.[38] Such self-irony is intrinsic to Shakespeare's wordplay. Thus, 'How every fool can play upon the word!' exclaims Lorenzo at Lancelot Gobbo's punning on 'The Moor', a moronic word for fool itself: 'I think the best grace of wit will shortly turn into silence, and discourse grow commendable in none only but parrots' [*Merchant, 3,5,34–9*]. The master's exasperation at a servant's fooling with the name of the Tudor martyr Thomas More reveals how contemporaries could be expected to understand 'There is more in it' [*As You, 4,3,158*] whenever Shakespeare played upon a word. Similarly, 'By Heaven, thou echo'st me', swears Othello at Iago's blank repetition of his questions, 'As if there were some monster in thy thought!' [*Othello, 3,3,110*]. In such reflections on his own cultural poetics we can hear the writer meditating, I therefore propose, not only on his utopian dream of separating art from mimesis, representation from presence, language from power, but on their tragic indivisibility, in that 'doubled or enfolded act of (re) cognition that makes art possible' on the liminal terrain 'occupied by aesthetics before aesthetics emerge', or rather, when the aesthetic and political have yet to be divorced.[39]

In Chapter 1 of *Free Will*, 'Picture of Nobody', I track this pre-Kantian nucleus of *willed nonentity* or interested disinterestedness in Shakespeare's own recorded words, when in a pair of legal disputes about real estate his testimony appears to parry his questioners by giving them back exactly what they came to hear. Biographers detect a chill aloofness in these legal depositions, as though the records communicate the speaker's impatience with realty, a resentful recognition of his failure to transcend the 'parchment bonds' [*Richard II, 2,1,64*] of property and personhood. But reading them as forms of *biographeme*, the quantum narrative that encapsulates a writer's entire work, I key them to the queer improvisatory time wasting by which his text successfully evades the impatient pressure of sovereignty on the space of the play, and to the passive power with which it turns a 'commanded performance to a commanding' one.[40] Among his repertoire of possibilities in an emerging liberal realm, where the self was starting to be formulated as active, assertive, voluntaristic, it suited this most elliptic of writers to *refrain* from authorization of his intellectual property, and to pay lipservice, like some legal non-person, to princely patrons as ultimate owners of his meaning, I conclude. Here Shakespeare's reluctance to tangle with the Behemoth of the monstrous new 'paper machine' becomes crucial. For it was this self-surrender as a kind of vapid and innocuous 'William Nemo' that covered Shakespeare's convenient postponement of the royalties of printed authorship, his discreet erasure in the theatre company's collective line-up, and self-denying ordinance to drown his own book.

The notion that the power of Shakespearean weakness emanates from an abandonment to non-being in the traumatizing confine of the royal court has been literally *animated* by the recent focus on the meaning of the creature as the 'extimate' animalistic double of the sovereign. 'Thou hast seen a farmer's dog bark at a beggar ... And the creature run from the cur?' instances the ruined king, 'There thou might'st behold the great image of authority' [*Lear*, *4,6,150*]. In exposing the arbitrariness of self-authorizing power it would indeed seem that Shakespeare anticipates the existentialist doctrine of the Nazi jurist Schmitt, lately refined by Derrida and Giorgio Agamben, that sovereign presence is constituted in agonistic embrace of its bestial shadow in 'bare life'.[41] Greenblatt thus identifies an 'unlikely emblem' of Shakespeare's own artistic freedom and scope to flout the law in the condemned prisoner Barnardine, 'a creature unprepared' for execution, who obdurately insists he 'will not die today, for any man's persuasion' [*Measure*, *4,3,52–61*].[42] And Julia Lupton regards this creaturely condition of non-existence as not simply 'the flip-side' of absolutism but the genesis of a distinct Shakespearean creativity spurred by *ressentiment* at the *cringe* of intimidated vassalage. Thus, 'First my fear, then my curtsy, last my speech', specifies 'our bending author' in one of his menial-like epilogues [*2Henry IV, Epi,1*]; and a theme of *Free Will* is how such asides ironize the bowing and scraping to sovereign violence, as the performer pledges 'to please you every day' in wily acknowledgement that 'By swaggering could I never thrive' [*Twelfth, 5,1,386–95*].[43]

In Shakespeare, observes Lupton, the creature is 'actively passive or, better, *passionate*, perpetually becoming created, subject to transformation at the behest of arbitrary commands'.[44] This genealogy of Shakespearean *jouissance* recalls Nietzsche's intuition that 'joy' is an effect not simply of the binding force of cruel power but also 'of the ecstatic *unbinding* of power from a signifier … the exuberance of an uncontrollable expenditure'.[45] Increasingly, the dramatist relates this affirmation of difference over repetition to the actor's drive to surpass the text of the play itself, and the escape from the master–slave dialectic to the 'infinite jest' [*Hamlet, 5,1,171*] when 'your clowns speak … more than is set down' [*3,2,35*]. Thus, 'This is miching *malhecho*', complains Prince Hamlet, when the players exceed their scripted parts [*3,2,124*]; and in 'Welsh roots', the second chapter of *Free Will*, the passive aggression of the creaturely voice that answers power back with the delinquent alterity of such a *bad echo* is found to be embodied in Shakespeare's dependent relations with his own Tudor overlords, the vice-regal Herbert dynasty whose 'British' imperial mythology his plays appear to rehearse. Turning the postcolonial cliché of Celtic repression around, however, this essay draws on recent historians who define the Tudor state as in reality a Welsh colonization of England, to commence from the surprise that whenever Shakespeare stages Anglo-Welsh exchanges it is the *English* who are the dominated.

In 'Welsh roots' Fluellen's force-feeding of Pistol with a leek is taken to be paradigmatic of the writer's subjection to unionist ideology, and his mimicry of the 'jolly Briton' as a ribald debunking of its pretensions. Shakespeare emerges, on this reading, as humorously sceptical of the farrago of a 'British' empire, a wry queering he metadramatized in the *Bildung* drama of the Latin lesson of *The Merry Wives of Windsor*, where a pert young William sabotages the *imitatio* of the *Pax Romana* by literally echoing Sir Hugh Evans's irritable cry for a 'peace' in his Welsh master's voice. This truant Will teaches us what 'any schoolboy knows, that nothing can be more insolent or subversive than a slightly ironic exact repetition'.[46] Classicist Mary Beard has in fact argued that such cheeky 'doublespeak' was 'a mechanism of control' over tyrannical power the Romans themselves taught the world.[47] So, though *Free Will* returns throughout to Shakespeare's squirming dependency relations with his Herbert patrons, the chapter concludes that the dramatist remained similarly disrespectful of their grand *translatio imperii*, and by sending the gabbling 'Romanitas' of 'Great Britain' 'cackling home to Camelot', insinuated to these 'British' earls that, like the good soldier he gave the border name of Williams, he would 'have none of [their] money' [*Henry V, 4,8,62*].

Shakespeare's interest in echo and repetition tends to be associated with the assertion of authorial sovereignty or some higher order. But the argument of *Free Will* is that it is by such self-duplication and reflexivity that Shakespearean drama instead struggles to escape from power relations into symbolic form, even as the debris of its own conditions of production obtrude into the text like the acoustic event of an actual echo, or those relics of defunct royalty that haunt the modern world. If sovereignty and servility are locked in agonistic embrace on this stage, therefore, a pre-aesthetic idea of autonomy can be detected in the dramatist's relation to the classical tradition of mimesis as semblance, a cagey non-compliance that ironically parallels the famous maxim by the Herberts' relation Sidney, that poetry is above copying, because 'the poet, disdaining to be tied to any such subjection ... doth grow in effect another nature'.[48] So it is significant that in *Julius Caesar*, the drama about inauguration we think Shakespeare wrote in 1599 to inaugurate the Globe playhouse, cries of 'peace, freedom, and liberty!' [*Julius, 3,1,111*] reverberate within the monumental irony of the building's imitation imperial design. Critics have long remarked how this metadramatic representation of Caesar's foundational murder is literally composed out of echoes, with words and names recycled, and philosophers have equally been fascinated by its sense of history as eternal recurrence. In Chapter 3, 'O world', I therefore consider this repetition compulsion to be a creative reflex of Shakespeare's creatural accommodation to the architectonics of the Globe's pseudo-antique façade, and what it signified: the unlucky intrusion of some unseen originating political presence into the aesthetic space of the new playhouse, of the Lords' factual *Room* into the play's fictive *Rome*.

Julius Caesar stages the contest between a charismatic and a constitutional politics, critics concur. But 'O world' refers this conflict back to the play's opening report of the river trembling 'To hear the replication' of the applause 'Made in her concave shores' [*1,1,45–6*], and asks, 'Did the Globe have a ghostly echo?' The entire play, I conjecture, can be read as a test of 'A canopy most fatal' [*5,1,87*] to the acoustic and sightlines of a 'room' that is felt to be too much like the grand type of absolutist theatre whose 'wide walls encompass but one man' [*1,2,158*]. Schmitt's political theology has inspired recent commentators to hear in these echoes the servile repetition of 'a monarch's voice' [*3,1,275*]. But with this sacrificial foundation play, in which Shakespeare, as we might say, truly becomes Shakespeare, the dramatist seems instead to exploit the chiasmic poetics of repetition as a condition of revolution, using them to undo myths of anterior origin and to warn those performing under these theatrical 'heavens' that the fault 'is not in our stars, / But in ourselves, that we are underlings' [*1,2,141–2*]: a culpability he associates with the hypocritical face-mask worn by Roscius, when the veteran Roman actor collaborated with the dictator Sulla. So, although the Globe stage is dwarfed by the triumphal pillars which bestride 'the narrow world / Like a Colossus' [*1,2,136*], it is by the echo-effect of its critique that *Julius Caesar* prevents the playhouse from becoming an officially authorized pulpit, and that the dramatist evades the fate of his court poet Cinna, who is beaten to death for dreaming he consorts with kings.

'Who ever knew the heavens menace so?' asks Shakespeare in his precautionary first Globe play; and the answer – 'Those that have known the earth so full of faults' [*1,3,44–5*] – reveals a practical man of the theatre unexpectedly ambivalent about the cultural and ideological implications of 'the wide arch of the ranged empire' [*Antony, 1,1,33*] now imposed upon his stage. So in Chapter 4, 'Denmark's a prison', I view *Hamlet* as the great refusal of the absolutist system symbolized by such triumphal façades. There the complaint about Denmark being one of the worst dungeons in the world [*2,2,242*] might look a contrarian way to greet the future King James and his Danish family, until the neoclassical aesthetic developing at the real contemporary court of Elsinore is taken into account. But once the absolutism of James's manic brother-in-law King Christian IV is considered as a model for the united Stuart kingdom, the play's metatheatrical references to this solar monarch start to look like signals of Shakespeare's own life-choice, and his negative professional positioning in response to the epochal invitation which around 1600 was tempting so many of his colleagues among the 'tragedians of the city' [*2,2,316*] to migrate to such continental courts.

Historians now tell us that there was indeed 'something rotten in the state of Denmark' [1,4,90]. But it took Shakespeare to identify the rottenness of this absolutist experiment as a prologue to the Stuart century and a deadly menace 'Unto our climature and countrymen' [1,1,106:16]. Thus the Player's fencing of Hamlet's order to 'reform' [3,2,34], and the 'damnable faces' [231] pulled by its actors, make their play-within-the-play a symbolization of the writer's own cautiousness about the impending state takeover of his profession, even as the Prince's tribute to the Clown – 'How absolute the knave is!' [5,1,126] – heralds a grudging monarchic consecration of the rival form of absolutism in art. 'The King is a thing ... Of nothing' [4,2,26], this tragedy of non-cooperation thereby insists. For by demystifying the Baroque 'king effect' Shakespeare's Danish drama puts out the Sun King's light, according to this interpretation, as the dramatist grounds his own aesthetic sovereignty not in monarchy's 'dying voice' [5,2,298] but in the popular acclamation of that 'whole theatre of others' behind him [3,2,25]: the people's body at the Globe.

'Speak ... Speak ... Speak again' [*King Lear*, 1,1,64–89]: beginning with this injunction, Chapter 5 of *Free Will* extends this account of Shakespeare's refusal of sovereignty, to consider *King Lear* as a staging of the challenge to *speak freely by command* which confronted the dramatist when the players were, after all, co-opted to proclaim the Stuart monarch's 'Free and Absolute' power. Critics have recently revived the naive notion that Shakespeare now flattered the king, like some literary Goneril or Regan, by penning dramas that mouth James's ramblings about the lord's anointed, and so laboured to ensure 'the persistence of sacral kingship throughout the Stuart era'.[49] But Lear's thunderclap that 'we have divided in three our kingdom' is directly analogous, I propose, to the charter with which this 'wisest fool' triangulated London's acting troupes in 1603; while in the youngest daughter's performative aside – 'What shall Cordelia speak?' [59] – can be heard her creator's own predicament during this investiture crisis, when the new absolutist monarchy collided with the rival absolutism of art. Shakespeare's 'darker purpose' [1,1,34] in *King Lear* is therefore not only the eclipse of sovereignty but a depersonalization of his own work. The outcome, however, is a true tragedy of divestment, a symbolic self-castration in which the play performs both the deconsecration of the Ubuesque king and sees the 'poor fool hanged' [5,3,304] himself.

Shakespeare's stripping of his dramaturgy down to the stark 'bare life' of the Cinderella story with *King Lear* is a *reductio ad absurdum*, I infer in 'Great stage of fools', through which *askesis* rehearses the negative aesthetic of later modernist artworks, as the anorectic expression of a passive aggression towards reality. As in other versions of the self-harming folktale recycled in absolutist states, the depersonalizing body politics of Shakespeare's 'Cinderella' tragedy encode the aesthetic repulsion from a court society in which 'tattered clothes' are condemned while 'Robes and furred gowns hide all' [4,6,158-9]. But seen by light of feminist theories of abjection, when the king and jester follow the noncompliant daughter into the night of self-annihilation the mortification of these 'hunger artists' foreshadows the auto-immune crisis that for Adorno results from the subtractive logic of all 'anti-art', as it 'indicts superfluous poverty by undergoing its own, yet indicts this asceticism as well'. *King Lear* is its author's profoundest critique of his own Ubu-like 'abject position', of the perverse power of weakness, the queer art of failure, and the absolutism of the autonomous artwork, I conclude. For centuries before Samuel Beckett, the famished *lessness* of *King Lear* means that here, as Adorno wrote of abstraction, the refusal to speak to order 'terminates in a complete impoverishment: the scream, or the destitute, powerless gesture, literally the syllables "da-da"'.[50]

At the close of *King Lear* the looking-glass for which the king calls is thought to have reflected King James at the Whitehall performance, in his guise as his own court fool. If so, absolute power and absolute art terminate in this reflection. The mirror can therefore stand as a symbol of Shakespeare's own mimetic relation to the united Stuart kingdom, for the glass carried onstage in his next tragedy, *Macbeth*, is expressly said to reflect those 'That twofold balls and trebles scepters carry' [4,1,136-7]: James and Christian in the Hall of Hampton Court, at the first great official assembly after the 1605 Gunpowder Plot. This mirroring is again often viewed as a Schmittian homage to divine right, since it figures in a masque of the Stuart dynasty that the Witches devise for Macbeth. But in Chapter 6 I take as a starting-point the embarrassment that the eighth Stuart ruler was in fact James's beheaded mother, Mary Queen of Scots. In order to succeed to his double inheritance the king had traitorously connived in her execution; so by reflecting the face of the murderer back upon itself, I deduce, this diabolical mirror poses the vital question of such duplicity: 'What is a traitor?' [4,2,46].

Shakespeare's obsession with doubleness arises in *Macbeth* from the play's barbaric circumstances, I propose in 'Double trouble', as a meditation upon the duplicitous origins of the newly united British kingdom. So it is not surprising that, following Derrida, critics have become alert to the mirror logic with which this drama dating from the doubling of a state deconstructs the distinction between authorized and unauthorized violence that is 'the mystical foundation of authority'.[51] But rather than flattering this double-headed Stuart monstrosity, I conclude, the duplicating 'double ... trouble' [4,1,10] of a play that 'palters with us in a double sense' [5,10,20], 'in every point twice done, and then done double' [1,6,15], works apotropaically, like the Gorgon painted in the same year for the Medici by Caravaggio, forcing us to confront the occult affinity of 'good' and 'bad' violence, yet also the necessity to yield to the hard imperative of choice. As Kantorowicz observed, when he perceived the Witches' clairvoyant ball to contain a prophecy of the later revolutionary scission of 'The King's Two Bodies', what Shakespeare thereby offers Britain's dual monarchy is a representation superior to the reality that intrudes upon it, a supra-sovereignty that exceeds its national foundation, and that inspired the German critic himself to oppose both Schmitt and Hitler. For if Schmitt's incarnational political theology pulls the aesthetic back towards consciousness of 'real presence', what Kantorowicz's reading of *Macbeth* contributes to Shakespeare studies is consciousness of real – or royal – *absence*.

If the metatheatrical mirrors brought into *King Lear* and *Macbeth* betray acute unease in the Jacobean Shakespeare with the play as royal command performance, a castrating investiture, they also figure the illusionistic picture frame to which theatre was reduced at the absolutist court. In *Antony and Cleopatra*, which was also likely put on for the state visit of King Christian to London in 1606, the whole drama is therefore 'windowed' by the instruction of courtier Philo to 'Behold and see' the legendary lovers 'transformed' to a 'gipsy' and 'a strumpet's fool' [1,1,9–13], and art-minded critics regard what ensues as an anamorphic 'turning picture': Shakespeare's attempt to compete with Baroque painting and the Apollonian spectacle of the Stuart masques. In Chapter 7, however, I argue that this tragedy should, instead, be viewed as a calculated equivocation before the scopic regime of absolutism, and a tactical surrender to the perspective technology focused on the sovereign only in order to subvert it. Antony's fear of being 'subdued / To penetrative shame' [4,5,74–5] in Caesar's 'imperious show' [4,16,24] voices the aversion of the King's Men, in this interpretation, to being 'shown / For poor'st dimunitives' [4,12,37] by 'mechanic slaves' in Masonic aprons who 'uplift' them 'to the view' [5,2,205] using the scenic machinery at Whitehall, as the play confounds this royal theatre of illusion with the creaturely worldliness of the riverside Globe, imaged as Cleopatra's 'little O o'th'earth' [5,2,79].

Critics automatically identify the visual slant of *Antony and Cleopatra* with the new ways of seeing inculcated by the absolutist state, but the play in fact exploits the visual technology of absolutism to reflect on what 'seeing like a state' implies, I propose in 'Your crown's awry'.[52] As a King's Man, Shakespeare may himself have 'bor[n]e the canopy' [Sonnet 125] on one of the triumphal arches at King James's coronation in 1604. But starting from the supposition that this work was framed to slot into a similar proscenium 'arch / Of the ranged empire' [1,1,35] erected in the Banqueting House for the masques designed by Inigo Jones, this chapter regards the play as a *turn* of the perspective technology back on itself, which exploits its equidistance between the playhouse and the palace, or the styles of Mannerism and the Baroque, to reverse the social and visual hierarchies of the sovereign point of view. Again there is an analogy, I therefore infer, between Shakespeare's ironic submission to the rules of pictorial illusion and the painting of Velàzquez, a master of perspective who similarly portrayed the likes of Cleopatra's maids and eunuchs at the Spanish court in magnified scale, but the king diminished, like a puppet reflected in the mirror at the back. As servitors of the sovereign, both the painter and playwright bowed to the imperative of the absolutist look, I conclude, but then 'overflowed the measure' [1,1,1] of their official commission, to deny that the vantage of the royals was the viewpoint of the picture or the play.

At the close of *Antony and Cleopatra* the playwright seems to speak through the palace slave, and to be resigned to deferring the freedom of an autonomous aesthetic until after his own lifetime, and that of the monarchy he serves: 'Your crown's awry. / I'll mend it, and then play' [5,2,309]. If this *détournement* implies that such a representational space cannot be long in coming, his next Roman drama, *Coriolanus*, nevertheless stages the obstruction to the emergence of a modern public sphere caused by the persisting personal presence of aristocratic patrons, the men of arms who blocked the stage in the London playhouses. Chapter 8, 'Like an eagle in a dovecot', therefore begins with the complaints made against Coriolanus that 'All places yield to him as he sits down' [*4,7,28*], and that by waving his feathered 'hat in scorn' [*2,3,156*] he interferes with 'the beam of sight' [*3,1,267*], to consider the play's insistent theatre metaphor in light of ongoing debate over whether Shakespeare's stage remained subdued to the incarnational logic of sovereignty, as Schmitt maintained, or completed the transfer of sovereignty, as Kantorowicz and Habermas proposed, from the personal body of the king to the collective body of the people. How far do these dramas chart the transformation of subjects into citizens? Or in the somatic imagery to which the Citizens of the play themselves keep returning: to what extent does the exiguous fleshly sovereignty for which Coriolanus *stands* remain on the body politic as 'a sore' [*3,1,234*] or unhealed scab?

With its protagonist isolated like 'a lonely dragon' [*4,1,31*], *Coriolanus* is the last of a sequence of Shakespearean dramas, *Free Will* notes, that record the expulsion of the obsolete overlord from the stage of the Globe as an aesthetic necessity, but then feature antiheroes who vent murderous hate on the 'detestable town' [*Timon, 4,1,33*] that drove them out. Its turnaround, when the ex-patron becomes a player at the great house of his foe, can thus be keyed to the conflict between the 'two authorities' [*Coriolanus, 3,1,112*] of court and commerce in Jacobean theatre, and the futility of Coriolanus's efforts to 'stand / As if a man were author of himself' [*5,3,35–6*] to his creator's discovery that by fleeing the market for the mansion the artist escapes economic demand only to perform by political command. So this tragedy can be regarded as an anticipation of Bourdieu's analysis of the 'absolute' artists of the aesthetic movement, who were trapped in the double bind of 'dominated dominators', as creatures of the political elite that sponsored their 'art for art's sake'.[53] In particular, its climax, when the warrior kneels 'like a dull actor' [*5,3,40*] to his mother Volumnia, reads like an expression of the author's prostration as 'a creeping thing' [*5,4,11*] in the Wiltshire mansion of Mary Herbert, Countess of Pembroke, whose reported letter informing her son that 'We have the man Shakespeare' revealed how the dramatist was coerced into speaking with 'a beggar's tongue' [*3,2,17*], by producing such an 'unnatural scene' [*5,3,184*] as this unperformed play about performance, *Coriolanus* itself.

'Cut me to pieces … Stain all your edges on me' [*5,6,112–13*]: Coriolanus's last words to his destroyers become in this account an Orphic statement of the author's own submission to the system of textual patronage governed by his imperious backers, the 'Incomparable Pair' of earls, William and Philip Herbert, to whom his Folio would be dedicated. For Shakespeare seems with this circumcision to recognize how, despite his misgivings at the literary sovereignty instituted by print technology, in the 'interpretation of the time' [*4,7,50*] his 'cut' pages would penetrate far beyond both the palace *and* playhouse to reach 'a world elsewhere' [*3,3,139*]. This project of an art that transcends sovereign selfhood, of 'sweet airs that give delight and hurt not' [*Tempest, 3,2,131*], is the subject of the Epilogue of *Free Will*, which relates how, for all his awareness of what Agamben calls 'the dark mystery of sovereign power' that the king *never* dies, Shakespeare persists in staging the spectacle of 'A begging prince' [*Richard II, 1,4,250*] who kneels for forgiveness, 'and henceforth / Begs mercy of the play'.[54] The opening here is therefore Gonzalo's utopian prospectus in *The Tempest* of ruling as king of a technologically innocent state with 'no sovereignty' [*2,1,148*], which his cynical companions mock as an 'impossible matter' [*88*], but that I suggest prefigures the thinking of Derrida and others about our need to 'be cheerful' [*4,1,147*] in expectation of the renunciation of sovereignty that is attempted in these late plays over and again:

ALONSO: But O, how oddly will it sound, that I
            Must ask my child for forgiveness!
PROSPERO: There, sir, stop.
            Let us not burden our remembrance with
            A heaviness that's gone.

                                   [*Tempest, 5,1,200–3*]

Shakespeare's romances presage our anxiety about losing the future, 'No Sovereignty' proposes, but then tantalizingly return us to the vision of an Arcadian 'golden age' [*2,1,167*] 'When earthly things made even / Atone together' [*As You Like It, 5,4,98–9*], an intimation that 'the time of universal peace is near' [*Antony, 4,6,4*] which may have dated from the 'balmy time' [*Sonnet 107*] when the poet's Herbert patrons retained him to add 'a Greek

invocation' to *As You Like It* [2,5,59] to celebrate the succession of King James. The sonnets also supposedly inspired by this
earthly paradise confirm Sidney's axiom that poets alone deliver
a golden world; yet Shakespeare transcended that absolutist aesthetic by humanizing himself in them not as a sovereign author
but as tongue-tied 'Will', 'an unperfect actor on the stage' [Sonnet
23] of the Globe.[55] There the Arcadian programme was reflected
in the series of Jacobean plays he wrote with classical settings, a
journey back to the Greece from where 'We came into this world
like brother and brother', made in hope of going out 'hand in hand,
not one before another' [*Errors, 5,1,427*]. Like the Greece imagined
by Hölderlin or Heidegger, the 'varying shore' [*Antony, 4,16,11*] of
this pre-Christian world remains haunted by a sovereign 'heaviness
that's gone', a tyranny with which Shakespeare now associates the
machinery of his own stage. But it is the theatre of these last plays
that itself provides a solution, *Free Will* concludes, to the question
they pose concerning technology, in the immanence of an art so
humanly 'warm' [*Winter's Tale, 5,3,109*] that the audience grants it
the royal 'pardon' [*Tempest, Epi.19*] that it craves.

   In Paul Auster's 2009 novel *Invisible* the poet protagonist discovers too late that the pact he makes with his princely patron
implicates his art in crimes of state terrible enough 'to curdle your
blood'; but his story has Shakespearean authority when he realizes he is in a play, 'and *all the men and women are merely players*'
[*As You, 2,7,139*]. Later, Auster's Prospero-like controller retires
to a Caribbean island populated by 'blue-eyed Africans' that is 'a
laboratory of human possibilities'; and *The Tempest* haunts the
novel as a paradigm for the conspiracy theory Schmitt calls political
romanticism: the idea that, just as 'Prospero holds the "mechanical
play" of the drama in his hands', so we are helpless in the hands of
'a secret power exercised "behind the scenes" ... an invisible power
of free subjectivity'.[56] *Invisible* thus testifies to the pervasiveness in
our culture of the notion of Shakespeare as the absent presence of a
secret sovereignty. At its most freakish this is the power complex or
fascist mindset that impels the delusion that the plays were written
by some mystery aristocrat. For as David Rieff regrets in his sombre
meditation on the death of Susan Sontag, one of the hardest things
for us to conceive is a writer who can express human *unimportance*
and still remain compassionate: 'How to do that and at the same
time fully take in the real measure of one's own insignificance?'[57]

Yet it is towards the realization of this impossible project of 'voluntary servitude'[58], and against a godlike sovereignty exercised by some 'old fantastical Duke of dark corners' [*Measure, 4,3,147*], be he authoritarian lawgiver or literary author, that these plays about all the different faces of human failure, struggle, I conclude, as Shakespeare dreams for us an art in which sovereignty is so dissolved that it 'will leave not a rack behind' [*Tempest, 4,1,156*].

Notes

1 Aristotle, *Poetics*, 1453b1–4, trans. Stephen Halliwell (Chapel Hill, NC.: University of North Carolina Press, 1987), p.45; Georg Wilhelm Hegel, *Hegel's Aesthetics: Lectures on Fine Art*, trans. T.M. Knox (Oxford: Oxford University Press, 1975), p.11; Terry Eagleton, *William Shakespeare* (Oxford: Blackwell, 1986), pp.1 and 99.

2 Peter Holbrook, *Shakespeare's Individualism* (Cambridge: Cambridge University Press, 2009), p.23.

3 Karl Marx quoted in S.S. Prawer, *Karl Marx and World Literature* (Oxford: Oxford University Press, 1976), p.310. For 'justice', 'right', 'toleration' and 'liberty' as Milton's 'keywords', see Annabel Patterson, *Milton's Words* (Oxford: Oxford University Press, 2009).

4 Claude Lefort, *Democracy and Political Theory* (Oxford: Oxford University Press, 1988), p.19; Chantal Mouffe, *The Democratic Paradox* (London: Verso, 2005), pp.1–2.

5 Stephen Greenblatt, *Will in the World: How Shakespeare Became Shakespeare* (London: Jonathan Cape, 2004), p.374.

6 Debora Kuller Shuger, *Political Theologies in Shakespeare's England: The Sacred and the State in 'Measure for Measure'* (Basingstoke: Palgrave, 2001), pp.2, 47, 56–7, et passim. For an 'old historicist' reading which remains Whiggishly oblivious to the fashion for political theology, see Andrew Hadfield, *Shakespeare and Republicanism* (Cambridge: Cambridge University Press, 2005).

7 Carl Schmitt, *Political Theology: Four Chapters on the Concept of Sovereignty*, trans. George Schwab (Chicago: University of Chicago Press, 1985), p.5. For a recent discussion of Schmitt's influence on the contemporary school of American legal realists, see David Cole, 'Are We Stuck with the Imperial Presidency?', *New York Review of Books*, 7 June 2012, 62–4.

8 Patrick Cheney, *Shakespeare's Literary Authorship* (Oxford: Oxford University Press, 2008), pp.3–4, 63 and 113–14.

9 William Hazlitt, 'Coriolanus', in *The Characters of Shakespeare's Plays* (Cambridge: Cambridge University Press, 1955), p.59.

10 Daniel Dennett, *Elbow Room: The Varieties of Free Will Worth Having* (Cambridge, Mass.: MIT Press, 1984), p.169.

11 Simone Weil, 'On Personality', in *The Simone Weil Reader*, ed. George Panicha (New York: McKay, 1977), p.331.

12 Saidiya Hartman, *Scenes of Subjection: Terror, Slavery, and Self-Making in Nineteenth-Century America* (Oxford: Oxford University Press, 1997), p.115.

13 James VI and I, 'Song, the first verses that ever the King made' (1582), in *The Poems of James VI of Scotland* (2 vols, Edinburgh: William Blackwood, 1955–58), vol. 2, p.132.

14 Matthew Arnold, 'Shakespeare', in *The Poems of Matthew Arnold*, ed. Kenneth Allott (London: Longman, 1965), p.48; Isaiah Berlin, 'Two Concepts of Liberty', in *Four Essays on Liberty* (Oxford: Oxford University Press, 1969), p. 127.

15 Hazlitt, op. cit. (note 9), p.59. For a recent variation on Hazlitt's reading, see the influential reading of Richard Helgerson, which places Shakespeare foremost among the champions of absolute monarchy, in *Forms of Nationhood: The Elizabethan Writing of England* (Chicago: Chicago University Press, 1992), p.244.

16 Ortega y Gasset, *Ortega y Gasset: Velázquez, Goya, and the Dehumanization of Art*, trans. A. Beeching (New York: Littlehampton, 1972), p.88.

17 Arifa Akbar, 'The Virgin Queen, the Serpent and the Doctored Portrait: Artist Painted Elizabeth I Holding a Snake – Then Lost His Nerve', *The Independent*, 5 March 2010, 10.

18 A particularly egregious instance of this tendency to portray the dramatist as a fawning toady of the monarchy was televised to coincide with the Golden Jubilee celebrations of Queen Elizabeth II: James Shapiro's *The King and the Playwright: A Jacobean History* (BBC 2012).

19 Theodor Adorno, *Aesthetic Theory*, trans. and ed. Robert Hullot-Kentor (London: Continuum, 2004), p.331; 'Reconciliation Under Duress', in *Art and Politics*, trans. Ronald Taylor (London: Verso, 1977), p.160.

20 Pierre Bourdieu, *The Rules of Art: Genesis and Structure of the Literary Field*, trans. Susan Emanuel (Cambridge: Polity Press, 1996), p.101.

21 Stephen Greenblatt, *Shakespearean Negotiations: The Circulation of Social Energy in Renaissance England* (Oxford: Clarendon Press, 1988), pp.29–30.

22 Wayne Koestenbaum, *Humiliation* (New York: Picador, 2011), pp.7–9 et passim.

23 Wayne Macauley, *The Cook* (London: Quercus, 2012). p.42.

24 'Mellifluous and honey-tongued Shakespeare': Francis Meres, *Pallas Tamia* (1598), quoted in Samuel Schoenbaum, *William Shakespeare: A*

Documentary Life (Oxford: Clarendon Press, 1975), p.140; 'Melicert': Henry Chettle (1603), quoted in Katherine Duncan Jones, *Ungentle Shakespeare: Scenes from a Life* (London: Thomson Learning, 2001), p.129; 'our pleasant Willy', Edmund Spenser, 'The Tears of the Muses' (1591), quoted in Ernst Honigmann, *Shakespeare: The 'Lost Years'* (Manchester: Manchester University Press, 1985), pp.71–2.

25 Michel Foucault, *Abnormal: Lectures at the Collège de France, 1974–1975*, trans. Graham Burchell (New York: Picador, 2003), p.13.

26 'Power's ode': Michel Foucault, '25 February 1976', in *'Society Must Be Defended': Lectures at the Collège de France, 1975–76*, trans. David Macey, ed. Mauro Bertini and Allesandro Fontana (London: Allen Lane, 2003), pp.172–7; 'freedom to roam': Michel Foucault, 'Dream, Imagination and Existence', in *Dream and Existence: Michel Foucault and Ludwig Binswanger*, trans. and ed. Keith Hoeller (Atlantic Highlands, NJ.: Humanities Press, 1993), pp.53–4. For a stimulating commentary on this return to the subject, see Eric Paras, *Foucault 2.0* (New York: Other Press, 2006), pp.101–23 et passim.

27 J. Hillis Miller, '"Don't Count Me In": Derrida's Refraining', in Allison Weiner and Simon Morgan Wortham, *Encountering Derrida: Legacies and Futures of Deconstruction* (London: Continuum, 2007), p.49.

28 Michel Foucault, *History of Madness*, trans. Jonathan Murphy and Jean Khalfa (London: Routledge, 2006), p.14; George Puttenham, *The Arte of English Poesie*, eds G.D. Willcock and A. Waller (Cambridge: Cambridge University Press, 1936), p.203. For the classic account of the poetics of chiasmus, see Alastair Fowler, *Conceitful Thought: The Interpretation of English Renaissance Poems* (Edinburgh: Edinburgh University Press, 1975); and for the association of this poetics with the Sidney circle, see William Engel, *Chiastic Designs in English Literature from Sidney to Spenser* (Farnham: Ashgate, 2009), in particular Chapter 3: 'Echo in Arcadia: Sidney's Legacy', pp.41–71: 'Sidney, and his sister after him, conceived and accomplished [coherence] through rhetorical mnemonics, of which chaiasmus is a constitutive part' (p.42). For the figural excess of Sidney's sonnet sequence as a premonition of the perverse inverted sovereignty theorized by Georges Bataille, see Fred Botting and Scott Wilson, *Bataille* (Basingstoke: Palgrave, 2001), pp.59–67. For an overview, see Judith Dundas, '*Paronomasia* in the Quip Modest: From Sidney to Herbert', *Connotations*, 2 (1992), 223–33; and for the theological use of echo effects, see Heather Asals, *Equivocal Predication: George Herbert's Way to God* (Toronto: Toronto University Press, 1981).

29 Jonathan Culler (ed.), *On Puns: The Foundation of Letters* (Oxford: Blackwell, 1988). See also Walter Redfern, *Puns* (Oxford: Blackwell, 1984).

30 Søren Kierkegaard, *Repetition and Philosophical Crumbs*, trans. M.G. Piety (Oxford: Oxford University Press, 2009), pp.20 and 38.

31 Judith Butler, *The Psychic Life of Power: Theories of Subjection* (Stanford: Stanford University Press, 1997), p.104.

32 Richard Wilson, *Secret Shakespeare: Studies in Theatre, Religion, and Resistance* (Manchester: Manchester University Press, 2004); 'Obsessive' mimic: René Girard, *A Theater of Envy: William Shakespeare* (Oxford: Oxford University Press, 1991), p.4; 'ritually induced states': Annette Kehnel, 'The Power of Weakness: Machiavelli Revisited', *German Historical Association Bulletin*, 33:2 (2011), 3–34, here 32.

33 Miller, op. cit. (note 27), p.49.

34 Jacques Derrida, *Specters of Marx: The State of the Debt, the Work of Mourning, and the New International*, trans. Peggy Kamuf (London: Routledge, 1994), p.18.

35 Jacques Derrida, *Points ... Interviews, 1974–1994*, ed. Elizabeth Weber, trans. Peggy Kamuf (Stanford: Stanford University Press, 1995), pp.149–50.

36 Jacques Derrida, quoted Jean-Luc Nancy, 'The Free Voice of Man', in Philippe Lacoue-Labarthe and Jean-Luc Nancy (eds.), *Retreating the Political*, ed. Simon Sparks (London: Routledge, 19976), p.54.

37 Richard Wilson, *Will Power: Essays on Shakespearean Authority* (Hemel Hempstead: Harvester, 1993), p.21.

38 Judith Halberstam, *The Queer Art of Failure* (Durham, NC: Duke University Press, 2011), pp.120–1.

39 Mark Robson, 'Defending Poetry, or, Is There an Early Modern Aesthetic?' in John Joughin, ed., *The New Aestheticism* (Manchester: Manchester University Press, 2003), pp.119 and 127. For the inseparability of politics and aesthetics in the early modern period, see Victoria Kahn, *Wayward Contracts: The Crisis of Political Obligation in England, 1640–1674* (Princeton: Princeton University Press, 2004), pp.6–24.

40 'A commanded performance': Luke Wilson, *Theaters of Intention: Drama and the Law in Early Modern England* (Stanford: Stanford University Press, 2000), p.170.

41 Carl Schmitt, *The Concept of the Political*, trans. George Schwab (Chicago: University of Chicago Press, 1996), p.27: 'the specific political distinction to which political actions and motives can be reduced is that between friend and enemy'; Giorgio Agamben, *The State of Exception*, trans. Kevin Attell (Chicago University Press, 2005), p.12: 'the sovereign, who decides on the exception, is, in truth, logically defined in his being by the exception'; Jacques Derrida, *The Beast and the Sovereign: Volume 1*, trans. Geoffrey Bennington (Chicago: University of Chicago

Press, 2009), p.60: 'The beast and the sovereign ... a couple, a duo or even a duel, but also an alliance, almost a hymen ...'.

42 Stephen Greenblatt, *Shakespeare's Freedom* (Chicago: University of Chicago Press, 2010), p.13.

43 Julia Lupton, *Citizen-Saints: Shakespeare and Political Theology* (Chicago: Chicago University Press, 2005), p.164; an earlier version appeared as 'Creature Caliban', *Shakespeare Quarterly*, 51 (2000), 1–23.

44 Ibid., p.161.

45 Botting and Wilson, op. cit. (note 28), p.113, referring to Friedrich Nietzsche, *On the Genealogy of Morals*, trans. Walter Kaufmann and R.J. Hollingdale (New York: Vintage Books, 1969), p.40.

46 Miller, op. cit. (note 27), p.49.

47 Mary Beard, 'It was satire', *London Review of Books*, 26 April 2012, 16.

48 Sir Philip Sidney, *A Defence of Poetry*, ed. J.A. Van Dorsten (Oxford: Oxford University Press, 1966), p.23.

49 Shuger, op. cit. (note 6), pp.55–6 and 66 et passim.

50 Adorno, op. cit. (note 19), pp.39 and 50.

51 Jacques Derrida, 'Force of Law: The "Mystical Foundation of Authority"', trans. Mary Quaintance, in Jacques Derrida, *Acts of Religion*, ed. Gil Adidjar (London: Routledge, 2002), pp.230–98, esp.268–72.

52 'See like a state': James C. Scott, *Seeing Like a State: How Certain Schemes to Improve the Human Condition Have Failed* (New Haven: Yale University Press, 1999).

53 Pierre Bourdieu, *The Rules of Art: Genesis and Structure of the Literary Field*, trans. Susan Emanuel (Cambridge: Polity Press, 1996), pp.77–80.

54 Giorgio Agamben, *Homo Sacer: Sovereign Power and Bare Life*, trans. Daniel Heller-Roazen (Stanford: Stanford University Press, 1998), p.93; 'henceforth / begs': Rainer Maria Rilke, 'The Spirit Ariel (After reading Shakespeare's *Tempest*)', in *Rilke: Selected Poems*, trans. J.B. Leishman (Harmondsworth: Penguin, 1964), p.74.

55 Sir Philip Sidney, *A Defence of Poetry*, in *Miscellaneous Prose of Sir Philip Sidney*, ed. Katherine Duncan Jones (Oxford: Clarendon Press, 1973), p.78.

56 Paul Auster, *Invisible* (London: Faber & Faber, 2009), pp.241, 280 and 295; Carl Schmitt, *Political Romanticism*, trans. Guy Oakes (Cambridge, Mass.: MIT Press, 1985), pp.78–9. Schmitt is particularly paranoid about 'secret societies and secret orders, Rosicrucians, freemasons', the 'silent ones in the land' he associates with the placeless 'spirit of the Jew': *The Leviathan in the State Theory of Thomas*

Hobbes, trans. George Schwab (Westport, CT: Greenwood Press, 1996), p.60.

57 David Rieff, *Swimming in a Sea of Death: A Son's Memoir* (London: Granta, 2008), p.157.

58 'Voluntary servitude': Étienne de la Boétie: 'The Discourse of Voluntary Servitude', trans. Harry Kurz, in *The Politics of Obedience and Étienne de la Boétie*, Étienne de la Boétie and Paul Bonnefon (London: Black Rose, 2007).

1

The picture of Nobody

Shakespeare in the time of the political

Bare life

At the end, 'his nose was as sharp as a pen' as he 'babbled of green fields' [*Henry V, 2,3,15*]. In September 1615, a few weeks before Shakespeare began to make his will and a little over six months before his death, Thomas Greene, town clerk of Stratford, wrote a memorandum of an exchange biographers treasure as the last of the precious few records of the dramatist's spoken words: 'W Shakespeares tellyng J Greene that I was not able to beare the enclosinge of Welcombe'.[1] John Greene was the clerk's brother, and Shakespeare, according to previous papers, was their 'cousin', who had lodged Thomas at New Place, his Stratford house. So the Greenes had appealed to their sharp-nosed kinsman for help in a battle that pitted the council against a consortium of speculators who were, in their own eyes, if 'not the greatest ... almost the greatest men of England'.[2] The plan to enclose the fields of Welcombe north of the town was indeed promoted by the steward to the Lord Chancellor, no less. But the predicament for Shakespeare was that it was led by his friends the Combes, rich money-lenders from whom he had himself bought 107 acres adjacent to the scheme. This land was his daughter Susanna's inheritance, and he had raised her interest in its development by investing in a half-share of the tithes on Welcombe's corn and hay. Critics like to read into Prospero's vision of 'nibbling sheep and flat meads thatched with stover' [*Tempest, 4,1,62–3*] 'Shakespeare's figurative return home'.[3] But at the close of his life, the dramatist was pitched into the thick of the epoch-marking conflict that was tearing this English idyll apart, for he now had to weigh his rental income from arable farming against the potential profits from those sheep.[4]

In his last days the great dramatist of indecision had to make a momentous decision. For the certain losers from sheep farming on Stratford's 'flat meads' would be the tenants, who when 'woolly breeders' [*Merchant, 1,3,79*] ate fields, in a notorious image from More's *Utopia*, must 'depart away' with babes and chattels on their backs.[5] Shakespeare had set these wrenching words in *Sir Thomas More*, where More's phrase about the destitute with babes and baggage at their backs was reassigned, however, to asylum-seekers [*Add.II, 81–2*]. When it came to evictions on his own turf his last recorded utterance that 'I was not able to bear the enclosing' is harder to read. Was his parting word on the most divisive social problem of the age that he could not *bear* or *bar* the change? Did he regret he had not barred the enclosure? Or that he could not bear its cost? And was the 'I' who he said 'could not bear the enclosing' even Shakespeare, indeed, or Greene? It seems more than chance that the Bard's valediction is such a bar to understanding we cannot tell whether he could not *prevent*, *endure* or *carry* the enclosing. We know he was aware of such ambiguities because he had a joke that sheep 'make me cry "baa"' [*Two Gents, 1,1,91*]; his Macbeth would sooner bar the door than 'bear the knife' [*Macbeth, 1,7,16*]; and he has Antigonus abandon a bairn in bearing-cloth before he is eaten by a bear [*Winter's, 4,1,105*]. But was Shakespeare, as a landowner and interested party, unable to stop, suffer or support the barring of his neighbours? In what did this lack of success consist? We cannot find our bearings. For as Terence Hawkes comments, 'an entire spectrum of potential meaning' is offered by the indeterminacy of these famous last words, as if their weakness and indecision were signifiers of some irresolvable confusion not only over the barring of real estate, but the *bearing* on the writer of his own life and times:

> Plurality invests all texts of course, but none more so than this. Its very subject guarantees it a talismanic, even votive status in our culture which offers to propel the words beyond the page. They seem to present, after all, a record of oral utterance, of actual speech on the Bard's part which, at this date, might almost lay claim to the aura of last words, significant beyond the context of their saying.[6]

Whatever their meaning Shakespeare's last words seem to speak of a profound failure. Yet in his critique of speech act theory Jacques Derrida opened a new itinerary for criticism by connecting art precisely with the experience of failure or ineptitude, and with the counter-intuitive idea that what is most powerful is 'often the most disarming feebleness'; so as a sign of the queer power of weakness, we might perhaps consider Shakespeare's reported statement that 'I was not able to bear the enclosing' as what Roland Barthes termed a biographeme: that quantum of truth that embodies a life's work.[7] For 'Who would fardels bear?' asks his Hamlet [*Hamlet*, 3,1,75]; 'I'll bear / Affliction till it do cry out', responds Gloucester [*Lear*, 4,6,75]; and Macbeth: 'bear-like I must fight the course' [*Macbeth*, 5,7,2]. But 'I had rather bear with you than bear you', sighs Touchstone [*As You*, 2,4,8]; and 'He's a lamb indeed that "baas" like a bear', sneer the Citizens of Coriolanus [2,1.10]. *Baring*, in all its multiple connotations of comportment, endurance, exemption, exposure, orientation and prevention, seems to have been this writer's habitual mode. We would thus surely like to know what the author of such lines thought about the condition of *bare life*, for human beings cannot bear too much reality, quips Hawkes, after T.S. Eliot, which is why they tell tales to paper over the cracks.[8]

Shakespeare span many sad stories about the 'bare / ruin'd choirs' [Sonnet 73] and 'thorny point of bare distress' [*As You*, 2,7,94], caused by England's textile-driven capitalist revolution. Yet when his townsmen gave him a leading part to play in this historic tragedy, it appears he almost literally sat on the fence, retreating behind a barrier of words into what Stephen Greenblatt calls the double consciousness with which an actor hides from view, and echoing his questioners with what they already knew, or even had themselves just said.[9] And this impression is reinforced by an earlier interview when Shakespeare had tried to calm their fears. For on 17 November 1614 Thomas Greene called on the great man at his London house in Blackfriars. But what the town clerk did not know, as Shakespeare and his son-in-law Dr. John Hall gave reassurances about going with the flow of events, was that on 28 October the poet's pen had signed a secret covenant to secure his own compensation 'for all such loss detriment or hindrance' as he might suffer 'by reason of any Enclosure':

> At my cousin Shakespeare, coming yesterday to town, I went to see him how he did. He told me that they assured him they meant to enclose no further than to Gospel Bush and so up straight (leaving out part of the dingles to the field) to the gate in Clopton hedge, and take in Salisbury's piece. And that they mean in April to survey the

land and then to give satisfaction, and not before. And he and Mr Hall say they think there will be nothing done at all.[10]

Perhaps his cousin Greene called 'to see how he did' because Shakespeare was already ill, and so too infirm to join the fight. Certainly, his reported attitude seems of a piece with the wish that warms his plays, to 'laugh this sport o'er by a country fire' [*Merry Wives, 5,5,219*]. Yet when the town clerk returned to Stratford he learned that 'the survey there was passed', despite his cousin's certainty that it would not take place until spring, and by the first days of December the trenches were being dug for the fences. Embarrassingly, when Greene tried to halt the developers on the 10th he went looking for their lawyer at Shakespeare's New Place, though it would be a month before lawyers tipped him off about the secret pact.[11] Biographers wring their hands at this sequence of events, which 'reveals a hitherto unseen side to the playwright of the people ... quietly hedging his bets', in Anthony Holden's words, 'by doing clandestine deals with the enemy'.[12] 'Either Shakespeare was lied to or he was lying', as Greenblatt admits.[13] So was he 'disinterested, or was he a schemer?' wondered Dennis Kay: 'Was he duplicitous or naive?'[14] Peter Levi feared the moneymen were 'too sharp for him'; and René Weiss thinks him too 'casual'; but Park Honan accepts his 'wish to protect the value of his assets' with the tired excuse that 'he had earned some rest'.[15] Likewise, while allowing that enclosure would be in his financial interests, Peter Ackroyd exonerates his reluctance to align himself as the result of a temperamental ambivalence: 'He seems to have been incapable of taking sides and remained studiedly impartial in even matters closest to him'.[16] Thus, as Greenblatt sums up a sorry story, 'Shakespeare stayed out of it, indifferent to its outcome perhaps. He did not stand to lose anything, and did not choose to join in a campaign on behalf of others who might be less fortunate'.[17]

If the spy Marlowe was transfixed by how much theatrical and political *plotting* had in common, the property-owner who called England a 'blessed plot' [*Richard II, 2,1,50*] liked to pun on the *topos* that made his old plays exchangeable for a New Place. So his ambiguity over this plot of green fields has become an epitome for his biographers of Shakespeare's famed disinterestedness. Yet it is the *interest* in his disinterest that is a focus of the most unforgiving treatment of the business, when a suicidal Shakespeare is portrayed in Edward Bond's 1973 drama *Bingo*. 'You read too much into it', Bond's playwright tells William Combe, as though addressing his later critics: 'I'm protecting my own interests. Not supporting you, nor fighting the town'. The banker knows, however, that Shakespeare's covert indemnity means he will never lift a finger against the plan. Thus, 'Be noncommittal', Combe slyly urges, 'or say you think nothing will come of it. Stay in your garden. It pays to sit in a garden.'[18] Bond sets his play in the bleak midwinter of the Christmas after Shakespeare struck his deal, when the town council begged him and other freeholders to prevent 'the ruin of the borough', and the confrontation turned violent as two aldermen mandated to fill the ditch were roughly thrown into it by Combe, who 'sat laughing on horseback and said they were good football players' but 'puritan knaves'.[19] In *Bingo* one of the protestors who cry for liberty is shot dead in the snow, while Shakespeare frets about the ice in his own soul: 'I must be very cold ... Every writer writes in other men's blood.'[20] These winter words may well be melodramatic, but they underline Bond's message, which is that Shakespeare's creative freedom, as the sovereignty of an artist who sits serenely cultivating his own garden, is the aesthetic interest earned from a deadly non-commitment:

> I howled when they suffered, but they were whipped and hanged so that I could be free. That is the right question: not why did I sign one piece of paper ... Stolen things have no value. Pride and arrogance are the same when they're stolen. Even serenity.[21]

'It pays to sit in a garden': for Bond Shakespeare's serenity in his country garden was the stolen fruit of a ruthless privatization. From the opposite ideological perspective Jonathan Bate agrees it was this private place, and the selfishness of 'keeping to oneself', that sustained the public plays. Just as Montaigne retreated from the French court 'to read books in his tower and cultivate his vegetables', observes Bate admiringly, so 'the key to Shakespeare' is that he 'kept his counsel and retired – possibly a great deal earlier than most biographers imagine – to his garden at New Place'. This eco-critic therefore salutes 'Shakespeare the Epicurean' as a follower of the philosopher Epicurus, whose 'garden was private property' and whose quiet advice to 'hide thyself' disconnected happiness from citizenship. If the refusal to participate in civic life was what the Greeks termed *idiocy*, Shakespeare was the greatest 'militant idiot', enthuses Bate.[22] The insistence here that an autonomous and autotelic literature grounded in private property is nevertheless *non-political* calls to mind Baudelaire's characterization of 'art-for-art's-sake' as a 'puerile utopia'.[23] But it also reinforces Hawkes's point that the really pressing question prompted by the steely self-containment portrayed in *Bingo* is not the naive one about how a man who wrote such plays about the tragedy of sovereign self-centredness could 'behave as he did in the face of suffering humanity. The more probing enquiry asks how could he not?'[24]

'How long have I been dead?' asks Bond's Shakespeare before he kills himself. It is a question that haunts every biography of a writer who, in the closing words of James Shapiro's *1599: A Year in the Life of William Shakespeare*, 'held the keys that opened the hearts and minds of others, even as he kept a lock on what he revealed himself'.[25] W.H. Auden thought a poet ought to 'Sing of human unsuccess / In a rapture of distress'.[26] But in Shakespeare's case his indifference to unsuccess is the more unsettling in the enclosure conflict because of the social relief organized by his neighbours, who mustered on behalf of the protests the festive 'welcome and protection' [*Lear*, 3,6,85] he invoked in his plays when they 'paid the participants, furnished them with food and drink, and provided music for their amusement'.[27] Thus the draper Arthur Cawdrey assured Combe 'he would never consent without the Town', and 'had rather lose his land than their good wills'.[28] The Cawdreys were recusants with cause to regret 'No night is now with hymn or carol blessed' [*Dream*, 2,1,102]. But the 'good will' they mobilised did in fact defeat the enclosers, when a day after their men had been mocked a carnival troop of women and children marched out at night and levelled the ditches. Combe persisted in depopulating Welcombe; but the Borough lodged a staying-order, and in April 1616 he was finally vanquished when the Lord Chief Justice, Sir Edward Coke, commanded him to 'set his heart at rest, he should neither enclose nor lay down his common arable land so long as he [Coke] served the King'.[29] Shakespeare, or the human shell in which the writer resided, passed away on 23 April, leaving nothing at all in his will to his Greene 'cousins', yet bequeathing grasping Combe his ceremonial sword. And Katherine Duncan-Jones concludes that this 'selfish landowner's view' was of a piece with his minimal bequest to the poor and failure to set up a charitable trust.[30] Truly, the hospitable name of Welcombe was a misnomer for the frosty scene of Shakespeare's own farewell.

Silence in court

We are all familiar with the Proustian notion that the artist puts the best of himself into his art; but the shock of the Welcombe controversy is that this possible glimpse of the worst side of Shakespeare provides such a contrast to the way we like to picture the man whose plays speak to us so urgently of the plight of 'poor naked wretches' and the hospitality owed to 'houseless poverty' [*Lear*, 3,4,26–9]. It does, however, contextualize the problem his plays confront of squaring sovereignty with democracy. As the entrepreneurial investor operates behind scenes as an invisible agent, the episode even seems to be a paradigm of Shakespearean dramaturgy, where an almost modernist investment in the aesthetic in terms of a decision that never comes is consistently foreclosed, as this case was decided by the Lord Chief Justice, via recourse to the archaic power of the king. The very name of Welcome figures in this sense a tension that drives so many Shakespeare plays, between the symbolic *representation* of some impersonal abstract ideal and the embodied *presence* of a concrete personal reality. That Coke, the great champion of the normative Common Law, upheld the community by invoking the exception of royal prerogative therefore only confirms the mysterious workings of the political theology that, in the eyes of recent critics, the whole of Shakespearean drama is designed to adumbrate: 'that what is abolished internally, the *shelter* of the rule of law, returns in the real of the exception as *exposure* to the pure force of law'.[31] Thus, though it looks as if Shakespeare died playing for time in the greatest conflict of his age, sympathetic commentators can take heart from the fact that this delaying tactic proved shrewd: thanks to the sovereign decision of the Lord Chief Justice, in the end there would indeed be 'nothing done' at all.

'There will be nothing done': taken out of context Shakespeare's words read like a premonition of Samuel Beckett's 'Nothing to be done'. So in *Bingo* they are ironized when the dramatist dies repeating the question, 'Was anything done?' And Bond's bitter aftertaste is shared by biographers, who are forced to concede that while the battle for Welcombe was a 'victory for the men, women and children of the borough who rose against a rapacious local grandee' it was the owner of New Place who did nothing at all.[32] Such is the fastidiously *refraining* Shakespeare, too, of Charles Nicholl's *The Lodger*: a searching study of the only other extant documentary record of the Bard's own voice, his testimony in the 1612 Mountjoy case, when he withheld the facts from the Court of Requests with a similar taciturnity or tact. The stakes in this Jacobean French farce were not nearly so high: a dowry he had brokered for the 1604 marriage of his London landlord's apprentice to a daughter of the Huguenot house. But his testimony in the courtroom, when he claimed under oath not to be able to remember the sum, was flatly contradicted by a subsequent witness, who stated he had gone recently 'to Shakespeare to understand the truth', and learned that 'as he remembered' it was 'about £50', to leave the identical suspicion that (as the judge solemnly advised the jury on a similarly uncomfortable occasion when Beckett himself took the stand) the dramatist 'does not strike one as a witness on whose word one would place a great deal of reliance':[33]

> He went 'to Shakespeare to understand the truth': something many have done since … This seems to imbue [Shakespeare's] deposition with a note of betrayal, a refusal to involve himself. He was probably the only person who could swing the court … But he does not. Caution prevails: a man must be careful what he says in a court of law. In his failure to remember, his shrug of non-involvement, he sides with the unforgiving father and against the spurned daughter. And so the deposition, a unique [sic] record of Shakespeare speaking, contains also this sour note of silence. He follows the example of his own Paroles … whose last words are, 'I will not speak what I know' [*All's Well*, 5,3,263]. 'Mr Words' has spoken enough.[34]

'He can say nothing touching any part or point': for Nicholl, this last entry in the legal record sums up not merely Shakespeare's excessive obedience in the Mountjoy proceedings to the customary order, 'Silence in court', but the cold-hearted detachment that characterizes all his deeds and works, an indifference sealed in the hurried, perfunctory signature appended to his deposition: 'Willm Shaks'. It is with this 'frozen gesture' of a scrawl 'abruptly concluded with an omissive flourish' that Nicholl opens and closes *The Lodger*, since its carelessness seems to him to epitomize the callous aloofness of the unsatisfactory witness he calls 'the gentleman upstairs': 'The pen blotches on the 'k' and tails off … It will do. It will get him out of that courtroom, away from all these questions and quarrels … The signature attests his presence at that moment, but in his mind he is already leaving'. In an earlier study the biographer had expressly praised Christopher Marlowe as a 'non-commitant', who belonged 'to both sides, and to neither'; but here his last glimpse of a busy Shakespeare bidding curt good day to the litigants evokes an entire lifetime of emotional and moral withdrawal: 'He walks down to the wharf at Westminster Stairs to catch a boat downriver. He does not know if he will see them again, and we do not know if he did.'[35] But Nicholl is, of course, not alone in discerning in Paroles his creator's self-portrait as the 'actor with nothing inside'.[36] His picture of a calculating non-combatant matches the image of 'Ungentle Shakespeare' that has become standard ever since Bond's play was produced, of the shifty tax-evader in that upstairs room, who has seen and heard everything but lives out the artful dodging of Matthew Arnold's sonnet: 'We ask and ask – Thou smilest and art still, / Out-topping knowledge'.[37]

In 1975 Samuel Schoenbaum could still pity the genius 'of superhuman powers' as a 'baffled mortal' when faced by the 'sordid and mercenary' scandal in the court of law.[38] But Ackroyd reflects a recent impatience when he complains that the Mountjoy case shows how whenever he is called to account Shakespeare stays noncommittal, immunising himself from queries with studied neutrality: 'He withdraws; he becomes almost invisible'.[39] Thus it sounds here as though the dramatist was again simply happy to repeat whatever was put to him. So he regularly features in biographies now as an 'Unpolitical Man', whose shirking of the weight of his own time is a slipperiness that could only serve what Bond calls 'the Goneril society'.[40] Shakespeare's playing dead to his interrogators has become the biographical equivalent, in fact, of his most famous character's hesitation about killing Claudius, and in hostile critiques, of Hamlet's sadistic postponement of revenge until he can 'trip him that his heels may kick at heaven' [*Hamlet, 3,4,93*]. As Margreta de Grazia writes, the question 'great minds have been asking' for centuries is 'How could this diabolic desire be reconciled with the nobility and decency of Hamlet's character?' But the analogy with his Prince of Hesitation also associates Shakespeare's depersonalization with the answers that 'our most sophisticated literary critics' devise when they recast the old question, and account for Hamlet's delay 'in terms not of his inability to perform his dead father's command, but of his inability to *refuse* to do so'.[41] Then the poet's silence in court could be heard as a key to a dramaturgy stalled by the weight of such responsibility, like the self-suppressing reticence his editors ascribe to Beckett:

as if so much suffering witnessed had put a cap forever on a merely personal expression ... as if, perhaps, the sight of so much brutal activity had confirmed him for ever in his inclination to a – however paradoxically rigorous and positively charged – *passivity*.[42]

Like John Donne preaching to startled congregations that he was not all there, Shakespeare's seemingly characterological absenteeism has become the ironic hinge connecting the author to his works.[43] Yet as Greenblatt remarks, the notion of his superhuman invisibility has to reckon with the fact that this writer famous for anonymity ended his last unaided play with a magus abdicating his art to return home not to lord over his neighbours but to die, and that, in contrast to Machiavelli or Montaigne, he never did retreat in his writing onto the Olympian heights of some ivory tower, nor ever 'showed signs of boredom at the small talk, trivial pursuits, or foolish games of ordinary people'.[44] His, in every sense, *ruling idea* that the world is but 'A stage where every man must play a part' [*Merchant, 1,1,78*] never meant Shakespeare ceased to dream of a freedom stripped of sovereignty over others, or of a service without servitude. And his withdrawing 'bearing' does take on a less reprehensible quality in light of theoretical debates about the decision, the aesthetic and the political, and the tension between action and acting that he himself prefigures whenever he has the player in the middle of a speech explain how he 'must pause till it come back' [*Julius, 3,2,104*]. Then Shakespeare's active passivity can be seen to underpin an entire *dramatics of attention*, dedicated to the proposition that, as Derrida demurred, undecidability does not mean indecision, but the 'suspense and suspension that freely decides to apply – or not – a rule' according to the infinite task of an impossible justice yet to come. What J. Hillis Miller says about Derrida's own *refrain* of 'don't count me in' has, indeed, a Shakespearean resonance:

> Derrida expresses the concept of an absolute right not to answer, associated by him especially with democracy and with its concomitant, literature, in its modern sense as the right to say or write anything and not be held responsible for it ... This gesture of refraining is Derrida's fundamental and defining act, his ground without ground.[45]

For Derrida the interest in an impossible justice was the dis-interest of sovereignty that goes by the name of deconstruction. 'The subject desists', in this philosophy; and such *desistance* does seem to bring us closer to a writer whose entire work presents itself as kind of memorial reconstruction, a recollection in which 'The play's the thing' to arrest the rush to judgement, and 'catch the conscience of the King' [*Hamlet, 2,2,581*] of sovereign selfhood.[46] Thus a poststructuralist criticism that follows the unstoppable Derrida and Gilles Deleuze in ruminating upon Herman Melville's scrivener Bartleby for continually responding 'I would prefer not to', finds in Shakespeare's actively passive 'inability to refuse' a decision to be undecided that *neither refuses nor accepts anything*, yet that thereby amounts, as Giorgio Agamben says of the cussedness of the pen-pusher, to a 'formula of potentiality'.[47] The dramatist then becomes the author of 'Jewish' texts in which 'we will never know exactly what took place', since the 'something after' [*3,1,80*] sovereignty thankfully never shows up, but in which this very incompleteness shows there can be 'fulfilment in non-fulfilment'.[48] So the Shakespeare who emerges killing time from this weak messianicity is another awkward customer whose writing might well be a 'representation of a historical state of emergency that requires a decision', but whose queer strength 'lies not in resolving the historical crisis (as we see from Hamlet's indecision) but in making it powerfully real'. As Victoria Kahn remarks, if sovereign is he who decides the exception in the charismatic state, Shakespeare's staging of the homologies between acting and action can be viewed as a refusal either to obey or reject sovereignty, whether of the self or state, and so as a veritably 'decisive indecisiveness'.[49] The whole of Shakespearean theatre thus becomes, in this Hebraicizing thinking, a dismantling of literary authorship or rendering of sovereign selfhood inoperative:

> I'll join with black despair against my soul
> And to myself become an enemy.
>
> [*Richard III, 2,2,36–7*]

Historian Paul Veyne likens Shakespeare to Michel Foucault for his 'sceptic renouncement' of a self-presence that would make sense of the world.[50] For at a time when humanist patrons such as Hamlet are ordering the actors to 'Suit the action to the word, the word to the action' [*Hamlet, 3,2,16*], it seems Shakespeare takes pride in sabotaging 'the name of action' [*3,1,90*] by splitting signs from things and redacting his own words, 'the magical stuff he could always produce, and can still produce if he chooses', but which, in

Nicholl's account, 'increasingly he does not'.[51] The recent 'Jewish' critical move has therefore been to affiliate these works with the Baroque *Trauerspiel* studied by Walter Benjamin, in which the sovereign who 'holds history like a sceptre in his hand' is incapable of deciding the state of emergency, as dramas about unkingly rulers such as Richard II, whose vacillation heralds the passage of sovereignty into the body of the people in the age of parliaments and peacemakers.[52] For those who follow Benjamin, such a theatrics of hesitation thereby aligns these texts with the epochal divestment of majesty described by Ernst Kantorowicz in *The King's Two Bodies*, when the incarnational fiction that 'the king never dies', because the immortal office survives the mortal man, became the symbolic instrument to transfer royal power from the king's natural body to the corporate body of the Crown, and so to establish that 'there is more reality in such theatrical appearances (of the court and the theatre) than in our everyday reality'.[53] Thus in *Shakespeare and Impure Aesthetics* Hugh Grady describes Shakespearean drama as given over to the same logic of allegorical deferral as the *Trauerspiel*, and proposes that its creator anticipated Kant's utopian conception of the lying counter-factuality of the aesthetic as a harbinger of the white lie of universal peace. For if his pre-aesthetic inhibitions are still betrayed by the resounding silence of 'what is *not* attempted by Shakespeare – a head-on critique of the power structure of his society', his playhouse is 'already an aesthetic space', in this neo-Kantian critique: 'an autonomous sphere of fanciful, pleasure-giving cultural production'.[54]

Read in the light of Kantian theories of the public sphere developed after Benjamin by thinkers like Jürgen Habermas, Shakespeare's fabled impersonality can be seen as prophetic of the Enlightenment project to secure a space for critical thought free of executive power, or rather of what Terry Eagleton terms *the ideology of the aesthetic*, where 'Disinterestedness means indifference not to others' interests, but to one's own'.[55] That the creator of vacillators like Richard distrusted the simulcral ghostliness of the emergent public sphere, however, and remained conflicted about the overthrow of the *ancien régime* of personal presence by one of impersonal representation, is implied by the frequency with which he exposed as inauthentic fictive substitutions for 'The King himself': 'Another king! They grow like Hydra's heads ... What art thou that counterfeit'st the person of a king?' [*1Henry IV, 5,4,24–8*].[56] For as René Girard and others insist, Shakespeare's agenda is actually 'to postpone for the whole duration of the lengthy Elizabethan play' a sovereign outcome that the investiture crisis never leaves in doubt.[57] So an opposing analysis has emphasized how 'A substitute shines brightly as a king' in these plays, 'Until a king be by' [*Merchant*, *5,1,93–4*], in a scenario which anticipates the realpolitik of Carl Schmitt that 'the norm is destroyed by the exception'.[58] In particular, Schmitt's book *Hamlet or Hecuba*, where the Nazi lawyer argued that the Prince of Denmark finally asserts his 'sacred blood right' over the effete constitutionalism of the aesthetic, when he gives Fortinbras a sovereign's 'dying voice' [*5,2,308*], has been hailed by those who insist that in its 'resistance to representation' this drama 'leads in the direction of absolutism', and upholds the political theology that 'There's such divinity doth hedge a king' [*4,5,122–3*] that 'the cease of majesty' [*3,3,15*] must jeopardize 'the whole social and cosmic order'.[59] As Eric Santner puts it, the implication of this counter-reading is that Shakespeare's staging of the separation of the king's two bodies does not therefore simply reveal the emperor naked, but rather makes us realize how much more of the moribund 'royal remains' malinger in our own body politics of authority or authorship than we had ever imagined or desired.[60]

Between Schmitt and Kantorowicz, presence and representation, twenty-first-century Shakespeare studies sometimes sound like an unconscious reprise of the celebrated debate by the philosophers Martin Heidegger and Ernst Cassirer at Davos in 1929 over the primacy of being or symbolic forms. For on the one hand the recent turn to political theology has thrown into relief the many different ways in which these plays stage the 'fundamental impasse' that 'putting the People in the place of the King cannot ultimately be done', since 'democracy and sovereignty are at the same time in contradiction and inseparable from each other'.[61] Yet on the other, the rupture of sovereignty by exposure to the other from which time comes has been the preoccupation of Derrida and his followers; so what a Derridean approach does is return us to the Shakespearean aesthetic as a *great refusal* of sovereignty, and to the artwork as 'the medium of a subjective spirit', in Theodor Adorno's definition, 'thrown back upon itself'.[62] It does this by highlighting the problem posed by Shakespeare of *his own literary sovereignty*, as an unhappy function of that affectless and differentiated 'psychical distance' that in a classic article of 1912 the psychologist Edward

Bullough called 'the filtration of sentiments when we are overcome by a feeling that "all the world's a stage"'.[63] So, rather than associating these plays with such a singular overview as that of the invisible author, *Free Will* proposes that Shakespeare remained in humble quest of a *creaturely sovereignty* that may have eluded him, but that he always dreamed would 'give delight and hurt not' [*Tempest, 3,1,131*]. It certainly remains possible, as I concluded my book *Shakespeare in French Theory: King of Shadows*, that the taciturn 'gentleman upstairs' *decided* to 'keep mum to keep peace' in the Mountjoy affair, knowing that silence is golden whenever speech is enforced.[64] 'Faith, I know more than I'll speak', his Paroles discloses [*255*]. Yet such canniness about his own self-centredness and sovereign immunity also hints at how 'Mr Words' was *interested in disinterest* in more ways than one.

A neutral heart

'Who can be ... Loyal and neutral in a moment?' [*Macbeth, 2,3,105–6*]: the writer who based his great tragedy of hesitation on the paused consciousness when the man of action stood 'like a neutral to his will and matter' and 'did nothing' [*Hamlet, 2,2,461*], was clearly interested in disinterest as an act, a performative way of mediating between the public and the private, or the subject and his times. Though it is usual to claim that the disinterestedness which would become the basis of the aesthetic was unavailable to a society conditioned to find experience 'productive, purposeful', we can in fact trace in these texts the great paradigm shift in the idea of disinterest itself from a public concept – as when Richard declares that 'impartial are our eyes and ears' [*Richard II, 1,1,115*]; the Lord Chief Justice esteems 'impartial conduct' [*2Henry IV, 5,2,36*]; and the Duke assures Angelo that 'In this I'll be impartial; be you judge' [*Measure, 5,1,165*] – to the private one with which York acquiesces in a political revolution: 'I cannot mend it ... But since I cannot ... I do remain as neuter' [*2,3,152–8*]; or by which Gloucester's tip-off comes 'from one that's of a neutral heart, / And not from one opposed' [*Lear, 3,7,48*].[65]

As Sean Gaston has shown, the modern concept of disinterest, impartiality or freedom from prejudice as an essentially private state of mind was well advanced in Shakespeare's England, where Bacon's belief that the law should 'disinterest' the refractory individual such as the duellist in his own interest was giving way to the Cartesian notion, affirmed by Milton, that 'The mind is it own place, and in itself / Can make a Heav'n of Hell, a Hell of Heav'n'.[66] But what the patently vested interests in his references imply, and Macbeth's question, 'Who can be both loyal and neutral?' under-lines, is that Shakespeare had long anticipated Hobbes's post-Cartesian awareness that *disinterest can never be disinterested* because indifferentism is itself governed by 'different passions' or 'prejudices of opinion'.[67] The dramatist thus became the best critic of the *performance of disinterest* that conditioned his own literary sovereignty. For to abstain and 'be neutral with him', as one of his two noble kinsmen remarks of their attitude to the actual sovereign, is as rebellious as 'to oppose' [*Two Noble, 1,2,100*].

Considering the difficulty of steering a middle course when the Stuart state split apart a generation later, and hopes for 'composing a third way' were swept aside by the discovery that 'No neutrality is admitted, both parts resolve that those who are not with them are against them', Shakespeare's interest in disinterest looks his-torically determined.[68] As Girard writes, his 'plague on both your houses' [*Romeo, 3,1,99*] 'must not be void of political significance'; and historians have in fact found that since 'the great majority of Catholics were neutral' all through the Civil War, over half the gentry of the dramatist's Catholic-leaning West Midlands shared the pacifism of the squire who protested that 'I never had any inten-tion of taking up arms of neither side, my Reason leads me to both King and Parliament'. Belligerents scorned schemes to construct 'a middle way of accommodation' as the apathy of those who 'love their pudding at home better than musket and pike abroad'. But Shakespeare appears with his own indifferentism to have prepared the discursive ground for neutralists like Sir James Vaughan, who agonized how 'to secure himself from trouble, at the same time doing no harm to the king and country, but as much good as he could to both'.[69] Francis Barker complained that in the world-historical choice between king and parliament 'Shakespeare never seems quite to know which he supports', but that he always escapes this predicament with 'a commitment to domination', of which 'sovereignty is a polite form'. Like Schmitt acting as 'Hitler's Crown Jurist', on this dark view, Shakespeare ultimately decides for the decision. Yet the dramatist's Hobbesian awareness of the partiality of a 'neutral heart' suggests he was fully alive to the self-motivated interest in such disinterestedness when he made the antisocial consequences of the sovereign subject 'the subject of tragedy'.[70]

Shakespeare had a professional interest in the way that 'enterprises of great pitch and moment ... lose the name of action' [*Hamlet, 3,1,86–8*]. Long ago Caroline Spurgeon related this fascination with circling inaction to the negative dialectic by which 'currents turn awry' [89] in an image which recurs in his plays of the swirling River Avon; as Mary Crane detects a palindromic 'to and back' [*Antony, 1,4,46*] thinking wired into the Bard's brain.[71] Less fancifully, Peter Platt attributes Shakespeare's chiastic backtracking to a 'culture of paradox' in Elizabethan law; while Paola Pugliatti thinks the oppositional contrarianism inculcated by the grammar school technique of arguing both sides – *in ultramque partem* – was what freed this punster from determinacy, as it promoted a type of ambidextrous logic-chopping known as 'Probation' that required a distrust of settled positions or received ideas: the 'probing' mind perceives all possibilities while postponing final solutions. Whatever the psychological origin, then, for these critics it was his affirmative openness to the event, a capacity to be 'all to all' [*Macbeth, 3,4,91*] signalling a queer sense of the doubleness of the world, which allowed Shakespeare, as the deconstructor of determinacy, to put meaning in suspense, for 'drama *is* conflict and antithesis'.[72] So the chameleon-like playwright was a forerunner, on this view, of those Civil War writers whose verbal anamorphoses, negativities, and 'words of avoidance', honed to outwit the censors in the time of emergency, had the unintended bonus, according to Annabel Patterson, of generating the modern concept of literature as *itself* a permanent state of exception, a discursive liberty 'with rules all of its own'.[73]

Pugliatti distinguishes what she terms the dramatist's 'probationary' strategy from the 'rabbit/duck' deadlock of contradictory gestalts that for earlier critics reduced the dramatist to perpetual paralysis. The Shakespeare we glimpse in such accounts resembles rather an improvising musician, who never forgets his 'inability to refuse' the *performance as event*. Thus Patricia Parker relishes how his preposterous '*arsie-versy*' wordplay turns sequence, sequitur and succession into endless possibility; as Kiernan Ryan believes his polysemic quibbling crucial to keep a vital 'breathing space open and hold clock time at bay for both the actors and audience'. For Ryan, from the instant when Egeon is reprieved from execution in

The Comedy of Errors Shakespeare creates 'breathing space' by *extemporizing* or 'speaking out of time', so as to evade closure and ensure there remains, as his clown Touchstone says, 'much virtue in If' [*As You*, 5,4,92], for 'procrastination is the thief of time'. Thus, Hamlet's improvisation on the arts of delay must proceed in the guise of a fool whose antic disposition and equivocation allow him 'to stall tragedy and postpone catastrophe'.[74] And these critiques of Shakespeare's work as a Sheherazade-type filibuster, like his cagey ambiguity in the real-time drama of the courts, do appear to be borne out by the theatrical 'pause' [*Hamlet*, 2,2,466] with which he sustains the impossibility that 'What's to come is still unsure' [*Twelfth*, 2,3,45], and so requires faith in the performance as a *happening*; like those 'serenely puzzling' final lines about unfulfilled desire, delay, deferral, and again the need to *bear* the weight of given time, in his definitive curtain-call or final comeback, which critics compare to Wittgenstein's maxim that 'Wherein we cannot speak, therein we must be silent', and that Nicholl quotes at the end of *The Lodger* as the ultimate dramatic tease, 'before the characters walk off':[75]

O you heavenly charmers!
What things you make of us! For what we lack
We laugh, for what we have, are sorry; still
Are children in some kind. Let us be thankful
For that which is, and with you leave dispute
That are above question. Let's go off
And bear us like the time.

[*Two Noble*, 5,6,131–7]

The readiness is all

'There is no literature without a *suspended* relation to meaning', Derrida airily advised; but pursued by his 'bear', Shakespeare exits from the stage of history without ever giving *anyone* a satisfactory account.[76] As Shapiro writes, he had seen enough judicial suppression to know the risks if he did not play safe in this way, since of all the major dramatists of his generation he alone avoided a run-in with the authorities: 'He had seen Thomas Kyd broken by torture on the rack, Christopher Marlowe probably assassinated, Ben Jonson imprisoned'.[77] In particular, it was the horrific fate of Marlowe, according to Harold Bloom, that stunned Shakespeare into becoming 'the major master of ellipsis in the history of the theatre', with 'dumb thoughts speaking in effect' [Sonnet 85], so 'we have to interpret what he leaves out'.[78] Critics date the liberation of this Shostakovich-like survivor, therefore, to his improvisation of a suspended consciousness in the dying days of Queen Elizabeth that is enacted in *Julius Caesar*, the play about the 'tide in the affairs of men' [4,2,270] where Brutus realizes that 'Between the acting of a thing / And the first motion, all the interim is / Like a phantasma or a hideous dream' [2,1,63–5]. For it is there, in imaging openness to the coming event in terms of a player poised before 'the acting of a thing', but ready to 'bear' the prompt of given time, that Shakespeare first analogizes the absolutism of the autonomous 'I' to that of the absolutist ruler, and, in a conceptualization paralleling the act of regicide, deconstructs the aporetic contradictions of the sovereign self. This Shakespearean sensation of the 'interim' is, in fact, a striking anticipation of Derrida's famous discussion of the interval between presence and the present that Plato termed the *khôra*:

> An interval must separate the present from what it is not in order for the present to be itself, but this interval that constitutes it as present must, by the same token, divide the present in and of itself, thereby also dividing, along with the present, everything that is thought on the basis of the present, that is every being ... In constituting itself, in dividing itself dynamically, this interval is what might be called *spacing*, the becoming-space of time or the becoming-time of space.[79]

Brutus's anticipation of Caesar's assassination is often misconstrued as though it was here that Shakespeare instantiates the interiority of sovereign selfhood, and as if the gap the Roman confronts 'Between the acting of a thing / And the first motion' was a premonition of Eliot's modernist sensation that 'Between the motion / And the act / Falls the shadow'. But Christopher Pye has pointed out that this hiatus has to be read not as the mere space between thought and action but 'an undoing of the act as such' that has 'the nature of an insurrection' [69] against agency itself; and Paul Yachnin notes how the shift from action to inaction was an essential move in the disempowerment of Shakespearean theatre as politically innocuous.[80] For this revolution inside 'the state of man' [67] seems to have given the writer the idea of playing itself as such a rebellion, a revolt against sovereignty, within which, as Hamlet sees, 'a man's life's no more than to say "one"' in the succession of other parts. With this 'interim' [*Hamlet, 5,2,75*] it is as if Shakespeare puts '"nothing" at the structural centre of the text', observes Eagleton.[81] So this instant of 'tongue-tied patience' [Sonnet 140] should not be confused with the separation of the aesthetic from the community, still less with the ipseity of sovereign presence, the mastering '"I can" or power of a self to constitute itself'.[82] Rather than such self-presence, the self exposed in these untimely Shakespearean meditations seems to shadow the active inaction that, in a hypnotic riff on mind, body and the tempi of thinking, *The Philosopher's Touch*, François Noudelmann attributes to pianistic improvisation:

> This is not some partitioning of public and private activities. Rather, it is a negotiation between the time of the now and the times of the imag- ination, of writing, and of feeling ... Playing the piano is part of these discrete temporalities, which escape any discourse of mastery ...[83]

A pianist improvises, according to Noudelmann, not to master reality but to explore in the time of the cadenzas his ambivalence towards the time of the real. Likewise, in Shakespeare's representa- tion of presence he never loses sight of the self as performance or the play as event. In fact, shortly after Brutus's hesitation, Antony *pre- tends* to 'pause' [*Julius, 3,2,104*] by being similarly lost for words. This is the kind of pose that made Derrida suspicious of theories of performativity, as implying a further level of mastery 'which neu- tralizes the event, that is to say, what happens'. But Shakespeare's performance theory always involves the stage fright generated by fear of loss that is precisely the opening towards the event Derrida commended as 'a force without power'.[84] For there is no per- formativity in these plays that is not haunted by this failure. The unmastering entailed in such a prevaricating 'interim', the castrating aporia when the actor dried, and 'like a neutral to his will matter, / Did nothing', seems in fact to be keyed to specific conditions at the Globe, where 'we often see the orb below as hush as death' [*Hamlet, 2,2,461–7*] in 'patient expectation' [*Julius, 1,1,40*] of what comes next. Thus, even as it recollects itself, the Shakespearean self is turned towards the other for a prompt, or begging to be released from its own part 'With the help of your good hands' [*Tempest, Epi.10*]. For if the actor who recalls the 'full disgrace' of being 'out' of his part [*Coriolanus, 5,3,41–2*] is to be believed, it was with the opening of the new house in 1599 that Shakespeare grasped

the paradoxical potential of 'a character suspended for virtually
the whole length of a play' *in wait* for a 'motive and cue' [*Hamlet,*
2,2,538] he is unable to refuse.[85]

'This silence ... shall be most my glory, being dumb' [Sonnet 83]:
Shakespeare always values 'tongue-tied simplicity' over the 'rattling
tongue / Of saucy and audacious eloquence', and punctuates his
plays with scenes of 'fearful modesty' as the performers 'shiver and
look pale, / Make periods in the midst of sentences, / And throttle
their practised accents in their fears' [*Dream, 5,1,102–3*]. Each new
beginning, theorized Richard Helgerson in *Self-Crowned Laureates,*
'brings a renewal of self-presentational presence'; but the 'thing of
nothing' [*Hamlet, 4,2,26–8*] exposed by the halting 'interim' of the
actor's discomposing loss of words in the plays Shakespeare wrote
for the Globe is the ipseity of sovereignty itself. So, rather than
defying sovereignty with the finality of a 'bloody period' [*Othello,*
5,2,366], he would put 'the promis'd end' [*King Lear, 5,3,263*] on
indefinite hold with all the patient tactics of delay: 'banishment, disguise, exile, trading of identities, and, in *Hamlet,* the active powers
of indecision'.[86] As Derrida intuited, the reason 'the time is out of
joint' [*Hamlet, 1,5,189*] from this instant on Shakespeare's stage is
therefore because, by defying the *telos* of 'a good end' [*4,5,181*], and
leaving so much to be desired in the to-come of what has yet to be
revealed, 'the rest' [*5,2,300*] is held for ever in reserve: 'It won't be
long. But how long it is taking.' All that matters is to 'Bear free and
patient thoughts': [*King Lear, 4,6,80*]: 'to have understood a call (or
an order, desire or demand)' of the other.[87] Just as, for Derrida, the
dimension of the *à-venir* was a messianic opening through which
no messiah will ever enter, and for the late Heidegger all thinking was a kind of waiting, so in the veritably 'late' Shakespeare,
'The end crowns all / And that old common arbitrator Time / Will
one day end it' [*Troilus, 4,7,106*]; which means that instead of
self-presence, as every bluffing actor knows, 'The readiness is all'
[*Hamlet, 5,2,160*].

'I will be patient ... I will not be myself ... I am all patience ... I
will be patient; outwardly I will' [*Troilus, 5,2,45–63*]: Derrida was
like Benjamin in reading the vigil of the 'guard of patience' [*53*] in
Shakespearean theatre as 'an opening in the passage of time' at the
midnight hour, when 'time stands still like the tongue of a scale:
"'Tis now the very witching time of night"' [*Hamlet, 3,2,358*].[88]
So, for deconstruction Shakespeare's given time becomes not only

the interminable Beckettian waiting-game of the Jacobean tragedies, where, as Frank Kermode saw, 'everything tends towards a conclusion that does not occur', and even death is 'terribly delayed', but a protraction of 'the wholesome end' [*King Lear, 5,3,263*] that puts in limbo everything written for the Globe, as though these characters had all the time in the world.[89] Rather than ever being entirely present, Troilus, Othello, Macbeth, King Lear and even Prospero are *beside themselves* with the necessity for patience. As Hélène Cixous perceived, the quotidian question 'What is it o'clock?' [*Julius, 2,1,191; 2,2,114; 2,4,24; 5,3,108*] therefore becomes the most imperative issue on this stage; so what also hangs about the endlessly unopened door, the uncanny *attentisme* of such a 'strange-disposéd time' [*1,3,33*], in these accounts, is a troubled impatience with the illusion of abstracted presence Descartes registered when he inaugurated the very idea of an absent-minded disinterest: 'I will now shut my eyes, stop my ears, and withdraw my senses'.[90]

Shakespeare was, of course, not the first to pathologize the infuriating silence of the 'Spartan dog' [*Othello, 5,2,371*] who hides himself behind impenetrable lies, as Katharine Eisaman Maus demonstrates in her study of interiority. But what was novel in plays he wrote after 1599 was a sense that the interior life is a danger to the exterior precisely because its space of freedom stays stubbornly unrepresentable, as Hamlet avows: 'I have that within which passes show' [*Hamlet, 1,2,85*]. So Maus relates how Shakespeare adopted the ancient analogy of childbirth and artistic labour, but deepened the commonplace of being 'great with child to speak' by gesturing to the opacity of the womb, where fecundity is 'dependent on its hiddenness'.[91] There were suspect affinities, Maus notes, between this recourse to the dark abyss of literary sovereignty and Christian tactics of secrecy, especially the Jesuit survival trick of verbal equivocation.[92] And its unaccountable diving and weaving were in fact keyed to the apparently *pointless* mode of delivery that a crypto-Catholic such as Ben Jonson disliked in Shakespeare himself, precisely because its facile articulacy seemed to be so *purposely* free of purpose:

> I remember the players have often mentioned it as an honour to Shakespeare, that in his writing (whatsoever he penned) he never blotted out line. My answer hath been, 'Would he had blotted a thousand!' ... He was, indeed, honest, and of an open and free nature; had an excellent phantasy, brave notions, and gentle expressions,

wherein he flowed with that facility that sometime it was necessary he should be stopped.[93]

Jonson, who considered 'rashness of talking should not only be retarded by the guard, and watch of our heart, but be fenced in', and himself 'rewrote Shakespearean inwardness as secrecy', was appalled by this writing of the self to infinity, the garrulousness it was easy to mistake for careless talk.[94] As Wittgenstein also objected: 'His pieces give me an impression as of having been *dashed off* by someone who can permit himself *anything* so to speak. And I don't like it.'[95] But for a post-structuralism that prizes an 'unstaunchable textual productivity', as Adorno did Beckett's *Endgame*, as the 'resistant art of modernity', it is just this 'omissive flourish' by a creator of language that never stops that generates the Tourette-like subjectivity effect Joel Fineman termed Shakespeare's perjured 'I': presence in *misrepresentation*.[96] Like Nicholl, Finemann detected this perjury in the dash with which the poet docked his signature to 'Willm Shakspere' or 'Wm Shakspē' documents, a self-abbreviation that betrayed the hypocritical 'relation between "Will" and "writing"'. For the penman who 'never blotted a line' was the same botcher who conceded that 'What wit sets down is blotted straight with Will' [*Lucrece, 1299*], so knew his letters were blotched and deconstructed by the speed with which he signed himself a 'Will in overplus' [Sonnet 135]. As Jonathan Goldberg reminds us, in Shakespeare's six surviving signatures he never spells his name the same way twice, as though his only sense of being is in the protocols of a secretary hand.[97] That manual grasp on collective identity fits a writer for whom community was sealed by the handclasp and loss of agency by a severed hand.[98] So we might imagine Shakespeare as one of those authors, like Sartre, who transcend the body/mind dualism by writing in public; for Jonson's anecdote suggests a 'Will' who works as if his cursive handwriting has neither beginning nor end, but is truly a *free hand*: 'frozen in static motility, between a departure always initiated and an arrival prospectively postponed in anticipation of a destination forever deferred'.[99]

Always running on, the 'Free Will' theorists celebrate for this flight into potentiality, the irresponsible supplementation of an 'open and free nature', comes to resemble the Derrida who in a valedictory interview revealed how he never stopped writing so as to stave off death: 'This is not a striving for immortality; it's something structural. Each time I let something go, each time some trace leaves me, "proceeds" from me ... I live my death in writing.' Whenever 'I leave a piece of paper behind, I go away, I die', the dying philosopher reflected.[100] And the elective affinity is increased by Derrida's memory in *Paper Machine* of the calligraphic crisis in which he generated endless drafts with the archaic implement of 'a special drawing quill', before reluctantly 'putting a stop to them' in type, a final 'signal of separation, of severance, the official sign of departure for the public sphere'.[101] Critics stress the ontological tension in Shakespeare of 'author's pen' and 'actor's voice' [*Troilus, Pro.24*]; and Patrick Cheney sees this hybridity behind his entire strategy of 'counter-authorship'.[102] But Derrida's reminder of how even modern writers might imagine their manumission as an escape from the dead hand of a sovereign authority instrumentalized in the technology of mechanical writing, suggests Shakespeare's multifarious signatures, unreadable equivocations, destroyed manuscripts and undocumented biography might all be traces of his 'free hand' within the early modern textual economy; as if he always intended to leave no paper behind – to remain not simply another invisible controlling author but a *paperless person* – at the very moment when, as his greatest literary contemporary Miguel de Cervantes was similarly fearing, the engine of literature was becoming the monstrous new monarch of the 'paper machine'.

Paperless person

Towards the end of *Don Quixote* the Doleful Knight wanders into a busy Barcelona printing-house, 'where he saw in one place drawing of sheets, in another Correcting, in this Composing, in that mending: Finally, all the Machine that is usual in great Presses'. Here he is introduced to the Author, 'a good comely proper man' but 'somewhat ancient', whom he wishes luck before asking about the book being printed: 'they answered him that it was called *The second part of the Ingenious Knight, Don Quixote de la Mancha*'. What is disconcerting to modern readers is how the Don instantly wants his book 'turned to ashes'.[103] For as Carlos Fuentes observed, this representation of representation is surely the first time a character ever learns he is himself to become a literary product and is condemned to be a mere fiction. Thus, 'The act of reading is both the starting point and the last stop on Don Quixote's route'. For Fuentes, this episode of spooky foreboding, printed a year *after* Cervantes's death, marked the life-threatening depersonalization of literature, as it is where 'reality loses its defined frontiers, feels itself displaced, transfigured by *another* reality made out of paper and words. Where are the limits between Dunsinane Castle and Birnam Wood?' Only Shakespeare foresees the coming of the book, Fuentes believed, with the same troubled misgivings about literary posthumousness as make *Don Quixote* so *sorrowful*, and only the dramatist shares the novelist's desire to be relieved of his own sovereignty. So when Cervantes leaves open the page of his volume where the reader knows himself read and the writer written, it is easy to imagine that these two who died on the same date in 1616 were one and the same man, that 'Will Shakespeare, the comedian with a thousand faces, wrote *Don Quixote*'.[104] For what these two exact contemporaries both foresee is that the figurative birth of the sovereign author will mean the actual death of the writer himself.

Fuentes likens the Sad Knight to the Black Prince, who, confronted by the Moloch of print, also knows he is a 'paper ghost' *written* out of mere 'Words, words, words' [*Hamlet, 2,2,192*]. But the alarm at book technology that for the novelist announces 'the existence of a thing called literature' had been rung by Shakespeare in 1613 with an even closer parallel to Cervantes, when the page Fidele played by Innogen was asked to identify his missing master, and the time-frame of *Cymbeline* was punctured with a similar uncanny reply: 'Richard du Champ'. For editors tell us that this French 'champion' translates as Richard Field, the printer of Shakespeare's own poems and his Stratford schoolmate, while Fidele is the very anagram of a *faithful page*. At the time of *Cymbeline* the King's Men had just occupied the playhouse alongside Field's printing-shop in Blackfriars, where, as Adrian Johns notes, 'the topography of print could be measured in feet'.[105] Thus, no wonder that this most bookish play turns on the trope of printing as parenting; nor that its text is where a future Folio is first projected as 'the world's volume' [*3,4,137*]. The novelistic literariness of *Cymbeline* flags Shakespeare's prescience about the questions concerning print technology and artistic sovereignty in the emerging literary field. But what makes Shakespeare so resemble his Spanish double is the melancholy with which he laments the loss of the service epitomized by the faithfulness of his impossible master/page. For Richard Field would, in fact, never print him again. And without 'such another master' as this oxymoronic sovereign creature to usher his words into the definitiveness of print, Shakespeare's page would never recover its *fidelity* to life:

> There is no more such masters. I may wander
> From east to occident, cry out for service,
> Try many, all good; serve truly, never
> Find such another master.
>
> [*Cymbeline, 4,2,372–6*]

'All that he hath writ / Leaves living art, but page, to serve his wit': the play on 'page' on his memorial tablet underline what the bust above celebrates, and critical fashion would restore: the image of Shakespeare as the *master* poised quill in hand over his masterpiece, absorbed in that rapt scene of writing Jonson so resented and his editors Heminge and Condell evoked when they recalled 'His mind and hand went together, and what he thought, he uttered with that easiness that we have scarce received from him a blot in his papers'.[106] This is the Bard generated by the First Folio as 'a figure for Art itself', existing, as Leah Marcus puts it, 'in lofty separateness from the vicissitudes of life', yet in trance-like communion with the future ages; and enshrined in portraits like Virginia Woolf's, when her Orlando bursts in on 'a rather fat, rather shabby man' sitting at the servants' table, who looks right through him with 'eyes globed and clouded,' as he 'turned his pen in his fingers, this way and that way ... and then, very quickly, wrote half-a-dozen lines'.[107] And it is the popular myth of the absent-minded genius who devours reality that inspires films like *Shakespeare in Love* and *Molière*, where a love affair cues *Twelfth Night* or a month in the country *Le Bourgeois Gentilhomme*.[108] Yet the Stratford memorial also hints at Cervantine *disenchantment* with the deadliness of a paper personality, when in the image of *Cymbeline*, it insists print leaves the dramatist's 'living art' with *but* a page 'to serve his wit.' For 'Living art' is what is lost by the bookmen in *Love's Labour's Lost* to buy the sepulchral eternity of print [*1,1,1–14*], as if Shakespeare experienced directly the historic reversal that has been described by Foucault, when instead of immortality writing began to bring about the author's death.[109] So this is a tribute that adds a sharp twist to the critics' debate about whether Shakespeare ever intended his 'living art' to be *engraved*, for it confirms how at the time of his passing even his close colleagues sensed the playwright's paper sovereignty to be the eclipse of his player's humanity, experiencing the painful birth of the immortal author in Derrida's and Fuentes's terms, as the death of the mortal wit.

Together with Fidele's lost faith, Shakespeare's Stratford 'graving' throws a shadow over the theory influentially floated by Lukas Erne in *Shakespeare as Literary Dramatist*, that the playwright always desired publication of his words, and had them printed as expertly as possible, until some point about 1602 when he began to *authorize* the novel idea of a folio of collected Works. Erne admits, however, that the primary push for publication came not from Shakespeare but from 'printers, publishers, and booksellers' eager to cash in on 'an enterprise with little or no prestige'; for, as John Kerrigan stresses, it was book producers who were invested in 'customizing' plays to make them readable.[110] And what the tomb and *Cymbeline* seem to mourn is in fact the falling-away of the dead and blackened page, the printed materiality that demands the human sacrifice of theatre's 'Golden lads and lasses', who 'must, / As chimney-sweepers, come to dust' [4,2,262]. Thus, the Shakespeare who emerges from recent studies of his literary authorship is a penman who can never forget the reality that, together with soot, wormwood and urine, his ink is 'made of gall' [1,1,102].[111] And as his book and grave loom closer, so Shakespeare's apprehension about the stigma of print deepens, we deduce, and the print-shop becomes, as it does for Cervantes, not the house of life but a place of death, to add to the other perils of representation, in an age when, if the author shows his own face, he does so shyly as the trailing snail, 'whose tender horns being hit / Shrinks backward in his shelly cave' [*Venus, 1033*]. So, though Cheney glimpses 'the author at work, crafting his text out of other texts' in Ulysses' citation of 'the author's drift' [*Troilus, 3,3,108*], and Hamlet's of 'the satirical slave' he reads [*Hamlet, 2,2,196*], Richard Hillman rightly demurs that, at these two Shakespearean instants when authorship is highlighted, it is precisely 'by being withheld'.[112] For if this performer was indeed destined to be made to 'speak in print' [*Two Gents, 2,1,169*], he was also one who early grasped the get-out that the definitiveness of 'Print gave books and authors new ways to make their anonymity visible', to *hide in full view*.[113]

Our humble author

'Thus far, with rough and all-unable pen / Our bending author hath pursued the story': what is striking about Shakespeare's own idea of authorship, it emerges from those few occasions like the one in the Epilogue of *Henry V* when he takes a bow, is how his authority is 'bent' by the same bonds of subjection he gave his protagonists, who in scene after scene he imagines in an attitude not of regal self-determination or intentionality, but of 'rough and all-unable', wily yet cringing, peasant-like subservience. We like to imagine that 'Printing opened up a world previously undreamed of, in a sense of liberating writers from the constraints of aristocrats', *authorizing* an emancipation which had 'already been happening in the theatre with its paying audience'.[114] But whenever Shakespeare refers to 'the author', we notice, it is either in a traditional context of culpability – as Hamlet is said to be the 'most violent author / Of his just remove' [*Hamlet, 4,5,76*] – or the dozen times he uses the word in a modern literary sense, of authorial evasion – as when Malvolio 'will read politic authors' to 'baffle Sir Toby' [*Twelfth, 2,5,141*]. At a time when, as Johns recounts, the credibility gap opened up by printing is being bridged by a new book culture of goodwill and trust, Shakespeare's authors remain for ever associated with hermeneutic crisis, like that 'strange fellow' who makes spymaster Ulysses 'strain' at his 'drift', that contrary to the myth of literary authorship, 'no man is the lord of anything ... Till he communicate his parts to others' [*Troilus, 3,3,90–111*].[115]

On the Shakespearean stage where books are seen as promiscuously 'sluttish', as they 'wide unclasp the tables of their thoughts / To every ticklish reader [*4,6,61–2*], characters who 'read much' are invariably depicted as myopic, misguided or treacherous, like Cassius and Brutus [*Julius, 1,2,22*].[116] So, when Troilus swears love by 'truth's authentic author' [*Troilus, 3,2,168*]; French 'authors faithfully affirm' the law [*Henry V, 1,2,43*]; or Gower retails 'what mine authors say' [*Pericles, 1,1,20*], credit is precisely what is *strained*, as in these plays, we discover, there is no 'author in the world / Teaches such beauty as a woman's eye' [*Love's, 4,3,291:17*]. Bent double in his *bearing* of subservient humility, 'our humble author' [*2Henry IV, Epi.23*] is as much a 'crooked figure' for this writer as his contorted text [*Henry V, Pro.15*]. So, like the Foucault who objected that although 'We are accustomed to seeing the author as a genial creator ... The truth is quite the contrary: the author is a functional principle by which, in our culture, one impedes the free circulation of fiction', it seems Shakespeare can never forget the constriction of his scene of writing, nor how 'Our bending author' is obliged to bow to the authorising institutions, even as his servile pen is subjected to the discourse of 'the story'.[117] For though Jeffrey Knapp imagines him 'bending' material to his sovereign will with the same power to 'mangle' as the king, just as the later Foucault saw the body as much *forming* as deformed, the passive implication is confirmed when in *Hamlet* he represents his twisted conditions of production, and has the rascally fellow who speaks the Prologue to *The Mousetrap* insist not only on the collective ownership of the play, but on the cravenly subjected 'stooping' required to produce it on demand: 'For us and for our tragedy, / Thus stooping to your clemency / We beg your hearing patiently' [*3,2,133–5*].[118]

Caught between stage and page, playing and playmaking, when he takes a bow Shakespeare comes forward, says the enigmatic 'Never Writer to the Ever Reader' of *Troilus and Cressida*, expressly 'not in confidence' of *either* 'author's pen or actor's voice' [*Pro.23*]. Editors like to believe that Shakespeare in fact himself spoke his curtain speeches in solo yet self-effacing cameo roles. And Shapiro contended that the Epilogue of *2 Henry IV*, which finishes by affirming 'I will bid you good night, and so kneel down before you – but to pray for the Queen', is 'the closest we get' to the author revealing his true or singular self, for there what commenced with Shakespeare 'modestly curtsying' abruptly shifts as he catches himself and then 'explains to his audience that while it may look as if he's kneeling "before them", he's not; he's kneeling in prayer for Elizabeth'. Like the makers of *Shakespeare in Love*, which has a 'self-schooled, self-scanned, self-honoured, self-secure' Bard authorized by Gloriana's gala appearance on the stage of the Globe, Shapiro saw no contradiction between his capitalist entrepreneur, 'who offers himself as a merchant' to his audience of investors, and this unctuous grovelling to feudal authority.[119] The Foucauldian news that there are 'no moments of pure, unfettered subjectivity' had been famously registered, however, when Greenblatt concluded *Renaissance Self-Fashioning* with the admission that although he had set out 'to understand the role of human autonomy' in shaping identity, he discovered instead that 'fashioning oneself and being fashioned by cultural institutions – family, state, religion – were inseparably intertwined'.[120]

Greenblatt's Nietzschean reflexiveness remains a good starting-point for approaching the doubly 'crooked' figure of 'our humble author' that forms and *reforms* by its excessive bowing and scraping in attendance on command. So in *Secret Shakespeare* I keyed Shakespeare's recurring allegiance test, in which subjects are suborned to present their own subjection, to the 'Bloody Question' of a loyalty divided between Queen and Pope that conditioned the writer's subject position in this age of vows, as one (like the composers Byrd, Dowland and Tallis) born into a Catholic milieu who *resisted the resistance* to Elizabeth's 'war on terror' whilst making a drama out of the silent refusal to be put on oath. There was a structural affinity, I maintained, between Shakespeare's tragic truth games and the enigmatic interplay of gazes painted by Caravaggio, who in pictures such as *The Calling of St Matthew*, where no one will meet Christ's eye or answer his call, repeats over and over the hermeneutic puzzle of a self *performing secrecy*, as Leo Bersani and Ulysse Dutoit put it: 'presenting and withdrawing itself' as if the viewer was being solicited by 'a desire determined to remain hidden.'[121] For the compulsion with which both painter and playwright return to such scenes of invigilation and interpellation confirms how these artists on the threshold of modernity see their imperative *calling* as the inescapable presentation of presence itself:

> What shall Cordelia speak? Love, and be silent ...
> Then poor Cordelia!
> And yet not so, since, I am sure, my love's
> More ponderous than my tongue ...
> Unhappy that I am, I cannot heave
> My heart into my mouth.
> [*King Lear*, 1,1,60; 75–7; 90–1]

'Now, our joy ... what can you say ...? Speak ... speak again ... mend your speech' [81–93]: as Stanley Cavell writes in an aside on asides, it is in staging the problem of performative utterance that here *the dramatist speaks*, for 'Doesn't it figure ... that it is Shakespeare who creates, as the first aside in *King Lear* – Cordelia's perplexity over what to say or to do – a question of ambiguity between speaking and silence, which the aside ... precisely embodies?' For Cavell, the theatrical convention in which words are at once 'overheard and unheard' metadramatizes Shakespeare's performative crisis by 'suggesting that this is the condition of words of the play as a whole'.[122] Thus, at the instant when the first rule of art is promulgated that to be an 'authentic author' it is necessary to 'look in thy heart and write!' Shakespeare makes a drama out of his resistance to the imperative 'That I ... Must, like a whore, unpack my heart with words', by demonstrating (like Brecht prevaricating before the Committee on Un-American Actitivities) that while 'you would pluck out the heart of my mystery' [*Hamlet, 2,2,561–3; 3,2,336*], 'You cannot, if my heart were in your hand' [*Othello, 3,3,176*].[123] So *Shakespeare in Love* got him exactly inside-out when Tom Stoppard imagined his incessant toying with different signatures to be symptomatic of writer's block, for what these execution metaphors make plain is how this most elliptic of writers identified 'windy suspiration of forc'd breath' [*Hamlet, 1,2,79*] with the torture rack and false confession, and self-expression with guts spilled on the scaffold.[124] By contrast, it is the playmaker's reluctance to *present* himself as the author and owner of his meaning, qualified by his actor's recognition that 'all the men and women are merely players' who 'have their exits and their entrances' [*As You, 2,7,141–2*] prescribed for them in advance, that makes his texts such apt illustrations of Foucault's theory that this 'Visibility is a trap'.[125]

The 'masked philosopher' who traced psychiatry to confession connected his desire to 'write without a face' to a sensation in Vichy France that 'the obligation of speaking was both strange and boring. I often wondered why people had to speak.'[126] Yet for Foucault, the fact that 'resistance is never in a position of exteriority to power' is not a double bind, for in his theory 'resistance relies upon the situation against which it struggles'. So it is his insight that 'the will not to be governed' is born from 'recasting a power that constitutes me as the power I oppose', that may offer a key to Shakespeare's 'sweet and witty soul', the 'honey tongue' with which the poet is said to have acquitted himself in his 'exits and his entrances', despite associating sycophancy with spaniels salivating over candy.[127] Thus, rather than searching for an authentic Shakespeare, it may be best to recall his image of himself as 'our bending author' who bows to the power that he bends; and to do so by considering how he images his *calling* not as the self-advancing 'trick of singularity' [*Twelfth,*

2,5,132] of literary authorship, 'As if a man were author of himself'
[*Coriolanus*, 5,3,36], but as the order to look sharp for the king.
For ever patiently attendant on 'the motive and the cue' [*Hamlet*,
2,2,538], Shakespeare is a writer who exists, as Jacques Lacan
observed of his Hamlet, always 'in the hour of the Other'; and
it seems indicative that while Jonson flaunts his 'presence in the
tiring house, to prompt' the player like a puppeteer, Shakespeare,
who never once refers to the prompter or 'book-holder', fills his
plays with terror that 'Like a dull actor ... I have forgot my part'
[*Coriolanus*, 41], even as his sense of timing remains that of those
old stagers resigned to 'put on manly readiness, / And meet in the hall
together' [*Macbeth*, 2,3,128], since, 'correspondent to command'
[*Tempest*, 1,2,299], they know that the first rule of their 'quality'
[194] is that the show must go on: 'When my cue comes, call me,
and I will answer' [*Dream*, 4,1,196].[128] So, if *Secret Shakespeare*
defined his drama as a great refusal of the pressure to perform, the
theme of *Free Will* is how Shakespeare turned from that negative
intention to a more positive theatre of attention, from an attitude of
mute desistance or refraining to a restructuring of the subject in a
posture of *bearing*, on the player's professional understanding that
'The weight of is sad time we *must* obey' [*King Lear*, 5,3,322].

Miching malecho

'Speak the speech, I pray you, as I pronounced it to you – trippingly
on the tongue' [*Hamlet*, 32,1]: with its suggestion of tripping them
as he plans to trip Claudius, Hamlet's instructions to the Players, so
often misinterpreted as his creator's own artistic manifesto, reminds
us how Shakespeare analysed his situation in terms not of free will
or self-determination, but of the 'forced breath' the Prince himself
so resents. This is a setting for what Judith Butler calls 'excitable
speech', after the legal term for utterances made under duress.
'Whereas some critics mistake the critique of sovereignty for the
demolition of agency', Butler proposes that 'agency begins where
sovereignty wanes'.[129] So how did this excited writer understand the
symbolic revolution by which the new cult of author as agent broke
free of the old culture of calendar custom and court ceremonial?
Dialectically; and time and again he dramatized the transition 'from
the commanded performance to a commanding performance' as an
interpellation like that at Elsinore where, as Pierre Bourdieu noted,

the surprise is that artistic independence has to be instituted under the tutelage of a royal who oversees the play like some master of revels, thereby confirming that Shakespeare did not always 'display towards external restraints the impatience that for us appears to define the creative project'.[130]

While he would eventually owe his freedom of expression to entrance fees paid by a public of increasingly diverse origin, early modern impresarios like Philip Henslowe could 'mould the taste of the age', which was why on the Shakespearean stage, Bourdieu argued, the modern literary field was inaugurated *in deference to rather than defiance of* the medieval licensing regime, and why, even as he gained autonomy, the dramatist protested ever more loudly his indebtedness to patrician patrons. Like the art-for-art's-sake it foretold, in this account, the birth of the author involved not simply a move 'from a system of patronage to one of commerce', or from use to exchange value, but a double rupture with both power and profit. So, for Bourdieu, the institution of the author commenced with a sweet Shakespearean refusal to reduce theatre to either capitalist commodity or political propaganda, when the playwright offered perfect proof of the sociologist's Nietzschean theory that *constraint makes freedom possible*.[131]

Shakespeare's will to freedom, in Bourdieu's reflexive logic, was as much in relation to pressures of the public playhouse as the princely patron. This is an interpretation that also chimes with the Marxist explanation of the genesis of the idea of the autonomy of art as a reaction to the early capitalist economy, when the artist remained the only worker whom the division of labour passed by through assertion of the privileges of the guild, the institution by which handicraftsmen secured prices and monopolized supply. According to this account, art was arrested at the handicraft stage of production because early modern artists continued to work for courts, and reacted feudally to the division of labour by affirming their exemption from the coercions of means–ends demand. So, claims for the autonomy of art emerged in the feudal sphere as brakes on the changes the market was bringing courtly society. In his *Theory of the Avant-Garde* Peter Bürger thus likened such a self-interested and calculatedly 'relative autonomy' to the far from 'idiotic' strategy of withdrawal of the noble *honnête homme* from the court in absolutist France.[132] This mercantilist scenario is familiar from the history of art. But it is also minutely substantiated by Andrew Gurr in *The*

Shakespeare Company, where the dramatist's queerly convoluted posture is attributed to the irony of a joint-stock company with a 'democratic, non-authoritarian management', which continued to pretend 'Motley's the only wear' by flaunting the antiquated feudal livery of a troupe of travelling players.[133]

If the Lord Chamberlain's Men persisted in being so 'motley-minded' [*As You, 2,7,44; 5,4,40*], that was because the 'customary suits' [*Hamlet, 1,2,78*] of a feudal household fitted their family type of firm, with joint ownership of assets, including play-texts, properties, costumes, and from 1599 the Globe itself. This marriage of convenience mimicked City livery companies, which also operated under royal charter, and of which the actors Heminge and Condell were Freemen (allowing them to enlist boys as 'apprentices'). Clinging to the charade of household service looks like 'a hypocrite's dressed-up version' of the lucrative commercial reality, Yachnin writes; and the childlike subservience signified by the royal patent became a dangerous double bluff after 1603, Gurr stresses, 'when the most democratic organisation in England came under the patronage of King James, the most despotic figure in the country'.[134] But the bad faith of such mock dependency was the dramatist's anxiety from the start, for whenever he imagined a stage it was never a public playhouse but always the hall of a palace.[135] So, from the Induction of *The Taming of the Shrew*, when the Lord has his page Bartholomew dressed 'like a lady' to mime 'her' love [*Ind., 1,102*]; to the grand finale of *The Tempest* when Prospero, 'last of the great house lords', directs his boy-player Ariel to present 'calm seas' [*5,1,318*], Shakespeare's *given time* is always a forced one when some sovereign or seducer programmes a theatre of desire.[136] Thus Venus, a 'lovesick Queen' who so resembles a geriatric Elizabeth, sets the scene for a lifetime of passive aggression towards the patronage system in which he thrived, when in Shakespeare's poem she implores the infantilized Adonis to cease behaving like a dumb statue: 'But when her lips were ready for his pay / He winks, and turns his lips another way' [*Venus and Adonis, 89; 175*]. For in these works 'the politics of mirth' always necessitate a similar winking performance of compliant but backhanded subjection:[137]

LORD: There is a lord will hear your play tonight;
          But I am doubtful of your modesties,
          Lest, over-eyeing of his odd behaviour –
          For yet his honour never heard a play –

> You break into some merry passion,
> And so offend him; for I tell you, sirs,
> If you should smile he grows impatient.
> A PLAYER: Fear not, my lord, we can contain ourselves
> Were he the veriest antic in the world.
>
> [*Shrew, Ind.*, 1,89–97]

With its sardonic 'over-eyeing' of the obtuseness of its lordly patrons, the play-within-the-play set up for the tinker Sly condenses all the irony of the Shakespearean gambit to 'contain ourselves' within the rules of the new art game without renouncing the 'merry passion' of a former stage. For though he knows the proverb 'Service is no heritage' [*All's Well*, 1,3,20], Shakespeare's primal performative scene is always a similarly feudal test of loyalty to such a lord and master. So, rather than adopting the devil's motto, 'Non Serviam', striving 'to please you every day' [*Twelfth*, 5,1,395] is, as David Schalkwyk shows, 'the informing condition of everything he wrote'.[138] More specifically, the physical act of *kneeling* is what Bourdieu would term his *hexis*: the hyper-correction that *embodies* his overdetermined social relations, and is thus 'at the heart of Shakespeare's dramatic explorations', but in which, as Meredith Ann Skura observes, the actor's power *over* as well his dependence on his audience is literally articulated. Kneeling in a Byzantine performance of selflessness, 'the player proudly secures the spotlight for himself and gets what he wants by being obsequious'.[139] And Shakespeare's knowing references to the body politics of courtly bowing, curtseying and kneeling suggest that this self-prostration is never without consciousness of how the compulsion to serve the other is what produces his sense of himself:

> Hearts, tongues, figures, scribes, bards, poets, cannot
> Think, speak, cast, write, sing, number – hoo! –
> His love for Antony. But as for Caesar –
> Kneel down, kneel down, and wonder.
>
> [*Antony*, 3,2,16–19]

The physical act of kneeling embodies the paradoxical power of weakness for Shakespeare. And in an important essay Julia Lupton relates the cringing self-abjection that defines his stance towards the great with the 'creaturely life' that Benjamin and Schmitt considered 'the flip side of the political theology of absolute sovereignty' that was developing around 1600. Just as Benjamin found Kafka's stories to be haunted by the abject figure of the hunchback 'who bows his head far down on his chest', Lupton considers the degraded passivity of the 'creature Caliban' before the arbitrary inflictions of Prospero to be symptomatic of a peculiarly Shakespearean submissiveness, 'at once sullen angel and pensive dog'. In absolutist doctrine the king is like God in his creative jurisdiction, since his subjects are his creatures. But it is Caliban's very creatureliness that excites *his own creativity*, in melancholy response to his subjection. So as Lupton points out, in his wonder at the 'Sounds and sweet airs' [*3,2,138*] of Prospero's creation, this creature is a created thing 'on the verge of creating'. 'Thou shalt have cramps, / Side stitches that shall pen thy breath up' [*1,2,128*], the cruel master threatens his slave. But in the body politics of this '*cramp* that *pens up breath* with its suturing *side-stiches*', what the creature is on point of creating is a suffocating, claustrophobic response, an inverted kind of sovereignty born of an 'oppressive sense of internal constraint':

> The pinches and cramps that Prospero visits upon Caliban ... may simply manifest the passion born of enforced service, the stinging nettles of resentment as it flowers on the body of the creature inhabiting the edge of symbolization. The aches and pains caused by Prospero's commands are the primitive equivalent of Hamlet's 'stings and arrows of outrageous fortune' [*Hamlet, 3,1,60*]. They are the passionate inscription ... of the slave's rejection of his master's rule.[140]

It seems apt that the document that places Shakespeare nearest the action in a world of power is the Treasurer's account of the payment of the King's Men for 'waiting and attending on His Majesty's service', hanging about in the wings, at the epoch-marking 1604 Somerset House peace negotiations with Spain, for which, biographers infer, he was paid with the silver bowl he entrusted to his daughter Susanna in his will.[141] For like Kafka in Benjamin's critique, Shakespeare's default position is truly that of a *waiter*: always gesturing to the other, or hovering on the threshold in 'prostrate and exterior bending' [*Henry V, 4,3,276*], with Jain-like deference lest he cause inadvertent harm, he is 'at home in distorted life', since 'even if he did not pray – and this we do not know – he still possessed in the highest degree ... "the natural prayer of the soul": attentiveness'.[142] That attentiveness on the alert is the subject of one of the most brilliant recent works of criticism, *Shakespeare in Parts*, where in 'a history of the cue' Simon Palfrey and Tiffany Stern show

how the practice of distributing Elizabethan actors with cue-scripts consisting only of roles generated a veritable 'thinking in parts', and subordination of the individual to the play. To a Shakespearean actor, far more than to his modern successor, we are reminded, the cue is his 'approaching moment, it is a call to arms'. The fact that early modern actors were therefore so acutely reliant on cues, produced, these critics argue, a contingent sense of timing and a partible conception of succession uncannily like those of our own postmodern philosophers of *l'attente*:

> Shakespeare's sense of what made a role might be is conditioned by his experience of playing parts, and so by a repeated confrontation with suddenness ... that strange nervousness that comes from knowing that 'something' is coming, but not quite knowing what or when it will arrive.[143]

Like an heir in a premodern system of tanistry, or partible inheritance, Shakespeare 'in parts' knows his own place. So, in the radical negativity of the master/slave dialectic that informs recent interest in sovereign power and bare life, his actor's punctual acceptance that 'Men must endure / Their going hence, even as their coming hither' [*King Lear*, 5,2,9–10] is perhaps a symptomatic expression of that pleasure-in-pain which Lacan referred to as 'jouissance', and Georges Bataille as the miracle of an incumbency weighed down so profoundly it becomes 'relieved of the heaviness that the world of utility imposes, of the tasks in which the world of objects mires' it.[144] Such an impossible attentiveness would indeed seem 'to render one without personality, without the very qualities upon which relations with the other are grounded'; yet read in the context of the inoperative power of *attendance*, as one after another Shakespearean lover or tyrant demands to know 'What revels are in hand? Is there no play / To ease the anguish of a torturing hour?' [*Dream*, 5,1,36], it is as if the official cover for the Elizabethan playhouse – that it was essential for the actors 'to use and practice stage plays' so 'they might be better prepared to show such plays before Her Majesty' – was the vital grit that irritated this writer into creation.[145]

Recent studies like Shapiro's *1599* have returned us to the old idea of Shakespeare as a veritable *gentleman in waiting*, who wrote for specific court occasions; while Leeds Barroll even infers that he wrote *only* on official assignment, and that if he received no commission 'simply did not wish to write plays'.[146] Thus in *Hamlet* the actors oblige their domineering Maecenas by rehearsing the marmoreal *Dido, Queen of Carthage* Marlowe composed for the Children of the Chapel as his only coterie production and 'caviare to the general' [*2,2,418*]. But as Robert Weimann comments, the evasiveness of the Player's response to the Prince's condescending ordinance about 'reforming' the troupe's old tendency to 'split the ears of the groundlings' – 'I hope we have reformed that indifferently with us, sir' – cues the 'unworthy antics' of their eventual court appearance, which, far from abiding by Hamlet's order for 'temperance', 'smoothness', 'modesty' and 'discretion', is its opposite: 'miching *malecho*', or *bad echo*, with 'inexplicable dumb-shows', and such a 'whirlwind of passion ... strutted and bellowed' that to the exasperation of their host, 'The players cannot keep counsel, they'll tell all' [*3,2,1–32; 124–8*].[147] The echo, Derrida taught us, is the place of 'la différance', that supplementation produced in an interval of space and time that Heidegger reined back into the 'finally proper name' where he insisted being was situated.[148] So nothing in Shakespeare more fully reveals his critical resistance to his given situation in the economy of the sovereign and the servant, nor better vindicates, against Derrida's reservations, Butler's performative theory that speech will always exceed the censor by which it is constrained, than this irrelevantly echoing 'impertinence':

> Speech is constrained neither by the specific speaker nor its originating context ... [but] has its own temporality in which it remains enabled precisely by the contexts from which it breaks. This ambivalent structure at the heart of performativity implies that the terms of resistance and insurgency are spawned by the powers they oppose.[149]

As Polonius earlier expostulated, such histrionics are 'too long' for a play [*2,2,478*]. So, like Heidegger recuperating being from time, Erne proposes that it is the sheer linguistic excess of later Quartos and Folio that constitutes their sovereign *literariness*, confirming Shakespeare as a master who intended such embarrassing riches only for the page.[150] Yet the problem with such a recuperation is how it defines authorship in the intentionalist and textualized terms of the novel; whereas what the collision of humanist 'matter' and popular 'impertinency' [*King Lear, 4,6,168*] in the character of Hamlet himself seems to mark, as Weimann shows, is the 'bifold authority' [*Troilus, 5,2,144*] of a playmaker who is always a player, a company sharer who is only incidentally a printed poet, even as he lives out the tensions between successive regimes of presence and representation. Above all, what the restored Victorian portrait of the Bard as self-serving literary entrepreneur ignores is how this 'willing over-supplier of words' Jonson likewise installed 'for all time' as a monarch of wit, remained 'our humble author', whom it suited to take his bow in the anonymity of the collective line-up as a punctual servant of the age's residual authorising powers. For Shakespeare, it seems, resigning the ownership of his own meaning founds an alternative notion of agency in the decommissioned power of weakness, a limited liability that recognizes how the one who acts does so to the extent that 'he or she is constituted as an actor and, hence, operating within a linguistic field of enabling constraints': 'My tongue is weary; when my legs are too, I will bid you good night, and so kneel down before you – but, indeed, to pray for the Queen' [*2Henry IV, Epi.28–30*].[151]

With printless foot

'If you look for a good speech now, you undo me; for what I have to say is of mine own making, and what indeed I should say will, I doubt, prove mine own marring': it is the self-deconstructing posture of Shakespeare's claim to be the maker and purveyor of his own meaning that it advances in self-cancelling reverse, backing into the limelight by harking back to service in the great house, as cap-in-hand on the doorstep it proffers 'First my fear, then my curtsy, last my speech' [*1–6*]. Thus, Douglas Bruster and Weimann discuss how with his threshold prologues and epilogues Shakespeare honoured the group dynamics of the great hall, imaging the troupe 'capitalizing on the good will that the performances' leading actors generated by having these actors continue on through the closing of the dramatic frame'.[152] So, although first among equals, he nonetheless affirmed that, as Stanley Wells reminds us, he would remain the pre-eminent *company man*, who worked 'exceptionally closely with fellow actors ... for no other dramatist had so long a relationship with a single company', nor such amiable relations with other writers. Wells's roguish *Shakespeare & Co.* therefore concludes that to situate this good companion in his theatrical neighbourhood 'only enhances our sense of what made him unique'.[153] Likewise, Bart Van Es pinpoints *A Midsummer Night's Dream* as the watershed where he realized the supreme advantage of his *collective identity*, in being at once a player, sharer and writer in a communal fellowship exempt from market pressure. So, like the king with two bodies, Shakespeare's sovereignty arose, on this view, from his dispersed and multiple personality in a corporate organization, and the golden opportunity the 1594 Lord Chamberlain's warrant afforded him, to be seen, whether writing singly or with others, as, in Knapp's words, 'many in one'.[154]

As Emerson wrote, Shakespeare proves 'the greatest genius is the most indebted'.[155] Such accounts are similar to Bourdieu's thesis that reconstructing the professional world of the artist 'allows us to understand the labour he had to accomplish, both against these determinations and thanks to them, to produce himself as the creator, that is, the *subject* of his own creation'.[156] But the question they prompt is also Bourdieu's, about what it was the writer gained from merging his individual interest in the faceless impersonality of a corporate brand. Scholars usually interpret his resistance to the 'intrusion of the author' onto the stage as proof he was so comfortable working in the collective ethos of the theatre he was simply 'indifferent to such individuation'.[157] But as Erne reminds us, this dramatist was still keenly aware of literary property, concerned about reputation, proud of his name.[158] So what, again, was Shakespeare's interest in disinterestedness? The answer the plays supply is that it was *the escape from his own sovereignty* that gave him limitless ability and freedom to write as he liked. In a co-operative where for one of the band to roar too loudly, his Peter Quince solemnly warns, 'were enough to hang us all' [*Dream, 1,2,72*], mutual 'good will' between performers and patrons was secured by subduing the writer's intentions and identity to his métier 'like the dyer's hand' [Sonnet 111]; by 'our good Will', the implied personality behind the scenes, never stepping out of collective line: 'If we offend it is with our good will. / That you should think we come not to offend / But with good will' [*Dream, 5,1,108–10*]. For as John Davies of Hereford poeticized in a salute of 1610 to 'Our English Terence' that remains the most acute analysis of the queer cultural politics of Shakespearean sovereignty, this 'reigning Wit' governed as a benevolent constitutional monarch in the premodern textual polity, precisely by exercising the power of weakness with his waiting, and like the gentleman-usher that he literally was, letting others take credit for his words:

Some say (good *Will*) which I, in sport, do sing,
Had'st thou not played some Kingly parts in sport,
Thou had'st been a companion for a *King*;
And been a King among the meaner sort.
Some others rail; but, rail as they think fit,
Thou hast no railing, but, a reigning Wit:
And honesty thou sow'st, which they do reap;
So, to increase their Stock which they do keep.[159]

Shakespeare displaced his authorial sovereignty 'in sport', if this encomium is to be believed, and by excelling so much in the 'Kingly parts' of moribund monarchy, like Julius Caesar or Old Hamlet, this 'reigning wit' was able to maintain the fiction that 'All for your delight / *We are not here*' [114–15]. For if texts began to have authors, as Foucault theorized and Quince fears, to the extent that authors became subject to punishment, Shakespeare's signature vanishing-act, his reduction to the missing person who is a cipher of the world's 'good will', also records the coincidence that (as Derrida countered) the 'Strange Institution' of literature commenced around 1600 as 'the right to say everything'. Thus, if this originator of modern authorship ensured freedom of expression by depersonalization, hiding his face in the crowd or being dragged to the chair, this modesty finessed the problem that prior to the instauration of a modern public sphere the literary field had no ground of authorization other than royal or aristocratic patronage. For 'How is it possible to answer for literature?' if it now bows to no sovereign authority yet demands by definition a 'charter as the wind' [*As You*, 2,7,48]: 'A paradox: liberation makes it an institution that is an-institutional, wild and unconditional'.[160]

To Lacan's accusation of irresponsibility in 'not recognising the impasse he himself attempts on the Other by playing the dead man', Derrida proposed that modern literature's claim to the sovereign silence of a privileged secrecy entailed not irresponsibility but rather a mutation in the concept of responsibility.[161] And it is the vertigo of this process that does seem to be negotiated in *A Midsummer Night's Dream*, the play above all that identifies interpersonal 'good will' and the power of weakness as preconditions of a self-constituting literature, when in its closing pact with the audience the actor playing Puck takes upon his fictive persona responsibility for a text that is 'No more yielding' to authority 'than a dream'. On the understanding that the 'play needs no excuse' if its creator is presumed 'dead' [*5,1,341–3; Epi.15–16*], Shakespeare's 'powerless theatre' thus leaps its own aesthetic groundlessness to assert the 'right to say everything, if only in the form of a fiction'.[162] So, although Woolf conjectured that Shakespeare marks the point when, because 'the playwright is replaced by the man who writes a book', he personifies the cultural discovery that 'Anon is dead', the pretence that 'We do not come … We are not here', suggests that for the artisanal playmaker who was author of the *Dream* there was life in the old Anon yet.[163]

In Shakespeare's Athens free speech is gained by absenting authorial presence, since '*We do not come*, as minding to content you, / Our true intent is' [*5,1,113–14*]: 'Therein lies literature's secret, the … power to keep undecidable the secret of what it says … The secret of literature is the secret itself … "the play's the thing" [*Hamlet, 2,2,581*]'.[164] So, if it is secrecy about its origins and intentions that grants literature a permit 'to say everything', that freedom may well explain why Shakespeare's self-deconstruction extends to the paradox that he was too *self-interested* a company man, with too much at stake in corporate identity, to push his name, too privileged by ties that went beyond a contractual framework to be the single author of any constraining book, as Richard Dutton infers.[165] The early modern system of textual patronage exalted aristocrats as presumed readers; so perhaps Shakespeare did fret that the religion of the book might be not only subjectifying but 'inherently elitist', as Knapp argues, and instead offered up his own literary sovereignty as a Eucharistic sacrifice to the 'mass entertainment' of the democratic stage.[166] For true sovereignty 'must subordinate no one', as Derrida put it, 'that is to say, be subordinated to nothing or to no one': it must 'lose all memory of itself and all the interiority of itself'.[167]

Whatever the political theology, by playing dead to literary sovereignty in a perpetual postponement, like his own Black Prince, Shakespeare escaped the dangers as well as the obligations of his royalties; and the one occasion he claimed author's rights was to signal he was 'much offended' with William Jaggard, the printer of the Folio, for publishing a volume in his name.[168] Such desubjectivization is not quite the same as the Hölderlin-like autodeconstruction we associate with Eliot's modernist doctrine that all art is 'an escape from personality'. But nor is it merely a type of *cosmesis*, a strategy to survive by the trivializing of oneself.[169] For if we take 'our good Will' to be one of the founders of the modern institution of authorship, we have to recognize that what happens in this writing is also a form of *creative* unselfing: 'a continual surrender of himself to something more valuable ... a continual self-sacrifice, a continual extinction of personality'.[170] Shakespeare's writing already goes beyond literary authorship, that is to say, as if in answer to Derrida's injunction that 'What must be thought ... is this inconceivable and unknowable thing, a freedom that would no longer be the power of a subject, a freedom without autonomy': 'Marry, if he that writ it had ... hanged himself ... it would have been a fine tragedy' [*Dream, 5,2,342–4*].[171]

Confronted by unproven murder accusations, Luke Wilson has intriguingly recounted, Elizabethan juries habitually shifted liability from the accused to a fictional killer named after the offending weapon, such as Thomas Staff, or simply non-existence, like William Nemo; which sounds the perfect alias for Shakespeare.[172] With his own lethal-sounding surname, the dramatist's self-erasure, his drive to hide himself in full view, has indeed been decoded by Greenblatt as a burial 'inside public laughter' of the terror which gripped him of an actual trial and condemnation. Having been traumatized by witnessing public hangings and eviscerations at Tyburn, the 'genially submissive' yet 'subtly challenging' writer staged his disappearance, on this view, 'to ward off vulnerability'.[173] Thus, in contrast to Caravaggio, who paints his own decapitation in picture after picture, the death of the author serves here a purely symbolic effacement, for 'given enough rope to hang himself, Shakespeare submits instead to an aesthetic closure'.[174] There are parallels, then, in such interpretations, between this particular William Nemo and a modernist writer such as Thomas Mann, who also put his guilt in plain view. Thus, 'How he terrifies me', wrote Rilke of the author of the Epilogues, 'This man who draws the wire into his own head, and hangs himself / Beside the other puppets, and henceforth / Begs mercy of the play'.[175]

The William Nemo known as Shakespeare hides his own responsibility behind a show of non-existence. Such ludic self-annulment is enacted by the fictional Williams of the plays and poems, 'self-deprecating cameos like Hitchcock's brief appearances in his films', a crafty procession, typified by the bumpkin of *As You Like It*, in which Shakespeare associates the shy volunteering that 'My name is Will' [Sonnet 136] 'with inarticulate, humble life obliterated by the textualized world of his betters', as Phyllis Rackin remarks.[176] Yet Mark Thornton-Burnett also notes the persistence of an illiterate underclass that 'agitates for proper acknowledgment' in these texts; and such is the creaturely resentment implied when these sweet Williams cheek their masters, accuse the king to his face or skive at Hinkley fair [*2Henry VI*, 5,1,21].[177] For what these winking Wills all personify is the truant evasion of the textualized world of authority that Shakespeare makes the story of his life: the great refusal that underlies his recalcitrance towards the sovereignty instituted in the printed fix of literary authorship itself. So, as A.D. Nuttall concludes, in his own eloquently posthumous book, *Shakespeare the Thinker*, while his name did become a selling point, because the public certainly cottoned on to 'the fact that Shakespeare was the man behind the plays', the writer himself appears to have feared his own typographic afterlife as a deadly freezing, 'a cryogenic perpetuation' of something he had imagined to be 'mobile' and alive.[178]

'When he is gone, and his Comedies out of sale', warned the 1609 Quarto of *Troilus and Cressida* darkly, 'you will scramble for them, and set up a new English Inquisition'.[179] Assuredly, Shakespeare was the author of his own authorship, who produced himself as the 'subject of his own creation'; but this inquisitorial metaphor hints how he also had cause to see himself as the 'tongue-tied unlettered clerk', mumbling 'Amen' to every 'form of well-refinèd pen' [Sonnet 85]. And so far from being indifferent to the coming 'paper machine', he littered his texts with sinister references to the tyrannical violence of penning, imprinting, impressing, branding, binding, and engraving: the morbid techniques of publishing that, as Goldberg argues, 'throw into question any identification of the *system* with a sovereign author', and mark aversion to the inscription of a name in *characters*.[180] 'Remember / First to possess his books', Caliban therefore reiterates, when plotting to assassinate his master, 'for without them / He's but a sot ... Burn but his books' [*Tempest*, 3,2,86–90]. Prospero's other slave Ariel then diverts the plotters by distracting their 'catch' [*112*] with one of his 'sounds and sweet airs' [*131*], an echo-song that seems caught up, however, in the infinite recession of the dramatist's own mimetic relations with the invisible hand of bookish sovereignty, and the actorly readiness with which his 'sweet sprites bear / The burden' [*1,2,383*], seeing that the words they 'troll' [*3,2,112*] – 'Thought is free' [*Twelfth Night, 1,3,59*] – are also the opening line of the first poem of the premiere publication of his own royal master, King James:[181]

> STEPHANO (*Sings*): Thought is free.
> CALIBAN: That's not the tune.
> ARIEL *plays the tune on a tabor and pipe.*
> STEPHANO: What is this same?
> TRINCULO: This is the tune of our catch, played by the
> picture of Nobody.
>
> [*Tempest, 3,2,118–22*]

Though he called upon him only sparingly, the old legal figment of Nobody, a subject without an identity, was much on Shakespeare's mind as an Odyssean figure for the disavowal of subjective authorial responsibility, recent critics show.[182] The slipperiness of Nobody, for a culture poised between presence and representation, was that he was always busy becoming Somebody; and when he was gone Shakespeare would himself fast mutate into just such a sovereign entity: 'an institutionalized residue' coating a proper name, pressed by the 1623 *Works* 'into the author he never was or wanted to be'.[183] But this waiting writer who dreaded the definitiveness of the book as his tombstone, like those brass-lettered graves which spell 'the disgrace of death' for the bookmen of *Love's Labour's Lost* [*1,1,1–3*]; and who blackened his most bookish character with the 'inky cloak' [*Hamlet, 1,2,78*] of the letter that kills, avoided 'the Graver' come to 'outdo the life' until the very last.[184] And even as his 'project gather[ed] to a head' [*Tempest, 5,1,1*], when the forthcoming Folio was in his head as 'a book of all that sovereigns do', he fretted that 'He's more secure to keep it shut than shown' [*Pericles, 1,1,137–8*]. 'O, like a book of sport thou'lt read me o'er', Shakespeare seemed reluctantly to foresee; 'But there's more in me', he also knew, 'than thou understand'st' [*Troilus, 4,7,123–4*]. So, until the very end, the creator of 'the world's volume' [*Cymbeline, 3,4,137*], who was such an unsatisfactory witness in his time, aborted his 'birth' as an author by deconstructing his own sovereign selfhood, intent on nothing more wilfully than that 'Deeper than did ever plummet sound / I'll drown my book' [*Tempest, 5,1,56*], as though to truly measure out his lines upon the shore 'with printless foot' [*34*], or 'like a face drawn in sand on the edge of the sea'.[185]

Notes

1 Thomas Greene, memorandum September 1615, repr. in E.K. Chambers, *William Shakespeare* (2 vols, Oxford: Clarendon Press, 1930), vol. 2, p.143. Chambers thought the 'I' of the note was Greene himself; but the consensus is that it refers to Shakespeare, since as Edgar Fripp logically objected: 'Why should Shakespeare tell John Greene, Thomas Greene's brother, what John Greene had long known and Shakespeare perfectly well knew was known to him? And why should Thomas Greene, in his confidential note-book, then enter such an inane memorandum?': Edgar Fripp, *Shakespeare Man and Artist* (2 vols, Oxford: Oxford University Press, 1938), vol. 2, p.814, n. 4.

2 Thomas Greene, quoting William Combe, memorandum 10 December 1614, quoted Mark Eccles, *Shakespeare in Warwickshire* (Madison: University of Wisconsin Press, 1961), p.137 (not in Chambers).

3 Maurice Hunt, 'Old England, Nostalgia, and the "Warwickshire" of Shakespeare's Mind', *Connotations*, 7 (1998), 159–80, here 177: quoting John Russell Brown in conversation.

4 For the details of Shakespeare's 1602 purchase of the 107 acres in Old Stratford and Welcombe, see Màiri Macdonald, 'A New Discovery about Shakespeare's Estate in Old Stratford', *Shakespeare Quarterly*, 45 (1994), 87–9.

5 Thomas More, *Utopia*, trans. Ralph Robinson, ed. Richard Marius (London: Dent, 1994), pp.26–7.

6 Terence Hawkes, 'Playhouse-Workhouse', in *That Shakespeherian Rag: Essays on a Critical Process* (London: Methuen, 1986), pp.10–11.

7 Jacques Derrida, 'This Strange Institution Called Literature: An Interview with Jacques Derrida', trans. Geoffrey Bennington and Rachel Bowlby, in *Acts of Literature* (London: Routledge, 1992), pp.33–75, here p.59; cf. Judith Halberstam, *The Queer Art of Failure* (Durham, NC: Duke University Press, 2011), p.2; Roland Barthes, *Sade, Fourier, Loyola*, trans. Richard Miller (New York: Hill & Wang, 1976), pp.2–3: 'failing, losing, forgetting, unmaking, undoing, unbecoming, not knowing may in fact offer more creative, more cooperative, more surprising ways of being in the world'.

8 Hawkes, op. cit. (note 6). p.21.

9 Stephen Greenblatt, *Will in the World: How Shakespeare Became Shakespeare* (London: Jonathan Cape, 2004), p.155.

10 Thomas Greene, memorandum 17 November 1614, repr. in Chambers, op. cit. (note 1), pp.142–3.

11 Thomas Greene, memorandum 10 December 1614, rpr. ibid., p.143.

12 Antony Holden, *William Shakespeare* (London: Little, Brown & Co., 1999), p.315.

13 Greenblatt, op. cit. (note 9), p.383.
14 Dennis Kay, *William Shakespeare: His Life and Times* (New York: Twayne, 1995), p.27.
15 Peter Levi, *The Life and Times of William Shakespeare* (London: Macmillan, 1988), p.334; René Weiss, *Shakespeare Revealed: A Biography* (London: John Murray, 2007), p.347; Park Honan, *Shakespeare: A Life* (Oxford: Oxford University Press, 1998), pp.389–90.
16 Peter Ackroyd, *Shakespeare: The Biography* (London: Chatto & Windus, 2005), pp.478–480.
17 Greenblatt, op. cit. (note 9), p.383.
18 Edward Bond, *Bingo* (London: Eyre Methuen, 1974) scene 1, pp.6–7. For Shakespeare's deployment of the 'plot' metaphor, see Roy Eriksen, *The Building in the Text: Alberti to Shakespeare and Milton* (Philadelphia: University of Pennsylvania Press, 2001), pp.112–17.
19 Thomas Greene to Arthur Mainwaring, 23 December 1614 quoted in Holden, op. cit. (note 12), p.314; Eccles, op. cit. (note 2), p.137.
20 Bond, op. cit. (note 18), scene 5, p.42.
21 Ibid., scene 6, p.48.
22 Jonathan Bate, '"Hide thy life": The Key to Shakespeare', *Times Higher Education Supplement*, 6 August 2009, 40–2, here 42. For this critic's uncomplicated celebration of the separation of the aesthetic from reality, see also *The Genius of Shakespeare* (London: Picador, 1997), pp.320–1.
23 Charles Baudelaire, quoted in Michael Hamburger, *The Truth of Poetry: Tensions in Modern Poetry from Baudelaire to the 1960s* (Manchester: Carcanet Press, 1982), p.5.
24 Hawkes, op. cit. (note 6), pp.21–2.
25 Ibid., scene 6, p.50; James Shapiro, *1599: A Year in the Life of William Shakespeare* (London: Faber and Faber, 2005), p.373.
26 W.H. Auden, 'In Memory of W.B. Yeats', in *W.H. Auden Selected by the Author* (Harmondsworth: Penguin, 1958), p.67.
27 Roger Manning, *Village Revolts: Social Protest and Popular Disturbances in England, 1509–1640* (Oxford: Clarendon Press, 1988), pp.90–1.
28 Eccles, op. cit. (note 2), p.61.
29 Manning, op. cit. (note 27), p.92; Eccles, op. cit. (note 2), p.138.
30 Katherine Duncan-Jones, *Ungentle Shakespeare: Scenes from His Life* (London: Thomson Learning, 2001), p.262.
31 Eric Santner, *The Royal Remains: The People's Two Bodies and the Endgames of Sovereignty* (Chicago: University of Chicago Press, 2011), p.24. For an acute account of the surprising interactions of equity and the common law in the Shakespearean period, see Lorna

Hutson, 'Not the King's Two Bodies: Reading the "Body Politic" in Shakespeare's *Henry IV*, Parts 1 and 2', in *Rhetoric and Law in Early Modern Europe*, ed. Victoria Kahn and Lorna Hutson (New Haven: Yale University Press, 2001), 166–98.

32 Bond, op. cit. (note 18), scene 6, p. 50; Weiss, op. cit. (note 15), p. 348.

33 Justice O'Byrne summing up in Sinclair v. Gogarty, *The Irish Times*, 24 November 1937, quoted in James Knowlson, *Damned to Fame: The Life of Samuel Beckett* (London: Bloomsbury, 1996), p. 259.

34 Charles Nicholl, *The Lodger: Shakespeare on Silver Street* (London: Allen Lane, 2007), pp. 271–2.

35 Ibid., pp. 3 and 272–3; 'non-commitant': Charles Nicholl, 'Faithful Dealing: Marlowe and the Elizabethan Intelligence Service', in *Marlowe, History and Sexuality*, ed. Paul Whitfield White (New York: AMS Press, 1998), p. 11.

36 Nicholl, op. cit. (note 34), p. 267.

37 'Ungentle Shakespeare': Duncan-Jones, op. cit. (note 30); Matthew Arnold, 'Shakespeare', in *The Poems of Matthew Arnold*, eds Kenneth and Miriam Allott (London: Longman, 1965), pp. 48–9.

38 Samuel Schoenbaum, *William Shakespeare: A Documentary Life* (Oxford: Oxford University Press, 1975), p. 213.

39 Ackroyd, op. cit. (note 16), p. 464.

40 Cf. Thomas Mann's 1918 'Reflections of an Unpolitical Man', with its disastrous defence of German spiritual inwardness (*Innerlichkeit*); Bond, 'Introduction', op. cit. (note 18), p. ix.

41 Margreta de Grazia, *'Hamlet' without Hamlet* (Cambridge; Cambridge University Press, 2007), pp. 158–9 and 170–1.

42 Dan Gunn, 'Introduction', *The Letters of Samuel Beckett, Volume II: 1941–1956* (Cambridge: Cambridge University Press, 2011), p. lxvi.

43 John Donne, *The Sermons of John Donne*, eds G.R. Potter and E.M. Simpson (Berkeley: University of California Press, 10 vols, 1953–1962), vol. 3, p. 110.

44 Greenblatt, op. cit. (note 9), p. 389.

45 Jacques Derrida, 'Force of Law: The "Mystical Foundation of Authority"', in *Acts of Religion*, ed. Gil Anidjar (London: Routledge, 2002), pp. 253–4; Jacques Derrida and Maurizio Ferraris, *A Taste for the Secret*, trans. Giacomo Donis (Cambridge: Polity Press, 2001), p. 27; J. Hillis Miller, '"Don't Count Me In": Derrida's Refraining', in Allison Weiner and Simon Morgan Wortham, eds, *Encountering Derrida: Legacies and Futures of Deconstruction* (London: Continuum, 2007), pp. 55 and 57.

46 'The subject desists': Philippe Lacoue-Labarthe, *Heidegger, Art and Politics*, trans. Christ Turner (Oxford: Basil Blackwell, 1990), p. 83.

47 Herman Melville, 'Bartleby, the Scrivener', in *Tales, Poems, and Other*

Writings, ed. J. Bryant (New York: Modern Library, 2002); Jacques Derrida, *The Gift of Death*, trans. David Wills (Chicago: Chicago University Press, 1995), pp.74–81, here p.75; Giorgio Agamben, *Potentialities: Collected Essays in Philosophy*, trans. Daniel Hellert-Roazen, (Stanford: Stanford University Press, 1999), p.235. For a commentary, see Arne de Boever, 'Agamben and Marx: Sovereignty, Governmentality, Economy', *Law and Critique*, 20:3 (2009), 259–79. For Deleuze's admiration of Bartleby, see David Couzens Hoy, *Critical Resistance: From Poststructuralism to Post-Critique* (Cambridge, Mass.: MIT Press, 2005), pp.9–10. By contrast, Slavoj Žižek sees only 'passive aggressivity' in Bartleby: see *The Parallax View* (Cambridge, Mass.: MIT Press, 2006), p.384,

48 'Fulfilment in non-fulfilment': Jean-François Lyotard, 'Jewish Oedipus', *Driftworks*, trans. Roger McKeon (New York: Semiotext(e), 1984), p.52; 'We never know exactly': Emmanuel Levinas, *Proper Names*, trans. Michael Smith (London: Athlone Press, 1996), p.110; 'something after': *Time and the Other*, trans. Richard Cohen (Pittsburgh, PA: Duquesne University Press, 1987), pp.72–3.

49 'Killing time': Kiernan Ryan, *Shakespeare's Comedies* (Basingstoke: Palgrave, 2009), Chap.1; 'Sovereign is he who decides': Carl Schmitt, *Political Theology: Four Chapters on the Concept of Sovereignty*, trans. George Schwab (Chicago: Chicago University Press, 2005), p.5; Victoria Kahn, 'Hamlet or Hecuba: Carl Schmitt's Decision', *Representations*, 83 (2003), 83.

50 Paul Veyne, *Foucault: His Thought, His Character*, trans. Janet Lloyd (Cambridge: Polity Press, 2010), p.137.

51 Charles Nicholl, 'Cardenio's Ghost', in *Traces Remain: Essays and Explorations* (London: Allen Lane, 2011), p.101.

52 Walter Benjamin, *The Origin of German Tragic Drama*, trans. John Osborne (London: Verso, 1998), pp.65 and 156. For this 'Benjamesque' reading of Shakespeare, see Richard Halpern, 'The King's Two Buckets: Kantorowicz, *Richard II*, and Fiscal Trauerspiel', *Representations*, 106 (2009), 67–76; and Zénon Luis-Martínez, 'Historical Drama as Trauerspiel – *Richard II* and After', *ELH*, 75 (2008), 673–705.

53 Ernst Kantorowicz, *The King's Two Bodies: A Study in Medieval Political Theology* (Princeton: Princeton University Press, 1997); 'there is more reality in theatrical appearances': Santner, op. cit. (note 31), p.45.

54 Hugh Grady, *Shakespeare and Impure Aesthetics* (Cambridge: Cambridge University Press, 2009), pp.9–11 and 95–6.

55 Terry Eagleton, *The Ideology of the Aesthetic* (Oxford: Basil Blackwell, 1990), p.39. See Immanuel Kant, 'What Is Enlightenment?'

in Lewis Beck (ed.), *Kant: On History* (Indianapolis: Bobbs-Merrill, 1963); and the extended critique of 'critique' by Jacques Derrida, 'Parergon', in *The Truth of Painting*, ed. Geoff Bennington and Ian McLeod (Chicago: University of Chicago Press, 1987), pp. 15–147.

56 For a Schmittian reading which argues that Shakespeare's commoners (or his theatre audience) are actually the *victims* of the revolution in representation, that favours only a privileged elite (including the actors themselves), see Oliver Arnold, *The Third Citizen: Shakespeare's Theater and the Early Modern House of Commons* (Baltimore: Johns Hopkins University Press, 2007).

57 René Girard, *A Theater of Envy: William Shakespeare* (Oxford: Oxford University Press, 1991), p. 273.

58 Carl Schmitt, op. cit. (note 49), pp. 12 and 31–2.

59 Carl Schmitt, *Hamlet or Hecuba: The Intrusion of the Time into the Play*, trans. David Pan and Jennifer Rust (New York: Telos Press, 2009), pp. 54–6; 'resistance to representation': Jonathan Goldberg, 'Shakespearean Inscriptions: The Voicing of Power', in Patricia Parker and Geoffrey Hartman (eds), *Shakespeare and the Question of Theory* (London: Methuen, 1985), pp. 116–37; 'leads in the direction of absolutism': Debora Shuger, *Political Theologies in Shakespeare's England: The Sacred and the State in 'Measure for Measure'* (Basingstoke: Palgrave, 2001), p. 79; 'jeopardises the whole social and cosmic order': Richard McCoy, *Alterations of State: Sacred Kingship in the English Reformation* (New York: 2002), p. xii.

60 Santner, op. cit. (note 31), pp. 46–7.

61 'Putting the people in place of the King': ibid., p. 92, quoting T.J. Clark, *Farewell to an Idea: Episodes from a History of Modernism* (New Haven: Yale University Press, 1999), p. 47; 'democracy and sovereignty': Jacques Derrida, *Rogues: Two Essays on Reason*, trans. Pascale-Anne Brault and Michael Naas (Stanford: Stanford University Press, 2005), p. 100. For a sharp discussion of the 'aporetic embrace' of sovereignty and democracy in Derrida's thinking, see Pheng Cheah, 'The Untimely Secret of Democracy', in Pheng Cheah and Suzanne Guerlac (eds.), *Derrida and the Time of the Political* (Durham, NC: Duke University Press, 2009), pp. 74–96.

62 Theodor Adorno, *Notes to Literature*, trans. Shierry Weber Nicholsen (2 vols, New York: Columbia University Press, 1991), vol. 1, p. 42.

63 Edward Bullough, '"Psychical Distance" as a Factor in Art and an Aesthetic Principle', *British Journal of Psychology*, 5 (1912), 87–117;

64 Richard Wilson, *Shakespeare in French Theory: King of Shadows* (London: Routledge, 2007), p. 260.

65 'Productive, purposeful': Charles Whitney, 'Ante-Aesthetics: Towards

a Theory of Early Modern Audience Response', in *Shakespeare and Modernity: Early Modern to Millennium*, ed. Hugh Grady (London: Routledge, 2000), p.42.

66 Sean Gaston, *Derrida and Disinterest* (London: Continuum, 2005), p.34; John Milton, *Paradise Lost*, ed. Gordon Teskey (New York: Norton, 2005), Book 1, ll. 254–5, p.10.

67 Thomas Hobbes, *Leviathan; or, The Matter, Forme, & Power of a Commonwealth Ecclesiastical and Civill*, ed. Richard Tuck (Cambridge: Cambridge University Press, 1996), p.31.

68 'A composing third way': Sir Edward Dering; and 'No neutrality is admitted', both quoted in Trevor Royle, *Civil War: The Wars of the Three Kingdoms, 1638–1660* (London: Little, Brown, 2004), p.178.

69 Girard, op. cit. (note 57), p.199; 'The great majority of Catholics': K.J. Lindley, 'The Part Played by Catholics in the English Civil War', unpub. Manchester PhD (1968), pp.iv–v; 'I never had any intention …': Jonathan Langley to Sir Francis Otterley and Henry Bromley; 'a middle way': Thomas Knyvett to Katherine Knyvett; 'love their pudding': Sir Robert Poyntz to the Duke of Ormonde; Sir James Vaughan of Trawscoed, all quoted in Charles Carlton, *Going to the Wars: The Experience of the British Civil Wars, 1638–1651* (London: Routledge, 1992), pp.290–1.

70 Francis Barker, *The Culture of Violence: Essays on Tragedy and History* (Manchester: Manchester University Press, 1993), p.71; Catherine Belsey, *The Subject of Tragedy: Identity and Difference in Renaissance Drama* (London: Methuen, 1985).

71 Caroline Spurgeon, *Shakespeare's Imagery and What It Tells Us* (Cambridge: Cambridge University Press, 1958), pp.97–9 and frontispiece; Mary Thomas Crane, *Shakespeare's Brain: Reading with Cognitive Theory* (Princeton: Princeton University Press, 2001), esp. pp.32–3. See also Ira Clark, *Rhetorical Readings, Dark Comedies, and Shakespeare's Problem Plays* (Gainesville: University of Florida Press, 2007), pp.41–56, where it is suggested that chiasmus provides Shakespeare with a model for a Solomonic concept of justice; and William Engel, *Chiastic Designs in English Literature from Sidney to Shakespeare* (Farnham: Ashgate, 2009), pp.96–7, where chiasmus is presented as the 'symbolic form' of a Mannerist 'memory theatre' which allowed Shakespeare to remain 'mindful of the gods'.

72 Peter Platt, *Shakespeare and the Culture of Paradox: Studies in Performance and Early Modern Drama* (Burlington, VT: Ashgate, 2009); Paola Pugliatti, *Shakespeare the Historian* (Basingstoke: Macmillan, 1996), pp.43–5 and 47. Pugliatti provides a valuable historical survey of the literature on Shakespearean ambivalence that commences with A.P. Rossiter's 1951 lecture on 'Ambivalence:

the Dialectic of History', printed in *Angel with Horns and Other Shakespeare Lectures*, ed. Graham Storey (London: Longmans, 1961). For the tradition that Shakespeare's ambivalence originated in the Tudor schoolroom technique of arguing on both sides of the question, see Joel Altman, *The Tudor Play of Mind* (Berkeley: University of California Press, 1978); Rosalie Colie, *Paradoxica epidemica* (Princeton: Princeton University Press, 1966); and Madeleine Doran, *Endeavors of Art* (Madison: University of Wisconsin Press, 1954). On Shakespeare as an equivocal or interrogative text, see Norman Rabkin, *Shakespeare and the Common Understanding* (London: Collier-Macmillan, 1967), and 'Rabbits, Ducks, and *Henry V*', *Shakespeare Quarterly*, 28 (1977), 279–96.; R. Grudin, *Mighty Opposites: Shakespeare and Renaissance Contrariety* (Berkeley: University of California Press, 1979); Jonathan Dollimore, *Radical Tragedy: Religion, Ideology and Power in the Drama of Shakespeare and His Contemporaries* (Brighton: Harvester Wheatsheaf, 1984); and Steven Mullaney, 'Lying Like Truth: Riddle, Representation and Treason in Renaissance England', *ELH*, 47 (1980), 32–47, repr. in *The Place of the Stage: License, Play, and Power in Renaissance England* (Chicago: Chicago University Press, 1988), pp. 116–34.

73 'Words of avoidance': Annabel Patterson, *Milton's Words* (Oxford: Oxford University Press, 2009); 'rules of its own': *Censorship and Interpretation: The Conditions of Writing and Reading in Early Modern England* (Madison: University of Wisconsin Press, 1984), pp. 4–18. For a similar historicist take on seventeenth-century literary ambiguity, see Lois Potter, *Secret Rites and Secret Writing: Royalist Literature 1641–1660* (Cambridge: Cambridge University Press, 1989), pp. 38–71.

74 Patricia Parker, *Shakespeare From the Margins: Language, Culture, Context* (Chicago: Chicago University Press, 1996), p. 28; Kiernan Ryan, *Shakespeare* (3rd ed., Basingstoke: Palgrave, 2002), pp. 121 and 124.

75 Nicholl, op. cit. (note 34), p. 278.

76 Derrida, op. cit. (note 7), p. 48.

77 Shapiro, op. cit. (note 26), pp. 142 and 153.

78 Harold Bloom, *The Anatomy of Influence* (New Haven: Yale University Press, 2011), p. 49.

79 Jacques Derrida, *Margins of Philosophy*, trans. Alan Bass (Chicago: University of Chicago Press, 1972), pp. 3–27, here p. 13.

80 T.S. Eliot, 'The Hollow Men'; Christopher Pye, *The Vanishing: Shakespeare, the Subject, and Early Modern Culture* (Durham, NC: Duke University Press, 2000), pp. 112 and 150–1; Paul Yachnin, *Stage-Wrights: Shakespeare, Jonson, Middleton and the Making of*

Theatrical Value (Philadelphia: University of Pennsylvania Press, 1997), passim.

81 Terry Eagleton, *William Shakespeare* (Oxford: Blackwell, 1986), p. 70.

82 Pheng Cheah and Suzanne Guerlac, 'Introduction: Derrida and the Time of the Political', in Cheah and Guerlac, op. cit. (note 61), p. 16.

83 François Noudelmann, *The Philosopher's Touch: Sartre, Nietzsche, and Barthes at the Piano* (New York: Columbia University Press, 2012), pp. 35–6 and 39.

84 'That which neutralizes the event': Jacques Derrida, 'As If It Were Possible: "Within Such Limits"', in *Paper Machine*, trans. Rachel Bowlby (Stanford: Stanford University Press, 2005), pp. 90–1; 'a force without power': 'Performative Powerlessness: A Response to Simon Critchley', *Constellations*, 7:4 (2000), 466–68, here 468. For Shakespeare's stage fright as a form of 'narcissistic' terror of exposure, see Meredith Anne Skura, *Shakespeare the Actor and the Purposes of Playing* (Chicago: Chicago University Press, 1993).

85 Greenblatt, op. cit. (note 9), p. 302.

86 Richard Helgerson, *Self-Crowned Laureates: Spenser, Jonson, Milton and the Literary System* (Berkeley: University of California Press, 1983), p. 13; 'banishment, disguise, exile': John Orr, 'The Hidden Agenda: Pierre Bourdieu and Terry Eagleton', in *Reading Bourdieu on Society and Culture*, ed. Bridget Fowler (Oxford: Basil Blackwell, 2000), p. 128.

87 'It won't be long': Jacques Derrida, *Specters of Marx: The State of the Debt, the Work of Mourning, and the New International*, trans. Peggy Kamuf (London: Routledge, 1994), p. 4; 'to have understood a call': Jacques Derrida, quoted in Jean-Luc Nancy, 'The Free Voice of Man', in Philippe Lacoue-Labethe and Jean-Luc Nancy, *Retreating the Political*, trans. Simon Sparks (London: Routledge, 1997), p. 54.

88 Benjamin, op. cit. (note 52), p. 135.

89 Frank Kermode, *The Sense of an Ending: Studies in the Theory of Fiction* (Oxford: Oxford University Press, 1966), p. 82.

90 Hélène Cixous, '"What Is It O'Clock?" or The Door (We Never) Enter', trans. Catherine MacGillivray, in *Stigmata: Escaping Texts* (London: Routledge, 1998), pp. 57–83, esp. pp. 57–63; René Descartes, *Meditations on First Philosophy*, trans. John Cottingham (Cambridge: Cambridge University Press, 2003), p. 24. And see Stephen Booth, *'King Lear', 'Macbeth', Indefinition, and Tragedy* (New Haven: Yale University Press, 1983); and Nicholas Royle, *How to Read Shakespeare* (London: Granta, 2005), pp. 34 and 37.

91 Katharine Eisaman Maus, *Inwardness and Theater in the English Renaissance* (Chicago: Chicago University Press, 1995), pp. 4 and 190; 'great with child to speak': Sir Philip Sidney, 'Astrophel and

Stella', 1, l.13, in *The Poems of Sir Philip Sidney* (Oxford: Clarendon Press, 1962), p.165.

92 Ibid., pp.15–24.

93 Ben Jonson, *Timber, or Discoveries*, in *The Works of Ben Jonson*, ed. C.H. Herford and P. and E. Simpson (11 vols, Oxford: Oxford University Press, 1925–52), vol. 8, pp.583–4.

94 Ibid.; 'rewrote Shakespearean inwardness': Yachnin, op. cit. (note 80), p.111.

95 Ludwig Wittgenstein, *Culture and Value*, ed. G.H. von Wright, trans. Peter Winch (Oxford: Blackwell, 2006), p.98.

96 'Unstaunchable flow': Terry Eagleton, op. cit. (note 81), p.1; 'resistant art': Lorenz Jäger, *Adorno: A Political Biography*, trans. Stewart Spencer (New Haven: Yale University Press, 2004), pp.188–9; Joel Fineman, *The Subjectivity Effect in Western Literary Tradition: Essays Towards the Release of Shakespeare's Will* (Cambridge, Mass.: MIT Press, 1991), pp.169 and 214. For a terrifying Žižekian riff arguing for the 'rashness' of Shakespeare's decisionism, see Ewan Fernie, 'The Last Act: Presentism, Spirituality and the Politics of *Hamlet*', in *Spiritual Shakespeares*, ed. Ewan Fernie (London: Routledge, 2005), pp.186–211, esp. p.194.

97 Jonathan Goldberg, *Shakespeare's Hand* (Minneapolis: Minnesota University Press, 2003), p.129.

98 For Shakespeare's valorization of the handclasp and terror of the severed hand, see Katherine Rowe, *Dead Hands: Fictions of Agency, Renaissance and Modern* (Stanford: Stanford University Press, 1999), p.83.

99 Fineman, op. cit. (note 96), p.168. For writing in public as a transvaluation of the Cartesian opposition, see the meticulous analysis in Kevin Kopelson, *Neatness Counts: Essays on the Writer's Desk* (Minneapolis: University of Minnesota Press, 2004), pp.62–3, 114–15 et passim.

100 For the 'hypocrisis' of writing as misrepresentation, see the brilliant deconstructionist reading of Donne, *John Donne Undone* by Thomas Docherty (London: Methuen, 1986), pp.89–119. Jacques Derrida, *Learning to Live Finally: The Last Interview*, trans. Pascale-Anne Brault and Michael Naas (Basingstoke: Palgrave Macmillan, 2007), pp.32–3.

101 Derrida, op. cit. (note 84), p.20.

102 Robert Weimann, *Author's Pen and Actor's Voice: Playing and Writing in Shakespeare's Theatre* (Cambridge: Cambridge University Press, 2000); Patrick Cheney, *Shakespeare, National Poet-Playwright* (Cambridge: Cambridge University Press, 2004).

103 Miguel de Cervantes, *The History of Don Quixote of the Mancha*,

trans. Thomas Shelton (London: 1620; repr. 4 vols., London: David Nutt, 1896), vol. 4, chap. 62, p. 195.

104 Carlos Fuentes, 'Cervantes, or The Critique of Reading', in *Myself with Others: Selected Essays* (London: Andre Deutsch, 1988), pp. 53–4, 58, 63 and 69–70.

105 Adrian Johns, *The Nature of the Book: Print and Knowledge in the Making* (Chicago: Chicago University Press, 1998), p. 68.

106 Henry Condell and John Heminge, 'To the great Variety of Readers', repr. in William Shakespeare, *The Norton Shakespeare*, ed. Stephen Greenblatt, Walter Cohen, Jean Howard and Katharine Eisaman Maus (New York: Norton, 1997), p. 335.

107 Leah Marcus, *Puzzling Shakespeare: Local Reading and Its Discontents* (Berkeley: California University Press, 1988), p. 24; Virginia Woolf, *Orlando: A Biography* (London: Penguin, 2006), p. 20.

108 See Robert Gottlieb, 'Lit-Flicks', *New York Review of Books*, 54:14, 27 September 2007, 20–2.

109 Michel Foucault, What Is an Author?' trans. Josué V. Harari, in *The Foucault Reader*, ed. Paul Rabinow (Harmondsworth: Penguin, 1984), pp. 106–7.

110 Lukas Erne, *Shakespeare as Literary Dramatist* (Cambridge: Cambridge University Press, 2003), p. 33; John Kerrigan, 'The Editor as Reader: Constructing Renaissance Texts', in James Raven, Helen Small and Naomi Tadmor (eds), *The Practice and Representation of Reading in England* (Cambridge: Cambridge University Press, 1996), pp. 102–24. Kerrigan also emphaizes the role of the reader in deconstructing the author.

111 For the noxious constituents of ink, see Margreta De Grazi and Peter Stallybrass, 'The Materiality of the Shakespearean Text', *Shakespeare Quarterly*, 44 (1993), 281–2.

112 Patrick Cheney, *Shakespeare's Literary Authorship* (Cambridge: Cambridge University Press, 2008), p. 15; Richard Hillman, *Self-Speaking in Medieval and Early Modern English Drama: Subjectivity, Discourse, and the Stage* (Basingstoke: Macmillan, 1997), p. 133.

113 'Print gave books and authors': John Mullan, *Anonymity: A Secret History of English Literature* (London: Faber & Faber, 2007), p. 286.

114 David Bergeron, *Textual Patronage in English Drama, 1570–1640* (London: Ashgate, 2006), p. 142.

115 Johns, op. cit. (note 105), pp. 31–7.

116 Frederick Kiefer, *Writing on the Renaissance Stage: Written Words, Printed Pages, Metaphoric Books* (Newark: University of Delaware Press, 1998), p. 292.

117 Foucault, op. cit. (note 109), pp. 118–19. Cf. Clare Connors, 'Derrida

and the Fiction of Force', *Angelaki*, 12:2 (2007), 13: 'It's deliberately orotund this chorus ... as well as excessive, in its very humility. It needs to invoke pardon, since it's a crooked not a perfect figure.'

118 Jeffrey Knapp, 'Religious Pluralization and Single Authorship in Shakespeare's Histories', in Andreas Höfele, Stephan Laqué, Enno Ruge and Gabriela Schmidt (eds), *Representing Religious Pluralization in Early Modern Europe* (Berlin: Lit Verlag, 2007), pp. 168–9. For an incisive account of the Nietzschean concept of embodiment, and Foucault's evolving notion of the body as both formed and forming, see Hoy, op. cit. (note 47), pp. 57–69.

119 Shapiro, op. cit. (note 26), p. 41; Matthew Arnold, 'Shakespeare', in *The Oxford Authors: Matthew Arnold*, eds Miriam Allott and Robert Super (Oxford: Oxford University Press, 1986), p. 8.

120 Stephen Greenblatt, *Renaissance Self-Fashioning: From More to Shakespeare* (Chicago: Chicago University Press, 1980), p. 256.

121 Leo Bersani and Ulysse Dutoit, *Caravaggio's Secrets* (Cambridge, Mass.: MIT Press, 1998), pp. 8–9; Richard Wilson, *Secret Shakespeare: Studies in Theatre, Religion, and Resistance* (Manchester: Manchester University Press, 2004).

122 Stanley Cavell, 'The Interminable Shakespearean Text', in *Philosophy The Day After Tomorrow* (Cambridge, Mass.: Harvard University Press, 2005), p. 57. Where Cavell's interpretation differs from the one offered here, however, is in his emphasis on Shakespeare's staging of 'stifled speech' and 'suppressed expression' (p. 58).

123 Sidney, op. cit. (note 91), l, 14.

124 For the association of self-expression with torture and execution, see Elizabeth Hanson, *Discovering the Subject in Renaissance England* (Cambridge: Cambridge University Press, 1998); Maus, op. cit. (note 89); and Wilson, op. cit. (note 121).

125 'Visibility is a trap': Michel Foucault, *Discipline and Punish: The Birth of the Prison*, trans. Alan Sheridan (Harmondsworth: Penguin, 1977), p. 200.

126 'Masked philosopher': 'Le Philosophe masqué,' anonymized interview with Christian Delacampagne, *Le monde dimanche*, 6 April 1980, 1 and 17, quoted in David Macey, *The Lives of Michel Foucault* (London: Hutchinson, 1993), p. 426: 'For someone like me, and I am not a great author, but simply one who manufactures books, one likes [the books] to be read for their own sake'; 'To write without a face': Michel Foucault, *The Archaeology of Knowledge*, trans. Alan Sheridan (London: Tavistock, 1972), p. 17; 'speaking was strange and boring': 'An Interview with Stephen Riggins' (Toronto, June 1982), in *Michel Foucault: The Essential Works: 1: Ethics*, ed. Paul Rabinow (London: Allen Lane, 1997), pp. 121–2: 'Silence may be a much

more interesting way of having a relationship with people ... This is
something that I believe is really worth cultivating. I'm in favour of
developing silence as a cultural ethos.'

127 'Resistance is never in a position': Michel Foucault, *History of Sexuality*,
vol. 1, *An Introduction*, trans. Robert Hurley (Harmondsworth:
Penguin, 1980), pp. 94–5; 'Resistance relies': 'Sex, Power, and the
Politics of Identity' (interview with B. Gallagher and A. Wilson,
Toronto, June 1982, originally pub. in *The Advocate*, 400 (7 August
1984), op. cit., 1997 (note 126), p. 168: 'For instance ... the medical
definition of homosexuality ... which was a means of oppression, was
a means of resistance as well, since people could say, "If we are sick,
why do you condemn us?"'. 'Honey tongued': Francis Meres, *Palladis
Tamia: Wit's Treasury* (London: 1598), ff. 281v–2, repr. in Samuel
Schoenbaum, op. cit. (note 38), p. 140. For the 'tactfully suppressed
grievance that Shakespeare did not love dogs as he should', because
he associated sycophancy with spaniels licking candy, see William
Empson, *The Structure of Complex Words* (London: Chatto and
Windus, 1951), p. 176.

128 Jacques Lacan, 'Desire and the Interpretation of Desire in *Hamlet*', ed.
Jacques-Alain Miller, trans. James Hulbert, *Yale French Studies*, 55/6
(1977), 11–52, esp. 18–19; Ben Jonson, 'Induction', *Cynthia's Revels*,
in *Ben Jonson*, ed. C.H. Herford and Percy Simpson (11 vols, Oxford:
Clarendon Press, 1925–52); for the 'book-holder' as prompter, see
Andrew Gurr, *The Shakespearean Stage* (Cambridge: Cambridge
University Press, 1992), pp. 208–11.

129 Judith Butler, *Excitable Speech: A Politics of the Performative* (London:
Routledge, 1997), pp. 15–16.

130 'From commanded performance': Luke Wilson, *Theaters of Intention:
Drama and the Law in Early Modern England* (Stanford: Stanford
University Press, 2000), p. 170; Pierre Bourdieu, 'Intellectual Field and
Creative Project', trans. Sian France, in *Knowledge and Control: New
Directions in the Sociology of Education* (London: Collier-Macmillan,
1971), pp. 161–4.

131 Ibid., p. 162; 'from a system of patronage': Kathleen McLuskie and
Felicity Dunsworth, 'Patronage and the Economics of Theater', in *A
New History of Early English Drama*, eds John Cox and David Scott
Kastan (New York: Columbia University Press, 1997), pp. 423–40,
here p. 426.

132 Peter Bürger, *Theory of the Avant-Garde*, trans. Michael Shaw
(Minneapolis: University of Minnesota Press, 1984), pp. 36–7. Bürger
provides an invaluable overview of the voluminous German literature
on the problem of the autonomy of art in early modern society: see in
particular pp. 112–13.

133 Andrew Gurr, *The Shakespeare Company, 1594–1642* (Cambridge: Cambridge University Press, 2004), p. 19.

134 Yachnin, op. cit. (note 80), p. 66; Gurr, op. cit. (note 133), p. 88.

135 For discussions of this paradox, see Alvin Kernan, *Shakespeare, the King's Playwright: Theater in the Stuart Court, 1603–1613* (New Haven: Yale University Press, 1995), pp. 178, 180 and 195; and Richard Wilson, 'The Management of Mirth: Shakespeare *via* Bourdieu', in op. cit. (note 64), pp. 123–39.

136 'Last of the great house lords': Skura, op. cit. (note 84), p. 201. For Ariel as a boy-player, see David Mann, *The Elizabethan Player: Contemporary Stage Representations* (London: Routledge, 1991), p. 41.

137 For the official side of this bargain, see Leah Marcus, *The Politics of Mirth: Jonson, Herrick, Milton, Marvell, and the Defense of Old Holiday Pastimes* (Chicago: Chicago University Press, 1986).

138 David Schwalkwyk, *Shakespeare, Love and Service* (Cambridge: Cambridge University Press, 2008), p. 1. For Shakespeare's grounding in a service economy, see also Elizabeth Rivlin, *The Aesthetics of Service in Early Modern England* (Evanston: Northwestern University Press, 2012), chap. 1.

139 Pierre Bourdieu, *Language and Symbolic Power*, trans. Gino Raymond and Matthew Adamson (Oxford: Polity Press, 1991), pp. 81–9; Skura, op. cit. (note 84), pp. 144, 171 and 285, n. 94.

140 Julia Lupton, *Citizen-Saints: Shakespeare and Political Theology* (Chicago: Chicago University Press, 2005), pp. 164–5 and 168–71; an earlier version appeared as 'Creature Caliban', *Shakespeare Quarterly*, 51 (2000), 1–23.

141 Repr. in Schoenbaum, op. cit. (note 38), p. 199. For Shakespeare as a 'waiter', see Ernest Law, *Shakespeare as a Groom of the Chamber* (London: G. Bell, 1910): 'All things considered, everything points to the main function of Shakespeare and his fellow actors having been very much what is said to be that of the modern gentleman-usher at the court of St. James – to stand about' (p. 31).

142 Walter Benjamin, 'Franz Kafka: On the Tenth Anniversary of His Death', in *Illuminations*, trans. Harry Zohn (London: Jonathan Cape, 1970), pp. 133–4.

143 Simon Palfrey and Tiffany Stern, *Shakespeare in Parts* (Oxford: Oxford University Press, 2007), pp. 84 and 121. For the psychological implications of the Elizabethan reliance on the 'cue-line', see Murray Cox and Alice Theilgard, *Shakespeare as Prompter: The Amending Imagination and the Therapeutic Process* (London: Jessica Kingsley, 1994), pp. 110–11 et passim.

144 Lacan quoted and discussed in Eric Santner, *On Creaturely Life:*

Rilke, Benjamin, Sebald (Chicago: University of Chicago Press, 2006) p.39; Georges Bataille, *The Accursed Share: An Essay on General Economy*, trans. Robert Hurley (New York: Zone Books, 1993), p.243. For an incisive commentary on the aptness to Elizabethan literature, and specifically to the Petrarchan sonnet sequence, of Bataille's notion of sovereign abjection as 'a force folded back on itself probing the limits of its own mode of existence', see Fred Botting and Scott Wilson, *Bataille* (Basingstoke: Palgrave, 2001), pp.53–67 (here p.56).

145 'To render one without personality': David Rieff, *Swimming in a Sea of Death: A Son's Memoir* (London: Granta, 2008), p.100; Privy Council minute, 19 February 1598, *Acts of the Privy Council*, ed. J.R. Dasent (32 vols, London: H.M.S.O., 1890–1907), vol. 28, p.327.

146 Leeds Barroll, *Politics, Plague and Shakespere's Theater* (Ithaca: Cornell University Press, 1991), p.17.

147 Weimann, op. cit. (note 102), pp.153 and 161.

148 Derrida, op. cit. (note 79), pp.13 and 27.

149 Butler, op. cit. (note 129), pp.40 and 129.

150 Erne, op. cit. (note 110), pp.234–41.

151 'Willing over-supplier': Gurr, op. cit. (note 133), p.14; Ben Jonson, 'To the memory of my beloved, the author,' repr. in William Shakespeare, op. cit. (note 106), p.3352; Butler, op. cit. (note 129), p.16.

152 Douglas Bruster and Robert Weimann, *Prologue to Shakespeare: Performance and Liminality in Early Modern Drama* (London: Routledge, 2004), pp.40 and 153. See also Tiffany Stern, *Rehearsal from Shakespeare to Sheridan* (Oxford: Clarendon Press, 2000), p.116.

153 Stanley Wells, *Shakespeare & Co.* (London: Allen Lane, 2006), pp.4–5, 27 and 231. The collaborative and even intermarried guild-like mutuality of Shakespeare's company has likewise been emphasized by Roslyn Knutson in *Playing Companies and Commerce in Shakespeare's Time* (Cambridge: Cambridge University Press, 2001); and by William Ingram in 'Neere the Playe Howse: The Swan Theater and Community Blight', *Renaissance Drama*, 4 (1971), 53–68; and 'The Globe Playhouse and Its Neighbours in 1600', *Essays in Theatre*, 2 (1984), 63–72.

154 Bart Van Es, 'Company Man: Another Crucial Year for Shakespeare', *Times Literary Supplement*, 2 February 2007, pp.14–15; Jeffrey Knapp, *Shakespeare Only* (Chicago: University of Chicago Press, 2009), p.33.

155 Ralph Waldo Emerson, *Representative Men*, ed. Pamela Schirmeister (New York: Marsilio, 1995), p.188.

156 Pierre Bourdieu, *The Rules of Art: Genesis and Structure of the Literary*

Field, trans. Susan Emanuel (Cambridge: Cambridge University Press, 1996), p.104.

157 'Intrusion': Jeffrey Masten, *Textual Intercourse: Collaboration, Authorship, and Sexualities in Renaissance Drama* (Cambridge: Cambridge University Press, 1997), p.108; 'indifferent to such individuation': David Scott Kastan, *Shakespeare and the Book* (Cambridge: Cambridge University Press, 2001), p.78.

158 Erne, op. cit. (note 110), p.2.

159 John Davies of Hereford, 'To our English Terence, Mr. Will. Shakespeare', repr. Chambers, op. cit. (note 1), vol. 2, p.214.

160 Derrida, op. cit. (note 7); Jacques Derrida and Elizabeth Roudinesco, *For What Tomorrow ... A Dialogue*, trans. Jeff Ford (Stanford: Stanford University Press, 2004), p.127.

161 Jacques Lacan quoted in Elisabeth Roudinesco, *Philosophy in Turbulent Times: Canguilhem, Sartre, Foucault, Althusser, Deleuze, Derrida*, trans. William McCuaig (New York: Columbia University Press, 2008), p.150. See also Benoît Peeters, *Derrida: A Biography*, trans. Andrew Brown (Cambridge: Polity Press, 2012), p.169.

162 'Powerless theatre': Yachnin, op. cit. (note 80), pp.12–13 and 21; Jacques Derrida, 'The Future of the Profession or the University Without Condition (Thanks to the "Humanities" what could *take place tomorrow*)', in *Jacques Derrida and the Humanities: A Critical Reader*, ed. Tom Cohen (Cambridge: Cambridge University Press, 2001), p.27. The claim that the aesthetic groundlessness of Shakespearean theatre ushers in the condition of modernity as a permanent crisis of meaning had been made by Hugh Grady in *Shakespeare's Universal Wolf: Studies in Early Modern Reification* (Oxford: Clarendon Press, 1996).

163 Virginia Woolf, 'Reading at Random: Anon' (1940), quoted in Hermione Lee, *Virginia Woolf* (London: Chatto & Windus, 1996), p.750.

164 Jacques Derrida, *Geneses, Genealogies, Genres and Genius: The Secrets of the Archive*, trans. Beverley Bie Brahic (Edinburgh: Edinburgh University Press, 2003), pp.18–19.

165 Richard Dutton, 'The Birth of the Author', in *Texts and Cultural Change in Early Modern England*, eds Cedric Brown and Arthur Marotti (Basingstoke: Macmillan, 1997, pp.153–78, here p.161.

166 Jeffrey Knapp, *Shakespeare's Tribe: Church, Nation, and Theater in Renaissance England* (Chicago: The University of Chicago Press, 2002), p.54.

167 Jacques Derrida, 'From Restricted and General Economy: A Hegelianism Without Reserve', in *Writing and Difference*, trans. Alan Bass (London: Routledge & Kegan Paul, 1985), p.265.

168 Thomas Heywood, 'Epistle' (to the printer Nicholas Okes), *An Apology for Actors* (London: 1612), quoted in Schoenbaum, op. cit. (note 38), pp. 219–20.

169 For the self-deflating trope of 'cosmesis', see Frank Whigham, *Ambition and Privilege: The Tropes of Elizabethan Courtesy Theory* (Berkeley: University of California Press, 1984), p. 116.

170 T.S. Eliot, 'Tradition and the Individual Talent', in *Selected Essays* (London: Faber and Faber, 1932), pp. 17 and 21.

171 Derrida, op. cit. (note 61), p. 152.

172 Wilson, op. cit. (note 130), pp. 175–7 and 217–19.

173 Greenblatt, op. cit. (note 9), pp. 152 and 155.

174 Richard Wilson, 'The Kindly Ones: The Death of the Author in Shakespearean Athens', op. cit. (note 64), p. 160.

175 Rainer Maria Rilke, 'The Spirit Ariel (After reading Shakespeare's *Tempest*)', in *Rilke: Selected Poems*, trans. J.B. Leishman (Harmondsworth: Penguin, 1964), p. 74. For Thomas Mann's strategic 'hiding in full view', see Michael Maar, *Bluebeard's Chamber: Guilt and Confession in Thomas Mann*, trans. David Fernbach (London: Verso, 2003).

176 Phyllis Rackin, *Stages of History: Shakespeare's English Chronicles* (Ithaca: Cornell University Press, 1990), p. 244; 'ironically self-deprecating cameos': Skura, op. cit. (note 84), p. 139.

177 Mark Thornton-Burnett, *Masters and Servants in English Renaissance Drama and Culture: Authority and Obedience* (Basingstoke: Palgrave, 1997), p. 147.

178 A.D. Nuttall, *Shakespeare the Thinker* (New Haven: Yale University Press, 2007), pp. 377–8.

179 'A never writer to an ever reader', 'Preface', *Troilus and Cressida* (London: 1609). For the implications, see in particular Joseph Loewenstein, *Ben Jonson and Possessive Authorship* (Cambridge: Cambridge University Press, 2002), pp. 26–9.

180 Jonathan Goldberg, *Voice Terminal Echo: Postmodernism and English Renaissance Texts* (London: Methuen, 1986), p. 97.

181 'Thought is free': James VI and I, 'Song, the first verses that ever the King made' (1582), in *The Poems of James VI of Scotland* (2 vols, Edinburgh: William Blackwood, 1955–58), vol. 2, p. 132.

182 See Wilson, op. cit. (note 130), pp. 259–60; and Richard Halpern, '"The Picture of Nobody": White Cannibalism in *The Tempest*', in *The Production of English Renaissance Culture*, ed. David Lee Miller, Sharon O'Dair and Harold Weber (Ithaca: Cornell University Press, 1994), pp. 262–92.

183 'Institutionalised residue': Terry Cochran, *Twilight of the Literary: Figures of Thought in the Age of Print* (Cambridge, Mass.: Harvard

University Press, 2005), p.232; 'the author he never was': Kastan, op. cit. (note 153), p.71. See also Nora Johnson, *The Actor as Playwright in Early Modern Drama* (Cambridge: Cambridge University Press, 2003), p.166 et passim: 'The notion of the individual author may indeed be "mythical", then as now, but early modern England was no more immune than we are to the creation of myths'.

184 'To The Reader,' repr. in William Shakespeare, op. cit. (note 106), p.3346: 'This figure, that thou here seest put, / It was for gentle Shakespeare cut; / Wherein the Graver had a strife / With Nature, to outdo the life ...'.

185 Michel Foucault, *The Order of Things: An Archaeology of the Human Sciences*, trans. anon. (London: Tavistock, 1970), p.387.

2

Welsh roots

Shakespeare's brute part

He cut our roots in characters

[Cymbeline, 4,2,51]

We have the man Shakespeare

'We have the man Shakespeare with us':[1] Lady Mary Herbert's
reported message to her son William, third Earl of Pembroke,
roots the dramatist firmly within the Welsh personal politics that
might have shaped his professional career. But it also grounds the
radical correction they make to traditional criticism: that throughout his work Shakespeare identifies Wales not with the uprooted
or dispossessed, dominated and despised by 'English' colonialism,
but with the dominators and possessors, *as itself the root of imperial power*. The countess's boast can thus stand as a frame for the
dramatist's ironic stance towards his own creative circumstances.
For the proprietorial claim by the imperious sister of Sir Philip and
daughter of Sir Henry Sidney, 'greatest of the Presidents of Wales',
reminds us sharply how his patronage relations – which demanded
a servile dedication of his published Works to 'The Most Noble
and Incomparable Brethren, William Earl of Pembroke, &c ... and
Philip, Earl of Montgomery, &c ...' – locked his writing into the
'British' imperialism and unionism that were the mythic patrimony
of this Welsh elite.[2] The very idea of Shakespeare as 'The Bard'
seats him mystically, of course, among the *beirdd cefn gwlad*, poets
elevated by the gentry to sing the Old Song of the Welsh. But the
startling revision made by recent research on Shakespeare and his
patrons has been a realization not only of the prominence his plays
give Anglo-Welsh relations but also of how false the critical cliché
of the subjugation of 'Poor Taffy' by the *saesneg* is made to look

by the power and prosperity of this sixteenth-century 'Wales of the squires, with the great house of Herbert rising newly minted from their ranks'.[3]

In the Peasants' Revolt of 1549 'a great number of the commons up about Salisbury in Wiltshire plucked down Sir William's Herbert's park about his new house' at Wilton, the vast trophy estate he had been awarded by his brother-in-law Henry VIII, resisting his rack-renting and enclosure. But this Tudor *condottiere* marched from Glamorgan with his Welsh 'affinity', and attacking his English tenants 'did put them down, overrun and slay them', as the boy king Edward VI gasped, as if they were foreign vermin, in a foretaste of the Highland Clearances 'or even of the National Parks in America'.[4] Then he turned his Welsh army onto the Cornish Catholic 'tag rag' opposing the Protestant Prayer Book with a ferocity that 'burned deep into the memory' of a people 'who lost everything they fought for, since by the end of the century the Cornish language was to be little more than a memory'.[5] These were the achievements for which Herbert was made Earl of Pembroke, and of which Sidney was surely thinking when staying at Wilton a generation later he wrote the heartless story in *Arcadia* of the slaughter of the 'mad multitude' of 'unruly clowns' who rise against King Basilius.[6] And when in 1613 he bought his Blackfriars Gatehouse in London beside their Baynard Castle, Shakespeare would look out on the Herberts' ferocious badge of a wyvern and javelins that commemorated their pig-sticking of the peasants.[7] These brute facts about the atrocious foundation of the Herbert family fortunes need therefore to be remembered in any consideration of Shakespeare and his patrons, since what they illustrate is the terrifying personal politics of his subordination to his Welsh overlords. For despite a postcolonial mythology of 'English' domination, such were in fact the origins of the so-called 'British' empire during Shakespeare's lifetime: appropriation, dispossession and indeed massacre – *by the Welsh* in their newly acquired territories.

Shakespeare's posture towards his Welsh patrons can be viewed as an indicator of the entire relation of his art to power, and of his preoccupation with the paradoxical strength of weakness. For the 'Welsh correction' in recent criticism has involved a rediscovery of the intrusive expansionism of Tudor Wales, and the recognition that in the newly united 'British' isles it was the Principality that now became the heartland. Thus Megan Lloyd's *Speak It in Welsh: Wales and the*

Welsh Language in Shakespeare complicates ethnic stereotypes by examining how the plays are created out of 'an amalgam of ethnicities, like the monarch for whom Shakespeare was writing': Elizabeth, a 'red-haired queen with a Welsh nurse', Blanche Parry, who spoke the tongue of her Tudor forebears and raised Welsh to official status.[8] And Philip Schwyzer's revelatory *Literature, Nationalism and Memory in Early Modern England and Wales* takes this redress of anachronistic assumptions further by reversing the expected hierarchy, and reminding us how the very notion of an empire of 'Great Britain' was invented by England's Welsh and Scottish ruling elites 'largely without native English participation'.[9] So this revision turns tables on postcolonial criticism, to present us with a Shakespeare who is *himself* in a subaltern position, as subject of 'a Welsh *reconquista*' and author of a series of plays in which 'it is apparently the English who must relinquish their old identity and go by the name of Britons'.[10] Thus, if this latest twist in post postcolonial scholarship suggests his earliest admirers might have meant it literally when they imagined the 'Bard of Avon' among the 'harpers and crowthers' of the Tudor eisteddfod, what recent studies like Schwyzer's and Willy Maley's collection *Shakespeare and Wales* ask us to question is the extent to which his works are held hostage to the messianic 'British' political theology, and the degree to which his Welsh promoters were justified to imagine they had 'the man Shakespeare'.[11]

In their tribute to 'our singular good Lords' the King's Men John Heminge and Henry Condell cravenly likened the 1623 Folio to the 'milk, cream, fruits' and 'leavened cake' with which their underlings regaled the Herberts at Wilton, Cardiff Castle and the Welsh 'capital' Ludlow, where their father's and grandfather's courts were so imposing 'a young man might learn there as much good behaviour and manners as should have stuck to him for ever'.[12] That would be Milton's route with *Comus*. And such was the scenario when, as 'Lord President of the Dominion and Principality of Wales and the Marches' – or '*llygad hol Cymru*: the eye of Wales' – the second Earl launched a theatre company with a unionist agenda likely to appeal to the future James I, a venture Marlowe slyly betrayed with his effort however, by having *his* Earl of Pembroke fail to guard the favourite or save Edward II from Rice Ap Howell's 'Welsh hooks'.[13] Shakespeare's offering for Pembroke's Men chimed more with the Herberts' Roman ambitions. But the end-of-empire *Titus Andronicus* was hardly a fanfare for the *imperium* they projected onto 'the darling of Wales', the Pembrokeshire Robert Devereux, Earl of Essex, in his genocidal Irish campaigns.[14] Essex would very soon fall out with the Herberts.[15] So when Shakespeare was commissioned by the Earl's Denbighshire agent, the brother-in-law of the Earl of Derby, Sir John Salusbury of Lleweni, to produce an elegy after Essex's execution, 'The Phoenix and the Turtle' was studiedly obscure; although that obscurity has not prevented speculation that the poet rose to be the 'Bard of Lleweni' penning additional grovelling verses to his host:

> Go blaze abroad the pride of Britain's soil,
>   For virtue, manhood, and for courtesy,
> The only pearl which all proud Wales doth foil,
>   For kindly favour and sobriety,
> Kind unto all, both high and low degree,
>   To rich and poor is worthy Salusbury.[16]

Shakespeare's lucky escape from questioning when his company was suspected of reviving a play about Richard II, probably his own, as a reveille for the Essex Revolt is one of the great mysteries of his biography. But he was likely being shielded by another Herbert kinsman and theatre-lover, the Monmouth-based crypto-Catholic Earl of Worcester.[17] Yet by the time he welcomed the Scottish monarch to Wilton in 1603, as the Countess preened, with an updated *As You Like It* heralding the new state of union, 'When earthly things made even / Atone together' [*5,4,98*], Shakespeare's escapology had developed into a game of artful but persistent evasion of these self-proclaimed 'Great Britons'.[18] Oscar Wilde mischievously proposed that the love-object of the Sonnets was a Welsh boy-player named Willy Hughes. But biographers have preferred the feckless William Herbert – '*colofn y deyrnas*: the pillar of Wales' – as the patronizing but patronized 'Mr WH' to whom the poet is supposed to have declared his exasperated love.[19] If so, these poems, with their images of the Herberts' Black Mountains remembered as a country of 'heart-stopping beauty and unrelenting rain', could stand not only for a bankrupt patronage relationship, but an entire lifetime of conflicted emotions about the myths and magic of this imperial Wales:[20]

> Full many a glorious morning have I seen
> Flatter the mountain tops with sovereign eye,
> Kissing with golden face the meadows green,

Gilding pale streams with heavenly alchemy;
Anon permit the basest clouds to ride
With ugly rack on his celestial face,
And from the forlorn world his visage hide,
Stealing unseen to west with his disgrace.

[Sonnet 33]

Mad as a mad dog

'Where is princely Richmond now? / At Pembroke, or at Ha'rfordwest in Wales': the first mention in *Richard III* of the myth of Tudor 'Britain' marshals a roster of those of 'great name and worth' who beached with 'the Welshman' Harri Tudur on his 'glorious morning' at Milford Haven, which doubles a century later as a homage to Shakespeare's own network of sponsors: 'Sir Walter Herbert, a renownèd soldier, / Sir George Talbot, Sir William Stanley, / Oxford, redoubted Pembroke, Sir James Blunt, / And Rhys-ap-Thomas with a valiant crew ... And towards London do they bend their power' [*4,4,407; 4,5,6–14*]. Among those who came from Cheshire under Stanley, if his father's application for arms is trusted, was Shakespeare's great-grandfather. So although *Richard III* may have been toured by Pembroke's Men, it also exaggerated the role of the Stanleys at Bosworth to flatter these Earls of Derby, the 'Kings' of Celtic Man, who were both the dynasty's and dramatist's backers. With Stanleys to the North, Talbots in the Marches, Rhys-ap-Thomas West and the Herberts South, the last invasion of England, this roll-call proclaims, makes the playhouse a Tudor protectorate. Such magnates, 'clustering thick along the critical Irish road ... were some of the richest in contemporary Europe', and in the Atlantic economy they 'moved resolutely into every conceivable avenue of advancement, from the Court to smuggling and piracy', including theatre patronage.[21] But the awkward fact that an identical muster of Marcher Lords and Welsh gentry would so soon after head up Essex's rebellion explains why forging a new Atlantic 'British' identity became ever more problematic for Shakespeare as the Tudor age ended calamitously with 'the Mayor and all his brethren' staring anxiously westwards from 'the peaceful city' at the 'General of our gracious Empress ... from Ireland coming', while the Earl rallied his 'valiant crew' and 'set on' implacably 'to London' [*Henry V, 5,0,14–33*].

In his study of 'The Question of Britain,' *Between Nations*, David

Baker interprets this famously backhanded compliment as a plea to 'conqu'ring Caesar' [28] to save 'Englishness' from 'barbaric Gaels'.[22] But this unthinking reading overlooks that fact that Essex 'came from the Welsh borders', where most of his veterans would 'steal unseen to west with his disgrace', and that 'his chief steward Sir Gelli Meyrick was a fiery Celt who knew personally the tenants of his master's Welsh lands'. And what recent criticism instead suggests is that flanked by his army of 'boisterous Welsh henchmen', the Earl is actually being identified with the Roman dictator crossing the Rubicon with his legions of Gauls, the Celtic mercenaries of a bellicose Atlantic 'Britain' that was at odds with a pacifist City of London, which still saw its trading prospects in the traditional terms of Europe and the East.[23] In fact, this ominous return from Ireland seems uncannily prophetic of Cromwell's (whose surname should have been that of his Glamorgan great-grandfather Morgan Williams), while Shakespeare's ambivalence towards this Celtic empire sounds strikingly like Andrew Marvell's:

And now the Irish are ashamed
To see themselves in one year tamed;
  So much one man can do
  That does both act and know.[24]

Essex's Atlanticist and Celtic affiliations make his coup look less like a feudal throw-back than an ill-timed attempt to force the birth of a 'British' empire by Caesarean section. In fact, historians now regard Essex and his Welsh 'band of brothers' as 'premature Jacobeans' who were counting on the King of Scots to seize his inheritance with Danish guns; and, with James VI indeed poised to strike, Shakespeare evidently sensed how easily England's unofficial republic would fall prey to the despotic personal rule of an archipelagic monarchy like that of the king's Danish in-laws, as imaged in *Hamlet*.[25] For the future did, of course, belong to a North Atlantic 'British' maritime federation strung from the American colonies to Hanover. Schwyzer therefore echoes Derrida in observing that one way Shakespeare does join the bards is in his spooky awareness of the ways in which the present is ghosted by 'what is past and what is yet to come (or come back)'.[26] The legend that America had in truth been named after its supposed Welsh discoverer apMeurig-apMeuryk-Ameriks might be far-fetched; and the Welsh colony of Cambriol in Newfoundland doomed; but 'Welsh intellectuals concentrated in force behind naval growth, American colonization, and empire'.[27] So in *Henry V* the conqueror who will emerge out of the Irish Sea like another Tudor has a 'British' imperial future on his side that explains why, despite English resentment and Welsh prejudice, it is the Celts in this drama, as in *Richard III*, who do all the uprooting and have the last laugh:

> Remember whom you are to cope withal:
> A sort of vagabonds, rascals and runaways,
> A scum of Britons and base lackey peasants,
> Whom their o'ercloyèd country vomits forth
> To desperate ventures and assured destruction,
> You sleeping safe, they bring to you unrest;
> You having lands and blessed with beauteous wives,
> They would distrain the one, distain the other ...
> If we be conquered, let *men* conquer us,
> And not these bastard Britons, whom our fathers
> Have in their own land beaten, bobbed, and thumped.
>
> [*Richard III*, 5,6,45–63]

'When the bull comes from the far land ... To be an earl again in the land of Llewelyn, / Let the far-splitting spear shed the blood of the Saxon': the problem for sceptics of the myth of the once and future 'British' empire, like Polydore Vergil, was that such Druidic war-cries about 'The Bull of Anglesey' avenging Saxon oppression came true.[28] Schwyzer prefers to think the genocidal thirst for blood running over Charing Cross that was tied to Tudor claims to be tools of 'British' ethnic cleansing, as foretold by Merlin or Geoffrey of Monmouth, was never serious.[29] But born in Pembroke and exiled to Brittany, with his Welsh accent Henry VII was a true son of Owain Glyndŵr, and may well have mistaken Winchester for Camelot. For the banner he flew at Bosworth and St Paul's was indeed the Red Dragon of Cadwaladr, and the son he sent as Prince of Wales to Ludlow, which killed him, was named Arthur. So, if this bloodlust was play-acting it worked, as Welsh historian Gwyn Williams quipped: 'England opened up like the rose it now bore as its badge, and the Welsh poured in'.[30] And as John Kerrigan shows in *Archipelagic English*, such symbols mattered when triangulating the new conglomerate of 'Great Britain'.[31] The Cecils do seem sincere, therefore, in regretting having altered their name from Sitsilt, 'that house of Wales' which came from Herefordshire with the Tudors; for, as Williams observed, if the Welsh were junior partners in the new amalgamated condominion, as 'the old inhabiters of the isle of Britanny' they were the intellectual seniors in 'the bureaucracy of colonialism', and in fabricating 'the imperial *British* identity by which the state lived'.[32]

'Why, this is lunatics! This is mad as a mad dog!': the pun given to his Welsh parson Sir Hugh Evans in *The Merry Wives of Windsor* [4,2,124] hints how Shakespeare regarded the fantasy that it was Welshmen under Prince Madog who first colonized the New World.[33] But it was the Welsh John Dee, a fabricator of this 'mad' Atlantis, who conjured the term 'British Empire', Hereford-born Richard Hakluyt who charted its voyages, London Welsh Inigo Jones who Romanized its style, John Donne of the Carmarthen Donnes who charted its imagined corners and Elizabeth Tudor who personified its power. More to the point, it was lawyers like the Cecils who ran the administration, and merchants such as the Middletons who reoriented the economy westwards towards America. It was also Sir Thomas Middleton, a Montgomery patron of his namesake the playwright, who funded the 1630 *Beibl bach* which, by putting the Scriptures into the hands of the people, was the greatest single factor in preserving Welsh.[34] Yet Sir Thomas is satirized by his protégé as Sir Walter Whorehound, the tycoon who brings his Welsh-speaking whore to London in *A Chaste Maid in Cheapside*: a play read by Lloyd as a classic of the Anglocentric genre by which Welsh speakers must be comic and under English control, entertaining yet harmless.[35] Happy to script Sir Thomas's evangelical Lord Mayor's Show, Middleton clearly resented his domineering Welsh father figures. This fraught Oedipal struggle of the Welsh Dispersion can therefore highlight the surprise of the latest criticism, which is Shakespeare's wary yet creaturely submission to the 'British scum' he consistently presents as perhaps 'the dominators among the dominated' (in Pierre Bourdieu's acute phrase), but all the same the dominators.[36] In fact, 'the question of Wales' Shakespeare poses again and again in his plays is, *Who is the dominated and who the dominator?*

Eat, look you, this leek

FLUELLEN: I peseech you heartily, scurvy lousy knave, at my
desires and my requests and my petitions, to eat, look
you, this leek. Because, look you, you do not love it,

nor your affections and your appetites and your
digestions does not agree with it, I would desire you
to eat it.

PISTOL: Not for Cadwallader and all his goats.
FLUELLEN: There is one goat for you. [*He strikes Pistol*].

[*Henry V, 5,1,20–6*]

The symbolic rape of Captain Fluellen's force-feeding of the leek
to the abject Pistol enacts the body politics of Anglo-Welsh Tudor
exchanges, and illustrates the inappositeness of a zero-sum critique
on the postcolonial model, with Wales as a subaltern minority culture
reduced to silence by a dominant England. That was the analysis prevailing until recently, however, fronted by Stephen Greenblatt's compelling view of the Histories as variants of the Conquistadors' precept
that 'Language is the instrument of empire'. 'By yoking together
diverse peoples' into 'The King's English', the New Historicist indict-
ment ran, Shakespeare's Henry V 'tames the last wild areas in the
British Isles ... doomed outposts of a vanishing tribalism'.[37] This
darkly Foucauldian account might apply to the Northumberland
of Hotspur, whose 'speaking thick' in the Geordie accent even
his mother calls 'his blemish' [*2Henry IV, 2,3,24–5*]. But fortified
by R.R. Davies's nationalist essay 'Colonial Wales', the approach
was applied to the Welsh in a prize cultural materialist article by
Jonathan Dollimore and Alan Sinfield. There the very *visibility* of
Wales in the Histories was discounted as the paradoxical signifier of
a cunning English 'aesthetic colonization'. Compared to the Ireland
of the 'shag-hair'd crafty kern' [*2Henry VI, 3,1,367*], 'Wales must
have seemed the most tractable issue', this counter-intuitive reason-
ing went, 'for it had been annexed in 1536, and the English ... legal
system imposed ... permit[ing] only English speakers to hold office',
in 'an effortless incorporation' that the Shakespearean text is said to
callously perpetuate, since ever after 'jokes about the way Fluellen
pronounces the English language have ... been an adequate way of
handling the repression of Welsh language and culture'.[38]

The subaltern theory of Celtic repression in the *Henriad* would
be a test case for postcolonial Shakespeare criticism. Dollimore
and Sinfield had difficulty explaining the irruption of Essex into
Henry V, however, because they could never imagine the 'internal
colonialism' of the Acts of Union to be multi-directional, nor that
when it came to 'the greatest upheaval in the land market Britain
had yet seen' Welsh grabbers might themselves have been the

'alien intruders'.[39] The same blind spot about 'English' colonialism blurs Willy Maley's influential polemic 'This sceptered isle',
which also underestimates how much Essex's 'Roman' triumph
terrorizes peace-loving Londoners. Maley, who sees the 'Brutish'
empire as 'Shakespeare's', is hard on the English for eliding England
with 'Great Britain'; but he effaces precisely what the dramatist
stresses, namely the investment of the Welsh in getting the English
to swallow their 'British' roots.[40] But Wales is neither a Tibet nor
a Peru. So such off-loading of colonial responsibility belongs with
a victim mentality or grievance culture that came to look like bad
faith in the triumphalist days of the 'Celtic Tigers'. As T.M. Devine
complained in *Scotland's Empire*, 'Modern Ireland tends to suffer
acute historical amnesia when the role of the Irish in the British
Empire is considered. Yet the Irish of all descriptions entered
enthusiastically into the business.' And likewise: 'So intense was
Scottish engagement with empire that it affected almost every nook
and cranny of Scottish life'.[41] A *British* empire had been falsely
identified with England by postcolonial critics; but the subtitle
of *Shakespeare and Wales*, 'From the Marches to the Assembly',
confidently announced why it had become so timely for a similar
impartial truth commission about 'The Bard' and Britain.

Even nationalists now acknowledge that the 'tribalism' that Henry
VIII's Acts of Union suppressed was in reality feudal bondage, since
prior to unification 'the Welsh were second-class citizens ... not
allowed to live in towns, trade, carry arms, or marry the English'.
Thus, far from Wales being reduced to an 'internal colony', this
revisionism goes, unification freed the Welsh from 'a status equivalent to apartheid or the condition of the Palestinians', for it was the
united kingdom that 'gave the Welsh equality with the English not
only in England, but also in Wales'.[42] Thus, it was Marcher unionist Arthur Kelton who concocted the cracked farrago of a British
translatio imperii, the Tudor descent from the Trojan Brutus (and
Osiris), Clifford Davies points out, for 'only in Wales was anything
made' of the fact that Elizabeth's surname was 'Tyder' (or strictly,
Meredith). This '"British" propaganda had little resonance', Davies
notes, outside Wales.[43] So the problem for postcolonial critics who
see Shakespeare's Welsh characters as 'unruly subjects', an '"external" enemy' of 'Britain' that has to be cruelly suppressed, is not only
that, as Baker concedes, they implicitly endorse an Anglocentric
telos, investing the text with a 'subordinating power to which they

think it must aspire', but also that they are so out of sync with Welsh historians who contend that, far from Wales being downtrodden, in these decades 'British imperial energy ... was Welsh Britain transfigured'. A sentimentalism soured by subsequent Celtic rancour looks perverse when set against evidence that a union that 'went through in jubilation' ushered in 'a kind of golden age for Wales', an institutional 'Paradise', in which the Welsh 'peopled the Inns of Court and colonized the law', as 'The Welsh language surged forward into long-lost districts'. And the notion that, thanks in part to Shakespeare, 'Wales was silently absorbed into Greater England' defies the reality that 'An integrated Britain becomes visible first in the migration of the Welsh to the centre of power', as Williams observed, and that it was Cymrophile sentiments about the 'Worthiness' and centrality of Wales which were those 'echoed by Shakespeare':

> From this period dates Shakespeare's sympathetic image of the Welshman – garrulous, comic, but brave, honourable and congenial; Pistol, after all, eats the leek ... From the middle of the fifteenth century nothing could stop the Welsh, particularly those who had taken the winning side.[44]

The self-pity for Wales as 'England's first colony' is a prime example of what Jeremy Black calls 'The Curse of History': the maudlin obsession with 'the ancient wrong' whereby a group's identifying characteristic is its victim's curse, and the emphasis is on 'the endless ill' of the original sin, rather than potential reconciliation.[45] But this myth is contradicted by an actual colonization that was indeed 'spectacularly successful': the Welsh occupation of Tudor England. For 'the century ending as Shakespeare wrote ... had seen a wave of emigration from Wales into England', Williams reminds us, as the Welsh, 'especially Welsh gentry, settled all over the island', and 'a large contingent lighted in the capital', making it the largest Welsh city.[46] A parallel, at which Shakespeare glanced in *Love's Labour's Lost*, was the takeover of Paris by similarly pushy Protestants, the Basque carpetbaggers of another Henry, the King of Navarre. If there was any anxiety about Tudor empire building, it came from English towns like Worcester, explains Penry Williams, which lost their liberties to the Council of Wales.[47] Thus as Joan Fitzpatrick has argued, it is significant that, contrary to the traditional idea that Shakespeare undermines Glyndŵr's prophecies, and degrades the

Welsh language, he depicts even 'the infamous Welsh rebel' as 'very much in control', and bilingualism as a source of political power, for whenever he is on the stage the 'great magician' [*1Henry IV, 1,3,83*] is, in fact, 'the only person present who understands everything that is said'.[48]

While Spenser is preoccupied with Celtic resistance to the Elizabethan state in Ireland, Fitzpatrick writes, Shakespeare's far more nuanced representation of Celtic alterity embraces Welsh cultural power when he ensures 'Welshness is given a voice ... in a specifically English space'.[49] In particular, it is 'the Welsh colonization of English professions' that the dramatist registers, with characters who constitute a cross-section of the Tudor regime: an army captain, a schoolmaster-parson, the ex-courtiers Glyndŵr and Belarius, and a line of kings from Henry VIII and his father back to Cymbeline, including a Henry V whose claim, 'I am a Welshman' [*Henry V, 4,1,51*], when Pistol assumes that his accent must be Cornish, emphatically endows 'Harry Monmouth' [*2Henry IV, Ind.29*] with a Welsh blood, as Schwyzer notices, which entered the royal line only when his widow Katherine of France married Owain Tudur.[50] Like the Cecils, Shakespeare's governing elite is avid for the *Romanitas* of Welsh affiliation, and Anne Boleyn, who smiles at an 'emballing' for Caernarvonshire, is content to sleep with Henry VIII to become a 'Marchioness of Pembroke' [*Henry VIII, 2,3,47–63*]. So the correction in twenty-first-century studies of Shakespeare and Wales has been a move away from the reductionism of 'The Curse of History' to the recognition that if there is domination of Welsh or English in these plays, *it is the English who are the ones anxious at being dominated.* And nobody has made this 'post post-colonial' turn more pressing than Terence Hawkes, inventor of the 'Presentist' vogue, and Wales's foremost Shakespearean critic.

Cackling home to Camelot

'What must surely now be sensed, in our post-devolution present, is that Welshness and its concerns throbs with a powerful, if occluded, pulse in the vasty deep of these plays', and 'its muffled beat invades and disrupts the steps by which they march': Hawkes's Derridean agenda, he states in *Shakespeare in the Present*, has been to deconstruct the plays to show that 'There never was a static, unified clearly defined England, absolutely distinct and separable from a static, unified and clearly defined Wales'.[51] His invocation of Glyndŵr's portentous line about 'spirits from the vasty deep' [*1Henry IV, 3,1,51*] reveals, however, how hard it has been to reverse the sovereign 'English' ideology without falling into an equally essentialist Welsh Anglophobia ghosted by Celtic racists like the wartime nationalist Caudillo Saunders Lewis. The precariousness of the balance is worryingly on display in Hawkes's intimidating essay 'Bryn Glas', which celebrates the atrocity of 'Blue Hill', on the border of A.E. Housman's elegized England, where the Shropshire lads in their hundreds were butchered by Glyndŵr's forces in June 1402, and as squeamishly reported early in *1 Henry IV*, suffered in death 'Such beastly shamelessness' from 'those Welshwomen ... as may not be / Without much shame retold' [*1,1,42–6*].

Recent critics who revisit this primal scene of Celtic revanchism echo Schwyzer's disquiet at the 'terrifying ethnic chauvinism', but treat the text's euphemizing of the Welsh 'Bacchae' as a neutralizing of English paranoia.[52] For Hawkes, however, Shakespeare's very circumlocution about the hate speech describing those 'cut roots', when the corpses had their genitals stuffed into their mouths and their noses up their anuses, is itself a sign of his lily-livered English weakness. The castration of the Shropshire boys at the hands of Welsh women thus provides a perfect pretext for outing Shakespeare as an effete and inauthentic Londoner, 'promoted in a context of institutionalised homosexuality', as part of the Victorian empire's cult of pseudo-manliness, whose 'conquering Englishness' wilts from its own 'effeminacy', as flaunted by a decadent Falstaff, or enacted in the 'Bard's' own sexual relations with his Welsh 'Willy'. This queer take on the body politics of the *Henriad* might have been prompted by *My Own Private Idaho*, a film that made Hal a boy prostitute. But what makes Hawkes's deconstruction so disturbing is how the response to 'an English nationalism once more anxious to impose itself' apparently involves such cruel relish for a *literal dismembering*, for 'the appalling sound of blades being whetted on the stones of Bryn Glas':

> The importance of the events derives not only from ... a decisive and brutal battle in which a large number of English were slaughtered by the Welsh ... Bryn Glas and its consequences release that most disturbing of spectres: a militant feminine and feminising force, with a bloody knife in its hand, an incomprehensible tongue in its head, and

with English manhood, the English language and (on both counts) English reality in its sights.[53]

Hawkes's postcolonial critique is a prime instance of the way Shakespeare's own subaltern situation has been misread through the distorting lens of later history. But to quote Holofernes – who may have the head of the dramatist's own Welsh schoolmaster – 'This is not generous, not gentle' [*Love's, 5,2,617*]. For the 'blue remembered hills' in this interpretation are not Housman's homoerotic 'land of lost content' but a waste land haunted by the 'unappeased spectre of a subverting, transforming, and unmanning Wales', an 'importunate ghost' that, as Gower warns of Fluellen, remains capable of mutilating their manhood if the English get too close: 'You thought because he could not speak English in the native garb he could not therefore handle an English cudgel. You'll find it otherwise.' 'We do. We will', nods Hawkes at Gower's threat to 'let a Welsh correction teach you a good English condition' [*Henry V, 5,1,67–9*], thereby ironizing Housman's famous line about a Welsh 'air that kills'.[54] And this threat of a mugging is of a piece with the bullying essentialism the argument shares with *Braveheart* and other films of the Celtic Revenge, in a formula that equates Englishness with homosexuality and homosexuality with effeminacy, and relies upon the familiar unexamined chiasmus that the only permitted targets of unthinking homophobia are now English, and of socially acceptable racism, gays.[55]

Hawkes's commendable plan to disrupt the sexual differences upon which English domination is supposed to rest thus collapses into mere inversion, where his Aberdaugleddyf – the Welsh name for Milford Haven – figures the openness of the 'Bard's' back passage to Celtic penetration, the violent 'oscillation between coming in and going out, ingestion and excretion, penetration and ejaculation', through which Shakespeare gets his comeuppance.[56] No one, surely, has ever written with cruder disrespect about the cultural policeman Hawkes likes to call 'The Old Bill'. But in this 'story of willies' the 'Bard's' Welsh honorific is the 'cudgel' with which to beat him, since the aggression of this Welsh iconoclasm springs from sour resentment that 'one of the main agencies promoting [a] barren, emptied Welsh culture may be the promotion, through and on behalf of a militant English-speaking world order, of the plays of Shakespeare'.[57] And for all the virtuosity with which Hawkes riffs upon themes of borders, colonialism, language, sexuality and roots, it is this resentful dead-end in postcolonial Celticity that closer attention to Shakespeare's impatience with his own subservience to the ideology of a 'British' empire helps us to escape.

From a post-devolution Welsh perspective, according to Hawkes, a Shakespeare play is itself 'the ailment' it 'helps us to diagnose', so culpably is the text to be associated with the Anglo-Saxon *imperium* that culminates in the *Pax Americana*.[58] But Shakespeare's resistance to his Welsh patrons suggests the opposite possibility: that the plays themselves offer the best deconstruction of the 'British' World Order that they have been made to represent. Proof that this dramatist was committed to deconstructing the gendered dichotomies of English law and Welsh lore, or Anglo-Saxon masculinity and Celtic mystery, comes indeed in another 'story of willies' that meditates explicitly on 'British Empire' as a specifically Welsh construction, and then advertises its own delinquency towards any such 'Roman Britain'.[59] The interlude in *The Merry Wives* where young William Page is examined in uncontrollably obscene Latin by the Welsh parson Evans was probably added to the text after the clown Robert Armin (who specialized in Celtic cameos like the Welsh Knight in his hit *Two Maids of Moreclack*) joined the company in 1599.[60] It was Armin who was given Shakespeare's only lines about Merlin, when as Lear's Fool, in a play that sends 'British' politics 'cackling home to Camelot' [*King Lear, 2,2,76*], he predicted that if all the prophecies of King Arthur's Welsh wizard were to come true, 'Then shall the realm of Albion / Come to great confusion' [*3,2,89–90*]. And it is to a state of 'great confusion' that the pompous Sir Hugh reduces the 'realm of Albion' when he struggles to impose his 'British' imperialism on Shakespeare's wayward Willy.

'God defend me from that Welsh fairy', cries Falstaff in *The Merry Wives*; but the fat knight is outdone by Sir Hugh's Celtic magic: 'Well, you have the start of me. I am dejected. I am not able to answer the Welsh flannel.' An incomer who 'makes fritters of English' has the last word in Shakespeare's Windsor, as the citizens wend home to 'laugh this sport o'er by a country fire' [*5,5,78; 136; 150; 219*]. Yet this tolerant hospitality concludes a plot that always threatens to bring racial and religious tensions between migrants and locals in the Berkshire town to a bloody climax. And the play-within-the-play on educating William in his Latin roots has enough of that latent aggression to read like a résumé of its author's own restiveness at Stratford Grammar School, and thus as a reflexive commentary on his earliest exposure to 'British' *Romanitas*. Often interpreted as a textbook case of hegemonic domination, Will Page's dysfunctional education is, in fact, a study in what Judith Halberstam terms 'The Queer Art of Failure', and a paradigm of its author's sly servility towards history's winners.[61] A vagrant 'O', nothing, or zero between the acts, this naughty truancy from a farce which reveals 'the multiple forms violence can take' deserves, therefore, to be considered Shakespeare's sabotage of Tudor ideology of the master race or tongue, and an epitome of his refractoriness towards his patrons, those Welsh powers who hectored their English subjects with manic myths of Trojan origins and 'Roman' peace.[62] For though Justice Shallow recalls playing 'Sir Dragonet in Arthur's show' at Mile-End [*2Henry IV, 3,2,257*]; and Mistress Quickly is sure Falstaff dies 'in Arthur's bosom' [*Henry V, 2,3,9*]; 'the dismissive treatment of matters Arthurian' in the Histories is well figured by the hopelessness of the boy Arthur in *King John*; and the only time Shakespeare ever sang of Arthur, the ballad of the Round Table had the fat knight urinating and reaching for his chamber pot: '"When Arthur first in court" – [*Calls*] Empty the Jordan – [*Sings*] "And was a worthy king"' [*2Henry IV, 2,4,28*].[63]

Unwillingly to school

With its Windsor setting, *The Merry Wives* seems designed to show how, as Bourdieu wrote in his essay 'The King's House', the features of 'the dynastic state can be deduced from the model of the house'.[64] But originally staged, it is thought, for a Whitehall St George's Day feast, and commissioned by the company patron and Lord Chamberlain, George Carey Lord Hundson, whose knighting at Windsor it riskily travesties when the madam Mistress Quickly impersonates the Queen of the Fairies to declaim the Garter motto, *Honi soit qui mal y pense* [*5,5,66*], this farcical carry-on from the Histories takes facetious aim at the heart of the Order 'which, with its Arthurian associations, had been made a vehicle for the glorification of the national monarchy established by the Tudors'.[65] It thereby suggests how the Spenserian myth that these 'Britons' incarnated 'Arthur's anti-Roman heroics' was coming to look 'inherently *foolish*. Indeed, belief in Arthur's return had long standing as a measure of folly'.[66] For with a Welsh pedant leading his infant charges in a fairy ring around the rogue Falstaff, who is meant to exemplify 'fair knighthood's bended knee' [69], the action comes as close as anyone surely dared to exposing the absurdity of Britain's 'imperial theme' [*Macbeth, 1,3,129*]. And it is the pedagogical playlet featuring just William that not only illustrates how the clerks who create this state 'make themselves by making the state' but allows us to say of the authorial William what Bourdieu said of Gustave Flaubert, that what gave the creator of *Sentimental Education* the freedom to become the best 'socioanalyst of Flaubert' was his ambivalence as the 'inheritor' of equal but contradictory amounts of cultural and economic capital:[67]

> The dual orientation of Flaubert's father, who invested both in the education of his children and in real estate, corresponds to the indeterminacy of the young Flaubert, faced with various equally probable futures. Everything happened as if his position in his family and the position of his family predisposed Flaubert to experience the force of the contradictions inscribed in the position of the writer and the position of the pure artist, where these contradictions attained their highest degree of intensity.[68]

Shakespeare's vignette of educating William in the British *translatio imperii* can be read as a template for his concept of creative autonomy because it confirms how, as Bourdieu suggests, the rules of art ground the aesthetic as a form of answering power back; a recalcitrance like that oddly endorsed in the primer for Tudor teachers, Roger Ascham's *Schoolmaster*, which disparaged obedience to 'time and custom' as like eating acorns with swine.[69] Thus, although he pays the fees, in *The Merry Wives* the businessman George Page is right to suspect his son 'profits nothing in the world at his book' [*4,1,12*], for the scene highlights the boy's conflicted position between Celtic myths and Anglo-Saxon maths. As Bourdieu notes of *A Sentimental Education*, to perpetuate itself patrimony requires that inheritance inherits the heir: but there are heirs who 'refuse to be inherited by their inheritance'. The trouble with Shakespeare's William, then, is the same as when Flaubert's Frédéric 'refuses to get in line ... He wants to inherit without being inherited'.[70] The boy's dilatory lack of empire-building application is the first thing we discover about him, in fact, when he enters with 'satchel / And shining morning face, creeping like snail / Unwillingly to school' [*As You, 2,7,144*], dragged by Margaret, his archetype soccer mum, who has postponed more pressing affairs to forcibly 'bring my young man here to school' [*4,1,6*]. And signed with Shakespeare's own name, the travesty interpellation that ensues will prove a master class in the echoing 'counter-speech' or 'redoubling of injurious speech' which, in her analysis of hate speech, Judith Butler applauds as the creaturely reversal accomplished by 'talking back':

> The present context and its apparent 'break' with the past are legible only in terms of the past with which it breaks. The present context does, however, elaborate a new context for such speech ... The revaluation of terms such as 'queer' suggests that speech can be 'returned' to its speaker in a different form, that it can be cited against its originary purposes, and perform a reversal of effects.[71]

In this Elizabethan version of the school run, Mistress Page is determined to have her son tested on his Latin grammar. But no wonder the truant creeps along so reluctantly if, as biographers believe, his tutor Evans is based, like Holofernes, on the dramatist's own Welsh schoolmaster Thomas Jenkins, who had trained at the prototype Merchant Taylors' Grammar School under the great grammarian Richard Mulcaster.[72] For Jenkins, a graduate of St John's, Oxford, when it was a hotbed of aspiring Jesuits, was a zealot in an academy that underwrote investment by fathers like Page with an economy of discipline and punishment in which the symbolic violence of Latin was imprinted upon the body by the actual violence of a thrashing. At a time when Latin was increasingly seen as a dead language, and in a 'Galilean revolution' the vernacular swept everywhere but schools, Shakespeare's ribbing of those who still 'spake in Latin' [*1,1,150*] has to be seen as a reaction to that imprinting.[73] As Parson Evans warns his squirming pupil: 'If you forget your "*qui*"s and your "*que*"s, and your "*quod*"s, you must be preeches' [*66*]. 'To be whipped – what's his fault?' 'The flat transgression of a schoolboy' [*Much Ado, 2,1,192–3*]. According to Henry Peacham, schoolmasters beat boys' backsides to keep their own hands warm.[74] But if Shakespeare, who opened so many plays contrasting 'tongue-tied simplicity' with 'the rattling tongue of saucy and audacious eloquence' [*Dream, 5,1,102–4*], ever afterwards associated the terror of castration with a silencing by Welsh power, that might have been because his sense of theatre was complicated by a deep psychological resistance to performing such 'Roman' lessons in the discourses of 'British' domination:

EVANS: Come hither, William. Hold up your head.
                  Come.
MISTRESS PAGE: Come on, sirrah. Hold up your head. Answer
                  your master. Be not afraid.

[4,1,14–16]

Complete with an emasculating mother, there is a trace of some traumatic humiliation in this 'circumfession' that goes a long way to explain why Shakespeare's castration anxiety is triggered by hearing in the rise of a Welsh accent the threat of his Master's voice.[75] We can hear Hawkes's knives being sharpened on those stones at Bryn Glas. And William's ur-act of Shakespearean refusal is put in context by anecdotes of sadistic schoolmasters like Mulcaster, who was supposed to treat every whipping as a mock marriage 'between this boy's buttocks and Lady Birch', thus literalising the boys' euphemism for a flogging: 'Marrying the master's daughter'.[76] So critics notice how the pederastic economy of exposed posteriors haunts *The Merry Wives*, as when Falstaff rues being 'paid for [his] learning', when disguised as 'Mother Prat' (or 'Bum'), Windsor becomes his schoolroom: 'Since I play'd truant, and whipped top, I knew not what 'twas to be beaten' [4,2,158; 4,5,50; 5,1,22]. As Alan Stewart recounts in *Close Readers: Humanism and Sodomy in Early Modern England*, the homoerotic 'breaching' of privates involved in publicly flaying adolescent boys' bare bottoms meant the value of Latin as a Roman rite of passage into manhood was *fundamentally* uprooted by the ritual itself.[77] There was thus a painful contradiction in this pedagogical exploitation of gendered parts that Shakespeare made the excruciating focus of Will's young life. For Evans's Welsh corrections imperil the very 'British' masculinity into which Latin grammar was supposed to be the discursive initiation, when his pronunciation reduces the lesson to hilarity by miniaturizing the foundation stones of the Eternal City, and infantilizing the manly roots of the imperial *Pax* itself:

EVANS: I pray you peace – What is *'lapis'*, William?
WILLIAM: A stone.
EVANS: And what is 'a stone', William?
WILLIAM: A pebble.
EVANS: No, it is *'lapis'*. I pray you remember in your prain.
WILLIAM: *'Lapis'*.
EVANS: That is good William.

[4,1,26–31]

William's doubling back of the Welshman's imperial 'peace' is a model of Shakespearean abjection, an ur-act of radical negativity worthy of Georges Bataille, for whom, the moment he accedes to the sovereign phallus, the creature releases excess energy in a golden shower of the elementary bodily waste. For, ever since he had the Spaniard Armado salute the pedant Holofernes and the curate Nathaniel as 'Men of peace' [*Love's*, *5,1,32*], Shakespeare had been taking the Tudor 'peace' for a laugh. So here, taking '*la piss*' out of the Roman *Pax*, William Frenchly answers back in his Master's voice. The allusion may be to the recent Gallic peace, the 1598 Edict of Nantes. But the small boy's '*pee ball*' exposes what he may yet lack, as the clergyman menacingly intones: 'Remember, William, the vocative is *caret*': the Latin root for 'missing' Mistress Quickly mishears as a phallic 'carrot' [*45*]. 'By gar, I will cut all his two stones', the French Doctor Caius threatens Sir Hugh himself [*1,4,98*], who then promises to 'knog your urinal' [*3,1,75*]; and in a po-faced Lacanian decrypting Elizabeth Pittenger solemnizes that William is constructed as a subject of humanist discourse by this playing upon his *rootlessness*, and the castration fears that transfix Windsor's husbands, which Falstaff acts out in drag, and that Evans now arouses with his Welsh '*p*'s' and '*q*'s', warning his pupil 'he'll lose his keys (*quies*) to the [female] case (*quaes*) and his cods (*quods*) … to peebles'.[78]

In mirthless decoding by gender critics, the sovereign discourse of classical pedagogy masters its uprooting by gendering a grammar where it is woman who is the only sanctioned 'fuckative case': an 'O – *vocative* – O', as William mimics back, like Falstaff's duplicate love letters to Windsor wives. So Master Page lives up to his name, Pittenger infers, by submitting to Evans's print culture of 'mechanically reproduced pages', as the lessons of textbooks like William Lily's *Short Introduction to Grammar* are 'inscribed in / on the boy's body,' and the 'standardized education that reinforces mechanical reproduction' locks into the 'mechanisms that enforce reproductive sexuality'.[79] Imprinted with identikit roles, ideas and norms by the Tudor national curriculum, on this Orwellian view, which leaves no scope for autonomous individuation, William will grow up a mechanical repetition of all the other Pages in the book. What such a dismal reading of the page cannot hear, of course, is the joyous creative havoc wreaked by William's verbal resistance to interpellation with his cod Welsh '*p*'s and '*q*'s, the *positive* negativity of his rooting for excess. For as Gilles Deleuze put it, and the play shows,

'What a will wants is to affirm its difference. In its essential relation with the "other" a will makes its difference an object of affirmation.'[80] So, if it was to Shakespeare's Herbert patrons that Tudor England most owed its classical cult of chiasmus, as early as *Love's Labour's Lost*, and the mimicry of another master by the ignoramus Dull, Shakespeare had shown how their language of empire might be undone by their own insolent trick of repetition:[81]

> HOLOFERNES: Most barbarous intimation! Yet a kind of
> insinuation, as it were in *via*, in way, of
> explication, *facere*, as it were, replication, or
> rather *ostentare*, to show, as it were, his
> inclination after his undressed, unpolished,
> uneducated, unpruned, untrained, or rather
> unlettered, or ratherest unconfirmed, fashion, to
> insert again my '*haut credo*' for a deer.
> DULL: I said the deer was not a 'auld grey doe', 'twas a
> pricket.
>
> [*Love's, 4,2,12–18*]

Sir Hugh's exasperated cry for 'peace' is an instance of Butler's 'excitable speech': language 'imagined to wield sovereign power' that fails as a performative when it 'excites' a chain of profane resignifications.[82] So a politically correct gender criticism is as deaf to the *excitement* of cocky Will's 'peace' offering as it is to the devious way mimicry has always operated as a challenge to imperialist metanarratives. Likewise, in a depressing heteronormative reading, David Landreth contends that 'those deviant meanings' and 'swerving' homoerotic choices are crushed by Margaret Page's obliviousness: 'Mrs Page cannot control the bawdy, but she can, by ignoring it', prevent her William becoming a 'lecherous translator', or 'the object of pederasty'.[83] Yet to reduce the lippy pupil to a mere textual effect like this, or the passive subject of imprinting, which was the aim of the Tudor grammar school, is to suppress the *jouissance* of his creative misconstructions, the naughtiness of his *ressentiment*. Shakespeare himself, so it is said, 'had been in his younger years a schoolmaster in the country'; and the legend challenges us to speculate what kind of pedagogue he would have been.[84] If William's queer Latin lesson is anything to go by, the dramatist's instruction would have been like that of the eighteenth-century teacher praised by Jacques Rancière in *The Ignorant Schoolmaster*, who encouraged pupils to 'get lost' in their very confusion, rather than cramming them with knowledge and 'having them repeat it like parrots', on the subversive principle he announced: 'I must teach you that I have nothing to teach you'.[85] Shakespeare's lessons would have been classes, that is to say, in the radical negativity of his own plays, where by staging again and again the grotesque act of foundational violence he subtly registers his bemusement at the Ubu-esque instantiation of 'Brutish' power, considering it was such 'a brute part to kill so capital a calf' [*Hamlet, 3,2,95*].

William's Latin lesson is a paradigm of the Ubu-like stupidity Shakespeare apparently learned from his classical education in 'skill-contending schools' [*Lucrece, 1018*], the 'Brute part' of 'utt'ring foolish things', like the original Brutus, so as to be esteemed 'As silly jeering idiots are with kings' [*1812*], that made this 'unlettered clerk' the 'major master of ellipsis in the history of theatre', as Harold Bloom puts it, with 'dumb thoughts, speaking in effect' [Sonnet 85].[86] For what the pornographic 'Story of "O"' teaches 'naughty' Will is the sheer impertinency of the 'British' union of Welsh and English, a roguish intractability, when the two tongues are combined, to Roman law and Latin logic that comes to the rescue when he is compelled to attend. It is now axiomatic, of course, to hear in this young wag's mimicry of Welsh '*p*'s' only the racism that divides Windsor between insiders and outsiders, yet another instance, like the jokes about Fluellen, of the 'internal colonialism' by which Welsh language and culture were negated.[87] But such an automatic postcolonial response ignores the Tudor context of Latin, as a cultural instrument of 'British' empire and the Roman road to *Welsh* empowerment. And it overlooks the point that, as with Pistol's leek, it is the Welsh man of authority who is here the colonist imposing 'British roots' with a threat of real violence. For as Chris Holcomb remarks in a sensible study of the early modern joke, 'Jests about the Welsh could be seen as a way to manage that threat, yet they would always presuppose the power of the people they target'.[88]

'Sir Hugh, persuade me not, I will make a Star Chamber matter': from the first words of *Merry Wives*, and Shallow's fury at Falstaff's poaching, the Welsh priest is identified not only with Tudor power but its 'benevolence to make atonements and compromises' [*1,1,1; 27–8*]. That split is revealed when he braces himself to fight Caius, who is itching to 'cut his throat' [*1,4,95*], by misquoting 'Come live with me and be my love' [*3,1,13–22*]: a 'correction' of Marlowe, the 'dead shepherd' [*As You*, *3,5,82*] murdered on royal orders in a similar imbroglio. The allusion suggests how Shakespeare could empathise with a Welshman who is 'at odds with his own gravity ... so wide of his own respect' [*3,1,45–9*]. For if ribaldry at their pronunciation was habitual in courts and colleges, that merely indicates the status of Welsh intellectuals as 'dominated dominators' in the translation of 'Roman' empire via Tudor education.[89] So something more creative or congenial than mere colonialism happens when a 'Welsh correction' is exploited by a cheeky chap who only wants to be excused, and he hears Welsh cries for 'peace' as provocations to take a different kind of 'leak' [*1Henry IV*, *2,1,20*]. Doubtless all Renaissance education was 'intensely dialogic'; but if so, this was just *asking for trouble* the dramatist seems to smile, for the *détournement* of sexual and political ordering disordered by the deviations it produces is a perversity that critics see running through his play.[90] So, in this paradigm of the Bartlebian politics of the power of weakness, we observe how Shakespeare's *civil* disobedience will always retain the facetious euphemism of the boy who asks to leave the room. For as the linguistic medium for imperial *translation*, Welsh Latin is here simply allowed to undo itself, disintegrating all the messianic 'madness' of 'Roman Britain' into its echoing contradictions, as though the entire deranged plot of *Cymbeline* was revenge for those interminable mornings with Master Jenkins.[91]

Lads of peace

'He is a better scholar than I thought he was' [*4,1,69*]: it is hard to read his mother's relief at educating William without hearing Ben Jonson's sneer at Shakespeare's 'small Latin and less Greek'.[92] Indeed this lavatorial interruption of a drama which opens in Latin jokes about the 'Justice of Peace', sees the French doctor crowned 'Castalian King Urinal' [*2,3,29*], and ends with Falstaff threatening to 'piss my tallow' [*5,5,12*], could serve as a test of the applicability of Bourdieu's sociology to the dramatist, as its text offers such a rich illustration of the 'thick description' the sociologist advocated. For this story of William is a microcosm of a play that strikes critics as the most socially embodied of Shakespeare's worlds: where the community is solidly rooted in 'town planning, diurnal activities, and local customs', and the plot unfolds in a location whose backdrop, the Garter Inn, still exists.[93] With its Vermeer-like itemization of the material 'spaces (coffers, closets, bakeries), objects (hodge-pudding, venison pasties), and practices (laundering, distilling, physic)' of early modern urban civilisation, *The Merry Wives* is one of the most detailed inventories ever compiled of the matrix of practical acts and cultural preferences that mesh, according to Bourdieu, to make an individual *habitus* or social world.[94] But the suffocating ideological weight of this material makes it the more striking that if Latin is the instrument of 'British' empire of his Welsh masters, in Shakespeare's mind it is also the misappropriated medium for such conscientious objection.

When William is marched to school he is briefly reprieved by the surprise that there is 'no school today', as the authorities have declared "'Tis a playing day' and 'let the boys leave to play' [*4,1,7–9*]. Together with his father's name, William's holiday therefore confirms the connection with the Queen's feast on 23 April: St George's Day, and Shakespeare's birthday. So when his mother persists in her son being tested on 'questions in his accidence' [*13*], the grammatical accidents that befall this unseasonable homework can be related to customs like 'barring the schoolmaster' detailed by François Laroque, which 'involved pupils locking the master out of the classroom', thus 'enacting a reversal of authority' and readmitting him only if granted a holiday.[95] For Pittenger, William's misrule is thus an instance of the carnival ruse which works on Hal's safety-valve logic that 'If all the year were playing holidays, / To sport would be as tedious as to work' [*1Henry IV, 1,2,182–3*]. Considering 'what happens to little boys' on red-letter days, she frowns, it is 'no wonder William hangs his head'. The feminist critic can see only a paedophile victim, and so it never occurs to her that when he shies away the inattentive William may well be smirking. The politically correct critique is oblivious to Shakespeare's signature theme of *the power of weakness*. No contestation is imaginable in such a scenario.[96] Laroque, however, cites John Aubrey's fond recollection of boys carrying their captain 'in ribbons, his schoolfellows following with drum and fiddle to a feast at the schoolhouse'; and it is with such a festive reversal that William will in fact turn the page.[97]

When Will reappears at the end of the play it is with head held high as a fairy page in a wedding presided over by the 'Fairy Queen' that has Caius paired with '*un garçon*', Slender with 'a great lubberly boy', and the master garbed as a 'Welsh fairy' [*5,5,78; 170–88*].[98] These boy-brides figure what Hawkes unthinkingly equates with castration: that in Shakespeare's playhouse, '*all* marriages are same-sex unions'. Thus, even as it represents the reproduction of family identity in the Tudor national curriculum, '*The Merry Wives* marks resistances to that production', and by celebrating the pederastic economy of men and boys makes identity even harder to control.[99] There is a fore-taste here, therefore, of that 'alternative pedagogy' of artful stupidity Halberstam celebrates for its queer non-reproductive disruption of the trans-generational logic of Oedipal transmission, since for Tudor 'history boys' like Shakespeare and Marlowe Latin was not only a public language of imperial power but a private language of sexual desire, 'homosexual desire in particular'.[100] 'All losers are the heirs of those who have failed before them', rejoices Halberstam; and with this perverse pedagogy Shakespeare seems to concur.[101] For as Georgia Brown puts it, Latin proved to be a bonding ritual far beyond the intentions of the government inspectors, since with its homoerotic subtexts the classical literature that was drummed into these first-generation English grammar school boys 'instilled many kinds of literacy', including enough 'emotional literacy' to universal-ize their wandering minds and hands.[102] So it is that in Shakespearean Windsor the master language meets its *accidental* match in the mother tongue spoken not by the Virgin Queen of the Castle, but by Dame Quickly, another kind of 'quean, an old cozening quean!' [*4,2,149*], who can have 'nothing to do with marriage'.[103]

'I pray you remember in your prain': with William's lesson Shakespeare anticipates Bourdieu's theory of social action, as he reflects upon the socialization by which norms are internalized. But as he queers this serious subject of his own subject formation, and the master–servant relation that came to dominate his plays, his lavato-rial subtext posits a 'subjugated knowledge' which also confirms Foucault's gleaming irony that it was its own classic texts about same-sex desire that subverted the grammar school the instant they were translated by boys into the vernacular: 'Universities, schools, and so on, cannot function with such friendships. [So] when they started to grade schools with hundreds of boys, one of the problems was how to prevent them having sex … [and] the Jesuits knew very well that this was impossible.'[104] In *The Merry Wives* love therefore really does go towards 'love as schoolboys from their books, / But love from love, toward school with heavy looks' [*Romeo, 2,1,201–2*], when from 'vocative' to 'fuckative,' 'peace' to 'piss', Shakespeare's primal pedagogic scene of creeping 'unwillingly to school' is played out in the dialectic between opposing libidinal pulls of books and looks, empire and desire, literacy and orality, or classroom and urinal, as personified by the parson and the hostess. For though she is now housekeeper to the Doctor, the pantomime Dame carries into Windsor all those 'immodest words' and 'gross terms' [*2Henry IV, 4,3,70–3*] from the Boar's Head tavern that Hal had banished in the Histories, and which now return irrepressibly, like embarrassing bodily emissions, the second time as farce.[105]

'Peace' making on the King's House, William's Latin lesson marks out a benevolent context for Shakespeare's irreverent idea that history repeats itself as the remainder that time has 'caused to belch up' [*Tempest, 3,3,56*]. Nothing the pedant declaims can repress Quickly, in any case, when she translates his Latin with louche gags on the genitive case she insists is 'Jenny's case', or genitals, and the '*horum*' she takes for his whore: 'You do ill to teach the child such words. He teaches him to hick and to hack, which they'll do fast enough of themselves, and to call "whorum". Fie upon you!' [*4,1,52–8*]. Everything we know suggests Evans is 'given to fornications, and to taverns, and sack', as she hints [*5,5,148*]. But as Patricia Parker exults, in the role-reversals of this barring game it is the madam who usurps the lectern and her sluttish 'mother tongue' which initiates the wag into 'a lazy vagrancy, a prodigality of synonyms'. For Parker, the Fat Lady's gabby case, 'so openly known to the world' [*2Henry IV, 2,1,31*], is the 'fuckative O' of English itself, an insatiable mouth endlessly receptive to vulgarity and so 'subversive of the entire system of instruction, a dangerous supplement to the closed humanist economy of translation'.[106] Initiation rites such as Latin are less about inheriting than excluding, Bourdieu theorises: separating the public parts exhibited in the schoolroom from the private parts exposed in the toilet.[107] But the intertext from which *Merry Wives* cannot be separated is that of the polymorphous erotic confusion of that Eastcheap backroom where William's other role-model, the poetry-rapping Fenton, a 'gentleman of no having' who is so cocksure in his buttons because he 'knows too much', has kept such queer 'company with the wild Prince and Poins' [*3,2,61*]:[108]

> He capers, he dances, he has the eyes of youth; he writes verses, he speaks holiday, he smells of April and May. He will carry't, he will carry't; 'tis in his buttons he will carry't.
>
> [*3,2,56–9*]

Shakespeare's comedy will crown Quickly the Queen because her cultural power will prove greater than the Welsh master's, more empowering for William than even his father's monetary investment. Evans calls her 'Oman', when she Englishes '*pulcher*' as 'polecats' or translates beauty into brothels: 'Oman, art thou lunatics? Hast thou no understanding for thy cases and the numbers of the genders?' [*4,1,25;65*]. But it is precisely her 'understanding for the cases of genders' (seven in Latin) that makes Quickly such an omen of Shakespeare's cross-dressed comedies, with their Cesarios and Ganymedes.[109] 'Our bending author' [*Henry V, Epi.2*] will also prove a poor scholar and lecherous translator. That is what comes of the sodomitic subculture of an old quean's 'Molly-house'.[110] In tutoring Will, the naughty madam therefore takes the pain from gain with the salacity of another kind of writing on the Tudor wall: the graffiti in the school latrine. 'There is extensive literary and non-literary evidence that the early modern English did not hesitate to write on walls', Juliet Fleming solemnly confirms: 'Political commentary, erotic fixation, personal slander are recognizable as appropriate for graffiti writing'.[111] Thus, the Elizabethan desks of Stratford's grammar school are coarsely incised with graffiti by boys with tales to tell, who refused to be inherited. And William, it is a safe bet, is one of those with such a story, for in *The Merry Wives of Windsor* English graffiti trumps Latin grammar with just such 'talking back'. The master marks it down when a pupil mimics his 'fuckative – O' and grades it at nought, like the privy nothing 'That's a fair thought to lie between a maid's legs' [*Hamlet, 3,2,107*]. But the 'nothing' that will free Will, and that gives him his brass, is the omen of that big 'O' Mistress Quickly promises, and that awaits him outside the school gates: his probable future filling that glorious 'wooden O', the voraciously demanding 'cock-pit' [*Henry V, Pro.11–13*] of the great Globe itself.

'Peace your tattlings! ... I pray you peace ... Prithee, hold thy peace' [*21; 25; 62*]: with Jenkins for a hectoring tutor, a Welsh grandmother in Alys Griffin, and a manager, it is said, in his wife's relation Davy Jones – who was paid 13s 4d by Stratford in 1583 for staging the 'pastime at Whitsun' when 'pageants of delight were played' [*Two Gents, 4,4,166*] – young Shakespeare was well qualified for the messianic role the Herberts foisted upon him as their Bard for 'the time of universal peace' [*Antony, 4,6,4*].[112] Yet judging by his incontinent Will, he could not help taking the 'piss' whenever

he heard these 'British' claim that 'Never was a war did cease, /
Ere bloody hands were washed, with such a peace' [*Cymbeline,*
5,6,484–5]. So, if his blank Page is a self-portrait, Shakespeare's
reply to the messianism that would see him as 'Bard of Britain'
was like that of *The Life of Brian*: 'He's not ... he's a very naughty
boy'. Schwyzer describes the tricky process of 'making safe (for
the English) the highly volatile material of Welsh prophecy' as 'an
anxious negotiation at an anxious time'.[113] But Will's urinating on
the Tudor myth also initiates the equally 'British' *anti-imperialism* of
Dad's Army, of empire's answering-back in *Monty Python*. 'He cut
our roots in characters': as research helps us see, the alphabet soup
Innogen cooks up from 'British' roots in *Cymbeline* [*4,2,51*] epito-
mizes the hospitality with which these plays turn Celtic threats of
castration and ethnic violence into a peace, like that of the Windsor
Host, *that passes understanding* in being so multi-confessional and
supra-national: 'Peace, I say, Gallia and Gaul, French and Welsh ...
Follow me, lads of peace, follow, follow, follow' [*Wives, 3,2,81–94*].

Chosen to conclude the 1623 Folio on the word 'peace', with
its Pembrokeshire locale *Cymbeline* can be read as Shakespeare's
swansong as the Bard of Avon, his final dues to the Herberts and
the Welsh elite who had imposed on him their own idea of a Roman
Pax.[114] Yet if it rains on their 'British ensign' and 'crooked smokes'
in this passing-out parade that could be because the plot seems
to be based on the cosmic joke that these 'Roman Britons' have
been too busy fixing 'peace and plenty' for themselves [*5,5,237;
5,6,442–77*] to attend to the truly Good News in that 'gracious
season' [*402*] when the adventitious 'decree went out from Caesar
Augustus, that all the world should be taxed' [Luke, 2:1]. 'Hath
Britain all the sun that shines?' the play therefore asks. For though
they do pay the tax in the end, the irony is that in their obliviousness these 'Britons' from the time of Christ will never know about
the Saviour who is among those 'livers out of Britain' they resist
[*3,4,136–9*]. King James's messianic programme to combine British
Empire with European Union was always such a contradiction,
and in *Cymbeline* his *Pax Britannica* is put in global perspective by
these allusions to the coincidental coming of the actual Prince of
Peace.[115] We 'cannot delve him to the root' [*Cymbeline, 1,1,28*]; but
this Shakespeare who cuts our national roots is therefore more truly
radical than the patriotic 'Bard' digging for his 'British' origins, and
one whose 'brute part' speaks to us like that of the soldier he gave

the border name of Williams, who not only rejects Fluellen's patronizing tip but refuses to take the King's shilling: 'I will have none of your money' [*Henry V, 4,8,62*].

Notes

1 Samuel Schoenbaum, *William Shakespeare: A Documentary Life* (Oxford: Oxford University Press, 1975), p.126; M.G. Brennan, '"We Have the Man Shakespeare With Us": Wilton House and *As You Like It*', *Wiltshire Archaeological and Natural History Magazine*, 80 (1986), 225–7.

2 'Greatest of the Presidents of Wales' (Sir Henry Sidney): A.H. Dodd, *Studies in Stuart Wales* (Cardiff: University of Wales Press, 1971), p.25; Dedication to the 1623 Folio repr. in *The Norton Shakespeare*, ed. Stephen Greenblatt, Jean Howard, Katharine Eisaman Maus and Walter Cohen (New York: Norton, 1997), p.3348.

3 Gwyn A. Williams, *When Was Wales?: A History of the Welsh* (Harmondsworth: Penguin, 1985), p.115.

4 John Paston, 25 May 1549, and the journal of Edward VI, quoted in Adam Nicolson, *Earls of Paradise: England and the Dream of Perfection* (London: Harper Collins, 2007), p.68; 'National Parks in America': ibid., pp.68–9. As well as enclosing large tracts of the county, the Herberts increased rents 'more than five-fold' when they took over their Wiltshire estates: see Anthony Fletcher, *Tudor Rebellions* (Harlow: Longman, 1968), p.65.

5 Julian Cornwall, *Revolt of the Peasantry 1549* (London: Routledge & Kegan Paul, 1977), p.206. For Herbert's campaign of terror in the West Country, see pp.197–200; 'tag rag': p.198.

6 Philip Sidney, *The Countess of Pembroke's Arcadia*, ed. Maurice Evans (Harmondsworth: Penguin, 1977), pp.380–1; for a commentary, see Stephen Greenblatt, 'Murdering Peasants: Status, Genre, and the Representation of Rebellion', in Stephen Greenblatt (ed.), *Representing the English Renaissance* (Berkeley: University of California Press, 1988), pp.1–29, esp. pp.15–19.

7 For the sinister class aggression of the Welsh wyvern and javelins, see Nicolson, op. cit. (note 4), pp.70–1.

8 Megan Lloyd, *'Speak It in Welsh': Wales and the Welsh Language in Shakespeare* (Lanham, Md: Rowman and Littlefield, 2007), pp.49 and 94.

9 Philip Schwyzer, *Literature, Nationalism, and Memory in Early Modern England and Wales* (Cambridge: Cambridge University Press, 2004), p.25.

10 Ibid., pp.24 and 43.

11 'Harpers and crowthers': BL, Lansdowne MS. 111, fo. 10, quoted in Dodd, op. cit. (note 2), p.13; Willy Maley and Philip Schwyzer (eds), *Shakespeare and Wales* (London: Ashgate, 2010).

12 'A young man might have learned': quoted Dodd, op. cit. (note 2), p.52.

13 'Eye of all Wales': Penry Williams, *The Council in the Marches Under Elizabeth I* (Cardiff: University of Wales Press, 1958), p.276; Christopher Marlowe, *Edward II*, SD, scene 20, 45, in *Christopher Marlowe: The Complete Plays*, ed. Frank Romany and Robert Lindsey (London: Penguin, 2003), p.475.

14 'The darling of Wales': Dodd, op. cit. (note 2), p.81.

15 For the quarrel between Pembroke and Essex, which dated from 1595, see Williams, op. cit. (note 13), pp.287–8.

16 Christ Church Ms. 184, XXI, ll. 7–12, repr. and discussed in Tom Lloyd-Roberts, 'Bard of Lleweni? Shakespeare's Welsh Connection', *The New Welsh Review*, 6:3 (1993–14), 11–18, here 15. For 'The Phoenix and the Turtle' and Sir John Salusbury of Lleweni in Denbighshire, see E.A.J. Honigmann, *Shakespeare: The 'Lost Years'* (Manchester: Manchester University Press, 1985), pp.91–113; For Sir John Salusbury and the Welsh politics of the Essex Revolt, see J.E. Neale, *The Elizabethan House of Commons* (London: Jonathan Cape, 1949), pp.111–28, esp. pp.118–19; and Williams, op. cit. (note 13), pp.289–97.

17 For Shakespeare, 'The Phoenix and the Turtle', and the Earl of Worcester in the aftermath of the Essex Revolt, see John Finnis and Patrick Martin, 'Another Turn for the Turtle: Shakespeare's Intercession for Love's Martyr', *Times Literary Supplement*, 18 April 2003, 12–14. The Worcester earldom was another branch of the Herberts, who had married into the semi-royal Somerset family. The Earl of Worcester had inherited most of the Herbert lands in South Wales: see Williams, op. cit. (note 13), p.234.

18 For the theory that Shakespeare revised *As You Like It* for a 1603 performance at Wilton House, see Nicolson, op. cit. (note 4), pp.144–9.

19 'The pillar of the Welsh realm': Emyr Humphreys, *The Taliesin Tradition* (London: Black Raven Press, 1983), p.53. For William Herbert as the most plausible 'Mr W.H.' see Katherine Duncan-Jones, 'Introduction', *The Arden Shakespeare: The Sonnets* (London: Thomas Nelson, 1997), pp.55–69.

20 'Heart-stopping beauty and unrelenting rain': Nicolson, op. cit. (note 4), p.51.

21 Williams, op. cit. (note 3), p.122.

22 David Baker, *Between Nations: Shakespeare, Spenser, Marvell, and the Question of Britain* (Stanford: Stanford University Press, 1997), p.28.

23 'From the Welsh borders ... Sir Gelli Meywick ...': Robert Lacey, *Robert, Earl of Essex: An Elizabethan Icarus* (London: Weidenfeld & Nicolson, 1970), p.275; 'Boisterous Welsh henchmen': Baker, op. cit. (note 22), p.54. For the Elizabethan City of London's traditional East-bound trading priorities, and their conflict with an emerging Atlantic economy, see Robert Brenner, *Merchants and Revolution: Commercial Change, Political Conflict, and London's Overseas Trade, 1550–1653* (Cambridge: Cambridge University Press, 1993).

24 Andrew Marvell, 'An Horatian Ode upon Cromwell's Return from Ireland', ll. 73–6, in *The Poems and Letters of Andrew Marvell*, ed. H.M. Margoliouth (2 vols, Oxford: Clarendon Press, 1927), vol. 1, p.89.

25 'Band of brothers': Neale, op. cit. (note 16), p.120; 'premature Jacobeans': Mervyn James, 'At the Crossroads of the Political Culture: The Essex Revolt, 1601', in *Society, Politics and Culture: Studies in Early Modern England* (Cambridge: Cambridge University Press, 1986), p.426. See also Andrew Hadfield, *Shakespeare and Republicanism* (Cambridge: Cambridge University Press, 2005), esp. Chap.6, 'The Radical *Hamlet*'.

26 Schwyzer, op. cit. (note 9), p.135, n. 15; Jacques Derrida, *Specters of Marx: The State of the Debt, Mourning, and the New International*, trans. Peggy Kamuf (London: Routledge, 1994), esp. p.25.

27 Williams, op. cit. (note 3), pp.115 and 123.

28 J.F. Rees, *Studies in Welsh History* (Cardiff: University of Wales Press, 1965), pp.30–1; W. Garmon Jones, 'Welsh Nationalism and Henry Tudor', *Transations of the Honourable Society of Cymmrodorion*, 1917–18, 1–59; 'The Bull of Anglesey': Alison Plowden, *The House of Tudor* (London: Weidenfeld and Nicolson, 1976), p.1.

29 Schwyzer, op. cit. (note 9), pp.20 & 30.

30 Williams, op. cit. (note 3), p.117.

31 John Kerrigan, *Archipelagic English: Literature, History, Politics, 1603–1707* (Oxford: Oxford University Press, 2008). And see Marcus Merryman, *The Rough Wooings: Mary Queen of Scots, 1542–1551* (East Linton: Tuckwell Press), p.42: 'Henry VIII, unsurprisingly, also believed the Brut story. When Polydore Vergil in 1513, on completion of the manuscript of his *History of England*, first requested the honour of dedicating it to him, the king robustly refused'.

32 Thomas Cecil, Earl of Exeter, letter to Thomas Allington, 13 November 1605, BM Harleian MSS 324, fols 32–32b: 'My lord, my father [Lord Burghley], alterying the writing of his name maketh many that are not well affectyd to our house, to dowbt whyther we rightly discended of that howse of Wales, because they wryte their names Sitsilt and our name is wrytten Cecyll. My grandfather write it Syssell, and so I

mervayle what moved my lord, my father, to alter it'. But when Robert Cecil was offered a family tree by his Welsh genealogist, he replied testily: 'I desire none of these vain toys, nor to hear of such absurdities': quoted in Baker, op. cit. (note 22), p.54. 'Old inhabiters': quoted Dodd, op. cit. (note 2), p.76; Williams, op. cit. (note 4), pp.115 and 123.

33 See Lloyd, op. cit. (note 8), p.78.

34 Dodd, op. cit. (note 2), p.46.

35 Lloyd, op. cit. (note 8), p.149.

36 Pierre Bourdieu, 'Field of Power, Literary Field and Habitus,' trans. Claud DuVerlie, in *The Field of Cultural Production*, ed. Randall Johnson (Cambridge: Polity Press, 1993), p.164.

37 Stephen Greenblatt, 'Invisible Bullets', in *Shakespearean Negotiations: The Circulation of Social Energy in Renaissance England* (Oxford: Clarendon Press, 1988), p.56.

38 Alan Sinfield, *Faultlines: Cultural Materialism and the Politics of Dissident Reading* (Oxford: Clarendon Press, 1992), p.125.

39 'Alien intruders': Dodd, op. cit. (note 2), p.76; Williams, op. cit. (note 3), p.122.

40 Willy Maley, '"This sceptred isle": Shakespeare and the British Problem', in John Joughin (ed.), *Shakespeare and National Culture* (Manchester: Manchester University Press, 1997), pp.83–108, esp. pp.100–1; and '"A Thing Most Brutish": Depicting Shakespeare's Multi-Nation-State', *Shakespeare*, 3 (2007), 79–101.

41 T.M. Devine, *Scotland's Empire and the Shaping of the Americas, 1600–1815* (Washington: Smithsonian Institute, 2003), p.xxvii.

42 'Internal colony': John Davies, *A History of Wales* (Harmondsworth: Penguin, 1990), p.225; 'Freed the Welsh from bondage': John Owen, 'Tudors', *Times Literary Supplement*, 11 July 2008, 6.

43 Clifford Davies, 'A Rose by Another Name', *Times Literary Supplement*, 13 June 2008, 14–15; 'Her Majesty whose name is Tyder': George Owen of Henllys, *Description of Pembrokeshire* (London: 1603), quoted ibid., 15.

44 'Unruly subjects ... "external" enemy ... Wales silently absorbed': Maley, op. cit. (note 40), pp.99 and 104; 'the subordinating power': Baker, op. it. (note 22), p.22; 'British imperial energy ... was Welsh' etc.: Williams, op. cit. (note 3), pp.114–15, 121, 124–5, 127.

45 Jeremy Black, *The Curse of History* (London: The Social Affairs Unit, 2008); 'the ancient wrong ... the endless ill': 'The Shropshire Lad: XXVIII: The Welsh Marches', in A.E. Housman, *The Collected Poems of A.E. Housman* (London: Jonathan Cape, 1939), pp.44–5: 'The sound of fight is silent long / That began the ancient wrong; / Long the voice of tears is still / That wept of old the endless ill. In my heart

it has not died, / The war that swept the Severn side; / They cease not fighting, east and west, / On the marches of my breast.'

46 Baker, op. cit. (note 22), pp.52–4.

47 Williams, op. cit. (note 13), pp.197–204.

48 Joan Fitzpatrick, *Shakespeare, Spenser and the Contours of Britain: Reshaping the Atlantic Archipeligo* (Hatfield: University of Hertfordshire Press, 2004), p.132. For the idea that Shakespeare belittles Glyndŵr as a displacement of contemporary anxieties about the Irish rebel O'Neill, see in particular Christopher Highley, *Shakespeare, Spenser, and the Crisis in Ireland* (Cambridge: Cambridge University Press, 1997), pp.87–95.

49 Ibid.

50 'Welsh colonization': Williams, op. cit. (note 3), p.122; Schwyzer, op. cit. (note 9), p.127.

51 Terence Hawkes, 'Bryn Glas', in *Shakespeare in the Present* (London: Routledge, 2002), p.44.

52 Schwyzer, op. cit. (note 9), p.24. Cf. Baker, op. cit. (note 22), pp.51–2: 'The castrating Welshwomen are twice removed and doubly mediated ... We hear only Westmorland's report of them ... The menace of Wales is well buried in the *Henriad*.'

53 Hawkes, op. cit. (note 51), pp.33–4.

54 A.E. Housman, 'A Shropshire Lad: XL: Into my heart an air that kills', op. cit. (note 45), p.58.

55 Thus Hawkes describes Jean Genet as a 'homosexual and transvestite' (p.24), whereas the crew-cut writer, who never dressed in drag, was so obsessed by his macho image that he destroyed a photograph showing him with hair as long as Rimbaud's: Edmund White, *Genet* (London: Chatto & Windus, 1993), pp.241 and 367.

56 Terence Hawkes, 'Aberdaugleddyf', op. cit. (note 51), p.52.

57 Ibid., p.63.

58 Ibid.

59 But for a brilliant account of Keynes's Shakespearean allusions in his theory of the dichotomy between Anglo-Saxon logic and Celtic magic in *The Economic Consequences of the Peace*, where Lloyd George is depicted as a 'Welsh *witch*' seducing the Presbyterian Woodrow Wilson, see Martin Harries, *Scare Quotes from Shakespeare: Marx, Keynes, and the Language of Reenchantment* (Stanford: Stanford University Press, 2000), pp.132–50, esp. p.148.

60 Charles Fever, *Robert Armin: Shakespeare's Fool: A Biographical Essay* (Kent, Ohio: Kent State University Press, 1961), pp.16–17 and 49.

61 Judith Halberstam, *The Queer Art of Failure* (Durham, NC: Duke University Press, 2011).

62 Veronika Pohlig, '"These Violent Proceedings" – Francis Ford's "Frenzy" and the Pains of Governing Merry Wives', *Shakespeare Jahrbuch*, 143 (2007), 101.

63 'The dismissive treatment of matters Arthurian': Richard Hillman, 'Shakespeare's Arthurian Misfortunes', in *Shakespeare, Marlowe and the Politics of France* (Basingstoke: Palgrave, 2002), p.68.

64 Pierre Bourdieu, 'From the King's House to the Reason of State: A Model of the Genesis of the Bureaucratic Field', originally 'De la maison du roi à la raison d'Etat: un modèle de la genèse du champ bureaucratique', *Actes de la recherche en sciences socials*, 18 (1997), 55–68, trans. Richard Nice and Loïc Wacquant in *Pierre Bourdieu and Democratic Politics*, eds Loïc Wacquant (Cambridge: Polity Press, 2005), p.31. For the dating of the play, see Barbara Freedman, 'Shakespearean Chronology, Ideological Complicity, and Floating Texts: Something Is Rotten in Windsor', *Shakespeare Quarterly*, 45 (1994), 190–210; and Leslie Katz, '*The Merry Wives of Windsor*: Sharing the Queen's Holiday', *Representations*, 51 (1995), 77–93.

65 Frances Yates, *Astraea: The Imperial Theme in the Sixteenth Century* (Harmondsworth: Penguin, 1977), p.109. For the connection with the St George's Day feast, see in particular Schoenbaum op. cit. (note 1), pp.145–6; and Helen Hackett, *Shakespeare and Elizabeth: The Meeting of Two Myths* (Princeton: Princeton University Press, 2009), pp.23–4.

66 Hillman, op. cit. (note 63), p.53.

67 Hackett, op.cit. (note 65), pp.45–6; Pierre Bourdieu, *The Rules of Art: Genesis and Structure of the Literary Field*, trans. Susan Emanuel (Cambridge: Polity Press, 1996), pp.3–4.

68 Pierre Bourdieu, 'Flaubert's Point of View', trans. Priscilla Parkhurst Ferguson, originally pub. *Critical Inquiry*, 14 (1988), 539–62, in *The Field of Cultural Production: Essays on Art and Literature*, ed. Randal Johnson (Cambridge: Polity Press, 1993), p.202.

69 Roger Ascham, *The Schoolmaster*, ed. Lawrence Ryan (Ithaca: Cornell University Press, 1967), p.145. For the ideological and poetic implications, see Richard Helgerson, *Forms of Nationhood: The Elizabethan Writing of England* (Chicago: Chicago University Press, 1992), pp.28–31.

70 Bourdieu, op. cit. (note 68), p.11.

71 Judith Butler, *Excitable Speech: A Politics of the Performative* (London: Routledge, 1997), pp.14–15.

72 T.W. Baldwin, *William Shakespeare's Small Latin and Lesse Greeke* (2 vols, Urbana: Indiana University Press, 1944), vol. 1, pp.478–80.

73 William Bouwsma, *The Waning of the Renaissance: 1550–1640* (New Haven: Yale University Press, 2000), p.5.

74 Quoted in Ivy Pinchbeck and Margaret Hewitt, *Children in English Society: From Tudor Times to the Eighteenth Century* (London: Routledge & Kegan Paul, 1969), p.39.

75 For 'circumfession' as a 'circling around' the conflict of the individual with a mechanized and textualized universal law, see Jacques Derrida, 'Circumfession', in *Jacques Derrida: A Biography*, trans. Geoffrey Bennington, pp.3–313, esp. pp.65–74: 'Circumcision, that's all I've ever talked about' (p.70).

76 William Barker, 'Introduction' to Richard Mulcaster, *Positions Concerning the Training Up of Children* (Toronto: Toronto University Press, 1994), p.lxv.

77 Alan Stewart, *Close Readers: Humanism and Sodomy in Early Modern England* (Princeton: Princeton University Press, 1997), p.102. For the classic account of the Latin lesson as a brutal rite of passage from the female household into masculine violence, see Walter Ong, 'Latin Language Study as a Renaissance Puberty Rite', in *Rhetoric, Romance and Technology: Studies in the Interaction of Expression and Culture* (Ithaca: Cornell University Press, 1971), pp.113–41.

78 Elizabeth Pittenger, 'Dispatch Quickly: The Mechanical Reproduction of Pages', *Shakespeare Quarterly*, 42 (1991), 389–408, here 404.

79 Ibid., 398 and 405.

80 Gilles Deleuze, *Nietzsche and Philosophy*, trans. H. Tomlinson (London: Athlone Press, 1983), p.9.

81 See William Engel, *Chiastic Designs in English Literature from Sidney to Shakespeare* (Farnham: Ashgate, 2009), pp.120–30.

82 Butler, op. cit. (note 71), p.14.

83 David Landreth, 'Once More into the Preech: The Merry Wives' English Pedagogy', *Shakespeare Quarterly*, 55 (2004), 420–49, here 441.

84 John Aubrey, repr. in Samuel Schoenbaum, *Shakespeare: A Documentary Life* (Oxford: Oxford University Press, 1977), p.58.

85 Jacques Rancière, *The Ignorant Schoolmaster: Five Lessons in Intellectual Emancipation*, trans. Kirsten Ross (Stanford: Stamford University Press, 1991), pp.3 and 15.

86 Harold Bloom, *The Anatomy of Influence* (New Haven: Yale University Press, 2011), p.55.

87 See, for example, R.S. White, *The Merry Wives of Windsor* (Hemel Hempstead: Harvester, 1991), p.51; Sinfield, op. cit. (note 38), pp.124–5. The problem was first considered in W.J. Lawrence, 'Welsh Portraiture in Elizabethan Drama', *Times Literary Supplement*, 9 November 1922, 724.

88 Chris Holcomb, *Mirth Making: The Rhetorical Discourse on Jesting in Early Modern England* (Columbia, SC: South Carolina University Press, 2001), p.105.

89 For Welsh 'annexation' of the Tudor education apparatus, see
    W.P. Griffith, *Learning, Law and Religion: Higher Education and
    Welsh Society, c. 1540–1640* (Cardiff: Cardiff University Press, 1996),
    p.93; and Prys Morgan, 'Wild Wales: Civilizing the Welsh from the
    Sixteenth to the Nineteenth Centuries', in *Civil Histories: Essays
    Presented to Sir Keith Thomas* (Oxford: Oxford University Press,
    2000), p.269.

90 'Intensely dialogic': Linda Woodbridge, 'Afterword: Speaking with
    the Dead', *PMLA*, 118:3 (2003), 597–603, here 601; for the struc-
    tural deviancy of *The Merry Wives of Windsor*, see Wendy Wall,
    'Unhusbanding Desires in Windsor', in Richard Dutton and Jean
    Howard (eds), *A Companion to Shakespeare's Works: III: The
    Comedies* (Oxford: Blackwell, 2003), p.387, quoting Jonathan
    Dollimore, *Sexual Dissidence: Augustine to Wilde, Freud to Foucault*
    (Oxford: Oxford University Press, 1991), p.160.

91 For British mimicry of the Roman Empire see Willy Maley,
    'Postcolonial Shakespeare: British Identity Formation and *Cymbeline*',
    in *Shakespeare and Race*, eds Catherine Alexander and Stanley Wells
    (Cambridge: Cambridge University Press, 2000), p.147.

92 Ben Jonson, 'To the memory of my beloved, The Author', repr. in
    William Shakespeare, op. cit. (note 2), p.3351.

93 White, op. cit. (note 87), p.2.

94 Wall, op. cit. (note 90), p.380.

95 François Laroque, *Shakespeare's Festive World: Elizabethan Seasonal
    Entertainment and the Professional Stage*, trans. Janet Lloyd
    (Cambridge: Cambridge University Press, 1991), p.60. Based on Keith
    Thomas, 'Rule and Misrule in the Schools of Early Modern England',
    The Stenton Lecture 1975, and Reading 1976.

96 Pittenger, op. cit. (note 78), 396–7 and 399. For a similar reading,
    which sees William 'assaulted by an adult harangue involving coarse
    sexual euphemisms', see Maurice Hunt, 'The "Warwickshire" of
    Shakespeare's Mind', *Connotations*, 7:2 (1998), 159–80, here 175.

97 Laroque, op. cit. (note 95), p.61.

98 Pittinger, op. cit. (note 78), 407.

99 Wall, op. cit. (note 90), pp.378 and 386.

100 Halberstam, op. cit. (note 61), p.13; 'homosexual desire in particu-
    lar': Bruce R. Smith, *Homosexual Desire in Shakespeare's England:
    A Cultural Poetics* (Chicago: Chicago University Press, 1994), p.84.
    See also Stephen Orgel, *Impersonations: The Performance of Gender
    in Shakespeare's England* (Cambridge: Cambridge University Press,
    1996), pp.55–6 and 66–7.

101 Halberstam, op. cit. (note 61), p.121.

102 Georgia Brown, 'Marlowe's Poems and Classicism', in *The Cambridge*

126 *Free Will*

Companion to Christopher Marlowe, ed. Patrick Cheney (Cambridge: Cambridge University Press, 2004), p.107. For the tendency of classical education to universalize homoerotic desire, see also Claude Summers, 'Homosexuality and Renaissance Literature, or the Anxieties of Anachronism', *South Central Review*, 9:1 (1992), 2–23, and '"Hero and Leander": and the Arbitrariness of Desire', in Alan Downie and J.T. Parnell (eds), *Constructing Christopher Marlowe* (Cambridge: Cambridge University Press, 2000), pp.134–5.

103 Jonathan Goldberg, *Sodometries: Renaissance Texts, Modern Sexualities* (Stanford: Stanford University Press, 1992), p.143.

104 'Subjugated knowledge': Michel Foucault, *Society Must Be Defended: Lectures at the Collège de France, 1975–1976*, trans. David Macey (London: Picador, 2003), p.7; 'Universities, schools, and so on': 'Sex, Power, and the Politics of Identity', trans. B. Gallagher and A Wilson, in *Michel Foucault: Ethics: The Essential Works: 1*, ed. Paul Rabinow (London: Allen Lane, 1997), pp.170–1.

105 See Steven Mullaney, *The Place of the Stage: License, Play, and Power in Renaissance England* (Chicago: Chicago University Press, 1988), p.87.

106 Patricia Parker, *Literary Fat Ladies: Rhetoric, Gender, Property* (London: Methuen, 1987), pp.28–9.

107 Pierre Bourdieu, *Language and Symbolic Power*, trans. Gino Raymond and Matthew Adamson, ed. John Thompson (Cambridge: Polity Press, 1991), p.117.

108 Landreth, op. cit. (note 83), pp.449 and 447.

109 Goldberg, op. cit. (note 103), pp.164–5 and 173–5. See also Heather Findlay, 'Renaissance Pederasty and Pedagogy: The "Case" of Shakespeare's Falstaff', *Yale Journal of Criticism*, 3 (1989), 229–38. And for the boy-player as object of homosexual excitement, see especially Mary Bly, *Queer Virgins and Virgin Queans on the Early Modern Stage* (Oxford: Oxford University Press, 2000), p.61.

110 For the Elizabethan prehistory of the homosexual 'molly house' see Alan Bray, *Homosexuality in Renaissance England* (London: Gay Men's Press, 1982), p.85; and Rictor Norton, *Mother Clap's Molly House: The Gay Subculture in England 1700–1830* (London: Gay Men's Press, 1992), pp.18–20.

111 Juliet Fleming, *Graffiti and the Writing Arts of Early Modern England* (London: Reaktion Books, 2001), pp.57–8.

112 For Davy Jones, who married first Elizabeth, daughter of the Shakespeares' business associate Adrian Quiney, and in 1579 Frances Hathaway, see Mark Eccles, *Shakespeare in Warwickshire* (Madison: Wisconsin University Press, 1961), p.83.

113 Schwyzer, op. cit. (note 9), p.24.

114 See Ronald Boling, 'Anglo-Welsh Relations in *Cymbeline*', *Shakespeare Quarterly*, 51:1 (2000), 33–66, esp. 64–5.

115 For the tension between the two narratives of the birth of Christ and 'British' origins, see Robin Moffet, '*Cymbeline* and the Nativity', *Shakespeare Quarterly*, 13 (1962), 207–17. And for the contradictions of James's twin projects of 'British' and Christian Union, reflected in *Cymbeline*, see W.B. Patterson, *King James VI and I and the Reunion of Christendom* (Cambridge, Cambridge University Press, 1997), pp. 36–41 and 49–57.

3

O World

The echoes of Rome in Julius Caesar

Every like is not the same

Tuesday July 3 1600. We heard an English play; the theatre was constructed in the style of the ancient Romans, out of wood. It was so
built that spectators could very easily see from every part.[1]

Two things that struck visitors to the Elizabethan playhouses were
their similarity to Roman amphitheatres and the fact that, as Swiss
tourist Thomas Platter reported in 1600, this should have meant
'everyone has a good view'.[2] Scholars debate the extent to which
these unroofed venues did in fact imitate the ancient Roman arenas,
and whether Shakespeare's 'wooden O' [*Henry V, Pro.14*] was constructed to be a 'Theatre of the World', modelled as a multi-sided
polygon on the designs by Vitruvius in *De Architectura*. The theory
that when he erected the first London playhouse in 1576 James
Burbage 'knew something of Vitruvian theory', calling this building
the Theater because that had been the word for a playing space; and
that when in 1599 his sons reassembled its timbers as the Globe
they reproduced a replica of the Roman amphitheatre, 'closer to its
spirit than any other Renaissance adaptation', is disputed.[3] But the
notion of the Globe as a spooky imitation of the cruel ring where
'so many lusty Romans / Came smiling' [2,3,78] to feast on blood, is
supported not only by the logic that a circular construction named
after the world '*must* have been based' on the stadium where, as
Roman historian Livy recorded, 'plays and games were looked upon
pell mell, without difference' of rank.[4] It is also prompted by the
fact that the play we think Platter saw, and that Shakespeare probably wrote for the inauguration of the Thames-side playhouse, was
a tragedy about the foundation of the Roman empire that opens
with a panorama of walls, battlements, towers, smoking chimneys

and windows, like one of the topographical views of early modern London, before zooming in on a great assembly beside a river, where an echo of 'universal' applause makes us believe this tiered arena must indeed be a likeness of that 'wide and universal theatre' [*As You*, *2,7,137*], 'the great globe itself' [*Tempest, 4,1,152–3*]:

> MURULLUS: Many a time and oft
> Have you climbed up to walls and battlements,
> To towers and windows, yea to chimney-tops,
> Your infants in your arms, and there have sat
> The livelong day with patient expectation
> To see great Pompey pass the streets of Rome.
> And when you saw his chariot but appear,
> Have you not made an universal shout,
> That Tiber trembled underneath her banks
> To hear the replication of your sounds
> Made in her concave shores?
>
> [*1,1,36–46*]

Did the shouts from the Globe create a ghostly echo? And if so, did Shakespeare exploit or resist that unexpected 'replication'? Since every echo is an anachronism, John Hollander has described *all* Shakespearean drama as 'an implicit echo chamber', or 'irony machine', the mnemonic reboundings from which 'define the tragic contingencies of those who give them voice'.[5] But editors remind us how disturbed the Elizabethan idea of dramatic authorship was by the inaccuracy of memorial textual reconstruction. And despite being the fanfare for a theatrical revolution, *Julius Caesar* is a play unusually plagued by the negativity of echoes, both real and imagined, by the split between the original and its 'replications', and also by misgivings as to 'whether revolution be the same' if 'there be nothing new, but that which is hath been before ... in some antique book' [Sonnet 59]. Its creator appears to sense here, more acutely than anywhere else in his work, that every beginning is *always already* haunted, that 'Time is come round, / And where I did begin, there shall I end' [*5,3,23*], since 'The presence of the present is derived from repetition and not the reverse'; for he knows the Rome in which the play is set is not simply a city of stones but the capital of the art of memory, where nothing is lost in the conflation of the primeval and the present, because as Freud will put it, 'the oldest structures coexist with the latest'.[6] Yet, as if in reaction to such 'archive fever', in this foundational Globe play Shakespeare seems to resist all myths of origins, to be relieved that 'every like is not the same', and to be committed to an almost post-structuralist notion of 'Repetition as a nonoriginary origin ... repetition which moves forward'.[7]

If Elizabethan science taught that 'An Echo's nothing but a forc'd rebound / Or airy repercussion of a sound', classicizing poets like Sir Philip Sidney nevertheless insisted on the *productivity* of such repercussions.[8] And the echoes of Rome appear to strike the author of *Julius Caesar* as both literal and figurative. For he also anticipates what Edgar Allan Poe and Karl Marx will each hear inside the Eternal City's walls: that '"Not all" – the Echoes' of its violent history have been silenced, since 'Prophetic sounds and loud, arise forever / From ... all Ruin', to 'rule / With a despotic sway'; so the difficulty in escaping the vicious circle of mimetic repetition will be that whenever its successors launch a revolution against the old order, 'they conjure up the spirits of the past and borrow from them names, battle cries and costumes, to present the new scene of world history in time-honoured disguise'.[9] If Shakespeare did write *Julius Caesar* for the inception of the Globe, it has always therefore seemed to critics that Shakespeare 'had something in mind' in filling it with such literally preposterous anachronisms as 'the strange disposèd time' [*1,3,33*] of a chiming clock.[10] But what they have perhaps not considered enough is how this uncanniness relates to the struggle the play explores of a repetition that moves *forward*. For alarmingly for the consecration of a house named and shaped to be a microcosm, every time Shakespeare invokes 'the revolution of the times' [*2Henry IV, 3,1,45*] he envisages the indisposition of a spiralling declension, a *mal archive* like the acoustic depreciation of actual echoes: as in Hamlet's 'fine revolution' of cannibalized corpses [*Hamlet, 5,1,83*]; or Antony's prescience that 'The present pleasure, / By revolution low'ring, does become / The opposite of itself' [*Antony, 1,2,113–15*].

Shakespeare is said to have a 'pious regard' for historical accuracy in his first Globe play, where the panorama that circumscribes the action has the quality W.G. Sebald ascribed to all such pre-cinematic visual simulacra, of creating the impression of 'being at the centre' of history.[11] Yet the circle, ring, or zero is always 'an O without a figure' [*Lear, 1,4,168*] waiting to be filled in his work, and therefore like the virgin Globe itself, potentially *naughty*. So the first declaration he likely wrote for the 'wooden O' [*Henry V,*

Pro.13] made Marx's wry point about all revolutions being acted in the worn-out shoes and second-hand clothes of the *ancien régime*: 'In respect of a fine workman I am but, as you would say, a cobbler' [*1,1,10*]. Thus, with the belching body-politics of a shoemaker's holiday, Shakespeare introduces the idea of modernity as a repeat performance, dating from the days of Rome, played out between kings and the actors who expropriate (literally in Elizabethan London) their obsolete regalia. Chiasmus in Shakespeare always 'announces and projects a signifying difference'; and, as Jacques Derrida intuited, 'Marx's love of Shakespeare' was inspired by the mad anachrony of such 'hauntology', and by the endeavour to rise above slavish repetition the nineteenth-century philosopher located in texts such as *Julius Caesar*, where the terrifying spirit of the old sovereignty keeps on coming back, and 'having expired returns', as Brutus anticipates: 'Well; then I shall see thee again?'; and the ghost grimly affirms, 'Ay, at Philippi' [*4,2,336*].[12]

In the circular world of *Julius Caesar*, as Theodor Adorno wrote of Richard Wagner's opera house at Bayreuth, 'every step forwards is a step back into the remote past'.[13] So Marx identified a return of repressed monstrosity haunting the streets where Shakespeare's Roman spectators sit in 'patient expectation' of something new that will begin by coming back. Yet if modernity finds it so hard to transcend what Eric Santner calls the 'after twitches' of the old corporeal sovereignty, Jeffrey Mehlman has also stressed how even as it strives to forestall the coming revolution, repetition cannot help but bring it on.[14] As the Tribunes remind these 'cruel men of Rome' how often they have *already* 'replicated' the archaic ceremonies of this 'present sacrifice' [*2,2,5*], in which they 'now strew flowers in his way / That comes in triumph over Pompey's blood' [*49*], these holidaymakers therefore also await the small mercy or saving grace in Marx's theatricalization of revolution, that if modernity is to be the handed-down reproduction of cast-off royal remnants, its *déjà vu* will be repeated like the metamorphosis of the voice in the interval of the echo itself: contrapuntally, both like and unlike, inside and outside, subservient yet *with a difference*, 'the first time as tragedy, the second time as farce'. For as Gilles Deleuze remarked in *Difference and Repetition*, such is the paradoxical 'secret vibration' of all such popular festivals: 'they repeat an "unrepeatable". They do not add a second or third time to the first, but carry the first to the "nth" power':[15]

FLAVIUS: Why dost thou lead these men about the streets?
COBBLER: Truly, sir, to wear out their shoes to get myself into
             more work. But indeed, sir, we make holiday to see
             Caesar and to rejoice in his triumph.
MURULLUS: Wherefore rejoice? What conquest brings he home?
             What tributaries follow him to Rome
             To grace in captive bonds his chariot wheels?
             You blocks, you stones, you worse than senseless
             things!

                                                    [*1,1,27–33*]

With their transmigrating 'soles', these down-at-heel workers who await Caesar want tragedy repeated farcically, like the shoemaker's belch. They are old hands at refashioning redundant sameness, with as much vested in holidaymaking as the author himself. So critics see the Cobbler as a portrait of the artist whose homophonous puns will likewise break with imitation to restore bad *souls*, for with his doubling, self-splitting play on the concept of the King's Two Bodies, Shakespeare's logic-chopper is a gatekeeper of the naughtily echoing 'wooden O', the gaping vaginal 'awl' or nothing [*21*] by which, he says, he lives. And it does sound like the son of the Stratford tanner speaking for a nascent public sphere, when this enterprise is grounded on the radical foundation that 'As proper men as ever trod on neat's leather have gone upon my handiwork' [*24–5*]. But from sacred 'holy day' to secular 'holiday', the body language of this shoemaker's festival thus also literalizes what Santner terms the *investiture crisis* generated by such a transmission of sovereignty from the royal to the republican body, personal presence to personifying representation, or politics to aesthetics, when the political theology that had legitimated office in the age of sacral kingship was subjected to an equally radical uncertainty, as 'with the old sartorial and behavioural codes gone, bodies were less legible', and '*suddenly every body bore political weight*':[16]

FLAVIUS: Hence, home, you idle creatures, get you home!
             Is this a holiday? What, know you not
             That being mechanical, you ought not walk,
             Upon a labouring day without the sign
             Of your profession?

                                                    [*1,1,2–5*]

Why do intellectuals make so much of shoemakers? asks Jacques Rancière. The answer he gives in *The Philosopher and His Poor* is that the shoemaker figures as the archetypal artisan, who because his work never advances beyond mere repetition can appreciate only spectacle, and understands neither art nor tragedy. The first thinker to break this stereotype, according to Rancière was Wagner, when he made the shoemaker Hans Sachs his Meistersinger.[17] Yet in *Julius Caesar*, far from being such a senseless 'block', the 'naughty knave' who cobbles new meanings out of redundant forms initiates a duel between living voices and the 'stones of Rome' [*3,2,221*], and an objection to the affront that the space of representation might belong more to 'A statue than a breather' [*Antony, 3,3,21*], that will agitate all of Shakespeare's later tragedies, as if this investiture crisis on the threshold of the modern public sphere, where everyone will find a 'place in the commonwealth' [*40*], indeed heralds a democracy to come composed out of the liberty of redistributed signs. But in this particular rite of spring we are still reminded of the earlier failures to escape sovereign power, like that when the ancestors of these merrymakers did 'from the streets of Rome / The Tarquin drive' [*2,1,53*]. Thus in René Girard's pessimistic reading, by emphasizing the regression of the sacrificial cycle and mob-like reciprocity of mimetic desire, *Julius Caesar* exposes the copycat violence of theatre itself; for this is not the first time, and nor will it be the last, as the Tribunes object, when the victors present the new scene of history in a false façade Marx laughingly called 'resurrected Romanity': as Marjorie Garber quips, this story shows Rome's story was an old story 'even when it was new'.[18]

'There was a Brutus once' Brutus is reminded, who deposed King Tarquin 'to keep his state in Rome' [*1,2,160–1*]. This founding father was Brutus's ancestor Lucius Junius Brutus, so a poster exhorting his namesake to use the same sacrificial violence is hung 'Upon old Brutus' statue' [*1,1,146*], making the king-killer the object of another cult. Its author Cassius aims to inspire heroic action as did 'Aeneas our great ancestor' [*1,2,114*]; and critics notice how all this recursive emulation centres on cultic statues, like those 'decked with ceremonies' for Caesar's triumph [*1,1,63–4*]; his 'statue spouting blood' in Calpurnia's dream [*2,2,85*]; or 'Pompey's statue, / Which all the while ran blood' when Caesar died [*3,2,183*], as if Rome is a necropolis entirely in thrall to the agonistic mode of *imitatio*, where the finest tribute paid a person will be to 'Give him a statue with his ancestors' [*3,2,46*]. The play thereby makes contact with an ancient controversy over the image lately revived by Rancière,

Giorgio Agamben and others, that was exemplified by Pliny the Elder's insistence that a statue should *only* represent an ancestor, rather than being treated as an artwork.[19] By situating the action in an arena encircled with statues, then, Shakespeare clearly marks its position in the transition from a regime of auratic presence to one of representation. For the simulation of patriarchal models was still pervasive in the Renaissance, we are told; and researchers suggest that, like the palace of some absolutist ruler, the 'marble mansion' [*Cymbeline, 5,5,181*] of the Globe was indeed ornamented with busts of pagan gods and heroes.[20] But if the nightmare spectres in *Julius Caesar* hark back to Roman worship of funeral effigies, the play implies how much these simulacra provoked Baudrillardian disquiet at such a faith in fakes out of the 'antique book', and determination that if the new house was to be as much a copy as Rome had been, the line of resistance to these haunted foundations would be to follow the saucy Cobbler, and by refashioning the semblances into something less imposing but more serviceable, get 'into more work' [*1,1,28*].[21]

Our lofty scene

'My heart laments that virtue cannot live / Out of the teeth of emulation' [*2,3,12–13*], sighs Shakespeare's Soothsayer; and his distress at mimetic rivalry would seem to have choric status in this tragedy that anticipates our own anxiety that the mimetic *agon* with Rome is 'the foundation of the modern political sphere', and that 'it is *imitatio* that governs the construction of the modern'.[22] For it is this colonnade of blood-soaked statues which links Rome's sacrificial project to the décor of the Globe. So when Caesar is in turn killed beneath Pompey's statue, the play's strangely disposed time allows playgoers their own flash of premonition, a veritable *coup de théâtre*, through which to glimpse their participation in the procession of 'conquests, glories, triumphs, spoils' [*3,1,180*] by which, as Walter Benjamin shuddered, our 'rulers step over those lying prostrate'.[23] For here, in what is often seen as one of 'the most metadramatic moments in the canon', Shakespeare seems to ponder proleptically on the 'representational deadlock' analysed by Santner in his account of Louis David's great depiction of unintended revolutionary consequences, his painting of the slaying of another king-killer, the *Death of Marat*, where modern art sets itself the task

of representing the body that would 'incarnate the empty place of
the king ... to *incarnate* in some ostensibly new way the *excarnated*
principle of sovereignty', but then confronts the shattering realisa-
tion of how problematic it will be for the revolution to abstract
itself from sovereign violence, to avoid a 'defiling contact with the
flesh that one has torn free from the king's sublime physiology and
claimed for the People':[24]

CASSIUS: How many ages hence
            Shall this our lofty scene be acted over
            In states unborn and accents yet unknown!
BRUTUS: How many times shall Caesar bleed in sport,
            That now on Pompey's basis lies along,
            No worthier than the dust!
CASSIUS: So oft as that shall be,
            So often shall the knot of us be called
            The men that gave their country liberty.

                                                    [*3,1,112–19*]

Like Marat, Shakespeare's revolutionaries intend to be authors of a
'lofty scene' that abstracts 'peace, freedom, and liberty' [*111*] from
the carnal matter of the dead sovereignty. They look forward to the
Enlightenment aesthetic ideology that would assert the disinterestedness and transparency of representation as emancipation from the
political, and their notion of a 'lofty scene' indeed alludes to the
balcony in the tiring-house of the Elizabethan playhouse, where elevated actions were played. But Caesar's execution has in fact taken
place below, on 'such slippery ground', as Antony complains, 'That
this foul deed shall smell above the earth / With carrion men, groaning for burial' [*3,1,192; 277–8*]; and what the tragedy actually stages
is the impossibility of converting the fleshly matter of the body politic
into such a 'lofty' aesthetic 'sport'. Thus the bloodthirsty shouting in
the arena makes its very foundations *tremble* with 'replications'
returning with a vengeance, as the spectators 'make a ring about
the corpse' [*3,2,155*]. Despite the aesthetic fantasy of 'excarnating'
sovereign power from the body of the king, this first text performed
at Shakespeare's riverside circle ripples with the irony of such unwelcome returns: lines belched in quotes like the Soothsayer's 'Beware
the ides of March' [*1,2,18; 3,1,1; 4,2,70*]; phrases that shift meaning,
such as 'grace his wheels', which recurs as 'grace his heels' [*1,1,33;
3,1,121*]; words that ring changes like Antony's 'Honourable men';

or catastrophic namesakes like those of Brutus and Cinna [*3,2,79–96; 121; 148–50; 203*]; as if the author of this play about difference and becoming was truly testing the echo in these pseudo-Roman walls, expanding the ever wider circumference of unintended consequences into the plasticity and impurity of contaminated theatrical space, 'In states unborn and accents yet unknown'. 'A mender of bad soles' [*1,1,14*], then, like the Cobbler, Shakespeare couldn't be broader about his own way of proceeding with the psychic foundations of his worn, soiled, and malodorous gift.

With its self-consciousness that 'the eye sees not itself / But by reflection' [*1,2,54–5*], *Julius Caesar* is preoccupied by the interplay of repetition and difference, and the shock that, as Brutus says when Caesar invites his killers to drink his wine eucharistically 'like friends', 'every like is not the same' [*2,2,128*]. Such self-reflexiveness about the return of the archaic, and the *mise en abyme* of its own chain of signifiers, connects this turn-of-a-century drama with the cult of the ruin Benjamin described, when he wrote how the Antique was 'the mirror within whose frame' the Baroque recognised itself, but that since this was a concave mirror, reflection 'was not possible without distortion'. For like the *Trauerspiel* the critic was describing, Shakespeare's play puts history on stage 'in the form of the ruin', only to retrieve from the stucco pediments and fake pillars the material for its reinvention, as 'The legacy of antiquity constitutes, item for item, the elements from which a new whole is mixed'. To Benjamin, the classical *bric-à-brac* of its theatre was the imperial debris against which the Baroque grasped its historicity, through an 'exuberant subjection of antique elements in a structure which ... would in destruction still be superior to the harmonies of antiquity'. Taking a leaf from Aby Warburg, who thought projection of 'the image in the clouds' to be the logic of Mannerism, Benjamin theorized that the Baroque discovered its own *ars inveniendi* in a fantasia of order imposed on such sovereign relics.[25] On this view, the early modern aesthetic was initiated in the endless substitutions of allegory. But tellingly for the belching Cobbler of old soles in *Julius Caesar*, the critic located the mainspring of this aesthetic in the contrarian inventiveness, a creaturely truancy from similitude, of the echo itself, as a form of *langue* or state of exception outside denotation or the law. Thus, for Benjamin, the fortunate linguistic fall of Shakespeare's era was precisely its discovery 'That every like is not the same':

In the anagrams, the onomatopoeic phrases, and many other examples of linguistic virtuosity, word, syllable, and sound are emancipated from the context of traditional meaning and are flaunted as objects which can be exploited for allegorical purposes. The language of the baroque is constantly convulsed by rebellion on the part of the elements which make it up.[26]

Everyone knows Shakespearean Rome is a city 'of orators and rhetoricians ... where the art of persuasion is cultivated, for better or worse, to an extent unparalleled in any other society', for here 'language is power'.[27] But critics also notice how this world of warring words is like the *Trauerspiel* in having fallen into the ruin and contagion of historical language, in which a word must always 'communicate *something* (other than itself)'.[28] So Frank Kermode remarks that, while its characters claim to be orators, Shakespeare's meaning in this play about rhetoric is as riddling as the omens and oracles that punctuate the plot, as if 'clarity was less and less his way'. Kermode believes the dramatist made words reverberate here to tantalize audiences with their importance 'while disclaiming all authority'.[29] And A.D. Nuttall gives this *fort/da* withholding game or echo-trick its Latin name: *occultatio*, the figure of deniability whereby 'information is cocooned in disclaimers', as Antony tempts the mourners with Caesar's will: 'Which pardon me, I do not mean to read' [*3,2,128*]. '*Occultatio* is everywhere' in this work, Nuttall asserts.[30] But Nicholas Royle has a more affirmative term for this revisionary playback: there is a portentous *to-effect* to *Julius Caesar*, he thinks, an endless supplementation that is its opening *to* tomorrow. With its uncanny counterpoint of duplicated scenes, speeches, words and names, this allusive play about mimicry and performance, which stages the impossibility of either an exact repetition or originary difference, is therefore a demonstration of the echo-like *ghosting* that Royle calls the *iteraphonic*:

> Where criticism has talked about 'mirror scenes', or one speech or phrase or character or episode 'echoing' another *Julius Caesar* seems to inscribe a thinking of 'theatrical derangement' in terms of what we might call the iteraphonic ... The opening scene is itself spooked when we learn that Murullus and his fellow Tribune Flavius are 'put to silence' [*1,2,275*]. But the iteraphonic also interrupts, overturns and disposes the sequentiality of acts and scenes ... It is no longer a question of saying that one scene or speech 'echoes' an earlier one, in the 'strange disposèd time' of the iteraphonic.[31]

If the Globe of 1599 is a place of the echo, Shakespeare's echo allusions show him invested like his Cobbler in recycled material, and what Derrida called the 'differential vibration' of 'writing in the voice', the 'call to come' that 'happens in multiple voices'.[32] A technical interest in how to make 'the church echo' [*Shrew, 3,3,52*], or 'start an echo with the clamour of thy drum' [*John, 5,2,168*], 'fetch shrill echoes from the hollow earth' [*Shrew, Ind.2,46*], and make crowds 'applaud to the very echo, / That should applaud again' [*Macbeth, 5,3,55*], informed this writer's notion of 'Rumour ... double, like the voice and echo' [*2Henry IV, 3,1,92*]. So his idea of a 'musical confusion / Of hounds and echo in conjunction' [*Dream, 4,1,107*], when 'babbling echo mocks the hounds' [*Titus, 2,3,17*], or 'Echo replies / As if another chase were in the skies' [*Venus, 695–6*], drew on the oppositional poetics with which contemporaries turned 'the affirmative role of the pastoral echo' into 'hideous echoes' to make 'the woods "Eliza" to resound'.[33] Shakespeare was alive, then, to the *jouissance* when walls 'make verbal repetition ... And twenty echoes twenty times cry so' [*Venus, 831*]. Yet in *Julius Caesar* he also marked how this adventitious playfulness was liable to be annexed to sovereign will, when, as Benjamin wrote, 'the harmless effusion of an onomatopoeic natural language ... the echo, the true domain of the free play of sound, is taken over by meaning'.[34] Later, when Iago parrots Othello it therefore sounds 'As if there were some monster' of intention in the repetition [*Othello, 3,3,111*]; and Hamlet will decry bad timing in 'The Mousetrap' as a '*malecho*' [*Hamlet, 3,2,124*] or deliberate *bad echo*. So in his first Globe text it is as if Shakespeare found in the accidental errancy of the 'replication of your sounds' the cue for his own struggle against sameness from *inside* the logic of mimesis, and in the dialogic deformation of a naughty malignant echo the irony of aesthetic mediation written on the Roman wall: that every obstruction will produce its own revolt.

Room enough

'When Caesar says "Do this", it is performed' [*1,2,12*]: starting at the Globe, it is as if some 'theatrical derangement' pushed Shakespeare into offering an entire play about performative speech, and that he reacted to this imperative by dramatising the impossibility of a command performance as either a perfect repetition or foundational event. Thus the most echoing line in *Julius Caesar*, notes Royle, is the mundane quotidian inquiry 'What is't o'clock?' [*2,3,114*].[35] And via the insane anachronism of its chiming clock, 'What time is it?' does seem a question Shakespeare's ill-disposed timetable is designed to prompt, as if cued by the future anteriority of its own 'antique book', Plutarch's contrapuntal *Parallel Lives*.[36] With Pompey's nemesis bearing the 'palm' [*1,2,176*], the games that start this play thus rerun the Roman carnival with which subsequent successor regimes manufacture consent in previous Shakespearean plays.[37] But, as when Henry V returns triumphant from *his* Gallic wars, and 'The Mayor and all his brethren, in best sort, / Like to the senators of the antique Rome ... Go forth and fetch their conqu'ring Caesar' [*Henry V, 5,0,25–8*] – itself an echo of Marlowe's translation of Lucan's *Pharsalia* – this 'real' Caesarean play for power owes more to the Elizabethan 'theatre state' than ancient Rome.[38] So from the first performance at the Globe, it would seem, Shakespeare is already opportunistically grasping how in this repeat *mis-en-scène* 'The time is out of joint' [*Hamlet, 1,5,189*].

In *Julius Caesar* Shakespeare's Roman triumph is said to reprise Elizabeth's Armada parade, when imitating the ancient Romans to intimidate Roman Catholics, she rode into the City of London in a chariot 'with four pillars behind to have a canopy, on top whereof was an imperial crown'. Then too officials ordered the crowds to wear 'best apparel' [*8*]; streets were decorated with patriotic banners; and the porch of St Paul's was transformed into a triumphal arch with Spanish flags for trophies [*1,2,280*].[39] The 'conscious classical parallel' with the empire structured Elizabeth's festivals because the regime projected its power as a Roman *renovatio*, and English poets 'thought of these shows as "triumphs"'.[40] So the question with which the Tribunes attempt to puncture this festive time with historical time could not be more *timely*: 'Is this a holiday?' Will this latest repeat be primitive sacrifice or progressive sport, another princely tragedy or a popular farce? The question foretells what the Situationist Guy Debord theorized in a section of *Society of the Spectacle* which reads like a synopsis of *Julius Caesar*, where he proposed that the Renaissance art of festival was in fact merely the strategy of the absolutist *triumphator* to stop the clock with the sovereignty of his own *coup d'état*, squaring the circle with the fake singularity of a standstill designed merely to superimpose his own totalizing imitation of Roman space on historical time:

The Renaissance, which finds its past and its legitimacy in Antiquity, carries with it a joyous rupture with eternity ... [But] this constant monopolization of historical life by the State of the absolute monarchy ... brings into clear view the irreversible time of the bourgeoisie. The bourgeoisie is attached to *labour time* ... [when] all social life has already been concentrated within the ornamental poverty of the Court, the tinsel of the state administration which culminates in 'the vocation of the king'; and all particular historical liberty has had to consent to its defeat, [as] the temporal game of the nobles is consumed in their last lost battles, the wars of the Fronde.[41]

Debord's idea of absolutism as a *chronotope*, an arresting of time in space, reminds us how repetition was the master code of Renaissance power, until it was smashed by the linear time of the bourgeoisie. When the puritanical Tribunes try to abort the play's opening by ordering 'idle creatures ... home' they therefore interpose a counter time-frame, fraught with the sectarian violence of 1599, the first of numerous irruptions by Elizabethan actuality into the fictive time on stage. With its references to arbours, orchards, pleasure gardens, walks and brothels in the delinquent 'suburbs' on 'this side' of the river [2,1,284; 3,3,236], this pioneer Bankside work is intensely aware of its material foundations; and recent critics follow Derrida in reading these topical allusions as 'the contretemps of ironic consciousness' which the text maintains towards its own liminal conditions of production.[42] But they do so knowing that the process analysed by Benjamin, whereby fascism and communism blur distinctions between reality and representation, either by aestheticizing politics or politicizing art, was well under way at the time of the first performance, when poets welcomed the contemporary state onto the stage as readily as princes exploited the theatre 'to turn the state into a spectacular work of art'.[43]

Benjamin's differentiation between a communism that makes art political and fascism that makes politics artistic has come to seem false in the light of his own messianic violence, and as his irrational politics have been scrutinized both strategies appear like a failure of the very aesthetic mediation that the echoes in *Julius Caesar* affirm. One of the sharpest accounts of Shakespeare's 'anti-historical arbitrariness' was indeed made in response to Benjamin, by the political theologian Carl Schmitt, when he argued that since *all art is political* it is precisely the invasion of the magic circle of the play by an anachronistic contemporary reality 'that encompasses the playwright, actors, and audience' which generated tragedy in the works performed at the Globe. Because this theatre 'did not set up an opposition between the present of the play and the lived actuality of a contemporary present', anachronisms were the crucial 'structurally determining *intrusions*', Schmitt countered, which gave Shakespeare's drama its dream logic, 'with all the condensations and displacements' of 'real events' that could never be displayed. Though this decisionist thinker was hostile to the aesthetic, as the harbinger of parliamentary democracy and precursor of liberal economic thought, he thus understood how Shakespearean theatre yearns for a condition of pure play, and aims to clear 'a space for itself within which a certain freedom is maintained' from both its occasion and its source.[44] Schmitt was writing about *Hamlet*. But his analysis applies equally to *Julius Caesar*, when he continues that it is because of the irruption of 'real historical time' into the fictional time of the stage that a Shakespearean drama 'does not completely exhaust itself as a play':

> It contains components that do not belong to the play and, in this sense, it is imperfect as a play. There is no closed unity of time, place, and action, no pure internal process sufficient to itself. It has ... openings through which historical time breaks into the time of the play, and through which this unpredictable current of ever-new interpretive possibilities flows into the otherwise so genuine play ... They disturb the unintentional character of pure play and, in this respect, are a *minus*. Nevertheless, they ... are a *plus*, because they succeeded in elevating [the play] to tragedy.[45]

For Schmitt, the traumatic reality that 'projects into the drama' like a 'dark area' or 'shadow' over the Globe, but that by disturbing the fiction in this nightmare way operates as the play's unconscious, as if *to highlight the difference of the aesthetic* from the political by hiding in plain view, is the Elizabethan succession crisis. This 'concrete taboo' can 'be explained by the time and place of the original performance', when the players were sponsored by Essex's conspirators, who pinned their hopes on King James, son of Elizabeth's enemy Mary Stuart.[46] What interests the thinker who detested the text-immanent criticism of German scholarship, however, is not this banal context but the *resistance* it precipitates in the negative form of the play, which is truly *tragic* because, unlike the *Trauerspiel*, it refuses to mimic its situation: that actuality is 'the mute rock upon which the play founders, sending the foam of genuine tragedy

rushing to the surface'.[47] Such a post-Freudian critique is similar to
that of Jacques Lacan, who in the same postwar years ('when we
were troubled why no one had assassinated Hitler'), was pushing
his own collaboration alibi: that 'suspended in the time of the
Other', *Hamlet* hides its guilt 'in full view'.[48] Likewise, Schmitt
decodes Shakespeare's anachronisms and metatheatre as means to
foreground the pressure of sovereign power on the play and *the*
repression by the play of power: 'it is the real play itself repeated
before the curtains'.[49] Thus, it as if in spite of himself, this old Nazi
was affirming resistance to Hitler. But whatever its own determinant
in the shadows of German history, his non-mimetic theory of the
aesthetic as a supplement or reflex to the political, which intrudes
like an iceberg into the fictional space of the play, offers an intriguing perspective on the reverberant return of repressed sovereignty
with the surplus poetic justice of *an echo* in *Julius Caesar*. For no
play of Shakespeare's is more concerned with the articulation of
temporal difference through the intrusiveness of what Jonathan Gil
Harris has brilliantly termed 'untimely matter'.[50]

The narrow world

The value of Schmitt's critique of Shakespearean anachronism,
according to Santner, is that it reveals how the dramatist 'found
a way to *stage* the remainder' of sovereignty, royal remains that
spook the thinking of philosophers like Derrida and Agamben
about the mutual attraction of the sovereign and the beast.[51] For
what time is it, the play asks, in this echo chamber where it is 'Rome
indeed, and room enough' for 'but only one man' [1,2,156]? From
the instant the Tribunes 'Disrobe the images' [63], the text's punning
on 'Rome and room' underscores how *Julius Caesar* is preoccupied
with the secularization of the space of representation generated by
the Reformation, but also with the uncanny return of incarnational
Catholic theology, when the *Rome* of the state intrudes into the
room of the stage. Confident that 'We princes are set on stages'
Elizabeth made this interstitial space her personal territory, when
her tinsel show imitated the Caesarian triumph simulated across
Europe by Renaissance artists like Mantegna.[52] If Shakespeare came
to London about 1588, he must have witnessed Gloriana in all her
scavenged pomp. Yet what is striking about his Roman triumph
is how, in line with Schmitt's thesis, he resists temptations to put

power on display, and keeps pageantry out of sight, as if Caesar is
more imposing in absence than presence, or when dead than alive.
Perhaps the dramatist grasped what historians have stressed, that
these dynasties were already living more in 'the spirit of Caesar'
[2,1,167] than in person; for the *occultatio* of his play about the
power of spectres in the society of spectacle is how the great com-
municator Caesar appears so little on stage.[53] As Lisa Hopkins complains, considering *Julius Caesar* stages events of world-historical
import, 'it is remarkable how little we actually see'.[54]

Schmitt calls the interpolations of real time into Shakespeare's
aesthetic space 'doors through which the tragic element of an actual
event enters into the world of the play', and he attributes these
openings to the non-mimetic concept of representation governed
by personal authority in a playhouse that remained 'a part of the
present in a society that perceived its own actions as theatre',
because 'Society too was on the stage', and embodied in the charismatic person of the sovereign as a *deus ex machina*.[55] This door
metaphor is keyed to Schmitt's political theology, with its reactionary nostalgia for the Pontifex Maximus, an 'authoritarian person
or an idea that as soon as it is represented also personifies itself'.[56]
But the occulting figure is very pertinent to *Julius Caesar*, where
as Hélène Cixous poeticizes, the question 'What is it o'clock' is
associated with a 'door we never enter', and history is 'at the door',
though we are kept in the dark about exactly who it is 'that knocks'
[2,1,60–9; 308].[57] For this drama seems to be wary about the actual
doors of its imposing Roman tiring-house, material signifiers of the
occluded yet menacing presence of its political backers, in that other
time of clandestine conspiracy, with its anachronistic delusions of
Tacitean grandeur. Thus the first Globe play is haunted by the spectrality of the spectacle, by the sensation that royal strings are being
pulled from behind the republican scenes, in some spooky Rome
behind the 'room'.

In Schmitt's account of the evolving English public sphere,
Shakespearean tragedy originated from the 'enigmatic concatenation
and entanglement of indisputably real people ... a reality externally
given, imposed and unavoidable', in the aesthetic space of the play.
These intruders were the play's shadowy 'angels': the plotters of
Essex's ill-starred revolt.[58] But the suspicion that the performance
is being supervised by a personal power 'hiding in full view' is also
grounded in a technical flaw intrinsic to classical theatre whenever its

circle was pressed into concave shape by fixed scenery or ceremonial doors. For whenever Shakespeare reflected on Rome's triumphal 'O', it emerges, what puzzled him was the practical problem of how so many 'dolts' and 'poor'st diminutives' could glimpse what sovereignty so teasingly withheld. Thus, 'Let him take thee / And hoist thee up to the shouting plebeians' in Caesar's procession, Antony taunts Cleopatra [*Antony*, *4,13,33–7*]. Marlowe had no trouble visualizing 'Caesar riding in the Roman street ... in his triumphant car'.[59] But spectating the triumphal march of Renaissance power as a theatre practitioner, we might infer, Shakespeare could never follow 'the swelling act / Of the imperial theme' [*Macbeth*, *1,3,126*]. For as Brutus and Cassius struggle to grasp what is happening behind the stage, he stresses not the unimpeded sightlines of Rome's spherical 'O' but a towering intrusion that appears just like the pillared tiring-house at the new Globe, since it 'gets the start' of the play and diminishes a potentially 'majestic world' to a 'narrow world', where to make any sense of its 'applauses' the 'amazed' actors must now 'peep about':

CASSIUS: Ye gods, it doth amaze me
          A man of such a feeble temper should
          So get the start of the majestic world,
          And bear the palm alone! ...
          Why, man, he doth bestride the narrow world
          Like a Colossus, and we petty men
          Walk under his huge legs, and peep about ...
                        [*Julius Caesar, 1,2,130–8*]

'What means this shouting? I do fear the people / Choose Caesar for their king' [*179*]: according to Jonathan Goldberg this is the only scene in Shakespeare when the onstage action depends on the unseen space behind the scenes, as if the subject of the play was revealed to be its own self-censorship.[60] Such dependence on what is heard but not seen is the more startling if we recall that it was precisely at the time of *Julius Caesar* that dramatists started to abandon the idea of auditors and to imagine their work as 'play'd to take spectators' [*Winter's, 3,2,35*]. Previously, playwrights 'said they wrote for ears whereas players merely offered shows'. But with the inauguration of the Globe they became 'concerned to offer "shows" to the "beholder" who gradually became a "spectator"'.[61] When Thomas Heywood described Roman theatres in his 1612 *Apology for Actors*, 'Every such was called a *Circus*', he thus explained, because it was 'Globe-like and merely round'.[62] With a capacity of three thousand, the London eye put visitors in mind of such a Roman arena because it too had the democratic potential of the circus, where 'each became Chief Spectator'.[63] In *As You Like It*, Shakespeare advertised the inclusiveness of the 'wide and universal theatre' of 'the wide world' [1,3,132] with a *Romany* spell 'to call fools into a circle' [2,5,53]. Yet it is surely a sign of disquiet with the eventual squared-off imperial bluntness of 'the antique world' [2,3,57] that the play he devised for its consecration should register not only a disruptive echo but the frustration of those positioned below the tiring-house, who have to 'peep about' to discover why the truly 'understanding' groundlings 'applaud to the very echo, / That should applaud again':

> *Shout [within]. Flourish*
> BRUTUS: Another general shout!
> I do believe that these applauses are
> For some new honours that are heaped on Caesar.
> [1,2,133–5]

Rather than placing the Senators onstage in this scene, the architecture of the 'majesty world' in fact asks us to imagine these baffled auditors, as Cassius rails, *beneath* the pillars and behind the arch in the concavity of the Lords' Room, the 'lofty scene' [3,1,113] or gallery of the tiring-house where 'the breed of noble bloods' [1,2,151] sat peering 'o'er the stage'.[64] Ben Jonson and others record how at the Globe those of 'the best respect' [59] on this balcony lorded over the players 'in gratifying proximity to the action'.[65] Their impaired relation to the actors seems to be described, however, along with the Globe's echo in *Troilus and Cressida*, where Achilles is warned 'no man is the lord of anything' until it is 'formed in th'applause' of the spectators who 'like an arch, reverb'rate the voice again' [3,3,110–16]. In their ornamental subjugation to a 'great Rome' [2,2,187] behind the scenes the lords relied on the applause of the groundlings to follow what was going on. So, far from offering privileged space for elite playgoers, the Lord's roomy loft was in a position of subordination beneath the imperial arch, precisely like that of the Senators in Shakespeare's Rome. 'Smothered to death in darkness' by the imposition of Elizabethan power over the stage, a literal materialization of Schmitt's 'dark shadow', these parliamentarians, who paid a steep 6d for a cushioned seat, were in a fix as 'narrow' as that of Cassius and Brutus, for while they could hear everything rebounding off the 'wide walls' [*1,2,156*], they could see nothing but the actors' backs.[66]

Rheumy and unpurged

'When could they say till now, that talked of Rome, / That her wide walls encompassed but one man?' [*155–6*]: visitors to the Globe were as struck as Shakespeare's republicans by the Caesarean echoes in its Roman walls. Humanists like Johannes de Witt indeed assumed that since they 'resembled Roman work' the London amphitheatres were deliberately pierced with 'wooden columns painted in excellent imitation of marble' to resurrect the Coliseum 'as it stood in the days of its imperial splendour'.[67] Thus by naming its stage the *proscenium* and its tiring-house a *frons scaenae*, these tourists implied they thought this was an absolutist arena, 'suitable for entertainment of a Roman Emperor of the modern kind'.[68] Research suggests De Witt and his illustrator Aernout van Buchel in fact identified the playhouses with a picture of the Coliseum published by Justus Lipsius in *De Amphitheatro*, where the emperor is 'sitting by himself because he is the central point'.[69] Significantly, the Dutch Stoic philosopher is also thought to be the source for Caesar's claim to a marbleized and timeless 'constancy'.[70] It is a cliché that a testing of such Stoicism is one of the motifs of Shakespeare's Roman plays, and that a writer who made his living from actors' bodies was unlikely to admire the Stoic's rock-like resolution commended in that 'antique book'. But in 1599 this anti-Stoicism had urgent and material specificity. For when he looked about the playhouse, what Shakespeare evidently envisaged was the interfering yet stellar position that such a motionless, central and solitary eminence might indeed soon come to occupy:

> CAESAR: The skies are painted with unnumbered sparks
> They are all fire, and every one doth shine:
> But there's not one in all doth hold his place.
> So in the world: 'tis furnished well with men,
> And men are flesh and blood, and apprehensive;
> Yet in the number I do know but one
> That unassailable holds on his rank,
> Unshaked of motion ...
>
> [*3,1,63–70*]

Caesar's 'thrasonical brag' [*As You Like*, *5,2,31*], seconds before
he is assassinated, that he personifies 'Olympus' [*74*], and is as
'constant as the Northern Star, / Of whose true fixed and resting
quality / There is no fellow in the firmament' [*60–2*], situates his
hubris pointedly beneath the Globe's canopy or 'heavens' with
its gilded galaxies and gods. And the novelty of his absolutism
is highlighted when he scorns the 'Low crooked curtsies, and
base spaniel fawning' supposed to mutualize the sovereign and
his creature, exclaiming: 'If thou dost bend and fawn ... I spurn
thee like a cur' [*43–6*]. Shortly, Shakespeare will have Hamlet
similarly contrast the humanist cosmology of 'this goodly frame,
the earth', and its 'excellent canopy ... brave o'erhanging' and
'majestical roof fretted with golden fire', with the creaturely flux
of its 'foul and pestilent congregation of vapours'. The Prince's
'fretting' over the failure of the audience to live up to a Vitruvian
design based on the triangulations of the zodiac – the *homo ad
quadratum* idea illustrated in the *Architectura*, of a circumference
squared by a 'godly' male body as 'the beauty of the world' in
'form and moving ... like an angel' [*Hamlet, 2,2,289–7*] – signals
the divorce of his classicizing court aesthetic from that 'whole
theatre of others' [*3,2,25*] in the arena beside the Thames.[71]
For the Prince, all that is solid melts into air, as the public space
of the people's theatre degrades his absolutist ideal of the 'high
and palmy state of Rome' [*1,1,106:6*] into a state of *rheum*: the
'vile contagion' of 'rheumy and unpurged air' [*2,1,265*] effused
by the reeking breath of the audience, that 'semiotic and somatic
vibrancy' Santner calls 'the flesh of the world', and into which,
so *Julius Caesar* forecasts, the 'roomy' space of the Globe would
always be liable to dissolve.[72]
    Critics usually follow Hamlet in blaming the obstructive 'vapours'
of Shakespeare's playing space on the masses, and what they term
'the collective halitosis of democracy'. But Richard Halpern counters that in *Julius Caesar* the creaturely element of breath starts to
congeal only when 'Fierce fiery warriors fight upon the clouds, / In
ranks and squadrons and right form of war, / Which drizzled blood
upon the Capitol' [*2,2,19–21*]. In Halpern's analysis the 'contest
between the material, rhetorical, theatrical, and even interpretive
practices of its two public spheres', the Senate House and Forum,
figures the opposition between the alternative historical trajectories
of the early modern stage. So this apparent allusion to the fractious

nobles perched 'in ranks and squadrons' beneath the Globe's masque-like 'heavens' implies that if the Elizabethan playhouse serves as the prototype for Habermas's liberal public sphere, where from a Schmittian perspective like that of Antony, everything gets said and nothing gets decided, it also demonstrates how easily this space of domination-free discourse 'can become encumbered by its repressed other', collapsing, as it does notoriously in Schmitt's narrative, into a decisionist decision for the sheer arbitrariness of the decision.[73]

The inaugural scene acted under the painted sky of London's new amphitheatre will have the commoners ordered to pray 'to intermit the plague' they incur by strewing garlands and hanging banners on the Capitol [*1,1,49–68*]. There is thus a sickly density to the incense-laden fumes in *Julius Caesar* that prefigures the 'smoky light' and 'stinking tallow' of papal Rome in *Cymbeline* [*1,6,110*]. In this tragedy foul obscuring air is associated with the myopic body-politics of genuflecting servility. It is the opaque medium of the incarnational theology that occludes the transparency of a truly representative system, as, in Santner's analysis 'The "mass" that is unleashed' by way of the displacement of the king's body 'metastazies *within* each individual', to '"crowd" out the self from within'.[74] Thus, while Shakespeare's universal 'O' might well have been the most *roomy* space in London for its Roman scale, with its persisting tendency to trap the pestilential 'humours of the dank morning' [*2,2,261*], its 'stinking breath', 'sweat' and 'bad air' [*1,2,244–8*], and its playgoers so prone to 'weep tears' [*1,1,57*], it yet appears from the somatic fluids of *Julius Caesar* to be a *rheumy* assembly of the blind and lame, where disabling 'rheumatic diseases' [*Dream, 2,1,105*] are still endemic, and the slavish submission of 'base spaniel fawning' and 'Low-crooked curtsies' [*3,1,43*] continues to serve the mystery cult of charismatic sovereignty. As Clifford Ronan remarks in his study of power and symbolism in the Elizabethan Roman play, such contorted body language was dictated by the 'antic' space in which it was performed, for these 'stage Romes brought ancient Roman experiences directly into the Tudor-Stuart ken':

> Triumphalist bending and bowing of the subjects were enforced at court by Elizabeth and the Stuarts alike, in imitation of customs rooted in pagan Roman Antiquity – and the liturgy of Roman Catholicism. Communicants knelt in both Tudor and Stuart times.[75]

'Room for Antony ... Stand back; room, bear back' [*3,2,166–8*]; 'must I give way and room?' [*4,3,39*]; 'room ho!' [*5,4,16*]: if this echo-play about Roman power designed for 'the mighty space of our large honours' [*4,3,25*] puns so much on the princes' *room* and people's *rheum*, that may be because it picks up from Roman rhetoricians an intense practical concern with the spatial volume required for the clarity of the actor's voice. *Julius Caesar* is literally a play about pressure to 'give way and room' [*4,2,93*], in which the Roman overhanging of the Globe is itself a physical obstacle to the actor's struggle 'to keep his state in Rome' [*1,2,161*], and the political theology concretized in 'the wide arch of the ranged empire' [*Antony 1,1,33*] is what gets in the way. For here it is Vitruvius's image of godlike man squaring the circle to bestride 'the narrow world / Like a Colossus', as in that 'antique book', which threatens to overpower the space of the stage: 'the king as actor, constant, unchanging, unique, a single star unmoving'.[76] So this play concentrates on the problem for every theatre 'constructed in the style of the ancient Romans', that, as Stephen Orgel explains in *The Illusion of Power*, the logical end of any Vitruvian design, with the monocular vanishing-point perspective at which Caesar aims, was monopolization of the grand central position by the body of the sovereign, as both the star actor and 'Chief Spectator'. In the triumphal squared-off proscenium to which Caesar aspires it might be true that 'everyone has a good view', but what they see remains for ever 'constant', because these 'wide walls encompass but one man' [*1,2,158*]:

> For Sebastiano Serlio, the most important interpreter of Vitruvian principles ... the primary audience was the monarch ... The royal seat was [therefore] placed directly on stage ... After 1605, when perspective settings were introduced, the monarch became the center of theatrical experience another way ... In a theater employing perspective, there is only one focal point, one perfect place from which the illusion achieves its fullest effect ... this is where the king sat ... only the king has a perfect seat.[77]

If Caesar's pontifical boast of 'Olympian' fixity implies Shakespeare may have known about Palladio's 1585 Teatro Olimpico, with its permanent perspective set figuring an ancient city, 'What time is it?' he appears to ask, when a 'genuine antique reproduction', like his own classical tiring-house, comes to tower over the play? When the academicians of Vicenza built their Olympic arena as 'a deliberate "copy" of an ancient Roman theatre', with its *all'antica proscenio* 'encrusted with statues of local worthies' wearing togas, they found 'one can only pretend to be an ancient Greek or Roman' in classical garb for so long 'before contemporary needs begin to take precedence'.[78] Ironically, their Vitruvian architecture, with its Olympian statues and starlit ceiling that were supposed to mirror the republic of letters, bankrupted the Academy, and so 'the prince, Leonardo Valmarana, paid for it'.[79] As Bruce Smith recounts, artistic decisions became political choices whenever Renaissance theatres obeyed the 'antique book', because 'Roman theatre positioned the actors in front of a façade that dominated the theatre'. Hence, the conflict between the square and the circle, or 'what ancient audiences and modern audiences imagined the playing space to be', was between 'an organic, intuitive sense of space and a constructed, rational sense of space'.[80] So, though *Julius Caesar* is often read as a text in which the collapse of the Roman Republic anticipates the crisis of parliament, and its citizens experience the disenfranchisement of the audience, Caesar's claim to statuesque immobility reveals more urgently how Shakespeare perceived his theatre might *itself* collude in the triumphal march of absolutism, if the open sightlines of its circular auditorium led eyes only towards the 'marble constancy' of some imperial arch, which, to create the illusion of centralizing timelessness, could only ever be viewed the same way.[81]

Because the Teatro Olimpico was so soon obsolete, Shakespeareans are hostile to the notion that 'the dead hand of Vitruvius' ever touched the Globe, where actors performed in a popular tradition that remained 'intensely alive'.[82] Yet it is the menace of that dead hand and the resistance to it that seem to haunt the first play for this house, where the reinvention of the antique circus has become a source of anxiety because its 'Romanity' threatens to engross the theatre, puncturing the boundary between state and stage, politics and play. Thus Heywood's narrative of how 'Julius Caesar, successor to Pompey's greatness, exceeded him' by building 'an amphitheatre in the field of Mars which as far exceeded Pompey's' as his had previous stages, reveals why Shakespeare might top-out the new Globe with a scene where workmen discard their 'rule' and 'leather apron' to 'rejoice in his triumph' [*1,1,7–30*]. In *An Apology for Actors* Caesar conquers in a war of theatres, when his 'Basses, Columns, Pillars, and Pyramids were of hewed Marble, the coverings of the stage ... [that] we call the heavens were Geometrically supported by a Giant-like Atlas'.[83] There is, in fact, no authority for this picture of Caesar's arena, which was an aquatic stadium.[84] Instead, when Heywood adds that above the pillars of this 'model of the firmament', with its 'stars, signs, & planets', soared a 'turret ... from which an ensign of silk waved continually', it becomes clear that his fantasy about 'this sumptuous and gorgeous building' is based on the Bankside playhouse.[85] Like the characters of *Julius Caesar*, Heywood is using the analogy with the Roman theatre to 'think of the world' [1,2,301]. Consciously or not, the actors' apologist is 'royalizing', as Ronan puts it, 'the world' of the Globe, for such architecture was 'the incarnation' of the Roman as 'royal / divine'.[86]

An *Apology for Actors* confirms how, with its 'Giant-like' carving above the stage of 'Hercules and his load' [*Hamlet, 2,2,345*], Shakespeare's 'world' was 'ornamented, perhaps very elaborately, in the baroque manner' that was the preferred décor for absolutist rulers, an association that may have extended to the curtain covering the tiring-house door, as Hercules with his 'massy club' [*Much Ado, 3,2,121*] was a stock subject of tapestries in royal courts.[87] The demigod who killed his wife and children personified sovereign violence in Renaissance iconography, according to Eugene Waith. Thus it had been as a clubbed Hercules that Caesar was said to have taken to the boards, according to Heywood, in one of the unluckiest episodes of Roman confusion of presence and representation, when 'carried away with the violence' of the part, he slew another actor 'dead at his feet, and after swung him (as the poet said) about his head'.[88] This anecdote would cue a spate of nervy Stuart plays on the hermeneutic circle when stage-struck Caesars projected fact into fiction despite disclaimers that any resemblance to real people was accidental, and ''tis not in us to help it'.[89] As Schmitt smiled, Shakespeare would 'not have been averse to prefacing his dramas with such a statement'.[90] But the legend of Hercules may already have perturbed the dramatist when he had his Athenian tragedians prevent Bottom from reminding Theseus of his cousin 'Ercles' by acting in the 'tyrant's vein' [1,2,19–36]. For as Richard Dutton acutely perceives, Heywood's *Apology* suggests allusions to the Globe's Herculean dimensions and decorations in *Julius Caesar* and *Hamlet* constitute a highly self-conscious sequence, in which the dramatist is questioning his own relationship to power by 'profoundly rethinking the fundamentals of his profession'.[91]

References to the contradiction between the circular auditorium and flat tiring-house imply that in *Julius Caesar* the admonition to 'think of the world' was as much aimed at the actors of the Globe as the characters in the play. And what that thinking involved was ironic *trembling* at the 'replications' of the 'fixed and resting' arch which now bestrode the theatre *unshaked of motion*, and dictated that whatever play or genre was performed the spectators would always see the same façade. Critics like to imagine Shakespeare invariably associated Rome with superhuman *constancy*, like that of this columned backdrop: the constancy Portia indeed images as 'a huge mountain 'tween my tongue and heart' [2,4,7] blocking what is said. Yet as Robert Miola notices, in *Julius Caesar* 'formal constancy' [2,1,227] begins for the first time to appear disturbingly rigid *and* superficial, as if to signify both immovability and falsity. Rather than consecrating a frontage of official permanence, then, what this exploratory Globe offering reveals is a writer who, as if pitching his quaking name to rebound against that Roman wall, conjures a room of 'restless movement ... astir with people' out of the trembling voices, rheumatic bodies, and shaking spears of human actors who, as he constantly reminds us, are 'not stones, but men' [3,2,139].[92] Such is the human stuff, 'shaked of motion', the play suggests, that 'binds subjects to that space of representation' where the body of the king has been displaced.[93] So *Julius Caesar* is the most *shaken* play in the canon, a text disarranged by the *tumultus* said by the Romans to erupt like a *tumour* whenever the body politic was agitated.[94] From a Globe 'well furnished' to be a 'constant' imitation of 'the stones of Rome', Shakespeare would thereby exploit the adventitious echo to generate a non-mimetic world of human *difference* for a company and an audience made not of stone but of 'flesh and blood, and apprehensive' [3,1,67] about the return of the repressed sovereignty from out its tomb.

Under his huge legs

By incorporating as its 'inescapable visual focus' a permanent scenic wall that would always resemble 'the gates of Rome' [3,2,269] the concave Globe repeated an old confusion between a political forum and the people's circus.[95] In his study *From Art to Theatre* George Kernodle was therefore able to trace the playhouse façade with its columns and canopy to the imperial triumph by way of the centralized archways of royal entries. 'Most of all', Kernodle affirmed, the Globe had 'the appearance of a triumphal arch'; a claim recently restated by the British Museum Director Neil MacGregor: 'Shakespeare's plays were performed in front of what was in effect a permanent temporary triumphal arch'.[96] This genealogy looks literally one-sided, and recent theatre historians have sharply debated whether the tiring-house had an equalizing pair or centralizing trio of openings. The consensus, however, is that it was at the Globe that the ceremonial impact of a three-door *frons scenae* was indeed first experienced; and as Andrew Gurr points out, in *Julius Caesar* the Globe's outsize posts are also identified with Caesar's imperial girth, when it is said that 'We petty men / Walk under his huge legs, and peep about'.[97] Experts calculate that the double Herculean pillars 'of the world' [*Antony, 1,1,12*] fronting Shakespeare's stage were at least as monumental and obtrusive as the pair of Corinthian columns depicted in the De Witt drawing of the Swan. So the actors made to 'peep about' these gigantic 'Pillars of Hercules' would certainly have felt dwarfed by the tumorous arched construction, with its marbleized balconies, busts, caryatids, obelisks, pillars and urns, so inauspiciously reminiscent, as Cassius suggests, of those vainglorious 'gilded monuments of princes' [Sonnet 55] that covered Elizabethan graves.

The same Southwark craftsmen who created the tombs at Westminster to proclaim the Globe motto that 'All the world's a stage' [*As You, 2,7,138*] fabricated the arches put up to welcome James I into London in 1603, upon one of which, literally supporting 'the canopy' [Sonnet 125], Shakespeare may himself have been obliged to perch. Thus, there is a theory that the Roman arcade with its three ceremonial openings erected for the Chamberlain's Men in 1599 copied the gilded columns, starry vault and balustrade of the Abbey tomb of their late patron, the Queen's cousin Lord Hunsdon.[98] If so, it was truly the dead hand of the old regime that reached from out the grave. Another inspiration may have been the storied chapel screens in Elizabethan 'prodigy houses', with doorways topped by the royal coat of arms. Either way, such sepulchral architecture would be apt for *Julius Caesar*, where each half ends in a state funeral, and it is said 'The heavens themselves blaze forth the death of princes' [*2,2,31*]. But if the boundary between the court and theatre was a site of anxiety, the tomb-like hanger of the Globe frontage, with which the actors were now stuck, must have seemed a monumental *momento mori* when it came to plays like *As You Like It* or *Twelfth Night*.[99] For the 'cheerful muddle' of vernacular and antique styles in Tudor 'Roman' architecture put a brave face on a profound cultural ambivalence, according to Alastair Fowler, as these overwrought triumphal forms incorporated both the idea of the Renaissance as a *renovatio* of the defunct *imperium* and 'deep uneasiness' in those who walked beneath them about the hubris of totalitarian power.[100]

Art historians insist that Shakespeare's plays were 'written to be performed in Great Halls' like that at Hatfield, where the gallery opposite the screen was 'the "circle" seating the Cecils and their most honoured guests', the royal party, and where actors 'would have enjoyed the advantages and the artificiality of a proscenium arch'. As Timothy Mowl admits, however, this elitist theory requires us to believe Shakespeare was as devoted to elaborate scenery as any 'Edwardian actor-manager'.[101] So it overlooks how his drama generates energy resisting such a frame. For what is clear is how Shakespeare understood the political impact of the kind of pictorial staging Antony describes, where 'windowed in great Rome', the actor is 'subdued to penetrative shame' before 'the wheeled seat / Of fortunate Caesar' [*Antony, 4,14,72–6*]. And if Fowler is correct to claim that until the nineteenth century the Roman triumph was the prime model not only for official ceremony but for theatrical design, the alarm that rings in *Julius Caesar* confirms how from the first day at the Globe Shakespeare distanced his work from such architecture, by making a song and dance out of the refusal to auspicate this centralizing portico of power.[102] For from the Arch of Constantine to the gates erected to admit Henri of Navarre as King of France, 'the wide arch' was always a mark of annexation, never complete 'without an effigy of Hercules' between pillars as a signifier of the Herculean choice between Virtue and Pleasure.[103] Thus, as historians remind us, the symbolism to which Shakespeare was compelled to respond at the Globe had an inescapable teleological thrust:

> The central aspect of any royal entry is that civic space presents itself to be 'read' by the monarch like a text … Specific features of the city, along with its overall identity, are presented as submissive to the royal presence as if they had only been waiting for that moment to arrive to fulfil their destiny, all with a view to demonstrating that his triumph is the only possible outcome of time itself, that everything past and present has been converging on it.[104]

To a generation trained to read the royal entry as a frontispiece, the Globe tiring-house, with its Herculean iconography, proclaimed the victory of authority over art, power over pleasure, for after a century of such parades, as Kernodle pointed out, the triumphalism of this 'show façade was known all over Europe' to be the 'symbol of the throne and of political order'.[105] In a recent study of Inigo Jones, Vaughan Hart indeed connects the 'Pillars of State' built into the playhouse specifically to the family that would shortly inherit the English throne, since 'The use of the antique column ... was central to the public identity of the Stuart monarchy right from the start'.[106] So, while Jonson would adopt the classical *frons scenae* for the title-page of his *Workes*, complete with an inset of a Roman amphitheatre featuring an English tiring-house, it seems perversely inauspicious for Shakespeare to inaugurate the Southwark building with a prologue that amplifies Puritan objections to 'the gorgeous Playing place called a Theatre', as though deliberately problematizing the absolutist 'replications' of this pillared construction, and prophesying future trouble from permitting such a 'fixed' portal to 'soar above the view of men' [*1,2,73*].[107] For preoccupied as this tragedy of soothsaying and prediction is by the prolepsis of its own liminal space, and by the prophetic *importance* of all arches, casements, corners, doors, gates, lintels, sills and thresholds, this refusal to bless the foundation-stone is itself *portentous*:

> FLAVIUS: Go you down that way towards the Capitol;
> This way will I. Disrobe the images
> If you do find them decked with ceremonies ...
> Let no images be hung
>   With Caesar's trophies.
>
>   [*1,1,62–8*]

A canopy most fatal

'Certain of the noblest-minded Romans ... stay for me in Pompey's Porch ... All this done, / Repair to Pompey's Porch ... That done, repair to Pompey's Theatre' [*1,3,120–52*]: the corner-stone Globe play keeps reverting to the fact that its story took place in Rome's first permanent theatre, which Pompey built not only for shows but as a place for the Senate to meet beneath a giant portico, 'as if the theatre could be explained away as a kind of annex'.[108] This debut thus draws attention to the portentousness of its own 'goodly frame': the unprecedented *roominess* of its own 'porch', which in Hollar's 1647 *Long View of London* extends over half the second Globe towards the south-west, at almost the exact angle dictated by the midsummer sun. John Orrell concluded from this view that the effect would be to throw the actors into permanent shadow.[109] No wonder, therefore, characters in the play argue over the direction of the sun, Casca insisting that 'Here, as I point my sword, the sun rises' [2,1,160], since the sheer size of this 'excellent canopy' puts them all in the shade. Indeed, 'the extent of the heavens ... would seem to make extra lighting imperative on such a stage'.[110] The contract for the Fortune theatre, modelled on the Globe and dated January 1600, actually calls the canopy 'a shadow or cover'.[111] And these are the terms the Senators use to describe the 'portentous things' that 'so conjointly meet' when they stand 'Against the Capitol' [1,3,20–31], as if by confusing outdoor and indoor space, the seen and unseen, the tiring-house has itself become the screen for all the actors' fears about interference in the theatre by the court.

Theatre historians struggle to square the apparent size of the Globe's 'shadow-roof', 'jutted eaves' and 'unwieldily massive' pillars with the sightlines of its galleries, and have even been forced to conclude that 'people whose view was impaired by the "shadow" were obliged to make the best of it'.[112] As Jerry Brotton therefore suspects, the arras through which Hamlet stabs Polonius betrays a deep professional concern at the paraphernalia of the tiring-house façade, with what its Roman iconography implies, and 'what lurks behind its glittering seductive surface'.[113] For instead of safely mediating violence, the wall now simply works as an architectural form of *occultatio*, to shield the perpetrators from the consequences of their acts. In *Julius Caesar*, therefore, we are expressly told it is the ominous 'shadow' of this 'brave o'erhanging' which causes the diminished underlings creeping below to be disturbed about the invasion of their space: 'Either there is civil strife in heaven, / Or else the world', Casca avers, 'Who ever knew the heavens menace so?' [1,3,11;44].

Critics emphasize how Shakespeare images a Rome whose instabilities can be equated with those of England; but in *Julius Caesar* Roman fixtures also figure as 'instruments of fear and warning / Unto some monstrous state' [1,3,70–1] overwhelming the playhouse itself.[114] Thus, if the 'stones of Rome' acquire unprecedented specificity here, as Shakespeare projects 'a symbolic geography consisting of city walls, the Capitol, the Forum, private houses, and battlefields, all reinforced by recurrent metaphors of space', that might be because of a sense at the Globe that 'This disturbèd sky / Is not to walk in' [1,3,38–9].[115] Cassius certainly views the 'heavens' as having grown as 'prodigious' as Caesar [1,3,76]; while Brutus, who cannot now tell the time by 'the progress of the stars' [2,1,2], connects the protruding ceiling directly to Caesarean power, saying these 'shadows seem / A canopy most fatal, under which / Our army lies ready to give up the ghost' [5,1,86–8]. Theatre specialists no longer consider the Globe, despite its columns, discovery-space and ceremonial central door, as a step towards the indoor, candlelit and illusionistic picture-frame stage. As David Bevington concludes, such theories about the evolution of the inner stage seem unlikely precisely because of the difficulty that such a penumbral enclosure would create in terms of sight lines and hearing.[116] But in *Julius Caesar* the 'fatal canopy' that doubles for 'Pompey's porch' does obtrude darkly over what Robert Weimann terms 'the popular *platea*' platform, as if to make the state and stage as identical as they had been in Pompey's theatre.[117] For if there was never any risk that absolutism would capture the 'wide and universal' stage, the actors of 1599 had no way of knowing. Like the lethal arras in *Hamlet*, the concave canopy of *Julius Caesar* seems instead a concrete signifier of the confusion of action with acting, of the contamination of the space of representation by the politics of presence. The Globe is said to have been the first Elizabethan playhouse designed by actors for acting. If so, *Julius Caesar* sounds like their sudden second thoughts about the Roman constitution of a playhouse for which they could blame only themselves: 'The fault, dear Brutus, is not in our stars, / But in ourselves, that we are underlings' [1,2,141–2].

In *Julius Caesar* the idea of the actor's greatness 'seems to reflect an attitude towards the Elizabethan theatre itself', writes Anne Barton, for 'the actors are no longer frail shadowy figures ... they are the creators and guardians of history'.[118] But to come out of the shadows the history they must create and guard, Shakespeare's pun implies, is that of their own 'room'. So, rather than amplifying the echoes of Republican Rome in Elizabethan London, like other plays, what his tragedy demonstrates is how the actors might be engulfed by this 'replication'. Thus, the circular Globe was 'an acoustical auditorium', we are told, 'intended to serve word and ear more than image and eye', where 'nothing interrupted the resonance of words spoken on stage from reaching every part'.[119] Yet Shakespeare inaugurated this new world of words not by proving how the perfect orb 'in his motion like an angel sings' [*Merchant, 5,1,60*], but by having the actors 'think of the world' as a space of performative crisis and interpretive chaos, where 'the earth [is] so full of faults' [*1,3,45*].[120] As critics always point out, this work that is supposed to ground 'the world' on firm foundations is in fact a tragedy of errors, that from the irruption of the logic-chopping plebs 'without the sign' of trades [*SD,1,1,1;4*], to the invocation of 'hateful Error' after the politicians have 'misconstrued everything' [*5,3,66; 84*], turns on the misrecognitions when characters 'construe things after their own fashion, / Clean from the purposes of the things themselves' [*1,3,34*]. Along 'Pompey's basis', now 'soaked with Caesar's blood', we are told, 'The people ... Do stand but in a forced affection' to 'this ground' [*3,1,115; 4,2,256–7*].[121] Yet the blame for the *misconstruction* of this echo chamber, Shakespeare appears to be continually reminding the players, lies not in a building 'so full of faults', but in their own complicity with power.

A cliché of Shakespeare studies 'is that the real hero of the Roman plays is Rome'.[122] But as Shakespeare thinks on his 'O world' [*3,1,20*] in *Julius Caesar* there is indeed a war between Rome and the Romans, royal and popular sovereignty, for its opening is sabotaged not only by what blocks the view but by what cannot be heard. Considering how Protestantism had promoted an aural sensibility, it is striking that, as Mark Robson details, from this point on 'the ear is treated with ambivalence' by Shakespeare, or suspected of being poisoned.[123] This suspicion is all the more startling if we take Weimann's point that a dramatist needed to stay 'close to a culture of voices'.[124] For here the 'feeble tongue' [*2,1,312*] strains to 'become the mouth as well' as the 'sound' of Caesar [*1,2,146*]; and if one Senator tells another 'Your ear is good' [*1,3,42*], they need to 'buy men's voices' [*2,1,145*] to 'let but the commons hear' [*3,2,130*], when all that can be heard is 'a bustling rumour, like a fray' [*2,4,19*]. 'Had you a healthful ear to ear of it' [*2,1,318*], Brutus assures the palsied Ligarius, 'to hear and answer such high things' [*1,2,170*], his words would not be so 'mistook' [*50*]. But the difficulty for this interpretive community is that its voices are distorted 'To sound more sweetly in great Caesar's ear' [*3,1,50*], whilst from his entry, crying against '*Loud Music*', or bidding 'every noise be still' to hear the Soothsayer 'shriller than all the music', Shakespeare has the dictator 'turned to hear' [*1,2,1–18*], or struggling to be heard. Caesar in fact misses the thrice-repeated warning to 'Beware the ides of March' [*1,2,1–26*] because of his deafness. 'Come on my right hand, for this ear is deaf' [*214*], he hisses to Antony. Caesar's deaf left ear is a Shakespearean invention. But it becomes metonymic of the corporeal dimension of sovereignty blocking the possibility of representation which seems to result, in this play of Chinese whispers, from the tragicomic inability of the speaker to exchange power with the people:

CASSIUS: But soft, I pray you. What did Caesar swoon?
CASCA: He fell down in the market-place, and foamed at mouth, and was speechless.
BRUTUS: 'Tis very like: he hath the falling sickness.
CASSIUS: No, Caesar hath it not; but you and I
           And honest Casca, we have the falling sickness.
CASCA: I know not what you mean by that, but I am sure Caesar fell down. If the tag-rag people did not clap and hiss him, according as he pleased and displeased them, as they use to do the players in the theatre, I am no true man.

                                                          [*1,2,249–58*]

'He did shake … this god did shake' [*1,2,123*]: in *Julius Caesar* it is the anachronistic and embarrassing fleshly presence of the man who would be king that blocks the transmission of power within the body politic, as Caesar's palsied tremors reduce the tongue 'that bade the Romans / Mark' to shuddering like 'a sick girl' [*1,2,127–30*]. 'Fear and trembling' was the sensation with which Kierkegaard said people responded to the teleological suspension of the ethical in the Abrahamic call to sacrifice; and Santner describes the modern tragic universe as just such a space of excitation, in which the body parts dismembered from the old sovereignty manifest a 'semiautonomous vitality' that, 'beginning with a series of minor tics and twitches, expands into a grand epileptic dance'.[125] So in this seismic drama, where even the 'Tiber tremble[s]' [*1,1,44*], as 'bondmen tremble' [*4,2,98*], Caesar's epilepsy is thus only the most convulsive of the 'strange eruptions' when 'the sway of earth / Shakes like a thing unfirm'. Here 'It is the part of men to fear and tremble / When the most mighty gods by tokens send / Such dreadful heralds' [*1,1,44; 1,3,3; 54; 76*]. Shakespeare, it is said, specialized as an actor in playing the parts of 'palsied eld' [*Measure, 3,1,36*], and if so, one can imagine that the quivering Caesar was his *pièce de resistance*.

In *The Uncanny* Royle has brilliantly proposed that with *Hamlet*, the 'spear-shaking' dramatist would amplify the earthquake metaphor from reports of the time 'A little ere the mightiest Julius fell' into an entire apocalyptic seismology of 'feared events, / As harbingers preceding still the fates, / And prologue to the omen coming on' [*1,1,106:6–16*]. For there the undead 'burst their cerements' and the sepulchre gapes 'ponderous and mighty jaws' [*1,4,31*] in a landslide that 'bodes some strange eruption' [*1,1,68*] in meaning itself, after the 'old mole' of revolution has undermined 'the cellarage' [*1,5,153–66*] in what Royle terms 'a kind of irremediable disturbance or perversion of the performative'.[126] Thus, '*Hamlet* "twitches"', in Santner's terms, under pressure of historical forces that the play 'cannot metabolize with aesthetic means'.[127] But in the earlier play 'the sway of the earth' already portends the logical and temporal slippages of such an uncanny causality, when the Romans likewise quake in borrowed boots. As Joseph Candido comments, the rumbling of '*Thunder*' and '*Thunder still*' that assaults our ears throughout its opening scenes materialises 'a powerful yet *unseen* element', the vibration of 'a gnawing edginess or tension', a condition of shivering *nerves* that seems to unhinge causality, sequence, and sense itself, in this drama of discontinuous *non sequiturs*, where day no longer follows night, and 'The noise of battle hurtle[s] in the air' [*2,2,22*].[128]

Thunder was suggested at the Globe by cannonballs rolled across the tiring-house floor, from which lightning shot on wire.[129] What the 'tempest dropping fire' [*1,3,10*] showed in its premiere work was thus identified with the unaccountable acoustic of this new 'Rome', as though the entire structure of the playhouse had become 'untimely matter'. So it may not be chance that the most quoted line in the play has become Antony's cry to be heard: 'Friends, Romans, countrymen, lend me your ears' [*3,2,70*]. Caesar's funeral begins with Brutus and Cassius dividing the listeners to be audible; and it is punctuated by attempts to hear above 'shouts and clamours' [*48*]: 'I will hear ... I will hear ... Silence. Be patient ... Peace, silence ... Peace, ho! ... Stay, ho, and let us hear ... We'll hear him ... What does he say? ... Peace, let us hear ... Peace, ho! Let us hear him ... Marked ye his words? ... Now mark him ... Read the will, we'll hear it ... We will hear ... We'll hear it ... Peace there, hear the noble Antony. We'll hear him, we'll follow him, we'll die with him' [*8–12; 50–69; 109–14; 135–44; 198*]. After this cacophony, Caesar's

mourners will therefore 'burn his body in the holy place' [243] of
the old kings, as though incited by the very 'stones of Rome to rise
and mutiny' [221] against their own republican inheritance.
Caesar's obsequies end fulfilling Antony's prediction that his
spirit will 'with a monarch's voice / Cry "havoc!"' [3,1,275], as
the mob screams to 'fetch fire / Pluck down benches! / Pluck down
forms, windows, anything' [3,2,246–8], in a frenzy often interpreted
as prophetic of how 'The great globe itself' [Tempest, 4,1,153]
would be razed to the ground. So, as the Plebeians are incited to
light brands to burn Caesar's body along with the building, the play
seems to prefigure Hobbes's famous characterization of democracy
as 'in effect, no more than an aristocracy of orators, interrupted
sometimes with the temporary monarchy of one orator'; and to
confront the fundamental impasse affecting all modern procedures
of representation that Santner locates in David's painting of Marat's
corpse: 'that putting the People in place of the King cannot be done',
because the old sovereign violence will always resurface in the new
forms of popular sovereignty.[130] For Casca's scorn at how 'the rabblement' uttered 'such a deal of stinking breath because Caesar
refused the crown that it had almost choked Caesar' [1,2,243–6],
situates the 'havoc' incited by 'a monarch's voice' expressly within
'these confines' [275], as though the tumult within the 'universal
world' [Henry V, 4,1,67; 4,8,10] of the new amphitheatre simply
concretized the cross-purposes that Shakespeare had always associated with an actor's catastrophic disorientation, 'When creeping
murmur and the poring dark / Fills the wide vessel of the universe'
[4,0,2–3], and 'they clap and hiss' as they use to do 'in the theatre':

Like one ...
That thinks he hath done well in people's eyes,
Hearing applause and universal shout,
Giddy in spirit, still gazing in a doubt
Whether these peals of praise be his or no.

[Merchant, 3,2,141–5]

A monarch's voice

In its awareness of spatial and acoustic volumes in 'the wide vessel
of the universe', Julius Caesar is Shakespeare's most roomy play.
But between the Lords' Rome and yard's rheum, Senate and Forum,
or what the patricians can hear but not see, and the plebeians see

but not hear, a gap opens for a demagogue with 'a monarch's voice' to appropriate the tumult, with the result that Caesar's funeral marks not the end of carnage, 'but a terrible new beginning', while the 'rites of burial' [5,5,76] solemnized by the guards who carry Brutus's body merely legitimise a martial law that is worse than the disease it was imposed to cure.[131] Agamben observes that *tumult* and *tumour* are so etymologically connected that when law and lawlessness coincide in an individual, as they do in Antony, 'the juridico-political system transforms itself into a killing machine'.[132] Such is the auto-immune crisis that consumes the orator Cicero, the crown jurist for the state of emergency, but a time-server whose Delphic legal opinion causes 'those that understood' his *obiter dicta* to smile and shake their heads [1,2,277]. The text is resoundingly silent on what it was Casca heard Cicero say in that room beyond the stage. But Suetonius recorded how it consisted of a version of Schmitt's *raison d'état*: that if the assassination 'were done when 'tis done, then 'twere well / It were done quickly' [*Macbeth, 1,7,1*], 'but in all things to preserve piety'; a mystification of emergency powers similar to the political theology of Brutus, when he endorses the murder as a sacrifice to end sacrifice, 'Let's be sacrificers, but not butchers' [2,1,166], itself a variant of Caesar's decisionist maxim (cut from the Folio after Jonson pretended to think it absurd), that 'sovereign is he who decides the exception': 'Know Caesar doth not wrong but with just cause' [3,1,47].[133]

'Those that understood ... smiled': by stressing the contrasting theatre experiences of those in the Lord's 'room' or 'rheumy' yard, Girard alleges, Shakespeare exploits the ironic gap between the ignorant lynch-mob and understanding elite, but 'does not perceive the irony' of his own role as author of the play.[134] Students of Jonson know the tension caused by zoning of the theatre by class rose 'at points of highest visibility' such as the Lord's Room, but that Shakespeare's rival disavowed the inside information claimed by 'the politique Picklock of the Scene'.[135] Perhaps Jonson played Casca; for in *Julius Caesar* the disingenuousness of an elite profession of innocence suggests its author was alert to such deniability, and so alarmed that the Janus-face of his profession had been aggravated by the structure of the playhouse he made a play out of the differentials between those inside and outside the loop. For as Smith explains, while the ideal space of early modern acoustics was certainly a circle, for auditors on the ground or in the galleries of the 'wooden O', its 'O factor' of circumambient sound was sabotaged by the tendency of the 'overhanging' concavity to 'reverb'rate the voice again' [*Troilus, 3,3,110–16*]. By reducing the actor to uttering 'a feeble tongue' [*2,1,312*], the 'fatal canopy' of the deranged Globe thus had a distracting effect which itself put the speaker into a false position of hypocritical *occultatio* between the groundlings and the great:

> Experience in the reconstructed Globe has demonstrated that [the] actor ... commands greatest *acoustical* power near the geometric center of the space beneath the canopy. The canopy also demonstrates the excellent acoustics enjoyed by occupants of the Lords' Room ... [where] one could hear and be heard: the canopy would have projected the lords' voices as well as the actors'. Thanks to the absence of a roof over the yard, however, auditors in the yard and the galleries would have found themselves in a perceptibly different relationship to the auditory events going on all around. In a cylindrical space applause sounds on the left and right, not all around ... Performers in the Globe have commented on the way audience response can start in one part of the theater and spread laterally to the rest.[136]

With its 'highly reverberant acoustics', Smith concludes, it is no surprise that plays written for the Globe's 'O world' betray acute alertness to volume 'in capturing, holding, and guiding an audience's attention'.[137] Bevington speculates that this reflexiveness actually arose from the about-face when the intrusion of the 'Lord's Room' forced actors 'to play fully in the round', since 'they would not wish to neglect their wealthiest patrons in the most expensive seats'.[138] But in the fault-finding laboratory of *Julius Caesar* the practical effect of such a reorientation is that voice and volume separate, as spectacle comes at the expense of sense in the 'rheumy' arena, even as sound comes at cost of sight to the nobles in their pillared 'Room'. So though critics view this tragedy as a play about the *vox populi* of the 'turbulent demotic crowd', it is the actor's duplicity before this 'bifold authority' [*Troilus, 5,2,146*] on which it turns.[139] As P. Jeffrey Ford notes, if Shakespeare's Roman plays are so alarmed about 'the effect of bloody spectacles on those who observe them', that is because they associate 'the effect of violent stage spectacle with the effect of the violent act of power'.[140] Shakespeare's writing was energised by the interplay of poetry and power, 'When in one line two crafts directly meet' [*Hamlet, 3,4,185:9*].[141] But in *Julius Caesar* it looks as if the untimely fabric of the Globe has generated a 'madness of discourse' [*Troilus, 5,2,142*], leaving the actor in the self-divided position of playing the fool to the groundlings whilst declaiming in tragic mode to his backers behind. In this crisis of lying *occultatio*, the player king has indeed been primed for a guilty critique of the 'double business' of his own craft:

> And like a man to double business bound
> I stand in pause ...
>
> [*Hamlet, 3,3,39–42*]

Arrested 'in pause', Brutus reflects on how 'Between the acting of a dreadful thing / And the first motion, all the interim is / Like a phantasma' [*2,1,63–5*]; and critics regard this paused consciousness on the eve of decision as a watershed in the history of drama, when 'something new' emerges: a mental crisis about performance, as the author weighs up what happens when the actor loses the plot, the seizing-up of mental operations before the order to do something 'dreadful'. This was the Shakespearean hiatus that persuaded even Schmitt 'to acknowledge (more or less unwillingly) the irreducibility of the play *as play*'.[142] But what is pointed about this 'interim' is that Shakespeare's man of *inaction* compares his stasis to the Roman state of emergency known as the *iustitium*, when the senate mandated its officers to take all necessary measures to preserve the state from tumult, and as Agamben relates, an extra-mural non-place was created by suspending sovereignty: 'a zone of anomie in which all legal determinations – above all the very distinctions between public and private – were deactivated'.[143] So, when Brutus imagines 'The genius and the mortal instruments / Are then in counsel, and the state of man, / Like to a little kingdom, suffers then the nature of an insurrection' [*66–9*], it is as if theatre is expropriating for its exemption what Agamben calls the *mana* of the *iustitium* as a caesura, a legal standstill, to assert its own state of permanent emergency; an interregnum stretched to the limit as, inspired by Pyrrhus, whose blade 'seemed i'th'air to stick' [*Hamlet, 2,2,459*], the Prince delays enacting his 'dreadful thing' over an entire play. As Girard admits, if the public bays for a sovereign decision Shakespeare must oblige; but he can turn this chore into protracted havering over his predicament.[144] Thus we might speculate that the reason why *Hamlet* is such a 'Romanized play' is because it was the 'high and palmy' classical theatre that first prioritized '*the question*' for the actor of whether or not 'to take arms'

[*3,1,58–61*] on stage, by letting political presence into the aesthetic representation.[145]

Shakespeare had raised the Aristotelian dilemma of whether 'we must leave the killing out' [*Dream, 3,1,12*] in his 'antic' burlesque of 'Pyramus and Thisbe'. What we detect there, Girard deduces, is the dramatist's 'extreme sensitivity to the hazardous nature of his craft'.[146] So in *A Midsummer Night's Dream* the actors milk frantic laughter from use of a lion mask as the face of symbolic violence in the play they perform to euphemize the real violence of Duke Theseus, Herculean lion-slayer, rapist and tyrant. Schmitt described the distorting dialectic of presence and representation on Shakespeare's stage as exactly such a 'dream-frame', whereby 'images and figures, events and situations are interwoven in a dream-like way', just 'as people and realities merge in a dream'.[147] But *Julius Caesar* is as conscious as the Athenian comedy of the two-faced aesthetic ideology that will use these 'antique fables' and 'fairy toys' [*5,1,3*] to 'Stir up the ... youth to merriments' [*1,1,12*] to efface its own violence; for Brutus will defend Caesar's assassination as just such an immunizing strategy: 'as subtle masters ... Stir their servants to an act of rage', after which the killers will 'be called purgers, not murderers'. 'Our course would seem too bloody', he avers, 'To cut the head off and then hack the limbs', by slaughtering Antony. But while he intends not to 'hew' Caesar 'as a carcass fit for hounds' [*2,1,162–9*], the text's verbal seepage from the sporting 'order of the course' [*1,2,27*] to the carnality of the actual corpse, its wounds 'Weeping as fast they stream forth blood' [*3,1,200*], proves there can be no such quarantine of 'the cruel issue' of 'this corse' [*294*].

In *Julius Caesar* the 'royal remains' that haunt the modern public sphere with the uncanny dimension of their fleshly materiality will 'smell above the earth ... groaning for burial' [*3,1,277–8*], as though the perturbation over Caesar's decaying corpse is a working out of the sequence described by Elaine Scarry in *The Body in Pain*: 'At particular moments when there is a crisis of belief ... the sheer material factualness of the human body will be borrowed to lend that cultural construct the aura of "realness"'.[148] Theatre historians prefer to regard the Globe as a civilizing step away from the sacrificial logic of such sovereign violence, as the first London amphitheatre where animal baiting did *not* take place.[149] But in his *Stage, Stake, and Scaffold* Andreas Höfele argues that this separation did

not mean the Bankside playhouse could escape the contamination
that went with 'the typological kinship' of adjacent buildings, and
that famously deceived Hollar into mislabelling the Globe the 'Bear
Baiting'.[150] In *Julius Caesar*, moreover, the lions have escaped the
circus to stalk the streets [*1,3,20*]; and Cassius therefore poses the
predicament of the sovereign predator in the liberal society, when
he claims Caesar 'were no lion, were not Romans hinds', and 'would
not be a wolf', but that the 'Poor man ... sees the Romans are but
sheep' [*103–5*].

In its obsessive recursion to the incarnational somatic metaphor
of the sacrificial corpse, and its structural fidelity to 'the order of the
course', Shakespeare's grounding 'goat song' keeps contact with the
spring festival of the Lupercalia that was meant to be the pretext for
Caesar's *coup*: the 'holy chase' [*1,2,10*] when 'mischief' ran 'afoot'
to 'Take what course' [*3,3,248*] it would, as naked youths raced to
eat raw flesh of 'a carcass fit for hounds', in a re-enactment of the
founding of the city by the wolf-boy Romulus. Scott Wilson believes
this atavistic rite, which structures its action even as the tragedy
announces 'a break from the underlying myth into something more
modern', was 'probably incorporated unconsciously' by the dramatist.[151] But it seems rather to deliberately highlight the affinity of
the sovereign and the beast, for, as Agamben comments, that the
victor is clothed as a wolf-man is decisive for the Lupercalia, since
a werewolf is *'neither man nor beast'*, but the outlaw, 'who dwells
paradoxically within both'. During such feasts men behave and
dress as animals, on this view, to reassert the lawlessness at 'the very
heart' of the law itself.[152] In *Julius Caesar*, therefore, the play can
be said to 'leave no ceremony out' [*1,2,13*] from the Lupercalia, as
Shakespeare allows the play to run its sacrificial 'corse' in the exception that is the sovereignty of the stage itself:

> [T]his lupization of man and humanization of the wolf is at every
> moment possible in the *dissolution civitatis* inaugurated by the state
> of exception. This threshold alone ... is the always operative presup-
> position of sovereignty.[153]

Shakespeare's Rome is fixated on the proximity of the sovereign and
the animal, and by the 'royal remains' its citizens pretend to have
overthrown. Thus, Antony, who enters *'stripped for the course'* [*SD,
1,2*], wins the race because he drinks 'The stale of horses, and the
gilded puddle / Which beasts would cough at ... Yea, like the stag'

[*Antony,* *1,5,62–5*]. As Georges Dumézil explained, 'the Luperci seem to represent the one exception to that permanent and public religion within which the whole life of society is set' because their consumption of uncooked flesh attests the priority of sovereign violence.[154] Francis Barker once objected that in his Roman plays Shakespeare occludes Elizabethan violence by displacing it onto 'another time, in another place, among other people'.[155] But it seems instead a sign of the failure of any such distantiation, and of theatre's inability to erase the 'savage spectacle' [*3,1,225*] of its origins, that in *Julius Caesar* the playing with the 'corse' should insistently record the actor's trauma at being 'at the stake / And bayed about with many enemies' [*4,1,48–9*], set on by spectators like a stag harried by the pack, who 'fawned like hounds' before striking 'like a cur' [*5,1,42*]. Thus, far from being the pure aesthetic realm Brutus plans, in this first Globe play the 'circle in which an audience entraps the player' remains a ring of shame, as the circuit around the 'corse' reconfigures 'the founding form of what we like to think "entertainment"', in Terence Hawkes's words, as a 'wheel of fire' [*Lear, 4,7,47*] with sacrifice its core, in which the victim 'cannot fly, / But bear-like ... must fight course' [*Macbeth, 5,7,1–2*]:[156]

> Here wast thou bayed, brave hart,
> Here thou didst fall, and here thy hunters stand
> Signed in thy spoil and crimsoned in thy lethe.
> O world, thou wast the forest to this hart;
> And this indeed, O world, the heart of thee.
>
> [*3,1,205–9*]

A cavern dark enough

'One can weep for many things', sneered Schmitt, but Shakespearean tragedy originates only from a circumstance 'that exists for all concerned – an incontrovertible reality for the author, the actors, and the audience'.[157] In Antony's cry of 'O world' we can hear a lament, therefore, not so much for hunted Caesar as for the collusion of the 'wooden O' with sovereign beasts. Brutus's hesitation over enacting 'the dreadful thing' would be stretched with *Hamlet* into an interminable interlude fixated upon whether 'the play's the thing' [*3,1,581*] for real or only in jest. It is suggestive that the king of that play is named, however, after the emperor who had himself triumphed like the first Brutus, by slyly performing the 'antic

disposition' [*1,5,173*] of a 'silly jeering idiot' [*Lucrece, 1812*]. For if
Roman theatre had kept slaughter offstage, its decorum was belied
by its games, where Claudius vied with his nephew Nero in the
shows he staged 'to feast on carnage'. So no wonder Hamlet aspires
to the 'soul of Nero' [*Hamlet, 3,2,364*]; for what recurs when he
plots to kill his uncle is Seneca's tale that Nero had Claudius poisoned 'while happily watching the comedians'.[158] 'Seneca cannot
be too heavy' [*2,2,382*], opines Polonius, having himself 'play'd
once', when he 'did enact Julius Caesar' [*3,2,90–3*]. But the Stoic
philosopher who banished violence from his tragedies was himself
'suicided' by Nero; and Goldberg and others infer that it is this
Roman theatre of cruelty which teaches Hamlet that the mediation
of the performance may be only a convenient screen for sovereign
violence: 'It is in the closet, after all, that Polonius, once again,
enacts the part of Julius Caesar; he falls to an actor who, having
avoided the role of Nero, has instead become Brutus'.[159]

In *Julius Caesar* the state of play is what the impresario Maecenas
planned for Caesar Augustus when he predicted that 'you will live
in a theatre where the spectators are the whole world'.[160] Like
Schmitt, Goldberg attributes this heightened sense of spectacle, the
feeling that there can be no hiding backstage if the closet where the
players retire is another show, to the interference of James, with
his Augustan belief in himself as a royal actor.[161] The limits of this
reading, however, are that the tragedy predates James's succession
and that it overlooks the anxiety with which, as John Drakakis
counters, Shakespeare presents the playhouse as 'an unstable institution proceeding gingerly into a terrain fraught with political
danger ... the precarious position of the Globe'. So *Julius Caesar* is
not so much a star-struck homage to the actors, Drakakis objects,
than 'an unmasking of the politics of representation'.[162] This alienation effect ensures that though these Romans 'see themselves as
glorious actors on the stage of history,' the player Caesar becomes is
a bombastic poseur, 'subject to an actor's defeats'.[163] So in contrast
to Shakespeare's usual reliance on what Manfred Pfister terms a
'producer figure' to personify theatre's shaping energies (imagined
as some 'well-governing individual of the upper orders'), his idea of
the actor at this moment of insecurity is no longer a free agent, still
less a *Johannes fac totum*.[164] For never is Shakespeare's apprehension about his workplace more acute than when he glances over
his shoulder at its Roman wall, and breaks Brutus's vacillation by

having him adopt the identical posture of Stoic 'constancy' to which
Caesar aspired:

> Let not our looks put on our purposes;
> But bear it as our Roman actors do,
> With untired spirits and formal constancy.
>
> [2,1,224–6]

In Brutus's imagination the Roman actor can 'be a statue of
himself', putting on an act of frozen immobility, as Caesar 'put it
on' [3,2,165] 'like a colossus'.[165] That might have been the 'formal
constancy' put upon the Globe actors if they had made themselves
agents of those real conspirators sitting in the Lord's Room, with
their Stuart affiliations as absolute as the monarch they opposed.
But when Brutus starts to adopt the same role as Caesar the play
exposes the affinity of the sovereign and his foes, for in this tragedy
of treason the part of the 'true man' [1,2,258] is always an act. So
trapped between republicanism and royalism, Rome and rheum, or
tragedy and farce, the Globe player will be contorted in a posture
of chronic bad faith. But to find a pattern for this *occultatio* he has
only to look about him at the architecture, and recall the time when
the great Roscius was an actor and the most celebrated performer
in all Rome. The example was not auspicious, as Shakespeare often
warned. Thus, imprisoned in 'Julius Caesar's ill-erected Tower' of
London [*Richard II*, 5,1,2], his Henry VI had consoled himself
reading; but no sooner had the king opened his book than the monstrous Richard Crookback loomed before him like the Roman actor
Roscius playing the butcher who relishes the silence of the lambs:

> So first the harmless sheep doth yield his fleece,
> And next his throat unto the butcher's knife.
> What scene of death hath Roscius now to act?
>
> [*3Henry VI*, 5,6,8–10]

Richard's identification with the legendary Roman actor Roscius,
crowns his career as 'Shakespeare's arch player'.[166] So critics primed
on Benjamin's dark aphorism about fascism turning politics artistic
are wise to the way Shakespeare toys with the actor's collusion in
state violence with scenes like the killing of Henry VI, as well as to
the exhibitionism that seems to compel him to return to the abattoir
where the dumb beast offers its 'throat unto the butcher's knife' as
a primal scene of aesthetic betrayal.[167] The recent critical interest

in the sovereign and the beast suggests the legend might not, then, be so fanciful that has this playwright, for whom 'political struggle occurs discursively over the meanings of blood', as a butcher's son, who 'when he kill'd a calf would do it in high style, and make a speech'.[168] For whatever the origin of this repetition compulsion, Hamlet's joke about Polonius being 'kill'd i'th'Capitol' in the role of Caesar, 'It was a brute part to kill so capital a calf' [*Hamlet, 3,2,105*], implies that the slaughterhouse was always identified by Shakespeare with the crisis of mediation the Prince exploits, when the arras provides cover for the 'rash and bloody deed' with which the 'rash intruding fool' is stabbed [*3,4,26–30*]. And whether or not this 'killing the calf' recalls some grim pantomime, with a bucket to catch the blood of the animal despatched behind the cloth, it seems there was an analogy for Shakespeare between his family 'bleeding business' [*3,1,168*] and the massacre of innocents behind drapes in the mystery plays he likely watched as a boy, and that, as Weimann points out, demanded a reaction, whether of relish or of revolt.[169] Thus, when the players descend on Elsinore and threaten to 'out-Herod Herod' [*3,2,12*], it is ominous that, like the mountebank Richard III, they are immediately compared to the Roman actor whose aesthetic of violence was the classic demonstration of the Faustian pact between history and histrionics, and whose career epitomised the scandal when the time of the stage was ruptured by the time of state:

POLONIUS: My lord, I have news to tell you.
  HAMLET: My lord, I have news to tell you. When Roscius was
                  an actor in Rome.
POLONIUS: The actors are come hither, my lord.
                                      [*Hamlet, 2,2,372–5*]

Hamlet's allusion to the Roman actor is glossed as mockery of Polonius for staleness, and scant attention is given to the Renaissance reputation of Roscius, as the first entertainer to be knighted, for separating himself from his public in the service of power. Robert Greene thought of him, however, as 'like Aesop's crow, being pranked with the glory of other's feathers'; or as a strangler of superior talents, given that 'Asterides seeing Roscius' gestures durst never after come on the stage'.[170] And when Quintus Roscius Gallus was mentioned by contemporaries it was as the Roman Gustaf Gründgens, a Mephistophelean impersonator of pimps and parasites whose phenomenal annual earnings of 600,000 sesterces were capped in 82 BC when he was given his title by his keenest fan Sulla, in a stunt timed to distract from the dictator's massacres.[171] Not coincidentally, however, it was in these days of terror that Roscius imported on stage the other invention for which he became infamous: the 'formal constancy' of the face-mask from Greek theatre. Plays had formerly been acted at Rome in wigs alone; but according to Latin critics, masks were introduced by Roscius to hide a nervous twitch with which he was afflicted during the proscription; and Cicero, who had been his lawyer, acidly remarked that there were some who did not speak any more highly of the actor, 'even with his mask on'.[172] The great showman thought so well of his profession that he wrote a treatise comparing the stage to politics.[173] But when Roscius was an actor, as Hamlet must have known, theatre was perverted by a two-faced careerist whose life and art were paradigms of artistic prostitution; whose irresistible rise to favour with his prince had been at the price of the literal death of his public; and whose innovation of the theatrical mask had been a crude attempt to smother interpretation by concealing the guilt-stricken rictus produced by his own collusion in the politics of despotism.

In *Hamlet* the mask of Roscius seems inseparable from the calculation of the players, and it is not chance that from the instant the Ghost materializes with its 'beaver up' [*1,3,228*], in the play that shows more than any other the '*visor effect*', as Derrida termed it, by which 'we do not see who looks at us', the face-mask is associated with the representational impasse that goes with ambiguity and prevarication.[174] In *Julius Caesar*, too, it is the 'pale companions' of melancholia [*Dream, 1,1,15*] who appreciate how their best plan will be to forge an alliance with theatre, and 'bear it' like 'our Roman actors'. Brutus's rehearsal note to the plotters, who have 'hats plucked about their ears / And half their faces buried in their cloaks' [*73–4*], when not forced by rheum 'To wear a kerchief' [*314*], to take their lead from the 'muffled' [*SD. 86*] players like Roscius, and 'find a cavern dark enough / To mask the monstrous visage' of the conspiracy in 'smiles and affability' [*82*], is the most sinister view of his art in Shakespeare, and baffles critics who assume his idea of the play always works to glorify the stage. In fact, the image of the Roman actor in *Julius Caesar* introduces what Barton admits is a 'decline in the dignity of the theatre' in the 1600s, personified by the cynical player 'who has sheltered behind a noble mask', as though it was a 'tiring-house of the imagination'.[175] Thus the first thing Brutus says about himself is how, unlike Antony, who 'loves plays' [*1,2,204*], he is 'not gamesome': 'If I have veiled my look, / I turn the trouble of my countenance merely upon myself' [*30*]. What he instead admires is the facelessness of the 'veiled' comedian, because it rigidifies a dissimulated meaning; and his entire story develops as if it was Shakespeare's reaction to Cicero's condemnation in his treatise *De Oratore* of the occultation of the face-mask worn by Roscius.

When the senators argue that Cicero's 'silver hairs / Will purchase us a good opinion', Brutus is adamant to 'leave him out' [*143–52*]; and among the father-figures deposed in *Julius Caesar* special malice is reserved for the lawyer with the 'ferret ... eyes' [*1,2,187*], who is soon dead 'by order of proscription' [*4,3,178*]. Yet, as Andrew Hadfield notes, 'The absence of Cicero's voice serves only to draw attention to his writings'.[176] For while his opinion on the state of emergency may sound Greek, in *De Oratore* and *Brutus* he in fact urged rhetorical transparency, in preference to the lies of the actor, who causes 'laughter when he wills it, or if he wills, tears; so the passer-by will always know a Roscius is on stage'. Persuasion 'depends on the eyes', the old advocate insisted, which was why 'better critics would never applaud Roscius when he wore his mask', and why the player who mouthed without eye-contact was 'turning his back on his audience'. When Roscius was an actor, Cicero lamented, the politics of the republic were corrupted by 'stagy gestures borrowed from the theatrical profession'.[177] Thus, nothing could be further from the proto-Enlightenment Ciceronian ideal than the masks adopted by Brutus's hit-men when they 'hide their faces / Even from darkness'.[178] 'Cocooned in disclaimers', their *occultatio* does what he deplored, by separating auditors from spectators. Thus, whether or not the play was orchestrated by the Essex rebels from their 'Lord's Room', Shakespeare's image of the actor as a butcher performing the 'bleeding business' in the mask of a high style *embodies* the treason of the players. As Christian Jouhard has remarked, what such scenes flag is that the seventeenth-century alliance between absolutism and theatre does not allow the performers to assert aesthetic autonomy, because by screening its violence they merely aestheticize the materiality of politics: 'They give to the brutality of its effects, the reality of its violence, the coherence of a narrative'. In short, the theatre simply 'contributes to the autonomization of politics ... by producing it as art'.[179]

The purpose of playing, according to Shakespeare's Athenian tyrant Theseus, will be to 'ease the anguish' of the 'torturing hour' of rendition and interrogation [*Dream* 5,1,36–7]. So when Roscius was an actor for the dictator in the days of Roman terror he established the pattern for the artist in the type of spectacular theatre state that intrigued the dramatist. That was certainly the sceptical view of the Roscian stage taken by disillusioned *aficionados* like Cicero, for whom the eclipse of classical theatre with propagandist 'pomp ... triumph ... and revelling' [1,1,19] was an index of the overthrow of republican institutions by Asiatic despotism. To Renaissance scholars, Smith points out, Cicero was the best guide to classical theatre precisely because he was so astute about the political power of plays and players, and peppered his writings with anecdotes about audiences howling their rage or adoration at the politicians.[180] Thus the nemesis of classical drama arrived, according to the orator, in 55 BC, with the trumpets and massed choirs which inaugurated Pompey's 17,500-seat Theatre, when Roscius's elderly partner Clodius Aesopus was hauled out of retirement to whisper the dedication, which was drowned by the crowd's clamour to see the parade of 600 lions, 150 leopards, 18 elephants, and 'for the first time on any Roman stage, a rhinoceros!'[181]

It was from Pompey's games that Cicero dated the corruption of Roman citizenship, and he demanded to know what the pleasure was in seeing 'some poor slave torn to pieces by a mighty beast, or fine animal impaled upon a spear?'[182] Thus, when Roscius was an actor, in Cicero's dejected account, nothing was sadder than to see the last of the old tragedians offer up their reputations in homage to the kind of tyrant they had once performed, trooping beside captives and gladiators in processions such as Pompey's triumph, when the generalissimo was 'carried in a great jewelled chariot drawn by white horses' behind 'innumerable waggonloads of plunder, above which towered a statue of his adversary, Mithridates, King of Pontus, made of solid gold'.[183] In the eyes of theatre-lovers, Pompey literally annexed the stage to the state with his over-mighty porch. So it is no wonder *Julius Caesar* 'came to mark the perceived decline of a critical, debating public and its replacement by ignorant masses' in the age of modern advertising, considering how the play opens with a report of the spectators thronging 'To see great

Pompey pass the streets of Rome' [1,1,41], and ends with the future Caesar Augustus planning his own triumph to celebrate 'the glories of this happy day' [5,5,80].[184] And as they push into the palace over the corpses of vanquished Amazons, Old Hamlet, or the dictator himself, Shakespeare's thespians know as well as the Prince of Denmark that when Roscius was an actor in Pompey's 'universal' theatre, he set the stakes in this system of bread and circuses, feasting with the victors on his royal road to fame. When Roscius was an actor, these stage players suggest, the comedian's mask was a face of shame.

Great reckoning in a little Rome

'Age, thou art shamed': there is a sense of shame in *Julius Caesar* about the 'wide walls' of the new 'room' [1,2,151] that may have been triggered by the players' move from Burbage's Theater to the Globe, but that extends to the entire company, including the author himself. In Santner's account, the shame of being stuck in 'technique, artifice, mediation, self-reflexivity' is written into the modern aesthetic from the outset, due to art's 'failure to reach its object' of purifying itself from the carnality of sovereignty.[185] And such shame is certainly attached to the play's scapegoat, the unluckily named court poet Cinna, whose first words are that 'I dreamt tonight that I did feast with Caesar'. The writer is in his own porch when he relates how 'things unlucky charge my fantasy. / I have no will to wander forth of doors, / Yet something leads me forth' [3,3,1–4]. This phantasmal banquet is Caesar's first spectral reappearance. But it recalls the dead dictator's last supper invitation to his killers 'go in and taste some wine with me ... like friends' [2,2,26–7]. Cinna's somnambulism has therefore seemed to critics to offer a key to the 'driven quality and peculiar inevitability' of the play.[186] In Schmitt's terms, the poet's unwillingness suggests how sovereign power diverts artistic intention with the charm of the seducer. It reprises previous liminal episodes that hover on the border between inside and outside in this play of fatal footfalls, as Shakespeare ambiguates the distinctions between private and public, and a domain 'removed, hidden and personal is recuperated as a site of public action'.[187] But the 'something' that compels the power-hungry poet to abandon his study for the street is the most drastic instance in the text of the way historical reality seeps into the aesthetic space. For as reclusive Cinna is made 'to wander forth of doors' he is drawn across a similarly dangerous doorstep as the commoners who voluntarily leave their homes to applaud Caesar; Brutus who opens his gate to conspiracy; or Caesar himself when he stands within his porch and declares, 'Danger knows full well / That Caesar is more dangerous than he ... And Caesar shall go forth' [2,2,28].

If *Julius Caesar* stands as a critique of its own relations to power, it reminds us that as Adorno wrote, 'every immanent critique pulses with the force of a position's commitments to where that position "cannot afford to go"'.[188] So editors point out that this superstition about entering the public domain has a truly ghostly echo, for Shakespeare here quotes Christopher Marlowe, who in some of his last lines before his own murder had his doomed Guise reiterate the same brag: 'Yet Caesar shall go forth ... Thus Caesar did go forth, and thus he died.'[189] In *Massacre at Paris* Marlowe touched a similar theatrical nerve as *Julius Caesar*, when he had Guise mask the Bartholomew's Day rioters as *players*. Shakespeare in turn always associated his rival's nemesis with the violence of representation, reflecting how 'When a man's verses cannot be understood ... it strikes a man more dead than a great reckoning in a little room' [*As You*, 3,3,9–12]. Cinna's sacrifice thus echoes that of Ramus, the Sorbonne rhetoric professor stabbed for his bad texts in Marlowe's massacre. Shakespeare's poet will likewise die when he loses the security of his 'little room', and in the most deadly echo, his name makes him a sacrificial *sinner*. As the plotters escape 'like madmen through the gates of Rome' [3,2,257], Antony thus makes the uncanniness of all these gateways and lintels explicit when he pictures Caesar's lifeblood 'rushing out of doors to be resolved' [173]. 'Rushing out of doors to be resolved' with a decisive meaning in the public forum, the characters of the play thereby seem to enact their creator's own trepidation below the Roman arch of his new stage, abreacting the conflicting attraction and repulsion before the allure of a charismatic politics he cannot help but fret over, as when nearing the end he has yet another pushy versifier presume to feast with princes, only to be ejected by the men of violence in contemptuous disgust: 'What should the wars do with these jigging fools?' [4,2,188].

If Shakespeare opened the Globe with such misgivings about 'warnings and portents / Of evils imminent' [2,2,80], Cinna's sleepwalking into the portal of power has lately assumed metatheatrical

status as a warning not only to the actors but to all thinkers tempted
to trespass on political *importance*. As Alan Sinfield infers, this
dream can be decoded as 'the nightmare of modern intellectuals:
that they are invited to become significant in government'. Thus,
just as Brutus's decision seems to enact Shakespeare's own inability
to transcend sovereignty, the poet's fantasy of feasting with Caesar
has come to figure the dramatist's guilty excitement at the summons
to collaborate with the power that 'constructs, entices, and destroys
him'. In Sinfield's imaginary staging the entire tragedy would thus
be Cinna's nightmare scenario: 'He would fall asleep and dream
Julius Caesar', but 'he would look like "Shakespeare"'.[190] This
reading accords with the demeaning Renaissance function of the
poet as lickspittle. As Gary Taylor notes, 'Shakespeare's poets are
defined by their relationship to a patron: Cinna is "a friend" to
Caesar'.[191] But in *Shakespeare and the Poet's Life* Gary Schmidgall
has discerned a growing tension in this relationship around 1600,
underlined by Cassius's characterization as the new type of satirical
writer who 'reads much' yet detests plays [1,2,202], and by Caesar's
irritation at 'sweet words' and 'lowly courtesies' [3,1,36–42].[192] In
Julius Caesar, moreover, something unprecedented happens to the
poet on the way to the Forum, which is that instead of waiting on
the monarch as expected, he is suddenly made to answer to the mob:

FIRST PLEBEIAN:	What is your name?
SECOND PLEBEIAN:	Whither are you going?
THIRD PLEBEIAN:	Where do you dwell?
FOURTH PLEBEIAN:	Are you a married man or a bachelor?
SECOND PLEBEIAN:	Answer every man directly.

[3,3,5–9]

'What is my name? Whither am I going? Where do I dwell? Am I
a married man or a bachelor?' [13–14]: it would be easy to hear
in the poet's parrying of the plebeian's questions Shakespeare's
own chariness towards the construction of modern authorship as
a function of market economics and consumer demand. The future
Globe will be a revolutionary forum for people's power, this face-
off might imply. In his polemic 'Bardicide' Taylor therefore claims
Shakespeare here goes out of his way to warn that it is the public,
not the prince, the artist has to fear.[193] He had skirted the death of
the author in *A Midsummer Night's Dream*, where 'The riot of the
tipsy bacchanals / Tearing' the singer Orpheus is one of the shows

offered Theseus, together with 'The Battle with the Centaurs' sung by a eunuch, and the muses mourning some versifier 'late deceased in beggary' [5,1,44–53], who sounds like the dead poet Greene. As Girard notices, in all three amusements a poet happens to be victimized, whether castrated, lynched or starved.[194] Such immolations thus literalize the duke's cutting critique of Quince's script: 'if he that writ it had hanged himself … it would have been a fine tragedy' [5,1,342–4]; and the callousness with which Shakespeare's onstage audiences shred play after play as 'the silliest stuff' [207]. Likewise, in *Timon of Athens* a craven Poet who sings about his patron's 'Magic of bounty' [1,1,6] is told to go hang himself or drown [5,1,101]. But like the 'poor harmless fly' killed for 'his pretty buzzing melody' in *Titus Andronicus* [3,2,63], these poets crushed by the intrusion of real time into the time of their art are all victims of patrician spite. What is new in *Julius Caesar* is that now it is proletarians who make the sacrifice of the artist a matter of life or death:

FOURTH PLEBEIAN:	Tear him for his bad verses, tear him for his bad verses.
CINNA:	I am not Cinna the conspirator.
FOURTH PLEBEIAN:	It is no matter, his name's Cinna. Pluck but his name out of his heart, and turn him going.
	[3,3,29–33]

As Taylor remarks, the only precedent for the murder of Cinna is when Jack Cade's peasants hang the Clerk of Chatham 'with his pen and inkhorn about his neck' [2Henry VI, 4,2,96]. This Roman mob is, moreover, further demonized when it victimizes Cinna not as in Plutarch, in error, but for his 'bad verses'. So according to Taylor Shakespeare makes the groundlings 'vulgar interlopers' in a scenario where 'the poet is unmistakeably innocent … the popular reading of the poet unmistakeably mistaken'.[195] In any art claiming to be disinterested every disavowal is an avowal, Taylor avers. But what this reading overlooks is how the author admits as much by having Cinna 'dwell by the Capitol' [3,3,24]. Following immediately upon Antony's incitement to let 'Mischief … Take what course [it] wilt' [3,2,248], the poet's social arrivisme thus chimes with Caesar's invitation to 'Sleek-headed men' [1,2,194] to 'revel long a-nights' [2,3,116], and the rabble-rouser's addiction, as 'a masquer and a reveller' [*5,1,62*], 'To sports, to wildness, and much company' [*2,1,189*]. So 'Fortune is merry', boasts Antony, and 'will give us anything' [*3,3,255–60*], as the rioters ransack Rome. Though we never do hear Cinna's verses, Sinfield is thus surely correct to see the poet's mugging as a penalty for imagining his art could find a place beside the 'plays' and 'music' politicians love [*1,2,204*]. Thomas Betteridge concurs that if this poet is another of Shakespeare's self-portraits, a work that has playgoers heckling Caesar, and that begins by projecting theatre as a space of equal access and free debate, seems to collapse with Cinna's murder in recoil from the early modern public sphere, as though in surrender to the absolutist realities of its age:

> Antony makes the Plebeians into the easily led, irrational and revolting audience that fills the works of opponents of Shakespeare's theatre – a spectral fantasy of the Globe's audience – or image of the future ... *Julius Caesar* is haunted by the spectre of theatrical power distorted and corrupted by men like Antony.[196]

Sole of the age

'He must be taught, and trained, and bid go forth': the theatrical imagery of Antony's disdain for Lepidus, as 'A barren, mean-spirited fellow, one that feeds / On objects, arts, and imitations, / Which, out of use, and staled by other men, / Begin his fashion', and abuse of his former ally 'But as a property' [*4,1,35–40*], suggests a condescending attitude to the audience on the part of the management of the Globe. Critics often assume that Shakespeare shared this 'disgust with the stage', which Paul Yachnin relates to the 'shift towards private legitimation' sealed when the Chamberlain's Men received royal warrant in 1603.[197] Contemporary reports of Globe performances confirm how playgoers were indeed swayed like 'The many-headed multitude' of the play 'when eloquent Mark Antony' has spoken.[198] Yet now the cliché of the populace as 'irrational, cruel, fickle, and easy to manipulate' is framed within a wholly novel theatrical context, when for the first and last time Shakespeare installs on stage the one piece of architectural furniture which concretized the political theology of divine right, was crucial to manipulation of public opinion and facilitated the official strategy that the citizen must be 'trained, and bid go forth'.[199] For though Antony marvels 'How I had moved them' [*3,2,260*] when the mob runs amok, the text of the Forum scene makes clear the turning-point in fact comes when the speaker is raised to the elevated vantage of the preacher, and 'Antony ascends to the pulpit' [SD:62]. As the Arden editor annotates this stage-direction, Shakespeare uses the word 'pulpit' only six times, all in these scenes, and then with an incongruousness which implies 'that Rome, and thus the stage, is about to become a place of preaching'.[200]

Of all the 'untimely matters' in Julius Caesar it is the installation of 'the public chair' [60] or official 'pulpit' that introduces the greatest derangement of Shakespeare's playhouse yet attracts least comment. This blind-spot about 'the keystone of the arch of government' is not surprising, however, when as Peter McCullough writes in his study of court sermons, 'use of the pulpit as a government mouthpiece' has for so long been overlooked, 'a bizarre gap in the historiography of the greatest preaching age'.[201] Yet Shakespeare not only insists on the state apparatus of the tribune in the Folio stage directions, as each speaker 'Goes into the pulpit', but highlights the power of speaking ex cathedra, with successive ascents to the chair marked by crowd commentary: 'The noble Brutus is ascended. Silence' [11]; 'Let him go up into the public chair. / We'll hear him. Noble Antony, go up' [60]. Editors infer that these voice-overs covered the actors' climb to the podium, which may have been 'some porch-like projection', or simply the balcony of the Lord's Room, fitted to resemble the 'removable pulpits' lined with heraldic sounding-boards erected in the royal chapels.[202] Doubtless this stage rostrum would also have been draped like London pulpits, with 'red velvet embroidered with gold' to trumpet the privilege Brutus institutes when he ordains: 'I will into the pulpit first ... What Antony shall speak I will protest / He speaks by leave and by permission' [3,1,238–41].[203] As a tiring-house within the tiring-house, the canopied lectern from which Brutus and Antony declaim thus constitutes a Baroque model for the future Globe itself, indenting the democratic circle of the 'wooden O' into what, in his study of the St Paul's pulpit, Millar MacLure calls a 'forum for the great and the would-be great to express their views'.[204]

In early modern England the pulpit embodied the intrusion of the 'royal remains' into the public space. So the first thought of Shakespeare's Senators after they seize power is to rush 'to the common pulpits' [3,1,79]. They are adopting the tactics of Elizabeth, who 'when she had any business to bring about amongst the people, used to tune the pulpits, as her saying was, to have some Preachers in or about London, ready to cry up her design'.[205] As McCullough has shown, the pulpit was the 'state mouthpiece' of the Tudors, with the Whitehall Preaching Place, where five thousand occupied the bear-pit, 'a later-day Coliseum' that buttressed royal supremacy 'by emphasizing that ancient architectural symbol of imperial power ... the elevated royal tribune'.[206] In *Julius Caesar* the pulpit is in fact located in the marketplace, like the Cheapside pulpit of St Paul's, where the sermons 'were major civic events attended by a host of dignitaries', and in 1599 preachers were playing a key part in the real-life Essex plot.[207] This piece of 'untimely matter' is therefore the most blatant symbol of the infiltration of real time into the time of the stage, clinching Gil Harris's account of the multitemporality of Shakespearean theatre, and Schmitt's theory that 'the conditions of the context within which the play was written have been brought into the play'.[208] For with rival rhetorical styles Brutus and Antony display all the discursive force with which preachers 'cobbled souls' as they 'tuned the pulpits' to 'agitate the multitude', in William Camden's phrase about the Essex camp, 'under colour of hearing Sermons'.[209] So, as Brutus professes 'love to Caesar', and Antony praises 'honourable men' [*3,2,18; 80*], it sounds as if this play that opens with the commoners exhorted to 'Assemble all the poor men' to 'weep tears' into the river [*1,1,56*] is indeed 'tuned' to contemporary sermons, like the one delivered by Essex's chaplain at St Paul's:

> Preaching on Matthew 22:21 ('Render unto Caesar that which is Caesar's') ... he cited the example of the Roman author Seneca, tutor and advisor to the emperor Nero ... It was obvious the candidate for the role of Seneca would be Essex ... while the Queen herself would be cast in the role of Nero.[210]

In *1599*, his study of the year of *Julius Caesar*, James Shapiro speculates there was a hitch in the building of the Globe, when its shareholders delayed signing the lease for the site because they were detained at court. 'There was a powerful incentive to linger at Richmond', Shapiro explains: Lancelot Andrewes was to preach the sermons there for Lent. It was the Bishop's support for Essex's Irish campaign that inspired the just war argument in *Henry V*, Shapiro argues, for it was with 'Andrewe's cadences ringing in his ears' that the dramatist returned to London 'to sign off on the Globe'. Listening to the Ash Wednesday sermon in the queen's chapel, Shakespeare is said to have nodded to its doctrine 'aligning Church and State', a political theology to which he subscribed by likening Elizabeth to an everlasting clock in the epilogue he 'dashed off' for a revival of *As You Like It* the night before. *1599* thus typifies the way these texts are read as celebrations of absolutism, as no irony is detected in a speech that wishes Elizabeth might revolve for ever, 'beginning in the ending' on her 'Circular' course.[211] But repetitious circles were much on Shakespeare's mind in the spring of 1599. And if the royal pulpit taught him anything, his Roman play suggests, it was that no circle was so perfect that it was not 'full of faults'.

With *Julius Caesar* Shakespeare built the echoing rhetoric of Rome into the fabric of his art. But if the Lord's Room serves as his pulpit, what is significant is that in the play it is also the locus of ultimate misunderstanding, when the lookout up 'above' [*SD*, 5,3,24] misreports the battle, and having 'misconstrued everything' [33], Cassius takes his own life. So to the end of this tragedy, the ill-omened anachronism of the Globe's Roman architecture is the occasion of interference, misconstruction and unintended consequences, when both the actors and audiences interpret 'clean from the purposes of the things themselves'. This Lord's 'Rome' was a literal projection of 'untimely matter' into the performers' room, the derangement of the perfect playing space by the political pressures of 1599. But whether or not these haunted ruins were imposed upon the actors, what the echo-effect of *Julius Caesar* discloses is a writer who, far from merely mimicking the political debates of such a 'republican moment', creates a drama out of the great creative *refusal* of any such intrusion of his time into the time of the play.[212]

'Courtiers of beauteous freedom' is how Shakespeare ironized Caesar's murderers in *Antony and Cleopatra* [2,6,17], as though he always conceived of freedom as a sovereign gift. *Julius Caesar* thus stages the difficulty of releasing the public sphere from the malingering notion that the sovereign 'was authority inasmuch as he made it present, embodied it in his personality'.[213] But it was Nietzsche, resenting his own servitude to Wagner, who read Brutus's treason as figuring Shakespeare's impatience with such subjection, and Cinna's murder as a measure of his self-contempt: 'This should be translated into the soul of the poet'.[214] In Wagner the alliance between the artist and the artisan lasted only until the shoemaker became a Meistersinger. But what Nietzsche grasped was how Shakespearean tragedy was constituted not through repetitious bondage to its originating presence, but the negation of that instant in the Cobbler's philosophy 'That every like is not the same'. As even Schmitt conceded (despite detesting the idea that 'the gods of theatre are different from those in the forum and the pulpit'), Shakespeare's freedom lay in representing history as a ground *to be negated*.[215] According to Hollander such *metalepsis*, the emancipation of the echo from mere repetition, means that 'the whole Renaissance is a transumption of antique culture, and the very concept of being reborn is a misconstruction'. So, if *metalepsis* is a figure of creative misconstruction, a 'taking hold of something to revise it upward', then *Julius Caesar* can be considered Shakespeare's most *metaleptic* work.[216] For in this play of psychic foundations devised to cement the cornerstone of a new era, the dramatist who was conscripted alongside the shoemakers to bear the weight of his sad time in the triumphal march of power made a creaturely treading upon *his own sovereignty* the indestructible sole of the age:

> Were't aught to me I bore the canopy,
> With my extern the outward honouring,
> Or laid great bases for eternity
> Which proves more short than waste or ruining?

> [Sonnet 125]

Notes

1 'Tuesday 3 July 1600': Anonymous Vatican MS, quoted in John Orrell, *The Human Stage: English Theatre Design, 1567–1640* (Cambridge: Cambridge University Press, 1988), p.45.
2 Thomas Platter, *Thomas Platter's Travels in England*, trans. Clare Williams (London: Jonathan Cape, 1937), p.167.
3 For the shape of the Globe, see John Orrell, 'Beyond the Rose: Design Problems for the Globe Reconstruction', in Franklin Hildy (ed.), *New Issues in the Reconstruction of Shakespeare's Theatre* (New York: Peter Lang, 1990), where a twenty-sided polygon was conjectured (p.95); Julian Bowsher and Pat Miller, *The Rose and the Globe Playhouses of Shakespeare's Bankside, Southwark: Excavations 1988–91* (London: Museum of London, 2009), who favour sixteen or eighteen sides (p.126); and Gabriel Egan, 'The 1599 Globe and Its Modern Replica: Virtual Reality Modelling of the Archaeological and Pictorial Evidence', *Early Modern Literary Studies*, 5 (2004), 1–22. Frances Yates, *Theatre of the World* (London: Routledge and Kegan Paul, 1969), pp.103 and 125; cf. Orrell, op. cit. (note 1), p.128: 'In naming their "Theater" in Shoreditch John Brayne and James Burbage

appealed to classical models ... Their amphitheatre was "Roman" in association, and to some extent in spirit.' See also Siobhan Keenan and Peter Davidson, 'The Iconography of the Globe', in J.R. Mulryne and Margaret Shewring, *Shakespeare's Globe Rebuilt* (Cambridge: Cambridge University Press, 1997), pp.148–9: 'In christening their new playhouse "the Globe" it may be expected that the Burbages commissioned a decorative scheme intended to foster an emblematic conception of the theatre as a microcosm ... a theatre of the world'.

4 '*Must* have been based': Yates, op. cit. (note 3), p.134.

5 John Hollander, *The Figure of Echo: A Mode of Allusion in Milton and After* (Berkeley: University of California Press, 1981), p.44. See also Max Nänny, 'Textual Echoes of Echoes', in Andreas Fischer (ed.), *Repetition in Language and Literature* (Tübingen: Gunter Narr Verlag, 1994), pp.115–43.

6 'The presence of the present': Jacques Derrida, *Speech and Phenomena*, trans. David Allison (Edmonton: North Western University Press, 1972), p.52; Sigmund Freud, *Civilization and Its Discontents*, trans. James Strachey (London: Hogarth Press, 1961), p.17. For the idea that the beginning is *always already* haunted, see Sigmund Freud, *The Psychopathology of Everyday Life*, trans. Alan Tyson (Penguin: Harmondsworth: 1976), pp.339–76. Cf. Martin Heidegger, 'In essential history the beginning comes last': *Parmenides*, trans. André Schuwer and Richard Rojcevicz (Bloomington: Indiana University Press, 1992), p.1. For the English history of the poetics of repetition, see Phyllis Portnoy, 'Ring Composition and the Digressions of *Exodus*: The Legacy of "The Remnant"', *English Studies*, 82:4 (2001), 289–307.

7 Jacques Derrida, *Archive Fever: A Freudian Impression*, trans. Eric Prenowitz (Chicago: University of Chicago Press, 1996); John Caputo, *Radical Hermeneutics: Repetition, Deconstruction, and the Hermeneutic Project* (Bloomington: Indiana University Press, 1987), p.139.

8 Francis Quarles, *Divine Fancies: Digested into Epigrams, Meditations, and Observations* (London: 1633), 2:89, quoted in William Engel, *Chiastic Designs in English Literature from Sidney to Shakespeare* (Farbham: Ashgate, 2009), p.41.

9 Edgar Allan Poe, 'The Coliseum', ll. 34–9; Karl Marx, *The Eighteenth Brumaire of Louis Bonaparte*, in Karl Marx and Friedrichs, *Selected Works* (New York: International Publishers, 1968), p.15.

10 'Something in mind': Sigurd Burckhardt, *Shakespearean Meanings* (Princeton: Princeton University Press, 1968), p.5. There is a reverberant critical literature on anachronism in *Julius Caesar*: see Jonas Barish, 'Hats, Clocks and Doublets: Some Shakespearean Anachronisms',

Shakespeare's Universe: Renaissance Ideas and Conventions, ed. John Mucciolo (Aldershot: Scolar Press, 1996), pp.29–36; John Velz, 'The Ancient World in Shakespeare: Authenticity or Anachronism', *Shakespeare Survey*, 31 (1978), 1–12; and Matthew Wikander, 'The Clock in Brutus' Orchard Strikes Again: Anachronism and Achronism in Historical Drama', in *The Delegated Intellect: Emersonian Essays on Literature, Science, and Art in Honor of Don Gifford*, ed. Donald Morse (New York: Peter Lang, 1995), p.149. In his numerological interpretation of the play, Steve Sohmer points out that, by retaining the Julian calendar, 'the Elizabethans were compelled to live, work and worship in Caesar's time', so 'England became a national anachronism': *Shakespeare's Mystery Play: The Opening of the Globe Theatre, 1599* (Manchester: Manchester University Press, 1999), pp.20 and 77.

    Other notorious Shakespearean anachronisms include the mention of Aristotle in *Troilus and Cressida* and [2,2,167]; of 'the Turk' and Nero in *King Lear [3,4,92; 3,6,6]*; and of a pistol in *Pericles* [1,1,166]. In chap.3 of *Stages of History: Shakespeare's English Chronicles* (London: Routledge, 1991), 'Anachronism and Nostalgia', pp.86–145, Phyllis Rackin accounts for such anachronisms as projections by which the imaginary world of the play 'invades the time-frame of the audience' with an effect 'no less striking than that of a character stepping off the stage to invade the audience's physical space' (p.94). By contrast, Thomas Greene interprets anachronism as the invasion of the fictive world by the factual at the intersection between 'the text's revelation of its date and the text's destiny to be dated': 'History and Anachronism', in *The Vulnerable Text: Essays on Renaissance Literature* (New York: Columbia University Press, 1986), p.218. The term 'anachronism' has been dated to 1629 in Herman L. Ebeling, 'The Word "Anachronism",' *Modern Language Notes*, 52 (1937), 121. See also Patricia Elizabeth Easterling, 'Anachronism in Greek Tragedy', *The Journal of Hellenistic Studies*, 105 (1985), 110.

11 'Pious regard': M.W. MacCallum, *Shakespeare's Roman Plays* (London, 1910), p.86; W.G. Sebald, *The Rings of Saturn*, trans. Michael Hulse (London: Vintage, 1992), p.124: Sebald is describing the historical panorama of the Battle of Waterloo.

12 Chiasmus 'announces and projects a signifying difference': William *Chiastic Designs in English Literature from Sidney to Shakespeare* (Farnham: Ashgate, 2009), p.4; Jacques Derrida, *Specters of Marx: The State of the Debt, the Work of Mourning, and the New International*, trans. Peggy Kamuf (London: Routledge, 1994), pp.10–11.

13 Theodor Adorno, *In Search of Wagner*, trans. Rodney Livingstone (London: New Left Books, 1981), p.95.

14 Eric Santner, *The Royal Remains: The People's Two Bodies and the Endgames of Sovereignty* (Chicago: Chicago University Press, 2011), p.246 et passim; Jeffrey Mehlman, *Revolution and Repetition* (Berkeley: University of California Press, 1977).

15 'Theatricalization of history': ibid., p.5; 'The first time as tragedy': Marx, op. cit. (note 9), p.15; Gilles Deleuze, *Difference and Repetition*, trans. Paul Patton (London: Continuum, 2004), p.2.

16 Santner, op. cit. (note 14), pp.xi–xii and 4, quoting Sara Melzer and Kathryn Norberg (eds), 'Introduction', *From the Royal to the Republican Body: Incorporating the Political in Seventeeth- and Eighteenth-Century France* (Berkeley: University of California Press, 1998), pp.10–11. For the semantic and ideological play on 'souls', see Maurice Hunt, 'Cobbling Souls in Shakespeare's *Julius Caesar*', in Beatrice Batson (ed.), *Shakespeare's Christianity: The Protestant and Catholic Poetics of 'Julius Caesar', 'Macbeth', and 'Hamlet'* (Waco, Tex.: Baylor University Press, 2006).

17 Jacques Rancière, *The Philosopher and His Poor*, trans. John Drury, Corinne Oster and Andrew Parker (Durham, NC: Duke University Press, 2004), pp.22–3, 46–7 and 58–69.

18 René Girard, *A Theater of Envy: William Shakespeare* (Oxford: Oxford University Press, 1991), p.223; Marx, op. cit. (note 9), p.16; Marjorie Garber, *Shakespeare's Ghost Writers: Literature as Uncanny Causality* (London: Methuen, 1987), p.56.

19 'Structures of emulation': Coppélia Kahn, *Roman Shakespeare: Warriors, Wounds, Women* (London: Routledge, 1997), pp.88–96. See Ernst Kantorowicz, *The King's Two Bodies: A Study in Medieval Political Theology* (Princeton: Princeton University Press, 1997), pp.427–37. But for a discussion of how Kantorowicz obfuscates the darker side of sovereignty, see also Giorgio Agamben, *Homo Sacer: Sovereign Power and Bare Life*, trans. Daniel Heller-Roazen (Stanford: Stanford University Press, 1998), pp.91–103; and Jacques Rancière, *The Emancipated Spectator*, trans. Gregory Elliott (London: Verso, 2009), pp.112–13.

20 See T.M. Greene, *The Light of Troy: Imitation and Discovery in Renaissance Poetry* (New Haven: Yale University Press, 1982), p.1; Keenan and Davidson, op. cit. (note 3), pp.150–2. For the clashing political symbolism of such statues, see T.J.B. Spencer, 'Shakespeare and the Elizabethan Romans', *Shakespeare Survey*, 10 (1957), 30–1: 'It was the busts of the Twelve Caesars that decorated almost every palace in Europe'; and J.W. Lever, *The Tragedy of State: A Study of Jacobean Drama* (London: Methuen, 1971), p.61: 'Certainly they did; but then one hardly expect to find statues of Brutus in the palaces of Renaissance princes, any more than to see portraits of Lenin in the Pentagon'.

21 'Exercise in the classical ... classicizing decoration': Jean Wilson, *The Shakespeare Legacy: The Material Legacy of Shakespeare's Theatre* (Stroud: Sutton Publishing, 1995), 158.

22 Philippe Lacoue-Labarthe, *Heidegger, Art and Politics*, trans. Chris Turner (Oxford: Blackwell, 1990), p.78.

23 Walter Benjamin, 'Theses on the Philosophy of History', in *Illuminations: Essays and Reflections*, trans. Harry Zohn (London: Jonathan Cape, 1970), pp.258 and 263.

24 'One of the most meta-dramatic': Meredith Anne Skura, *Shakespeare the Actor and the Purposes of Playing* (Chicago: Chicago University Press, 1993), p.184; Santner, op. cit. (note 14), pp.91–2. For anachronicity and Shakespearean 'counter-time' see Jacques Derrida, 'Aphorism Countertime', trans. Nicholas Royle, in *Acts of Literature*, ed. Derek Attridge (London: Routledge, 1992), pp.414–33, esp. pp.423–6, 429 and 432–3

25 Walter Benjamin, *The Origin of German Tragic Drama*, trans. John Osborne (London: Verso, 1998), pp.91 and 177–9.

26 Ibid., pp.207–8.

27 'Of orators and rhetoricians': Anne Barton, '*Julius Caesar* and *Coriolanus*: Shakespeare's Roman World of Words', in *Shakespeare's Craft*, ed. Philip Highfill (Carbondale: Southern Illinois University Press, 1982), p.24; 'language is power': Gayle Greene, '"The Power of Speech / To Stir Men's Blood": The Language of Tragedy in Shakespeare's *Julius Caesar*', *Renaissance Drama*, 11 (1980), 68–9.

28 Walter Benjamin, 'On Language as Such and on the Language of Man', in *Walter Benjamin: Selected Writings, 1913–1926*, eds Marcus Bullock and Michael Jennings (Cambridge, Mass.: Belknap Press, 1996), p.71. Cf. Marion Trousdale, *Shakespeare and the Rhetoricians* (Chapel Hill: University of North Carolina Press, 1982), p.25: for the Renaissance, 'God's word is substance; it is ontologically real. But in man language is accident, not substance'. See also Barbara Baines, '"That every like is not the same": The Vicissitudes of Language in *Julius Caesar*', in Horst Zander (ed.), '*Julius Caesar*': *New Critical Essays* (London: Routledge, 2005), pp.139–53.

29 Frank Kermode, *Shakespeare's Language* (London: Penguin, 2000), pp.87, 92 and 95.

30 A.D. Nuttall, *Shakespeare the Thinker* (New Haven: Yale University Press, 2007), pp.187 and 191.

31 Nicholas Royle, 'The Poet: *Julius Caesar* and the Democracy to Come', *In Memory of Jacques Derrida* (Edinburgh: Edinburgh University Press, 2009), pp.1–20, here pp.8–12, originally published in *The Oxford Literary Review: Angles on Derrida: Jacques Derrida and Anglophone Literature* (2003), 47–51.

32 'Differential vibration ... writing in the voice': Jacques Derrida, 'Dialanguages', in *Points ... Interviews, 1974–1994*, trans. Peggy Kamuf et al. (Stanford: Stanford University Press, 1995), p.140; 'call to come ... multiple voices': 'Psyche: Inventions of the Other', trans. Catherine Porter, in *Reading de Man Reading*, eds Lindsay Waters and Wlad Godzich (Minneapolis: Minnesota University Press, 1989), p.62.

33 Hollander, op. cit. (note 5), p.15.

34 Benjamin, op. cit. (note 25), p.210.

35 Royle's haunting essay is itself a revisiting of Hélène Cixous's dreamlike meditation on *Julius Caesar*, 'What Is It O'Clock? or The Door (We Never Enter)', trans. Catherine MacGillvray, in *Stigmata: Escaping Texts* (London: Routledge, 1998), pp.57–83.

36 For the atemporality inculcated by the humanist cult of Plutarch, see Kahn, op. cit. (note 19), pp.91–2.

37 Cf. Stephen Greenblatt, 'Invisible Bullets', *Shakespearean Negotiations: The Circulation of Social Energy in Renaissance England* (Oxford: Clarendon Press, 1988): 'Royal power is manifested to its subjects as in a theatre': p.65.

38 Christopher Marlowe, 'Lucan's First Book', in *Christopher Marlowe: The Complete Poems and Translations*, ed. Stephen Orgel (London: Penguin, 2007), ll. 481–95, pp.196–7. For the 'theatre state' see Clifford Geertz, 'Centers, Kings, and Charisma: Reflections on the Symbolics of Power', in *Culture and Its Creators: Essays in Honor of Edward Shils*, eds Joseph Ben David and Terry Nichols Clark (Chicago: University of Chicago Press, 1977), p.177; 'Playing for power': Richard Beacham, *Spectacle Entertainments of Early Imperial Rome* (New Haven: Yale University Press, 1999), chap.2.

39 'Imitating the ancient Romans': John Stowe, *Annales* (London: 1631), p.751; 'Made with four pillars', V. von Klarwill (ed.), *The Fugger News Letters* (2nd series, London: 1926), pp.184–5, both quoted in Roy Strong, *The Cult of Elizabeth* (London: Thames and Hudson, 1977), p.120.

40 Gordon Kipling, 'Triumphal Drama: English Civic Pageantry', *Renaissance Drama*, 8 (1977), 37–56, here 38–9; Strong, op. cit. (note 39), pp.122 and 128.

41 Guy Debord, *Society of the Spectacle* (Detroit: Black and Red, 1977), 139–40. Cf. the discussion of sovereignty as a 'mode of temporalization' in Eric Santner, *On Creaturely Life: Rilke, Benjamin, Sebald* (Chicago: University of Chicago Press, 2006), pp.66–9.

42 Jacques Derrida, 'Aphorism Countertime', trans. Nicholas Royle, in *Acts of Literature*, ed. Derek Attridge (London: Routledge, 1992), p.431; Nicholas Royle, op. cit. (note 24), pp.3–6. For the concept of

the 'chronotope' as a spatializing of time, see Clifford Ronan, *'Antike Roman': Power Symbology and the Roman Play in Early Modern England, 1585–1635* (Athens: University of Georgia Press, 1995), pp. 11–35.

43 Walter Benjamin, 'The Work of Art in the Age of Mechanical Reproduction', trans. H. Zohn, *Illuminations* (London: Fontana Collins, 1973), p. 244. See David Norbrook, *Poetry and Politics of the English Renaissance* (rev. ed., Oxford: Oxford University Press, 2001), pp. 4, 13, 64, 132 and 160: 'Spenser's vision had a harsh Machiavellian realism. He had no illusion about the power of art … unless it was aided by political action' (p. 132).

44 Carl Schmitt, *Hamlet or Hecuba: The Intrusion of the Time into the Play*, trans. David Pan and Jennifer Rust (New York: Telos Press, 2009), pp. 24–5, 36–7 and 48. Schmitt's interpretation of anachronism as an intrusion of real historical time into the fictional space of the play contrasts with Phyllis Rackin's belief that anachronism instead serves to obliterate history: 'Breaking the frame of historical representation, anachronisms dissolve the distance between past events and present audience in the eternal present of dramatic performance': in *Stages of History: Shakespeare's English Chronicles* (Ithaca: Cornell University Press, 1990), p. 94. As Royle smartly ripostes, 'Whom does she think she is addressing with these words?': op. cit. (note 24), p. 6.

45 Ibid., p. 44.

46 Ibi., pp. 16–17, 20, 24 and 44.

47 Ibid., p. 49.

48 Jacques Lacan, 'Desire and the Interpretation of Desire in *Hamlet*', trans. James Hulbert, ed. Jacques-Alain Miller, *Yale French Studies*, 55/6 (1977), 11–52, here 50–2.

49 Schmitt, op. cit. (note 44), p. 43.

50 Jonathan Gil Harris, *Untimely Matter in the Time of Shakespeare* (Philadelphia: Pennsylvania University Press, 2009).

51 Santner, op. cit. (note 14), p. 157.

52 Frances Yates, *Astraea: The Imperial Theme in the Sixteenth Century* (London: Routledge & Kegan Paul, 1975).

53 Anthony Brennan, *Onstage and Offstage Worlds in Shakespeare's Plays* (London: Routledge, 1989), p. 272. For an exhaustive consideration of Elizabeth's politics of self-presentation, see Kevin Sharpe, *Selling the Tudor Monarchy* (New Haven: Yale University Press, 2009).

54 Lisa Hopkins, *The Cultural Uses of the Caesars on the English Renaissance Stage* (Aldershot: Ashgate, 2008), p. 41.

55 Schmitt, op. cit. (note 44), pp. 41 and 48.

56 Carl Schmitt, *Römischer Katholizismus und politische Form* (Stuttgart: Klett, 1984), pp. 35–6, quoted and trans. Johannes Türk,

'The Intrusion: Carl Schmitt's Non-Mimetic Logic of Art', *Telos*, 142 (2008), 85.

57 Cixous, op. cit. (note 35), esp. pp.57–63.

58 Schmitt, op. cit. (note 44), p.45.

59 Christopher Marlowe, *Edward II*, 1,173–4, in *Christopher Marlowe: The Complete Plays*, ed. Frank Romany and Robert Lindsey (London: Penguin, 2003), p.406.

60 Jonathan Goldberg, *James I and the Politics of Literature: Jonson, Shakespeare, Donne, and Their Contemporaries* (Stanford: Stanford University Press, 1989), pp.169–70.

61 Andrew Gurr, *Playgoing in Shakespeare's London* (Cambridge: Cambridge University Press, 2004), pp.107–111.

62 Thomas Heywood, *The Actors' Vindication* (London: W.C., 1658), p.20.

63 'Each became Chief Spectator': M.C. Bradbrook, *The Rise of the Common Player* (London: Chatto and Windus, 1962), p.100; 'nothing interrupted': Yates, op. cit. (note 3), p.124.

64 Everard Guilpin, *Skialetheia*, Epigram 53, 'Of Cornelius', quoted in Gurr, op. cit. (note 61), p.147.

65 Ibid., p.136.

66 Thomas Dekker, *The Gull's Hornbook* (1609), chap.6: 'How a Gallant should behave himself in a Play-house', repr. ibid., p.228.

67 'Roman work': diary of Johannes de Witt, quoted in Andrew Gurr, *The Shakespearean Stage, 1576–1642* (Cambridge: Cambridge University Press, 1992), p.132; 'the Colosseum as it stood': John Gleason, 'The Dutch Humanist Origins of the De Witt Drawing of the Swan Theatre', *Shakespeare Quarterly*, 32 (1981), 324–38, here 328.

68 Orrell, op. cit. (note 1), p.51.

69 Gleason, op. cit. (note 67), 335.

70 See in particular Robert Miola, *Shakespeare's Rome* (Cambridge: Cambridge University Press, 1983), pp.98–9.

71 Cf. Yates, op. cit. (note 3), pp.188–9: 'To the cosmic meanings of the ancient theatre, with its plan based on the triangulations of the zodiac, was added the religious meanings of the theatre as a temple ... The Globe was a magical theatre, a cosmic theatre ... designed to [represent] ... the drama of the life of man within the Theatre of the World'; and John Orrell, *The Quest for Shakespeare's Globe* (Cambridge: Cambridge University Press, 1983), p.149: 'A detailed knowledge of the *Architectura* would hardly be necessary to suggest such an intention; the idea was widely illustrated and vivid enough to appeal in its own right. On the other hand, we can be certain that Inigo Jones, in his schematic design for a man-centred anatomy theatre prepared for the Barber-Surgeons Company in 1636, used *ad quadratum*

procedures to develop its oval plan ... an enlightening *post facto* analogue of the Globe.' For Hamlet's 'excellent canopy' as a reference to
the superstructure of the Globe, see also Nevill Coghill, *Shakespeare's
Professional Skills* (Cambridge: Cambridge University Press, 1964),
pp. 8–9; and Harold Jenkins, 'Introduction' and note, *Hamlet: New
Arden* (London: Methuen, 1983), pp. 2–3 and 257.

72 Santner, op. cit. (note 14), p. 4 et passim; quoting the philosopher
    Maurice Merleau-Ponty.
73 'Halitosis of democracy': Brents Stirling, *The Populace in Shakespeare*
    (New York: Columbia University Press, 1949), p. 66; 'how easily the
    space': Richard Halpern, *Shakespeare Among the Moderns* (Ithaca:
    Cornell University Press, 1997), pp. 75 and 79.
74 Santner, op. cit. (note 14), p. 96.
75 Ronan, op. cit. (note 41), pp. 54 and 56.
76 Goldberg, op. cit. (note 60), p. 166.
77 Stephen Orgel, *The Illusion of Power: Political Theater in the English
    Renaissance* (Berkeley: University of California Press, 1975), pp. 7 and
    10–11.
78 Eugene Johnson, 'The Architecture of Italian Theaters Around the
    Time of William Shakespeare', *Shakespeare Studies*, 33 (2005), 42.
79 D.J. Gordon, 'Academicians Build a Theatre and Give a Play: The
    Accademia Olimpica', in *The Renaissance Imagination: Essays and
    Lectures by D.J. Gordon*, ed. Stephen Orgel (Berkeley: University of
    California Press, 1975), p. 265.
80 Bruce R. Smith, *Ancient Scripts and Modern Experience on the
    English Stage, 1500–1700* (Princeton: Princeton University Press,
    1988), p. 61.
81 For statements of such views of the politics of the play, see for example
    Ian Donaldson, '"Misconstruing Everything": *Julius Caesar* and
    Sejanus', in *Shakespeare Performed: Essays in Honour of R.A. Foakes*
    (Newark: University of Delaware Press, 2000), pp. 90–1; and Andrew
    Hadfield, *Shakespeare and Republicanism* (Cambridge: Cambridge
    University Press, 2005), pp. 182–3.
82 D.F. Rowan, 'Inigo Jones and the Teatro Olimpico', *The Elizabethan
    Theatre: VII* (Basingstoke: Macmillan, 1980), 65–81, here 79 and 81.
83 Heywood, op. cit. (note 62), p. 20.
84 For the design of Caesar's *naumachia* in the Campus Martius, see
    Beacham, op. cit. (note 38), pp. 79–80.
85 Pindar, fragment 169: 'The *nomos*, sovereign of all ... Leads with the
    strongest hand, / Justifying the most violent. / I judge this from the
    works of Hercules': quoted in Giorgio Agamben, op. cit. (note 19),
    pp. 30–1: 'What is decisive is that the poet defines the sovereignty of
    the *nomos* by means of a justification of violence'; Heywood, op. cit.

(note 62), pp.20–1. Richard Dutton points out that Heywood had misread Ovid, who in fact stated that *no* flag flew from 'the marble house': see '*Hamlet, An Apology for Actors*, and the Sign of the Globe', *Shakespeare Survey*, 41 (1988), 41.

86 Ronan, op. cit. (note 42), p.69.

87 'In the Baroque manner': Walter Hodges, *The Globe Restored: A Study of the Elizabethan Theatre* (London: Ernest Benn, 1953), p.81. For the unfortunate absolutist associations of Hercules, see Rebecca Olson, '*Hamlet*'s Dramatic Arras', *Word and Image*, 25:2 (2009), 143–53, here 143; and Andrew Gurr and Mariko Ichikawa, *Staging in Shakespeare's Theatres* (Oxford: Oxford University Press, 2000), p.59.

88 Eugene M. Waith, *The Herculean Hero in Marlowe, Chapman, Shakespeare and Dryden* (London: Chatto & Windus, 1962), p.17; Heywood, op. cit. (note 62), p.22.

89 Philip Massinger, *The Roman Actor*, 1,3,139–40, in Philip Edwards and Colin Gibson (eds), *The Plays and Poems of Philip Massinger* (5 vols, Oxford: Clarendon Press, 1976), vol. 3, p.33.

90 Schmitt, op. cit. (note 44), p.35.

91 Dutton, op. cit. (note 85), p.39.

92 Miola, op. cit. (note 70), pp.79 and 99.

93 Santner, op. cit. (note 14), p.4.

94 For the etymological connection between *tumult* and *tumour*, see Giorgio Agamben, *State of Exception*, trans. Kevin Attell (Chicago: Chicago University Press, 2005), p.42.

95 'Inescapable visual focus': John Ronayne, '*Totus Mundus Agit Histrionem*: The Interior Decorative Scheme of the Bankside Globe', in Mulryne and Shewring, op. cit. (note 3), p.124. For the confusion between theatre and circus, see Beacham, op. cit. (note 38), pp.8–9 and 139–42.

96 George Kernodle, *From Art to Theatre: Form and Convention in the Renaissance* (Chicago: Chicago University Press, 1944), p.151; Neil MacGregor, *Shakespeare's Restless World* (London: Allen Lane, 2012), p.257.

97 Andrew Gurr, 'Staging at the Globe', in Mulryne and Shewring, op. cit. (note 3), p.164: 'The stage posts figured in the language and images used in the plays more strongly than we now recognise. Julius Caesar's power over the conspirators invites a gesture to the two posts when we are told that he "doth bestride the narrow world / Like a colossus …".' For the thesis that the Globe possessed three entrances, with a central ceremonial door, see Andrew Gurr and Mariko Ichikawa, 'Stage Doors at the Globe', *Theatre Notebook*, 53:1 (1999), 8–18; and Andrew Gurr, 'Doors at the Globe: The Gulf between the Stage and

Page', *Theatre Notebook*, 55:2 (2001), 59–71; and for the opposing argument, see Tim Fitzpatrick, 'Shakespeare's Exploitation of a Two-Door Stage: *Macbeth*', *Theatre Research International*, 20:3 (1995), 207–303; 'Stage Management, Dramaturgy and Spatial Semiotics in Shakespeare's Dialogue', *Theatre Research International*, 24:1 (1999), 1–24; and 'Playwrights with Foresight: Staging Resources in the Elizabethan Playhouses', *Theatre Notebook*, 56:2 (2002), 85–116; and Tim Fitzpatrick and Wendy Millyard, 'Hangings, Doors and Discoveries: Conflicting Evidence or Problematic Assumptions?', *Theatre Notebook*, 54:1 (2000), 2–23.

98 Wilson, op. cit. (note 21), pp. 84–5. For the classicism of funerary monuments of Gerard Johannsen (Gheerart Janssen), the sculptor of Shakespeare's own tomb, see Timothy Mowl, *Elizabethan and Jacobean Style* (London: Phaidon, 1993), pp. 32–4: 'The Fleming Gerard Johannsen was ... working from his yard in Southwark to deliver imperial Rome ... [He] did not take the capital and the English nobility by storm with a mass of grotesque detail ... but by a rich, colourful assemblage of accurate Roman detail ... All the Roman trappings of death are far more authentic than any Roman trimmings these Earls might have gathered around them when they were alive.'

99 For tiring-house decorations as foci of anxiety about court interference, see Olson, op. cit. (note 87), 145.

100 'Cheerful muddle': Ronayne, op. cit. (note 95), p. 126; Alastair Fowler, *Triumphal Forms: Structural Patterns in Elizabethan Poetry* (Cambridge: Cambridge University Press, 1970), p. 28. For political ambivalence towards the triumphal arch, see also Marina Dmitrieva-Einhorn, 'Ephemeral Ceremonial Architecture in Prague, Vienna and Cracow in the Sixteenth and Early Seventeenth Centuries', in J.R, Mulryne and Elizabeth Goldring (eds), *Court Festivals of the European Renaissance: Art, Politics and Performance* (Aldershot: Ashgate, 2002), pp. 363 and 383.

101 Mowl, op. cit. (note 98), pp. 149–50: 'Much time and money has been spent scouring the South Bank for the foundations of Shakespeare's Globe Theatre, when up to twelve authentic Elizabethan and Jacobean theatres survive intact with their backdrops in great houses like Hatfield' (p. 146); and 'Too many literary critics have staked their reputations on the idea that Shakespeare was a dramatic minimalist for these Great Halls and their screens to be accepted for what they really were, the ideal theatres of their day ... Far more could be achieved indoors with complex roof beams to suspend ropes and pulleys and a gallery with a high parapet over the stage, than could be contrived in open-air theatres like the Globe' (p. 150).

102 Fowler, op. cit. (note 100), p.27. For the question of imagery and English political reality, see Alan Sinfield, *Faultlines: Cultural Materialism and the Politics of Dissident Reading* (Oxford: Oxford University Press, 1992), pp.80–5.

103 Margaret McGowan, 'The Renaissance Triumph and Its Classical Heritage', in Mulryne and Goldring, op. cit. (note 100), pp.31 and 37.

104 Nick Myers, 'Hercule Gaulois, Great Britain's Solomon – Myths of Persuasion, Styles of Authority', in *The Stuart Courts*, ed. Eveline Cruickshanks (Stroud: Sutton Publishing, 2000), p.30.

105 George Kernodle, 'The Mannerist Stage of Comic Detachment', in *The Elizabethan Theatre, III*, ed. David Galloway (Waterloo: University of Waterloo, 1973), p.121.

106 Vaughan Hart, *Inigo Jones: The Architect of Kings* (New Hanen: Yale University Press, 2011), pp.57 and 127.

107 'The gorgeous playing place': John Stockwood, sermon preached in 1578, quoted in E.K. Chambers, *The Elizabethan Stage* (4 vols, Oxford: Oxford University Press, 1923), vol. 4, pp.199–200.

108 Smith, op. cit. (note 80), p.21.

109 Orrell, op. cit. (note 71), pp.152–5. Although Hollar's *View* depicts the second Globe, as rebuilt in 1613, Orrell persuasively argues that the dimensions of the tiring-house were identical in the 1599 building: p.122. See also Andrew Gurr, 'The Playhouses: Archaeology and After', *Shakespeare*, 7 (2011), 405–6.

110 Wilson, op. cit. (note 21), p.79.

111 Repr. ibid., p.75.

112 Hodges, op. cit. (note 87), pp.31–2.

113 Jerry Brotton, 'Ways of Seeing in *Hamlet*', in '*Hamlet*': *New Critical Essays*, ed. Arthur Kinney (London: Routledge, 2002), p.170.

114 Gordon McMullan, *The Politics of Unease in the Plays of John Fletcher* (Amherst: University of Massachusetts Press, 1994), pp.95–6.

115 Miola, op. cit. (note 70), pp.112–13.

116 David Bevington, *This Wide and Universal Theater: Shakespeare in Performance Then and Now* (Chicago: Chicago University Press, 2007), p.26.

117 Robert Weimann, *Shakespeare and the Popular Tradition in the Theater: Studies in the Social Dimension of Dramatic Form and Function* (Baltimore: Johns Hopkins University Press, 1978), p.246 et passim.

118 Anne Barton (Righter), *Shakespeare and the Idea of the Play* (London: Chatto & Windus, 1962), p.157.

119 'Everyone a spectator': M.C. Bradbrook, *The Rise of the Common Player* (London: Chatto and Windus, 1962), p.100; 'nothing

interrupted': Yates, op. cit. (note 3), p.124; Orrell, op. cit. (note 71), p.140.

120 For the supposedly perfect acoustic of the Globe as a realization of the Neo-Platonist idea of the 'proportionate structure of the cosmos', see Orrell, ibid.

121 See Naomi Liebler, *Shakespeare's Festive Tragedy: The Ritual Foundations of Genre* (London: Routledge, 1995), pp.88–9.

122 Hadfield, op. cit. (note 81), p.167. Cf. Charles Wells, *The Wide Arch: Roman Value in Shakespeare* (Bristol: Bristol Classical Press, 1993), p.15; Geoffrey Miles, *Shakespeare and the Constant Romans* (Oxford: Clarendon Press, 1996), pp.1–2.

123 Mark Robson, 'Looking with Ears, Hearing with Eyes: Shakespeare and the Ear of the Early Modern', *Early Modern Literary Studies*, 7:1 (2001). See also Reina Green, 'Poisoned Ears and Parental Advice in *Hamlet*', *Early Modern Literary Studies*, 11:3 (2006). For the more familiar argument that Shakespeare endorsed the Protestant promotion of performed speech in place of visual distraction, see Grace Tiffany, '*Hamlet* and Protestant Aural Theater', in Batson, op. cit. (note 16).

124 Robert Weimann, 'Mimesis in *Hamlet*', in Patricia Parker and Geoffrey Hartman (eds), *Shakespeare and the Question of Theory* (London: Routledge, 1991), p.276.

125 Søren Kierkegaard, *Fear and Trembling*, trans. John Minford (London: Penguin, 2005); Santner, op. cit. (note 13), pp.192–3

126 Nicholas Royle, 'Mole', in *The Uncanny* (Manchester: Manchester University Press, 2003), pp.241–55, here p.251.

127 Santner, op. cit. (note 14), p.224.

128 Joseph Candido, 'Time ... Come Round', in Zander, op. cit. (note 28), pp.130–1.

129 Gurr, op. cit. (note 61), p.182; C. Walter Hodges, *The Globe Restored: A Study of the Elizabethan Theatre* (London: Ernest Benn, 1953), pp.30–1.

130 Thomas Hobbes, *The Elements of Law, Natural and Politic*, ed. J.C.A. Gaskin (Oxford: Oxford University Press, 1999), p.120; Santner, op. cit. (note 14), p.92, quoting T.J. Clark, *Farewell to an Idea: Episodes in the History of Modernism* (New Haven: Yale University Press, 1999), p.47.

131 Michael Neill, '"Exeunt with a Dead March": Funeral Pageantry on the Shakespearean Stage', in David Bergeron (ed.), *Pageantry in the Shakespearean Theater* (Athens: University of Georgia Press, 1985), pp.169–70.

132 Agamben, op. cit. (note 94), p.86.

133 Suetonius, *Life of Caesar*, xxx, translated and quoted in Nuttall, op.

cit. (note 30), p.190; Carl Schmitt, *Political Theology: Four Chapters on the Concept of Sovereignty*, trans. George Schwab (Chicago: Chicago University Press, 2005), p.36.

134 Girard, op. cit. (note 18), pp.249–53.

135 Jonathan Haynes, *The Social Relations of Jonson's Theater* (Cambridge: Cambridge University Press, 1992), p.71. For 'the emphasis on learning or judgement in prologues and the like after 1600', see in particular Leo Salingar, 'Jacobean Playwrights and "Judicious" Spectators', in *British Academy Shakespeare Lectures, 1980–89*, ed. E.A.J. Honigmann (Oxford: Oxford University Press, 1993), pp.231–53, here p.234.

136 Bruce Smith, *The Acoustic World of Early Modern England: Attending to the O-Factor* (Chicago: Chicago University Press, 1999), pp.213–14.

137 Ibid., pp.224–5.

138 Bevington, op. cit. (note 116), p.24.

139 Halpern, op. cit. (note 73), p.63.

140 P. Jeffrey Ford, 'Bloody Spectacle in Shakespeare's Roman Plays: The Politics and Aesthetics of Violence', *Iowa State Journal of Research*, 54 (1980), 21–46, here 24 and 48.

141 Robert Weimann, *Author's Pen and Actor's Voice: Playing and Writing in Shakespeare's Theatre* (Cambridge: Cambridge University Press, 2000), p.176.

142 'Something new': Stephen Greenblatt, *Will in the World: How Shakespeare Became Shakespeare* (London: Jonathan Cape, 2004), p.301; see also James Shapiro, *1599: A Year in the Life of William Shakespeare* (London: Faber & Faber, 2005), p.152; 'to acknowledge': Katrin Trüstedt, 'Hecuba against Hamlet: Carl Schmitt, Political Theology, and the Stake of Modern Tragedy', *Telos*, 153 (2010), 109.

143 Agamben, op. cit. (note 94), p.50.

144 Girard, op. cit. (note 18), pp.273–4.

145 'Romanized play': Ronan, op. cit. (note 42), p.162; and see Hopkins, op. cit. (note 29), p.40.

146 Girard, op. cit. (note 18), p.271.

147 Schmitt, op. cit. (note 44), p.24.

148 Elaine Scarry, *The Body in Pain: The Making and Unmaking of the World* (Oxford: Oxford University Press, 1985), p.14.

149 See Oscar Lee Brownstein, 'Why Didn't Burbage Lease the Beargarden? A Conjecture in Comparative Architecture', in Herbert Berry (ed.), *The First Public Playhouse* (Montreal: McGill-Queen's University Press, 1979), pp.81–96; and Orrell, op. cit. (note 1).

150 Andreas Höfele, *Stage, Stake, and Scaffold: Humans and Animals*

in Shakespeare's Theatre (Oxford: Oxford University Press, 2011), pp. 3–12, here p. 6.

151 Fred Botting and Scott Wilson, *Bataille* (Basingstoke: Palgrave, 2001), pp. 115–16.

152 Agamben, op. cit. (note 19), p. 105; 'the very heart': Agamben, op. cit. (note 94), p. 72. For the relations of the play to the Lupercalia, see Richard Wilson, *Shakespeare in French Theory: King of Shadows* (London: Routledge, 2007), pp. 178–85.

153 Agamben, op. cit. (note 19), p. 106.

154 Georges Dumézil, *Mitra-Varuna: An Essay on Two Indo-European Representations of Sovereignty*, trans. Derek Coltman (New York: Zone Books, 1988), pp. 27–37, here p. 28.

155 Francis Barker, *The Culture of Violence: Essays on Tragedy and History* (Manchester: Manchester University Press, 1993), p. 191.

156 'Circle in which the audience': Skura, op. cit. (note 24), p. 8: for animal-baiting imagery in *Julius Caesar*, see pp. 133, 186 and 210–11; 'founding form': Terence Hawkes, 'Harry Hunks, Superstar', in Terence Hawkes (ed.), *Shakespeare in the Present* (London: Routledge, 2002), p. 90.

157 Schmitt, op. cit. (note 44), p. 45.

158 'To feast on carnage': Dio Cassius, quoted Beacham, op. cit. (note 37), p. 189; 'While happily watching': Seneca, quoted ibid., p. 195.

159 Goldberg, op. cit. (note 60), p. 167.

160 'You will live as it were in a theatre': Dio Cassius, quoted Beacham, op. cit. (note 37), p. ix.

161 Goldberg, op. cit. (note 60), pp. 165 and 167–8.

162 John Drakakis, '"Fashion it thus": *Julius Caesar* and the Politics of Theatrical Representation', in Richard Wilson (ed.), *'Julius Caesar': A New Casebook* (Basingstoke: Palgrave, 2002), p. 87.

163 Skura, op. cit. (note 24), p. 185.

164 Manfred Pfister, *The Theory and Analysis of Drama*, trans. John Halliday (Cambridge: Cambridge University Press, 1988), p. 75; Douglas Bruster, *Quoting Shakespeare: Form and Culture in Early Modern Drama* (Lincoln: University of Nebraska Press, 2000), p. 115.

165 'A statue of himself': Skura, op. cit. (note 24), p. 184.

166 Ibid., p. 65.

167 See Richard Wilson, 'A Brute Part: *Julius Caesar* and the Rites of Violence', *Cahiers Elisabethains*, 50 (1996), 19–32.

168 'Political struggle occurs': Gail Kern Paster, '"In the spirit of men there is no blood": Blood as Trope of Gender in *Julius Caesar*', in Wilson, op. cit. (note 162); 'Whenever he killed a calf': John Aubrey, *Brief Lives*, ed. Oliver Lawson Dick (London: Secker & Warburg, 1949), p. 275.

169 'Behind the cloth': E.K. Chambers, *William Shakespeare* (2 vols, Oxford: Clarendon Press, 1930), vol. 1, p. 17, n. 4; Robert Weimann, *Shakespeare and the Popular Tradition in the Theater: Studies in the Social Dimension of Dramatic Form and Function* (Baltimore: Johns Hopkins University Press, 1978), pp. 67–8.

170 Robert Greene, *Francesco's Fortunes* (London: 1590), quoted in Park Honan, *Shakespeare: A Life* (Oxford: Oxford University Press, 1998), p. 157; *Mamillia* (London: 1583), quoted in *Writing Robert Greene: Essays on England's First Notorious Professional Writer*, ed. Kirk Melnikoff and Edward Gieskes (Farnham: Ashgate, 2008), p. 7.

171 Richard Beacham, *The Roman Theatre and Its Audience* (London: Routledge, 1995), pp. 155 and 245, n. 3.

172 W. Beare, *The Roman Stage* (London: Methuen, 1950), pp. 192–3.

173 Macrobius, *The Saturnalia*, trans. P.V. Davies (London: Heinemann 1969), p. 233.

174 'Visor effect': Jacques Derrida, *Specters of Marx: The State of the Debt, the Work of Mourning, and the New International*, trans. Peggy Kamuf (London: Routledge, 1994), p. 7.

175 Barton, op. cit. (note 118), pp. 140–1 and 156.

176 Hadfield, op. cit. (note 81), p. 171.

177 Cicero, *Brutus*, trans. H.H. Hubbell (Cambridge, Mass.: Harvard University Press, 1959), p. 253; *De Oratore*, trans. H. Rackham (Cambridge, Mass.: Harvard University Press, 1942), p. 177.

178 For Caesar as a failed old actor, see Skura, op. cit. (note 24), pp. 184–5.

179 Christian Jouhard, 'Power and Literature: The Terms of the Exchange 1624–42', in Richard Burt (ed.), *The Administration of Aesthetics: Censorship, Political Criticism, and the Public Sphere* (Minneapolis: University of Minnesota Press, 1994), pp. 73–4.

180 Bruce R. Smith, *Ancient Scripts and Modern Experience on the English Stage, 1500–1700* (Princeton: Pinceton University Press, 1988), p. 22.

181 Beacham, op. cit. (note 38), pp. 156 and 162.

182 Ibid.

183 Ibid., p. 157.

184 Halpern, op. cit. (note 73), p. 75.

185 Santner, op. cit. (note 14), p. 93.

186 Miola, op. cit. (note 70), p. 78.

187 Kahn, op. cit. (note 19), p. 80.

188 Theodor Adorno, *Against Epistemology: A Metacritique*, trans. Willis Domingo (Oxford: Basil Blackwell, 1982), p. 14.

189 Christopher, *Massacre at Paris*, 21,65/86, in Marlowe, op. cit. (note 59), p. 550.

190 Sinfield, op. cit. (note 102), pp. 25–7.

191 Gary Taylor, 'Bardicide,' in Wilson, op. cit. (note 162), p.198.

192 Gary Schmidgall, *Shakespeare and the Poet's Life* (Lexington: University of Kentucky Press, 1990), pp.130 and 149.

193 Taylor, op. cit. (note 191), pp.188–209, esp. pp.194–5.

194 Girard, op. cit. (note 18), p.240.

195 Taylor, op. cit. (note 191), pp.190–1.

196 Thomas Betteridge, *Shakespearean Fantasy and Politics* (Hatfield: University of Hertfordshire Press, 2005), pp.119–20.

197 'Disgust with the stage': Barton, op. cit. (note 118), p.155; Paul Yachnin, *Stage-Wrights: Shakespeare, Jonson, Middleton, and the Making of Theatrical Value* (Philadelphia: University of Pennsylvania Press, 1997), pp.77–9.

198 John Weever, *The Mirror of Martyrs, or the Life and Death of Sir John Oldcastle* (1601), repr. E.K. Chambers, *William Shakespeare* (2 vols, Oxford: Clarendon Press, 1930), vol. 2, p.199.

199 'Crowds are cruel': Taylor, op. cit. (note 191), p.192.

200 David Daniell, note to 3,1,80 ('Some to the common pulpits'), in William Shakespeare, *The New Arden Shakespeare: 'Julius Caesar'* (London: Thomson Learning, 1998), p.238.

201 Peter McCullough, *Sermons at Court: Politics and Religion in Elizabethan and Jacobean England* (Cambridge: Cambridge University Press, 1998), pp.1, 35 and 42.

202 'Porch-like projection': Hodges, op. cit. (note 87) p.60; 'removable pulpits': John Nichols, *The Progresses and Public Processions of Queen Elizabeth* (3 vols, London: 1823), vol. 2, p.413.

203 'Red velvet': Lupold von Wedel, 'A Journey Through England and Scotland in the Years 1584 and 1585', ed. and trans. Gottfried von Bulow, *Transactions of the Royal Historical Society*, New Series, 9 (1895), 262.

204 Millar MacLure, *The Paul's Cross Sermons, 1534–1642* (Toronto: Toronto University Press. 1958), p.168.

205 Peter Heylyn, *Cyprianus Anglicus* (1668), p.253, quoted in McCullough, op. cit. (note 201), p.59.

206 Ibid., pp.34, 42, 46 and 93.

207 Arnold Hunt, 'Tuning the Pulpits: The Religious Context of the Essex Revolt', in Lori Anne Ferrell and Peter McCullough (eds), *The English Sermon Revised: Religion, Literature and History, 1600–1750* (Manchester: Manchester University Press, 2000), p.90.

208 Gil Harris, op. cit. (note 50); Schmitt, op. cit. (note 44), p.20.

209 McCullough, op. cit. (note 201), p.102, quoting Richard Eedes, *Six Learned and Godly Sermons: Preached some of Them before the King's Majestie, some before Queenn Elizabeth* (London, 1604); 'under colour of hearing Sermons': William Camden, *The Historie of*

the Life and Reigne of ... *Queen Elizabeth* (London, 1630), quoted in Hunt, (note 207), p. 95.

210 Hunt, ibid., quoting 'The answeres or examination of John Richardson': Lambeth Palace Library, MS 2004 (Fairhurst papers), fol. 9.

211 Shapiro, op. cit. (note 142), pp. 85, 88–9 and 96. The text of the epilogue is produced in William Shakespeare, *As You Like It*, ed. Juliet Dusinberre (London: Arden Shakespeare / Thomson, 2006), pp. 351–2.

212 'Republican moment': Hadfield, op. cit. (note 81), pp. 167 et passim.

213 Jürgen Habermas, *The Structural Transformation of the Public Sphere*, trans. Thomas Burger (Cambridge: Polity Press, 1992), p. 13.

214 Friedrich Nietzsche, *The Gay Science*, trans. Walter Kaufmann (New York: Vintage Books, 1974), pp. 150–1.

215 Schmitt, op. cit. (note 44), pp. 43–4: 'intrusions ... are shadows ... around which the play timidly maneuvers'.

216 Hollander, op. cit. (note 5), p. 147.

4

Denmark's a prison

Hamlet *and the rules of art*

'It may be,' says a tall gentleman, who hurries on, carrying the light, 'that His Majesty, King Christian, will command you to play for him tonight. He is not well and his physicians have prescribed music. Therefore, members of the royal orchestra must be ready to perform at all times, day and night. I thought it best to advise you of this straight away.'

Peter Claire's feelings of dismay increase. He begins to curse himself, to berate his own ambition for bringing him here to Denmark, for taking him so far from the places and people he had loved. He is at the end of his journey and yet he feels lost. Within this arrival some terrifying departure lies concealed.[1]

So runs the world away

In Rose Tremain's *Music and Silence* the lamp which leads the young English musician Peter Claire through Denmark's royal palace makes his shadow expand 'upwards for a few seconds towards the ceiling before being swallowed by darkness'. This shadow is a symbol for the miraculous yet menacing scenario of the novel, which is the opportunity that opened in the 1600s for artists and performers to inflate their profits and prestige by taking salaried posts in Europe's new absolutist states. *Music and Silence* is inspired, in fact, by the well-documented Danish career of the real composer John Dowland. Yet directly Peter Claire is presented to his employer, King Christian IV warns him to beware the precedent: 'I suppose you know we had your Mr Dowland here … We would sit and blub, and Master Dowland would kill us with his furious look. I told my mother to take him to one side and say: "Dowland, this will not do and cannot be tolerated," but he told her music can only be born of fury and fire.' In this retelling of the legend of Saul and David, we infer, majesty meets its match in the rival monarchy of art. So the king sits enthralled, biting his elflock in emotion, as the lutenist plays Dowland's *Lachrymae*; and 'that enigma Dowland' haunts the novel, which turns on Christian's pawn of his 'angel' Claire to his nephew Charles I for £100,000.[2] This idea was doubtless cued by the rumour that Dowland was similarly exchanged, when Christian, 'coming over into England, requested him' of his brother-in-law King James, 'who *unwillingly willing* parted with him'.[3] But behind that story there also stands the new concept that the English musician personified, of the absolute sovereignty of an art beyond any such price.

Dowland would confound political absolutism with the opposing absolutism of art. In the novel Claire escapes the haunted castle, however, by eloping to Norfolk with a maid. And if this happy ending looks far-fetched that may be because such an escape from power defies absolutism's own rules of art, which are imposed with systematic callousness in Christian's *Vinterstue*, the magnificent Winter Room in which his throne is installed, amidst Rubens-like paintings depicting Denmark as Neptune's empire, above the cellar where his court orchestra sits shivering in the dark to create an illusion of the music of the gods. As Louis Marin explained in *Portrait of the King*, in the palace of the Sun King 'the Baroque effect' that sees everything 'the king ever does, says, and thinks', works only because 'something is hidden that luminous vision conceals in order to unfold itself': the 'nocturnal face of the royal sun', which is that of the artist '*suppressing himself*' in what he creates by negating his presence in the production of the spectacular personalized 'king-effect' of royal visibility.[4] Marin is here writing about Louis XIV and Racine; but his account of the absolutist 'king machine', which impresses by *repressing* its own means of production, might just as well have been describing the mechanical music-making at the 'fairytale' palace of King Christian IV:

> The position of the castle, surrounded by landscaped gardens and raised on miniature battlements with ornamental draw-bridges, gives it the delicate dreamlike character of a belvedere. Inside, Christian IV's arrangement of pipes, with ducts and vents which could be opened or closed apparently without human agency to let the music sound from orchestras hidden in cellars below, underscores the magical playfulness of the building. The architecture of the exterior, consisting of fantastic contours and clusters of turrets, lends the castle

a visionary atmosphere, which is redolent of the fanciful fairytale palaces Inigo Jones designed for the scenery of the English court masques.[5]

In 1603 Danish suzerainty over Hamburg was celebrated in festivities where the manic Christian did indeed dazzle as a Sun King. As Peter Burke notes, many of the innovations that featured in the fabrication of Louis XIV as the ultimate Baroque monarch were deployed in the Danish royal repertoire when, starting at his 1596 coronation, for which he designed his own crown, the 'engineer king' recruited an army of painters, poets and performers to legitimate his political theology of divine right. Thus, 'the number of portraits of Christian was remarkable for the time', but 'the king also commissioned tapestries representing his life as Louis was to do. In addition, over a hundred engraved portraits of Christian IV survive', and the medals struck for his wars prefigured the 'Eucharistic' rites of Versailles.[6] 'The power of the State was his central idea. The State was to lead, create and organise': and historians confirm that, long before Danish absolutism was officially proclaimed in 1660, Christian was recruiting designers like Jones to create a ceremonial type of court with classical façades, gilt furniture, allegorical ballets and orchestral music, so that by the 1600s Elsinore was already a model of the Baroque 'theatre state', with 'staff numerous and strictly organised, etiquette complex and regulated,' and 'an expensive festival culture of daylong processions, triumphs, and masquerades'.[7] With the king himself dancing in masques, 'Danish court culture was brilliant during the reign of Christian', we are reminded; and 'Copenhagen was a thriving artistic centre that provided enduring impetus to the courts of Protestant Europe'.[8] Thus at a single Dutch auction in 1621 Christian bought 350 pictures for a stupendous 50,000 guilders. With such distortion of the market, the advent of this Oldenburg cultural juggernaut truly opened a new horizon in the history of art. For as Paul Douglas-Lockhurst comments in the latest study, this new type of personal monarchy was effectively *made of money*:

> As a patron of the arts, Christian IV equalled or surpassed most of his European contemporaries. His success at enticing foreign painters and musicians to his court had less to do with the attraction of Copenhagen itself, however, than with the abandon with which he spent his personal funds. Christian bought talent, pure and simple.[9]

'Christian IV was well aware of the importance of music in creating an appropriate aura' for the '*rex splendens*', writes Douglas-Lockhurst, and at its peak 'the Danish "music royal" numbered some 76 singers, trumpeters, and other instrumentalists'.[10] So *Music and Silence* is right to present Dowland's encounter with the ruler whose talent-spotters scoured Europe as some terrifying new intrusion into seventeenth-century art. Yet what is so striking about the stand-off between the Scandinavian Maecenas and the English musician is how this prodigious new purchasing power produced such meagre returns. Thus the documents record that the annuity of 500 daler paid Dowland on appointment as royal lutenist in 1598 equalled an admiral's; but by 1600 the Treasury was advancing 600 daler to cover debts. Then in June 1601 we read that 'Johannes Dowland received 250 daler which is pay for six months. His Majesty graciously advanced him the money *which he will have to work for*'. The reason for this caveat is stressed in July 1603 when the English musician is paid his arrears, 'provided his Majesty will pay him the money, as he has been in England on his own commitments and much longer than his Majesty most graciously allowed him to be'. 'From now on the situation becomes desperate', Dowland's accounts reveal, as the salary is either forwarded or docked until efforts to get satisfaction end on 10 March 1606, with six days' pay and 32 daler for lute strings, as 'he has been discharged', we read: 'And he has had his agreed pay according to the appointment, which has now been terminated'.[11] Evidently, there was something literally unaccountable about English performers at the court of Denmark that makes the Controller's minute for 24 September 1602 look all too representative:

> As we want the English lutenist and dancer dismissed, we ask you to give them the pay which Dowland promised them in England; but you should keep the harp for which we paid. And as we have learnt that the English musicians who ran away have left an instrument and a viol de gamba in Elsinore, we ask you to appropriate them too if they are still there, so that we may have some compensation for the money they ran away with.[12]

Dowland's lute would come to occupy pride of place in the 1988 Council of Europe exhibition, 'Christian IV and Europe'.[13] When he had Hamlet reach for a symbol of resistance to the King of Denmark, Shakespeare therefore surely knew what he was doing by making it a musical instrument: 'O, the recorder. Let me see ... Why, look you now, how unworthily a thing you make of me! You would play upon me, you would seem to know my stops, you would pluck out the heart of my mystery, you would sound me from the lowest note to the top of my compass, and there is much music, excellent voice in this little organ, yet cannot you make it speak' [*Hamlet*, *3,2,334–9*]. Memoranda detailing the bureaucratic nightmare of the English players who fled Elsinore so hastily they left their instruments behind in fact offer an exact contemporary context for the work, above all others, which questions the service of art to power, and does so by staging, in this very location, Dowland's artistic refusal: "Sblood, do you think I am easier to be played upon than a pipe? Call me what instrument you will, though you can fret me, you cannot play upon me' [*339–1*]. Despite his Catholicism, we know that Dowland spied for English intelligence on Jesuit plots. But whatever political role he had in this shadowy world of espionage and entertainment, between the king and the comedians we can also see here the creator clearing his own *aesthetic* space. For what these archives expose is the mismatch between absolute monarchy and an equally absolute artist, the English composer's refusal to submit his introverted 'fury and fire' to the Baroque *mise-en-scène*. In *Hamlet*, too, the protagonist will pipe his own tune after the 'cry of players' [*255*] have fled the stage. For Shakespeare's tragedy of music and silence also figures the escape from the 'many confines, wards, and dungeons' of Denmark [*2,2,241–2*] as a pre-condition for an autonomous art:

> Ah ha! Come, some music, come, the recorders.
> For if the king like not the comedy,
> Why, then, he likes it not, pardie.
>
> [*3,2,268–70*]

How chances it they travel?

'So runs the world away' [*252*]: with its constant backward glances to the Globe theatre, *Hamlet* is a story like that of Dowland, of the flight from absolute power. So it cannot be chance that Shakespeare set his great drama of refusal at the court which in 1601 constituted the most organized cultural space in northern Europe, a showcase for what Burke calls 'the state bureaucratisation of art'; nor that its premise should be non-cooperation with the 'king effect' of just such a solar regime: 'How is it that the clouds still hang on you? ... Not so, my lord, I am too much i'th'sun' [1,2,66].[14] As Robert Weimann remarks, the culture shock that drives *Hamlet* is the discrepancy between the 'expectancy' of the star's performance in a spectacular state, as 'The courtier's, soldier's, scholar's eye, tongue, sword ... The glass of fashion and the mould of form', and the dissonant 'music' he perversely creates: 'Like sweet bells jangled out of tune, and harsh' [3,1,150–7].[15] Hamlet's lecture that 'the purpose of playing' is to hold 'the mirror up to nature' [3,2,20] is thus a manifesto for the neoclassical aesthetic which idealized the picture-frame of the court masques. Yet his carnivalesque 'antic disposition' [2,1,173] clashes so dementedly with his austere advice to the actors to subdue personality in the 'temperance', 'smoothness' and 'discretion' of a courtly theatre [3,2,7–15] that it is as if Hamlet's unhinged character is *itself* composed from the culture clash that he describes: ''tis most sweet / When in one line two crafts directly meet' [3,4,185:9]. The discontinuity between Hamlet's professed distaste for 'inexplicable dumb shows' and the 'miching mal echo' or pantomime he actually produces [3,2,10] is the tension, therefore, that runs throughout the text, as if this drama was deliberately designed to confound continental court ceremony with the lesemajesty of the English public playhouse, where, so we are reminded, 'the men are as mad as he' [5,1,142]. As Weimann writes:

> [T]he gap between Renaissance precept and performance practice is quite deliberately used ... It is no exaggeration to say that the element of contrariety pervasively informs what is most enigmatic, but highly effective, in the characterization of Hamlet. As perhaps nowhere else in Shakespeare's plays, the difference between a High Renaissance figuration and an antic practice is infused, not only into the double image of a protagonist, but into the tragic theme of an entire play.[16]

Despite his disgust at 'a robustious, periwig-pated fellow' [3,2,8], as soon as the actors depart Hamlet himself reverts to the manic singing, jigging and clowning he must have learned as a boy on the back of the court jester Yorick. So our interpretative question becomes the one that vexes King Claudius: 'And can you by no drift of circumstance / Get from him why he puts on this confusion, / Grating so harshly all his days of quiet / With turbulent and dangerous lunacy?' [3,1,1–4]. Thus, in the 'crafty madness' [8] of this version of the weak power of the legendary trickster – David, Brutus, Emperor Claudius or Amleth – it seems Shakespeare was metadramatizing his own evasion of absolutism's neoclassical aesthetic, with its imperious demand for decorum, reason, transparency and order, and his response to the advent of Stuart empire in the age-old strategy: 'I must be idle' [3,2,83]. And here the setting of this play was crucial to its cultural politics. For at the time of *Hamlet* it might have appeared that the most decisive event for the future of English culture had taken place in Oslo on 23 November 1589, when James VI of Scotland married Anne, the sister of the boy-king Christian, in St Hallvard's Cathedral. As Leeds Barroll points out in his biography of Anne, the impact of James's Oldenburg marriage has been largely ignored by Shakespeareans; but Denmark's rule extended north over all Norway; east over provinces in modern Sweden and the Baltic islands of Bornholm and Gotland; northeast over Iceland, Greenland, the Faeroes and Orkney; and south to the German duchies of Schleswig and Holstein. So, 'as one of the largest political entities on the early modern continent', the Danish Crown 'wielded tremendous international influence', and by the end of the sixteenth century its tolls on Baltic shipping and duties on Norwegian timber put the Danish monarchy among Europe's richest.[17]

Economists define this unstable maritime Oldenburg confederation, with its ruinous consumption of resources on arms, ships and fortifications, as the first fiscal-military empire and the epitome, therefore, of the illusoriness of the Baroque. Like the fairytale palaces of the self-advancing 'Builder King', Denmark appeared rich and powerful, but 'its wealth lay on the surface; its foundations were not solid', and its pretensions would be exposed by Christian's catastrophic interference in the Thirty Years War.[18] Yet as a young man Christian enjoyed a reputation as 'the wealthiest king in Christendom', with a personal fortune of one and a half million daler;[19] and the Oldenburgs could afford to cede James Orkney as Anne's dowry. So no wonder that in a letter to 'The People of Scotland' written as he sailed for Norway ('Leander-like' according to one his poems, but in a ship full of 'minions of his stable and bedchamber') James explained the reasons for his match 'were that I was alone, without father, mother, brother or sister, king of this realm and heir apparent of England ... my nakedness made me weak and my enemies stark'.[20] Nor that, having landed safely with Anne and her six siblings, he stayed six months, celebrating Christmas in Oslo before sleighing to Elsinore, where after a second Lutheran wedding he was edified with plays in Danish and Latin about Dido and Aeneas, and then attending the marriage on 19 April of Princess Elizabeth to the Duke of Brunswick. His Oldenburg relations would indeed make James feel strong, for Anne's other sisters would marry the Duke of Holstein and the Elector of Saxony. But for the dramatist, the meaning of these wintry northern nuptials must have been in the 'cracked gold' from those plays staged at Elsinore, when James's Danish marriage promised that 'He that plays the King shall be welcome' [2,2,308] in the palace as much as the king:

> Welcome good friends. – O my old friend! Thy face is valanced since I saw thee last. Com'st thou to beard me in Denmark? – What, my young lady and mistress. By'r Lady, your Ladyship is nearer heaven than when I saw you last by the altitude of a chopine. Pray God your voice, like a piece of uncurrent gold, be not cracked within the ring. – Masters, you are welcome all. [408–12]

Critics have lately become aware of how warily *Hamlet* reacts to an absolutism that could elevate a callow boy like Christian nearer to god 'by the altitude of a chopine' through its political theology that 'There's such divinity doth hedge a king' [4,5,120]. Yet considering the impending impact on Shakespeare's own creative project, it is astonishing how little the Oldenburg programme figures in their accounts. In Margreta de Grazia's 2007 monograph, setting out to correct 'a 200-year old tradition' of de-historicizing the play, the reigning King of Denmark is mentioned, for instance, not once.[21] Yet Hamlet's orders to Polonius to receive the actors 'after your own honour and dignity' – 'Good my lord, will you see the players well bestowed? Do you hear? – let them be well used' – register a golden opportunity for English performers, when the Oldenburg cultural network promised to lift 'the tragedians of the city' [2,2,315] out of the bear-pit of economic competition. Thus on 20 September 1589 the Governor of Carlisle notified the English embassy in Edinburgh that hearing of James's 'earnest desire to have Her Majesty's players repair unto Scotland to His Grace, I did forthwith despatch a servant unto them where they were in furthest Lancashire'. The Queen's Men were at the Earl of Derby's house at Knowsley; but a month later they were in the Scottish capital being 'used with great kindness and all courtesy' by the Earl of Bothwell while James sailed to fetch his bride.[22] Likewise, no sooner had Anne's sister Elizabeth been installed at Wolfenbüttel than members of the Admiral's Company were issued passports, and on Midsummer Night 1592 they were acting in the palace there for Duke Heinrich Julius.[23] As the author himself of nine plays published in 1594, it is tempting to see something of this Julius in Duke Theseus, who similarly celebrates his Amazonian marriage 'With pomp, with triumph, and with revelling' [*Dream, 1,1,19*]. The experience of Julius's player Robert Browne certainly suggests the scale of the inducements that must have tempted the author of *A Midsummer Night's Dream*.

An almost exact contemporary of Shakespeare, Browne first toured the Netherlands, and in 1590 headed a company at Leyden. The Brunswick gala, funded by the Duke's silver-mines, was his breakthrough, however; and by 1594 he was in Kassel, 'loaded with gold and silver' by Landgraf Moritz of Hesse.[24] Over the next thirty years Browne and his team would entertain such patrons as the Elector of Brandenburg in Potsdam, Henri IV at Fontainebleau, Archduke Albert in Brussels, Emperor Matthias in Regensburg, and Frederick and Elizabeth, the King and Queen of Bohemia, in Prague. But it was the Landgraf's funds that furnished the 'English comedians' with an aesthetic programme and a base for these ceremonial gigs, in the neoclassical shape of the Ottoneum, a court theatre Moritz built in Kassel in 1604, and named after his heir. Moritz had been inspired by a tour of French amphitheatres.[25] So, with a statue of 'Hercules and his load' [*2,2,345*] above the stage, the 480-seat Ottoneum appears to have been a 'cross between the Roman and English theatres'. But this 'comedy house built in the round' was intended to be 'designed according to the old Roman style' of Vitruvius, and its repertoire similarly mixed the contemporary and classical: *The King of Scotland and England*; *Tarquinio und Lucretia*; and the Landgraf's own *Otto the Protector*.[26] Browne had helped construct a similar court theatre for the Earl of Derby to produce his own plays at Knowsley in the 1590s; and he would later work on converting the royal Fencing School at Gdansk.[27] In 1600 he was back in London advising on 'the secret parts' of the Fortune playhouse, a project to which *Hamlet* refers, when the Prince ribs his friends: 'What have you ... deserved at the hands of Fortune that she sends you to prison hither?' This sparring about performing in 'confines, wards, and dungeons' [*2,2,230–7*] suggests that, however mouth-watering the invitations Browne brought from the continent, they must have been equivocally received: 'Gentlemen, you are welcome to Elsinore. Your hands, come. Th'appurtenance of welcome is fashion and ceremony' [2,2,353–4].

In the 1590s the marvel of Oldenburg state sponsorship was offering London players not just a variant of touring but a refuge from touring itself. One of those who may have been tempted to take the king's shilling was Christopher Marlowe, who, so Thomas Kyd informed the Privy Council, 'would persuade men of quality' to go to the Scottish court, where 'when I saw him last, he meant to be'.[28] The theory that the author of *Hero and Leander* and *Edward II* had the King of Scots in mind when he penned these works, and was waiting to embark for Edinburgh when he was murdered in Deptford, has been mooted by Charles Nicholl. The idea is intriguing not only because it explains 'a sudden access of Scottishness' in Marlowe's writing, but also because it hints at why Shakespeare might associate the Danish miracle with a massacre.[29] For 'What need the arctic people love starlight' Marlowe's doomed Gaveston asks, in an apparent reference to King Christian, 'To whom the sun shines both by day and night?' when similarly called north 'to live and be the favourite of a king'. Such was surely the career-move of which his creator dreamed when he had Faustus beg his infernal masters to 'let me an actor be', so as to be 'feasted' by 'noblemen' at 'courts of kings'. The doctor's schemes to attain 'the signory of Emden', 'serve the German Emperor' and 'banquet and carouse' at Wittenberg map a continental itinerary, in fact, which explains why this 'wonder of the world for magic art' devotes his precious time to theatricals, like that 'enchanted castle' he conjures for the Duke of Vanholt. Thus Faustus, who desires nothing more than 'with a solemn noise of trumpets' to 'Present before this royal Emperor / Great Alexander and his paramour', looks like a fantastic wish-fulfilling self-portrait of the London player that was made feasible when Oldenburg patronage inverted the terms of theatrical trade with the weddings of Christian and his sisters.[30] For then the prospects for entertainers, reported back by performers like Browne and Dowland, must indeed have seemed Faustian:

> When I came to the Duke of Brunswick he used me kindly and gave me a rich chain of gold, £23 in money, with velvet and satin and gold lace to make apparel, with promise that if I would serve him he would give me as much as any prince in the world. But from thence I went to the Landgrave of Hesse, who gave me the greatest welcome that

might be for one of my quality, who sent a ring into England for my wife valued at £20 sterling, and gave me a great standing cup with a cover gilt, full of dollars, with many great offers for my service.[31]

It took that fetishist art collector Jacques Lacan to deduce that the primary objects of desire in *Hamlet* are the fatally attractive foils, the 'French rapiers' with 'delicate carriages' [*5,2,109*], which are the stakes in the King of Denmark's lethal game.[32] So far as we know, however, Marlowe never was tempted enough to join 'the English comedians' in the courts of Europe, although his *Faustus* would be one of the plays Browne acted in Vienna for the Emperor.[33] And the frightening implications of picturing this new departure as a Devil's Pact are indeed borne out by the shock to the actors who put on *The Mousetrap* for Claudius, when the King rises and furiously terminates the show: 'Give me some light. Away. / Lights, lights, lights!' [*3,2,247*]. Having fled the court, Hamlet's players presumably resume their tour of northern Europe, like the real actors who played Elsinore at this time, when, as Jerzy Limon recounts, 'Denmark seems to have become the first important destination for English players' on the way towards Germany and Poland.[34] They would be following the path beaten by the troupe of Leicester's Men Frederick II hosted in 1586, whose wagons rolled on from Elsinore to the Elector of Saxony in Dresden. As feminist critics have been discovering, 'The interest in drama at the Danish court exerted a lasting influence' throughout Europe as the players shuttled along the patronage networks of Frederick's four Amazonian daughters.[35] Whether or not the twenty-two-year-old Shakespeare was in the company that played at the castle for old King Frederick, as some surmise, he would have heard about the family reunion for Christian's coronation when the feasts and fireworks fuelled a month of revels by the English troupers from Wolfenbüttel, who escorted the king carried in a litter dressed as an anti-pope.[36] Willem Schrickx has even surmised that Browne purposely 'visited England in the winters of 1600 and 1601 to supply his company with fresh play-scripts', which included *Hamlet*. This theory gains plausibility from the fact that two of the 'tumblers and instrumentalists' who performed at Elsinore in 1586, Thomas Pope and William Kempe, were Globe shareholders, and would later be joined by Browne, while a third, George Bryan, was also in Shakespeare's company, the Chamberlain's Men. All had toured together with Strange's

Men in Lancashire and other parts of the Stanley outreach since the 1580s.[37] So, although critics always interpret the arrival of the actors in Denmark in terms of the old insecurities of English touring, what was being touted in 1600, to form the professional and political unconscious of *Hamlet*, was not the 'primordial night-mare' of reverting to the 'primitive wanderings' of strollers but an entirely new type of official appointment, and a salaried commission in the absolutist state.[38] *Hamlet*, as James Marino demonstrates, was always a changeable text, revised to reflect the current priorities of Shakespeare's troupe.[39] Thus, the question carries real authorial urgency when Hamlet is informed how Rosencrantz and Guildenstern have overtaken the 'tragedians of the city' on the road from Wittenberg, and he demands to know, 'How chances it they travel?' when 'Their residence both in reputation and profit was better both ways' at home [2,2,305–18].

Something rotten

Under its solar sovereign, Copenhagen developed as a 'Northern equivalent of Rudolfine Prague' that was to be the inspiration to Anne, when she became patroness of the platonizing masque designs of Jones, the designer she summoned from Elsinore, and also to her son Prince Henry, when he pushed plans for a militant Protestant crusade.[40] But as the Norwegian historian Kenneth Robert Olwig points out, Anne 'would never have had virtual *carte blanche* to drain the royal treasury' with her 'taste for continental Renaissance spectacle', if her husband had not been equally inspired by the absolutist agenda he saw unfolding in his brother-in-law's federal state. Consulting academicians such as the astronomer Tycho Brahe, whom he presented with two guard-dogs, and honoured with a sonnet about the mystery of 'governing bodies', James 'met with much in Denmark that strengthened his belief that ... science and "natural law" should provide the foundation of government'. And in Denmark he also encountered a Nordic confederation that had 'succeeded in uniting a diversity of lands' just as he intended to unite the British archipelago, and was 'well on the path to the absolute rule' he desired.[41] Ominously, however, the first bitter fruits of James's Nordic winter were the trials on both sides of the North Sea of the so-called witches accused, in a classic case of abjection, of raising the storms that prevented Anne from sailing to marry him in Edinburgh. For it was Scandinavian folklore, sociologists deduce, that sparked the king's obsession with demonology, and initiated him into the continental fantasy of the Black Mass. Indeed, at the first trial it was even alleged the 'witches' had slipped between the bride and her incapable husband 'at Upslo [Oslo] on the first night of their marriage'.[42] So it is possible that Marlowe was deliberately toying with this royal paranoia in his dangerous play about feasting with monarchs after a Devil's Pact.[43]

If Shakespeare, who treated tales of Scottish witches and 'Lapland sorcerers' [*Errors*, 4,3,11] so equivocally, was ever tempted to follow Marlowe's alleged advice to take the royal road of northern favour, what is extraordinary is how with his Amleth plot he homed in on the Viking savagery of the Oldenburg saga, highlighting how the Danish state 'had only just emerged from turmoil that revolved around the same issues' as would 'bedevil James in Britain'. Thus the representational crisis in *Hamlet* pointedly reflects how 'These struggles turned on conflicting conceptions of what was representative of the polity. Was it the monarch, or a representative body?'[44] Without the Oslo wedding, Keith Brown has claimed, 'Shakespeare's tragedy would never have come to exist'. Yet even he concedes that such a *risqué* scenario was 'needlessly unpalatable', and would have been 'curiously shocking' to James and his family, as 'it is of the essence of *Hamlet* to present Denmark as a great international power' which now has the strength to 'crush even England itself'.[45] For eighteen months after his sister's wedding to the Scottish king, on 8 June 1591 the Danish Caesar had had himself acclaimed King of Norway in unprecedented absolutist terms, as he sat beneath Oslo's Akershus fortress 'on a throne glittering with gold and precious stones', by seven hundred Norwegian nobles, 'who one by one knelt to swear fealty'. Evidently, Shakespeare could not have selected a more urgent setting than that of *Hamlet* for a tragedy about a system that so dangerously combines the barbaric and Baroque, nor chosen a more topical location for a drama about the 'Election Trouble' when absolutist monarchy threatened to overturn elective norms.[46]

'This heavy-headed revel east and west / Makes us traduc'd and tax'd of other nations – / They clepe us drunkards, and with swinish phrase / Soil our addition; and indeed it takes from our achievements' [1,4,18:1–2]: Hamlet's report of drunken orgies at Elsinore, which features only in the second 1604 quarto, is assumed to be based on the bilious accounts of the 'Bacchanal entertainments' and 'drunken healths' that greeted the Earl of Rutland's 1603 embassy to Denmark.[47] Critics also connect the fact that 'above all, Christian was known as a drinker' to Shakespeare's later caricature of Antony as a drunken boor in the tragedy he wrote at the time of the king's return visit to London in 1606; and concur that in drinking toasts Claudius is likewise 'a truly royal Dane', as 'Christian was capable of downing forty goblets of wine in an evening', and for his coronation 35,000 glasses were requisitioned from the navy, whilst his father died of drink, and 'old Queen Sophia worked her way through two gallons of wine a day'.[48] In the most recent extenuation, however, Michael Srigley contends that the inserted 'speech of some dozen or sixteen lines' [2,2,517], about how this 'vicious mole of nature' undermines 'the pales and forts of reason' [1,4,8-12], is 'not so much an attack' on the Oldenburgs for their toping as a subtle defence, since Hamlet is saying a 'weakness for drink should not derogate from their achievements': by which he must mean the Arsenal Christian constructed in 1598, the ramparts of Copenhagen, and the coastal moles thrown up to repel the Swedes. Despite the scandalous 'dram of evil' [20] in their drinking, Shakespeare was happy, on this view, to raise a toast to the Danes' 'warlike state' [1,2,9], and down the king's 'god rus' as his own good 'rouse' [1,4,9]:[49]

So oft it chances in particular men ...
Carrying, I say, the stamp of one defect ...
Shall in the general censure take corruption
From that particular fault.

[1,4,6-20]

Shakespeare's damning praise for Christian's enterprise might seem less sinister if it were not for the cancerous burrowing of that 'old mole': the 'worthy pioneer' who 'Canst work i'th'earth so fast' that he brings down the entire edifice, as he 'courses through / The natural gates and alleys of the body' [1,5,66-7; 164]. There is in fact no way that this deadly 'mole', who betrays the subterranean rottenness in 'the pith and marrow' [1,4,18:6] of the body politic, can be anything but an intrusion and a melanoma, a diagnostic figure for the way the Danish 'engineer' will himself be undermined, or as the 1604 text puts it, 'Hoist with his own petard' [3,4,185:5], when his fatal inheritance erupts.[50] So, if *Hamlet* was 'Newly imprinted', in the words of the 1604 title-page, 'and enlarged almost as much again', because Shakespeare was asked to revise a text for the Danish visit, as Srigley proposes, that might well be the reason the Prince now became thirty, the same age as Christian. But this Jacobean reworking can hardly have been composed to flatter. Srigley suggests *Hamlet* was, in fact, revived at Greenwich in July 1606, when 'the King of Denmark would have watched a play in which the mirror was held up' to his inebriated and philandering court.[51] More plausibly, at Hampton Court on 6 August Shakespeare held a literal mirror up to James and his brother-in-law, when the kings of the two united kingdoms, 'That twofold balls and treble sceptres carry' [*Macbeth, 4,1,137*] as partners in the same imperial project, were reflected in the glass the Witches use to show 'double … trouble' [*4,1,20*] to Macbeth. But if the rewritten *Hamlet* was also revived for Christian's visit, the additions about 'This heavy-headed revel east *and west*' must have sounded, in the peculiar and uncanny future anterior tense assumed by Horatio, more like a panic, to English ears, than a panegyric:

And even the like precurse of feared events,
As harbingers preceding still the fates,
And prologue to the omen coming on,
Have heaven and earth together demonstrated
Unto our climature and countrymen.

[*1,1,106:14–18*]

Like the allusions to Christian's alcoholism, or the reference to 'a Dane-like barbarous sot' censored in the 1616 edition of Marston's *Jack Drum's Entertainment*, Horatio's warning about the 'disasters' in train for 'Neptune's empire' [*11–12*] also engulfing 'our climature and countrymen' were cut from the Folio, perhaps for fear of offending the king's nephew Prince Charles.[52] It only gains in impudence, however, if the play-within-the-play that causes offence to the Danish royals is, as Srigley concludes, taken as a self-reflexive mirror of Shakespeare's text. Then the dramatist does look certifiably 'mad' in his impertinence towards a family that was in the process of annexing England to its constellation of crowns. Yet *impertinence*, in the sense both of the *insolence* Hamlet shows the politicians and the *irrelevance* Guildenstern decries, when he begs him to put his 'discourse into some frame and start not so wildly' from the affair of the offending play [*3,2,282*], is, as Weimann contends, the very logic of this play, which does seem designed to show 'matter and impertinency mixed! Reason in madness!' [*King Lear, 4,6,168*].[53] So, 'Though this be madness, yet there is method in't' [*2,2,203*], as the wily old chancellor concedes. Indeed, once the Oldenburg aspect of *Hamlet* is recognized, the impertinence looks so indiscreet it seems it must have had some 'method', on the lines of the prince's own rationale for things done *rashly*: 'praised be rashness for it: let us know / Our indiscretions sometime serves us well / When our dear plots do pall' [*5,2,6–9*]. For if this play was staged with an eye to Denmark's maritime power, there can hardly ever have been a more rash presentation than a play set on these famous Danish battlements that advertises how (in an addition also cut in 1623) 'The very place puts toys of desperation, / Without more motive, into every brain' [*1,4,55:1–2*].

Shakespeare goes to conspicuous lengths in the *Hamlet* quartos to make Elsinore a vertiginous 'place of desperation'. Critics notice, for example, how their plots seem 'designed to express the anxiety felt by English subjects' at James's accession by echoing the 'secrets of the prison-house' [*1,5,14*] that had brought him the Scottish crown, when his handsome father Lord Darnley was murdered in his orchard: poisoned, it was alleged, by the Earl of Bothwell, the brutish lover of his wife, Mary Stuart; a scandal recalled when Gertrude compares the portraits of her husbands.[54] As Carl Schmitt theorized, 'the unhappy lineage from which James descended' appears to have been the 'terrible historical reality that shimmers through the masks and costumes of the stage play', as the 'concrete taboo' which was its essential yet inhibiting determinant.[55] This intrusive topicality is reinforced by the less-noticed fact that when Bothwell fled to Denmark, where he died insane, his gaolers were Eric Rosencrantz and Mörgens Guildenstern.[56]

As a future functionary of the very absolutist system he was depicting, with his Baltic drama Shakespeare was skating on very thin ice. For a tragedy that introduces the Danish court as a hotbed of adultery and incest, ruled by a fratricidal usurper, and haunted by a ghost crying out for the vengeance that will inexorably extinguish the entire royal house, can hardly be said to be currying any favours in Copenhagen. In 1599 the young Christian had sailed to 'the end of the earth' in the Arctic to assert his rights over Norway.[57] With some thirty visits there, the self-proclaimed 'Northern Star' was the first Danish ruler to tour his Norwegian colonies. Yet Shakespeare subverted this imperial triumph with a disaster-story that concludes in the reverse takeover of Denmark by Norway's 'delicate and tender' [4,4,9:38] Prince Fortinbras. So this was a drama that literally went far out of its way to provoke the hostile reaction Claudius gives *The Mousetrap*, that its author was fit only for England:

> I like him not, nor stands it safe with us
> To let his madness rage. Therefore ...
> ... he to England shall ...
> The terms of our estate may not endure
> Hazard so dangerous as doth hourly grow
> Out of his lunacies.
>
>   [3,3,1–7]

'Something is rotten in the state of Denmark' [1,4,67]: if we take its setting seriously, then from the opening of this Danish play, with its report of how 'young Fortinbras, / Of unimproved mettle hot and full, / Hath in the skirts of Norway here and there / Sharked up a list of landless resolutes' [1,1,94–7], Shakespeare seems *madly* determined to play upon the insecurities of the Oldenburg state, with its militarized economy, rebellious taxpayers, and sham Baroque façade. Thus, editors struggle to square the means by which Claudius steals the succession from Hamlet with the divine right dogma about the 'divinity' that 'doth hedge a king' [4,5,120] he utters just before he offers the crown to Laertes [201], and to reconcile the fact that the Prince is himself able to 'prophesy th'election lights / On Fortinbras', yet in an act of sovereign decision give him his 'dying voice' [5,2,297–8]. Likewise, in the Norwegian monarchy of the play it is the brother rather than the son who succeeds, despite being reported 'impotent and bed-rid' [1,2,29]. But historians point out that it was Christian who had plunged Scandinavia's ancient elective monarchies into just such constitutional confusion, with the very novelty of a coronation, when 'in contravention of the charter that he, like other Danish kings had had to sign', he was crowned by Bishop Peder Winstrup as 'the vicar of Christ. In this way, the ground was prepared for conflict between a powerful monarchy based on divine right and an aristocratic constitutionalism supporting traditional decentralized government.'[58] Audiences might well have construed this innovation as a pointer to England's future at this 'republican moment', when politicians like Raleigh were countering that 'the wisest way' for politicians to proceed when

Elizabeth died was 'to keep the Government in their own hands and set up a Commonwealth'.[59] For seen in the shadows cast by Danish absolutism, the twisted constitutionalism of *Hamlet* becomes both urgently topical and alarmingly specific.

In the only study yet to examine the actual contemporary Danish context of *Hamlet* in detail Gunnar Sjögren shows how Claudius's 'theatre state' does replicate many of the kitsch effects of Christian's coronation, such as the mock guard of actors led by the English acrobat Thomas Sackville, who cavorted as 'Switzers' [4,5,94] of the sacrilegious anti-pope.[60] Thus Andrew Hadfield speaks for a current consensus when he deciphers *Hamlet* as 'a coded warning' of 'the problems that James might bring with him to England – political instability, religious conflict, sexual scandal, corruption at court ... *Hamlet* stands as a distinctly republican play'.[61] But what no one has considered is why Shakespeare had the effrontery to insult James and his relations in this way, and to what possible purpose he demystified their self-made monarchy as 'not a crown neither', but one of these glitzy 'coronets' [*Julius Caesar, 1,2,237*]. As early as 1599 he had identified Christian with absolutist hubris, when he had Caesar claim an instant before his assassination to be 'constant as the Northern Star' [3,1,60]. But although historians now tell us that something was indeed rotten in the Baroque polity of Denmark, it seems that it took Shakespeare to ask his colleagues to 'Season your admiration for a while' [1,2,191], and look behind the façade:

> The King doth wake tonight and takes his rouse,
> Keeps wassail, and the swagg'ring upspring reels,
> And as he drains his draughts of Rhenish down
> The kettle-drum and trumpet thus bray out
> The triumph of his pledge.
>
> [*1,4,9–13*]

Method in the madness

'What was wanting in meat and other ceremony was helped out in gunshot and drink', sniped Dudley Carleton when Christian and his brother-in-law sailed into London in 1606, 'for at every health, of which there was twenty, the ship the kings were in made nine shot'. Terrified of an explosion, the gossip sneered, James gave orders 'at his own ships not to be annoyed with smell of powder, but store of good healths made him so hearty he bade them at last shoot and spare not, and very resolutely commanded the trumpets to sound him a point of war'.[62] It was in the play then acted for the kings, editors think, at Hampton Court that Shakespeare altered Scotland's defeated foes from Danes to Norwegians [*Macbeth*, 1,2,31], proving how tactful he could be if compelled. For by the time of *Macbeth* Christian's delusions of grandeur were being exposed in infamous incidents such as the 'disgusting shambles' recorded by John Harington, when the kings presided at a masque of Solomon, and Sheba 'overset her caskets into his Danish Majesty's lap and fell at his feet, though I rather think it was in his face. His Majesty then got up and would dance with the Queen of Sheba; but he fell down and was carried to an inner chamber and laid on a bed of state, which was not a little defiled with the presents of the Queen which had been bestowed on his garments, such as wine, cream, jelly, beverage, spices and cakes.'[63]

Historians concur that Christian personified the Janus-face of his entire regime, which combined the pomposity of the new type of ceremonial court with the 'hard-drinking, boorish life' of the patriarchal courts of his poor German cousins.[64] Typical of this ambivalence were the king's boast that he needed no guard and could 'spend the night with any of his subjects', and his prank of travelling as Captain Frederickson.[65] His sister may have been thrilled when Christian jumped on her incognito in London in 1614, but his brother-in-law was not amused; and his buffoonery almost wrecked the diplomacy in 1606 when he pointed cuckold's horns at the Lord Admiral Nottingham after seducing his wife.[66] Seen in this lurid light, Shakespeare's anamorphic drama, with its hesitation, hendiadys and exhortations to 'Look here upon this picture, and on this, / The counterfeit presentment of two brothers' [3,4,52–3] does begin to look like the dramatist's professional vacillation on the eve of the annexation of England, and a prescient warning about Europe's new northern gods. For King Frederick's grandson would indeed reign calamitously over the united kingdoms of Great Britain.

Around 1600, we could infer from Hamlet's bullying of the Players, the author of *Hamlet* confronted Dowland's dilemma, which is also the predicament of the performers in his play, of how far to collaborate with the triumphalist ceremonies of this incoming dynasty, and how much of their neoclassical aesthetic to admit into his work. Such, then, was the origin of what Weimann terms 'the profound crisis in representativity' which threatens in this tragedy to rupture the precarious 'synthesis between humanist learning and native practice'.[67] But if attention at the 'distracted Globe' [1,5,97] was so disturbed, such a short time after the new playhouse had opened in 1599, then that was more than an aesthetic issue, for it meant that the integrity of the literary field which Shakespeare had helped to shape was now menaced by the impending intrusion of an overwhelming new *political* power:

> Good now, sit down, and tell me, he that knows,
> Why this same strict and most observant watch
> So nightly toils the subject of the land,
> And why such daily cast of brazen cannon,
> And foreign mart for implements of war,
> Why such impress of shipwrights, whose sore task
> Does not divide the Sunday from the week:
> What might be toward that this sweaty haste
> Doth make the night-labourer with the day ...?
>
> [1,1,69–77]

The shiver of apprehension at Danish military preparations which runs through *Hamlet* can be explained as a reaction to the rumours that James would seize his English inheritance at the point of Christian's guns.[68] But if the play is so concerned that the power distracting the Globe 'bodes some strange eruption to our state' [68] that might also be because the drama the Prince demands when the players arrive in Elsinore is one that 'pleased not the million. 'Twas caviare to the general.' The Baltic delicacy underlines how Hamlet's predilection for this 'excellent play, well digested in the scenes, set down with as much modesty as cunning', runs snobbishly counter to the public preference for 'sallets in the lines to make the matter savoury' which had brought the house such profits. But then he also rejoices that there was in this play 'no matter in the phrase that might indict the author of affectation' or political intent. As 'whole-some as sweet, and by very much more handsome' than appealing [2,2,418–24], the work he seems to have in mind is Marlowe's neoclassical *Dido Queen of Carthage*, which might have inspired the amusements staged at Elsinore for James. If the Players do recite from this marmoreal tragedy, however, that must be because in staging Aeneas's recital of his 'tale to Dido' [426] as a play-within-the-play, Marlowe had signalled his own stifled situation at the court of Elizabeth, as one 'Too mean to be a companion to a queen' invited to 'sink at Dido's feet', on condition he will 'Look up and speak'.[69]

Acted by the boy-players of the Chapel Royal, *Dido* was itself one of those very closet dramas which, so we are told, have become the rage in the City, where 'an eyrie of children, little eyeases ... are most tyrannically clapped for't. These are now the fashion, and so berattle the common stages' [*326–9*]. Hamlet seizes on the parallel between this theatrical tyranny and Claudius's coup, complaining that 'their writers do them wrong to make them exclaim against their own succession' [*335–6*]: a reference to the spoofing of the adult professionals in satires the boys acted at the private Blackfriars theatre, like Jonson's *Poetaster*.[70] His sympathy is all the more seductive if, as has been proposed, the First Quarto title-page is taken seriously, and *Hamlet* was itself 'acted ... in the City' in 1600–1 at one of the inns like the Cross Keys, only to be upstaged by the boys.[71] For whatever its performance history, the 1603 version is clearly smarting with indignation on behalf of the Chamberlain's Men, that 'the principal public audience that came unto them, are turned to private plays and to the humour of the children'. So when Shakespeare had the players flee the metropolis, it might well have been because, as Joseph Loewenstein argues, he was indeed tempted to make a virtue of necessity, and develop Elsinore into an 'author's theatre'. According to this interpretation, the Prince voices Shakespeare's 'good riddance' to the London stage.[72] But Hamlet's neoclassical faddishness also reveals that for the Players the choice between England and Elsinore is false. For what they discover, when they are shouted off stage by a brutal, interfering and suspicious king, is that there is now no more place at a continental court than in the City for the 'gibes', 'gambols' and 'flashes of merriment' that in the good old days of Yorick (or King Frederick) 'were wont to set the table on a roar' [*5,1,175–7*].

'Bid the players make haste. / Will you two help to hasten them?' [*3,2,43–4*]: Hamlet's impatient orders to Rosencrantz and Guildenstern to speed the actors' preparations underlines how aesthetic values will be subordinated to political expedience in the absolutist state. No wonder then that when Hamlet sermonizes against the 'antic disposition', which 'though it make the unskilful laugh, cannot but make the judicious grieve', the First Player replies so guardedly: 'I hope we have reformed that indifferently with us, sir'. The Prince's diktat, 'O reform it all together' [*3,2,23–34*], aligns his cultural crusade with the Reformed religion of the Oldenburg courts. Jonathan Goldberg therefore reads this tense encounter as a premonition of Shakespeare's entrapment in absolutism's 'spectral domain of shadows' where 'playwright, actor, and represented all join to be caught and tangled'.[73] Yet the Player's reaction 'shows an extraordinary degree of reserve,' as Weimann puts it, which sounds all the more cagey when we consider 'the extraordinary newness' of this exchange between the professional performers and the royal connoisseur.[74] And it is around that professional reserve before the theatre preferences of a monarch, more than any sovereign's 'dying voice' in 'the election', that the politics of Shakespeare's succession play revolves.

Around 1600 Shakespeare was made an offer he could scarce refuse, we might conclude, to team up with Browne's continental company and serve the rising power. With a fleet expected to sail across from 'Neptune's empire' to assert James's claims to his English inheritance, the offer might have seemed a no-brainer. For when they 'returned home so generously rewarded and loaded with gold and silver', artists such as Dowland and Jones flaunted the glittering material rewards of Oldenburg employment.[75] But then they also revealed the artistic price of this emancipation from the laws of commerce, which was their submission to the triumphalist neoclassical aesthetic that the prince demands. So the mad impertinence of the reaction he encoded in his New Year drama implies that on the eve of England's Union with Scotland what Shakespeare detected in Oldenburg patronage, however gilt or laden with dollars, was not the loving wassail cup of a northern Hogmanay but a poisoned chalice:

Let all the battlements their ordnance fire.
The King shall drink to Hamlet's better breath,
And in the cup an union shall he throw
Richer than that which four successive kings
In Denmark's crown have worn. Give me the cups,
And let the kettle to the trumpet speak,
The trumpet to the cannoneer without,
The cannons to the heavens, the heaven to earth,
'Now the King drinks to Hamlet'.

[*5,2,208–16*]

King of shreds and patches

In *The Guns of Elsinore* Martin Holmes long ago noticed that the deafening cannonade which complements Claudius's hypocritical and homicidal toasts echoes the artillery greeting ships sailing up the Danish Sound, where Elsinore was the check-point for tolls levied on all vessels entering the Baltic, and that 'the platform' on which *Hamlet* opens [*1,2,213; 251*] refers to the threatening battery every traveller was forced to pass.[76] If so, this murderous gun-salute is an apt figure for the sinister ambivalence of the embrace await-ing those entertainers who braved Denmark's ceremonial court. As Limon shows, the 'Englische Komödianten' soon extended their circuit from Copenhagen as far as Vienna, and their first appear-ance in Gdansk was in August 1601.[77] Such is the Baltic geography of *Hamlet*; but there this new northern Europe is presented as one vast killing-field, where Fortinbras is admired by the protagonist for sending 'twenty thousand men ... to their graves', and the way he returns the compliment is to 'Bear Hamlet like a soldier to the stage' and 'bid the soldiers shoot' [*4,4,9:50–2; 5,2,340–7*]. As more and more critics sense, 'Hamlet, the prince of players, kills players', in Harold Bloom's words, since, from the moment Claudius instructs Voltemand and Cornelius as ambassadors to Norway, the play implies an analogy between actors and agents that concludes, with the ruthless despatch of Rosencrantz and Guildenstern, in making Hamlet the true heir of his homicidal uncle.[78] And even if the per-formers he employs are unlike Yorick in escaping with their lives, Hamlet's elitist strictures against the 'pitiful ambition in the fool' [*3,2,39*] are enough to throttle their careers.

Far from being Shakespeare's own artistic manifesto, Hamlet's patronizing 'advice' to the players as their self-appointed Maecenas would have made for 'a disastrous failure in the Elizabethan com-mercial theatre'.[79] But even at the court of Denmark – where life consists of nothing but rehearsals, 'in which one character tells one or more other characters how to act' – Hamlet's conceited platitudes about the humanist 'purpose of playing' [*3,2,19*] mask his plan to manipulate the stage to his own political purposes, and to sabotage the very performance he directs in his self-appointed role as a theatre intendant. Hamlet's maltreatment of his theatrical servants, as James Hirsh comments, thus exemplifies his callous Machiavellian realpolitik that "Tis dangerous when the baser nature comes / Between the pass and fell incensed points of mighty opposites' [5,2,61], and his hijack of their work is of a piece with his contemptuous abuse of Ophelia, harassment of Gertrude, exploitation of friends and humiliation of Osric: 'Hamlet poses as a friend to the players, but he actually sees them merely as pawns in his machinations ... He lures them into putting on a performance he fully intends to ruin', and during which 'he insults and demeans the actors' until he goads the king into obliterating their work. In the word Lacan made a focus of his *Hamlet* seminars, with his commission of *The Mousetrap* the Prince disposes of the play and its players as nothing more than *bait*:

> Never once does he express the slightest regret that his ploy will humiliate the players. They are merely 'baser' mortals ... Hamlet is so oblivious to the effect of his actions that he even asks Horatio, 'Would not this ... get me a fellowship in a cry of players?' [3,2,253–5]. But it is hard to imagine that this particular cry of players would offer a fellowship to someone who insulted them in public and turned their royal command performance into a fiasco ... It is not likely that the players will look back fondly on the pre-performance commands and insults inflicted upon them by this presumptuous, discourteous, and hypocritical prince.[80]

'I have of late – but wherefore I know not – lost all my mirth ... and indeed ... this goodly frame, the earth, seems to me a sterile promontory. This most excellent canopy the air, look you, this brave o'erhanging, this majestical roof fretted with golden fire – why it appears no other thing to me than a foul and pestilent congregation of vapours' [2,2,285–93]: if the schizoid prince does internalize Shakespeare's crisis of identity, the moment of *Hamlet* was a season of anxious authorial 'distraction' from the Globe and its 'foul and pestilent' crowds. It was the period of 'The War of the Theatres' when for 'tragedians of the city' the time was truly 'out of joint' [1,5,189]. Yet this spasm of disillusion is, of course, spat by Hamlet at the very groundlings the play will need to court, and is instantly followed by the nervous joke that 'if you delight not in man, what Lenten entertainment the players will receive from you', with the irruption into the Danish palace of the Londoners themselves [2,2,304]. For all the disdain of a High Renaissance aesthetic that considers their popular art 'monstrous' [528], this drama is permeated, as Anne Barton writes, by 'the time now past when Hamlet lived ... with actors, and learned speeches from their plays'.[81]

And in the end, as Francis Barker saw, Shakespeare enlisted all his own authority in defence of his play and on behalf of the players 'against contemporary power', and had the strength to make his Danish tragedy a great refusal of the absolutist state.[82] In *Hamlet* 'The play's the thing' [*581–2*]. And the source of that strength was the popularity of the actors themselves: 'For the law of writ and the liberty, these are the only men' [*384*].

The irony of the Players' patronized position in *Hamlet* is that Shakespeare's company never was driven from the city to the court, let alone to foreign exile, and that this play which could never have pleased royalty was applauded by that 'pestilent congregation' at the Globe. Thus, in his study of 'The Poets' War', James Bednarz emphasizes that while the picture of 'the harassed Chamberlain's Men as homeless tragedians' might have been a nightmare in 1601, in the event it would prove only 'an anxious joke'.[83] As Alfred Harbage calculated, the attempted *coup d'état* by the boys, which threatened to 'carry it away' from the Globe, never had a chance of dethroning the 'common players' [*334–44*], because in the year of *Hamlet* the ratio of attendance at public and private theatres was 50 to 1.[84] Thus, though Gabriel Harvey ranked the tragedy in 1601 among works which 'have it in them to please the wiser sort', by 1604 poet Anthony Scoloker was commending 'Friendly Shakespeare's tragedies' as models for a box-office hit: 'Faith, it should please all, like Prince *Hamlet*'.[85] It would therefore have come as no surprise to audience-friendly Shakespeare when John Dowland absconded from the gilded cage of Elsinore to his digs on Fetter Lane, the better to supervise the printing of his best-selling album *Lachrymae* himself.[86]

'How absolute the knave is!': Hamlet's aside about the Gravedigger, usually explained as a back-handed tribute to the verbal wit of the clown Robert Armin who played the part, is a grudging recognition of the playhouse as the antithesis of the court, and a quibble that fixes the equivalence between struggles in the English theatre and the Danish state.[87] The Prince senses that what will decide this duel between opposing absolutisms is the people's power: 'The age is grown so picked that the toe of the peasant comes so near the heel of the courtier he galls his kibe' [*5,1,126–30*]. As Pierre Bourdieu commented, unlike the theatre of the French court which, as Voltaire reminded the English critic who praised the naturalism of the line, "Not a mouse stirring" [*1,1,10*], was confined to a language as exalted as that of the persons to whom it was addressed, 'the Elizabethan dramatist owed his freedom of expression to entrance fees paid by a public of increasingly diverse origin'.[88] It may not be chance, therefore, that when he declares how 'He that plays the King shall be welcome; his majesty shall have tribute of me' [2,2,304–9], Hamlet's oath of allegiance to the Player King is in the old style of a Danish investiture, rather than the 1596 coronation, when subjects who paid no tax by compulsion swore to 'send the King presents, as to a friend'.[89]

'His majesty shall have tribute of me': Hamlet's salute records an instant in the transmission of sovereignty, like that we discern between the lines of Dowland's file, when absolute monarchy submits to absolute art, and the cultural field is first acknowledged by the field of power. Recent research finds there were indeed moments when the classical tragedies favoured by the 'judicious' had to make way at Elsinore for the crowd-pleasing antics of the clowns, who laughed 'to set on some quantity of barren spectators to laugh too' [3,2,36].[90] Thus, Christian had likely been present as a boy in 1585 when an English troupe performed in the courtyard and the locals broke down a wall to get in. If so, he had witnessed a public that gatecrashes into the play of *Hamlet* only once – when the offstage crowd, whose 'Caps, hands, and tongues applaud it to the clouds' as they acclaim Laertes king, force open the palace doors [4,5,103] – but which is always implied by the metatheatrical deference to that 'whole theatre of others' [3,2,25] set on to roaring at the Globe. So, although 'the Northern Star' had designed his own meretricious crown, and, in an ominous precedent for the English, deprived the Danish electors of their votes, Shakespeare's drama ends by invoking those 'That are but mutes and audience to this act', when Fortinbras revives the dishonoured Scandinavian custom of oath-taking, giving orders to 'call the noblest to the audience', and Horatio, picking up on the theatre metaphor, refers Hamlet's dying nomination not to sovereign decision but to the voices of the crowd:[91]

> Of that I shall have also cause to speak,
> And from his mouth whose voice will draw on more.
>
> [5,2,277;335–6]

'The King is a thing ... Of nothing' [4,2,26–7]: by his great refusal Shakespeare put out the Sun King's light. For in *Hamlet* neither the boy-players nor the sham king succeed in their plots to usurp the stage. Thus the first modern literary field was inaugurated by a deliberate demystification of the absolutist 'king effect'. And although Anne of Denmark and her sons would strive to impose the Baroque aesthetic upon them, like Shakespeare the English were more interested in seeing the purple face of 'his Danish Majesty' covered in custard-pie.[92] The 'monumental solidity' of the Baroque, art critics remind us, 'is imposing in both a literal and metaphorical sense, it presses down upon the viewer with its full visual exploitation of its heavy masonry', employing 'downward pressure' to 'cast dark shadows below'.[93] Danish Baroque was therefore built to impress. But Shakespeare, it appears from *Hamlet*, was not to be impressed. As Louis Montrose has written, in this 'metatheatrical tragedy of state' he seems instead 'to have been acutely sensitive to the power and danger entailed by the relationship of the commercial theatre to the court'.[94] And he was no more willing than the absconding Dowland to provide music from 'the cellarage' for the 'king machine', nor sit shivering in the dark as the 'nocturnal face' of the royal sun.

On 23 January 2009 fresh evidence was published to confirm that Shakespeare's apprehension about the rottenness of Denmark had been acute. The diary of one of Christian's bosom friends had just been discovered, and among state secrets were the details of a trip to Prague in 1597. The mission of this courtier named Rosencrantz was to slip poison into the goblet of the lover of the king's mother, Queen Sophia, during a banquet at the imperial court. The victim, who died after twelve hours in hideous convulsions, was none over than the royal astronomer, that truly great Dane who had inspired the Scottish king to poetry with glimpses of his supernova – the 'same star' to which Barnado points with perturbation in the play [*1,1,34*] – Tycho Brahe.[95] 'It is even suggested', one newspaper reported breathlessly, 'that Shakespeare used the alleged liaison as an inspiration for *Hamlet*'. 'Hamlet may have poisoned stargazer in mercury murder', was the headline in *The Times*.[96]

Whatever he knew about the murder of the 'stargazer', *Hamlet* suggests Shakespeare understood a marriage of a King of Scots to a Danish Princess was not so auspicious. He may in fact have heard how the very first Stuart masque had ended in the snow-bound streets of a freezing Oslo, when James, in an 'elegant blue suit' and 'preceded by six heralds in red velvet coats', and Anne, wearing a bridal gown of peach and parrot damask three hundred tailors had toiled to weave, rode in a silver coach from St Hallvard's Cathedral to their wedding breakfast in the castle of Akershus: 'As they drove from church James had arranged a curious spectacle for the entertainment of the people of Oslo. By his orders four young Negroes danced naked in the snow in front of the royal carriage.'[97] This cruel conceit might well have been inspired by Marlowe's sadistic fantasy in *Tamburlaine* of having 'naked negroes' draw 'thy coach ... as thou rid'st in triumph through the streets', and may have prompted Anne to stage her own *Masque of Blackness*.[98] But when the show was re-enacted by English actors at her coronation as Queen of Scots in Edinburgh, the black slaves had to be replaced by Scottish boys wearing chains and visors, 'to make them seem Moors', and 'all gorgeous to the eye'.[99] For in Oslo the cold had been so intense that before the banquet was over three of the African dancers died of hyperthermia. As *Hamlet* foretells, this tragic Danish prelude was the precursor of many such fatalities for the House of Stuart: 'As harbingers preceding still the fates, / And prologue to the omen coming on' [*1,1,106*]. Thus it was Shakespeare's historic role to expose the parading emperor as 'A king of shreds and patches' [*3,4,3*]. But, in the equally immortal words of another great poet of Elsinore:

> the Emperor marched on in the procession under the beautiful canopy, ... And he drew himself up still more proudly, while his chamberlains walked after him carrying the train that wasn't there.[100]

Notes

1 Rose Tremain, *Music and Silence* (London: Chatto and Windus, 1999), pp.3–4.

2 Ibid., pp.6 and 294.

3 Thomas Fuller, *The History of the Worthies of England* (London: 1662), quoted in Diana Poulton, *John Dowland* (London: Faber & Faber, 1972), p.2.

4 Louis Marin, *Portrait of the King*, trans. Martha Houle (Basingstoke:Macmillan, 1988), pp.72 and 79.

5 Description of Rosenberg in Steffen Heiburg (ed.), *Christian IV og Europa* (Copenhagen: Foundation for the Christian IV Year, 1988), the catalogue of the nineteenth Council of Europe exhibition, p.471 [trans. Christina Sandhaug]. Cf. Tremain, op. cit. (note 1), pp.15–16:

'Near the throne, a section of the floor can be raised or lowered by means of ropes. Beneath the trap is a grille and beneath that an assemblage of brass ducts or pipes let into the vaults of the cellar ... each one fashioned so sounds are transmitted without distortion into the space above, and all the King's visitors marvel when they hear it, not knowing whence the music can possibly come and wondering whether Rosenberg is haunted by the ghostly music makers of some other age.'

6 Peter Burke, *The Fabrication of Louis XIV* (New Haven: Yale University Press, 1992); 'State-Making, King-Making and Image-Making from Renaissance to Baroque: Scandinavia in a European Context', *Scandinavian Journal of History*, 22 (1997), 1–8, here 2–3.

7 Paul Palmer, *Denmark* (London: Macdonald, 1944), p.44; Sebastian Olden-Jørgensen, 'State Ceremonial, Court Culture and Political Power in Early Modern Denmark, 1536–1746', *Scandinavian Journal of History*, 27 (2002), 65–76, here 68–71. It is thought that Inigo Jones worked at the Danish court between 1603 and 1605, perhaps arriving in Copenhagen (where he is mentioned attending a banquet on 10 July 1603) in the embassy of the Duke of Rutland, and that he then entered the service of Queen Anne on the recommendation of her brother Ulric, who visited her in Edinburgh in 1604; though Jones's assistant John Webb recorded that it was Christian who personally 'sent for him out of Italy': see John Summerson, *Inigo Jones* (Harmondsworth: Penguin, 1966), pp.15–21; John Harris, 'Inigo Jones: Universal Man', in *Inigo Jones: Complete Architectural Drawings*, eds John Harris and Gordon Higgott (London: Royal Academy of Arts, 1989), p.13; and Michael Leapman, *Inigo: The Troubled Life of Inigo Jones, Architect of the English Renaissance* (London: Review, 2003), pp.21–2.

8 Mara Wade, *Triumphus Nuptialis Danicus: German Court Culture and Denmark: The 'Great Wedding' of 1634* (Wiesbaden: Harrassowitz Verlag, 1996), p.295. For Christian's own performances on stage, see Heiburg, op. cit. (note 5), pp.143–4.

9 Burke, op. cit., 1997 (note 6), 5; Paul Douglas-Lockhurst, *Denmark, 1513–1660: The Rise and Decline of a Renaissance Monarchy* (Oxford: Oxford University Press, 2007), p.191.

10 Ibid., pp.191–2.

11 Poulton, op. cit. (note 3), pp.52, 56 and 62–3.

12 Ibid. p.58.

13 *Christian IV og Europa: Kataloget er udgivet af Fonden Christian IV året 1988* (Copenhagen: Council of Europe, 1988), pp.124–32 (cat. 403).

14 Burke, op. cit. (note 6), p.58.

15 Robert Weimann, *Author's Pen and Actor's Voice: Playing and Writing in Shakespeare's Theatre* (Cambridge: Cambridge University Press,

2000), pp. 161–2. Cf. Thomas McAlindon, *Shakespeare and Decorum* (London: Macmillan, 1973), p. 14: 'a discordant combination of things unlike'.

16 Ibid. p. 161. Likewise, Harold Goddard notes how Hamlet's clownish behaviour sabotages his own directions for the performance of the play-within-the-play, in *The Meaning of Shakespeare* (Chicago: University of Chicago Press, 1951), pp. 366–7. And see David Wiles, *Shakespeare's Clown: Actor and Text in the Elizabethan Playhouse* (Cambridge: Cambridge University Press, 1987), pp. 57–9: 'When the players end the play, Hamlet's clown takes the stage and plays on … Like the clown in the public theatres, Hamlet sings as soon as the play is over, and probably also dances … The momentum of Hamlet's clowning sweeps him on and he demands music to accompany his manic fooling.' Cf. James Shapiro, *1599: A Year in the Life of William Shakespeare* (London: Faber & Faber, 2005), p. 323: 'In his verbal sparring, his intimate relationship with the audience, his distracting and obscene behaviour at the performance of "The Mousetrap" (where he cracks sexual jokes at Ophelia's expense and calls himself her "only jig-maker"), and his "antic" performance for much of the play, Hamlet appropriates much of the traditional comic part'.

17 Leeds Barroll, *Anna of Denmark, Queen of England* (Philadelphia: University of Pennsylvania Press, 2001), pp. 6–7. For details of the celebrations accompanying the Oslo marriage, see *Kongehyllest*, ed. J.J. Wolf and H. Gunnarsson (Oslo: Universitetsforlaget, 1991); and Lars Roar Langslot, *Christian IV: Konge av Danmark og Norge* (Oslo: J.W. Cappelens, 1997), pp. 38–9.

18 Thorkild Kjægaard, *The Danish Revolution: 1500–1800: An Ecohistorical Interpretation* (Cambridge: Cambridge University Press, 1994), pp. 9–11 and 13–25; Palle Lauring, *A History of the Kingdom of Denmark* (Copenhagen: Høst, 1973), p. 152; and T.K. Derry, *A History of Scandinavia* (London: George Allen & Unwin, 1979), pp. 102–3.

19 David Kirby, *Northern Europe in the Early Modern Period: The Baltic World, 1492–1772* (London: Longman, 1970), p. 200.

20 James Stuart, *The Poems of James VI of Scotland*, ed. James Craigie (2 vols, Edinburgh: Blackwood, 1955–58), vol. 2, p. 68; Thomas Fowler, quoted in Ethel Carleton Williams, *Anne of Denmark, Wife of James VI of Scotland: James I of England* (London: Longman, 1970), p. 19; Caroline Bingham, *James VI of Scotland* (London: Weidenfeld & Nicolson, 1979), pp. 117 and 120; David Bergeron, *Royal Family, Royal Lovers: King James of England and Scotland* (Columbia: University of Missouri Press, 1991), p. 53. There is a useful résumé of James's itinerary in Norway and Denmark in Alan Stewart, *The*

Cradle King: A Life of James VI & I (London: Chatto & Windus, 2003), pp.111–18.

21 Margreta de Grazia, '*Hamlet*' *without Hamlet* (Cambridge: Cambridge University Press, 2007); '200-hundred-year-old': p.5.

22 K.P. Wentersdorf, 'The Queen's Company in Scotland in 1589', *Theatre Research International*, 6 (1980), 33–6.

23 Willem Schrickx, 'English Actors at the Courts of Wolfenbüttel, Brussels and Graz During the Lifetime of Shakespeare', *Shakespeare Survey*, 33 (1980), 153–68, here 155.

24 'Loaded with gold and silver': Erhardus Cellius, *Eques auratus Anglo-Wirtembergicus* (Tübingen, 1605), quoted in June Schlueter, 'English Actors in Kassel, Germany, during Shakespeare's Time', *Medieval and Renaissance Drama in England*, 10 (1998), 238–61, here 244.

25 'English comedians': quoted Gerhart Hoffmeister, 'The English Comedians in Germany', in Gerhart Hoffmeister (ed.), *German Baroque Literature* (New York: Columbia University Press, 1983), p.146; for Moritz's 1602 tour of France, see Schlueter, op. cit. (note 24), 250.

26 'Comedy house': quoted Graham Adams, 'The Ottoneum: A Neglected Seventeenth-Century Theater', *Shakespeare Studies*, 15 (1982), 247; 'the old Roman style': quoted ibid. For the Ottoneum repertoire, see ibid., 244.

27 David George, 'The Playhouse at Prescot and the 1592–3 Plague', in Richard Dutton, Alison Findlay and Richard Wilson (eds), *Region, Religion and Patronage: Lancastrian Shakespeare* (Manchester: Manchester University Press, 2003), p.233; Jerzy Limon, *Gentlemen of a Company: English Players in Central and Eastern Europe, 1590–1660* (Cambridge: Cambridge University Press, 1985), pp.39–40, 50–1, et passim.

28 Thomas Kyd quoted in David Riggs, *The World of Christopher Marlowe* (London: Faber & Faber, 2004), p.139.

29 Charles Nicholl, *The Reckoning: The Murder of Christopher Marlowe* (London: Vintage, 2002), p.312. See also Lisa Hopkins, 'Was Marlowe Going to Scotland when He Died, and Does It Matter?' in J.R. Mulryne and Takashi Kozuka (eds), *Shakespeare, Marlowe, Jonson: New Directions in Biography* (Aldershot: Ashgate, 2006), pp.167–82.

30 Christopher Marlowe, *Edward II*, 1,16–17; *Doctor Faustus*, 3,2,76; 3,3,110–23; 1,5,24; 4,2,16; 4,1,11; 4,7,3; 3,3,32; 4,2,34–6: in *Christopher Marlowe: The Complete Plays*, ed. J.B. Steane (Harmondsworth: Penguin, 1969), pp.279, 295, 300, 303, 309, 307, 323 and 401.

31 John Dowland, quoted in *Grove's Dictionary of Music and Musicians* (London: Macmillan, 1980), vol. 2, p.755.

32 Jacques Lacan, 'Desire and the Interpretation of Desire in *Hamlet*', ed. Jacques-Alain Miller, trans. James Hulbert, *Yale French Studies*, 55/6 (1977), 11–52.

33 Schrickx, op. cit. (note 23), 166.

34 Limon, op. cit. (note 27), p.3. See also Albert Cohn (ed.), *Shakespeare in Germany in the Sixteenth and Seventeenth Centuries* (1865; rpt Wiesbaden: Martin Sandig, 1967); Emil Herz, *Englische Schauspieler und englisches Schauspiel zur Zeit Shakespeares in Deutschland* (Hamburg and Leipzig, 1903); and Ernst Brennecke, *Shakespeare in Germany, 1590–1700* (Chicago: University of Chicago Press, 1964). For more recent research, see Graham Adams, 'The Ottoneum: A Neglected Seventeenth-Century Theater', *Shakespeare Studies*, XV (1982), 243–68; Simon Williams, *Shakespeare on the German Stage, 1586–1914* (Cambridge: Cambridge University Press, 1990), pp.27–33; and Schlueter, op. cit. (note 24), 244–6.

35 Mara Wade, 'The Queen's Courts: Anna of Denmark and Her Royal Sisters – Cultural Agency at Four Northern European Courts in the Sixteenth and Seventeenth Centuries', in *Women and Culture at the Courts of the Stuart Queens*, ed. Claire McManus (Basingstoke: Palgrave, 2003), pp.49–80, here p.55.

36 Ibid., p.57; V.C. Ravn, 'English Instrumentalists at the Danish Court in the Time of Shakespeare', *Sammelbände der Internationalen Musikgesellschaft*, 7 (1905–6), 550–63; and 'Engelsk "Instrumentalister" ved det danske Hof paa Shakespeares Tid', *For Ide og Virkelighed*, Copenhagen, 1 (1890), 75–92. And see also Gunnar Sjøgren, 'Hamlet and the Coronation of Christian IV', *Shakespeare Quarterly*, 16 (1965), 155–60.

37 Schrickx, op. cit. (note 23), 160; Wiles, op. cit. (note 16), p.32. For the 1586 visit to Elsinore, see also Klaus Neiiendam, *Renaissanceteatret i Danmark* (Copenhagen: Det teater-videnskabelige Institute, Københavns Universitat, 1988), pp.89–93; Janne Risum, 'De tidligste teaterformer', in *Dansk Teaterhistorie: I: Kirkens og kongens teater*, eds Kela Kvam et al. (Copenhagen: Gyldendal, 1992), pp.9–56. And for the debate about whether a young Shakespeare himself visited Elsinore, see Gunilla Dahlberg, *Komedianttheatern i 1600-talets Stockholm* (Stockholm: Kommittén för Stockholmsforskning, 1992), p.33, n. 5. For the players' longstanding association as members of the Strange/Derby troupe, see Sally-Beth Maclean, 'In Search of Lord Strange: Dynamic Patronage in the North-West', in Phil Butterworth, Pamela King and Meg Twycross (eds), *According to the Ancient Custom: Essays Presented to David Mills: Medieval English Theatre: 29* (Lancaster: Folio, 2009), pp.42–59, esp.pp.49–50.

38 James Bednarz, *Shakespeare and the Poets' War* (New York: Columbia

University Press, 2001), 240–1. And for a similarly Anglocentric inter-
pretation, see also Alan Somerset, '"How Chances It They Travel?"
Provincial Touring, Playing Places, and the King's Men', *Shakespeare
Survey*, 47 (1994), 45–60.

39 James Marino, *Owning Shakespeare: The King's Men and Their
Intellectual Property* (Philadelphia: University of Pennsylvania Press,
2011).

40 Roy Strong, *Henry Prince of Wales and England's Lost Renaissance*
(London: Thames and Hudson, 1986), p.187.

41 James VI and I, 'That onlie essence who made all of noght', in *New
Poems by James I of England* (New York: Columbia University Press,
1911), p.26; Kenneth Robert Olwig, *Landscape, Nature, and the
Body Politic: From Britain's Renaissance to America's New World*
(Madison: University of Wisconsin Press, 2002), p.9.

42 Quoted in Stewart, op. cit. (note 20), p.125. See also Geoffrey Watson,
Bothwell and the Witches (London: Robert Hale, 1975); and Christina
Larner, 'James VI and I and Witchcraft', in *The Reign of James VI and
I*, ed. Alan Smith (New York: St Martin's Press, 1973), pp.74–90; and
Enemies of God: The Witch-Hunt in Scotland (London: John Donald,
1981).

43 Thomas Kyd quoted in Riggs, op. cit. (note 28), p.139.

44 Olwig, op. cit. (note 41), p.9.

45 Keith Brown, 'A Wedding in Oslo', *The Norseman*, 6 (1969), 141–2;
and 'Polonius and Ramelius', Letters, *Times Literary Supplement*, 13
June 2003, 17.

46 Frank Noel Stagg, *East Norway and Its Frontier* (London: George
Allen & Unwin, 1956), p.104; 'Election Trouble': Julia Lupton, 'The
Hamlet Elections', in *Thinking with Shakespeare: Essays on Politics
and Life* (Chicago: Chicago University Press, 2011), pp.69–95, here
p.78. Eschewing topical allusions to the Stuarts, in contradistinction
to Carl Schmitt's *Hamlet of Hecuba*, Lupton interprets the constitutional crisis in *Hamlet* in the exact opposite way to my sense of
it, as an interruption of divine right by election, which 'functions
precisely as what intrudes or breaks into the hereditary succession'.
But this involves a misunderstanding of the *exceptional* character
of Christian's coronation (see below, note 58), as itself a novelty
in breach of the normative elective rule (restated by the officiating
bishop) that the king receives '*from us* the Crown' (p.79).

47 'Bacchanal entertainments': Sir William Segar quoted in John
Stow, *Annales* (London, 1605), p.1437; John Dover Wilson, *The
Manuscript of Shakespeare's 'Hamlet' and the Problems of Its
Transmission* (Oxford: Oxford University Press, 1934), p.25. See
G. Young, 'Christian IV and *Hamlet*', *Times Literary Supplement*, 6

December 1928, 965, where it is proposed that the lines were omitted from the Folio in order not to offend Anne's brother.

48 Neville Davies, 'Jacobean *Antony and Cleopatra*', in '*Antony and Cleopatra*': *Contemporary Critical Essays: New Casebooks*, ed. John Drakakis (Basingstoke: Macmillan, 1994), p.142, originally pub. in *Shakespeare Studies*, 17 (1985), 123–58; and 'The Limitations of Festival: Christian IV's State Visit to England, 1606', in *Italian Renaissance Festivals and Their European Influence*, ed. J.R. Mulryne and Margaret Shewring (Lewiston, NY: Edwin Mellen, 1992), pp.320–5. For English reactions to the Danish tradition of court drunkenness, see also Olwig, op. cit. (note 41), p.6; Brown, op. cit. (note 45), 1969, 141–2; and Stewart, op. cit. (note 20), pp.113–14. See also Langslot, 'Christian IV og Shakespeare', op. cit. (note 17), pp.84–6.

49 Michael Srigley, '"Heavy-headed revel east and west": Hamlet and Christian IV of Denmark', in Gunnar Sorelius (ed.), *Shakespeare and Scandinavia: A Collection of Nordic Studies* (Newark: University of Delaware Press, 2002), pp.168–92, here pp.169–70.

50 For the complexity of the metaphor, see the brilliant chapter 'Mole' in Nicholas Royle's *The Uncanny* (Manchester: Manchester University Press, 2003), pp.241–55.

51 Srigley, op. cit. (note 49), pp.180 and 188.

52 See James Kilby, 'Marston's Drinking Danes', *Notes and Queries*, 10 (1963), 347.

53 Weimann, op. cit. (note 15), p.173.

54 Andrew Hadfield, *Shakespeare and Republicanism* (Cambridge: Cambridge University Press, 2005), p.198. See also Roland Mushat Frye, *The Renaissance 'Hamlet': Issues and Responses in 1600* (Princeton: Princeton University Press, 1984); Alvin Kernan, *Shakespeare, the King's Playwright* (New Haven: Yale University Press, 1995), pp.37–40; Howard Erskine-Hill, *Poetry and the Realm of Politics: Shakespeare to Dryden* (Oxford: Oxford University Press, 1996), pp.99–111. For a systematic reading of the play as an inauspicious reflection on the impending accession of James I, see Eric Mallin, 'Succession, Revenge, and History: The Political *Hamlet*', in *Inscribing the Time: Shakespeare and the End of Elizabethan England* (Berkeley: University of California Press, 1995), pp.106–66.

55 Carl Schmitt, *Hamlet or Hecuba: The Intrusion of the Time into the Play*, trans. David Pan and Jennifer Rust (New York: Telos Publishing, 2009), pp.16–18; see also Hadfield, op. cit. (note 53), p.202.

56 Robert Gore-Browne, *Lord Bothwell* (London: Collins, 1937), pp.409–11, 417–18 and 454.

57 Karen Larsen, *A History of Norway* (Princeton: Princeton University Press, 1950), p.282. For Christian's arctic voyage, see John Gade, *Christian IV, King of Denmark and Norway: A Picture of the Seventeenth Century* (London: Cassell, 1928), pp.82–94.

58 Kjægaard, op. cit. (note 18), p.201. For the change from election to coronation, see also Egil Kraggerud, *Kongehyllest* (Oslo: Oslo University Press, 1991), p.141.

59 'Republican moment': Hadfield, op. cit. (note 54), passim; 'Keep the government': Sir Walter Raleigh, quoted by John Aubrey, in *Aubrey's Brief Lives*, ed. Oliver Lawson Dick (London: Secker and Warburg, 1949), p.257. For discussions of Raleigh's republicanism, see Christopher Hill, *Intellectual Origins of the English Revolution* (Oxford: Clarendon Press, 1965), p.150; and C.A. Patrides (ed.), *Sir Walter Raleigh: The History of the World* (London: Macmillan, 1971), p.14.

60 Sjøgren, op. cit. (note 36), 157–8.

61 Hadfield, op. cit. (note 54), pp.189 and 204.

62 Dudley Carleton, *Dudley Carleton to John Chamberlain, 1603–1624: Jacobean Letters*, ed. Maurice Lee (New Brunswick: Rutgers University Press, 1972), pp.87–8.

63 Sir John Harington, *Nugæ Antiquæ* (2 vols, London, 1779), ed. Rev. H. Harington, vol. 1, p.134, and vol. 2, p.129; 'disgusting shambles': John F. Danby, *Poets on Fortune's Hill: Studies in Sidney, Shakespeare, Beaumont and Fletcher* (London: Faber & Faber, 1952), p.156.

64 Olden-Jørgensen, op. cit. (note 7), 68.

65 Gade, op. cit. (note 57), p.97; and see Burke, op. cit., 1997 (note 6), 22.

66 G.P.V. Akrigg, *Jacobean Pageant: The Court of King James I* (London: Hamish Hamilton, 1962), pp.80–1 and 83–4.

67 Robert Weimann, 'Mimesis in *Hamlet*', in *Shakespeare and the Question of Theory* (London: Routledge, 1985), pp.281–2.

68 See Stuart M. Kurland, '*Hamlet* and the Scottish Succession?' *Studies in English Literature 1500–1900*, 34 (1994), 293.

69 See Richard Wilson, 'Tragedy, Patronage, and Power,' in *The Cambridge Companion to Christopher Marlowe*, ed. Patrick Cheney (Cambridge: Cambridge University Press, 2004), pp.208–12.

70 The most enlightening analysis of the 'little eyases' exchange as it evolves from Q1 to Q2 and the Folio is in Bednarz, op. cit. (note 38), pp.240–56.

71 See Paul Menzer, 'The Tragedians of the City? Q1 *Hamlet* and the Settlements of the 1590s', *Shakespeare Quarterly*, 57 (2006), 164–82.

72 Joseph Loewenstein, *Ben Jonson and Possessive Authorship* (Cambridge: Cambridge University Press, 2002), p.101, sig. E3r.

73 Jonathan Goldberg, *James I and the Politics of Literature: Jonson, Shakespeare, Donne and Their Contemporaries* (Stanford: Stanford University Press, 1989), p.203.

74 Weimann, op. cit (note 15), pp.153 and 160. Cf. Mitchell Greenburg, *Canonical States, Canonical Stages: Oedipus, Othering, and Seventeenth Century Drama* (Minneapolis: University of Minnesota Press, 1994), p.xxvii: 'Certainly in this transitional period of European history, the theater situates itself as the privileged form of representation of the emerging absolutist states ... at once strictly supervised by political and religious authorities and yet also escaping, by the ambivalent nature of theater itself, a totally complicitous relation with institutional power'.

75 Quoted in Limon, op. cit. (note 27), pp.26–7: 'The amounts paid to the English players and musicians by their noble patrons was very high indeed ... Taking into account the fact that the players' living expenses were also covered by the court treasury, we can see that such contracts were very lucrative and sought after by the players, and that at least some of them "returned home generously rewarded and loaded with gold and silver" – as one of the accounts indicated. But salaries were not, of course, the players' only source of income. It should be remembered that in the summer theatrical season players retained by noble courts were allowed to visit other places ... [for] astonishingly high profits.'

76 Martin Holmes, *The Guns of Elsinore* (London: Chatto & Windus, 1964), p.51.

77 Limon, op. cit. (note 27), pp.14, 37 and 40. See also Gunnar Sjögren, 'The Geography of *Hamlet*', in Sorelius, op. cit. (note 49), pp.64–71.

78 Harold Bloom, *'Hamlet': Poem Unlimited* (Edinburgh: Canongate, 2003), p.54.

79 Annabel Patterson, *Shakespeare and the Popular Voice* (Oxford: Basil Blackwell, 1989), p.3. Likewise, Roy Battenhouse points out how commercially unviable Hamlet's ideal humanist theatre would be: 'The Significance of Hamlet's Advice to the Players', in *The Drama of the Renaissance: Essays for Leicester Bradner*, ed. Elmer Blistein (Providence: Rhode Island University Press, 1970), p.26.

80 Lacan, op. cit. (note 32); James Hirsh, 'Hamlet's Stage Directions to the Players', in *Stage Directions in 'Hamlet': New Essays and Directions*, ed. Hardin L. Aasand (Madison: Fairleigh Dickinson University Press, 2003), pp.48 and 59.

81 Anne Barton, *Shakespeare and the Idea of the Play* (London: Chatto & Windus, 1962), p.162.

82 Francis Barker, *The Culture of Violence: Tragedy and History* (Manchester: Manchester University Press, 1993), p.48: 'There has

been considerable debate as to whether the theatre underwrites, opposes or even "negotiates" state power, but here, at any rate, it appears to be enlisted against contemporary power (even if a compensatory romanticism – at bottom legitimatory – of Shakespeare's theatre, rather than the vagabond players', is at work)'.

83 Bednarz, op. cit. (note 38), pp.240–1.
84 Alfred Harbage, *Shakespeare and the Rival Traditions* (Bloomington: Indiana University Press, 1952), p.45.
85 Gabriel Harvey, manuscript note in copy of Speght's *Chaucer* (1598); and Anthony Scoloker, 'Epistle' to *Daiphantus, or the Passions of Love* (London: 1604), repr. in Edmund Chambers, *William Shakespeare* (2 vols, Oxford: Oxford University Press, 1930), vol. 2, pp.197, and 214–15.
86 Poulton, op. cit. (note 3), pp.60–1.
87 Shapiro, op. cit. (note 16), pp.248 and 323–4.
88 Pierre Bourdieu, 'Champ intellectual et projet créatur', *Les temps modernes*, 246 (1966), 868; 'Intellectual Field and Creative Project', trans Sian France, in *Knowledge and Control: New Directions in the Sociology of Education* (London Collier-Macmillan, 1971), p.162.
89 Kjægaard, op. cit. (note 18), p.201; quoting the words of the medieval Norwegian chieftain Asbjørn.
90 Wade, op. cit. (note 35), p.55.
91 For a similar interpretation, see Timothy Wong, 'Steward of the Dying Voice: The Intrusion of Horatio into Sovereignty and Representation', *Telos*, 153 (special issue on Carl Schmitt's *Hamlet or Hecuba*, 2010), 113–31: 'Horatio forces election to come to the fore and thereby establishes the conditions for the birth of sovereignty of the popular will' (129).
92 Leeds Barroll, op. cit. (note 17), pp.55–6. Although tantalized by Shakespeare's possible relations with Queen Anne, in *Politics, Plague, and Shakespeare's Theater: The Stuart Years* (Ithaca: Cornell University Press, 1991) Leeds Barroll argues that for his part King James was oblivious of the dramatist: pp.67–9.
93 Murray Roston, *The Soul of Wit: A Study of John Donne* (Oxford: Oxford University Press, 1974), pp.29–30.
94 Louis Montrose, *The Purpose of Playing: Shakespeare and the Cultural Politics of the Elizabethan Theatre* (Chicago: University of Chicago Press, 1996), p.103. For a bravura discussion of the fraught relations of the theatre to the court, framed by the operatic assassination of Gustav III of Sweden, see also Matthew Wikander, *Princes to Act: Royal Audience and Royal Performance, 1578–1792* (Baltimore: Johns Hopkins University Press, 1993).
95 For the supernova in Cassiopeia discovered by Tycho Brahe and 'yond

same star that's westward from the pole' mentioned by Barnado at 1,1,35, see Donald Olson, Marilynn Olson and Russell Doescher, 'The stars of *Hamlet*', *Sky and Telescope* (November 1998), 68–73,

96 Bojan Pancevski, 'Hamlet May Have Poisoned Stargazer in Mercury Murder', *The Times*, 23 January 2009, 36.

97 Williams, op. cit. (note 20), p.21. See also Dympna Callaghan, *Shakespeare Without Women: Representing Gender and Race on the Renaissance Stage* (London: Routledge, 1999), p.75.

98 Christopher Marlowe, *Tamburlaine the Great, Part Two*, in *Christopher Marlowe: The Complete Plays*, ed. Frank Romany and Robert Lindsey (London: Penguin, 2003): 'With naked negroes shall thy coach be drawn, / And as thou rid'st in triumph through the streets, / The pavement underneath thy chariot wheels With Turkey carpets shall be covered, And cloth of arras hung about the walls, Fit objects for thy princely eye to pierce' [*1,2,40–5*]. If *Hamlet* was connected in this way to King James's Danish marriage, it would be fascinating to relate this episode to the 'domination of blackness over whiteness' in the play which Peter Erickson has analysed in 'Can We Talk about Racism in *Hamlet*?' in *'Hamlet': New Critical Essays*, ed. Arthur Kinney (London: Routledge, 2002), pp.207–13, esp. p.212. For the connection between Anne's masque and her Oslo wedding, see Kim Hall, 'Sexual Politics and Cultural Identity in *The Masque of Blackness*', in Sue-Ellen Case and Janelle Reinelt (eds), *The Performance of Power: Theatrical Discourse and Power* (Iowa City: University of Iowa Press, 1991), p.4; and Suzanne Westfall, 'Theories of Patronage Theatre', in Paul Whitfield White and Suzanne Westfall (eds), *Shakespeare and Theatrical Patronage in Early Modern England* (Cambridge: Cambridge University Press, 2002), pp.34–5.

99 Quoted Alan Stewart, op. cit. (note 20), p.120.

100 Hans Christian Andersen, 'The Emperor's New Clothes', *Fairy Tales*, ed. Svend Larsen, trans. R.P. Keigwin (Odense: Flensted, 1950), pp.179–81.

5

Great stage of fools
King Lear *and the King's Men*

When the mind's free,
The body's delicate

[*King Lear, 3,4,13–14*]

The wisest fool

knowe ye that Wee of our speciall grace certeine knowledge &
mere motion have licenced and aucthorized and by these presentes
do licence and aucthorize theise our Servauntes Lawrence Fletcher
William Shakespeare Richard Burbage Augustyne Phillippes John
heninges henrie Condell William Sly Robert Armyn Richard Cowly
and the rest of theire Assosiates freely to use and exercise the Arte and
faculty of playinge Comedies Tragedies histories Enterludes moralls
pastorals Stageplaies, and suche others like as theie have already
studied or heareafter shall use or studie aswell for the recreation of
our lovinge Subjectes, as for our Solace and pleasure when wee shall
thincke good to see them duringe our pleasure.[1]

King James's 'fast intent' [*Lear, 1,1,36*] to divide in three his theatrical kingdom, trumpeted within days of his arrival in London with a
royal warrant chartering Shakespeare's company as the King's Men
on 19 May 1603, is often described as a fanfare for Stuart absolutism, and a decisive manoeuvre in the Jacobean reinvention of the
English monarchy. But the practical effect of this 'swift, thorough
and autocratic' move to incorporate the three leading acting companies in the 'several dowers' [42] of separate royal households, with
the Admiral's Men attached to the Puritan-tutored Prince Henry
and Worcester's Men assigned to the Catholic Queen Anne, was to
provoke an artificial competitiveness among the players by freezing
their corporate identities and imposing 'a durability they never had

under Elizabeth'.[2] This restructuring notionally put the companies on an equal footing; and analogies with James's similar triangulation of religion, to ensure that 'future strife / May be prevented now' [*41–2*], therefore soon emerged, as with 'oily art' [*225*] or 'saucy bluntness' [*2,2,89*] the sister troupes produced distinct repertoires tailored to the expectations of their different audiences. Critics have in fact noticed intensifying legalistic connotations to the idea of 'performance' itself in Shakespearean drama at this time, as the performance of a 'part' became enmeshed in the evolving law relating to contract, intention, promises, satisfaction, and service. But the terms of this theatre charter suggest that James's absolutist attitudes also introduced a new suspicion of performance, as 'an obligation amounting to coercion':[3]

EDMUND: My services to your lordship.
  KENT: I must love you, and sue to know you better.
EDMUND: Sir, I shall study deserving.

[*1,1,27–9*]

Under King James Shakespeare became increasingly concerned about having to perform 'such a part which never / I shall discharge … a part / Thou hast not done before' [*Coriolanus, 3,2,105–6*], yet this new interest in non-compliance seems in excess of the pressures of his commercial contract with his company, as though his concept of agency was being inflected by the absolutist agenda. For whether or not the King's Men were now encouraged to perform plays that accorded with James's own Anglican middle way, the 'darker purpose' [*34*] of the British Solomon's scheme to divide and rule London's theatre-land was effectively to extend his 'largest bounty … Where nature doth with merit challenge' [*51–2*], by favouring his preferred players with a 'third more opulent' [*74*] of the professional spoils, in return for 'cooperating to produce a more conservative royal authority'.[4] Queen Elizabeth's theatrical patronage had never favoured a monopoly, Leeds Barroll emphasizes, 'but when Shakespeare and his fellows now proceeded to present at court the first five or six plays in a row', the other two acting consortia must have been 'genuinely alarmed'.[5] And according to many critics, the King's Men duly obliged their new master when they 'entered wholeheartedly into the fiction' of his royal game, and with competitive entries such as *King Lear* ventriloquized James's patriarchal 'conception of the absolute king'.[6]

When he became 'His Majesty's Servant' with the title of Groom of the Chamber, the story goes, Shakespeare tied his work 'directly to the myth' of divine right James 'was citing as a way of authorizing' his 'Free and Absolute Monarchy', and henceforth wrote plays that 'served the specific interests of the Crown'.[7] The idea that this 'royal takeover' arose from the king's personal belief that actors should express his power, as the 'outward and visible signs of [his] sense of office', is disputed by some critics, however, who argue that the fact that the charter was so hurried suggests that 'someone must have intruded' the theatre onto the Crown agenda, 'a powerful intercessor' who was perhaps the pushy young William Herbert Earl of Pembroke who, to show him who loved him most, during the coronation 'actually kissed his Majesty's face'.[8] If the King's Men did owe their sudden elevation to such 'unruly waywardness' [295], that may explain the surprise omission from the patent of any mention of the Master of the Revels who had censored theatre under the Tudors. With further nudging from the Herberts, the Queen's Men would also be freed from the censor and placed under the poet Samuel Daniel. What bewilders scholars about these manoeuvres, therefore, is that it was just at this point of absolutist interference, when the acting companies were nationalized by royal decree, that their tripartite division seemed to promise the players emancipation, as the Elizabethan censorship system was relaxed and decentralized, and with niche markets the three sister companies were encouraged to go separate ways.[9] No wonder, then, that critics are puzzled by this 'somewhat careless' proclamation to launch a competition that was in reality a charade, for by shaking off 'The sway, revenue, execution' of the old Elizabethan Revels Office, and 'Conferring them on younger strengths', while still retaining 'The name, and all the additions' [135–7] of a royal patron, the monarch known as 'The Wisest Fool in Christendom' appears, as so often, to have been making himself truly the king of fools:[10]

FOOL: All thy other titles thou hast given away: that thou wast
           born with.
KENT: This is not altogether fool, my lord.
FOOL: No, faith, lords and great men will not let me; if I had a
           monopoly out, they would have part on't.

                                  [1,4,130–4]

James's actors' charter was an unprecedented abdication of cultural authority, since for the first time royalty 'asserted directly that the pleasures of playgoing were not just the monarch's but the people's'. As Andrew Gurr observes, 'That innovation called for redress'.[11] For the king had stumbled into a conceptual minefield strewn with opposing notions of patronage and representation. Such confusion over standards of censorship can perhaps be explained only by supposing 'that Stuart autocratic ambitions (at least in theatrical affairs) were matched by a degree of incompetence, or venality', Richard Dutton suggests.[12] Philip Finkelpearl in fact connects 'the comedians' liberty' to 'the chaos in the Revels Office'; and another explanation for the muddle is that it arose out of conflict between the Court and Council in the first days of the reign, and James's attempt 'to give himself freedom of action' against the old guard.[13] 'Full of changes' and 'unconstant starts' [287–98], the king was himself in the dark, it is said, about the power he was throwing away, when out of his 'mere motion' he divested himself of these 'cares of state' [48], and authorized the actors 'freely to use and exercise the art and faculty of playing'. Yet in liberating the London stage James had form, having overruled the Kirk of Scotland when it tried to block an Edinburgh season by 'certain English Comedians' in 1599, with a decree that 'all His Majesty's subjects, inhabitants within this said burgh may freely at their own pleasure repair to the said comedies and plays without any pain, censuring, reproach or slander to be incurred'.[14] In 1601 the English actors penetrated even further north to Aberdeen, 'where they received the title of the "King's Servants"', and the Freedom of the city, after performing 'the old play of *Macbeth*', biographers have imagined, before James. And these Freemen who were also royal servants included, so the legend goes, Shakespeare himself.[15]

King James's emancipation of the players was a *faux pas* that may have originated as a misguided attempt to transfer the familiarity of Scottish court culture to England, a cultural misunderstanding, like 'his easy relations with his Scottish court fools', that was 'one of many indications of the preservation of Edinburgh court *mores* in the new kingdom'.[16] But this false start surely also reflected the contradictions of his attempt to be both king and poet that Jane Rickard has analysed.[17] For the very 'first verses that ever the King made' as an aspiring poet aged fifteen had been a fanfare for just such intellectual freedom: 'Since thought is free, think what thou wilt'.[18] And it was in tune with that enlightened edict of artistic emancipation that the King's Men were to be liberated, it appeared in the division of the kingdom, from other authorities. Equipped with their royal patent they would henceforth be free to perform wherever the wind took them: 'as well within their now usual house called the Globe within the County of Surrey as also within the liberties and freedom of any other City, university town, or Borough whatsoever within our said Realms and dominions'.[19] In the days of the old queen Shakespeare dreamed that her successor would grant 'liberty / Withal, as large a charter as the wind' [*As You*, 2,7,47–8]. But now he had received just such a windy charter the work the king's servant made of the mixed signals concerning the sovereign and his creature James gave out hints how he was as baffled as the historians about the largesse of the gift:

> KENT: I thought the king had more affected the Duke of
>   Albany than Cornwall.
> GLOUCESTER: It did always seem so to us; but now, in the
>   division of the kingdom, it appears not which of
>   the dukes he values most; for equalities are so
>   weighed that curiosityin neither can make choice
>   of either's moiety.
>
>   [*1,1,1–6*]

Truth's a dog to kennel

'He hath ever but slenderly known himself. The best and soundest of his time hath been but rash' [*291–3*]: if Lear's division of his kingdom does metadramatize the uncertainty in which the dramatist was caught by the king's reorganization of the London theatre, with its contradictory orders to his new 'Servants' to 'freely' perform 'as well for the recreation of our loving Subjects, as for our Solace and pleasure', the confusion perhaps offers a professional context for one of the crucial questions in Shakespeare criticism: whether 'King James got his £10 worth?' for *King Lear*, as Alvin Kernan put it in *Shakespeare the King's Playwright*, when it was acted before him at Whitehall on St Stephen's night, 26 December 1606.[20] The fact that Lawrence Fletcher, a new sharer in the company and the only one listed ahead of Shakespeare in the patent, had been 'comedian to his Majesty' in Edinburgh, and so 'could only have been added on the king's instructions', is seen as proof the King's Men could not but fall in with the wishes of a ruler who once said anyone who hanged Fletcher would 'hang also', and had himself composed a masque and a treatise lecturing poets how to write.[21] And Ben Jonson's tribute, in his verses for the 1623 Folio, to Shakespeare as the 'Sweet Swan of *Avon*' whose 'flights upon the banks of *Thames* ... did take our *James*', is backed by another legend that might just confirm this level of royal involvement. 'That most learned Prince, and great patron of learning, King James', the story went when it was printed a century later, 'was pleas'd with his own hand to write an amicable letter to Mr. Shakespeare'.[22]

Jenny Wormald remarks that it was when James was fooling around with them that his English subjects became most worried; but if the king ever did write to the dramatist in 'his own hand', this gesture of friendship would seem to be a prime instance of the 'manipulative falsity' that Slavoj Žižek detects in all such protestations of amicability, which consists in the catch that 'somebody who is ready to damage me if I say no to him cannot really be devoted to my happiness, as he claims'.[23] For James had in fact warned Prince Henry never to fraternize with theatre folk, nor make 'your sporters your counsellors', and especially not 'Comedians and Balladines, for the Tyrants delighted most in them'.[24] So, when he arrived in London in 1603, the king came south with a confusing reputation as a monarch who claimed divine right, yet blurred 'the distinction between his roles as writer and king', when he 'engaged with other poets not only as a patron but also as a fellow poet'.[25] Perhaps it was because he was so nervous of the rival power of the dramatic poet that even in Scotland he therefore kept an eagle-eye on the English players, and plaintively protested that they mocked him as 'the poorest prince in Christendom'. Thus, 'It is regretted that the Comedians of London should scorn the king and the people of this land in their play', the English ambassador reported ominously from Edinburgh in 1598, 'and it is wished that the matter be speedily amended, lest the king and the country be stirred to anger'.[26]

By the time he was presented with *King Lear* James had probably 'already seen most of Shakespeare's plays then in existence', since now that he had the opportunity the king tried to attend every court performance, enjoying twenty plays in 1603–4 alone, including a *Henry V* from which the author took care to cut wry digs at 'Scots Captain Jamy' [*3,3,19*] and 'the weasel Scot' [*1,2,170*] who snaffles up England.[27] 'Our bending author' is how Shakespeare characterized his abject posture in the Epilogue inserted on that royal occasion. But a self-demeaning shot at 'smiling rogues', who 'Renege, affirm, and turn their halcyon beaks / With every gale and vary of their masters' [*2,2,65–71*], encapsulated the problem that now seemed to be staged in *King Lear*, with its language of service yet 'potentially sensational' opening lines, blurting out the names of the two real dukes of Albany and Cornwall – the Princes Charles and Henry – as rivals for the crown.[28] The problem was the oldest one of all for the artist, that 'Truth's a dog to kennel; he must be whipped out' [*1,4,95*]; but given extra urgency by King James's contradictory warranty to praise without praise, perform 'freely' for 'our Solace', and speak both what was expected yet also what was felt:

> Now, our joy ... what can you say to draw
> A third more opulent than your sisters? Speak.
>
> [*1,1,81–5*]

How to speak 'free and patient thoughts' [*4,6,80*] for a 'free and absolute monarch'? As the leading dramatist of the King's Men, Shakespeare rose to the perverse and irrational challenge of *speaking 'freely' by compulsion*, critics deduce, with a procession of plays that artfully negotiated the paradox of 'A love that makes breath poor and speech unable' [*58*]. Thus, with *Othello* at Hallowe'en 1604 he welcomed a pedantic know-all, it is suggested, by setting the story around the Battle of Lepanto, about which the king had written an epic in verse.[29] Then in *Measure for Measure* at Whitehall, on 26 December, Shakespeare created a Christmas comedy in which he even played the Duke himself, to broadcast 'what King James had written about state-craft'.[30] Likewise, when *Macbeth* was showcased at Hampton Court on 7 August 1606, before the monarch and his Danish brother-in-law King Christian IV, this 'royal play' provided 'a theatrical version' of James's tome about witchcraft by the lurid light of the Gunpowder Plot. 'James Stuart must have been enormously pleased', Kernan infers, since *Macbeth* was a perfect dynastic commemoration, 'celebrating his ancient lineage ... and making divine-right identical with sanity and nature'.[31] Shakespeare's ethic of hospitality was such that in *The Winter's Tale*, it is said, he gave 'a banquet worthy of the Banqueting House and a sop for the sovereign'.[32] Finally, with *The Tempest*, Shakespeare created what Stanley Wells calls 'a musical entertainment' for the rich and powerful, as he became, on this view, a slavish toady in the very role he seems all through his life to have despised as demeaning and hypocritical: the official laureate 'spending [his] fury on some worthless song, / Dark'ning [his] power to lend base subjects light' [Sonnet 100].[33]

On all the grand Jacobean gala occasions 'our bending author' was truly a royal favourite, whose 'great succession of Stuart plays' constituted 'one of the master oeuvres of European patronage art', it is proposed, comparable to Velázquez's canvases for the court of Spain, Monteverdi's operas in Venice or Molière's comedies at Versailles.[34] Recently, the picture of Shakespeare as such a court functionary has been given a varnish of Schmittian political theology by critics who view the plays as idealizations of sacred kingship. According to this interpretation, the plays affirm the terrifying affinity of art and power because they share Hölderlin's excitement, cited so often by Heidegger, that 'where danger threatens / That which saves from it also grows'.[35] Such readings are, by their own account, oblivious to works such as *King Lear* or *Measure for Measure* as *theatre*. So, 'What interests me is the obvious' avers Debora Shuger, which is that what might sound like 'interchangeable flattery' to modern ears was in fact the language of 'high Christian royalism'. Shakespeare endorsed the king's vision of himself as a 'sacral monarch', in this reading, and duly oriented his plays 'in the direction of absolutism'.[36] That the dramatist parroted the doctrine of the divine right is however by no means so obvious. For what this neo-conservative recuperation misses is that, from the first day that he became a King's Man, Shakespeare made the logical contradiction of performing freely to order, the double-bind of praising without praise, the subject of his work:

> LEAR: Tell me, my daughters –
> Since now we will divest us, both of rule,
> Interest of territory, cares of state –
> Which of you shall we say doth love us most?
>
> [1,1,46–9]

As flies to wanton boys

'They flatter'd me like a dog ... they told me I was everything' [4,6,96–102]: editors key *King Lear* to James's need to promote his absolutist project to unite his triple crown and restore a mythic British empire.[37] Certainly, the free speech the king so rashly gave the actors was soon curtailed, when Robert Cecil, the Machiavellian chief minister, assumed personal control of the bureaucracy of the stage. 'No one was better placed than Cecil to appreciate the increasing importance of pageantry and theatricals', Dutton explains.[38] And the idea that Shakespeare performed Stuart propaganda on command runs up against the 'intricate games he now played with realism', and the negative image of performance itself that darkens the work he devised for the new reign, which, as Anne Barton observes, represents the theatre as 'a thing devoid of value, as it is in Lear's bitter evocation of the play metaphor: "When we are born, we cry that we are come / To this great stage of fools" [4,6,183]'.[39] New Historicists have inferred that these plays square artistic freedom with a free or unlimited monarchy by prescribing 'a single law for the state and theater ... For Shakespeare ... it was his law, and the king's.'[40] Professional opportunism might, therefore, have encouraged the dramatist to identify his own symbolic 'royalties' with the real ones of James. Yet as Dutton shrewdly comments, 'this can hardly be the whole story', for it does not explain what 'drove Shakespeare to transcend his material, to write *King Lear* rather than *The Triumphs of Reunited Britannia*'.[41]

New Historicist critics liked to believe that in *King Lear* Shakespeare 'insists on the iconic nature of the monarch's body'.[42] Yet what complicates these Jacobean dramas is how each 'foregrounds the play's status as a piece of theatre – the extent to which it is a written text acted by paid actors speaking someone else's words', and an imposed chore that is felt to be 'cabined, cribbed, confined, bound in / To saucy doubts and fears' [*Macbeth*, 3,4,23–4].[43] As Luke Wilson puts it, these plays in which we hear the dramatist 'speaking out of the mouth of the character' reveal 'agency-for-another lurking behind agency-for-oneself'.[44] Thus, if *Measure for Measure* reflected James's conference of bishops on the 'great stage' at Hampton Court, the mirror was distorted by the perception of how, 'Dressed in a little brief authority', man 'Plays such fantastic tricks before high heaven / As makes the angels weep' [2,2,120–5].[45] If *Othello* honoured the royal author of *Lepanto* who was 'a Homer to himself', the homage was undercut by a story that is 'a pageant to keep us in false gaze' [1,3,19] stage-managed by Iago, a conspiracy theorist who abuses the other characters as his 'Players' [2,1,115], and whose name approximates to James.[46] If 'what the stained-glass in the Great Hall at Hampton Court did' for the Tudors, '*Macbeth* did ... for the Stuarts', the commission was ironized by a tragedy in which life itself appears no more than 'a walking shadow, a poor player / That struts and frets his hour upon the stage' [*5,5,23–5*].[47] And most perversely of all, if Shakespeare was such a celebrant of Jacobean absolutist political theology, in *King Lear* he anticipated the discursive paradoxes of modernism, with an entire drama constructed, from the moment Cordelia offers 'Nothing' [*1,1,86*] to the king, on the imperative Samuel Beckett called 'the obligation to express' when there is nothing to be said:

> The expression that there is nothing to express, nothing with which to express, nothing from which to express, no power to express, no desire to express, together with the obligation to express.[48]

'We cry that we are come / To this great stage of fools': Shakespeare returned to the same performative crisis throughout his career, when an aristocratic audience at first compels then condemns the antics of the 'poor player' as 'A tale / Told by an idiot full of sound and fury, / Signifying nothing' [*25–7*]. At a time when players were moving away from private patrons to public playhouses, he created a sequence of plays-within-plays that are callously disrupted by courtier spectators as 'the silliest stuff that ever I heard' [*Dream, 5,1,207*]. As Meredith Anne Skura comments in *Shakespeare the Actor*, whatever it was that had terrified Shakespeare whenever he 'Made [him]self a motley to view' [Sonnet 110] was 'of a piece with his ability to imagine the story of other beggars who cannot move their stony-hearted auditors'.[49] Thus the pathos of dependency seems to have been so intrinsic to his experience of performance that it is hard not to associate the dramatist himself with expressions like Antonio's: 'I hold this world but as the world ... A stage, where every man must play a part, / And mine a sad one' [*Merchant, 1,1,77–9*]. What overshadows the idea of the play in *King Lear*, however, is that here the players' entire universe is conceived as such a theatre of cruelty, in which 'As flies to wanton boys are we to the gods; / They kill us for their sport' [*4,1,37*].

When Shakespeare was commissioned to put power on display with a performance that began with loyal protestations like Kent's to 'Royal Lear / Whom I have ever honour'd as my king, / Lov'd as my father, as my master follow'd, / As my great patron thought on in my prayers' [*1,1,39–42*], it seems that his picture of his own profession was now soured by a self-lacerating sensation of the theatre as a paltry game to 'trifle with despair' [*4,6,33*], like Lear's mock trial, or Edgar's chicanery with his father's suicide attempt. As

Stephen Booth observes, in *King Lear* the cliché that 'All the world's
a stage' [*As You*, *2,7,138*] has suddenly become so fraught 'because
the play as play – as an event in the lives of its audience – is analogous to the events it describes', which, from the king's staging of his
love-test as a grand ceremonial pageant, seem to be pre-scripted,
'like the catastrophe of the old comedy', as Edmund jeers [*1,2,123*],
or 'An interlude!', in Goneril's derisive words [*5,3,90*]. 'What we see
Lear do during the test is what audiences do always' in prejudging
the case, Booth observes, but what is original is the dramatist's self-
consciousness about this hermeneutic circle.[50] For what the king's
daughters are required to undergo to meet these prior expectations,
supposedly of their own voluntary accord, is precisely the interpel-
lative ordeal to which the dramatist was now being subjected as an
official purveyor of words by royal appointment:

> Sir, I love you more than words can wield the matter;
> Dearer than eye-sight, space, and liberty;
> Beyond what can be valued, rich or rare;
> No less than life, with grace, health, beauty, honour;
> As much as child e'er lov'd, or father found;
> A love that makes breath poor, and speech unable;
> Beyond all manner of so much I love you.
>
> > [*1,1,53–9*]

Self-abasement was obligatory in a literary system still deferential to
textual patronage, and thereby locked into the Petrarchan discourse
of lover and beloved, suzerain and vassal, so copiously rehearsed
by Goneril and Regan. But the dramatist's concern about the particularly infantilized way in which the actor 'gets what he wants by
being obsequious to the audience' becomes so acute in *King Lear*
that Skura places it among a sequence of Jacobean 'flattery plays',
including the revived *Gorboduc*, the original *King Leir*, Jonson's
Sejanus (in which Shakespeare himself acted) and *Timon of Athens*,
which were put on 'in an attempt to warn James about his behaviour'.[51] For Maynard Mack, too, there is an abrupt realization in
King Lear of the performative significance of the archetypal tale of
'The Abasement of the Proud King', in which a king is 'made the
court Fool and compelled to take his food with the palace dogs', as
a *topos* highlighting the calculated hypocrisy to which the player is
reduced. Thus, when Lear's obliging daughters demean themselves
professing to be 'alone felicitate / In your highness' love' [*73–4*], it is

as if the Petrarchan erotics of cringing feudal servitude with which Shakespeare had presented himself in his Sonnets to the patron he addressed as the 'Lord of my love' are exposed as a sham and ploy to both 'rise and stoop at once'.[52] For in *King Lear* the sacrificial terms of 'organized dejection' with which the poet of the Sonnets prostrates himself 'all naked' in his 'tattered loving' [Sonnet 26], to show how 'civilizations transform torment into style', are *themselves* exposed as an insincere charade.[53] So it is impossible not to connect this self-shaming with the fact that what had altered for Shakespeare was that he had now become a King's Man *in truth*.

Shakespeare's revulsion from his conflicted desire 'to please you every day' [*Twelfth, 5,1,395*] may have been triggered by the sheer number of days on which the King's Men were expected to perform for James. The dramatist had probably been summoned to Wiltshire to take part in celebrations hosted by his Herbert patrons in Bath on the official Coronation Day, 25 July, the Feast of St James, 1603, for instance; and he was likely back there at Christmas to entertain the ambassadors presented to the new monarch, then holding court at the spa. And whether or not he did humour his Herbert hosts at nearby Wilton by inserting a topical masque about union for a gala night of *As You Like It*; or appeared in *A Midsummer Night's Dream* when the King's Men revived it on New Year's Day for nine-year-old Prince Henry; he was certainly in the official line-up in August 1604, when he and his colleagues were obliged to attend the Somerset House peace conference as glorified waiters upon the Spanish delegation. To lubricate this summit the diplomats showered bribes, and although biographers are unsure 'what form his "tip" may have taken', they speculate that the 'broad silver-gilt bowl' he bequeathed to his daughter Judith was the glittering prize bestowed for his smooth discretion over these eighteen days upon 'the man Shakespeare'.[54]

'What hast thou been? A serving-man, proud in heart and mind; that curled my hair; wore gloves in my cap' [*3,4,79–81*]: the dramatist had headed the list of the players issued with four yards of crimson cloth for the livery he wore the first time at the delayed coronation procession on 15 March 1604.[55] He probably had to pose beneath one of the triumphal arches heralding James as the new Augustus. But judging by the sonnets he wrote at this time which scorn these 'pyramids' [123] of 'smiling pomp' [124], Shakespeare felt no satisfaction in the 'obsequious' role he was forced to perform beside the Oswalds of the court: 'Were't ought to me I bore the canopy', he shrugs, 'With my extern the outward honouring? ... No, let me be ... in thy heart ... poor but free' [125]. His craven stooping in 'rustling silks' appears instead to have provided this conscripted 'serving-man' [88] with a problematic for *King Lear*, in the experience of one who remains 'poor but free' at heart. 'No troupe acted more for James', we are reminded, 'than the King's Men'. In the year preceding the tragedy about 'this great stage of fools' the Revels Office listed eleven court appearances by His Majesty's players.[56] Thus it is all the more telling that the drama Shakespeare devised at this instant of his greatest access to the royal palace should be his retelling of *Cinderella*, the most popular of all stories about rags to riches, and an archetypal affirmation of the power of weakness, yet itself the most crude and spare expression of the creaturely tatters to which truth is reduced in the world of the court. For the closer he came to the face of sovereign power, *King Lear* suggests, the more the dramatist, like La Fontaine in the Fables, was struck by its bestial snarl:

> Thou hast seen a farmer's dog bark at a beggar?
> And the creature run from the cur? There thou mightst
> behold the great image of authority: a dog's obeyed in office ...
> Through tattered clothes small vices do appear;
> Robes and furred gowns hide all.
>
> [4,6,150–9]

Fathers that wear rags

Recent reflections on 'bare life' by thinkers like Giorgio Agamben, Jacques Derrida and Eric Santner have allowed *King Lear* to be seen as Shakespeare's most piercing examination of the complicity of the 'creature' with the sovereign 'cur', the perverse logic of authority that requires abjection of 'unaccommodated man' as a 'poor, bare, forked animal' [3,4,99–100] to represent its power.[57] Yet ever since Coleridge noted that Shakespeare's play about the girl in 'tattered clothes' has the moral economy of a nursery-tale, critics have averted their eyes from its similarity to the stark and rudimentary *Cinderella*.[58] The likeness was not lost, however, on Freud, who also compared Lear's test to the casket scene in *The Merchant of Venice*, where Bassanio prefers 'meagre lead', that moves him 'more than eloquence' [3,2,104–6].[59] And in *Why Shakespeare?*

Catherine Belsey insists on the degrading resemblance 'between one of the grandest of all tragedies' and the homely story where 'a prince chooses between three sisters and opts for the youngest and humblest, making the right choice in spite of outward appearances'. In peasant tales like *Cinderella* or its English version *Cap o' Rushes* the correct choice is always the unassuming deferential one, Belsey observes, for 'humility and reticence are endorsed'. Thus, by applying folklore's magical 'law of threes', Shakespeare invites us to take sides with Cordelia, who in this genre could not have spoken other than she did, Belsey avers, when her tyrant king and father demanded to know 'what can you say to draw / A third more opulent than your sisters?' and with feudal exactitude she replied, 'I love your majesty / According to my bond' [*1,1,84–92*].

In Belsey's feminist critique Shakespeare's tragedy adopts the rags-and-riches theme on which *Cinderella* is itself based, where a daughter says she loves her father 'as meat loves salt', to probe the limits of language and the rule that 'Wherein we cannot speak, therein we must be silent', as by drawing on the folktale about the deceptiveness of words yet spoiling its happy end, '*King Lear* builds a monumental demonstration' of what lies outside of speech and so must *never* be spoken.[60] This reading highlights the play's dependence on 'A woman's story at a winter's fire / Authorized by her grandam' [*Macbeth, 3,4,64*]. But what it thereby effaces is precisely the dark thread of *intention*, the dirty secret Shakespeare learned from the 'curious tale' [*1,4,28*] of *Cinderella*, and wove into his own negative dialectic of investiture and divestment, sight and blindness, which is the irony that the *askesis* of sackcloth and ashes is always a form of exhibitionism and deliberate *aesthetic* choice. For other critics have noted an affinity between Cordelia's Trappism, Lear's disrobing, Edgar's dishevelment and the author's own discursive dismantling in the borrowed rags of a female taleteller beside the fire, Shakespeare's own conceited swelling with 'the mother' [*2,4,56*].[61] They recognize that his 'Cinderella' project shares with 'Poor Tom', who 'in the fury of his heart … eats cow-dung' [*3,4,120*], the masochistic destitution of a Counter-Reformation saint, on whose 'sacrifices', Lear is foolish enough to believe, 'The gods themselves throw incense' [*5,3,20*].[62]

King Lear is 'crossed' by the 'side-piercing sight' [*4,6,85*] of martyrdom. The king himself says that he cannot get 'crosses' [*5,3,277*] out of his eyes; and allusions to St Lucy's 'poor old

eyes' [*3,7,57*], St Catherine's 'wheel of fire', or St Juliana's boiling
in 'molten lead' [*4,7,47–8*] are truly from the Catholic *Theatre of
Cruelty*. Yet the hagiography of sacrifice is so compromised in this
play by narcissistic self-importance, as it had been when Isabella
flaunts 'Th'impression of keen whips ... as rubies' [*Measure,
2,4,101*], when Cordelia glories in being 'Most loved, despised'
[*1,1,252*]; Kent embraces 'cruel garters' [*2,4,7*], Lear calls 'execut-
ing fires' to 'singe my white beard' [*3,2,4–6*]; or Edgar mortifies
his 'bare arms' with 'Pins, wooden pricks, nails, sprigs of rose-
mary' [*2,3,15–16*], that it is as if Shakespeare is *double-crossing*
the same pseudo-martyrdom as John Donne: a chiasmic pose in
which 'self-crossing is not only linked to an *imitatio Christi*',
but as Thomas Docherty comments, 'to its seeming opposite: it
implies an activity of wounding oneself or "cursing"'.[63] For as
Maud Ellmann points out in *The Hunger Artists*, a study of the
dark continuities between fasting, martyrdom and writing, this
sacrificial crisis is one that aligns Cordelia with Lear, and implies
that it is precisely in her depersonalized non-compliance that this
classic anorectic is most her father's child. For with his '*hysterico
passio*' [*2,4,55*], Lear is himself a study in the inverted logic
of those whose infantilized anger against oppression is turned
against themselves:

> Like [the anorectic exhibitionist] King Lear ... gives up all his human
> superfluities in order to experience himself as bare forked animal.
> For Lear, too, is a hunger artist, and for this reason one could argue
> that Cordelia gives her father just what he is asking for, a vision of
> the 'nothing' at the heart of things. 'Nothing, my Lord.' Indeed, Lear
> pursues this nothing with the frenzy of an addict from the moment
> that he gives away his kingdom until he holds the lifeless body of his
> daughter in his arms.[64]

Ellmann's characterization of Lear as one of those 'Fathers that wear
rags' [*2,4,46*] to teach their 'pelican daughters' [*3,4,72*] the coun-
terintuitive logic of masochism, divestment and self-subjugation
invites us to rethink Shakespeare's drama of self-dismembering
in light of feminist and postcolonial investigations of internalised
oppression, such as Gayatri Spivak's essay 'Can the Subaltern
Speak?', which views Hindu suttee as a positive choice, or Elfride
Jelinek's novel *The Piano Teacher*, in which the protagonist solic-
its 'an inventory of pain' in resistance to fascism.[65] According to

Judith Halberstam, 'To be cut, to be bared, to be violated publicly', as was Yoko Ono in her 1965 happening 'Cut Piece', is a defiant depersonalization exemplifying the radical passivity of 'The Queer Art of Failure', for in such 'silence, stubbornness, self-abnegation, and sacrifice', we glimpse the undoing of being, where being is defined 'in terms of mastery, pleasure, and heroic liberation'.[66] Halberstam has no time for Deleuze's implicitly humanistic contention that 'the masochist's apparent obedience conceals a criticism and a provocation'; and instead finds an aesthetic of 'unbecoming' in the uncooperative illegibility of certain types of collage.[67] And suffused with images of sexual discharge, shit and vomit, *King Lear* does have affinities with 'Abject Art'. But what this queer theory of self-shattering does not quite engage is the continued egocentricity of the anti-social sulk, the self-regard in the histrionics of negativity that Shakespeare seems to look right through, when he presents radical passivity as mere radical chic, yet another imitative Jesuitical imposture:

LEAR: Ha! Here's three on's are sophisticated. Thou art the thing itself; unaccommodated man is no more than such a poor, bare, forked animal as thou art. Off, off, you lendings! Come, unbutton here.

FOOL: Prithee, nuncle, be contented; 'tis a naught night to swim in.

[3,4,98–102]

For Ellmann, 'self-starvation is above all a performance'. So Cordelia and her father are both performers who ask to be judged on their contrived *representation* of self-sacrifice, like those Irish hunger-strikers whose 'dirty protest' began with the daubing of their cells in excrement, or the protagonist of Kafka's story 'The Hunger Artist', who locks himself in a circus cage and starves to entertain the crowd. As with Hamlet's mousetrap, Ellmann proposes, this type of self-privation is necessarily staged, since 'Anorectics are "starving for attention"; they are *making a spectacle of themselves*'. With analogies to the death-drive of Andromache, the staging of martyrdom in *King Lear* therefore brings us much closer than anything in a fairy story to consciousness of the perverse sovereignty of self-immolation, and to awareness that 'the anorectic body ... depends upon the other as a spectator ... its emaciation, which seems to indicate a violent rebuff, also bespeaks a strange adventure in seduction'.[68] Like the suicidal potlatch of the immigrant riots discussed by Žižek, which torch the protestors' possessions, in this retelling the self-wasting economy of the Cinderella posture literally *cries out* to be decoded as a type of meta-linguistic or phatic gesture, the unbecoming and self-exposing emptiness of which functions 'to create a problem', and so signify as 'a test of the system'.[69] Shakespeare had, after all, built an entire career on the pretence of speaking to his patron 'In true plain words' as 'thy true-telling friend' [Sonnet 82], and on stage in 'russet yeas and honest kersey noes' [*Love's*, 5,2,413]. So he knew better than anyone how a self-abasing *Sachlichkeit* of 'Plainness and reluctance, the censure and apparent absence of rhetoric', is always demonstrative, and itself constitutes a fashion statement, as Cornwall sceptically remarks of Kent:[70]

> This is some fellow
> Who, having been praised for bluntness, doth affect
> A saucy roughness and constrains the garb
> Quite from his nature. He cannot flatter, he,
> An honest mind and plain, he must speak truth!
> An they will take it, so; if not, he's plain.
> These kind of knaves I know, which in this plainness
> Harbour more craft and more corrupter ends
> Than twenty silly ducking observants
> That stretch their duties nicely.
>
> [2,2,87–96]

'Nothing will come of nothing' [1,1,88], the king insists. Yet *askesis* is intended to generate meaning; and in Shakespeare the gesture of nothingness always signifies, as Kent knows: 'I can keep honest counsel, ride, run, mar a curious tale in telling it, and deliver a plain message bluntly' [1,4,28]. The queer power of this theatrics of anti-theatricality had been essayed by Marlowe, whose Tamburlaine also stages a truth-test for his three sons that is sabotaged when the youngest sissy boy refuses to co-operate, and is killed by his father for 'folly, sloth, and damnèd idleness'.[71] So, though a line of critics side with Cordelia, as if her sealing of her lips means she never speaks another word, her generic resemblance to the eponymous 'Cinders' alerts us to the attention-seeking ruse of 'plainness' which is the scarlet thread of all the 'Love Like Salt' narratives, in which a father's incestuous desire is thwarted by the daughter's 'dirty protest' in the protective smuts she cleans off for her prince: the self-dramatizing ploy 'To take the basest and most poorest shape

/ That ever penury, in contempt of man, / Brought near to beast' [2,3,7–9]. For as folklorists remind us, it was no accident that these peasant tales of the power of weakness, and the surprising victory of grime and indigence, were published in the Enlightenment France of Louis XIV, where the stain of incest could figure the tyranny of unlimited sovereignty, and its sublimation the *civilité* of the Sun King.[72] There were politic Aesopian reasons why a wise old Mother Goose brooded in the court culture of the absolutist state. And it is the recital of the *conte de fée* in the Paris salons of the 1690s that might offer a key to what Shakespeare made of the 'dirty secret' of *Cinderella* at Whitehall.

Donkey skin

Charles Perrault, the architect who first recorded *Cendrillon*, had been Colbert's aide for twenty years, historians remind us, 'suggesting and supervising cultural policies to glorify the king'.[73] Thus, the best gloss on *King Lear* may be Louis Marin's, when in his classic study of representation at Versailles, *Portrait of the King*, the semiotician analyses the tale known as *Donkey Skin*, and shows how this variation on the sight/blindness paradox, rewritten by Perrault, 'turns absolute power against itself'. What *Donkey Skin* tells the vicious, incestuous society of the court is 'the story of the desire of all power to be absolute', Marin considers. But when the princess flees marriage to her father in her animal disguise the 'path of the mask' also offers the tale-teller his own escape from the conundrum that 'The King must be praised without praise': 'Hide yourself well: / The skin is so frightful no one will believe / It encloses anything beautiful'. In *Donkey Skin* a threadbare vulgarity, 'like a dirty monkey', cloaks Perrault's nervous praise of Louis when monarchy is reconstituted as a happy family.[74] Like the Mannerist sartorial fashion of 'slashing' dresses, such is the 'distressed' *faux-naif* beauty of the *Contes de ma mère l'Oye*. But though she 'walks off with the fairy-tale prince', when Cordelia tries the same trick, her *prima donna* offer of 'love like salt' is *itself* what critics now take 'with a pinch of salt'.[75] And the reason for our scepticism is that Shakespeare shows how in the personalist politics of the Jacobean court, between the mirror and the map the fairy-tale mode of representation by self-disfigurement is *vain* in every sense:

LEAR: So we'll live
                         And pray, and sing, and tell old
                         tales, and laugh
          At gilded butterflies, and hear poor rogues
          Talk of court news ...
EDMUND: Take them away.

                                          [*5,3,11–19*]

'This king unto him took a peer, / Who died and left a female heir ...
With whom the father liking took, / And her to incest did provoke':
in the deliberately 'distressed' and 'slashed' *Pericles*, written soon
after *Lear*, Shakespeare again deployed the incest motif with 'a
song that old was sung' [*Pro.1; 21–6*], like *Cinderella*, to speak
the unspeakable about unnatural power.[76] There too the riddle of
telling truth to kings is posed as a deadly quiz, in which Pericles is
caught in a double bind that to win the princess he must guess the
forbidden love he dares not name. He knows 'Who has the book
of all that monarchs do is more secure to keep it shut than shown',
yet fears the king 'Will think me speaking though I swear to silence'
[*1,1,137–8; 1,2,19*], so is driven schizoid by the logical knot of what
he feels he ought to say. *Pericles* thus reads like a further baring of
King Lear, in which the old story sung 'On ember-eves and holy
ales' spells out what the tragedy encrypts: 'Bad child, worse father,
to entice his own' [*Pro.6; 27*]. Leaving father and child to their
'uncomely claspings' [*1,1,171*], this later yet cruder play is *King
Lear* as told by the suitors. For despite her vow never to marry
like her sisters to please her father, Cordelia had ended like King
Antiochus's daughter, abandoned by France 'To love [her] father
all' [*1,1,103*].[77] Shakespeare cut the information from the 1608
Quarto that she is deserted by her husband due to his troubles at
home, and in the Folio this Prince Charming simply vanishes, along
with 'the powers of France' [*Q SD:23*], to leave father and daughter
alone. But when Lear re-enters howling, 'with Cordelia dead in his
arms' [*SD:5,3,255*], like some perverted Pièta, as critics observe, we
see at last how these two absolutists of art and power have come to
deserve each other, even as the shock of their incestuous 'clasping'
freezes our affective reaction and stuns our aesthetic response. All
through his career Shakespeare plays upon the distinction between
'statues and breathers'.[78] But the trauma of this unbecoming art
is that it is now the spectators themselves who are struck into the
immobility of emotionless 'stones':

Howl, howl, howl, howl! O, you are men of stones:
Had I your tongues and eyes, I'd use them so
That heaven's vault should crack.

[5,3,256–8]

Presented nakedness

'And my poor fool is hanged' [304]: Lear's confusion of his dead
daughter with his clown clinches Cordelia's subliminal association
with the King's Men that began as with 'my young lady's going into
France', the Fool 'much pined away' [1,4,62–3]; and in the Folio
the king dies begging 'men of stone' to 'Look' at nothing [309],
like some mad Pygmalion, in a final self-reflexive image of the
stage. 'Free and absolute' power and 'free and absolute' art have
combined to produce what Frank Kermode calls this 'craftiest' of
endings, where Lear begs us to 'undo this button' [309], as if a
sovereign's order to his player to perform 'freely for our pleasure'
must undo them both.[79] Kent sees the dying man detained 'upon
the rack of this tough world'; and this metaphor of confession
extracted under torture reminds us of the cruel material context
of this representational impasse, in the 1606 Oath of Allegiance,
which, like Lear's truth game, either 'strangered' [1,1,204] or
promised freedom to James's Catholic subjects in return for words
of love.[80] In this scenario of abreaction 'those who watch Lear
die can imagine existence as a torture rack on which the old king
has now the good fortune of no longer being stretched', as Wayne
Koestenbaum writes in *Humiliation*.[81] But the 'rack' Kent says
God 'hates' [312] for stretching out 'the promised end' [262] also
alludes to the cloud machinery of 'this tough world' – the 'wooden
O' [*Henry V, Pro.13*] itself – and hence a self-incriminating taint
of collusion between the 'gorgeous palaces' and 'this great globe'
[*Tempest, 4,1,152–3*] returns this tragedy of vicious circles to its
author's reflexive question, and the performative quandary he posed
at the start: 'What have you done? … What have you performed?'
[4,2,4]. And in this other scenario, where as Koestenbaum says, 'we
might experience joy' watching Gloucester 'having his eyes jabbed
out', abreaction is superseded by something more like the *alchemy*
with which a writer like Jean Genet 'turns moral values upside
down' by eroticizing 'spit, stink, sperm', the 'vile' abjected 'jelly'
[3,7,86] that is the matter of his art:

Shakespeare humiliates the prior body of language – the poor body of English ... When [he] commits lexical excess (by coining new words, by larding a simple thought with plump, dense sounds and meta-phors, by hyper-enlivening every sentiment with figurative language), English becomes a body punctured by his violent actions. Example: 'The murmuring surge / That on th'unnumb'red idle pebble chafes / Cannot be heard so high' [*4,6,20–2*] ... This apex of virtuosity – lan-guage creaming, ascending, and thickening – this process alerts me to a violence committed symbolically, against English's body. Poetic intensity – linguistic bravado, musical compression – hurts the mother tongue. 'Good' language is hurt language. Bare, desiccated language – Samuel Beckett's – is also humiliated: shorn, Samson-like.[82]

'What shall Cordelia do? Love and be silent' [Q.*1,1,54*]; 'What shall Cordelia speak? Love and be silent' [F *1,1,59*]: as Stanley Cavell comments, the discrepancy between Quarto and Folio variants of Cordelia's first words seems to betray Shakespeare's alarm 'about what it is that speech does and what the absence of speech does, about why both can be lethal'.[83] Either way, it is the passive aggres-sion of her anorectic display of self-harm that effortlessly upstages her sisters' hyperbolic deployment of the inexpressibility *topos* that was the staple, Kermode notes, in eulogies of emperors and kings.[84] Critics have long viewed Cordelia's non-cooperation and refusal to enter into these panegyric games as a marker of Shakespeare's 'Bartleby' strategy, 'as if the author outside the play were asking himself what he should have his character say and deciding she should say nothing'.[85] But the 'pride and sullenness' they detect in the daughter's refusal to humour her father other than 'according to [her] bond' [*1,1,92*] can also be read, in light of King James's ultimatum to the stage, as the playwright figuring out the dead-end of what Žižek calls this Bartlebian 'gesture of subtraction', his suicidal Cinderella gambit to 'unbutton' and 'grime' the face of his art with 'filth', like those who with 'horrible object' and 'lunatic bans ... Enforce their charity' [*2,3,9–20*].[86] Throughout his career Shakespeare's refrain has been to revel in the perversity that 'This silence for my sin you do impute, / Which shall be most my glory, being dumb' [Sonnet 83]. But the shock of the nude in *King Lear* can only be viewed as Shakespeare's reflection on the dead-end of such an aesthetic of negativity, and on the 'sad fact' that, as Žižek observes of the shattering pointlessness of the immigrant riots, 'when the only choice is between playing by the rules and (self-)

destructive violence', opposition to power can only take the shape of the 'meaningless' gesture 'to shift / Into a madman's rags; to assume a semblance / That very dogs disdained' [5,3,185–7].[87]

'Our basest beggars / Are in the poorest things superfluous … If only to go warm were gorgeous, / Why nature needs not what thou gorgeous wear'st' [2,4,259–64]: with a scenario of fathers in 'rags' and a sovereign crowned with thorns, the plot of King Lear has been regarded as a reworking of Cinderella's midnight hour of disenchantment for the actor, his reversal from king to beggar as stripped of illusion he kneels for applause. 'The King's a beggar now the play is done', explains the King in the Epilogue to the 1604 All's Well That Ends Well; and such is the 'trick' of pretended weakness Lear mimics after Regan tells him to return to Goneril: 'Do you but mark … "On my knees I beg / That you'll vouchsafe me raiment, bed, and food"' [148–50]. But near the end it will be no such 'prank' [1,4,213] when he says to Cordelia, 'I'll kneel down / And ask of thee forgiveness' [5,3,10–11]. So as Skura observes, although there is no Epilogue to Lear, audiences must have recognized that its Fool takes up the bleak refrain from Feste's in Twelfth Night: that for the actors at the end of the show 'the rain it raineth every day' [3,2,75]. Thus Lear's self-exposure in 'houseless poverty' and 'loop'd and window'd raggedness' [3,4,27–32], 'makes this of all plays the most focused on the actor's body and hunger for recognition', and compels the auditors to respond like the king to the 'poor unfortunate beggar' [4,6,68], with appalled compassion.[88] Yet, as Koestenbaum perceives, the self-soiling incontinence of King Lear goes further than this by probing the darkest recesses of the histrionics of humiliation: 'Watching, I sense, first of all, that person's humiliation, and I'm struck by horrified commiseration. Next, I feel an urge to eject that person from my sight: get away from me, you vomiting freak.'[89]

Bad is the trade

In The Birth of Tragedy Nietzsche derived an aesthetic of negativity from the embrace of the repulsive and accursed, which is indeed how Lear reacts to the sight of Poor Tom, the 'Player-Beggar' who with 'hair elf(ed) in knots' acts out the socially embarrassing extremity of such theatrically 'presented nakedness' [2,3,10–11].[90] And by the end of King Lear 'it is if the play finally unleashes its grotesque violence against the audience themselves', comments Terry Eagleton, with relish, in *Sweet Violence*, his study of the idea of the tragic, 'rounding on them sadistically, and rubbing their noses in its revolting injustices until they are tempted to whimper that they can take no more'.[91] Thus, by baring its devices with gouged eyes, maimed limbs and 'roaring voices' [14], the 'horrible object' and 'side-piercing sight' [4,6,85] of the dirty protest that is *King Lear* 'enforces' [2,3,20] attention as offensively as the threats of any 'Tom o'Bedlam' [1,2,126] or stench of 'poor naked wretch' [3,4,29] pleading for relief so *persistently*, and in such a 'repellent, nasty, and noisy' way, that 'you pay him', as Skura winces, 'to go away'.[92] This radical poverty is the condition of 'abstract nakedness' in which Hannah Arendt thought the merely human loses all legal and expressive significance; but, as Ernst Kantorowicz detailed, and Shakespeare illustrates with his 'long procession of tortured kings', such wretchedness accords with the entire theatrics of posing, deposing, and exposing that signifies instead that it is '*the king that always dies*': those degrading rites of investiture which would, in fact, inspire the symbolic destitution of a sovereign art.[93]

In Kafka's story the hunger artist wearies the public with his exhibition of suffering, and eventually pines away, not through starvation but for lack of an audience, when the spectators hurry on to watch the lions feed. Ellmann deciphers this tale as a meditation on the self-induced predicament of the sovereign author: 'As the hunger artist starves his flesh, so Kafka emaciates his own prose, supplanting the fat novel ... with the skeletal apparatus of a writing machine'; thus 'The image of the starving artist seems to stand for the crisis of high art ... for the exclusion of artists from commerce and their proud refusal to be fed'. She cites the poem 'Fêtes de la Faim', in which Rimbaud limits the poet to a diet of stones, and Yeats's play *The King's Threshold*, where the bard goes on hunger strike to protest the king's neglect of poetry, to show how for modernism autonomy is ultimately self-consuming.[94] These texts thereby address what Theodor Adorno identified as the problematic of 'the artfulness of all anti-art', which arose when modern art's isolation from social function or economic support induced a sense of its futility, and the avant-garde artwork emerged as the attempt to criticize and overcome this writer's block. To be sure, *King Lear* is based upon the archetypal story of aesthetic subtraction, *Cinderella*. But to identify the drama only with the rebellion of the girl in cinders is to miss how it transcends what Adorno termed modernity's 'ideal of blackness', by turning away from the null point of poverty and bareness, and critiquing the self-centred sovereignty of such an aesthetic of impoverishment:

> To survive reality at its most extreme and grim, artworks that do not want to sell themselves as consolation must equate themselves with that reality ... Art indicts superfluous poverty by voluntarily undergoing its own; but it indicts asceticism as well and cannot establish it as its norm. Along with the impoverishment of means entailed by the ideal of blackness – if not by every sort of aesthetic *Sachlichkeit* – what is written, painted, and composed is also impoverished; the most advanced arts push this impoverishment to the brink of silence.[95]

Adorno's account of the 'unsolvable aporia' of the art that 'becomes allergic to itself' in its 'negation of the negative' is concerned with the autoimmunity of modernist works like those of Beckett, which internalize the social malnutrition of artistic self-sufficiency with the famished 'lessness' of an art that struggles to be about nothing but itself.[96] But what he writes about this *reduction ad absurdum* begins to apply, Peter Bürger argues in *The Theory of the Avant-Garde*, to courtly art in the period of *King Lear*, as the sustenance obtained by glorifying the prince is spurned by the self-consecrated artist who 'produces as an individual and develops a consciousness of the uniqueness of his activity'.[97] Keyed to its creator's life-long reluctance to personalize himself as such a solo performer, his courtly pretence of non-being, with its depleted language – 'Fie, fie, fie! pah! pah!' [4,6,126] – minimal morality – 'Ripeness is all' [5,2,11] – and attenuated characters – 'Nay he reserved a blanket, else we had been shamed' [3,4,63] – Shakespeare's great tragedy of autoimmunity and self-abnegation, in which it is as though 'this mouth should tear this hand / For lifting food to't' [16], because 'Humanity must perforce prey on itself, / Like monsters of the deep' [4,2,50], becomes in this context perhaps one of the earliest instances of the art that performs, in order to critique, the hunger of its own ruinous autophagy:

GENTLEMAN: This night, wherein the cub-drawn bear would couch,
The lion and the belly-pinchéd wolf
Keep their fur dry, unbonneted he runs,

> And bids what will take all.
> KENT: But who is with him?
> GENTLEMAN: None but the fool, who labours to out-jest
>   His heart-struck injuries.
>
> [*3,1,12–17*]

'Bad is the trade that must play the fool to sorrow, angering itself
and others' [*4,1,39–40*]: as Philip Schwyzer astutely comments,
King Lear cannot only be about 'denials, undoings, and evacua-
tions', since 'only a Dadaist would construct an aesthetic object
solely on the basis of refusals'.[98] So, whatever the source of its anger
and self-hate, in the negative dialectic of *King Lear* Shakespeare
responded to the bad business of speaking freely to order with a
Cinderella story about the art of defilement that held a mirror up
not only to the grime of 'The Wisest Fool', but the filth of the fool
himself. Editors speculate that at the first performance the Fool
did indeed proffer James the 'looking glass' for which Lear calls
[*5,3,260*], thus reversing the coxcomb and crown in an act of displacement that enacts the usurpation of the sovereign by the clown:
'The one in motley here, / The other found out there' [*1,4,127*].[99] If
so, this tense exchange gave a new twist to Shakespeare's dangerous
game of allowing what Carl Schmitt called the 'intrusion' of real
time into the time of the play, so as to negate the royal person and
'extract from the contemporary political situation the form that
could be intensified to the level of myth'.[100] But the 'glass-gazing'
[*2,2,16*] in Shakespeare's *fort/da* game is even more deconstructive
of His Majesty the Ego than this implies, for what it discloses is
the common destiny of the monarch and the mime who 'labours to
outjest' sovereignty's self-erasing 'injuries':

> LEAR: Make no noise, make no noise; draw the curtains. So, so,
>   so. We'll go to supper i'th'morning.
> FOOL: And I'll go to bed at noon.
>
> [*3,6,76–8*]

The folkloric mirror through which the play makes insolent contact
with the Basilisk-like royal person of the historical sovereign would
reappear before the king's eyes, with yet more injurious implications, in the ghostly procession of Stuart monarchs in *Macbeth*. And
though someone sensibly cut from the Folio Lear's pointed question,
'Dost thou call me fool, boy?' [*1,4,129*], the lament was allowed to
stand 'That such a king should play bo-peep, / And go the fools

among' [*1,4,154*].[101] Historians insist that no one seriously believed in the slumming games that the Stuarts performed with their plebeian subjects.[102] But there is enough Brechtian alienation in the Fool's anachronistic prediction that Merlin will prophesy the apocalyptic time when 'the realm of Albion' shall indeed 'come to great confusion' [*3,2,89*], to sense already the 'chronic apprehensions about being the King's servants' which made Shakespeare's allusions to the ruling dynasty that played an unnerving game of 'bo-peep' with the actors they commanded so 'distinctly edgy'.[103] For if *King Lear* revolves on the topsy-turvy swapping of the king's sceptre with the fool's dildo that Shakespeare had observed for himself as a King's Man in the mad world of the Jacobean court, what it surely also registers is the symbolic castration that necessarily goes, Žižek reminds us, with the investment in any such kingly role:

> If a king holds in his hands the scepter and wears the crown, his words will be taken as the words of a king. Such insignia are not part of my nature: I don't own them; I wear them to exert power. As such they 'castrate' me: they introduce a gap between what I immediately am and the function that I exercise. This is what the infamous 'symbolic castration' means.[104]

In her essay on 'The Aesthetics of Silence' Susan Sontag wrote of the art of 'impoverishment and reduction' as the product of a crisis in the relations between art and its consumers, when the artist is 'forced to take a position that is either servile or insolent. Either he flatters or appeases his audience, giving them what they already know, or he commits aggression against his audience, giving them what they don't want.'[105] In the years after offering *King Lear* at court the King's Men 'flaunted their freedom from sycophancy' with something like the latter contrariety, Gurr demonstrates; yet it was ironically their royal status that became their undoing, when the Stuart regime 'enveloped and finally swallowed them up completely'.[106] 'Let go thy hold when a great wheel runs down hill', counsels the court jester, 'lest it break thy neck with following it' [*2,4,66–7*]. But Shakespeare perhaps spoke more than he knew when he foretold how the king and his comedian would go into the dark night of history side-by-side, both victims of the Civil War: 'That sir which serves and seeks for gain … Will pack when it begins to rain, / And leave thee in the storm. / But I will tarry; the fool will stay, / And let the wise man fly' [*2,4,72–6*]. 'But goes thy heart with

this?' [*1,1,194*], asks the old king pitifully; for this beggarly service
was not, for sure, the heartfelt declaration of love the sovereign
might have expected from his creature when he proclaimed himself
the 'King of Fools'. But it was, perhaps, the wisest way to answer his
fool's errand, and obey 'The weight of this sad time', yet still 'Speak
what we feel, not what we ought to say' [*5,3,322–3*].

Notes

1 Royal Patent for the King's Men, 19 May 1603, repr. in Andrew Gurr,
   The Shakespeare Company: 1594–1642 (Cambridge: Cambridge
   University Press, 2004), p.254.
2 'Swift, thorough and autocratic': Glynne Wickham, *Early English
   Stages* (3 vols, London: Routledge, 1959–81), vol. 2 (1963), part
   1, p.92; 'durability they never had': Gurr, op. cit. (note 1), p.169.
   The assignment of the Lord Admiral's Men to Prince Henry and
   Worcester's Men to Queen Anne took place in February 1604, though
   they did not receive official patents until 1606 and 1609 respectively.
3 Luke Wilson, *Theatres of Intention: Drama and the Law in Early
   Modern England* (Stanford: Stanford University Press, 2000), p.301;
   see also pp.166–7.
4 'Cooperating to produce': Leonard Tennenhouse, *Power on Display:
   The Politics of Shakespeare's Genres* (London: Methuen, 1986),
   p.149.
5 Leeds Barroll, *Politics, Plague, and Shakespeare's Theater: The Stuart
   Years* (Ithaca: Cornell University Press, 1991), pp.47–8.
6 Alvin Kernan, *Shakespeare, the King's Playwright: Theater in the
   Stuart Court, 1603–1613* (New Haven: Yale University Press, 1995),
   pp.14 and 96.
7 'His Majesty's Servant': Samuel Schoenbaum, *William Shakespeare: A
   Documentary Life* (Oxford: Oxford University Press, 1975), p.195;
   'directly to the myth': Tennenhouse, op. cit. (note 4), pp.159–60;
   'Free and Absolute Monarchy': James Stuart, *The Trew Law of
   Free Monarches*, in *James VI and I: Political Writings*, ed. Johann
   Sommerville (Cambridge: Cambridge University Press, 1994),
   p.63. For the debate about the character of Stuart absolutism, see
   Johann Somerville, 'English and European Political Ideas in the Early
   Seventeenth Century: Revisionism and the Case of Absolutism',
   Journal of British Studies, 35 (1996), 168–94.
8 'Royal takeover': Gurr, op. cit. (note 1), p.169; 'outward and visible
   signs': Stephen Orgel, 'Making Greatness Familiar', in *Pageantry in
   the Shakespearean Theater*, ed. David Bergeron (Athens: University of

Georgia Press, 1985), pp. 22–3; 'someone ... a powerful intercessor': Barroll, op. cit. (note 5), pp. 35 and 41; 'actually kissed': report of the Venetian ambassador, Girolamo Scaramelli, *Calendar of State Papers Venetian* (35 vols and, London: Historical Manuscripts Commission, 1864–), vol. 10, pp. 76–7.

9 Janet Clare '"Greater Themes for Insurrection's Arguing": Political Censorship of the Elizabethan and Jacobean Stage', *Review of English Studies*, 38 (1987), 182. Clare speculates that the relaxation was possible because 'the government of James I had little to fear'. For the relative autonomy of the Queen's court, and the influence within it of the Herberts, see Leeds Barroll, 'The Court of the First Stuart Queen', in Linda Levy Peck, *The Mental World of the Stuart Court* (Cambridge: Cambridge University Press, 1991), pp. 204–6.

10 'Somewhat careless': Barroll, op. cit. (note 5), p. 43.

11 Gurr, op. cit. (note 1), pp. 168 and 170.

12 Richard Dutton, *Mastering the Revels: The Regulation and Censorship of English Renaissance Drama* (Manchester: Manchester University Press, 1991), p. 145.

13 Philip Finkelpearl, 'The Comedians' Liberty', in *Renaissance Historicism: Selections from 'English Literary Renaissance'*, ed. Arthur Kinney and Dan Colllins (Amherst: Massachusetts University Press, 1987), p. 199; 'To give himself freedom': Neil Cuddy, 'Reinventing a Monarchy: The Changing Structure and Political Function of the Stuart Court, 1603–88', in *The Stuart Courts*, ed. Eveline Cruickshanks (Stroud: Sutton Publishing, 2000), p. 72.

14 *Acts of the Privy Council of Scotland* (1884), vol. 6, p. 41, repr. in James Dibdin, *The Annals of the Edinburgh Stage* (Edinburgh: Richard Cameron, 1888), p. 23.

15 Ibid., p. 24; Frederick Gard Fleay, *A Chronical History of the Life and Work of William Shakespeare, Player, Poet and Playmaker* (London: J.C. Nimmo, 1886), p. 43.

16 'Easy relations with his Scottish court fools': Murray Pittock, 'From Edinburgh to London: Scottish Court Writing and 1603', ibid., p. 14.

17 Jane Rickard, *Authorship and Authority: The Writings of James VI and I* (Manchester: Manchester University Press, 2007), p. 47.

18 James VI and I, 'Song, the first verses that ever the King made' (1582), in *The Poems of James VI of Scotland* (2 vols, Edinburgh: William Blackwood, 1955–58), vol. 2, p. 132.

19 In Gurr, op. cit. (note 1), p. 254; cf. p. 171: 'Now equipped with their royal patents they could perform at whatever inn would take them'.

20 Kernan, op. cit. (note 6), p. 102; 'comedian to His Majesty': Park Honan, *Shakespeare: A Life* (Oxford: Oxford University Press, 1998), p. 300.

21 Gurr, op. cit. (note 1), p.168; 'The king heard that Fletcher, the player, was hanged, and told him and Roger Aston so, in merry words, not believing it, saying very pleasantly that if it were true he would hang them also': *Calendar of State Papers, Scotland*, vol. 2, p.676.

22 'Sweet Swan': Ben Jonson, 'To the memory of my beloved, the author', in William Shakespeare, *The Norton Shakespeare*, ed. Stephen Greenblatt, Walter Cohen, Jean Howard and Katharine Eisaman Maus (New York: Norton, 1997), p.3352; 'That most learn'd Prince': Anon. preface to *Collection of Poems ... By Mr. William Shakespeare* (London: Bernard Lintot, 1709), repr. in Schoenbaum, op. cit. (note 7), p.204.

23 Jenny Wormald, '*Basilikon Doron* and *The Trew Law of Free Monarchies*', in Peck, op. cit. (note 9), p.54; Slavoj Žižek, *How to Read Lacan* (London: Granta, 2006), p.14.

24 James VI and I, *Basilikon Doron* (London, 1603), p.127.

25 Rickard, op. cit. (note 17), p.45.

26 Quoted in Dutton, op. cit. (note 12), p.142; *Calendar of State Papers, Scotland*, vol. 2, p.749.

27 'He had already seen': Josephine Waters Bennett, '*Measure for Measure' as Royal Entertainment*' (New York: Columbia University Press, 1966), p.111; Gurr, op. cit. (note 1), pp.169 and 182.

28 'Potentially sensational': ibid., p.183.

29 Kernan, op. cit. (note 6), pp.60–1.

30 Bennett, op. cit. (note 27), p.137. For a survey of the tradition that the play's Duke Vincentio is identifiable with King James see Carolyn Harper, '*Twixt Will and Will Not: The Dilemma of 'Measure for Measure'* (Niwot, Col.: Colarado University Press, 1998), pp.28–33.

31 'Royal play': H.N. Paul, *The Royal Play of 'Macbeth'* (New York: Macmillan, 1950, pp.317–31; Kernan, op. cit. (note 6), p.88.

32 Julia Lupton, *Thinking with Shakespeare: Essays on Politics and Life* (Chicago: Chicago University Press, 2011), p.185.

33 'A musical entertainment': Stanley Wells, quoted in Vanessa Thorpe, 'Shakespeare's last masterpiece was secretly a musical', *The Observer*, 21 August 2011, 12. For Shakespeare's repudiation of the writer as courtier, see Gary Schmidgall, *Shakespeare and the Poet's Life* (Lexington: Kentucky University Press, 1990), pp.128–60.

34 Kernan, op. cit. (note 6), p.xxiii.

35 'Patmos', Friedrich Hölderlin, *Selected Poems and Fragments*, trans. Michael Hamburger (London: Penguin, 1998), p.231. For the relevance of Hölderlin's lines to the plays, see Ian Ward, *Shakespeare and the Legal Imagination* (London: Butterworths, 1999), p.193.

36 See Debora Shuger, *Political Theologies in Shakespeare's England: The Sacred and the State in 'Measure for Measure'* (Basingstoke: Palgrave,

2001), pp.1, 6, 56 and 79–80: 'because the play is a meditation on its political moment my book ... says nothing virtually nothing about imagery, irony, or characterization' (p.1). Shuger instead cites approvingly Carl Schmitt: 'all significant concepts of the modern theory of the state are secularized theological concepts': *Political Theology: Four Chapters of the Concept of Sovereignty*, trans. George Schwab (Cambridge, Mass.: MIT Press, 1985), p.36; and refers throughout to theologian John Milbank, whose citation of that maxim in *Theology and Social Theory* (Oxford: Blackwell, 1990) has become a rallying-call for Britain's Conservative Party. 'Interchangeable flattery': Sir Dudley Carleton reporting the parliamentary tributes to Queen Elizabeth's 'sacred spirit', 29 December 1601, quoted Shuger (p.56), from *The Journal of Sir Roger Wilbraham*, ed. Harold Spencer Scott, *The Camden Miscellany*, 10 (1902), pp.42–4.

37 See, in particular, Richard Dutton, '*King Lear, The Triumphs of Reunited Britannia*, and "The Matter of Britain"', *Literature and History*, 12 (1986), 139–51.

38 Dutton, op. cit. (note 12), p.145.

39 'Intricate games': Gurr, op. cit. (note 1) p.147; Anne Barton, *Shakespeare and the Idea of the Play* (London: Chatto & Windus, 1962), p.184.

40 Jonathan Goldberg, *James I and the Politics of Literature* (Stanford: Stanford University Press, 1989), p.239.

41 Richard Dutton, *William Shakespeare: A Literary Life* (Basingstoke: Macmillan, 1989), p.138.

42 Tennenhouse, op. cit. (note 4), p.135.

43 Thomas Betteridge, *Shakespearean Fantasy and Politics* (Hatfield: University of Hertfordshire Press, 2005), p.142.

44 Wilson, op. cit. (nore 3), p.177.

45 Cf. Peter Thomson, *Shakespeare's Professional Career* (Cambridge: Cambridge University Press, 1992), p.169: 'Seen in the context of James's first full year on the English throne, [*Measure for Measure*] is nothing short of a *caveat Rex* from the nation's leading playwright to the new monarch'.

46 'A Homer to himself': Gabriel Harvey's annotation to *Lepanto* quoted in Rickard, op. cit. (note 16), p.65. Barton sees Iago's plot as a 'ghastly play within the play': op. cit. (note 39), p.185.

47 'What the stained-glass': Kernan, op. cit. (note 6), p.77.

48 Samuel Beckett, *Proust and Three Dialogues* (London: John Calder, 1965), p.139.

49 Meredith Anne Skura, *Shakespeare the Actor and the Purposes of Playing* (Chicago: Chicago University Press, 1993), p.145.

50 Stephen Booth, *'King Lear', 'Macbeth', Indefinition, and Tragedy*

(New Haven: Yale University Press, 1983), p.64. Cf. Derek Peat, '"And that's true too": *King Lear* and the Tension of Uncertainty', *Shakespeare Survey*, 33 (1980), p.48: 'As Edgar has trifled with Gloucester, so Shakespeare has trifled with us'; and Jay Halio (ed.), 'Introduction', *The Tragedy of King Lear* (Cambridge: Cambridge University Press, 1992), p.22: 'The trick Edgar plays on his father's imagination is also the trick Shakespeare plays on ours – except that here he means us to be conscious of everything that is happening, including the way in which our imagination is being made to work'.

51 Skura, op. cit. (note 49), pp.168–71 and 294, n. 11.
52 Maynard Mack, *'King Lear' in Our Time* (Berkeley: California University Press, 1966), p.50; 'rise and stoop at once': Skura, op. cit. (note 49), p.216.
53 'Organized dejection': Wayne Koestenbaum, *Humiliation* (New York: Picador, 2011), p.43.
54 Barroll, op. cit. (nore 5), p.108; Ernest Law, *Shakespeare as a Groom of the Chamber* (London: George Bell, 1910), pp.59–60; Schoenbaum, op. cit. (note 7), p.246.
55 Ibid., p.196.
56 Ibid.
57 Laurie Shannon, 'Poor, Bare, Forked: Animal Sovereignty, Human Negative Exceptionalism, and the Natural History of *King Lear*', *Shakespeare Quarterly*, 60 (2009), 168–96, here 181; Eric Santner, *The Royal Remains: The People's Two Bodies and the Endgames of Sovereignty* (Chicago: Chicago University Press, 2011).
58 In Jonathan Bate (ed.), *The Romantics on Shakespeare* (Harmondsworth: Penguin, 1992), p.389. For *Cinderella* as an analogue of *King Lear*, see Wilfrid Perrett, *Palaestra: 35: The Story of King Lear from Geoffrey of Monmouth to Shakespeare* (Berlin: Mayer & Müller, 1904), pp.10–13; Geoffrey Bullough, *Narrative and Dramatic Sources of Shakespeare: VII: Major Tragedies* (London: Routledge & Kegan Paul, 1973), p.271; Laurence Coupe, '*King Lear*: Christian Fairy Tale', *English Review*, 6 (1996), 2–6; and Dennis Welch, '*Christabel, King Lear*, and the *Cinderella* Folktale', *Papers on Language and Literature*, 32 (1996), 291–314.
59 Sigmund Freud, 'The Theme of the Three Caskets', *The Penguin Freud Library: 14: Art and Literature*, ed. Albert Dickson (Harmondsworth: Penguin, 1985), pp.233–47.
60 Catherine Belsey, *Why Shakespeare?* (London: Palgrave, 2007), pp.45 and 62–3.
61 See for example, Leslie Thomson, '"Pray you, undo this button": Implications of "Un-" in *King Lear*', *Shakespeare Survey*, 45 (1992),

79–88. For the theme of divestment an its relation to the language of the play, see in particular, Maurice Charney, '"We put fresh garments on him": Nakedness and Clothes in *King Lear*', in *Some Facets of 'King Lear'*, eds Rosalie Colie and F.T. Flahiff (Toronto: University of Toronto Press, 1974), pp. 80–2.

62 See Julia Reinhard Lupton, *Afterlives of the Saints: Hagiography, Typology and Renaissance Literature* (Stanford: Stanford University Press, 1996), 62–4, 114–16 and 211.

63 Thomas Docherty, *John Donne Undone* (London: Methuen, 1986), p. 206.

64 Maud Ellmann, *The Hunger Artists: Starving, Writing and Imprisonment* (London: Virgo, 1993), p. 13.

65 Gayatri Chakravorty Spivak, 'Can the Subaltern Speak?', in *Marxism and the Interpretation of Culture*, eds Cary Nelson and Larry Grossberg (Champaign: University of Illinois Press, 1988); 'inventory of pain': Elfride Jelinek, *The Piano Teacher*, trans. Joachim Neugroschel (London: Weidenfeld & Nicolson), p. 217.

66 Judith Halberstam, *The Queer Art of Failure* (Durham, NC: Duke University Press, 2011), pp. 126, 130 and 145.

67 Gilles Deleuze, *Masochism: An Interpretation of Coldness and Cruelty*, trans. Jean McNeil (New York: Braziller, 1971), p. 77.

68 Ellmann, op. cit. (note 64), p. 17.

69 Slavoj Žižek, *Violence: Six Sideways Reflections* (New York: Picador, 2008), pp. 76 and 79.

70 Ifig Cocoual, 'Craft and Corrupt Plainness? *King Lear* as a Devious Defence of Dramatic Rhetoric', in *Lectures du 'Roi Lear' de William Shakespeare* (Rennes: Presses Universitaires de Rennes, 2008), p. 39.

71 Christopher Marlowe, *Tamburlaine the Great, Part Two*, 4,1,126, in *Christopher Marlowe: The Complete Plays*, eds Frank Romany and Robert Lindsey (London: Penguin, 2003), p. 211.

72 See Jack Zipes, 'Spells of Enchantment', in *Folk and Fairy Tales*, eds Martin Hallett and Barbara Karasek (Peterborough, Ontario: Broadview, 1996); Dorothy Thelander, 'Mother Goose and Her Goslings: The France of Louis XIV as Seen Through the Fairy Tale', *Journal of Modern History*, 54 (1982), 467–96.

73 Natalie Zemon Davis, *Society and Culture in Early Modern France* (Cambridge: Polity, 1987), p. 252.

74 Louis Marin, *Portrait of the King*, trans. Martha Houle (Basingstoke: Macmillan, 1988), pp. 138–65, here 138, 150 and 164; 'The king must be praised without praise': p. 69.

75 Cocoual, op. cit. (note 70), pp. 35–6.

76 For incest in *Pericles* as a figure for tyranny, and for James's desire to be 'free and absolute', see Constance Jordan, *Shakespeare's Monarchies:*

Ruler and Subject in the Romances (Ithaca: Cornell University Press, 1997), pp. 35–47.

77 See Philip Maguire, *Shakespeare: The Jacobean Plays* (Basingstoke: Macmillan, 1994), p. 101.

78 Schmidgall, op. cit. (note 33), p. 200.

79 Frank Kermode, *Shakespeare's Language* (London: Allen Lane, 2000), pp. 199–200.

80 For the contradictions in James's Oath of Allegiance, see John LaRocca, '"Who Can't Pray With Me, Can't Love Me": Toleration and the Early Jacobean Recusancy Policy', *Journal of British Studies*, 23 (1984), 22–36.

81 Koestenbaum, op. cit. (note 53), p. 42.

82 Ibid., pp. 42–3 and 102.

83 Stanley Cavell, 'The Interminable Shakespearean Text', in *Philosophy the Day After Tomorrow* (Cambridge, Mass.: Harvard University Press, 2005), pp. 54–5.

84 Kermode, op. cit. (note 79), p. 185.

85 Stephen Greenblatt, 'The Cultivation of Anxiety: King Lear and His Heirs', in *Learning to Curse: Essays in Early Modern Culture* (London: Routledge, 1990), p. 97.

86 'Bartlebian': Žižek, op. cit. (note 69), p. 214; 'gesture of subtraction': Slavoj Žižek, *The Parallax View* (Cambridge, Mass.: MIT Press, 2009), p. 382.

87 'Pride and sullenness': R.A. Foakes, *Hamlet versus Lear: Cultural Politics and Shakespeare's Art* (Cambridge: Cambridge University Press, 1993), p. 47; Žižek, op. cit. (note 69), p. 76.

88 Skura, op. cit. (note 49), pp. 147–8.

89 Koestenbauym, op. cit. (note 53), p. 20.

90 Friedrich Nietzsche, *The Birth of Tragedy*, trans. Shaun Whiteside (Harmondsworth: Penguin, 1993).

91 Terry Eagleton, *Sweet Violence: The Idea of the Tragic* (Oxford: Blackmail, 2003 pp. 139–40.

92 Skura, op. cit. (note 49), pp. 147–8.

93 Hannah Arendt, *The Origins of Totalitarianism* (New York: Harcourt Bruce, 1975), pp. 297 and 302; Ernst Kantorowicz, *The King's Two Bodies: A Study in Medieval Political Theology* (Princeton: Princeton University Press, 1997), p. 30. For a brilliantly illuminating discussion, to which I am indebted throughout, see Santner, 'Of Kings and Other Creatures', op. cit. (note 57), pp. 33–62.

94 Ellmann, op. cit. (note 64), pp. 66 and 70.

95 Theodor Adorno, *Aesthetic Theory*, eds Gretel Adorno and Rolf Tiedemann, trans. Robert Hullot-Kentor (London: Continuum, 2004), pp. 50–1.

96 Ibid., p.45. For Beckett's impossible project to create a work that refers to nothing but itself, see also Pascale Casanova, *Samuel Beckett: Anatomy of a Literary Revolution*, trans. Gregory Elliott (London: Verso, 2006).

97 Peter Bürger, *Theory of the Avant-Garde*, trans. Michael Shaw (Minneapolis: Minnesota University Press, 1984), pp.47–8.

98 Philip Schwyzer, 'The Jacobean Union Controversy and *King Lear*', in Glenn Burgess, Rowland Wymer and Jason Lawrence (eds), *The Accession of James I: Historical and Cultural Consequences* (Basingstoke: Palgrave Macmillan, 2006), p.44.

99 For accounts of Lear's mirror, see R.A. Foakes (ed.), *The Arden Shakespeare: 'King Lear'* (London: Nelson, 1997), pp.385–6. And for the connection with the Fool, see Allan Shickman, *English Literary Renaissance*, 21 (1991), 85–6.

100 Carl Schmitt, *Hamlet or Hecuba: The Intrusion of the Time into the Play*, trans. David Pan and Jennifer Rust (New York: Telos Press, 2009), p.49.

101 Where Paulina calls the king 'a fool' to his face in *The Winter's Tale* [*3,2,186*], the text was also allowed to stand. The implications are discussed in Irene Dash, *Wooing, Wedding, and Power in Shakespeare's Plays* (New York: Columbia University Press, 1981), p.134.

102 See Brian Weiser, 'Access and Petitioning During the Reign of Charles II', in *The Stuart Courts*, ed. Eveline Cruickshanks (Stroud: Sutton Publishing, 2000), p.205: 'Broadside ballads relate Henry VIII's drinking with a cobbler, and James V of Scotland roaming around the countryside. Shakespeare's Henry V, who donned a common soldier's garb to converse with his troops, provides a particularly famous example … [But] no one expected to meet the King in this fashion.'

103 Gurr, op.cit. (note 1), p.173.

104 Slavoj Žižek, *Organs without Bodies: On Deleuze and Consequences* (New York: Routledge, 2004), p.87. Cf. Jeffrey Mehlman, *Revolution and Repetition* (Berkeley: University of California Press, 1977), p.94: 'Much of the aftermath of structuralism may be read in terms of degrees of ambivalence toward the duplicity of castration: at once radical theory of *difference* and medium through which subject is made to adapt to structure'.

105 Susan Sontag, 'The Aesthetics of Silence', in *Styles of Radical Will* (London: Picador, 2002), p.15.

106 Gurr, op.cit. (note 1), p.193.

6

Double trouble

Regime change in Macbeth

Come like shadows

Four hundred years ago, on 7 August 1606 if its editors are correct, the first performance of *Macbeth* in the Great Hall at Hampton Court presented King James with Shakespeare's most 'mystical and legitimist' vision of state power, when the British monarch was offered his own reflection in a mirror brought on stage at the climax of a masque of his Stuart ancestors: '*A show of eight kings, the last with a glass in his hand*' [*SD: 4,1,127*].[1] Macbeth's report of the hall of mirrors opened by the Witches, where an 'eighth appears, who bears a glass / Which shows me many more', has persuaded scholars that the image fleetingly captured in the glass – presumably behind the reflected head of Macbeth himself – of some 'That twofold balls and treble sceptres carry' [*135–7*] is a double portrait of King James, as the new ruler of Scotland, England and Ireland, enthroned beside his guest and brother-in-law Christian IV, sovereign of the similar federated state of Denmark, Norway and Schleswig-Holstein.[2] Thus, Alvin Kernan infers that the King's Men staged *Macbeth* 'to display their patron's greatness to his fellow king', and that what divine right supporters did for the Tudors Shakespeare's troupe now achieved for the Stuarts, legitimating their regime with a triumphal procession that 'parades down time and across stage like a living family tree'.[3] So, as the symbol of the sinister collusion between the black arts of theatre and politics, the Witches' glass seems to confirm New Historicism's suspicion that in a system where 'power is constituted through theatrical celebrations of royal glory and theatrical violence visited upon enemies of that glory', Shakespearean theatricality is not set over against power 'but is one of power's essential modes'.[4]

The mirror was a signature prop of James, who told Parliament in 1609 that his own speech was 'such a Mirror, or Crystal, as through the transparentness thereof, you may see the heart of your King'; and Shakespeare's framing of the body of the monarch in the mirror of *Macbeth* has therefore come to be viewed as one of the definitive statements of Baroque court art, equivalent to the twin portrait of King Philip IV and his Queen Mariana in the mirror at the centre of *Las Meninas* by Velázquez.[5] But like that even more famous yet equally opaque reflection, the intangible image in Shakespeare's mirror appears to be far more mediated than a simple act of homage, since, as Michel Foucault observed of 'the two tiny silhouettes gleaming out from the looking-glass' in the painting, in so far as they are identifiable or visible at all these sovereigns are now 'the frailest and the most distant form of all reality' represented in the work of art. For just as the painter has asserted two levels of reality with the mirror in his picture, where the duplicated bodies of the royal couple are notional occupants of the space in which Velázquez or the viewer stands, so the dramatist has complicated his ostensible act of homage by superimposing the space of the play over that of the banqueting hall in which the house of Stuart is seated, and to similarly subversive effect. For as Foucault remarks, the mirror that seems to restore 'as if by magic' the absent presence of the sovereign as focus of the composition actually confirms that this king will now only come and go like a shadow, at the secondary level of his representations:

> In the realm of the anecdote, this centre is symbolically sovereign, since it is occupied by the king ... But perhaps this generosity on the part of the mirror is feigned; perhaps it is hiding as much and even more than it reveals. That space where the king and his wife hold sway belongs equally well to the artist and the spectator ... the king appears in the depths of the looking glass precisely because he does not belong to the picture.[6]

In the painting that is for ever named after the royal waiting women, rather than the royalty they serve, the seventeenth-century court artist negotiates the change of regime when sovereignty is stolen from the royal presence by representation itself; yet the medium for this act of usurpation is the very mirror that is the essential symbolic property of absolute power. Likewise, by putting charismatic power on display to itself at a state banquet, the masque of kings in *Macbeth* seems initially to seal the mimetic circularity by which, in recent critiques, 'Shakespeare's stagecraft collaborates with statecraft', and an art that appeals to a paranoid fascination with the violence it represents colludes with that violence, stimulating the desire to participate by inviting the spectators to approach the chamber of horrors, 'peep through the blanket of the dark', and 'look on death itself' [*1,5,51; 2,3,74*].[7] And this superficial reading is cued by what we know of the original performance, which was at the first state assembly, in the aftermath of the Gunpowder Plot, of those very judges and politicians who, as terrorism's intended targets, were now waging the king's own war of terror against his Catholic foes. By reflecting the reigning ruler in his pomp, after earlier denying Macbeth the banquet Banquo's ghost interrupts, and finally serving up to the incomer James his predecessor's framed head as though on a platter, it is therefore as if Shakespeare is literally *recapitulating* the archaic cycle of power, and offering the violence of the old order as a gift to the successor regime:

> He reinvigorates the signs and symbols associated with legitimate power … If Macbeth has appropriated the technology of punishment, in other words, the play's tribute to James comes as Shakespeare signals the reversal of Macbeth's reversal … by having Macduff hold up the severed head of the tyrant.[8]

After they reveal to Macbeth the 'horrible sight' of his Stuart successors, the Witches '*dance and vanish*', with a parting wish 'That this great king may kindly say / Our duties did his welcome pay' [*4,1,137–49*]. But the ambiguity about which 'great king' it is they served to welcome makes it all the more disturbing when, as Stephen Greenblatt notes, though the plot implicates them deeply in Macbeth's violence, there is no plan to punish them, nor 'sign the victors are even aware of their existence … when the threats they embody are absorbed' by the incoming regime.[9] Superimposition of Macbeth's head over that of James in the Witches' clairvoyant ball thus carries an additional prophetic twist when the old agents of terror go Scot free in the new civil order. So the notion that the author is here 'laying on flattery with a trowel' is undercut by the way that this Salome-like dance turns a king's command into a shocking surprise to 'Show his eyes and grieve his heart' [*126*].[10] Shakespeare had, after all, called his theatre a mirror to 'show scorn her own image', a 'glass / Where you may see the inmost part of you'

[*Hamlet, 3,2,21; 3,4,19–20*]. If James did see his head juxtaposed with Macbeth's it would thus clinch what Jonathan Goldberg terms the 'specular contamination' whereby this mirror of kings deconstructs the legitimacy of the successor state by its chiasmic equivocation: 'Such welcome and unwelcome things at once / 'Tis hard to reconcile', since 'So foul and fair a day I have not seen' [*1,3,36; 4,3,139*].[11] Far from validating his paranoia, this mirror masque would thereby expose the Scottish interloper as another Herod, by turning 'James's own strategy of equivocation against James', as Goldberg puts it, while 'relying on his self-deception to keep him from understanding the implications'.[12]

The intrusion of James's head into the Witches' ball would appear to constitute a most literal instance of the anachronistic projection of real time into the time of the play that Carl Schmitt considered the source of tragedy in Shakespeare. Though the Nazi jurist was thinking of *Hamlet*, the diabolical glass would seem to be the perfect instrument for his theory that it is by mirroring the person of the king that 'the play on stage could appear ... as theatre within theatre ... could magnify itself as a play without detaching itself from the immediate reality'.[13] Schmitt's belief that through such metatheatrical effects Shakespearean tragedy helped shape the regime by which it was itself shaped anticipated the New Historicist reading of *Macbeth*, *King Lear*, *Othello* and *Measure for Measure* as a sycophantic procession which 'leads in the direction of absolutism'.[14] The theorist of political theology considered that Shakespeare was committed to the myth of divine right, and in allusions like the one to touching for the 'King's Evil' as 'A most miraculous work in this good King' [*4,3,148*], to James Stuart in person as an embodiment of the principle that 'sovereign is who decides the exception'.[15] What Schmitt misses in Shakespeare, however, is the glassy imperviousness of his symbolization to the reality it reflects, and the indifference of the apparitions who are here identified with the theatre, and who come and go like 'shadows', or the imperturbable actors themselves, in the onward march of the play:

FIRST WITCH: Show.
SECOND WITCH: Show.
THIRD WITCH: Show.
ALL THE WITCHES: Show his eyes and grieve his heart
                      Come like shadows, so depart.
                                        [*4,1,123–7*]

A generation ago the New Historicist critique of Shakespeare's Jacobean dramas was cued by Stephen Orgel's belief that masques were allegories that 'gave a higher meaning to the realities of politics and power, their fictions created heroic roles for the leaders of society', and that with shows-within-shows like the one the Witches produce for Macbeth these works themselves 'express the developing movement toward autocracy'.[16] But more recent scholars have discovered that even court masques were 'more problematically implicated' in the Stuart regime than this, and that, as David Lindley insists, 'within the panegyric genre of the masque writers could do more than simply flatter the monarch and ventriloquise his politics'.[17] In fact Schmitt's personalist account of the intrusion of the real time of Stuart history into the fictive time on the stage had already been countered when his erstwhile fellow Weimar rightist Ernst Kantorowicz deduced that as they 'conjure up the uncanny ghostly procession of Macbeth's predecessors, whose last one bears the glass showing the long file of his successors', these 'midnight hags' [4,1,47] are doing exactly what London lawyers did prior to the Civil War, by projecting the fiction of a Crown that never dies, because it transcends each successive change of regime as 'a mystical person', whose temporary incumbent is disposable compared to 'the immortal body by succession'.[18] For Kantorowicz, then, the mirror was the symbol not of the play's passive mimetic servility towards the time that it reflects but rather of the play's active representational difference, and the transcendence of myths by symbolic forms.

Because it has been confused with his genuflecting 1927 bestseller on the medieval Hohenstaufen Emperor Frederick II, Kantorowicz's postwar masterwork *The King's Two Bodies* has been persistently misread by Shakespeareans as though it was merely yet another Schmittian legitimation of the *Führerprinzip*.[19] In fact, as Alain Boureau shows in a brilliant meditation on the political evolution of the historian, Kantorowicz's 1957 book 'inverted Schmitt's understanding of political theology', as here 'Political theology used the moment of the Incarnation as the model of a liberating fiction that affirmed the office of man above and beyond his natural existence'. Whereas for Schmitt the monarch is God on earth, Kantorowicz 'restored the emancipatory function of law: to create fictions that remove man' from such personal power.[20] So, while Schmitt stressed the *theology* in the term 'political theology' he invented, or the king's body natural, Kantorowicz came in the second half of his own schizoid double career, spent in Oxford and the United States, to emphasize the *political*, or the body politic. Thus, in his view, the mirror in *Macbeth* disclosed that 'the "head" of the body politic which, after all, was a mortal individual man ... was of relatively minor importance as compared to the immortal body corporate'. Ultimate authority was never to be confused, that is to say, with that of the temporary 'head of state'.[21]

'Uneasy lies the head that wears a crown' [*2Henry IV, 3,1,31*], says Shakespeare's usurping Henry IV; and the importance of Kantorowicz's reference to the decapitation of Charles I is how, contrary to Schmitt, he derived from such moments what Julia Lupton calls 'figures of collectivity' which 'exist beyond the king as a natural person and serve to limit his sovereignty'.[22] No wonder, therefore, in view of this analysis, that when the eighth spectre looms before him, Macbeth cries, 'Down! / Thy crown does sear mine eyeballs' [*128*]. For it may be that at this moment of Shakespeare's closest proximity to the face of Stuart power those royal spectators themselves recoiled in similar horror from the reflected heads, since like the mirror which shatters the king in *Richard II*, the glass held up in *Macbeth* carries the fatal sentence for the monarch, that 'A brittle glory shineth in this face. / As brittle as the glory is the face' [*4,1,277*]. Thus, far from deifying these northern interlopers in England's royal succession, the doctrine that 'The body is with the King, but the King is not with the body. The King is a thing ... of nothing' [*Hamlet, 4,2,25*], would be sharpened into the legal weapon to cut off the head of Christian's beloved nephew and James's son, when with the paradox that 'We fight the *k*ing to defend the *K*ing', the regicides pushed to its bitter, bloody, yet logical, conclusion what Kantorowicz himself admitted was 'that most unpleasant idea of the violent separation of the King's Two Bodies':

> Without [this idea] it would have been impossible for Parliament to summon, in the name of Charles I, King body politic, the armies which were to fight the same Charles I, king body natural ... Nor can the fiction of the King's Two Bodies be thought of apart from the events when Parliament succeeded in trying 'Charles Stuart ...' for high treason, and finally in executing solely the king's body natural without doing ... harm to the King's body politic – in contradistinction to the events in France, in 1793.[23]

Fair is foul

In *Portrait of the King* Louis Marin described how the Eucharistic doctrine of sacral kingship came in France to be disastrously identified with his body natural. But while at every *levée* the Sun King could declare '*L'état, c'est moi*', and claim his reflection in the Hall of Mirrors to be his inseparable 'second body', the Stuarts were prised from the Crown, according to Kantorowicz, by the revolution staged in *Richard II* and *Macbeth*, where 'Proud majesty' is made into 'a mockery king of snow' [*4,1,242–50*], as 'the King's body politic was retained, whereas the king body natural was, so to say, frozen out'.[24] As Greenblatt remarks, while it opens with Richard's agonized recognition that 'I live with bread, like you, feel want' [*Richard II, 3,2,171*], the king's real body was ruthlessly excised from Kantorowicz's book.[25] Victoria Kahn concurs that, contrary to its misinterpretations, 'The displacement of the body is, ironically, the message of *The King's Two Bodies*'.[26] For unlike critics who read Shakespeare as a Stuart publicist, Kantorowicz's take on the mirror dialectic of the King's Two Bodies was as justification for violent *resistance* to absolutism, and he traced the English version of the doctrine through the Catholic jurist Edmund Plowden, who had revived the medieval *doxa* that the king never dies to paper over his refusal to swear the oath of royal supremacy demanded by the Protestant Queen Elizabeth.

For a 'church papist' such as Edmund Plowden the fiction of the mystical monarchy was a legalism to render unto Caesar only that which was Caesar's.[27] It may be no accident, therefore, that Kantorowicz completed *The King's Two Bodies* during a comparable crisis of conscience, after he had left Berkeley having refused to take the loyalty oath imposed by the University of California in the anti-Communist McCarthyite purge. But its genesis had been in the Germany of Schmitt's state of emergency. In his 1957 Preface he in fact speaks of its relevance to 'the horrifying experience of our own time, in which whole nations, the largest and the smallest, fell prey to the weirdest dogmas in which political theologisms became genuine obsessions defying ... human and political reason'. He could hardly have expressed more strongly his disagreement with a Schmittian theologization of Nazi politics. Thus, this diehard conservative, who fought with the *Freikorps* as an agent of terror to suppress the

1919 German Revolution, stood by the deconstructive philosophy he discovered in Shakespeare: that the individual ruler has no claim on the loyalty owed to the spiritual empire, which stretches out, as Macbeth is shown, 'to the crack of doom' [*4,1,133*].[28]

Kantorowicz's messianic notion of allegiance to a sacred kingdom-to-come not of this world recalls his Jewish heritage. But its context was the self-styled 'Secret Germany' of poet Stefan George, whose cult of the mystical realm of the once-and-future king was maintained in contempt of the Weimar Republic.[29] And here the historian's history provides an object lesson on the problem that Shakespeare repeatedly stages in *Macbeth*, of the trouble, when the world-historical time comes, in making the 'due decision' [*5,4,17*]. For it was his mystique of an *ideal* sovereignty which compelled Kantorowicz to make the dismaying declaration, just a day in 1933 before being ejected by the new Hitler regime as a Jew from his professorship at Frankfurt, that 'if current events are not a grimace of that ideal but a path to its fulfilment, then it is of no consequence whether the individual will – may, rather – march along or step to one side instead of cheering. "Imperium transendat homine," Frederick II said and I would be the last to contradict him.'[30] This phantasm of the true Reich as a timeless procession was the same as the author of *The King's Two Bodies* derived from the Witches' glass; and hostile critics have likened his response to Shakespeare to the endorsement of the 1934 'Night of the Long Knives' by Schmitt.[31] But in proving the inability of philosophy to detach itself from politics, Kantorowicz's troubling personal story might explain why his esoteric scholarship still remains so influential, as it seems to have made him alive to one of the most disturbing implications of *Macbeth*, which is the 'double ... trouble' [*4,1,20*] humanism shares with the tyranny it opposes, the 'demonic complicity' symbolized in that satanic mirror between the terrorist and tyrant, or those who cast the dictator out and those who raised him up:[32]

> But for all this,
> When I shall tread upon the tyrant's head,
> Or wear it on my sword, yet my poor country
> Shall have more vices than it had before,
> More suffer, and more sundry ways, than ever,
> By him that shall succeed.
>
> [*4,3,45–50*]

In a fierce rereading from an opposite ideological perspective, Alan Sinfield was one of the first Shakespeareans to understand Kantorowicz correctly, in noticing that, while always seen as a tragedy of violence, what this play, which opens with a 'brave', 'worthy' and 'noble Macbeth' promoted by King Duncan for the 'bloody execution' of the rebel Macdonald [*1,2,16; 18;24; 70*], in fact stages is the instability of the distinction between an authorized and unauthorized violence, and that when Malcolm tests Macduff by purporting to be as cruelly despotic as Macbeth his duplicity serves to expose the resemblance of the tyrannicide and tyrant. Thus after Malcolm pretends his project is to invade the country for its riches and to 'cut off the nobles for their lands', we learn Macduff is prepared to let him rape, terrorize and 'forge / Quarrels unjust against the good and loyal, / Destroying them for the wealth' [*4,3,83–5*], so long as the present incumbent is eliminated. By envisaging Scotland under English occupation as another rogue state the tragedy thereby disrupts the claim on which the Crown's monopoly of violence is staked, that violence is good when it serves a prevailing power but evil when it resists.[33] Insisting from the start that 'Fair is foul, and foul is fair' [*1,1,10*], *Macbeth* would seem instead to be about the antinomy discussed by Walter Benjamin in his 'Critique of Violence', to which Schmitt and Kantorowicz were responding, between natural law which regards violence as perennial, and positive law which sees violence as the product of history; and to pose the conundrum that 'If natural law can judge existing law only in criticizing its ends, positive law can judge evolving law only in criticizing its means', so while 'natural law attempts by the justness of its ends to "justify" the means, positive law "guarantees" the justness of the ends through justification of its means'.[34]

Benjamin's insoluble antimony was also the starting-point for Francis Barker in *The Culture of Violence*. But there Barker maintained that the irresolvable contradiction is simply cancelled in *Macbeth*, 'a play of hurt and violence' and the most savage of the tragedies in both the brutality of its story and its symbolization of blood, by the mimetic terror unleashed within Shakespeare's text itself: '*Macbeth* has no compunction about the violence of its own resolution, even going so far as depicting actual battle ... The appearance [of legitimacy] is no doubt saved by this violence being ... a crushing victory for reparation', yet 'It is not just that violence is depicted, but that the text is instinct with violence in its very constitution'. Thus, if the dramatist 'never seems to know quite what he supports', and may have intended *Macbeth* 'as an argument against Absolutism', the bias the play does betray, Barker alleges, is a craven 'commitment to domination'.[35] Culture *is* violence, in this version of Benjamin's dark maxim that 'There is no document of civilization that is not a document of barbarism'; and the mirror frames the grimacing face of the tyrant Macbeth – like Caravaggio's severed head of the screaming Medusa, created, also in 1606, for the Medici rulers of Florence – as one of those cultural treasures 'carried along in the triumphal procession in which the present rulers step over those lying prostrate'.[36] Not for nothing, then, if it was performed by royal command to salute the regime change in Stuart England, does *Macbeth* both begin and end with a decapitation invoking the hangman's bloodcurdling cry, as his macabre trophy was held up 'to be the show and gaze o'th'time' [5,11,24], to 'Behold the head of a traitor':

> For brave Macbeth – well he deserves that name! –
> Disdaining fortune, with his brandished steel
> Which smoked with bloody execution,
> Like valour's minion
> Carved out his passage till he faced the slave,
> Which ne'er shook hands nor bade farewell to him
> Till he unseamed him from the nave to th'chops,
> And fixed his head upon our battlements.
>
> [1,2,16–23]

Opening with Macdonald's severed head impaled for Duncan by Macbeth, and closing with Macbeth's displayed by Macduff to Malcolm 'upon a pole' [5,11,26], where each time 'a supposedly saintly king lets another do his dirty work', what the reflecting play of mirrors in *Macbeth* reveals is how sovereignty is always, in Derrida's pun, the 'discourse of the capital': from the Latin for head, *caput*.[37] And whenever he crossed into the capital on London Bridge, biographers remind us, young Shakespeare would indeed pass beneath the spiked heads of his mother's Catholic relations Edward Arden and John Somerville, executed in 1583 for plotting to assassinate Elizabeth on behalf of Mary Queen of Scots.[38] So the conflicting signals about traitors and tyrants he took from those boiled and painted skulls must have reminded him each time how perilously close 'the state's machine of terror and taint of treason' had come to his own doorstep.[39] Someone strangled Somerville in his cell hours before the barbaric sentence was to be carried out. But the despatch of Arden had followed the appalling ritual prescribed for traitors: 'to be hanged and let down alive, and your privy parts cut off, and your entrails taken out and burnt in your own sight; then your head cut off, and your body divided in four parts, to be disposed of at Her Majesty's pleasure'.[40] Thus the equation of decapitation with castration enacted at the very start, when Macbeth disembowels and then beheads Macdonald – expressly like the hangman 'Which ne'er shook hands nor bade farewell' to the traitor he gutted with 'steel / Which smoked with bloody execution' – was impressed upon the writer as the condition of losing your head by witnessing your victimization *'in your own sight'*.

Destroy your sight

Lurid allusions to public executions in *Macbeth* are signs of how, as Schmitt writes, the time of the present forces itself into the virtual time of the play, and puts the spectator or critic who resists such anachronistic intrusions in the same position as the sovereignty that 'With barefaced power sweeps from sight' its crimes, 'Masking the business from the common eye / For sundry weighty reasons' [*3,1,120–7*]. So the possibility of Shakespeare's personal witness to these spectacles of punishment sparks similar interpretive questions to those posed by the paintings of Caravaggio, who also liked to update biblical or mythical decapitations as if happening in the present on a Renaissance scaffold, and to actualize such traumatic histories by inserting among participants the wide-eyed faces of his contemporaries, or in the hands of the future King David, and in the place of that of the disembodied monster, his own severed head. Thus, in shocking pictures of the decapitations of Goliath, Holofernes or Medusa, it is as if the painter associated an 'obscene fascination with the mechanics of violence' with his own aesthetic space, and the specific act of decapitation, Leo Bersani and Ulysse Dutoit argue in *Caravaggio's Secrets*, with the treachery implicit in his art, to the extent, in *The Beheading of St John the Baptist*, of symbolically *signing* the picture in the victim's blood.[41]

It would be easy to associate the horrific images of beheading staged in *Macbeth* or depicted by Caravaggio with those later modernist 'crimes of art' where 'terror is the logical endpoint' of the artist's own homicidal will to power; and Julia Kristeva has indeed spoken of the sadomasochistic intimacy into which we are tempted by *David and Goliath*, remarking that 'no one looks at a severed head except art lovers, voyeurs like you and me'. In *The Severed Head*, her meditation on 'capital visions', the theorist proposes that in presenting us with such an *eyeful* of extreme abjection, where sacrificial violence coincides with seduction, 'The thoroughly displayed beheading signals the end point of the visible', a literal *obscenity* beyond which 'There is nothing more to see'.[42] Regarding the pain of others to the extent of enacting the act of decapitation becomes, however, for Bersani and Dutoit, not an incitement to masturbatory voyeurism but an anxious probing of the psychotic origins of the work of art, an exploration which suggests that the artist's plan is instead to break the cycle of suffering by deconstructing the dichotomy of subject and object, violator and violated, and by questioning the murderous instrumental capacity of the slashing pen or brush:[43]

> Is this a dagger which I see before me,
> The handle toward my hand? Come, let me clutch thee,
> I have thee not, and yet I see thee still.
> Art thou not, fatal vision, sensible
> To feeling as to sight? Or art thou but
> A dagger of the mind, a false creation
> Proceeding from the heat-oppressèd brain?
> I see thee yet, in form as palpable
> As this which now I draw.
>
> [2,1,33–41]

'I see thee still, / And on thy blade and dudgeon gouts of blood' [45–6]: with its determination to 'Show ... Show ... Show' the 'gory locks' [3,4,50] of the severed head, *Macbeth* is a work that shares with seventeenth-century paintings a distress at the inability of art to sublate itself from 'the bloody business' of power [2,1,48], to cleanse the artist's hand of the stains which 'pluck out mine eyes' [2,2,57]. And in an essay on the depiction of such bloodshed in Renaissance art Svetlana Alpers concedes that there is 'a sequence of painters in the European tradition who are intrigued by killing, by slaying, by delving into the flesh'. But she similarly proposes that this 'troubling relationship between paint and flesh and blood, between the hand that wields a weapon and the hand of the painter', is problematized by the baring of technique, which 'makes us pause to look'. Thus when Titian highlights the flashing motion of the knife in his *Flaying of Marsyas*, or Rembrandt the blood-soaked gown in his *Lucretia*, these painters 'identify with both the slayer and the slain', and show us that the way for the artist 'to reflect on violent actions is to acknowledge that, albeit metaphorically, one engages in them oneself'.[44]

'Manner of painting makes a difference to the depiction of violence', Alpers affirms, because it is 'the painter's very involvement with the medium' that serves as art's 'antidote to violence'.[45] Caravaggio's pictures thus use the polished shield of Perseus to reflect the petrifying gaze of Medusa back on itself, as a representation of *the artist's own incrimination*; as Shakespeare's drama of decapitation likewise seems to do, when it expressly invites its spectators to 'Approach the chamber, and destroy your sight / With a new Gorgon' [2,3,73], by looking upon 'the very painting of your fear' [3,4,60]. The myth of the three Gorgons, Medusa, Euryale and Stheno, lies close to the *Macbeth* experience, where the scopic power of the 'weird sisters' to 'look into the seeds of time' [1,3,30;56] likewise stems from their ability to petrify with a look, 'an inversion of the human gaze that wants, precisely, to capture the horror of the other, to freeze it, to eliminate it'.[46] Not for nothing, therefore, have performers neutralized the uncanny reputation of this unlucky work by euphemizing it with superstitions. For though 'this defeat can never take place if the human fascination with the spectacle of violence is not deprogrammed', Bersani and Dutoit concede, with its dazzling game of mirrors Caravaggio's art permits what critics have begun to retrieve from the metatheatre of 'the Scottish play': a recognition of the reversibility of martyrs and monsters, or artists and assassins:

> Cutting into and shaping space: was Caravaggio interested in executioners as modes of self-representation? The executioner's gesture is not unlike that of the painter ... The represented looks solicited by the severed heads and helpless victims insist on the impossibility of detaching ourselves entirely both from real and imaginary scenes of violence ... But much of Caravaggio's work raises the question of whether Goliath's death was necessary ...[47]

Reflecting his own moment in scenes of historical violence, Caravaggio put his head upon the symbolic block, art historians infer, 'to prevent us from reading the scene merely *as* history'.[48]

Likewise, Shakespeare's mirroring of contemporary terror in his historical plays can be seen to expose the violent genealogy of his own culture. It thus seems a misperception when Barker accuses Shakespeare of always shifting the spectacle of violence onto 'another time, another place, among other people', seeing that the text he cites is the cruel interlude in *Titus Andronicus* where the Clown is hanged who petitions the Emperor in the name of 'God and St Stephen' [4,4,42]. For St Stephen was stoned to death for preaching; and this incident has since been connected to the tragedy of Richard Shelley, a naive Catholic liquidated after petitioning Elizabeth for religious toleration. To Barker, the atrocious episode was 'stunning, inexplicable, strange, *unheimlich*, and haunting'. But in 1993 his Marxian critique could not hear the pun of *Roman* Catholics on ancient Romans which testifies how Titus guarantees his own victimization by butchering the Goths, who are now seen as the images of the Protestant reformers martyred under the Catholic Tudor, 'Bloody Mary'.[49]

Critics are embarrassed by the fleshly materiality with which the time of sovereignty presses on the time of the stage through these allusions to the sufferings of Catholic martyrs. We can, of course, never know whether young Shakespeare stood in Smithfield to witness the old 'Roman' Arden hanged; or at Tyburn when the Jesuit Edmund Campion, who hid in Stratford on arriving from Prague, was hacked to pieces, and in the mêlée zealots tore off relics; though the tribute in *Macbeth* to the Thane of Cawdor echoes Catholic martyrology, when it is said that 'Nothing in his life / Became him like the leaving of it. He died / As one that had been studied in his death / To throw away the dearest thing he owed' [1,4,7–10]. But repeated references to 'The shape of love's Tyburn, that hangs up simplicity' [*Love's*, 4,3,49], where 'Romans' kiss the victim's wounds and dip 'their napkins in his sacred blood' [*Julius*, 3,2,129], suggest the dramatist remained alert to the symmetry between the theatre and the scaffold as institutions of sacrifice – 'the spectacle of the traitor on the platform of public execution and on stage' – which he surely witnessed at the Holywell gallows, in the shadow of his Shoreditch playhouse: 'The place of death and sorry execution / Behind the ditches of the abbey here' [*Errors*, 5,1,122].[50]

Editors connect the sentence passed on Egeon in *The Comedy of Errors* to the hanging of the exorcist William Hartley, an associate of Stratford's Jesuit schoolmaster Simon Hunt.[51] And even if

punning of a condemned *Syracusan* with *recusancy* is now inaudi-
ble, the affinity of 'this great stage of fools' [*Lear, 4,6,177*] to the
theatre of the Jesuit exorcists would have been blatant, Greenblatt
believes, to the earliest audiences.[52] Clearly, Shakespeare knew how
state terror worked at Tyburn, and in *Venus and Adonis* may have
penned an allegory to warn his young patron, Southampton, against
papist conspiracy, with a nightmare vision of a swine slicing his 'soft
groin' to castrate and eviscerate Adonis [*1116*]. This reads like a
report on the martyrdom of the Earl's priest, the 'beautiful English
youth' Robert Southwell, grotesquely cradled by the executioner
'in his own arms to where he was to be quartered'.[53] The Greek
word *martyr*, we register, means *witness*. But what returns with the
change of regime, along with the repressed record of the scene of
Tudor butchery, where 'so many smiling Romans' came to 'bathe
their hands' in blood [*Julius, 2,2,77–86*], is the dramatist's own
sense of the *untimeliness* of sacrificial violence: his eye-witness to
the uncanny reversal when yesterday's terrorists become tomorrow's founding-fathers, and, as Derrida observed, 'Armed repression
and state terrorism all of a sudden become "a war"', while 'the terrorists are from now on considered freedom fighters and heroes':[54]

> To this I witness call the fools of time,
> Which die for goodness, who have lived for crime.
>
> [Sonnet 124]

For Derrida, the ambivalence of the German word *Gewalt*, meaning
both unauthorized violence and sanctioned force, was not the
contradiction Benjamin thought, but an expression of the fact that
every state originates in the same treason and terrorism as, say, the
Israel of the Stern Gang.[55] As Sir John Harington quipped, 'Treason
doth never prosper ... For if it prosper, none call it treason.' So
this might explain why Shakespeare's witness to violence has itself
been effaced in the process of burying the originary violence of
the United Kingdom *Macbeth* describes.[56] For one consequence
of Elizabeth's succession by the son of the Catholic queen she sent
to death was that the National Poet's family links with Mary's
partisans became the scandal they remain, when James effaced the
matricidal foundations of his Protestant state. To be sure, there have
always been those, like the Catholic critic Richard Simpson, who
read the Bard's decision to 'leave the killing out, when all is done',
as a 'device to make all well' in a police state where 'doing it too

terribly were enough to hang us all' [*Dream, 3,1,13–15*]; and others like the Catholic writer Graham Greene who grieve how one scene is absent from Shakespeare's stage, where 'the martyrs are quite silent': 'The kings speak, the madmen and the lovers', yet 'How removed they are from the routine of the torture chamber'.[57] But it is only with the advent of political theology in studies of the plays that this apparent invisibility has come to seem a *creative* inhibition.

Francis Bacon, Greene observed, had been one of the lawyers taking notes as Catholic prisoners were racked, so the novelist would have supported the Baconian heresy if that had meant it was the author of the plays who faced the prisoners in the Tower.[58] But Greene had not noticed how when the Rackmaster Thomas Norton boasted he had stretched one priest 'a foot longer than God made him', Shakespeare gave Kent the rebuttal: 'He hates him much / That would upon the rack of this tough world / Stretch him out longer' [*King Lear, 5,3,312*].[59] Nor how when Gloucester is tortured and blinded to divulge 'Wherefore to Dover?' the Quarto text prints the question as 'Wherefore to *Douai*?': the training-school for Jesuit missionaries [*3,7,52*]. For it is only recently that critics have come to recognize how even the Comedies are haunted by this religious violence, in the 'constant allusions to burning at the stake, blinding, and hanging' which evoke the cruelties perpetrated on priests like 'Master Parson, *quasi* "pierce one"' [*Love's, 4,1,76*] – the Jesuit Robert Parsons – or 'the old hermit of Prague, that never saw pen and ink' at his show-trial [*Twelfth, 4,2,11*] because of his wounds – the tormented Campion.[60]

In 1988 Stephen Greenblatt could still reason that if such 'Martial Law in the Land of Cockaigne' aroused the same anxieties as maiming and executions on the scaffold that was likewise 'to set the stage for royal pardons to demonstrate a prince's mercy'.[61] Yet what the recent religious turn in Shakespeare studies allows us to perceive is how these hungry ghosts pleading from limbo to be remembered destabilize the absolutism of any such imposition, just as they repel us by crying for bloody revenge. For Campion, Greenblatt now realizes, 'was a fanatic, or more accurately, a saint. And saints, Shakespeare understood, were dangerous.'[62] In light of the critical interest in political theology, Hamlet's dilemma therefore becomes the 'Bloody Question' of a Counter-Reformation suicide-bomber: whether to suffer 'slings and arrows' of persecution, like a medieval saint, or take arms like the Jesuit, 'And by opposing, end them' [*Hamlet, 3,1,60–1*].[63] But the other question that resounds in these texts comes from collateral victims of this Jacobean war of terror, and is posed by Macduff's young son, when he and his mother are about to pay with their lives for Macduff's premature resistance, in the scene that counts as Shakespeare's 'Massacre of the Innocents': 'What is a traitor?':

MACDUFF'S SON:	What is a traitor?
LADY MACDUFF:	Why, one that swears and lies.
MACDUFF'S SON:	And be all traitors that do so?
LADY MACDUFF:	Everyone that does so is a traitor, and must be hanged.
MACDUFF'S SON:	And must they all be hanged that swear and lie?
LADY MACDUFF:	Every one.
MACDUFF'S SON:	Who must hang them?
LADY MACDUFF:	Why, the honest men.
MACDUFF'S SON:	Then the liars and swearers are fools, for there are liars and swearers enough to beat the honest men and hang up them.

[*Macbeth, 4,2,44–58*]

In every point twice done

In a much-quoted essay David Norbrook typifies the humanist response to *Macbeth* when he asserts that 'Shakespeare invents the scene of the murder of Lady Macduff and her son to bring home [how] Macbeth's rule strikes against the family', and thus to establish that 'virtuous forces must use violence. Macduff must not sheathe his sword ... The tyrannicide's dagger is redeemed by legitimacy.' But this account forgets Lady Macduff's bitter insinuation that her husband has betrayed his own wife and child and implication that with such 'liars and swearers' there are enough traitors to hang the rest. These lines are thought to refer to the Jesuit Henry Garnet, executed in May 1606 after equivocating on oath over knowledge of the Gunpowder Plot. But like Malcolm's dissembling, they do not authorize 'the foundation of a new and more stable order' so much as reveal the collusive 'family resemblance', in Steven Mullaney's acute phrase, 'between authority and its Other'.[64]

If it was commissioned to mark the monstrous union of the Tudor and Stuart states, of the lion and the unicorn, it is no wonder that *Macbeth* is so preoccupied with duplicity and duplication. As Derrideans object, what the humanist critics of *Macbeth* cannot recognize is that, like the strange new polity's two bodies, with its two countries, two invasions, two Cawdors, two feasts, two doctors, two kings, and two severed heads impaled on poles, the 'equivocation' of this doubled play about a duplex state – which 'palters with us in a double sense', 'in every point twice done, and then done double', duplicating 'double trouble' in such self-splitting and mutual incrimination [1,6,15; 4,1,10; 5,5,41; 5,10,20] – mirrors insurgency with counter-insurgency, victims with violators, so insistently it cannot simply be intended as a demonstration of the necessity of their war on terror designed to reassure the family of King James. Nothing in *Macbeth* can ever be so completely 'done' or finished.[65] Thus, critical consensus takes Lady Macduff seriously when she calls her husband a traitor, and endorses Jan Kott's belief that in this self-deconstructing scenario *everyone* is steeped in blood:

> The whole world is stained in blood ... 'There's daggers in men's smiles: the nea'er in blood, / The nearer bloody' [2,3,36–7]. Blood in *Macbeth* is not just a metaphor; it is real blood flowing out of murdered bodies. It leaves its stains ... But this blood cannot be washed off hands, faces, or daggers. *Macbeth* begins and ends with slaughter. There is more and more blood, everyone walks in it ...[66]

For a survivor of Hitler and Stalin, such as Kott, the 'double trouble' of *Macbeth* is the nightmare of the criminal state. Thus the chilling realization that, in killing Macbeth, Macduff steps into his role to become Malcolm's Macbeth, making the future a recurrence of the same, accords with recent readings which see 'one king slide into the other' in the hall of mirrors, as the 'family likeness' of Duncan and Macbeth is passed from Macbeth to James.[67] And here the question of what the real king saw in this endless contaminating duplication becomes key to the politics of the play, because, as editors recognize, there is a difficulty if this 'show of eight kings' is supposed to stabilise his claim to succeed one not 'of woman born' [4,1,96]. For the eighth Stuart ruler was in fact the very female through whom James's 'two-fold balls' descended, but whose absence from the scene was vital to his preserving them, the woman he had sacrificed to inherit the throne of England, and whose atrocious death, which made him as much an assassin as Macbeth in the eyes of her mourners, became synonymous with the barbarity of decapitation, when 'the first blow, as it fell, missed the neck and cut into the back of her head': his own mother, the martyred Queen of Scots.[68] Though he underrated how much she had been venerated, Schmitt was therefore correct to claim that, if Shakespeare's Jacobean tragedies are structured around an occluded historical displacement, 'this very concrete taboo concerns Mary Queen of Scots':

> The unhappy Stuart lineage from which James descended was more deeply involved than others in the fate of the European schism of belief. James' father was murdered; his mother married the murderer; the mother for her part was executed … a devotee to her Roman Catholic beliefs. The son, to avoid losing the throne of Scotland, had to ally himself with the Protestants. He had to put himself on good terms with his mother's enemy to the death, Queen Elizabeth, in order to win the throne of England. He was thus literally from his womb immersed in the schisms of his era.[69]

'When the executioner held up the dead woman's head', James might have recalled, as his ancestors rose from the grave with their 'gold-bound' hair 'blood-baltered' [*129–39*], 'the auburn tresses came apart from the skull and the head itself fell to the ground, for it was seen that she had chosen to wear a wig', since she was 'very grey and nearly bald'.[70] The Folio is evasive about whether Mary's phantom did appear on stage in the masque of kings in the haunted chamber at Hampton Court, where the ghost of that other repressed mother and figure of female abjection, Anne Boleyn, is said always to carry its own head. But if Mary is, as Schmitt thought, the Medusa-haired mother-figure and castrating queen of night who haunts the misogynistic phantasmagoria of *Macbeth*, what her matricidal son and heir would catch in her peripheral absent-presence would literally make 'each particular hair to stand an end' [*Hamlet, 1,5,19*]. For his mother's botched beheading was the fissure which both opened and blocked James's right to succeed, the violent breach in sovereignty that, as he plots to murder Duncan, Macbeth gasps is indeed the 'horrid image' which 'doth unfix my heir' [*1,3,134*]. In case we miss the connotations of unmanning in this ghoulishly somatic pun, at the very end Siward declares that 'Had I as many sons as I have hairs / I would not wish them to a fairer death' [*5,11,14*]. So, as David Scott Kastan glosses it, what this uncannily scalp-tingling wordplay emphasizes is how 'Both hairs and heirs may be unfixed by the knowledge of sovereignty's violent origins'.[71]

Towards the end, after he has supped so 'full with horrors' his 'slaughterous thoughts' no longer 'start' him, Macbeth will recall the 'taste of fear', when his blood ran cold 'To hear a night-shriek, and my fell of hair' would 'rouse and stir / As life were in't' [*5,5,9–14*]. And for sure, the uncanniness of this 'unfixed hair' must have unsettled Mary's heir, when the locks she had shorn before her hair was forever 'unfixed' were circulated as relics in Catholic houses, and her 'golden' tresses were depicted matted in a martyr's blood in plays like 'the Tragedy of the Queen of Scots publicly acted' in Paris, and tactlessly posted to James in 1604 by its author Antoine de Montchrétien.[72] One Jesuit drama even pictured the king addressing the bleeding stump of his mother's headless neck with memories of how he had hung upon it as an infant.[73] Vulva as visage in such a hallucination, Mary's severed head must truly have possessed for her son the 'absolute ugliness of the originary hole' of which Kristeva writes: 'Medusa is *abject* as primitive matrix of that archaic nondifferentiation in which there is neither subject nor object, only the sticky slimy ab-ject ... indissociable from the terror prompted by castration and death'.[74]

Like Marie Antoinette's, the blood-dripping head of King James's mother became for an entire generation what Kristeva calls 'the capital vision, with so excessive a vital, libidinal impact that it warrants an equally capital repression'.[75] For from the day of the queen's beheading, when the block and every scrap stained with her blood were burned, the son hoped, like Macbeth, that 'this blow / Might be the be-all and end-all'; and that his 'Bloody instructions' – where in a 'bloody and invisible hand' he had reassured her killers that he would 'never prefer my mother to the title' – would 'trammel up the consequence, and catch' with her 'surcease success' [*1,7,3–9; 3,2,49*].[76] Thus at the time of *Macbeth* Mary's tomb was being projected at Westminster, to 'erase his part in Mary's death'.[77] As David Howarth recounts, the queen's re-internment was meant 'to reconcile the irreconcilable', when the marble 'became the shroud to cover the horror of the execution of one sovereign by another'.[78] But 'to avoid a concourse in the place whence she had been expelled with tyranny', as the crypto-Catholic Earl of Northampton recorded, her remains were brought to the Abbey in 1612 under 'the blanket of the dark', and interred with 'a general repression of pageantry'. For in squeamish conflicted solicitude over his mother's mutilated body the king 'did not care to witness' it, and so 'guaranteed that psychologically it would remain unburied'.[79]

After succeeding to the English throne, James never 'let a day pass without lamenting that his mother's head fell, at the third stroke, by a villainous deed', the Venetian ambassador relayed, 'till those who, even by relationship, are stained with that blood grow fearful ... lest their end be a bloody one'.[80] But if he followed Shakespeare's Scottish ghost story, James would find reflected a king whose own bloody hands are what 'will ne'er be clean', and who is haunted by corpses that when their brains are out, 'rise again / With twenty mortal murders on their crowns, / And push us from our stools' [3,4,78; 5,1,37]. 'Sighted like the basilisk' [*Winter's*, 1,2,388], he would indeed see in his own reflection 'a new Gorgon'. And whether or not the spectre of his decapitated mother did 'sear his eyeballs', unseat him or make James's hair stand up, by returning to him his severed head that 'horrid image' assuredly 'unfixed his heir', for as prosecutor John Bradshawe reminded Charles I: 'No Kingdom has yielded more experience than your native Scotland concerning the deposition and punishment of offending Kings'.[81] Thus it seems that *Macbeth* would never let these Stuarts forget how much 'Blood hath been shed' and crimes 'performed / Too terrible for the ear' [3,4,74] to secure their succession. For if it was indeed the ghost of the tragic Queen of Scots which materialized at Hampton Court, mirroring her own son's scalp, then Shakespeare was daring something not done again until Schiller had Mary confront Elizabeth in the play staged at Weimar in 1801, after state violence had unmasked itself in French Revolutionary Terror, which was to double power on itself by bringing sovereignty *face to face* with 'the consequence' of its 'success':

> It will have blood, they say. Blood will have blood.
> Stones have been known to move, and trees to speak,
> Augurs and understood relations have
> By maggot-pies and choughs and rooks brought forth
> The secret'st man of blood.
>
> [3,4,121–5]

'Blood will have blood': *Sanguis sanguinem procreat*: the argument against Mary's execution in a minute penned by Lord Burghley weeks before her death was the one relished by Catholics themselves, when they exulted that a martyr's blood sows dragon's teeth.[82] And in another memo at this time the old Polonius listed 'the many horrible, detestable, and cruel acts committed in Scotland' as 'the reasons for which the King of Scots is unacceptable to the people of England'. These included the assassination of his father, Darnley, bombed to bits by his mother; the murder of his Regent, Moray; and the slaying of his grandfather, Lennox: 'things which bear such a show of cruelty and mortal hatred in this King, as without great show of an altered mind, the hearts of honest men in England will never be recovered'. As his biographer Alan Stewart remarks, when he came south in 1603 James 'would have his work cut out to win England over'.[83] For the doubled trouble with making this foreigner Elizabeth's heir by 'unfixing the hair' of his real biological mother, these notes make plain, was that the violent separation of a Queen's Two Bodies exposed the arbitrariness of power, the brute fact that as Sir Henry Saville declared at the time of James's English coronation, kingdoms were always 'first purchased by conquest'.[84] The execution of one anointed sovereign by another disclosed what Derrida calls 'the force of law': the logic that regime change can never be negotiated lawfully, since 'The origin of authority, the foundation or ground cannot by definition rest on anything but themselves'.[85]

James's openly 'claimed ancestral conquest as the ultimate sanction of his authority'; but his success in succeeding to the 'twofold balls' of his double-headed empire by conniving in his own mother's 'surcease' was too glaring an exposure of how 'The foundation of all states occurs in a revolutionary situation. It inaugurates a new law, but always in violence.'[86] And this faultline riving the foundation of the new dual polity was deepened when Mary had been held, like Duncan, in 'double trust': as both a sovereign and a guest of the English, 'Who should against [her] murderer shut the door, / Not bear the knife' [1,7,12]. So her prosecutors tied themselves in legal knots denying their own realpolitik; deposing that Mary had forfeited sovereignty by making Elizabeth her host; while the best precedent they could dig up was the execution of Conradin, the last of the Hohenstaufens.[87] It seems doubtful, therefore, that when proffered Macbeth's poleaxed skull, James would understand the implications of the homage: 'Hail, King, for so thou art. Behold, where stands / Th'usurper's cursed head' [5,11,20]; for not only was this monstrous totem an unlikely offering for a ruler who denied the right to resist any head of state, nor 'even Tyrannical kings'.[88] As his own disembodied reflection, the severed head of a King of Scots would also have confronted this 'secret'st man of blood' with his 'secretest' act of betrayal.

'In blood so far steep'd', these Stuart head-hunters were exposed in Shakespeare's mirror as indelibly tainted by their own accursed share, like that 'bloody child ... untimely ripped' from its mother's womb as the revelation of the hidden Neronian truth of Caesarean rule [3,4,135; 4,1,93; 5,10,16]. Thus, uncannily constructed to make 'Your bedded hair, like life in excrements, / Start up and stand on end' [*Hamlet, 3,4,112*], by reflecting back upon the Stuart state the petrifying Medusa head of its own violence, Shakespeare's play of monstrous doubleness actualized the royal spectators' terror of the return of the abjected and repressed, the horror that, for all their hope of burying the disappeared so that the 'Rebellious dead rise never' [4,1,112] – 'safe in a ditch' [3,4,25], or 'To leave no rubs nor botches in the work' [3,1,135], 'perfect, / Whole as the marble, founded as the rock' [3,4,21], where the corpse 'cannot come out on's grave' [5,1,54], like a tomb at Westminster itself – their bloody deeds would out: 'If charnel-houses and our graves must send / Those that we bury back, our monuments / Shall be the maws of kites' [3,4,70–2]. As Kott concluded:

> Macbeth dreams about a world in which ... all murders will have been forgotten; where the dead will have been buried once and for all, and everything will begin anew ... Macbeth's last hope is that the dead will not rise. But they do.[89]

Napkins enough

'When he was cut up and his bowels cast into the fire, and his head showed unto the people with these words, "Behold the head of a traitor," there was not heard any applause, or those that cried, "God save the King"':[90] the execution of Father Garnet *alias* Farmer for his alleged part in the Gunpowder Plot, three months before the royal performance of *Macbeth*, is the recognized source for the Porter's gallows humour about hanging the Jesuit 'equivocator' who 'committed treason enough for God's sake, yet could not equivocate to heaven'. 'Have napkins enough about you', the Porter jeers [2,3,5–10]. But the silence of the crowd that had witnessed Garnet hanged, drawn and quartered in front of St Paul's, and then rushed to soak napkins in his blood, throws a very different light on the relation of the drama to these events than the tradition that with *Macbeth* 'Shakespeare was paying tribute to the triumph of Stuart monarchy over its popish enemies'.[91]

Once the logic of its mirror reversal is recognized, the Porter's interregnum emerges as the alternative focus of a tragedy in which 'Murder and treason' each reflect the other, as the atrocity of the elderly priest's martyrdom is displaced onto Duncan's 'golden blood … his gashed stabs like a breach in nature', with the executioners, their 'hands and faces badged with blood', 'breeched with gore' and 'Steeped in the colours of their trade' [2,3,109–13]. Because Schmitt appears not to have registered the king's own guilt complex, and focused on James's embarrassment at Mary's culpability in his *father's* murder, he too viewed such anachronisms as tributes in which Shakespeare's play paid homage to the Scottish dynasty.[92] But the macabre irruption of the Jesuit's execution into *Macbeth* suggests how such uncanny intrusions work dialectically, and how, having been required to underwrite the state's paranoid war on terror, Shakespeare refused to join this blame game, but instead held up a mirror to the terror of the state itself.

'Faith, sir, we were carousing till the second cock' [23]: as a carnival figure the Porter of Glamis Castle is a topical link to the Bacchanalia of the Jacobean court. So it might be apt to give him a Scots accent, as his over-emphatic phallic jokes about red noses, sexual erections and urine make him not just Macbeth's alter ego but a spitting image of King James. Thus, 'who would have thought the old man to have so much blood in him' [5,1,33], Lady Macbeth winces in the tone of Garnet's executioners. For 'Farmer's' blood would soon seep uncontrollably from relics like the 'bladed corn' to which the Porter and the Witches refer, snatched from the basket in which the priest's head was carried, and supposed to preserve his 'perfect face, as if painted, upon one of the husks' [2,3,4; 4,1,71].[93] As Naomi Liebler writes in relation to *Julius Caesar*, where Antony 'locates both his credibility and feet' on 'slippery ground' [3,1,191] saturated in martyrs' blood, what Shakespeare illustrates with such grisly scenes is Derrida's axiom that all attempts to earth violence in some core or base are metaphysical illusions.[94]

Those who spiked it on the bridge could no more stem the semiotic haemorrhage from Father Garnet's skull than the Jesuit William Sankey could circumscribe Shakespeare's text, when one day during the 1640s at the English College in Valladolid he annotated

Macbeth for novices by underlining Malcolm's line, 'our country ... weeps, it bleeds' [4,3,41].[95] Rector Sankey may have understood the Witches' eerie war-cry that cues Macbeth's drum – 'Here I have a pilot's thumb, / Wrack'd as homeward he did come' [1,3,26] – to be an invocation of the most infamous Jesuit fetish, hacked from the 'pilot' of their mission, and inserted into the vaginas of menstruating girls during exorcisms: the thumb of Campion himself.[96] Baubo, the false phallus of the Eleusinian mysteries, is another monstrosity associated with the castrating Mother which her children prefer not to view, notes Kristeva.[97] But what the Rector could never censor was the implication in that 'devil's dildo' of the mutual violence duplicated by those Jesuitical 'bearded ladies' through their worship of such ghoulish relics:

> Double, double, toil and trouble,
> Fire burn and cauldron bubble.
>
> [4,1,10–11]

The stirrer of 'double trouble' in *Macbeth* was obsessed by the *doppelgänger* story of Cain and Abel, writes R.A. Foakes in his study *Shakespeare and Violence*, but always with a sense of the arbitrariness of God's empowerment of one brother and awareness of the likeness encoded in the sibling rivalry.[98] Likewise, René Girard finds Shakespearean theatre mirroring 'confounding contraries' [*Timon*, 4,1,20] of fratricidal desire, 'As two spent swimmers that do cling together / And choke their art' [1,2,8], until he loses patience with such mimetic rivalry, and focuses 'more and more on its ethical and human consequences, on the needless suffering that this madness produces'.[99] But the frustration of this binary 'reflex theory' for *Macbeth*, as Kastan complains, is that if nothing can ever be settled or 'safe' about our own discrimination between such polar opposites we are truly left in the indeterminacy of a hall of mirrors that is endlessly reflecting and yet 'signifying nothing' [5,5,28].[100] As Alpers remarks, Renaissance works of art depicting violence, like those innumerable images of martyrdom (and we might add *Macbeth*), are so unsettling precisely because they bewilder us with this nightmare vision of contaminating 'double trouble', yet still compel us to submit to the harsh imperative of choice:

> There is bad violence, such as the Massacre of the Innocents ... And there is good violence, such as Judith (heroically) beheading the general Holofernes. And there is some that falls in between, neither

good nor bad, such as Abraham with a knife raised to slay his son, Isaac, or St. Sebastian bound to a tree and pierced by arrows. How does one tell the difference? Can the artist in the painting of it show us the difference between violence that is justified and that which is not?[101]

'About suffering they were never wrong, / The Old Masters': Alpers begins her essay on violence in the age of Velázquez by citing the urgency of W.H. Auden's poem 'Musée de Beaux-Arts' to those who must live 'in terror's wake – New York, 9/11/01'.[102] So, as Derrida also asked after 11 September: How do we take sides in such a confusing time of 'double trouble' as that of international terror? The philosopher's answer, by which he distinguished deconstruction from the decisionism of Schmitt, gives us a vital purchase on *Macbeth*, when he affirmed that 'I would take the side of the camp that leaves a perspective open to perfectibility for *this world*'. Thus, with its decapitation of the Twin Towers of the capital, al-Qaeda would seem to have aimed to be a quintessential form of founding violence, Derrida conceded. But where it differed from political violence is that its actions *opened onto no future*, because it left '*nothing good* to be hoped for'.[103] *Terrorism has no future*: in this distinction we grasp the weight of the Macbeths' realization that despite their craving to 'feel now / The future in the instant ... never / Shall sun that morrow see', and we understand their terrible fatalism that 'Tomorrow, and tomorrow, and tomorrow / Creeps in this petty pace of time' [*5,5,19*], without a hope.

Macbeth is a play preoccupied by the rules of hospitality we owe to what 'tomorrow' and succession bring. In this tragedy that revolves around breaches of hospitality and broken feasts the state terrorists struggle, as they always do, to convince themselves that 'we'll talk tomorrow' [*3,1,23*], 'tomorrow ... we shall have cause of state' [*33*], 'Tomorrow we'll hear ourselves again' [*3,4,30*], that 'tomorrow, / And betimes' [*3,4,131*] they will be secure. But they remain stranded 'here upon this bank of time' [*1,7,6–8*], 'cabined, cribbed, confined' [*3,4,23*], in a perpetual 'tonight' where, for all the prophecies, it is for themselves, not their victims, that 'tomorrow' never comes, because, as Macbeth acknowledges, 'the life to come' is what 'I must not look to have' [*5,3,27*]. And so it is our openness to Malcolm's promise that 'What's more to do / Which would be planted newly with the time ... We will perform

in measure, time, and place' [5,11,30–9], that allows us in the end
to side with 'invincible hope', in Derrida's words, despite all its
betrayals and failures, and 'even in its most cynical mode', and
thereby to dream of some future justice when, as the new king
pledges, 'The time is free' [21].[104] Thus we see how the Adventism
of even *Macbeth* contributes to Shakespeare's vision of an art
divorced from power which will give 'delight and hurt not', in that
time to come when sovereignty has renounced its prison camps
and torture chambers, so as to 'leave not a rack behind' [*Tempest*,
3,2,131; 4,1,155].

'The time approaches / That will with due decision make us
know / What we shall say we have, and what we owe', assert
the freedom-fighters towards the end of *Macbeth*, this play that
urges us that 'Thoughts speculative their unsure hopes relate, /
But certain issues strokes must arbitrate' [5,4,16–20]. As Derrida
warned, quoting Kierkegaard, because there is no pure foundation
uncontaminated by violence, the instant of this 'due decision' is
'a madness'.[105] For yesterday's victims may indeed turn out to be
tomorrow's violators. But deconstruction is 'the thought of this differential contamination', the philosopher also maintained, 'and the
thought *taken by* the necessity of this contamination'.[106] So, like
Kantorowicz and Schmitt, we may well misrecognize the incom-
ers. And we must surely have misgivings when Malcolm pledges to
'reckon with your several loves' by getting 'even' [28]. Yet this evil
chance cannot be foreclosed, for it is only by staking the future on
'the perfectibility of public space' the regime change promises that
we can make any sense of historic violence, or share the optimism
felt, according to Marvell, by the 'due decision' of those suicidal revolutionaries – who might have known how they would themselves
end up on the scaffold, their excruciating sufferings prolonged by
the hangman, 'in conscious agony for as long as possible' – when
they beheaded King Charles:[107]

> So, when they did design
> The Capitol's first line,
> A bleeding head, where they begun,
> Did fright the architects to run:
> And yet in that the state
> Foresaw its happy fate.[108]

Coda

Terror, an old servant of Elizabeth, Shakespeare wrote in *Henry VIII*, would be inherited by King James along with Plenty and Peace [5,4,4]. For terror was 'a particular figure of state power', Alain Badiou points out, until the term 'terrorist' was first applied by the state to anti-Nazi resisters, then the Algerian NLF, and so to Palestinian fighters, to signify the opposite.[109] *Macbeth* is a drama which questions this reversal, refusing the spiritually mystified violence invested in the modern state. And as is well known, it was by reciting Shakespeare in light of such questioning that what Hitler called the clique of terrorist criminals in the George Circle steeled themselves for their July Plot. Thus, when he planted the bomb in the Wolf's Lair, Claus von Stauffenberg imaged himself in a Shakespearean tragedy in just the way his friend Kantorowicz saw the plays as blueprints for revolt.[110] On Easter Day 1944, we therefore read, he 'discussed Shakespeare ... and the future of Germany'; and a few days before 20 July he affirmed: 'He who has courage to act must know he will go down in German history as a traitor. But if he fails to act he will be a traitor to his own conscience'.[111]

The historian Joachim Fest believes nothing alienated the Plotters more from those they hoped to impress than this internationalism, as the heady idea of '"treason" for a higher moral purpose was an enigma' to Churchill's Britain.[112] Likewise, Golo Mann argued that the Plotters failed through 'thinking too much about history'.[113] Christians like Moltke and Bonhoeffer did fret over killing Hitler with what seems like seventeenth-century religiosity; and one fellow-conspirator described Adam Von Trott as looking so tragic he 'involuntarily called to mind the Droeshout portrait of Shakespeare'.[114] However, according to Hans-Georg Gadamer, himself ambiguously implicated in the Hitler regime, it was by reading Shakespeare that he and his friends from the George Circle liberated themselves from 'the old Prussian willingness to obey the state' enough to ask the question Stauffenberg would answer: 'Can one abolish despotism without violence?' And it was this supra-nationalism, identified by Kantorowicz in *Macbeth*, that was surely the most enduring legacy of the German reading of Shakespeare:

> I am perfectly willing to admit that my generation grew up under authoritarian conditions; but in my case it was very clear what I had

to do. I really wanted to go to the theatre and read Shakespeare … The liberation came in 1918, and the fact that I was reading Shakespeare was already a sign of new things. I am trying to tell you how in spite of everything I escaped the prevailing militarism.[115]

Notes

1 'Mystical and legitimist': David Norbrook, '*Macbeth* and the Politics of Historiography', in *Politics of Discourse: The Literature and History of Seventeenth-Century England* (Berkeley: University of California Press, 1987), p.116.

2 E.K. Chambers, *The Elizabethan Stage* (4 vols, Oxford: Oxford University Press, 1923), vol. 4, p.173; H.N. Paul, *The Royal Play of 'Macbeth'* (London: Macmillan, 1950); E.B. Lyle, 'The "Twofold Balls and Treble Sceptres" in *Macbeth*', *Shakespeare Quarterly*, 28 (1977), 516–19.

3 Alvin Kernan, *Shakespeare, the King's Playwright: Theater in the Stuart Court, 1603–1613* (New Haven: Yale University Press, 1995), p.77.

4 Stephen Greenblatt, 'Invisible Bullets: Renaissance Authority and Its Subversion: *Henry IV* and *Henry V*', in Jonathan Dollimore and Alan Sinfield (eds), *Political Shakespeare: New Essays in Cultural Materialism* (Manchester: Manchester University Press, 1985), p.33.

5 James I, *The Kings Maiesties Speech to Parliament, 1609* (London: Robert Barker, 1609), sig. A2v, quoted in Jane Rickard, *Authorship and Authority: The Writings of James VI and I* (Manchester: Manchester University Press, 2007), p.124. For the importance of mirror symbolism in the consolidation of absolutism, see in particular Timothy Murray, 'Richelieu's Theater: The Mirror of a Prince', *Renaissance Drama*, 8 (1977), 275–98.

6 Michel Foucault, *The Order of Things: An Archaeology of the Human Sciences*, trans. Anon. (London: Fstiella Routledge, 1970), pp.14–15. For a more recent interpretation, see de Diego, 'Representing Representation: Reading *Las Meninas* again', in *The Cambridge Companion to Velázquez*, ed. S.L. Stratton-Pruitt (Cambridge: Cambridge University Press, 2002), pp.149–69.

7 Leonard Tennenhouse, *Power on Display: The Politics of Shakespeare's Genres* (London and New York: Methuen, 1986), p.15.

8 Ibid., pp.15 and 130–2.

9 Stephen Greenblatt, Introduction to *Macbeth*, Norton Edition, ed. Stephen Greenblatt, Walter Cohen, Jean Howard and Katharine Eisaman Maus (New York: Norton, 1997), p.2561.

10 Anthony Holden, *William Shakespeare* (London: Little, Brown, 1999), p. 235.

11 Jonathan Goldberg, 'Speculations: *Macbeth* and Source', in *Reproducing Shakespeare*, ed. Jean Howard and Marion O'Connor (London: Methuen, 1987), p. 249.

12 Jonathan Goldberg, 'James I and the Theater of Conscience', *ELH*, 46 (1979), 381.

13 Carl Schmitt, *Hamlet or Hecuba: The Intrusion of the Time into the Play*, trans. David Pan and Jennifer Rust (New York: Telos Press, 2009), pp. 41 and 53.

14 'Leads in the direction of absolutism': Debora Kuller Shuger, *Political Theologies in Shakespeare's England: The Sacred and the State in 'Measure for Measure'* (Basingstoke: Macmillan, 2001), p. 79.

15 Carl Schmitt, *Political Theology: Four Chapters on Sovereignty*, trans. George Schwab (Cambridge, Mass.: MIT Press, 1985), p. 1.

16 Stephen Orgel, *The Illusion of Power: Political Theater in the English Renaissance* (Berkeley: California University Press, 1975), pp. 38 and 51. For a similar interpretation of ceremonial effects and state power, see also Herbert Lindenberger, *Historical Drama: The Relation of Literature and Reality* (Chicago: Chicago University Press, 1975), pp. 78–86.

17 David Lindley, 'Courtly Play: The Politics of Chapman's *The Memorable Masque*', in *The Stuart Courts*, ed. Eveline Cruickshanks (Stroud: Sutton Publishing, 2000), pp. 43 and 56.

18 Ernst Kantorowicz, *The King's Two Bodies: A Study in Medieval Political Theology* (rep. Princeton: Princeton University Press, 1997), pp. 312–13 and 387.

19 See David Norbrook, 'The Emperor's New Body? *Richard II*, Ernst Kantorowicz, and the Politics of Shakespeare Criticism', *Textual Practice*, 10 (1996), 329–57: 'The very act of personifying the state in corporeal, sacramental terms tended to work against a more radically abstract concept of the state' (p. 344); and Shuger, op. cit. (note 14). For a critique of this misreading of Kantorowicz, see Lorna Hutson, 'Imagining Justice: Kantorowicz and Shakespeare', *Representations*, 106 (2009), 118–42, esp. pp. 120–1.

20 Alain Boureau, *Kantorowicz: Stories of a Historian*, trans. Stephen Nichols and Gabrielle Spiegel (Baltimore: Johns Hopkins University Press, 2001), p. 106.

21 Kantorowicz, op. cit. (note 18), pp. 312–13.

22 Julia Lupton, *Thinking with Shakespeare: Essays on Politics and Life* (Chicago: University of Chicago Press, 2011), p. 213.

23 Kantorowicz, op. cit. (note 18), pp. 20–1, 23 and 39–41

24 Ibid. p. 21. Louis Marin, *Portrait of the King*, trans. Martha Houle

(Minneapolis: University of Minnesota Press, 1988). Kantorowicz's interpretation of *Richard II* is elaborated by David Scott Kastan in 'Proud Majesty Made a Subject: Shakespeare and the Spectacle of Rule', *Shakespeare Quarterly*, 37 (1986), 459–75.

25 Stephen Greenblatt, 'Introduction: Fifty Years of *The King's Two Bodies*', *Representations*, 106 (2009), 64.

26 Victoria Kahn, 'Political Theology and Fiction in *The King's Two Bodies*', *Representations*, 106 (2009), 97.

27 For Edmund Plowden's Catholic legalism, see Geoffrey de C. Parmiter, *Elizabethan Popish Recusancy at the Inns of Court: Bulletin of the Institute of Historical Research*, Special Supplement, 11 (1976), pp.6–7; Wilfrid Prest, *The Inns of Court under Elizabeth I and the Early Stuarts, 1590–1640* (London: Longman, 1972), p.179; and Alexandra Walsham, *Church Papists: Catholicism, Conformity and Confessional Polemic in Early Modern England* (Woodbridge: Boydell & Brewer, 1993), p.83.

28 Kantorowicz, 'Preface', op. cit. (note 18), p.xviii; William Chester Jordan,'Preface:1997,' ibid., pp. xi–xiii; Peter Hoffmann, *Stauffenberg: A Family History, 1905–1944* (Cambridge: Cambridge University Press, 1995), pp.64–5 and 312, n. 17.

29 For a monumental (though deeply hostile) recent American account, see Robert Norton, *Secret Germany: Stefan George and His Circle* (Ithaca: Cornell University Press, 2002), esp. pp.x–xvii, 434–5, 529–7, 689–5, 729–30 and 743–4.

30 Ernst Kantorowicz, letter to Stefan George on his sixty-fifth birthday, 12 July 1933, quoted ibid., p.735.

31 See Jordan, op. cit. (note 28), p.x, citing the review by Ernst Reibstein in *Zeitschrift der Savigny-Stiftung für Rechtsgeschichte* (Germanistische Abteilung), 76 (1959), 379. For Schmitt's Hobbesian justification of Hitler, see Tracy Strong, 'Foreword: Dimensions of the New Debate around Carl Schmitt', in Carl Schmitt, *The Concept of the Political*, trans. George Schwab (Chicago: Chicago University Press, 1996), pp.xiii–xxviii. And for Schmitt's influence, through his protégé Leo Strauss, over George Bush's neo-conservative 'War on Terror', see Anne Norton, *Leo Strauss and the Politics of American Enpire* (New Haven: Yale University Press, 2004), pp.35–40 et passim.

32 Christopher Pye, 'The Sovereign, the Theater, and the Kingdome of Darknesse: Hobbes and the Spectacle of Power', in *Representing the English Renaissance*, ed. Stephen Greenblatt (Berkeley: University of California Press, 1988), p.299.

33 Alan Sinfield, '*Macbeth*: History, Ideology, and Intellectuals', in *Faultlines: Cultural Materialism and the Politics of Dissident Reading*

(Oxford: Oxford University Press, 1992), pp.95 and 103; originally in *Critical Quarterly*, 28 (1986), 63–77.

34 Walter Benjamin, 'Critique of Violence', trans. Edmund Jephcott, in *Walter Benjamin: Selected Writings: I: 1913–1926*, ed. Marcus Bullock and Michael Jennings (Cambridge, Mass.: Belknap & Harvard University Press, 2004), p.237.

35 Francis Barker, *The Culture of Violence: Tragedy and history* (Manchester: Manchester University Press, 1993), pp.58–9, 65 and 79–1.

36 Walter Benjamin, 'Theses on the Philosophy of History', in *Illuminations: Essays and Reflections*, trans. Harry Zohn (London: Jonathan Cape, 1970), p.258.

37 Goldberg, op. cit. (note 11), p.249; Jacques Derrida, *The Other Heading: Reflections on Today's Europe*, trans. Pascale-Anne Brault and Michael B. Naas (Bloomington: Indiana University Press, 1992). The etymology dates at least from Varro, who explains that the Capitol was so called because when the temple of Jupiter was being built a skull was found buried on the site: *On the Latin Language*, trans. Roland Kent (2 vols, Cambridge, Mass.: Harvard University Press, 1958), vol. 1, p.39. Decapitation was later considered such an indignity that in Garrick's productions Macduff brandished his captured sword instead of Macbeth's head: Peter Holland, 'The Age of Garrick', in Jonathan Bate and Russell Jackson (eds), *The Oxford Illustrated History of Shakespeare on Stage* (Oxford: Oxford University Press, 2001), p.87.

38 Michael Wood, *In Search of Shakespeare* (London: BBC, 2003), p.95.

39 Ibid., p.95: 'So before the poet was out of his teens the state's machine of terror and a taint of treason had touched his family. And the cost of conscience was all too plain in the spectacle of their kinsman's tarred head displayed, as was the grim custom, on London Bridge, and his quarters on the gates of Warwickshire towns'.

40 Quoted Richard Simpson, *Edmund Campion: A Life* (London: John Hodges, 1896), p.436.

41 Leo Bersani and Ulysse Dutoit, *Caravaggio's Secrets* (Cambridge, Mass.: MIT Press, 1998), pp.94 and 98–9.

42 'Crimes of art': Frank Lettricchia and Jody McAuliffe, *Crimes of Art + Terror* (Chicago: Chicago University Press, 2003, p.23: Lentricchia and McAuliffe are responding to the claim made in *The New York Times* (16 September 2001) by the composer Karlheinz Stockhausen that the attack on the Twin Towers was 'the greatest work of art' (p.6); Julia Kristeva, *The Severed Head: Capital Visions*, trans. Jody Gladding (New York: Columbia University Press, 2012), pp.88–9.

43 Cf. Susan Sontag, *Regarding the Pain of Others* (London: Penguin,

2004): 'Let the atrocious images haunt us. Even if they are only tokens, and cannot possibly encompass the reality to which they refer, they still perform a vital function. The images say: This is what human beings are capable of doing – may volunteer to do, enthusiastically, self-righteously. Don't forget' (p.102).

44 Svetlana Alpers, 'Waiting For Death: Velázquez's *Mercury and Argus*', in *The Vexations of Art: Velázquez and Others* (New Haven: Yale University Press, 2005), pp.128–9.

45 Ibid., p.129.

46 Kristeva, op.cit., note 42, p.30.

47 Bersani and Dutoit, op. cit. (note 41), pp.94 and 98–9.

48 Ibid., p.91.

49 For the significance of the martyrdom of Stephen [Acts, 7:51–8], see the commentary by René Girard in *Things Hidden since the Foundation of the World*, trans Stephen Bann (London: Continuum, 2003), pp.170–4; Barker, op. cit. (note 35), pp.165–8 and 191. For the allusion to the punishment of Richard Shelley, see John Clause, 'Politics, Heresy, and Martyrdom in Sonnet 124 and *Titus Andronicus*', in *Shakespeare's Sonnets: Critical Essays*, ed. James Schiffer (New York: Garland, 1999), pp.225–6. And for the Goths as Protestant martyrs, see Jonathan Bate, '"*Lucius*, the Severely Flawed Redeemer of *Titus Andronicus*": A Reply', *Connotations*, 6:3 (1996/7), 339–3.

50 Steven Mullaney, 'Lying like Truth: Riddle, Representation, and Truth', in *The Place of the Stage: License, Play, and Power in Renaissance England* (Chicago: Chicago University Press, 1988), p.117.

51 See T.W. Baldwin, *William Shakespeare Adapts a Hanging* (Princeton: Princeton University Press, 1931); and *Shakespeare's Small Latine and Lesse Greeke* (2 vols, Urbana: University of Illinois Press, 1944), vol. 1, p.479.

52 Stephen Greenblatt, '*King Lear* and the Exorcists', in *Shakespearean Negotiations: The Circulation of Social Energy in Renaissance England* (Oxford: Clarendon Press, 1990), chap.4.

53 Quoted, Arthur Marotti, 'Southwell's Remains: Catholicism and Anti-Catholicism in Early Modern England', in *Texts and Cultural Change in Early Modern England*, ed. Cedric Brown and Arthur Marotti (Basingstoke: Macmillan, 1997), p.52. See also Richard Wilson, 'A Bloody Question: The Politics of *Venus and Adonis*,' in *Secret Shakespeare: Studies in Theatre, Religion and Resistance* (Manchester: Manchester University Press, 2004), pp.126–43.

54 Jacques Derrida, 'Autoimmunity: Real and Symbolic Suicides', in *Philosophy in a Time of Terror: Dialogies with Jürgen Habermas and Jacques Derrida*, ed. Giovanna Borradori (Chicago: Chicago University Press, 2003), p.104.

55 Jacques Derrida, 'Force of Law: The "Mystical Foundation of Authority"', trans. Mary Quaintance, in Jacques Derrida, *Acts of Religion*, ed. Gil Anidjar (London: Routledge, 2002), pp. 230–98.

56 Sir John Harington, *Epigrams*, quoted in Lacey Baldwin Smith, *Treason in Tudor England: Politics and Paranoia* (London: Jonathan Cape, 1986), p. 1.

57 Graham Greene, 'Introduction', *John Gerard: The Autobiography of an Elizabethan*, trans. Philip Caraman (London: Longmans, 1951), p. x.

58 Richard Simpson, 'The Political Use of the Stage in Shakespeare's Time', *New Shakspere Society's Transactions* (1974), 395; Greene, op. cit. (nore 57), p. xi.

59 Robert Parsons, *An Epistle of the Persecution of Catholics in England* (Douai, 1582), quoted in Michael Grieves, *Thomas Norton: Parliament Man* (Oxford: Blackwell, 1994), p. 272.

60 Stephen Greenblatt, 'Introduction' to *Much Ado About Nothing*, op. cit. (note 9), p. 1384.

61 Stephen Greenblatt, 'Martial Law in the Land of Cockaigne,' op. cit. (note 52), p. 137.

62 Stephen Greenblatt, *Will in the World: How Shakespeare Became Shakespeare* (London: Jonathan Cape, 2004), p. 110. For overviews of the 'religious turn', see Ken Jackson and Arthur Marotti, 'The Religious Turn in Early Modern Studies', *Criticism*, 46 (2004), 167–90; Graham Hammill and Julia Lupton, 'Sovereigns, Citizens, and Saints', special edition of *Religion and Literature*, 38:3 (2006); and Bruce Holsinger (ed.), 'The Religious Turn (to Theory) in Shakespeare Studies', *English Language Notes* (2006), 145–8.

63 Kantorowicz, op. cit. (note 18); Carl Schmitt, *Political Theology: Four Chapters on Sovereignty*, trans. George Schwab (Cambridge: Cambridge University Press, 1985); and see Jennifer Rust and Julia Lupton, 'Introduction: Schmitt and Shakespeare', in Schmitt, op. cit. (note 13), pp. ix–xii.

64 Norbrook, op. cit. (note 1), pp. 104 and 111–12; Mullaney, op. cit. (note 50), p. 126.

65 David Scott Kastan, '*Macbeth* and the "Name of King"', in *Shakespeare After Theory* (London: Routledge, 1999), pp. 166 and 174. For the chime of the syllable 'done' through the play, see Russ McDonald, *Shakespeare and the Arts of Language* (Oxford: Oxford University Press, 2001), pp. 158–9.

66 Jan Kott, *Shakespeare Our Contemporary*, trans. Boleslaw Taborski (London: Methuen, 1964), p. 90.

67 See Harry Berger, 'The Early Scenes of *Macbeth*: Preface to a New Interpretation', *ELH*, 47 (1980), 4; and Goldberg, op. cit. (note 11), pp. 251–2.

68 Antonia Fraser, *Mary Queen of Scots* (London: Weidenfeld and Nicolson, 1969), p.539; John Guy, *My Heart Is My Own: The Life of Mary Queen of Scots* (London: Harper Perennial, 2004), p.1. The implied presence of the 'untimely' executed mother suggests how much Robin Headlam Wells misses the point of the mirror masque when he claims that 'unlike Macbeth, James did not actually murder his way to the throne': see 'Historicism and "Presentism" in Early Modern Studies', *Cambridge Quarterly*, 29 (2000), 51.

69 Schmitt, op. cit. (note 13), p.27.

70 Fraser, op. cit. (note 68), p.539.

71 Kastan, op. cit. (note 65), p.170.

72 Antoine de Montchrétien, *Escossaise, ou le Desastre Tragedie* (Rouen, 1603), pp.52–3: 'Her hair of purest gold is bloodied', quoted in James Emerson Phillips, *Images of a Queen: Mary Stuart in Sixteenth-Century Literature* (Berkeley: University of California Press, 1964), p.221; Sir Ralph Winwood, *Memorials of Affairs of State in the Reigns of Queen Elizabeth and King James I* (2 vols, London, 1725), vol. 1, p.398, quoted in Frances Yates, 'Some New Light on "L'Escossaise" of Antoine de Montchrétien', *Modern Language Review*, 22 (1927), 292.

73 Jean de Bordes, *Maria Stuarta Trageodia* (1589), quoted Phillips, op. cit. (note 72), p.192. And see James Emerson Phillips, 'Jean de Bordes's *Maria Stuarta Trageoedia*: The Earliest Known Drama on the Queen of Scots', in *Essays Critical and Historical Dedicated to Lily B. Campbell* (Berkeley: University of California Press, 1950), pp.45–62.

74 Kristeva, op. cit. (note 42), p.31.

75 Ibid., p.82.

76 James VI to Robert Dudley, Earl of Leicester, 15 December 1586, in Robert Rait and Annie Cameron, *King James's Secret: Negotiations Between Elizabeth and James VI Relating to the Execution of Mary Queen of Scots, From the Warrender Papers* (2 vols, London: Nisbet, 1927), vol. 1, pp.248–9.

77 Jonathan Goldberg, *James I and the Politics of Literature: Jonson, Shakespeare, Donne, and Their Contemporaries* (Stanford: Stanford University Press, 1989), p.17.

78 David Howarth, *Images of Rule: Art and Politics in the English Renaissance, 1485–1649* (Basingstoke: Macmillan, 1997), p.166.

79 Henry Howard, Earl of Northampton, 12 October 1612, *Calendar of State Papers Domestic*, IX: 90; Jayne Elizabeth Lewis, *Mary Queen of Scots: Romance and Nation* (London: Routledge, 1998), p.66.

80 Giovanni Carlo Scaramelli to the Venetian Doge and Senate, 22 May 1603, *Calendar of State Papers Venetian*, X: 33.

81 Quoted in Geoffrey Robertson, *The Tyrannicide Brief: The Story*

of the Man who sent Charles I to the Scaffold (London: Chatto & Windus, 2005), p.185.

82 Quoted in Fraser, op. cit. (note 68), p.525; Simpson, op. cit. (note 40), pp.462–3. For the idea of blood as seed see also Claire Cross, 'An Elizabethan Martyrologist and His Martyr: John Mush and Margaret Clitheroe', *Studies in Church History*, 30 (1993), 278.

83 'Reasons for which the King of Scots is unacceptable to the people of England' (1586), *Historic Manuscripts Commission: Salisbury Papers*, vol. 3, pp.310–11; Alan Stewart, *The Cradle King: A Life of James VI and I* (London: Chatto and Windus, 2003), p.86.

84 Henry Saville in *The Jacobean Union: Six Tracts of 1604*, eds Bruce Galloway and Brian Levack (Edinburgh: Scottish Historical Society, 1985), p.196.

85 Jacques Derrida, op. cit. (note 55), p.244.

86 'Claimed ancestral conquest': Richard Helgerson, *Forms of Nationhood: The Elizabethan Writing of England* (Chicago: University of Chicago Press, 1994), p.38; Derrida, op. cit. (note 55), p.269.

87 See Phillips, op. cit. (note 72), p.124.

88 James Stuart, *A Remonstrance for the Right of Kings*, in *The Political Works of James I*, ed. Charles McIlwain (Cambridge, Mass.: Harvard University Press, 1918), p.206.

89 Harry Berger, 'The Early Scenes of *Macbeth*: Preface to a New Interpretation', *ELH*, 47 (1980), 4.

90 John Gerard quoted in Philip Caraman, *Henry Garnet, 1555–1606, and the Gunpowder Plot* (London: Longmans, 1964), p.439.

91 Peter Lake and Michael Questier, *The Antichrist's Lewd Hat: Protestants, Papists, and Players in Post-Reformation England* (Princeton: Princeton University Press, 2002), p.388. The stunned contemporary reactions to Garnet's execution also contradict Headlam Wells's naive assertion that James was perceived to be 'unusually humane' in his treatment of religious dissidents: op. cit. (note 68), 51.

92 Schmitt, op. cit. (note 11), p.56.

93 John Gerard, quoted in Caraman, op. cit. (note 90), p.444. See H.L. Rogers, 'An English Tailor and Father Garnet's Straw', *Review of English Studies*, 1965, 44–9; and Garry Wills, *Witches and Jesuits: Shakespeare's 'Macbeth'* (Oxford: Oxford University Press, 1995), pp.93–105.

94 Naomi Conn Liebler, *Shakespeare's Festive Tragedy: The Ritual foundations of Genre* (London: Routledge, 1995), p.90.

95 See Roland Mushat Frye, *Shakespeare and Christian Doctrine* (Princeton: Princeton University Press, 1963), pp.275–93.

96 See Wilson, op. cit. (note 53), pp.190–3.

97 Kristeva, op. cit. (note 42), pp.31–2.

98 R.A. Foakes, *Shakespeare and Violence* (Cambridge: Cambridge University Press, 2003), pp.25–7 et passim.

99 See René Girard, *A Theater of Envy: William Shakespeare* (Oxford: Oxford University Press, 1991), pp.325–6.

100 Kastan, op. cit. (note 65) p.181. For a brilliantly Empsonian riff on the complexity of the word 'safe' in the play, see Nicholas Royle, *How to Read Shakespeare* (London: Granta, 2005), pp.88–105.

101 Alpers, op. cit. (note 44), p.113.

102 Ibid., p.111.

103 Derrida, op. cit. (note 54), pp.113 and 167.

104 Ibid., p.114.

105 Derrida, op. cit. (note 55), p.255.

106 Ibid., p.272.

107 Robertson, op. cit. (note 81), p.339.

108 Andrew Marvell, 'An Horatian Ode upon Cromwell's Return from Ireland', ll. 67–72, in *The Poems and Letters of Andrew Marvell*, ed. H.M. Margoliouth (2 vols, Oxford: Clarendon Press, 1927), vol. 1, p.89.

109 Alain Badiou, 'Philosophy and the "War Against Terrorism"', in *Infinite Thought: Truth and the Return of Philosophy*, trans. Oliver Feltham and Justin Clemens (London: Continuum, 2003), pp.144–5. And for a recent critique of state terror, see Terry Eagleton, *Holy Terror* (Oxford: Oxford University Press, 2005), pp.42–67.

110 Adolf Hitler, quoted in Roger Manvell and Heinrich Fraenkel, *The July Plot: The Attempt on Hitler's Life in July 1944* (London: Bodley Head, 1964), p.155. For Stauffenberg's preoccupation with Shakespeare, see Hoffmann, op. cit. (note 28), pp.17, 24 and 235; and Michael Baigent and Richard Leigh, *Secret Germany: Claus von Stauffenberg and the Mystical Crusade Against Hitler* (London: Jonathan Cape, 1994), pp.98–9 and 107.

111 Quoted, Hoffmann, op. cit. (note 28), pp.235 and 243; Joachim Fest, *Plotting Hitler's Death: The German Resistance to Hitler, 1933–1945* (London: Weidenfeld & Nicolson, 1996), pp.240–1, and Peter Hoffmann, op. cit. (note 28), p.24.

112 Fest, op. cit. (note 111), p.209.

113 Golo Mann, *History of Modern Germany, 1789–1945* (London: Chatto & Windus, 1968), p.487.

114 Franz Josef Furtwängler, quoted in Christopher Sykes, *Troubled Loyalty: A Biography of Adam Von Trott* (London: Collins, 1968), p.339.

115 For the influence of the George Circle on Gadamer's reading of Shakespeare, see and also Jean Grondin, *Hans-Georg Gadamer*, trans. Joel Weinsheimer (New Haven: Yale University Press, 2003), p.51;

and for Gadamer's ambiguous relations with the Nazi regime, see Richard Wolin, *The Seduction of Unreason: The Intellectual Romance with Fascism from Nietzsche to Postmodernism* (Princeton: Princeton University Press, 2004), pp. 93–100.

7

Your crown's awry

The visual turn in Antony and Cleopatra

> Sometime we see a cloud that's dragonish,
> A vapour sometime like a bear or lion,
> A towered citadel, a pendent rock,
> A forked mountain, or blue promontory
> With trees upon't that nod unto the world
> And mock our eyes with air ...
>
> $\qquad\qquad\qquad\qquad\qquad$ [*Antony, 4,15,3–8*]

Unnoble swerving

When Ernst Gombrich analysed the Renaissance cult of anamorphosis in his 1960 study of the psychology of representation, *Art and Illusion*, he opened his discussion with a long quotation from *Antony and Cleopatra*. Antony's meditation upon 'a cloud that's dragonish' was cited to illustrate the art historian's thesis that sixteenth-century awareness of the subjective construction of 'the image in the clouds' generated 'an entirely new idea of art', in which 'the painter's skill in suggesting must be matched by the public's skill in taking hints'. Shakespeare's play was a record of this 'momentous change', it was claimed, when art liberated itself from its ritual context and 'appealed deliberately to man's imagination'; or, as Cleopatra declares in the terminology of the time, when artists first came to believe that 'nature wants stuff / To vie strange forms with fancy' [5,2,97]. By annexing Shakespeare's drama about the overthrow of the Roman Republic to art history, Gombrich thereby encouraged critics to consider *Antony and Cleopatra* as the dramatist's entry into the *paragone*, the Renaissance contest between poetry and painting, and as a work that 'mimics a perspective picture'.[1] What this art-historical interpretation left out, however, were the implications for Shakespeare's own stage and story of a pictorial mode of representation which works to 'mock our eyes with air'. Yet the play revolves precisely around the prospect of such a mockery, which Antony imagines as having an entire body politics requiring an ignoble contortion, a creaturely bending and turning, like that of some tortured animal or plant:

> ANTONY: Wouldst thou be windowed in great Rome and see
>   Thy master thus: with pleached arms, bending down
>   His corrigible neck, his face subdued
>   To penetrative shame, whilst the wheeled seat
>   Of fortunate Caesar, drawn before him, branded
>   His baseness that ensued?
> EROS: I would not see it.
>
> [4,15,72–7]

Antony's fear of having his 'corrigible neck' and limbs 'pleached' in the 'window' of the Roman show implies a distinctly guarded response to contemporary Italian art, which was indeed characterized by the human figure twisted into serpentine forms. Yet Gombrich's interpretation of *Antony and Cleopatra* was based on a belief that, as Martin Jay also argues, 'Shakespeare revels in visual metaphors and references' because he shared the achievement of perspective that 'made possible the liberation of art'.[2] This approach has recently been restated by Robert Weimann, who infers that Sebastiano Serlio's *Architettura*, the key Renaissance treatise 'speaking of Perspective things', and a volume that marked a 'resolute separation between a carefully designed imaginary space and the place of playing', must have been 'either known or of great potential interest' to the dramatist whose *Othello* was staged at Whitehall in 1604 behind 'a prototype proscenium arch'.[3] But the trouble with the words of Antony read as celebrations of such an autonomization is that they come from a scene not of self-actualization but self-annulment, and his attempted suicide, when defeated by Caesar, and betrayed he thinks by Cleopatra, he compares his fate to the sky at dusk. So the irony that this disastrous *peripeteia* is caused by a visual turnaround, and a sight that makes 'eyes sicken' [3,10,16], of the Roman's 'unnoble swerving' [3,11,49] to chase after the Egyptian queen 'like a doting mallard' [3,11,19] 'And leave his navy gazing' [3,13,11], suggests that rather than hitching his star to 'the Great

Revolution' of perspective, the dramatist is probing how such a 'windowing' might prove 'the world's great snare' [4,8,18] and a theatrical trap.[4] Far from liberation, in fact, the notion of pictorial illusion as a mode of vision which functions to 'seel our eyes', or obstruct 'our clear judgements, / Make us adore our errors' [3,13,112–15], by having the viewer 'pay his heart / For what his eyes eat' [2,2,236], like 'those poor birds that helpless berries saw' [*Venus, 604*] in the legend of Alexander's court painter Apelles, recurs throughout this play as a figure for the disenchantment of a round world made flat:

> The crown o'th'earth doth melt. My lord!
> O, withered is the garland of the war.
> The soldier's pole is fall'n; young boys and girls
> Are level now with men. The odds is gone
> And there is nothing left remarkable
> Beneath the visiting moon.
>
> [4,16,64–70]

Liquefaction in the Roman plays is always a sign of emasculation, and the melted globe of *Antony and Cleopatra* belongs to a recurring Shakespearean image cluster connecting 'sweets' that 'discandy' to a salivating court [4,13,22].[5] 'Let Rome in Tiber melt, and the wide arch / Of the ranged empire fall! Here is my space' [1,1,35], Antony therefore pronounces, in one of the play's many spatial metaphors alluding to the proscenium arch of the picture-frame stage. But later, 'authority melts from me', the renegade Roman says [3,13,90]; while 'Melt Egypt into Nile', Cleopatra exclaims [2,5,78], as if 'By the discandying of this pelleted storm' [3,13,168] the lovers do allow their story to be framed in Caesar's show. So painterly critics have long felt there is 'something deliquescent' in this play, in J.F. Danby's phrase, where 'pigments vividly opposed to each other on the canvas have to mix in the spectator's eye'.[6] Separating Antony's melancholy meditation from its cringing context, Gombrich thus tracked his 'dragonish' clouds back to Leonardo da Vinci's *Treatise on Painting*, where the Renaissance polymath similarly pondered the emancipating capacity of random shapes 'to rouse the mind to new invention', and proposed a kaleidoscopic method of picture-making which seemed to prefigure the dramaturgy of Shakespeare's play: 'You should look at walls stained with damp ... you will be able to see in these mountains, ruins, rocks, plains, hills and valleys ... an infinity of things you will be able to reduce to their complete and proper forms'.[7]

Despite Gombrich's encomium, critics have drawn attention to Shakespeare's intensifying concern at the tendency to 'invert th'attest of eyes and ears, / As if those organs had deceptious functions' [*Troilus, 5,2,122–3*], which may reflect 'the increasingly strained relations between the visual and the verbal' in the Jacobean period, and might indeed explain why *Antony and Cleopatra* hovers between 'near-simultaneous wonder and consciousness of deception that is formulated by one's response to an illusionist painting'.[8] Thus, for the protagonists of Shakespeare's post-revolutionary Roman tragedy, what Erwin Panofsky termed the 'systematic abstraction' of the perspective 'windowing' of reality is never enfranchising, but a ploy to 'Make your thoughts your prisons' [*5,2,181*].[9] Gombrich himself confirmed that the liberating potential of 'the beholder's share' was in fact soon cancelled, when the art historian Giorgio Vasari restored artistic sovereignty by praising Donatello for *intentionally* leaving his work 'rough and unfinished, so that from a distance it looked much better', and advised that 'Careful finish betrays the artisan. A true artist, like a gentleman, will work at ease.'[10] Designed to be appreciated only from the sanctioned position by a discerning elite, this was the 'stylish style' of 'effortless force' commended by Italian writers such as Aretino and Castiglione, and categorized with the term *la maniera* (from the Latin for 'handling': *manuaria*) that was first applied to the *free hand* of a Titian or Tintoretto, but which would repress its origins in *manumission* as this Mannerism was absolutized into the Baroque.

The Renaissance idea of a 'theatre' as a 'common beholding space' was always one that shared these absolutist affiliations with illusionist art, William West has lately emphasized, since its etymological root in *theory* implied that 'Distance rather than immersion offers the best position for understanding'; yet whenever this abstraction was put into practice theatre was programmed to reproduce the blind spots of perspective vision.[11] For if Leonardo had liberated the beholder with the manner 'where we see / The fancy outwork nature' [*2,2,200*], the connection with handicraft was already being effaced in words added to Vasari's *Lives* in 1568, where the relation between visual measure and patrician distance began to be codified. What makes the art-historical narrative of the irresistible rise of pictorial perspective so problematic, therefore,

when extended to a dramatist like Shakespeare, are the anti-manual
and authoritarian implications of the alignment it posits between
the virtuosity of the artist and the vantage of the viewer, as the
'literal-minded Philistine is excluded from the closed circle', we are
told, because 'he lacks the appropriate mental set' to decode the
brush strokes of a Titian.[12] In the play, moreover, this reordering
of vision is experienced as a function of the zero-sum game when
callow Octavius metamorphoses into Caesar Augustus, which
comes like an anamorphic reversal, and as a perfect illustration of
an idea which currently fascinates Shakespeareans, that the creature represents the flip-side of the sovereign, with the splaying of a
'pleached' and 'corrigible' Antony into 'penetrative shame':

> ANTONY: My good knave Eros, now thy captain is
>   Even such a body. Here I am Antony,
>   Yet cannot hold this visible shape ...
>
>   [4,15,12–14]

Three-nook'd world

Like Polonius humouring Hamlet about the appearance of a 'cloud
that's almost in shape of a camel' [*Hamlet, 3,3,367*], Antony struggles to grasp the abstraction that Shakespeare ascribes to the picture
of 'The Fall of Troy' in *The Rape of Lucrece*, where 'A hand, a foot,
a face, a leg, a head / Stood for the whole to be imagined', while
the subject 'Was left unseen, save to the eye of mind' [*1425–8*]. His
creator himself became adept at 'the new style that elaborates what
cannot be seen rather than what can' as 'something understood',
with a punning manner that would be vital to his projection of
psychological inwardness.[13] So we can assume we are meant to
think the general has seen the 'turning picture' drawn 'one way
like a Gorgon, / The other way's a Mars' [*2,5,117*] to which he is
compared. For these notes on illusionism do connect the play to
the haughty world of English collectors like the Earl of Arundel,
portrayed in his London gallery full of artworks by the likes of
Veronese. By the 1600s these self-styled *virtuosi* were competing
with the continental courts for the latest masterpieces, Linda Levy
Peck relates.[14] But to report, as did the diplomat Sir Henry Wotton,
that 'the limbs and muscles in a Tintoretto move', these grand
tourists had first to be let in on the secret that painting no longer

involved the 'reproduction of sharply illuminated objects, but the suggestion of three-dimensional space'.[15] So they had to internalize the habit of bending and turning to view the image from the prescribed angle and distance, 'Like perspectives, which rightly gazed upon, / Show nothing but confusion; eyed awry, / Distinguish form' [*Richard II, 2,2,18*], which when Shakespeare incorporated it as the frontispiece to *Antony and Cleopatra*, art-minded critics claim, made this his 'most anamorphic' play:[16]

> Nay, but this dotage of our general's
> O'erflows the measure. Those his goodly eyes,
> That o'er the files and musters of the war
> Have glowed like plated Mars, now bend, now turn
> The office and devotion of their view
> Unto a tawny front.
>
> [*1,1,1–6*]

Andrew Gurr has proposed that the 'concept of a "front" reflects a basic change' in theatre behaviour after 1600, since Jacobean playgoers 'would not have positioned themselves anything like so readily at the "front" of the stage for a play' as modern audiences, because they remained wedded to 'the expectation that plays are things to be heard rather than seen ... and it is natural for an audience to group themselves all around'.[17] Yet it is just such an optical turn from auditors to spectators which *Antony and Cleoptra* seems to negotiate, for with its fixation on a centred visual perspective, and regard for the 'graceful eyes which fronted' its performance [*2,2,64*], the play introduces itself as a process of refocusing to establish the optimum spatial 'measure' which, the tart courtier Philo complains, Antony's 'goodly eyes' have 'overflowed'. From Alberti onwards the trend in perspective treatises had indeed been towards an ever 'more complex and ambiguous relationship between the knower and the knowable'; but in *Downcast Eyes*, a study of western ocularcentrism, Jay describes the cult of anamorphosis (from *ana*, Greek for 'again', and *morphe*, 'form') as a *counter-reformation* or reaction to this information overload, which forced the viewer 'to reform a distorted picture' from the mandatory distance, and so as a tool of the 'seductive use' of playful spectacle for serious ends which was given its final twist in the theatre technology of seventeenth-century court masques.[18]

In *Antony and Cleopatra* it is the Nile which 'overflows the

measure', unlike the measured Tiber, as though this play is keyed
to the transition art historians describe, when 'the more mature
Baroque triumphs' over the playfulness of Mannerism, and 'works
up emotionalism into a magnificent theatricality' which then
hardens into 'an austere and clear-headed authoritarianism'.[19] The
play seems in fact to enact the idea that the Baroque differs from
Mannerism by sheer force. For from the cornucopian fantasia of
Arcimboldo, to the coercive colonnades of Bernini, as it froze into
a single viewpoint, perspective tipped into the totalizing optic of
an elite struggling to restrain the slippage from royal to popular
sovereignty, in Jay's analysis, and so became a key instrument of the
absolutist state. Thus the forcing of Mannerism into the 'achievement of the stupendous' known as the Baroque corresponds to the
imposition of divine right discourse studied by the Weimar thinkers Walter Benjamin and Carl Schmitt, when as soon as the world
has been represented its singular subject is centred as the sovereign
who presides over that representation, and must *decide* the correct
angle and distance from which it is to be perceived; so when 'the
monarch is identified with God, and has in the state a position
exactly analogous to that attributed to God in the Cartesian system
of the world'.[20]

Recent historians see the royal court as 'not the source so much
as the vehicle' though which the new 'windowed' ways of seeing
'established their commanding place'; yet what is inherently courtly
about Baroque art, according to Benjamin, is precisely its framing
of history around the sovereign as a godlike creator, for 'In this
picturesque period chronological movement is grasped and analysed in a spatial image. The image of the court becomes a key to
historical understanding. For the court is the setting.'[21] And in his
essay on the founder of the Society of Jesus, Roland Barthes likewise inferred that it was because the disciplined eye was crucial to
Counter-Reformation revanchism that Ignatius Loyola opposed
Protestant iconoclasm with 'a radical imperialism of the image'.[22]
This visual imperialism was a synecdoche, then, for the political
theology of the absolutist state, as the freedom of Mannerism was
bent and twisted into the resolution of the Baroque, a process of
closure Christopher Pye describes in his book *The Vanishing* as the
reality effect that at first constitutes the sovereign subject as the sole
subject of vision, but then subdues 'that masterful being to its own
annulment': a threat which assumes visual form by subjecting the

subject to the terror of infinitude. Pye is here analysing the vertiginous Dover Cliff episode in *King Lear*, where Edgar's verbal picture of how 'fearful dizzy 'tis to cast one's eyes so low' anticipates the spatial anxieties of *Antony and Cleopatra*, by visualizing both perspective space and the swooning tipping-point when subjective apprehension of the vanishing point 'exceeds itself and "the brain turns"':[23]

> ... I'll look no more,
> Lest my brain turn, and the deficient sight
> Topple down headlong.
>
> [*King Lear, 4,6,11–24*]

If Mannerism appealed to the Warburg school of art historians because its symbolization seemed to anticipate Surrealism, the entire movement of the Baroque can be interpreted as a regression to expression and presence from abstraction and representation. Thus, according to Gilles Deleuze, the Baroque expresses the attempt to circumscribe infinity in a fold, where light and dark, real and ideal, the infernal and the best of all possible worlds, are doubled in a single point of view, like two floors of the same house, that is ultimately 'joyful, not mournful or melancholic'.[24] Typifying this totalizing drive, court masques therefore aspired to *spatialize time*, so as to secure the intentionalist visual order for which a mirror was intended, as Hamlet asserts, to show 'the very age and body of the time his form and pressure' [*Hamlet, 3,2,23–4*]. As Jerzy Limon has recounted, the function of perspective scenery in a masque was therefore indeed to *fold* the brazen world of the spectators into the golden world on stage in a continuous plane, as parts of 'a created model of the universe', and so to harness the new visual technology to sovereign order, which was why Ben Jonson considered these spectacles to be 'mirrors of man's life'.[25] Transitional between the circular amphitheatre which required no illusion, and the proscenium box that represented infinite space when seen through the barrier between actors and audience that Diderot would call the 'fourth wall', each and every masque thereby traversed the passage from Mannerism to Baroque, Alexandria to Athens, or from the 'unworthy scaffold' of the *platea* to the 'swelling scene' [*Henry V, Pro.1–10*] of the *locus*, material world or 'world-as-stage' to the play world or 'stage-as-world', in Weimann's terms, by inducing its participants to flip from one convention to the other; just as Antony foresees his body twisted to shapeless 'baseness' when he is 'windowed' and 'penetrated' by the spectators of Rome.[26]

'The time of universal peace is near', declares Shakespeare's Octavius, in the Virgilianism of the Stuart court, giving a spatial stage-direction for this messianic epoch to be put on show: 'the three-nooked world / Shall bear the olive freely' [4,6,4–6]. The reference might be to the trio of alcoves behind the stage of the Globe, now reserved for royal entrances. But such would also be the visual turn of the court masque, where perspective made the phenomenal world look so ephemeral it appeared that 'life is a dream'. Shakespeare wrote the classic account of such a 'reformation' as an epiphany 'like bright metal on a sullen ground' [*1Henry IV*, 1,2,190] in the history of Prince Hal. This prodigal's claim to have 'turned away' his dreaming self [*2Henry IV*, 5,5,56] confirms how alert the dramatist was to 'the deep and pervasive commitment to forms of picturing' that was making the aesthetic into the private property, Octavio Paz has remarked, of the very few.[27] Yet the epistemological puzzle of the Prince's 'turning-picture' also reminds us how sceptical Shakespeare remained of 'ocular proof' [*Othello*, 2,3,361], and of the 'deficient sight' of modern selfhood. It cannot then be chance that pictorial perspective figures so often in his work as a brain-turning imposition: like 'sorrow's eye, glazed with blinding tears', which 'Finds shapes ... Looking awry' in *Richard II* [2,2,16–21]; the seeing 'perspectively' that so dazzles Henry V he 'cannot see many a fair French city for one fair French maid' [*Henry V*, 5,2,293–5]; the 'natural perspective' [*Twelfth*, 5,1,209] which finesses Sebastian's gate-crashing of Illyria; the 'scornful perspective' that 'Extended or contracted all proportions / To a most hideous object' when Bertram rejected Helena [*All's Well*, 5,3,49–53]; and most tellingly, the windowed 'perspective' of Sonnet 24, which means that 'through the painter must you see his skill / To find where your true image pictured lies'. It may be fanciful to believe, as optometrists deduce from his portraits, that Shakespeare himself suffered from strabismus, or a squint; but as John Kerrigan writes, the 'good turns eyes for eyes have done' in these fraught lines point up all the 'troubled counter-energies' of Shakespeare's concerns about pictures as products of astigmatism or even blindness:[28]

Yet eyes this cunning want to grace their art:
They draw but what they see, know not the heart.

The breaking of so great a thing

Unlike Jonson, Shakespeare did not write court masques 'but *embedded* them within his mixed-genre, socially inclusive plays'; and his response to the 'sovereign eye' [Sonnet 33] was always to question the *wryness* of perspective vision and the illusoriness of its 'regal phantasm' by insisting that 'eyes corrupt with over-partial looks' [Sonnet 137].[29] By valorizing the democratic 'gaze' and aesthetic sociality above aesthetic separation and the distanced 'look', he therefore prefigured what Jay describes as the 'oscillation between visual serenity and anxiety' in the theatre of the seventeenth century, typified by the way that for Racine light signalled more than visibility, it meant *le regard absolu*: 'the judging eye of God or the sun', and so of the Sun King.[30] If Pye and others are correct, Shakespeare had already exposed such a despotic form of vision as a kind of blinding, like that of Rembrandt's Samson, in *King Lear*; for, as theatre historians explain, it is because it insists the viewer sees things in the same way as the artist that monocular perspective inevitably carried such theological ramifications.[31] In fact, nothing better illustrates Pierre Bourdieu's dictum that categories of perception held by art lovers to be eternal are historical than the biopolitics of Stuart London, where the inculcation of a poetics of perspective was a true *rite de passage*, bewildering to outsiders but legible to the chosen few, as 'courtiers learned to decode the signs of power, distinction, and hierarchy in the gestures and accoutrements of bodies semaphorically on view'.[32] As Jen Boyle relates, the new 'imperialist looking' imposed a 'collective social imaginary' upon seventeenth-century cultural consumers that was tyrannically organized around the 'anamorphic experience'.[33] For they were embodying the phenomenon Svetlana Alpers calls the singular viewer as a genius in 'the matter of disdain'; an attitude of superciliousness thought to be personified by the painter Velázquez, in whose clean hands and glacial eye the art historian discerns 'something of Shakespeare's Coriolanus':

> A seventeenth-century *refrán* ... wittily juxtaposes painting (brush-work in the Venetian-Veláquez manner) and fighting. The saying goes, 'I keep my distance from paintings and from fights' ... It is an example of how court notions of the correct distance to view a painting spread out into the speech of the world at large. But it also suits Velázquez. One is reminded that he is said to have painted using a

brush with a long handle – hence stood back, as he did from strife. But there is a problematic side to [this distancing]. Conceived in this way, the detachment of the individual is accompanied by a distaste for the crowd ... the hostility to human community [...][34]

Ever since the German Romantics, art historians have defined the aesthetic in terms of distance, and praised painters like Velázquez for the 'cool and detached serenity' said to go with what Aby Warburg called the 'balancing evaluation of the aesthetic attitude'.[35] So the icy aloofness of the Spanish artist is said to be a function of his never 'overflowing the measure' of his dispassionate glance. The tenet of aesthetic distance between the audience and stage cultivated by seventeenth-century French dramatists such as Corneille and Racine has similarly been attributed to religious cooling in the aftermath of the Wars of Religion.[36] And Shakespeare continues to be analysed as a master of such 'psychical distance', who according to René Girard always meant the privileged elite 'to appreciate that distance', and opened *Antony and Cleopatra* with the disdainful Philo's direction to 'Take but good note, and you shall see in him / The triple pillar of the world transformed / Into a strumpet's fool. Behold and see' [*1,1,10–13*], because he was part of the world of power and possession, and shared its visual priorities.[37] With his injunction to 'Look where they come' [9], Philo has even been compared to the figure in painting of the period who controls our glance by looking out at us, as though the entire play was framed by the aesthetic credo of the Baroque state, *Ut pictura poesia*: as is the picture so is the poem.

As a Baroque court artist himself, so it is claimed, Shakespeare 'accommodated his aristocratic audience's tastes' by 'appropriating visual effects from masques, statuary, and portraiture'. In short, by exchanging his 'three-nooked world' for a two-dimensional picture when his play was staged at Whitehall, and even envisaging its action inserted into 'the wide arch', flanked by the Globe's emblems of Atlas and Hercules, which the architect Inigo Jones had erected in the Banqueting Hall for *The Masque Hymen* on Twelfth Night 1606, the dramatist created 'a flattering portrait of magnificence' in homage to King James.[38] Jones's sets for *Hymen* had indeed been flanked by triangular *periaktoi*: 'triple pillars' which were 'triple turn'd' [*4,13,13*] whenever the scene was 'transformed', just as Philo directs.[39] So it is tempting to conclude that Shakespeare did devise this counter-revolutionary Roman drama as a turning-picture to be slotted into the 'window' of that pre-existing frame. But what this assumption effaces is *the critical distance the work itself maintains* from the 'penetrative shame' of such an absolutist windowing, and how this tragedy can be appreciated as Shakespeare's sustained refusal of the concept of psychical distance that went with such a literally diminished single point of view:

CLEOPATRA: Know you what Caesar means to do with me?
DOLABELLA: I am loath to tell you what I would you knew.
CLEOPATRA: Nay, pray you, sir.
DOLABELLA: Though he be honourable –
CLEOPATRA: He'll lead me, them, in triumph?
DOLABELLA: Madam, he will. I know't.

[5,2,105–8]

In *Antony and Cleopatra* we are always conscious of two plays: the one we are watching and the other Caesar is preparing, which is pre-empted in such graphic descriptions that 'it comes to have the imaginative force of an event materially realized'.[40] Under the sign of its impending Whitehall transformation, therefore, the entire action unfolds like some antimasque or satyrs' play, 'branded in baseness' by the victor's prospective triumph. But as Margorie Garber writes, this expectation is deeply ironic because 'Caesar will never understand his own play', and his 'limited vision emphasizes the radical disjunction' between his designs and the actual play we see.[41] In its alertness to the 'turn' in pictorial perspective *Antony and Cleopatra* is a work that therefore seems to hesitate before its own transfer from the playhouse to the palace. For as Caesar imposes his dictatorial point of view on the 'courtiers of beauteous freedom' [2,6,17] who had been liberated by the assassination enacted in *Julius Caesar*, the inaugural Globe play, this sequel parallels the instauration of his *imperium* with that of a picture-frame stage, as if *itself* undergoing the counter-revolutionary turn from Mannerism to the Baroque, play to seriousness, and resolving the conflict between 'the stage with scenery and the stage for acting' in favour of the pictorial set.[42] As Bruce Smith comments, this tragedy will see Antony systematically 'aligned within a single perspective view'.[43] Yet it is precisely his future framing in the 'window' of the proscenium arch which the warrior resists, when he predicts that his 'visible shape' will be reconfigured to appear like a 'mangled shadow' [4,2,27] in the eyes of the 'million' spectators attending the Roman games to be staged by victorious Caesar, with a captive Cleopatra in the supporting role:

> ... she, Eros, has
> Pack'd cards with Caesar, and false play'd my glory
> Unto an enemy's triumph.
>
> [*4,15,16–20*]

'Is it not strange', asks Antony, that his rival 'could so quickly cut' the sea to Egypt; and Caesar's decisive 'celerity' is throughout associated with his redaction of the script [*3,7,20*], and with his Hamlet-like precautions to moralize his text, and ensure the actors 'Do not exceed / The prescript of this scroll' [*3,8,5–6*]. 'What needs more words?' the 'young man' [*3,11,63*] therefore protests after his 'bacchanals' with Antony [*2,7,122*]. Like Iago framing Othello, Caesar aims to window his 'great competitor' as 'a man that is the abstract of all faults' [*1,4,3–9*], since he knows that what 'appeared indeed' to be 'triumphant ... upon the river' will look 'monstrous' [*2,2,189–94*] when 'the common liar' speaks of it [*1,1,60*] in Rome. The master of measure, this 'wild disguise hath almost antick'd us all' [*2,7,122*], he winces after Pompey's feast. Like other Romans who separate speech from passion [*2,2,12*], or eschew 'too great an act' of 'garlands' or 'triumphal chariots' [*3,1,10*], calculating Octavius shares Hamlet's chilly humanist repulsion from 'anything so overdone' [*Hamlet, 3,2,18*]. 'I have eyes upon him, / And his affairs come to me on the wind', he therefore sneers [*3,6,62*]. It is the future emperor who in this twist of history thus heralds the pictorialism of the aesthetic point of view, and the Leviathan of the absolutist state which comes to figure the power abstracted from the sovereign body. So, 'Observe how Antony becomes his flaw', he orders, 'And what thou think'st his very action speaks / In every power that moves' [*3,12,34–6*]. As this vigilance implies, in a century that saw such advances in glass, spectacles, and artificial light 'the very ability to look and be seen in a social setting' meant that in addition to powers of illusion, absolutism was perfecting the surveillance system Shakespeare's Richard II terms 'the searching eye of heaven'. Under a Sun King, the lighting of festivity accompanied the festival of light:[44]

> ... when from under this terrestrial ball
> He fires the proud tops of the eastern pines,
> And darts his light through every guilty hole ...
>
> [*Richard II, 3,2,33–9*]

The little O o'th'earth

In his transformation from Octavius to Augustus, Mannerism to Baroque, Shakespeare's solar sovereign seems to augur the *enframing* or conquest of the world as picture that Heidegger called *technē*, and considered 'the foundation of the modern world view'.[45] Thus, 'Can he be there in person? 'Tis impossible', exclaims Antony, as 'This speed of Caesar's carries beyond belief'; but 'While he was yet in Rome', an insider explains, 'His power went out in such distractions as / Beguiled all spies' [3,7,56; 75–7]. So with his 'strange power' [57] of invisibility, omniscience, and ubiquity, Caesar is a forerunner of the Enlightenment watchfulness the historian Jean Starobinski termed '*puissance de voir*'.[46] What makes *Antony and Cleopatra* extraordinary, then, is that it anticipates this new instrumentalist 'order of light' as an *obstruction* of 'our clear judgements' and a *contraction* of space. For here the fall of the Republic figures as a collapsing of 'The sides of the world' [1,2,176], from rounded multi-dimensionality to the frontality of perspective, when 'the bulk o'th'world' [3,11,64] is 'Quartered' [4,15,58], then bisected with 'half to half the world opposed' [3,13,9] until 'The greater cantle' or angle 'of the world is lost' [3,11,6] and 'The little O o'th'earth' [5,2,79] is crushed. In *Antony and Cleopatra*, it seems, the war of the world is between the two regimes of sense concretized by the circular amphitheatre and proscenium arch. So it is suggestive that Jones's designs for *Hymen* featured just such an attack upon 'the world', when the curtain rose upon a globe coloured 'with countries' to figure 'the little world of man', which, as it descended, opened like a yawning jaw, to allow the actors from the real Globe who played the Humours and Affections to leap out and dance with Juno and her maids. Jonson's text glossed 'this terrestrial ball' as a political symbol, intended to signify that as 'parts of this world may dwell in one Center', so Juno would unite the Stuart kingdoms:

> She that makes *soules*, with *bodies*, mixe in love,
> Contracts the world in one, and therein IOVE;
> Is *spring*, and *end* of all things: yet, most strange!
> Her selfe nor suffers *spring*, nor *end*, nor *change*.[47]

The poetry of a body age 'cannot wither, nor custom stale' would reverberate in Cleopatra's 'infinite variety' [2,2,240]; but what may have struck her creator most about *Hymen* was its design for a world like 'a pair of chops' that 'grind the one the other' [*3,5,11–14*]. Since Jonson is said to have operated the winch to lower this 'microcosm', it is possible Shakespeare was himself one of the actors cooped inside this machine 'meant to quail and shake the orb' [*5,2,84*].[48] Certainly it is suggestive that he never again imagined the 'wooden O' [*Henry V, Pro.13*] as secure, for he must have recognised in this mechanical sphere a symbolic appropriation of his own Globe. Thus even Caesar admits he does not know 'What hoop should hold us staunch, from edge to edge / O'th' world' [*2,2,120–1*]; 'I am the man / Will give thee all the world', Menas brags [*2,7,61–2*]; and Antony fears 'I am so lated in the world that I / Have lost my way for ever ... who / With half the bulk o'th'world played as I pleased' [*3,11,3; 65*]. So, though the word 'world' occurs forty-two times in this play, over twice as often as in any other Shakespeare text, together with 'circle', 'earth', 'land', 'orb', 'round' and 'sphere' it carries the weight of 'the great globe itself' [*Tempest, 4,1,153*] in apprehension, as if forces exterior to the 'little O' threaten to 'make a sop of all this solid globe' [*Troilus, 1,3,113*], and 'th'affighted globe / Should yawn at altera-tion' [*Othello, 5,2,109*].[49] While there may be historical necessity, then, in Caesar's plan to reconfigure 'the three-nooked world', and 'Smite flat the thick rotundity o'the world' [*Lear, 3,2,7*], to suit his turning-machine, the *machina ductilis* of a two-dimensional *Pax*, even the great geometer shares the sense of anti-climax at the fea-tureless prostration to which 'the round world' of *Julius Caesar*, with its thunder, ghosts and lions, has thereby been reduced:

> The breaking of so great a thing should make
> A greater crack: the round world
> Should have shook lions into civil streets,
> And citizens to their dens: the death of Antony
> Is not a single doom; in the name lay
> A moiety of the world.
>
> [*5,1,14–19*]

A 'moiety' or share in the globe is in Antony's name because, we are reminded, he was 'the greatest soldier of the world' [*1,3,38*], 'the greatest prince o'th'world' [*4,16,56*], and his face 'lighted / The little O o'th'earth' [*5,2,78*]. In a clear allusion to the symbol of the playhouse, he is thus identified with the 'demi-Atlas of this earth' [*1,5,23*].[50] As Cleopatra is the 'day o'th'world' [*4,9,13*], they there-fore together constitute a theatre of the world; so it is hard not to read their defeat as that of the Globe players, for as she sighs, 'his reared arms / Crested the world. His voice was propertied / As all the tunèd spheres ... But when he meant to shake the orb, / He was as rattling thunder' [*5,2,81–5*]. We can, perhaps, hear a tribute to the actor Richard Burbage in this Marlovian hyperbole; and there might be an echo of some Globe feast in the toast of the 'world-sharers' to Bacchus, the god of drama: 'Cup us till the world go round, / Till the world go round!' [*2,7,67; 113*]. But 'Wilt thou be lord of the whole world?' [*58*], Menas incites Pompey, as Lepidus, who 'bears a third part of the world', staggers drunk [*86*]; and the thrust of all these metadramatic glances at the Globe as such a 'load' [*Hamlet, 2,2,345*] is to expose its vulnerability to takeover, as the 'senators alone of this great world' [*2,6,9*] fight among themselves. Thus 'the land bids me tread no more' [*3,11,1*], grieves Antony like some old trouper bidding farewell to the boards; and Enobarbus specifies that by meeting on Caesar's terms he threw away the 'absolute' power he had 'by land' [*3,7,42*]. So, 'Turn from me then that noble countenance', says his page, picking up the anamorphic figure, 'Wherein the worship of the whole world lies' [*4,15,85–6*]. The disillusion that 'The bright day is done, / And we are for the dark' [*5,2,188*], therefore seems prompted in this play by the conscription of the King's Men as masquers at Whitehall, and goes with a fatalistic surrender of 'the wide world's common space' [Sonnet 137] to the confining visual technology of Crown control:

> O sun,
> Burn the great sphere thou mov'st in; darkling stand
> The varying shore o'th'world!
>
> [*4,16,9–11*]

Shakespeare would repeat this premonition of 'the great sphere' in ashes on the bank of a darkened Thames in *The Tempest*. But here he pointedly attributes the melting of 'the crown o'th'earth' to the sovereign sun. So seeing Atlas and Hercules have crossed the river to the palace, he switches Antony's 'angel': from 'plumpy Bacchus' [*2,7,108*], who presides in Plutarch, to the Globe's 'daemon', when music 'under the earth' announces Hercules 'now leaves him' [*4,3,13*], as if 'the demi-Atlas' of the playhouse is 'afeard, as being o'erpowered' [*2,2,17–20*]. This regime change registers in the plot as a switch from the Mannerist arbitrariness of a game of chance, like the 'lots who shall begin' [*2,6,61*] when the Triumvirs banquet

Pompey, to the Baroque rules of a strict game of skill, from *alea* to *agôn*, as 'pack'd cards' prevail over 'the wounded chance of Antony' [*3,10,35*], proving 'Wisdom and fortune combating together, / If that the former dare but what it can, / No chance may shake it' [*3,13,79–81*]. Antony will thus stake his 'absolute soldiership' on 'chance and hazard' [*3,7,41–7*], despite being warned by the Soothsayer that 'If thou dost play with him at any game … He beats thee 'gainst the odds', and sensing his enemy's luck is stacked: 'The very dice obey him … If we draw lots, he speeds; / His cocks do win the battle still of mine / When all is to nought, and his quails ever / Best mine' [*2,3,34–9*]. Caesar, for his part, will shrug off setbacks as 'things done by chance' [*5,2,119*]. So, if *Antony and Cleopatra* is a wager in the *paragone* of word and image, its dice are loaded, because the match is always already decided, a march towards an unavoidable historical goal. As Leonard Tennenhouse puts it, 'In this manner of delivering the world over' to the world-picture of Augustus, Shakespeare makes it clear that 'a whole way of figuring power has been rendered obsolete'.[51]

'*Agôn* is vindication of personal responsibility; *alea* is a surrender to destiny', according to Roger Caillois.[52] The distinction seems apt for *Antony and Cleopatra*, where the transit from the aleatoric fantasia of Mannerism to the agonistic order of the Baroque is anticipated as the ineluctable outcome of the struggle, like that in Barthes's comparison of boxing and wrestling, between what Antony terms the 'sports' of 'better cunning' and 'chance' [*2,3,35*]. As Stanley Wells notes, it will be in the Late Plays that Shakespeare revives the illusion of happenstance, for there 'the logic of chance and fortune governs all'.[53] Such is the kind of romance to which Antony and Cleopatra aspire. No wonder, therefore, that Caesar refuses to be 'staged to th'show' [*3,13,30*] in single combat; nor that Cleopatra cries, 'In this dull world … The odds is gone' [*4,16,63–8*]. For the turn from Antony's 'glory' to Caesar's 'show' is here presented as a *fait accompli*, with the queen compelled to 'frame herself' the 'way she's forced to', and rehearsed in the role the victor calculates 'Would be eternal in our triumph' [*5,1,66*]. Thus Antony is justified in calling these programmed games 'false play', since they are the type of *trompe l'oeil* Johann Huizinga described in *Homo Ludens* when he explained how in the society of the spectacle, when power plays, 'it plays false' by instrumentalizing 'the purpose of playing' [*Hamlet, 3,2,19*], as if play is never a mere game.[54] Caesar leaves no doubt, in any case, that his culminating 'ostentation' [3,6,52] will be a purposeful play to end play, with himself as focal point:

> The wife of Antony
> Should have an army for an usher, and
> The neighs of horse to tell of her approach
> Long ere she did appear. The trees by th'way
> Should have borne men, and expectation fainted,
> Longing for what it had not. Nay, the dust
> Should have ascended to the roof of heaven,
> Raised by your populous troops ...
> We should have met you
> By sea and land, supplying every stage
> With an augmented greeting.
>
> [3,6,43–55]

Holes where eyes should be

Caesar's design for 'every stage' is that of the triumph London witnessed with the royal entry of March 15 1604, when James was compared with Augustus as he entered the city under seven arches in tableaux scripted by Jonson and other playwrights; although significantly not by Shakespeare. Latin slogans in this 'augmented greeting' proclaimed the Stuart the avenger of the other Ides of March; and Jonson cried up the absolutist symbolism of the arches, which were 'all with that general harmony so connexed as no one little part can be missing to the illustration of the whole'.[55] Critics regard this 'picturing' of public space as an annexation of the popular aesthetic to that of the court; and Jonson seized on its scenario as his own entrée to the world of the masque.[56] There beholders were indeed supposed to be petrified into worshippers by a design that organized visual experience, Stephen Orgel relates, around 'the single point in the hall from which the perspective achieved its fullest effect, the royal throne'. Captivated by this optical marvel, the court was meant to be transfixed into a 'visible emblem of the aristocratic hierarchy', for the closer one sat to him the better one's view, but 'only the king's place was perfect'.[57] With its switch from light to dark, and climactic dance when performers and spectators joined hands, a masque was thus the fulfilment of what Shakespeare's Caesar has in mind, and Jacques Rancière describes in *The Emancipated Spectator* as a Platonist *theatre to end theatre*:

Plato wanted to replace the democratic, ignorant community of theatre with a different ... choreographic community where everyone must move in accordance with the community rhythm fixed by mathematical proportion, even if that requires getting old people reluctant to take part in the community dance drunk.[58]

However laughable in its effects, a court masque was intended as 'a liturgy of state', in Roy Strong's phrase, so 'more like a ritual' than a play, according to Limon, in which 'the florescent monarch' was the source of light and action.[59] In Louis Marin's words, in this hall of mirrors 'The portrait of the king is not only the sun in the central place of the narrative, it is also the light spread ... on everything and everyone, *making* them be seen'; and in *Antony and Cleopatra* the 'imperious show / Of the full fortuned Caesar' [4,16,24] will be a similar post-dramatic model of the 'good theatre' that 'adopts Plato's prohibition of theatre for theatre'.[60] Recent critics like David Lindley detect irritation at this absolutist optic within the Stuart masques themselves, however; and when perspective was tested at Oxford in August 1605 officials 'utterly disliked' the set-up, and moved the king so far back in order to be seen that James complained he could not *hear* the play. Such was the kerfuffle over the appropriate 'measure' for viewing perspective scenery that Orgel thinks 'it was many years before the implications of this sort of theatre were realized in the drama, or indeed recognized at all'.[61] Shakespeare's text refers expressly to these debates, however, when Cleopatra objects that any representation of 'Our size of sorrow' will need to be 'Proportioned to our cause' [4,16,4–5]. And so disproportioned and 'awry' is Philo's framing of its lovers as a gypsy and a 'strumpet's fool' that *Antony and Cleopatra* looks from the start like Shakespeare's squinting recognition from inside the cramped confinement of Jones's microcosm of the occlusion that this type of *camera obscura* would bring to the 'huge sphere' of the Globe:

> To be called into a huge sphere, and not to be seen to move in't, are the holes where eyes should be which pitifully disaster the cheeks ...
> [2,7,13–14]

Anamorphosis is art in code, wrote Barthes in his essay on Arcimboldo, as 'its message is concealed ... and it is by an effort of distance that I receive another message which, like a decoding grid, allows me to suddenly perceive the "real" meaning'.[62] By framing his play as such an optical puzzle, critics argue, Shakespeare was thus pitching his work at playgoers of 'the judicious' type admired by Hamlet, just one of whom, the Prince avers, must 'o'erweigh a whole theatre of others' [*Hamlet, 3,2,24*]. He was supposedly competing in these new registers of singularity with Jonson, who just prior to *Hamlet* began to appeal to the 'happy judgements' of 'judicious friends'. Yet as Leo Salingar details, Jonson's inductions, referring his text to 'attentive auditors / Such as will join their profit with their pleasure / And come to feed their understanding parts', were part of a campaign to create an intellectual elite from the court and lawyers' Inns. Shakespeare's rival therefore offered his plays as anamorphic turning-pictures, which 'upon the view might, without cloud, or obscurity, declare themselves to the sharp and learned', because the 'effort of distance' or 'measure' was built into the privileged experience of the Jonsonian stage.[63] But what is notable about the older writer, Salingar reminds us in 'Shakespeare and the Italian Concept of "Art"', is that for this man of the theatre 'art' was always a lie. So he never participated in this snobbish vogue; and though Girard claims he winked up to the 'happy few' [*Henry V, 4,3,60*] in the Lord's Room, only referred to such a clique in the words of the Prince, whose talk of Marlowe's *Dido Queen of Carthage* as 'caviare to the general' [*2,2,418*], and preference for the 'judicious' over the groundlings with their love of 'inexplicable dumb shows and noise' [*3,2,9; 24*], gives his superciliousness 'a hint of fashionable affectation' which distinguishes it from both the playwright and the play.[64] In *Antony and Cleopatra*, moreover, nothing marks Caesar as the enemy of that theatre on the tumescent river more than his Hamlet-like disgust at the inability of its 'common' playgoers to 'perceive the total meaning' from the anchor of his own 'singular' point of view:

> This common body,
> Like to a vagabond flag upon the stream,
> Goes to and back, lackeying the varying tide,
> To rot itself with motion.
>
> [*1,4,44–7*]

With its snarl at the playhouse pennant, Caesar's contempt for 'This common body' reiterates Hamlet's complaint when, from his 'seat' in its gallery, the Prince of Denmark speaks of 'this distracted globe' [*Hamlet, 1,5,97*]. But unlike younger contemporaries, whose ideal of 'a full and understanding auditory' is, like Jones's, the exclusive membership of an academy or club, Shakespeare never forgets his prime 'understanders' are those 'vagabond' groundlings who *stand under* the stage, in that 'whole theatre of others' 'upon the stream', nor that as his punster Launce jokes, 'stand-under and under-stand is all one' [*Two Gents, 2,5,28*].[65] As Charles Whitney points out, in a scopic system moving to separate the knowing subject and fixed standpoint from the object of knowledge, which the new picture-frame stage would help install, his epilogues invoke only collective pleasure and audience response.[66] It cannot therefore be chance that so much depends in these paratexts on the appeal to 'Give me your hands' [*Dream, Epi.15*]. For it is in tune with *mutual understanding* that in *Antony and Cleopatra* the first lesson the Roman must learn from his Egyptian conquest is the alternative to the dictatorial princely look of the distracted plebeian *gaze*, when 'the city cast / Her people out upon her, and Antony, / Enthroned i'the market-place, did sit alone, / Whistling to th'air, which but for vacancy / Had gone to gaze on Cleopatra too' [*2,2,219–23*].

In the pre-Jacobean *Henry V* London had poured out her citizens like those of 'antique Rome' to 'fetch their conqu'ring Caesar in' [*5,0,248*]. But now it is the Roman show that is deserted, as the Alexandrians rush to the extramural theatre on the wharf. For only the law that nature abhors a vacuum could bar Cleopatra's drawing power when 'Antony sent to her' and 'She replied it should be better he became her guest' [*2,2,226*]. Thus if pictorial perspective is distrusted on this stage as 'a pageant to keep us in false gaze' [*Othello, 1,3,19*], the diffusion of the intersubjective 'gaze' is a force for resistance, for it means the singularity of a Coriolanus stays merely 'picture-like' until it has 'plucked all gaze his way' [*Coriolanus, 1,3,6*], as thankfully, eyes 'blunted with community' can 'Afford no extraordinary gaze / Such as is bent on sun-like majesty' [*1 Henry IV, 3,2,76–9*]. By opposing conflicting modes of vision, and valorizing the interactive communal gaze over the passive singular look, Shakespeare is thereby anticipating the contrast drawn by Jacques Lacan between the phallic eye of the sovereign subject, desiring specular plenitude in a mirror image of itself, and the diffused gaze in a field of pure monstrance.[67] For by the end of these tragedies the tyrant will be like 'our rarer monsters', a 'show and gaze o'th'time' [*Macbeth, 5,10,24*]; while Antony will delight gallery-goers and groundlings with a playfulness that, glancing at *Dido*, defiantly asserts theatre as a community of understanders going 'hand in hand':

> Where souls do crouch on flowers we'll hand in hand,
> And with our sprightly port make the ghosts gaze.
> Dido and her Aeneas shall want troops,
> And all her haunt be ours.

[4,15,51–4]

Their most absurd intents

Shakespeare consistently praises the reciprocity of 'The lovely eye where every gaze doth dwell' [Sonnet 5], 'Gilding the object whereupon it gazeth' [Sonnet 20], over the unilateralism of the prescriptive 'look'. As Paul Yachnin notes, his ideal theatre continues to be an 'interspecular community', with 'eye to eye opposed' [*Troilus*, 3,3,107] in the shared 'meeting of eyes'.[68] This is because he persists in conceiving vision as a quasi-linguistic exchange. Thus when Cleopatra reminds Antony how 'eternity was in our lips and eyes' [1,3,35], or Pompey the Elder 'Would stand and make his eyes grow' in hers [1,5,31]; Enobarbus recalls how her women 'tended her i'th'eyes' [2,2,213]; Antony fears she will 'mingle eyes / With one that ties his points' [3,13,158]; or Charmian closes her 'Downy windows' so that Phoebus will 'never be beheld / Of eyes again so royal' [5,2,307–8], the play affirms the Shakespearean paradox that 'There's language in her eye' [*Troilus*, 4,5,55]. Joel Finemann called this verbalization of vision 'Shakespeare's Perjur'd Eye', and described the Sonnets as a systematic revolt against the official literary doctrine of *ut pictura poesis*, in which 'poetry based on visual likeness' is made to give way to 'poetry based on verbal difference'. After the Sonnets, Shakespeare is never a 'visionary poet who identifies his "I" with his "eye"', Finemann concluded, 'instead, because he *speaks* ... his "I" is precipitated in or as the slippage between his eye and tongue'. Thus, 'what is odd about the eye' in Shakespeare's later works 'is that it is opposed to vision', as though he intuited that the single eye of perspective is, as Alpers writes, 'a dead eye', and its model of vision or painting 'is a passive one'.[69] And in *Antony and Cleopatra* we have it confirmed that this Shakespearean sensation of some fundamental inertia in pictorial representation is because for the 'absolute' actor of the Globe the speaking 'I' is still constructed in the 'public eye' of the 'common' stage:

CAESAR: Unto her
                   He gave the stablishment of Egypt; made her
                   Of lower Syria, Cyprus, Lydia,
                   Absolute queen.
MAECENAS: This in the public eye?
CAESAR: I'th'common showplace.

                                                    [3,6,8–12]

'I admit nothing but on the faith of the eye', asserted Francis Bacon.[70] But in Shakespeare's Egypt the 'absolute' monarchy that goes with this sovereign 'I' is given away in 'the public eye' of the 'common showplace'. So in a culture slipping towards a scopic regime where the eye of power puts subjects under surveillance, Cleopatra still glories in a decentred theatre optic that puts power on display. As Gary Schmidgall fancies, Antony is thus the type of drunken Whitehall politician ferried down to the Liberties, as the queen is of the brothel madam who beckons him east, 'to reel the streets at noon and stand the buffet / With knaves that smells of sweat' [1,4,20–1]: 'Their Alexandria is a seamless blend of Bankside tavern and whorehouse', which would make audiences 'feel completely at home' when acted at the Globe.[71] So Cleopatra clothes Antony as her travelling player: 'In his livery / Walked crowns and crownets'; and she confounds the absolutist doctrine that 'Nature wants stuff / To vie strange forms with fancy' with the materiality of the actor's body, for 't'imagine / An Antony were nature's piece 'gainst fancy / Condemning shadows quite' [5,2,89]. Her fleshly naturalism underlines the fact that the courtly cliché that the artwork 'tutors nature. Artificial strife / Lives in these touches livelier than life' is mouthed by Shakespeare's sycophants, like the pretentious Poet and Painter of *Timon of Athens* [1,1,37]; and that the Baroque maxim that 'life is a dream' is repeatedly undermined in these plays by the natural philosophy that 'over that art / Which you say adds to nature is an art / That nature makes' [*Winter's*, 4,4,90–2]. As Salingar points out, though Shakespeare is intensely interested in the rivalry of painting and acting, when it comes to a choice between art and life he always 'inverts the art critics' view', and puts acting on the side of life.[72]

Editors note that the only contemporary artist Shakespeare mentions is the quintessential Mannerist Giulio Romano. But Gombrich traced this reference to Vasari's *Life*, where it was said Jupiter so resented Romano depicting breathing bodies that he 'carried him off'.[73] So it is piquant when in *The Winter's Tale* we are told 'he would beguile nature of her custom' *if only* he had eternity, as 'that rare Italian master' [*5,2,87*] had in fact died in 1546. And it is in line with that ultimate creative defeat that in *Antony and Cleopatra* Shakespeare's intervention in the *paragone* is a statement of the deadliness of both poetry and painting compared to the live performance of the 'quick comedians' [*5,2,212*]; to the vitality of 'our quick minds' [*1,2,99*] which outshines any Roman 'celerity in dying' [*131*]; or to 'the fire / That quickens Nilus's slime' [*1,3,68*] as Cleopatra moulds the bodily 'clay, our dungy earth' [*1,1,35*], like a potter: 'Quick, quick. Good hands' [*5,2,38*], and the mature lovers 'quicken with kissing' [*4,16,40*]. So while Enobarbus's glance at 'that Venus where we see / The fancy outwork nature' makes critics think Shakespeare must have been familiar with pictures of 'What Venus did with Mars' [*1,5,18*] by painters like Botticelli or Veronese, the contrast the veteran makes in fact picks up the inexpressibility *topos* from Antony's impatience at the futility of such abstractions, 'There's beggary in the love that can be reckoned' [*1,1,16*], to insist on the *poverty* of painting compared to the liveliness of performance, its failure to attain its object or fulfil desire.[74] Shakespeare's most famous allusion to Renaissance 'picturing' is, in fact, a striking anticipation of the modernist fatigue at the separation from 'quick' life of the 'endless, meaningless objectivity produced by paint':[75]

> For her own person,
> It beggared all description. She did lie
> In her pavilion – cloth of gold, of tissue –
> O'er-picturing that Venus where we see
> The fancy outwork nature.
>
> [*2,2,203–7*]

Sir Philip Sidney had defined poetry as a 'speaking picture' or *ekphrasis*; but invisible in her own *ekphrasis*, Shakespeare's Cleopatra is unrepresentable in the 'golden world' of picture or poem. Constructed as a desired absence, she can, Phyllis Rackin and others perceive, *quicken* only with hand-clapping on a three-dimensional stage.[76] So critics mistake the play's allusions to paintings for celebrations of pictorialism, when they sound like subversions of what A.D. Nuttall termed 'the frigidly linear structure of the Roman world'.[77] For if Shakespeare had followed Mannerism into the abstraction of the Baroque, remarked the art historian John Shearman, he would have produced plays like Guarini's *Pastor fido*, where the fixation on frontality creates 'an entirely artificial drama peopled by "characters" so thin and depersonalized' they seem 'totally abstract'.[78] Instead, at the instant when perspective was being exploited to star 'the prince at the centre of the macrocosm in every enactment of Court ritual', the 'visual anchor' Cleopatra calls the 'Sole sir o'th'world' [5,2,116], it is as a 'pitiful *disaster*' that the lovers of *Antony and Cleopatra* invoke the stellar imagery of such an absolutist display.[79] For like a player peeping through holes in Jones's globe, Antony images his 'declining day' [5,1,38] as the effect called the 'glory': a corona eclipsed by clouds which signalled the turning-point of masques. With punning reference to the 'rack' on which 'all length is torture' [4,14,46], a term first used for Jones's cloud scenery in *Hymen*, Antony's stomach-churning ordeal is thus that of the actor hoist only to be lowered again in the 'rattling' machine:[80]

> Thou hast seen these signs,
> They are black vesper's pageants ...
> That which is even now a horse, even with a thought
> The rack dislimns, and makes it indistinct
> As water is in water.
>
> [4,14,7–11]

Strapped into this 'turning picture', like one of the actors in a Stuart masque, the 'old lion' [3,13,95] suffers the nauseating 'madness of vision' of the *Trauerspiel*, the German mourning play studied by Benjamin, where the 'tension between the world and its transcendence' experienced by nobles at the absolutist court issued in a visual deadlock 'bound up with the mirror-nature of the play'.[81] 'The shirt of Nessus is upon me' [4,13,43], Antony therefore rages, alluding to the trick when Hercules was poisoned; and as music signals the desertion of its angel, the play does come near to imaging itself as such a claustrophobic space. In fact, this suicide scenario has a specific ideology, reminding us how it suits the powerful to 'Tie up the libertine in a field of feasts; / Keep his brain fuming' [2,1,23], and that it is Caesar who benefits from Antony's 'lascivious wassails' [1,4,56], for every element of this dizzying spectacle would lodge in the royalist visual repertoire that evolved in the masques and Van Dyck's tenebrous portraits of Charles I.[82]

'Dissolve, thick cloud, and rain' [*5,2,298*] would be unintentionally monitory signifiers of Stuart political theology. More immediately, Antony's comparison of his 'wreck' to the 'rack' of a cloud machine prefigures Prospero's sermon upon the 'insubstantial pageant fading' that dissolves to 'Leave not a rack behind' [*Tempest, 4,1,154*], which Orgel reads as Shakespeare's *endorsement* of absolutism, evincing a 'profound understanding of court theatre and masques as expression of the monarch's will'.[83] This interpretation seems superficially to be supported by Antony's likening of his fall to 'black vesper's pageant': a reference to the earliest Stuart masque, *The Masque of Blackness* of 1605. For Jonson's text does confirm that what overwhelmed that show was Jones's design, which opened on an artificial sea. This was the first perspective set ever seen in England, and introduced the notion of the central vanishing-point as what Weimann terms 'a catalyst for a coherent and controlled laying out of theatrical space':

> [T]he scene behind seemed a vast sea and united with this that flowed forth; from the termination or horizon of which, being the level of the chair of state which was placed in the upper end of the hall, was drawn by the lines of prospective, the whole work shooting downwards from the eye; which decorum made it more conspicuous, and caught the eye afar off with a wandering beauty.[84]

Wave machines were constructed from silver cylinders which reflected the spectators as they revolved. So during *Blackness* the sovereign seated in state could glimpse his face 'As water is in water'. With its maritime setting and colonial allegory, in which nymphs of Niger, whom 'no cares, no age, can change', are bleached white by the solar James, this Egyptian masque therefore established the Platonist symbolism with which *Antony and Cleopatra* engaged. Thus, 'When such a spacious mirror's set before him', comments Maecenas of Caesar, 'He needs must see himself' [*5,1,53*]. But as the Moon ascended 'in a silver throne made of a pyramid', to beam on Queen Anne and her 'hieroglyphic' Ladies transported in a giant shell by 'sea-monsters, bearing twelve torch-bearers', these 'Alexandrian revels' excited 'immortal longings' [*5,2,280*] in the court with a scenography Shakespeare seems to have considered 'most absurd' [*5,2,22*].[85] As recent scholars emphasize, *Blackness* was put on by Anne to reassert her royal role, and may have been a signal about her Catholicism. If so, there would be no repeat, for, as Leeds Barroll recounts, its cool reception persuaded the queen to cease 'presenting these elaborate shows'.[86] The sarcasm of the gossip John Chamberlain that 'You cannot imagine a more ugly sight', confirms, in any case, what the dramatist surely glimpsed in this 'spacious mirror': that far from falling into line with the king, participants in a masque would always view its picture with 'double vision' and in 'contradictory ways'.[87] In Martin Butler's words, because the fixation on the sovereign's unique angle of vision marginalizes the viewpoints of performers and spectators, its grandiose design could never be 'the sum total' of the evening's show:[88]

> IRAS: I'll never see't! For I am sure my nails
>   Are stronger than my eyes.
> CLEOPATRA: Why, that's the way
>   To fool their preparation, and to conquer
>   Their most absurd intents.
>
> [5,2,219–22]

Give me mine angle

What Shakespeare gleaned from *The Masque of Blackness* confirmed his own instinct that the way 'To fool their preparation' was to pretend to submit to 'Their most absurd intents', judging by the reaction he slipped at the time into *Measure for Measure*: 'wisdom wishes to appear most bright / When it doth tax itself: as these black masks / Proclaim an enshield beauty ten times louder / Than beauty could, displayed' [2,4,78–81]. Thus, performed before the royal family, it is believed, at Christmas 1607, possibly at the behest of the Countess of Pembroke, whose translation of Garnier's *Marc Antoine* was a source, *Antony and Cleopatra* is likely to have been produced in response to just such a commission for the 1606 London visit of Anne's brother and James's brother-in-law, Christian IV of Denmark, when the two kings feasted on a barge of 'pinnacles and pyramids', as do Antony and Caesar.[89] Alvin Kernan has therefore argued that with this assignment Shakespeare produced 'not just propaganda but a true piece of theatrical magic', by orientalizing the 'shabby decadence of the Stuart court' into something as 'rich and strange as the beasts' of the Nile.[90]

According to Kernan's art-inspired interpretation, Shakespeare's strategy in *Antony and Cleopatra* is a vast exaggeration of scale: 'James and his court looked cheap and vulgar only so long as they

were confined to the realistic setting of the Thames'. Angle them
correctly, and 'English vices become Egyptian virtues ... Sex, drink,
idleness, luxury, waste' are expanded into 'a vision of beauty and
delight'. Thus, Kernan contends that Shakespeare shared the same
agenda as James, or as his Caesar: to magnify the illusion of power
'with all the taste and skill that the great Renaissance masters of the
métier contrived for their patrons in spectacle and masque'. This
critique locks into an analysis of the later plays as a showcase for
'royalism in the arts', which 'presents a Jacobean audience with a
mirror', and veils absolutist ideology in avant-garde forms.[91] But
it thereby turns the tragedy inside-out, since it ignores the *wryness*
with which this play about the 'size of dreaming' [5,2,97] reverses
such grandiosity by 'yawning at alteration' on the Stuart stage. For
while a masque elided the difference between illusion and reality
by angling its 'corrigible' spectators around a single point of view,
Shakespeare's tragedy swerves from such intentions by persistently
referring itself back to 'the common body' on that 'overflowing'
river, and with earthy jokes about 'your merry angling', truly
meeting its players half way:

CLEOPATRA: Come, you'll play with me, sir?
MARDIAN: As well as I can, madam.
CLEOPATRA: And when good will is showed, though't come too
                            short,
      The actor may plead pardon. I'll none now.
      Give me mine angle. We'll to th'river; there
      My music playing far off, I will betray
      Tawny-finned fishes.
                          [2,5,7–16]

With its 'transcendence of reality and dematerialization of the phenomenal', wrote Murray Roston, *Antony and Cleopatra* is the only
Shakespearean play truly belonging to the Mannerist tradition, since
in this drama 'petty limitations of perspective collapse or shimmer
away as in an El Greco painting'.[92] Likewise, in *Shakespeare and the
Mannerist Tradition* Jean-Pierre Maquerlot charts the dramatist's
trajectory in terms of the counterpoint Cleopatra relishes, symbolized by contrasts of place such as Westminster and Eastcheap.
Shakespeare remains a Mannerist artist, by this account, rather than
submitting to the decisiveness of the Baroque, by elaborating his
see-saw structures, with 'delight in ambiguous situation, equivocal

discourse and ambivalent behaviour', until in *Antony and Cleopatra* East and West equalize and the characters 'feast on the sublime and sordid alike'. George Kernodle had argued that the effect of perspective scenery, in which 'cloud machines came down, ships moved between rolling waves, and monsters rose', was to express the restlessness of the Mannerist age; but Maquerlot considers that because it stayed so alive to 'the beholder's share', Shakespeare's theatre could suspend opposing viewpoints in a perpetual stasis, like 'the swan's-down feather / That stands upon the swell at the full tide, / And neither way inclines' [3,2,47–9], in Antony's words at the wavering mid-point of the play, 'When vantage like a pair of twins appeared / Both as the same' [3,10,12–13].[93]

Macquerlot's theory of Mannerism as a style 'between extremes' draws on the revaluation of anamorphosis by Lacan, who decoded the elongated skull in Holbein's *The Ambassadors* as a symbolic castration of the Cartesian subject, decentring the desiring look with 'the inside-out structure of the gaze'.[94] It is a critique that thus invokes the distinction between representational drama that offers itself as a mimetic image of life, and presentational that foregrounds the signifier; and it chimes with Yachnin's thesis that Shakespeare's work stayed *socially* two-faced, catering for '*populuxe* consumption', which involved 'aspiration on the part of lower-class people and a "commoning" of the material markers of a higher class'. As purveyor of such a 'heavenly mingle' Shakespeare became a pioneer of a *populuxe* market, on this view, who exploited his intermediacy between court and city to 'add value to the goods' he produced, as the King's Men paraded their Whitehall connections to give playgoers the illusion that they too were 'courtly insiders'.[95] These theories thus explain why the battle in *Antony and Cleopatra* is as much between actors as armies, with the 'imperious show' sabotaged by the popularity of the playhouse. For here the frontality of the masque, in which the mirrored spectator will 'anchor his aspect, and die / With looking on his life' [1,5,33], is persistently offset by the 'thick rotundity' [*Lear*, 3,2,7] or 'greater cantle' of the Globe. The result is that so long as Antony can 'make space enough' [2,3,25] between his arena and that of Caesar the play remains a tragicomedy, as generically 'mingled' as its lovers' games [4,15,23], the 'mingle' of their grey hair with 'younger brown' [4,9,20], the 'mingle with rattling taborins' the general orders, 'That heaven and earth my strike their sounds together' [*37–8*], or the 'well-divided' rabbit/duck conundrum that Cleopatra credits to the man himself:

> Note him, good Charmian, 'tis the man; but note him!
> He was not sad, for he would shine on those
> That make their looks by his; he was not merry,
> Which seemed to tell them his remembrance lay
> In Egypt with his joy; but between both.
> O, heavenly mingle! Be'st thou sad or merry
> The violence of either thee becomes,
> So does it no man else.
>
> [*1,5,53–61*]

According to the anamorphic viewing, the equilibrium of *Antony and Cleopatra* is a function of a chiastic design that dovetails with settings at both Whitehall and the Globe. If its dual commission determined the 'two-facedness' of this Janus play, what its author therefore served up is said to be the Mannerist ideal, where multiple points of view are entertained, and the 'skill in suggesting' is matched by 'skill in taking hints'.[96] But other critics feel uneasy pinning the Mannerist label to Shakespeare.[97] And such is indeed the 'well-divided disposition' expressly assigned in the play to Caesar's sister Octavia when she is married to Antony, and becomes a spectator of her brother's show, with her 'heart parted betwixt two friends' [*3,6,77*], 'Praying for both parts' [*3,4,13*]. Antony assuredly hopes she will 'go between's' as 'reconciler' [*30*]. What the anamorphic version therefore overlooks is that Olivia finds 'no midway / 'Twixt these extremes at all' [*3,4,13–26*], no equidistance between 'Husband win' and 'win brother' [*3,4,18*]. As Garber objects, the approach that would balance opposing views 'in fact suggests a false analogy' with the stillness of a picture, as the 'violence of either' is not equalized: 'The play is not evenly divided in its emphasis between the lovers and the aspiring emperor', and the end is not greeted 'with an auspicious and a drooping eye'.[98]

As many critics as applaud the ambivalence of *Antony and Cleopatra* are alienated by the way that Shakespeare seems to deepen the fatalism of the 'foregone conclusion' he had explored in *Othello* [*3,3,428*], the play he wrote in seeming homage to King James's poem on the Battle of Lepanto. Jonathan Dollimore eloquently voiced this dismay, when he observed how the play's insistence on 'the strong necessity of time' [*1,3,42*] ends up mystifying power, by 'playing itself out in the wake of history, the dust of the chariot wheel'.[99] For Schmitt, however, what differentiated Shakespeare's tragedies from the indecisiveness of the *Trauerspiel* was precisely that they 'originated in direct contact with the London court, London public, London actors', and that their fatalism was dictated by their own 'unalterable reality'.[100] These plays had not therefore separated presence from representation; and Peter Holland has explained the positive implications of this openness to 'the common body' well: 'the actors aligned themselves with the audience', who saw them in a situation 'analogous to their own, rather than a totally fictive world'.[101] In *Antony and Cleopatra* this means that the struggle to be 'absolute master' [2,2,68] is a true war of theatres, a battle between the 'windowed' picture at Whitehall and the 'distracted' scaffold at the Globe that only one of the opposed playing spaces can win. So, as Antony foretells, the 'heavenly mingle' of equalities is doomed by the imperative to 'turn' towards the Crown:

> Where it appears to you this begins,
> Turn your displeasure that way, for our faults
> Can never be so equal that our love
> Can equally move with them.
>
> [3,4,33–6]

Ever since the Globe opened, Shakespeare had compared the pause 'between the acting of a dreadful thing / And the first motion' [*Julius*, 2,1,63] to the eternal stasis of a 'painted tyrant', in reaction to the stillness in the playhouse whenever 'we see ... the rack stand still, / The bold winds speechless, and the orb below / As hush as death' [*Hamlet*, 2,2,460–6]. The merciful relief of this subjectivizing 'interim' [5,2,74] had been an unintended consequence of the architectonics of the Bankside auditorium. But critics who picture 'Shakespeare's great anamorphic drama' as similarly suspended within such a temporizing hiatus underrate the necessity by which 'this dramatic oxymoron' is *itself* swept along in the Baroque turn of the tide.[102] Like the *Trauerspiel*, art historians remind us, Mannerism was only a transitional style of the brief era of equivocation that preceded the rise of absolute monarchy in the courts of vacillating rulers such as Rudolf II. So in *Antony and Cleopatra* it is likewise the capricious queen who delights in ambiguity, and treasures the turning picture which depicts 'a Fury crowned with snakes, / Not like a formal man' [2,5,40–1]. In this play, we infer, the aesthetic pause or interim which has come to mean so much to recent critics, and that with reference to Greek tragedy Lacan terms the zone between two deaths, is doomed to be swallowed up, along with the mixed body of the playhouse, in the enveloping night of the absolutist stage.[103]

It is the drama queen Cleopatra who thrives in the amphitheatre's suspended animation, the interregnum 'Like to the time o'th'year between the extremes / Of hot and cold' [1,5,51], and whose words are 'divided / Between her heart and lips' [4,15,32]. She thus shares, it is tempting to imagine, the indeterminacy of her creator, who is said by critics to 'leave unanswered the central questions' of the play by 'surrendering the production of meaning to his audiences', so it can be viewed 'one way like a gorgon, the other way like Mars'.[104] But it is because her ideal of 'the mean' [2,7,18], 'midway / 'Twixt these extremes' [3,4,19], is tied to her dream of an Antony 'propertied / As all the tuned spheres' [5,2,82], when he in fact 'reneges all temper' [1,1,8], and 'mocks the pauses that he makes' [5,1,2], that if 'she can guess what temperance should be' Cleopatra can never 'know what it is' [3,13,122]. Thus it will be the queen herself who breaks the deadlock by turning tail, 'like a cow in June' [3,10,14]. And just as Antony's men look for 'Some way to leave him' [3,13,200], so the text knows its middle way will be shattered by the 'boys', when the actors themselves rush from the playhouse to the palace, instead of waiting for the kings to come to them:

ANTONY: Authority melts from me of late. When I cried, 'Ho!',
           Like boys unto a muss kings would start forth,
           And cry, 'Your will?' – Have you no ears?

                                                    [3,13,86–93]

Kings of the earth

'Shadows, dreams, the actor and the play', according Anne Barton, are all 'degraded' in *Antony and Cleopatra*, which represents theatre, she asserts, as a place of 'emptiness and deceit', and the player as a cipher of 'futility and shame'.[105] Critics have long noted this tendency in the Jacobean Shakespeare to denigrate acting with images of futility and lies. Yet this disparagement is not anti-theatrical, for, as Antony's fury implies, it is aimed at the 'poor player / That struts and frets his hour upon the stage' [*Macbeth*, 5,2,217] when he prostitutes the stage in 'anti-plays' that divide the aesthetic community and diminish the performers.[106] As Meredith Anne Skura stresses, the alarm that rings in these works is not over theatre, but 'the ruler who uses theatre', and the ways theatre is betrayed.[107] Thus 'proud man / Dressed in a little brief authority' is personified by the actor who 'plays such fantastic tricks' in the mirror of the mighty as make his true admirers weep [*Measure*, 2,2,121–4]. Likewise, the spectators who 'cast their caps up and carouse' are only scorned as turncoats when they fawn like 'spanieled' courtiers and 'melt their sweets / On blossoming Caesar' [4,13,12–22]. These self-reflexive glances at changing conditions in Jacobean theatre explain why the crisis of allegiance occurs in this play with Enobarbus's fatalistic realization that 'loyalty well held to fools does make / Our faith mere folly' [3,13,41], and why Shakespeare makes this 'masterleaver' die not, as he does in Plutarch, of disease, but of a broken heart. Just as the fall of the prince is caused by indecisiveness in the world of the *Trauerspiel*, to which Antony succumbs, explains Benjamin, 'so does unfaithfulness characterize the courtier'.[108] Thus in this story the theme of professional betrayal and desertion is keyed to the sickening physical sensation of literally *turning* for the composition of a picture, and to the visual 'diminution' of the entertainer [3,13,197] who tags behind 'Caesar in his triumph' [138] so slavishly he looks no bigger than 'an Egyptian puppet' [5,2,204]:

> Vanish, or I shall give thee thy deserving
> And blemish Caesar's triumph. Let him take thee
> And hoist thee up to the shouting plebeians;
> Follow his chariot, like the greatest spot
> Of all thy sex; most monster-like be shown
> For poor'st dimunitives, for doits ...
>
> [4,12,32–7]

Recollections of actors 'enclouded' in Caesar's show suggest that what makes them seem 'monster-like' in *Antony and Cleopatra* is when the 'mechanic slaves / With aprons, rules, and hammers' who supervise the scenery 'Uplift [them] to the view' [5,2,205–8]. These remarks, always taken to belittle the 'smelly populace', thus sound more like asides about Jones and his technicians, as what nauseates Cleopatra is that she and her ladies will appear as much diminished as the onlookers will to her when she is 'shown / In Rome' [204].[109] Conflating the cloud machine with the 'thick breaths' of its mechanics, it is the picture-making operatives of 'Caesar's triumph' she scorns, not the playgoers of the Globe. There is a premonition here of Jonson's eventual contempt for those who 'cry up the Machine' that lifts 'The majesty of Juno in the clouds', as functionaries of a 'money-get, mechanic age'. The laureate would come to ridicule Jones as a malodorous cook, baffling 'politique Eyes' with a 'mere perspective of an Inch board'.[110] Likewise, Shakespeare's 'overflowing' actors dread their foreshortening when seen 'with the sober eye' of a 'Demurring' spectator like 'dull Octavia', with her 'cold and still conversation' [2,6,120], 'modest eyes' and 'still conclusion' [4,16,28–30], since her artistic ideal is the reverse of Pygmalion's, being more that of 'A statue than a breather' [3,3,21]:

> I will not wait pinioned at your master's court,
> Nor once be chastised with the sober eye
> Of dull Octavia. Shall they hoist me up
> And show me to the shouting varletry
> Of censuring Rome? Rather a ditch in Egypt
> Be gentle grave unto me! Rather on Nilus' mud
> Lay me stark naked, and let the waterflies
> Blow me into abhorring!
>
> [5,2,52–9]

'Rather make my country's high pyramides my gibbet / And hang me up in chains', retorts Cleopatra, at the prospect of being 'hoist' in an Egyptian masque. In Shakespeare's professional terms, she would prefer to act beside 'The kings o'th'earth' [3,6,68], amid 'flies and gnats' [3,13,169] on Bankside, than be strung up among the King's Men at Whitehall. She knows Antony's humiliation when he returned to court was his inability to 'play one scene of excellent dissembling, and let it look / Like perfect honour' [1,3,78]. For in 'th'world' of the playhouse the Globe performers' nightmare is to be 'laughed at' [2,2,35] or 'traduced for levity' [3,7,13] on an unfamiliar stage where they are blind to their own faults. So Shakespeare's paranoiac visual thematics of the 'Evil Eye' – the fear of the unseen look – here has a pressing occupational context in 'thoughts of horror' [5,2,62] about the chains and pulleys of the Stuart masque. For in this play which values the interactive gaze of the 'shouting plebeians' who 'crouch' in the playhouse pit above the censorious 'look' of a seated elite, a theatrical 'boggler' literally loses 'the world' by losing contact with audience response:

> You have been a boggler ever.
> But when we in our viciousness grow hard –
> O, misery on't! – the wise gods seel our eyes,
> In our own filth drop our clear judgements, make us
> Adore our errors, laugh at's while we strut
> To our confusion.
>
> [3,13,110–15]

With the creaturely image of blind game birds strutting in their filth, Shakespeare inscribes his own apprehension about a drama written for the 'kings' of the Globe ensnared in a golden cage at court. So if advocates of the courtly aesthetic were the *avant-garde* of the 1600s, Whitney comments, this refusal to be 'pinioned' by pictorial perspective might perhaps mark the writer as a cultural conservative, but it also situates him as the precursor of Brecht, whose 'alienation effect' linked life inside and outside the play by requiring the 'slippery people' [1,2,186] to look through the illusionistic stage.[111] In *Antony and Cleopatra* this anti-illusionism, which makes the play, as Weimann says, resistant to 'the symbolism of socially remote privilege', means that the contrast between the city and the suburb, the marble decorum of the 'imperious show' and the 'dungy earth' of the wharf, is in fact between competitive playhouse and palace presentations of *the play itself*.[112] For here it is by cheapening the court that the boy-player seduces the 'common body', and by 'commoning' the noble Roman with 'tears that live in an onion' [1,2,167] that a Burbage thrills the 'understanders' in the pit. The Prince of Denmark warned the players never to 'o'erstep the modesty of nature'. But it is precisely when their pantomime is 'overdone or come tardy off' that the lovers in *Antony and Cleopatra* 'set on a whole theatre' by making 'the unskilful laugh' [*Hamlet*, 3,2,20–42]. For like theatre-mad Achilles crying 'Excellent!' as mincing Patroclus mimics the heroes as near as 'extremest ends / Of parallels' [*Troilus*, 1,3,153–70] in a perspective set, a paying public prefers to see the 'strutting player' guy greatness than have it 'windowed' in some neoclassical arch:

> Contemning Rome, he has done all this and more
> In Alexandria. Here's the manner of't:
> I'th'market-place on a tribunal silvered,

Cleopatra and himself in chairs of gold
Were publicly enthroned.

[5,6,1–5]

Antony's enthroning of Cleopatra in the 'common showplace' would seem to make their 'Egyptian bacchanals' [2,7,98] synonymous with Shakespeare's Bankside 'field of feasts'. Yet it also hints how by 1607 the Globe might appear a 'vile world' [5,2,304], or a 'world … not worth leave-taking' [288], compared to the 'graver business' that 'Frowns at this levity' from Whitehall [2,7,115–16]. For though Shakespeare's play is usually thought to oppose Roman anti-theatricality and Egyptian theatricality, in a contest in which the 'exotic, foreign, stagy queen' defeats Roman historiography, this interpretation is overly schematic.[113] More acute is the analysis by Stephen Mullaney, who, while he never mentions *Antony and Cleopatra*, relates how its actors were being corralled by the incorporation of the Liberties. When the theatre moved to the suburbs 'a gap had opened in the social fabric', he explains, an opening where brothel and playhouse coexisted, which provided the Elizabethan drama with an 'anamorphic perspective' on the age. But by 1607 the old forms of licence were falling under Crown control. The upshot, Mullaney concludes, would be the abdication to royal power that the forced reconciliations of Shakespeare's Romances expressed.[114] But meanwhile it is the vertigo of this occupational 'turn' or professional betrayal which gives the final 'gaudy night' [3,13,185] of *Antony and Cleopatra* its gravity:

ANTONY: Love, I am full of lead.
        Some wine,
        Within there, and our viands! Fortune knows
        We scorn her most when most she offers blows.

[3,11,73–6]

What characterizes the heavy 'bacchanals' of *Antony and Cleopatra* is self-consciousness. For as Antony and his troupe 'make a jolly march' with 'hacked targets', and he orders trumpeters to blast the city 'Applauding our approach' [4,8,30–9], there is a pathos in this play about its own 'place i'th'story' [3,13,46], and a 'conspiracy with the audience' which stirs 'late Elizabethan memories of the *platea*', in Weimann's words.[115] In the old trouper's charge to his 'sad captains' to 'Fill all our bowls once more' and 'have one more gaudy night' [3,13,182], we can hear the author sounding 'These drums! These trumpets, flutes!' to let 'Neptune', or King Christian, hear 'we bid a loud farewell / To these great fellows' [2,7,126–8]. A similar sentimentality colours Cleopatra's memories of times 'I laughed him out of patience … and next morn … I drunk him to his bed; / Then put my tires and mantles on him, whilst / I wore his sword' [2,5,18–23]. Shakespeare had never denied the scandal in a trade which made 'greatness very familiar, if not ridiculous' in this fashion, as Wotton complained, for he had absorbed anti-theatricality into his plays.[116] But now he made the outrage a defiant swansong, as he harped upon the fact that the roisterers who dance with the royals at the palace vulgarize that royalty in the 'slime and ooze' [2,7,21] of their own 'varying shore': like the 'wrangling queen' [1,1,59] who hops 'forty paces through the public street' [2,2,234] to turn the geometry of angles into angling, or the 'brave Emperor' [2,7,97] who 'fishes, drinks, and wastes / The lamps of night in revel; is not more manlike than Cleopatra, nor the queen of Ptolemy / More womanly than he' [1,4,4–7].

A wonderful piece of work

'Now he'll outstare the lightning', sighs Enobarbus at Antony's defiance of Caesar's *son et lumière*, as if 'A diminution in our captain's brain / Restores his heart' [3,13,197–201]. Likewise Shakespeare's play seems to identify with everything in theatre that must have looked *diminished* in a perspective set. 'Mannerism is the scar left by expression in a language no longer capable of expression', Adorno reflected. He was referring to Mahler's jolting from marches to waltzes, as what is retrograde in his music clashes with what is revolutionary, and 'how they wear each other away' becomes its theme.[117] Such juxtaposition itself constituted a resistance to subjectivization.[118] Likewise, Smith hears wilful anachronism in the acoustic world of *Antony and Cleopatra*, which is unique in challenging the low-frequency that predominates as Shakespeare's troupe matures, by allowing Cleopatra to break the bass line, and by puncturing the sonority of its Roman scenes with 'drums and trumpets' from the playhouse of the 1590s, until 'Caesar re-enters to take control of the action … [and] the field of sound'.[119] The out-moded sound world of the play thereby amplifies the vulgarization of the Stuart court which tempts biographers to identify in its queen a portrait of the dead Elizabeth, who also liked to moor her barge beside the playhouses, so that 'A strange invisible perfume' would hit 'the sense / Of the adjacent wharfs' [2,2,218–19].[120]

Critics have long noted how *Antony and Cleopatra* lives in remembrance of things past.[121] As Tennenhouse writes, by endowing Cleopatra with the features of carnival Shakespeare makes this play into an elegy for the signs and symbols of Elizabethan sovereignty.[122] In fact, Enobarbus's report on Cleopatra's vessel recalls the equally impractical and symbolic galleon of 'rivelled gold', its masts 'hollow pyramides of silver plate', that Dido promises Aeneas in Marlowe's meta-play of the Chapel Royal, where that pseudo-antique toy was first performed. If *Antony and Cleopatra* is haunted by *Dido Queen of Carthage*, however, it is because Marlowe's Aeneas, whom the African queen also dresses as a player, points the way out of this infantilism by rejecting the dry dock of the Elizabethan court for the open waters of commerce at the Bankside Rose, or the body of the monarch for the body of the metropolis.[123] What saves *Antony and Cleopatra* from neo-Elizabethan nostalgia is therefore the self-reflexivity with which it affirms how it is the 'sweating labour' [1,3,93] of the toiling playhouse workers which not only keeps the 'seeming' ship afloat, but converts all this pragmatic tacking and trimming into art:

> Her gentlewomen, like the Neireides,
> So many mermaids, tended her i'th'eyes,
> And made their bends adornings. At the helm
> A seeming mermaid steers. The silken tackle
> Swell with the touches of those flower-soft hands
> That yarely frame the office.
>
> [2,2,212–17]

'Yare, yare', Cleopatra chivvies the maids she commands to 'Give me my robe. Put on my crown' [5,2,271–4]; and the nautical term confirms the impact made by Marlowe's symbolization of the Thames-side theatre as a ship, albeit of fools. Thus in *Antony and Cleopatra* a belief that if 'thou knews't / The royal occupation, thou should'st see / A workman in't' bestows sovereignty on this ship-shape house, where 'your soldier's dress' [2,4,5] is 'buckled well' because the 'queen's a squire / More tight at this than thou' [4,4,11–18]. As Yachnin notes, Shakespeare's grip on his real conditions of production is secured by this artisanal ethos, for his yardstick of value remains the 'monstrous labour [2,7,12] of his profession,

and the capacity of its waterside fraternity 'To do that thing ...
Which shackles accidents and bolts up change' [5,2,5].[124] So this
text is full of manual metaphors to do with cutting lace [1,3,71], or
patching cloth [2,2,55], as though 'mechanic compliment' [4,4,32]
is being paid to 'the tailors of the earth' [1,2,65] for their 'tires and
mantles' [2,5,22], and the myth of Hercules dressed by Omphale is
relocated to the wardrobe of the Globe. Thus, Eros, 'one that ties
his points' [3,13,159], is told by his master 'To do thus / I learned
of thee' [4,15,102–3]; for as Antony assures his dressers, the reason
'kings have been your fellows' is related to performance: 'I wish ... I
might do you service / So good as you have done' [4,2,13–19]. The
'contradiction between artisanal base and absolutist superstructure
characterized Shakespeare's dramaturgy even in his final plays',
Walter Cohen observes; while Weimann adds that self-awareness
about earning a living from leisure always translates Shakespearean
drama back into the world of work.[125] Yet all through these *works*
the menial labour involved in the production of the play *as play* is
valorized as what Herbert Marcuse called 'a counterforce against
aggressive and exploitative socialization'; and here it is her creator's craftiness in making obsequious 'bends' to Stuart monarchy
his own 'adornings' that validates Cleopatra's 'work-a-day' [1,2,47]
world:[126]

ANTONY: Would I had never seen her!
ENOBARBUS: O, sir, you had then left unseen a wonderful piece
            of work, which not to have been blessed withal
            would have discredited your travel.
                                              [1,2,138–40]

Transposing the 'Alexandrian revels' of the masque into 'th'common
showplace' where a queen dances 'in the public eye ... In the habili-
ments of the goddess' [3,6,12–18], and an emperor takes a 'turn of
tippling with a slave' [1,4,19], *Antony and Cleopatra* foregrounds
the double duty of the King's Men as private and public players with
a reflexivity that recalls Bourdieu's comment that Flaubert's fiction
'supplies all the tools necessary for its sociological analysis'.[127] It is a
function of the play's 'exploratory and analytical intelligence' that it
should be upfront about its mixed origins, but it is also a symptom
its contradictory commission.[128] In fact, the entire action could be
said to consist of variations on the performative predicament generated by incompatible pressures of the palace and the playhouse, as

from the entry of the courier with the news from Rome that 'grates' Antony, its creative dilemma is posed by what Cleopatra terms Caesar's 'powerful mandate': '"Do this or this ... Perform't, or else we damn thee' [*1,1,19*]. With such 'news the time's with labour' [*3,7,80*], so there is hardly a scene that does not turn on a letter, nor prove how 'bad news infects the teller' [*1,2,96*]. Thus, beaten for reporting 'good and bad together', Cleopatra's agent avoids being 'whipped with wire' [*2,5,54; 66*] by telling her what she wants to hear, and is duly rewarded: 'There's gold for thee. / Thou must not take my former sharpness ill' [*3,3,35*]. Yet 'The gold I give thee will I melt and pour / Down thy ill-uttering throat', the queen threatens [*2,5,35*]; and her chamberlain sums up the resulting crisis of representation: 'Good majesty, / Herod of Jewry dare not look upon you / But when you are well pleased' [*3,3,3*]. In the corridors of princes, 'Truth should be silent' [*2,2,112*], Enobarbus therefore concludes; and this wisdom is confirmed when, after pretending 'Who tells me true ... I hear him as he flattered' [*1,2,98–106*], Antony orders the emissary Thidias whipped, so he will be 'sorry to follow Caesar in his triumph' [*3,13,135*]:

ANTONY: What art thou fellow?
THIDIAS: One that performs
             The bidding of the fullest man, and worthiest
             To have command obeyed.
ENOBARBUS: You will be whipped.
                                  [*3,13,86–8*]

Throughout *Antony and Cleopatra* the same representational impasse seems to figure the dramatist's chafing at co-option into 'the royal occupation' of an entertainer at the court. Early on, for example, the Soothsayer, who tellingly earns his living reading hands, gives a master class in the old Shakespearean reticence, when he denies Cleopatra's maids particulars of their fortunes, clamming up with 'I have said' [*1,2,57*]. Later, however, this Egyptian 'charmer' [*Othello, 3,4,55*] wishes he had never left the riverside for Rome: 'Would I had never come from thence' [*2,3,11*]. This was perhaps as outspoken as the author dared to be about his own summons from the Liberty of Southwark to service at Whitehall. But in a study of the innumerable bit parts in the play, M.M. Mahood details how its dressers, messengers and slaves in fact provide discrepant viewpoints on the action by responding to vassalage with

the self-awareness of a chorus: 'In a play where almost every incidental character exists in dependence' these subordinates are thus
more than mere foils, for Shakespeare allows us to glimpse how the
logic of service works, by 'enabling us to see through the eyes of a
host of watchers and reporters'.[129] In literally *waiting* on their social
betters, the eunuchs, clerks and skivvies of *Antony and Cleopatra*
thereby acquire an 'extra dimension' as figures for the familiar irony
of the power of weakness the play deepens, the radical passivity of
the Shakespearean cringe which is explained by Antony's lieutenant
Ventidius:

> A lower place, note well,
> May make too bold an act ... and ambition,
> The soldier's virtue, rather makes choice of loss
> Than gain which darkens him.

> [3,1,12–15]

By th'height, the lowness, or the mean

In *Hamlet* and *King Lear* Shakespeare as 'minimus' pushed a theatrics of non-performance to the edge of professional suicide. With
Antony and Cleopatra, however, he explored the virtuous necessity of the 'choice of loss' and nominal compliance staged in the
Romances, where it is said that 'Kings are earth's gods', and 'Will
think me speaking though I swear to silence'. 'Prince, pardon me,
or strike me if you please', exclaims the wise counsellor in *Pericles*,
'I cannot be much lower than my knees' [1,146; 2,19–20; 51–2].
Likewise, submission to the pictorial turn here figures as a duty,
and when Antony berates himself it is in the technical terms of this
'royal occupation', in which he becomes 'A workman' [4,4,17],
pledging that though 'I have not kept my square', his work will
'be done by th'rule' [2,3,6–7], lest 'labour / Mars what it does'
[4,14,47]. From such perspectival allusions Lisa Hopkins guesses
Shakespeare must have been familiar with the pseudo-religion
of Freemasonry.[130] What supports this intriguing hunch is that,
according to his assistant Nicholas Stone, from 1607 to 1652 the
Grand Master of the English Lodge was none other than Jones,
whose designs frequently incorporated Masonic symbols, like
the triangles and compasses worn by Theory and Practice in the
masque *Albion's Triumph*.[131] As Frances Yates chronicled, Masons
always claim the ancient Egyptian geometry 'invented to cope with

inundations of the Nile' was transmitted to London from Scotland when James revived the English Lodge under Jones, whom they revere as 'undoubtedly a Freemason'.[132] If so, what is striking is the irreverent profanity with which, for all its talk of the human form as 'this mortal house' [*5,2,50*], this 'triple-turned' play about measuring the time and tide breaks the esoteric secrets of those supposed 'Egyptian' mysteries that sealed the 'great men's fellowship' [*2,7,10*], when it introduces the brotherhood of 'good fellows' [*4,2,20*] reeling in their cups:

> ANTONY: Thus do they, sir: they take the flow o'th' Nile
> By certain scales i'th' pyramid. They know
> By th'height, the lowness, or the mean, if dearth
> Or foison follow. The higher the Nile swells
> The more it promises ...
>
> [*2,7,16–20*]

Deferring to the supposedly invisible power of the Worshipful Fraternity, 'With greasy aprons, rules and hammers' [*5,2,205–6*], Shakespeare debunks Jones's secret society in his 'Egyptian' play by taking its egalitarian rigmarole for truth. This reversal of work and play climaxes in the 'heavy sport' [*4,15,32*] when Cleopatra heaves a dying Antony up to her 'monument': a 'secret house of death' [*4,2,83*], 'Proportioned' [*4,16,4–5*] to the 'high pyramides' [*5,2,60*], if Jones had an invisible Masonic hand in it, but at the Globe simply the tiring-house loft. A 'right gypsy', the queen always played 'fast and loose' [*4,13,28*]; and the 'commoning' by which she here transmutes Roman law into Romany lore foretells the risqué parody of Masonic ritual in *The Magic Flute*.[133] As in Mozart's opera, the esotericism of the 'Egyptian' mystery is restored in *Antony and Cleopatra* to the artisan milieu from which it came. But there is an even closer analogue to this demystification in Velázquez, who in meta-pictures depicting artistic process like *The Spinners* shows workers in large scale, and the royalty they themselves depict miniaturized, or like puppets in a tarnished mirror at the back. With no fewer than ten mirrors in his studio, the 'Prince of Painters' was supreme master of perspective and the singular manner, who aspired like Shakespeare to nobility. Yet as Alpers concludes, the effect of his reversal of social distinction was to disavow the myth of psychic distance, and to affirm the labour in the artwork he represented (in *The Spinners*, a tapestry copied from Titian):

At court Velázquez existed within a kind of prison ... But [he] took the 'cárcel dorada' and made it an enabling condition of his art. His sense of singularity is not only a quality of his paint, but an attribute his paint gives to human beings of whatever station. This might not have been Velázquez's own view of the world and of the crowd of people in it, but in his paintings, the singularity of Velázquez is not his alone.[134]

The golden cage of Baroque pictorialism turned the clowns and maids to non-being; but Velázquez restores these little people to life, for as Alpers observes, by reversing the court's perspective 'His painting equalizes ... he frees representation from any simple relating of importance and size'.[135] It is in this 'triple-turning' of pictorial illusion back upon itself that the analogy between Shakespeare's stage and contemporary painting therefore becomes significant. For in *Antony and Cleopatra* the captive queen likewise warns Caesar to look behind him in his triumph: 'behold / How pomp is followed! Mine will now be yours / And should we shift estates, yours would be mine' [5,2,146–8]. So unlike the Antony and Cleopatra of other Renaissance dramatizations, Shakespeare's lovers address menials and retainers as 'friends', and, while Caesar chides Octavia for resembling a 'market maid' [3,6,51], Cleopatra is proud to be 'No more but e'en a woman, and commanded / By such poor passion as the maid that milks / And does the meanest chores' [4,16,76]. Thus a play so concerned 'By th'height, the lowness, or the mean' of social and psychic space does turn in the end on 'diminution': but the opposite way to what had been prescribed. For as Judith Weill points out in her study of Shakespearean service, *Antony and Cleopatra* is one of a series of plays the dramatist wrote at this time which merge the fates of masters and servants when a household sinks like a 'Leak'd ... barque' [*Timon, 4,2,19*], as if his own divided sense of obligation had forced him to notice the motto inscribed over the gates at Whitehall: '*In servitude dolor, in libertate labor*': 'In service pain, in freedom toil'. He therefore makes slaves and masters mimic each other, Weill argues, because of an interest not only in the difference between service and servitude, the true friend and 'slave of no more trust / Than love that's hired' [5,2,55], but in the scams and ruses that allow dependants to 'survive by accommodation'; as Charmian pertly tells her mistress that she will 'sing but after you' [1,5,72]:

It is evident that both Enobarbus and Charmian practise a type of 'cosmesis' ... a strategy for camouflaging one's own vulnerability by trivializing oneself. Yet ... these servants are potentially liberating and creative flatterers [who] understand Cleopatra so well because within the great house ménage they share, they must employ similar skills.[136]

Singing a song of 'My master and my lord' [*5,2,122; 186*], the servants of *Antony and Cleopatra* make this play an extended exploration of Shakespeare's survival strategy of passive aggression in his golden cage, but also a showpiece for the art of answering the sovereign back in his own voice, 'sending him', as Cleopatra puts it, 'The greatness he has got' [*30*]. The effect, Weill argues, is to revalue the kind of wily accommodation featured in that most sardonic Shakespearean treatment of 'the beholder's share', when the old politician successively agrees with the domineering prince that 'yonder cloud' is 'like a camel', a weasel, or 'very like a whale'. 'They fool me to the top of my bent', Hamlet complains [*Hamlet, 3,2,346–53*]. But suppose that Polonius is being merely tactical, 'cautiously deferential' in adapting to the princely perspective, conjectures Weill, who finds the same crafty pliability in the 'rural fellow' Cleopatra claims 'brings me liberty' with his asps, when he speaks about a satisfied customer that 'makes a very good report o'th'worm' which killed her [*5,2,229–48*]. Shakespeare similarly converts the poison of flattery into the kiss of death by which Cleopatra enacts her resolution, in this account, when 'in her most startling act of imitation' she takes her cue from the artful peasant cunning of the snake charmer, and deceives Caesar into thinking she will disappoint her own claque and that 'He'll lead me in triumph'.[137] 'Though I am mad I will not bite' she laughs; but in fact her eagerness for the 'Poor venomous fool' to 'kiss' its victim becomes the key to the metadramatic 'hissing' of the entire play, and to its strategy of having creeping 'creatures / Turn all to serpents' [*2,5,78–9*]: 'O could'st thou speak, / That I might hear thee call great Caesar ass / Unpolicied' [*5,2,296–8*].

Sovereign creature

The worm turns in *Antony and Cleopatra* enough for the queen to be seen as that paradoxical thing, 'A most sovereign creature' [*5,2,80*], by her gaolers. Julia Lupton has argued that Shakespearean drama consistently works in this way to reverse the creative–destructive relation of the sovereign and the creature, releasing the creativity of the one 'produced or controlled by an agent, author, master, or tyrant', by figuring 'another model of humanity in the motif of the creature'. Caliban, cursing the master who sends adders to hiss him 'into madness' [*Tempest, 2,2,14*], is the archetype of such 'actively passive' servitude.[138] But Cleopatra's intuition that 'My desolation does begin to make / A better life' [*5,2,1*] is a similar affirmation of the creaturely sovereignty of 'bare life'.[139] Certainly, to hiss 'kiss' and 'ass' in his Augustan tragedy, yet still go 'unpolicied', was *her* creator's own Rabelaisian response to the cringing theatrics of Stuart power. Editors like to think that this 'most courtly' of Shakespeare's plays was commissioned as an 'imperial work in a special sense', acclaiming James 'the "Emperor" of Great Britain'.[140] But its hissing insinuation from within the Jacobean system instead suggests that, unlike Octavia, a 'creature' who is 'no such thing' [*3,3,39*], Cleopatra becomes 'a lass unparalleled' [*306*] precisely because she ruins the perspective of such a Roman triumph, not by refusing the turning picture, but by reversing its reversal, as the dramatist himself buckled under the absolutist rules of the new visual technology, the philosopher Christine Buci-Glucksmann maintains in her study of Shakespeare's 'tragedy of shadows', *the better to subvert them.*[141]

From representation to reality and back to representation: to 'triple-turn' Caesar's turning-picture, 'fool their preparation, and conquer / Their most absurd intents', means Cleopatra must exploit her 'sweet dependency' as 'fortune's vassal' [*26–9*] to play 'a noble act' such as Antony might 'rouse himself / To praise' [*275–6*]. Like the first English actresses, required to perform before perspective sets and shutters which produced 'a kind of pornographic painting brought to life', the queen pledges her captor she will 'Hang in what place you please', amid the 'scutcheons and your signs of conquest' of his *tableau vivant* [*131*], while knowing 'he words me, that I should not / Be noble to myself' [*5,2,187–8*].[142] What she has to gain from state subsidy in protective custody, her conqueror promises, will be intellectual freedom: 'If you apply yourself to our intents ... you shall find / A benefit in this change ... Therefore be cheered, / Make not your thoughts your prisons' [*122;180*]. 'Thought is free', James likewise poeticized; to which Jonson responded that a poet's role was therefore to be 'thy servant, but not thy slave'.[143] The emperor's suspicion, after he arrives too late for Cleopatra's *pièce-de-resistance*, that 'She levelled at our purposes, and, being royal, / Took her own way' [*325–7*], can therefore be read as Shakespeare's wishful-thinking about the limits of Crown control, and an apologia for the kowtowing to Stuart ideology with which the King's Men elbowed at this time to become 'dominated dominators', in Bourdieu's phrase, 'within the field of dominant power'.[144] For Cleopatra's staged suicide, 'her Egyptian revision of the Roman death', contrasts with Antony's botched efforts to 'play the Roman fool' [*Macbeth, 5,10,1*] precisely in its 'levelling' of its own artistic space:[145]

> He brings me liberty.
> My resolution's placed, and I have nothing
> Of woman in me. Now from head to foot
> I am marble-constant; now the fleeting moon
> No planet is of mine.
>
> [*5,2,237–41*]

Antony had dreaded 'bending down his corrigible neck' to be 'windowed' in the Roman show. But whether or not the author himself 'bore the canopy' [Sonnet 125] in such 'penetrative shame' on one of James's triumphal arches, along with the other King's Men assigned court cloth for their livery, it is tempting to include Shakespeare in the contract Cleopatra strikes to serve her vanquisher on condition he redeems her debts.[146] Viewed like this, the emperor's connoisseurship, 'coming to see performed the dreaded act' [*330*], after Charmian has arranged her 'tremblingly … trimming up the diadem / On her dead mistress' [*340*], looks like the consecration of an art exempted from the monarchy by the monarch himself.[147] As Hugh Grady comments, Antony is rescued from the stalemate of the *Trauerspiel* by the 'aesthetic possibilities' of the drama in which Cleopatra makes his character live: 'the legend of the two lovers, embodied meta-aesthetically in the play we are watching'.[148] Yet it is the sovereign's tardiness on the scene which puts this aspect in the shade, when he proves 'too sure an augurer', and the very spectacle he presaged comes true [*323*]. Cleopatra's dying posture, feeding the 'baby' viper 'That sucks the nurse asleep', has been described as a perverse Nativity painting; but with its invocation of Sirius, the 'eastern star' [*298*] that was supposed to herald a 'time of universal peace', but that in fact portended the Massacre of Innocents, it is also an ambiguous homage to the messianic political theology of the Stuart state.[149] 'Do this or this ... Perform't, or else', had been Caesar's ultimatum. Now, as he rushes into the monument, the future Augustus is presented with the 'solemn show' [*354*] he always 'purposed', and the work of art that greets him is 'All dead' [*319*], as breathless as a statue, and as perfect as a picture.

'What work is here, Charmian? Is this well done?' [*316*]: the question prompted by the still life of the dead queen regaled with 'crown and all' [*227–31*] carries irresistible biographical significance if *Antony and Cleopatra* was 'windowed' at Whitehall. Then, Cleopatra's cheating of the king's commission would take on meta-aesthetic status similar to that of the canvas reversed towards the viewer in Velázquez's own equally epochal staging of the princess and her maids. In this 'representation of representation', as Foucault termed it, the impertinent backside of the picture on which the artist portrays himself at work constitutes in its blankness an unprecedented refusal of the royal expectation, figured by a chamberlain entering the studio, to repeat the artistry of those Renaissance masterpieces by the likes of Titian which are sunk in shadow on the walls.[150] Instead the body of the king has been displaced by the vacancy of the painting. Likewise, and with comparable illusionism, Shakespeare has his queen decry the 'squeaking Cleopatra' who will 'boy' her 'greatness', in an allusion to George Chapman's *Tragedy of Byron*, where the Queen of France had lately been travestied 'in the posture of a whore' [*216–17*].[151] So, if King James saw himself reflected as the patron of *Antony and Cleopatra*, we might infer, it would have been with something like the negation of those monarchs elided from reality in the mirror of *Las Meninas*. For in Shakespeare's drama, too, all the rules of pictorial technology have been transcended by an art that gives itself leave 'To play till doomsday' [*231*], as the work we are watching defers just enough to correct the twisted slant of the Stuart crown, before asserting its own ever-living sovereignty:

> Downy windows, close,
> And golden Phoebus never be beheld
> Of eyes again so royal. Your crown's awry.
> I'll mend it, and then play –

> [*5,2,306–9*]

Notes

1 Ernst Gombrich, *Art and Illusion: A Study in the Psychology of Pictorial Representation* (London: Phaidon, 1960), pp.154 and 61. See also Ernst Gombrich, 'The Renaissance Conception of Artistic Progress', in *Norm and Form* (London: Phaidon, 1966), p.7. 'Mimics a perspective picture': Marguerite A. Tassi, 'O'erpicturing Apelles: Shakespeare's *Paragone* with Painting in *Antony and Cleopatra*', in *'Antony and Cleopatra': New Critical Essays*, ed. Sara Munson Deats (London: Routledge, 2005), p.297. For the history of anamorphosis, see Fred Leeman, *Hidden Images: Games of Perception, Anamorphosistic Art and Illiusions from the Renaissance to the Present* (New York: 1976); and Marie-Louise d'Otrange Mastai, *Illusion in Art: Trompe l'Oeil: A History of Pictorial Illusionism* (New York: Abaris Books, 1975).

2 Martin Jay, *Downcast Eyes: The Denigration of Vision in Twentieth-Century French Thought* (Berkeley: University of California Press, 1993), pp.44–5.

3 'Speaking of Perspective': Sebastiano Serlio, *The First Booke of Archirecture* (London: Robert Peake, 1611), F26; Robert Weimann, *Author's Pen and Actor's Voice: Playing and Writing in Shakespeare's Theatre* (Cambridge: Cambridge University Press, 2000), pp.186 and 189. For the court performance of *Othello* 'bordered by a prototype proscenium arch', see John Orrell, 'The Theaters', in *A New History of Early English Drama*, eds John D. Cox and David Scott Kastan (New York: Columbia University Press, 1997), pp.93–112, here p.95.

4 Gombrich, op. cit. (note 1), p.161.

5 See Caroline Spurgeon, *Shakespeare's Imagery and What It Tells Us* (Cambridge: Cambridge University Press, 1935), pp.194–5; C.H. Hobday, 'Why the Sweets Melted: A Study in Shakespeare's Imagery', *Shakespeare Quarterly*, 16 (1963), 3; Meredith Ann Skura, '"Dogs, Licking, Candy, Melting" and the Flatterer's False Glass', in *Shakespeare the Actor and the Purposes of Playing* (Chicago: University of Chicago Press, 1993), pp.166–9. For fluidity as the sign of effeminate subjugation, see Gail Kern Paster, *The Body Embarrassed: Drama and the Disciplines of Shame in Early Modern England* (Ithaca: Cornell University Press, 1993), pp.23–63, 79–84 and 98–9.

6 John F. Danby, *Poets on Fortunes Hill: Studies in Sidney, Shakespeare, Beaumont and Fletcher* (London: Faber & Faber, 1952), p.131.

7 Quoted Gombrich, op. cit. (note 1), p.159.

8 Weimann, op. cit. (note 3), pp.248–9; 'increasingly strained relations': Jonathan Baldo, *The Unmasking of Drama: Contested Representation in Shakespeare's Tragedies* (Detroit: Wayne State University Press,

1996), p.135; 'simultaneous wonder': Lucy Gent, *Picture and Poetry, 1560–1620* (Leamington Spa: James Hall, 1981), pp.61–2.

9 Erwin Panoksky, *Perspective as Symbolic Form*, trans. Christopher Wood (Cambridge, Mass.: Zone Books, 1991), p.3.

10 Gombrich, op. cit. (note 1), pp.162–5.

11 William West, 'The Idea of a Theater: Humanist Ideology and the Imaginary Stage in Early Modern Europe', *Renaissance Drama*, 28 (1999), 245–87, here 249.

12 Gombrich, op. cit. (note 1), pp.162–5; Anthony Blunt, *Artistic Theory in Italy* (Oxford: Oxford University Press, 1962), p.100. For a magisterial overview of the recall to order after the Mannerist 'liberation of space', see William J. Bouwsma, *The Waning of the Renaissance, 1550–1640* (New Haven: Yale University Press, 2000), pp.129–30 and 143–64.

13 'The new style': Anthony Dawson and Paul Yachnin, *The Culture of Playgoing in Shakespeare's England: A Collaborative Debate* (Cambridge: Cambridge University Press, 2001), p.78; 'Something understood': George Herbert, 'Prayer (I)', in *The English Poems of George Herbert*, ed. C.A. Patrides (London: Dent, 1974), p.71, l. 14.

14 Linda Levy Peck, 'Introduction', *The Mental World of the Jacobean Court* (Cambridge: Cambridge University Press, 1991), p.12.

15 Malcolm Smuts, *Court Culture and the Origins of a Royalist Tradition in Early Stuart England* (Philadelphia: University of Pennsylvania Press, 1987), pp.157–8; Lucy Gent, *Picture and Poetry, 1560–1620: Relations between Literature and the Visual Arts in the English Renaissance* (Leamington Spa: James Hall, 1981), pp.74–5; Roy Strong, *Henry Prince of Wales and England's Lost Renaissance* (London: Thames and Hudson, 1986), pp.109–10.

16 'Most anamorphic': Sara Munson Deats, 'Shakespeare's Anamorphic Drama: A Survey of *Antony and Cleopatra* in Criticism, on Stage, and on Screen', in Deats, op. cit. (note 1), p.1. See also Wylie Sypher, *Four Stage of Renaissance Style: Transformations in Art and Literature, 1400–1700* (New York: Doubleday, 1955), pp.171–2.

17 Andrew Gurr and Mariko Ichikawa, *Staging in Shakespeare's Theatres* (Oxford: Oxford University Press, 2000), p.8.

18 Ernest Gilman, *The Curious Perspective: Literary and Pictorial Wit in the Seventeenth Century* (New Haven: Yale University Press, 1978), p.14; Jay, op. cit. (note 2), pp.46–8. For illusionist spectacle as an instrument of absolutism, see especially José Antonio Maravall, *Culture of the Baroque: Analysis of a Historical Structure*, trans. Terry Cochran (Minneapolis: Minnesota University Press, 1986).

19 Arnold Hauser, *The Social History of Art: Two: Renaissance, Mannerism, Baroque* (London: Routledge, 1962), pp.94–5. For the

origins of the Baroque, the standard accounts remain John Rupert Martin, *Baroque* (New York: Harper & Row, 1977); and Germain Bazin, *The Baroque: Principles: Styles, Modes, Themes*, trans. Pat Wardroper (New York: Norton, 1968). But for more recent debate about its relations with Mannerism, and the borderline between the two styles, see Gauvin Alexander Bailey, *Between Renaissance and the Baroque: Jesuit Art in Rome, 1565–1610* (Toronto: Toronto University Press, 2003), pp.22–30.

20 'Achievement of the stupendous': Peter Davidson, *The Universal Baroque* (Manchester: Manchester University Press, 2007), p.11; 'the monarch is identified with God': Carl Schmitt, *Political Theology*, trans. George Schwab (Chicago: University of Chicago Press, 1985), p.46.

21 'Not the source': Macolm Smuts, 'Cultural Diversity and Cultural Change at the Court of James I', in Peck, op. cit. (note 14), p.106; Walter Benjamin, *The Origin of German Tragic Drama*, trans. John Osborne (London: Verso, 1998), p.92.

22 Roland Barthes, *Sade, Fourier, Loyola*, trans. Richard Miller (New York: 1976), p.85.

23 Christopher Pye, *The Vanishing: Shakespeare, the Subject, and Early Modern Culture* (Durham, NC: Duke University Press, 2000), pp.91–2.

24 Gilles Deleuze, *The Fold: Leibniz and the Baroque*, trans. Tom Conley (London: Continuum, 1992), p.85 et passim; 'ultimately joyful': Moyen Loerke, 'Four Things Deleuze Learned from Leibniz', in Sjoerd van Tuinen and Nianh McDonnell (eds), *Deleuze and the 'The Fold': A Critical Reader* (Basingstoke: Palgrave Macmillan, 2010), p.31.

25 Jerzy Limon, 'The Masque of Stuart Culture,' in Peck, op. cit. (note 14), pp.212–13 and 216–20. Cf. 'Athens must always be conquered afresh by Alexandria': Aby Warburg, quoted by Ernst Gombrich, *Aby Warburg: An Intellectual Biography With a Memoir on the History of the Library by F. Saxl* (Oxford: Phardon, 1986), p.214.

26 Robert Weimann, *Shakespeare and the Popular Tradition in the Theatre* (Baltimore: Johns Hopkins University Press, 1978), pp.75–89 et passim.

27 'Deep and pervasive': Christopher Braider, *Refiguring the Real: Picture and Modernity in Word and Image, 1400–1700* (Princeton: Princeton University Press, 1993), p.3; 'for the few': Octavio Paz, quoted in Bouwsma, op. cit. (note 12), p.148. For Shakespeare's suspicion of visual culture, see, in particular, Katharine Maus, 'Proof and Consequences: Inwardness and Its Exposure in the English Renaissance', *Representations*, 44 (1993), 30–43, esp.467; and

Patricia Parker, '*Othello* and *Hamlet*: Dilation, Spying and the "Secret Place" of Woman', *Representations*, 44 (1993), 70–90.

28 Jeffrey K. Aronson and Manoj Ramachandran, 'The Diagnosis of Art: Dürer's Squint – and Shakespeare's?', *Journal of the Royal Society of Medicine*, 102 (2009), 391–3; John Kerrigan, 'Between Michelangelo and Petrarch: Shakespeare's Sonnets of Art', in Yasunari Takada (ed.), *Surprised by Scenes: Essays in honour of Professor Yasunari Takahashi* (Tokyo: Kenkyusha, 1994), p. 158. Cf. Marcus Nordlund, *The Dark Lantern: A Historical Study of Sight in Shakespeare, Webster, and Middleton* (Gothenburg: Acta Universitatis Gothobergensis, 1999), p. 236: 'Anyone who puts his sanity at stake in grappling with the body of this Sonnet is bound to be at least perplexed'.

29 'Embedded': Ifig Cocoual, 'The Poetics and Politics of Storytelling in *The Winter's Tale*', in Delphine Lemonnier-Texier and Guillaume Winter (eds), *Lectures de 'The Winter's Tale'* (Rennes: Presses universitaires de Rennes, 2010), p. 36; Christopher Pye, *The Regal Phantasm: Shakespeare and the Politics of Spectacle* (London: Routledge, 1990).

30 Jay, op. cit. (note 2), p. 89.

31 David Evett, *Literature and the Visual Arts in Tudor England* (Athens: Georgia University Press, 1990), p. 190. For perspective as a form of blindness in *King Lear*, see the classic account in Marshall McLuhan, *The Gutenberg Galaxy: The Making of Typographic Man* (Toronto: Toronto University Press, 1962), pp. 11–17.

32 Pierre Bourdieu, *The Rules of Art: Genesis and Structure of the Literary Field*, trans. Susan Emanuel (Cambridge: Polity Press, 1996), p. 313; cf. John Berger, *Ways of Seeing* (Harmondsworth: Penguin, 1972), p. 16: 'Perspective makes the single eye the centre of the visible world. Everything converges on to the eye as to the vanishing point of infinity. The visible world is arranged for the spectator as the universe was once thought to be arranged for God'; 'bewildering to outsiders': Jay, op. cit. (note 2), p. 87.

33 Jen Boyle, *Anamorphosis in Early Modern Literature* (Farnham: Ashgate, 2011), pp. 46 and 51.

34 Svetlana Alpers, *The Vexations of Art: Velázquez and Others* (New Haven: Yale University Press, 2005), pp. 162–3.

35 Aby Warburg, note on Dürer (1912), quoted in Ernst Gombrich, *Aby Warburg: An Intellectual Biography* (London: Phaidon, 1970), p. 253. For the genealogy of Warburg's concept, see Michael Podro, *The Critical Historians of Art* (New Haven: Yale University Press, 1984), pp. 168–77. The notion of 'psychical distance' was simultaneously floated in an essay that has become a founding document of business

studies, by Edward Bullough, '"Psychical Distance" as a Factor in Art and as an Aesthetic Principle', *British Journal of Psychology* 5 (1912), 86–117.

36 See Andrea Frisch, 'French Tragedy and the Civil Wars', *Modern Language Quarterly*, 67:3 (2006), 286–313.

37 René Girard, *A Theatre of Envy* (New York: Oxford University Press, 1991), p.272.

38 For Philo and Enobarbus as equivalents of the *Sprecher*, the figure in a painting who looks out at the viewer, see John Greenwood, *Shifting Perspectives and the Stylish Style: Mannerism in Shakespeare and His Jacobean Contemporaries* (Toronto: University of Toronto Press, 1988), pp.53–4 and 80–1; and Cyrus Hoy, 'Jacobean Tragedy and the Mannerist Style', *Shakespeare Survey*, 26 (1973), 49–67, esp.63; 'accommodated his aristocratic audiences': Tassi, op. cit. (note 1), p.294.

39 Allardyce Nicoll, *Stuart Masques and the Renaissance Stage* (London: Harrap, 1938), pp.63–7; John Orrell, 'The Theater at Christ Church, Oxford, in 1605', *Shakespeare Survey*, 35 (1982), p.134.

40 Coppélia Kahn, *Roman Shakespeare: Warriors, Wounds, and Women* (London: Routledge, 1997), p.127.

41 Margorie Garber, '"Vassal Actors": The Role of the Audience in Shakespearean Tragedy', *Renaissance Drama*, 9 (1978), 87.

42 Peter Holland, *The Ornament of Action: Text and Performance in Restoration Comedy* (Cambridge: Cambridge University Press, 1979), pp.23–4.

43 Bruce Smith, 'Pageants into Play: Shakespeare's Three Perspectives on Idea and Image', in David Bergeron (ed.), *Pageantry in the Shakespearean Theater* (Athens: University of Georgia Press, 1985), p.230.

44 Jay, op. cit. (note 2), pp.88–9.

45 Martin Heidegger, 'The Age of the World Picture', in *The Question Concerning Technology and Other Essays*, trans. William Lovitt (New York: Harper Colophon, 1977), pp.115–34.

46 Jean Starobinski, *L'oeil vivant: Essais* (Paris: Gallimard, 1961), p.43; quoted in Jay, op. cit. (note 2), p.89.

47 Ben Jonson, *Ben Jonson: Works*, ed. C.H. Herford and Percy Simpson & Evelyn Simpson, 11 vols (Oxford: Clarendon Press, 1925–52), Vol. 7, p.232. D.J. Gordon, '*Hymenaei*: Jonson's Masque of Union', in *The Renaissance Imagination: Essays and Lectures by D.J. Gordon*, ed. Stephen Orgel (Berkeley: University of California Press, 1975), pp.159, 162 and 172.

48 For Jonson and the winching mechanism, see Nicoll, op. cit. (note 39), p.64.

49 Caroline Spurgeon, *Shakespeare's Imagery and What It Tells Us* (Cambridge: Cambridge University Press, 1935), p.352.

50 See Richard Dutton, '*Hamlet, An Apology for Actors* and the Sign of the Globe', *Shakespeare Survey*, 41 (1989), p.39: 'None of the allusions (to Atlas) is, as it were, redundant or arbitrary'.

51 Leonard Tennenhouse, *Power on Display: The Politics of Shakespeare's Genres* (London: Methuen, 1986), p.146.

52 Roger Caillois, *Man, Play and Games*, trans. Meyer Barash (Urbana: University of Illinois Press, 2001), p.18.

53 Roland Barthes, 'The World of Wrestling', *Mythologies*, trans. Annette Lavers (London: Jonathan Cape, 1972), p.15: 'Boxing is a Jansenist sport, based on a demonstration of excellence'; Stanley Wells, 'Shakespeare and Romance', in *Later Shakespeare*, ed. John Russell Brown and Bernard Harris (London: Edward Arnold, 1966), p.49.

54 Johan Huizinga, *Homo Ludens: A Study of the Play Element in Culture*, trans. Anon. (London: Routledge, 2003).

55 Jonson, op. cit. (note 47), vol. 7, p.90; see Gail Kern Paster, 'The Idea of London in Masque and Pageant', in Bergeron, op. cit. (note 43), pp.55–6: 'The *flamen martialis* which greeted James just before he left the city contrasted the present date of March 15 with Caesar's disastrous Ides of March ... James's procession through London ... is the beginning of the new *pax Augusta*'.

56 See Helen Moore, 'Jonson, Dekker, and the Discourse of Chivalry', *Medieval and Renaissance Drama in England*, 12 (1999), 121–65, esp.149; and Tracey Hill, '"Representing the awefull authoritie of soveraigne Majestie": Monarchs and Mayors in Anthony Munday's *The Triumphs of Re-united Britania*', in Glenn Burgess, Rowland Wymer and Jason Lawrence (eds), *The Accession of James I: Historical and Cultural Consequences* (Basingstoke: Palgrave Macmillan, 2006), pp.15–33, esp. pp.16–17.

57 Stephen Orgel, *The Authentic Shakespeare and Other Problems of the Early Modern Stage* (London: Routledge, 2002), p.58.

58 Jacques Rancière, *The Emancipated Spectator*, trans. Gregory Elliott (London: Verso, 2009), p.5.

59 'Liturgy of state': Roy Strong, *Art and Power* (Berkeley: University of California Press, 1984), p.40; 'more like a ritual': Jerzy Limon, 'Performativity of the Court: Stuart Masques as Postdramatic Theater', in Paul Cefalu and Bryan Reynolds (eds), *The Return of Theory in Early Modern English Studies* (Basingstoke: Palgrave, 2011), p.276; Rancière, op. cit. (note 58), p.7.

60 Louis Marin, *Portrait of the King*, trans. Marcha Honle (Basingstoke: Macmillan, 1988), pp.72 and 79.

61 Orgel, op. cit. (note 57), p.58. For the discrepancy between the prime

and optimum position for the king's chair of state, see Orrell, op. cit. (note 38), pp.136–8; and for resistance to the absolutist optic within the court masques themselves, see Martin Butler, 'Royal Slaves? The Stuart Court and the Theatres', *Renaissance Drama Newsletter*, Supplement 2 (Coventry: University of Warwick, 1984); and David Lindley, 'Courtly Play: The Politics of Chapman's *The Memorable Masque*', in Eveline Cruickshanks (ed.), *The Stuart Courts* (Stroud: Sutton Publishing, 2000), pp.43–58.

62 Roland Barthes, 'Arcimboldo, or Magician and Rhétoriqueur', in *The Responsbility of Forms: Critical Essays on Music, Art, and Representation*, trans. Richard Howard (New York: Hill & Wang, 1985), p.137.

63 Leo Salingar, 'Jacobean Playwrights and "Judicious" Spectators', *Renaissance Drama*, 22 (1991), 209–34; Ben Jonson, op. cit. (note 47), vol. 7, p.213. For Jonson's 'hermeneutic of secrecy' and his requirement for an 'in-group of "understanders"', see William Slights, *Ben Jonson and the Art of Secrecy* (Toronto: University of Toronto Press, 1994), pp.111–12 and 172.

64 Leo Salingar, 'Shakespeare and the Italian Concept of "Art"', in *Dramatic Form in Shakespeare and the Jacobeans* (Cambridge: Cambridge University Press, 1986), pp.1–18; Girard, op. cit. (note 36), p.272 et passim; Ben Jonson, *Every Man Out of His Humour*, 'Induction', 56–65 and 201–3, ibid., vol. 3, p.435. Cf. Jennifer Richards, 'Social Decorum in *The Winter's Tale*', in *Shakespeare's Late Plays: New Readings*, eds Jennifer Richards and James Knowles (Edinburgh: Edinburgh University Press, 1999), p.80: '*The Winter's Tale* ... appeals to the "bifurcation" of its audience into those who "belong" to a courtly "club" because they know how to read its signs, and those who are merely its admiring "victims"'.

65 'A full and understanding auditory': John Webster, *The White Devil*, ed. John Russell Brown (London: Methuen, 1960), 'To The Reader', p.1; William West, 'Understanding in the Elizabethan Theaters', *Renaissance Drama*, 35 (2006), 113–43. See also Mary Blackstone and Cameron Louis, 'Towards a Full and Understanding Auditory: New Evidence of Playgoers at the First Globe Theatre', *MLR*, 90 (1995), 556–71.

66 'Exclusive clientele': David Howarth, 'The Politics of Inigo Jones', in David Howarth (ed.), *Art and Patronage in the Stuart Courts* (Cambridge: Cambridge University Press, 1993), p.87; Charles Whitney, 'Ante-aesthetics: Towards a Theory of Early Modern Audience Response', in *Shakespeare and Modernity*, ed. Hugh Grady (London: Routledge, 2000), pp.47 and 51.

67 Jay, op. cit. (note 2), pp.363–4.

68 Dawson and Yachnin, op. cit. (note 13), p.80.

69 Joel Finemann, *Shakespeare's Perjur'd Eye: The Invention of Poetic Subjectivity* (Berkeley: University of California Press, 1986); pp.102–4; 'a dead eye': Svetlana Alpers, *The Art of Describing: Dutch Art in the Seventeenth Century* (Chicago: University of Chicago Press, 1983), p.36.

70 Francis Bacon, *The Great Instauration*, in *The Works of Francis Bacon*, ed James Spedding et al., 14 vols. (London: 1857–1864), vol. 4, p.30.

71 Gary Schmidgall, *Shakespeare and the Courtly Aesthetic* (Berkeley: University of California Press, 1981), pp.197–8.

72 Leo Salingar, *Dramatic Form in Shakespeare and the Jacobeans* (Cambridge: Cambridge University Press, 1986), p.14.

73 Ernst Gombrich, '"That rare Italian Master ..." Giulio Romano, Court Architect, Painter and Impresario', in *Splendours of the Gonzaga*, eds David Chambers and Jane Martineau (London: Victoria & Albert Museum, 1981), pp.83–5; see also Geoffrey Bullough, *Narrative and Dramatic Sources of Shakespeare* (8 vols, London: Routledge & Kegan Paul, 1975), vol. 8, p.150.

74 See for example Smith, op. cit. (note 43), p.230: 'Like Botticelli, Veronese, and other painters for whom the disarming of Mars was a favourite subject'. Cf. R. Shaw Smith, '*Antony and Cleopatra*, II.ii.204', *Shakespeare Quarterly* (1973), 92–3.

75 T.J. Clark, *Farewell to an Idea: Episodes from a History of Modernism* (New Haven: Yale University Press), p.48.

76 Phyllis Rackin, 'Shakespeare's Boy Cleopatra, the Decorum of Nature and the Golden World of Poetry', *PMLA*, 87 (1972), 201–12; repr. John Drakakis (ed.) *New Casebooks: 'Antony and Cleopatra'* (Basingstoke: Macmillan, 1994), pp.78–100, here pp.84–5. There is a large literature on Cleopatra's invisibility in her most famous scene. See Jonathan Gil Harris, '"Narcissus in thy face": Roman Desire and the Difference It Fakes in *Antony and Cleopatra*', *Shakespeare Quarterly*, 45 (1994), 418; Pauline Kiernan, *Shakespeare's Theory of Drama* (Cambridge: Cambridge University Press, 1996), pp.158–60; Alison Newton, '"At the Very Heart of Loss": Shakespeare's Enorbarbus and the Rhetoric of Remembering', *Renaissance Papers* (1995), 87–8; and Alison Thorne, *Vision and Rhetoric in Shakespeare: Looking through Language* (New York: St Martin's Press, 2001), p.166. In his fine book on ekphrasis, *Narrating the Visual in Shakespeare* (Farnham: Ashgate, 2009), Richard Meek comments: 'Within a narrative account that self-consciously denigrates its own powers of narration, Cleopatra is said to 'O'er-pictur[e] a picture of Venus in which the artist has outdone a work of art that was already better than life. But paradoxically this

remarkable "reality" – which we do not see – can only be depicted within the supposed inadequacy of Enobarbus' description' (p. 171).

77 A.D. Nuttall, *Shakespeare the Thinker* (New Haven: Yale University Press, 2007), p. 324.

78 John Shearman, *Mannerism* (Harmondsworth: Penguin, 1967), p. 91.

79 'Projection of the prince': Vaughan Hart, *Art and Magic in the Courts of the Stuarts* (London: Routledge, 1994), p. 84; 'visual anchor': Marvin Carlson, *Places of Performance: The Semiotics of Theatre Architecture* (Ithaca: Cornell University, 1989), p. 137.

80 See Salingar, op. cit. (note 72), p. 13.

81 Walter Benjamin, *Gesammelte Schriften*, eds Rolf Tiedemann and Hermann Schweppenhäuser (6 vols, Frankfurt: Suhrkamp Verlag, 1972), vol. 2, 1, pp. 134–6, quoted in Christine Buci-Glucksmann, *Baroque Reason: The Aesthetics of Modernity*, trans. Patrick Camiller (London: Sage Publications, 1994), pp. 67–8.

82 Malcolm Smuts, *Court Culture and the Origins of a Royalist Tradition in Early Stuart England* (Philadelphia: University of Pennsylvania Press, 1987), pp. 171–7.

83 Stephen Orgel, *The Illusion of Power: Political Theater in the English Renaissance* (Berkeley: University of California Press, 1975), p. 45.

84 Ben Jonson, *The Masque of Blackness*, quoted Nicoll, op. cit (note 39), pp. 58–60; 'a veritable catalyst': Weimann, op. cit. (note 3), p. 186.

85 Nicoll, op. cit. (note 39), pp. 58–60.

86 John Leeds Barroll, *Anna of Denmark Queen of England: A Cultural Biography* (Philadelphia: Pennsylvania University Press, 2001), pp. 99, 101 and 104; Davidson, op. cit. (note 20), p. 61.

87 'You cannot imagine a more ugly sight': John Chamberlain, quoted ibid., p. 102; 'A double vision': Lindley, op. cit. (note 61), pp 54–5. Referring to George Chapman's coded critique of James in *The Memorable Masque* of 1613, Lindley cites the dramatist's use of 'the anamorphic portrait to suggest the different perspectives that may be taken on his hero' in *Tragedie of Chabot, Admirall of France*: 'So men that view him but in vulgar passes, / Casting but laterall, or partiall glances / At what he is, suppose him weake … but stand free and fast, / And judge him … by the right laid line / Of truth' (*The Tragedie of Chabot, Admirall of France*, 1,1, ed. George Blakemore Evans (Woodbridge: D.S. Brewer, 1987), p. 72).

88 Martin Butler, *The Stuart Court Masque and Political Culture* (Cambridge: Cambridge University Press, 2008), p. 15. See also Russell West, 'Perplexive Perspectives: The Court and Contestation in the Jacobean Masque', *The Seventeenth Century*, 18 (2003), 33.

89 Neville Davies, 'Jacobean *Antony and Cleopatra*', in *Shakespeare Studies: 17* (1985), p. 123; 'The Limitations of Festival: Christian IV's

State Visit to England, 1606', in J.R. Mulryne and Margaret Shewring (eds), *Italian Renaissance Festivals and Their European Influence* (Lewiston, NY: Edwin Mellen, 1992), pp. 320–5. For the Pembroke connection, see Geoffrey Bullough, *Narrative and Dramatic Sources of Shakespeare: V: The Roman Plays* (London: Routledge & Kegan Paul, 1964), pp. 228–32. For Shakespeare's apparent comments on the preparations for *The Masque of Blackness*, see Josephine Waters Bennett, *'Measure for Measure' as Royal Entertainment* (New York: Columbia University Press, 1966), pp. 8–9 and 109–11.

90 Alvin Kernan, *Shakespeare, the Kings Playwright: Theater and the Stuart Court, 1603–1613* (New Haven: Yale University Press, 1995), pp. 122–31.

91 Ibid.; 'royalism in the arts': Gary Schmidgall, *Shakespeare and the Courtly Aesthetic* (Berkeley: University of California Press, 1981), p. 100; 'presents a Jacobean audience': Brian Gibbons, *Shakespeare and Multiplicity* (Cambridge: Cambridge University Press, 1997), p. 41.

92 Murray Roston, *The Soul of Wit: A Study of John Donne* (Oxford: Clarendon Press, 1974), pp. 194–5.

93 Jean-Pierre Maquerlot, *Shakespeare and the Mannerist Tradition: A Reading of Five Problem Plays* (Cambridge: Cambridge University Press, 1995), pp. 65–7, 169 and 177–8; George Kernodle, 'The Mannerist Stage of Comic Detachment', in *The Elizabethan Theatre, III*, ed. David Galloway (Waterloo: University of Waterloo Press, 1973), pp. 121–2. See also Greenwood, op. cit. (note 38); and Arnold Hauser, *Mannerism: The Crisis of the Renaissance and the Origin of Modern Art* (London: Routledge, 1965), pp. 344–5; and op. cit. (note 19), p. 157: 'The indissoluble union of naturalism and conventionalism suggests that the best approach to Shakespearian form is from the side of mannerism. The conscious mixture of comic and tragic motifs … the emphasis on the a-logical, the unfathomable and contradictory in life, the idea of the theatrical and dream-like quality, the compulsions and restraints of human life – all these are arguments for taking mannerism as the starting point of the analysis. The artificiality, affectation and mania for originality in Shakespeare's language are also manneristic and to be explained by the mannerist tastes of the age. His euphuism, his often overladen and confused metaphors, his piling up of antitheses, assonances and puns, his fondness for the complicated, intricate and enigmatic style, are all manneristic, as are also the extravagant, bizarre and paradoxical elements … [such as] the erotic trifling with the masculine disguise of girls played by boys'.

94 Jacques Lacan, *The Four Fundamental Concepts of Psychoanalysis*, ed. Jacques-Alain Miller, trans, Alan Sheridan (New York: Norton,

1981), pp. 88–9. 'Inside-out structure of the gaze': Christopher Pye, op. cit. (note 23), p. 93.

95 Alexander Bakshy, *The Theatre Unbound* (London: Unwin, 1923), passim; Paul Yachnin, '"The Perfection of Ten": Populuxe Art and Artisanal Value in *Troilus and Cressida'*, *Shakespeare Quarterly*, 56 (2005), 307. Yachnin introduced the idea of the 'populuxe theatre' in Dawson and Yachnin, op. cit. (note 13), pp. 38–65.

96 For a recent restatement of the anamorphic interpretation, see William Engel, *Chiastic Designs in English Literature from Sidney to Shakespeare* (Farnham: Ashgate, 2009), pp. 4–5; Paul Yachnin, *Stage-Wrights: Shakespeare, Jonson, Middleton, and the Making of Theatrical Value* (Philadelphia: University of Pennsylvania Press, 1997), pp. 12–13 and 21. See also Greenwood, op. cit. (note 38).

97 See Peter Platt, *Reason Diminished: Shakespeare and the Marvelous* (Lincoln: University of Nebraska Press, 1997), pp. 126–7 and 222, n. 14, for a useful survey of the literature.

98 Garber, op. cit. (note 41), p. 87.

99 Jonathan Dollimore, *Radical Tragedy: Religion, Ideology and Power in the Drama of Shakespeare and His Contemporaries* (Hemel Hempstead: Harvester, 1984), pp. 208 and 217.

100 Carl Schmitt, *Hamlet or Hecuba: The Intrusion of the Time of the Play*, trans. David Pan and Jennifer Rust (New York: Telos Press, 2009), pp. 36 and 45.

101 Holland, op. cit. (note 42), p. 29.

102 Deats, op. cit. (note 16), p. 3.

103 Jacques Lacan, *Seminar 8: The Ethics of Psychoanalysis* (London: Routledge, 2008), quoted and discussed in Julia Lupton, *Thinking with Shakespeare: Essays on Politics and Life* (Chicago: University of Chicago Press, 2011), pp. 92–3; see also Pye, op. cit. (note 23), p. 112.

104 Yachnin, op. cit. (note 96), p. 6.

105 Anne Barton, *Shakespeare and the Idea of the Play* (Harmondsworth: Penguin, 1967), pp. 164 and 167–9.

106 'Anti-plays' Garber, op. cit. (note 41), p. 83. See also Thomas Betteridge, *Shakespearean Fantasy and Politics* (Hatfield: University of Hertfordshire Press, 2005), p. 142.

107 Skura, op. cit. (note 5), p. 143.

108 Benjamin, op. cit. (note 21), p. 156. See Horst Weinstock, 'Loyal Service in Shakespeare's Mature Plays', *Studi Neophilologica,* 43 (1971), 446–73, here 465. In Plutarch Enobarbus dies of disease not a broken heart.

109 'Smelly populace': Brents Stirling, *The Populace in Shakespeare* (New York: Columbia University Press, 1949), p. 70.

110 Ben Jonson, 'Expostulation with Inigo Jones', op. cit. (note 47), vol.

8, pp.403–4. Jonson satirizes Jones as the Cook in the antimasque of *Neptune's Triumph*.

111 Whitney, op. cit. (note 66), p.46.

112 Weimann, op. cit. (note 3), pp.194–5. Cf. Schmitt, op. cit. (note 100), pp.40–1.

113 Alan Stewart, 'Lives and Letters in *Antony and Cleopatra*', *Shakespeare Studies*, 35 (2007), 98–9.

114 Steven Mullaney, *The Place of the Stage: License, Play, and Power in Renaissance England* (Chicago: Chicago University Press, 1988), pp.136–7.

115 Weimann, op. cit. (note 3), p.200.

116 'Something scandalous … characteristically absorbs': Yachnin, op. cit. (note 95), 315; 'greatness very familiar': Sir Henry Wotton, letter of 30 June 1613 recording the burning of the Globe, repr. in *The Norton Shakespeare*, ed. Stephen Greenblatt, Walter Cohen, Jean Howard and Katharine Eisaman Maus (New York: Norton, 1997), p.3339.

117 Theodor Adorno, *Mahler: A Musical Physiognomy*, trans. Edmund Jephcott (Chicago: University of Chicago Press, 1996), p.22.

118 Theodor Adorno, *Quasi una Fantasia: Essays on Modern Music*, trans. Rodney Livingstone (London: Verso, 1998, p.98.

119 Bruce R. Smith, *The Acoustic World of Early Modern England: Attending to the O-Factor* (Chicago: University of Chicago Press, 1999), pp.236–7 and 243.

120 For Elizabeth's game of mooring her royal barge beside the theatres on Bankside, see Helen Hackett, *Shakespeare and Elizabeth: The Meeting of Two Myths* (Princeton: Princeton University Press, 2009), pp.11–12.

121 See, for instance, Paul Yachnin, '"Courtiers of Beauteous Freedom": *Antony and Cleopatra* in Its Time', *Renaissance and Reformation*, 15 (1991), 1–20; and Robert Ornstein, 'The Ethic of the Imagination: Love and Art in *Antony and Cleopatra*', *Stratford-upon-Avon Studies*, 8 (London: Edward Arnold, 1967), ed. John Russell Brown and Bernard Harris, p.40.

122 Tennenhouse, op. cit. (note 51), p.146.

123 Christopher Marlowe, *Dido Queen of Carthage* in *Christopher Marlowe: The Complete Plays*, eds Frank Romany and Robert Lindsey (London: Penguin, 2003), 3,1,115–22, p.31. For Aeneas as a player, see Richard Wilson, 'Tragedy, Patronage, and Power,' in *The Cambridge Companion to Christopher Marlowe*, ed. Patrick Cheney (Cambridge: Cambridge University Press, 2004), pp.208–12.

124 Yachnin, op. cit. (note 95), 308.

125 Walter Cohen, *Drama of a Nation: Public Theater in Renaissance England and Spain* (Ithaca: Cornell University Press, 1985), p.388;

Weimann, op. cit. (note 3), p.196. For the costuming motif and the legend of Hercules and Omphale, see Robert Miola, *Shakespeare's Rome* (Cambridge: Cambridge University Press, 1983), pp.129–33.

126 Herbert Marcuse, *The Aesthetic Dimension: Toward a Critique of Marxist Aeshetics* (Boston: Beacon Press, 1978), p.5.

127 Bourdieu, op. cit. (note 32), p.3.

128 Graham Bradshaw, *Misrepresentations: Shakespeare and the Materialists* (Ithaca: Cornell University Press, 1993), p.104.

129 M.M. Mahood, *Playing Bit Parts in Shakespeare* (Cambridge: Cambridge University Press, 1992), pp.181 and 204.

130 Hopkins, 'Cleopatra and the Myth of Scotia', in Munson Deats, op. cit. (note 1), p.237.

131 Michael Leapman, *Inigo: The Troubled Life of Inigo Jones, Architect of the English Renaissance* (London: 2003, Review), pp.124–5; T.G. Findel, *A History of Freemasonry* (London: Asher & Co., 1866), p.117; Douglas Knoop and G.P. Jones, *A Handlist of Masonic Documents* (Manchester: Manchester University Press, 1942), pp.33–4.

132 Frances Yates, *The Rosicrucian Enlightenment* (London: Routledge & Kegan Paul, 1972), pp.257 and 263.

133 For Cleopatra's game of 'fast and loose', involving 'disappearing knots in a handkerchief', and her other circus tricks, see Charles Whitney 'Charmian's Laughter: Women, Gypsies, and Festive Ambivalence in *Antony and Cleopatra*', *The Upstart Crow*, 14 (1994), 67–88; and Lisa Hopkins, 'Cleopatra and the Myth of Scotia', in Munson Deats, op. cit. (note 1), pp.231–42.

134 Alpers, op. cit. (note 34), p.180. For Velázquez's collection of mirrors, see Martin Kemp, *The Science of Art: Optical Themes in Western Art from Brunelleschi to Seurat* (New Haven: Yale University Press, 1990), pp.9–10.

135 Ibid., p.177.

136 Judith Weil, *Service and Dependency in Shakespeare's Plays* (Cambridge: Cambridge University Press, 2005), pp.7, 92, 96–7 and 100.

137 Ibid., 99 and 103–4.

138 Julia Lupton, *Citizen-Saints: Shakespeare and Political Theology* (Chicago: Chicago University Press, 2005), pp.161 and 174.

139 See Giorgio Agamben, *Homo Sacer: Sovereign Power and Bare Life*, trans. Daniel Heller-Roazen (Stanford: Stanford University Press, 1998), esp. p.29.

140 Emrys Jones (ed.), 'Introduction', in William Shakespeare, *Antony and Cleopatra* (Harmondsworth: Penguin, 1977), p.46.

141 Christine Buci-Glucksmann, *Tragique del'ombre: Shakespeare et le*

maniérisme (Paris: Editions Galilée, 1990). See also Barbara Freedman, *Staging the Gaze: Postmodernism, Psychoanalysis, and Shakespearean Comedy* (Ithaca: Cornell University Press, 1991), pp. 4–5; and Andrew Gurr, *Playgoing in Shakespeare's London* (Cambridge: Cambridge University Press, 1996), p. 106.

142 Elizabeth Howe, *The First English Actresses: 1660–1700* (Cambridge: Cambridge University Press, 1992), p. 46.

143 James VI and I, 'Song, the first verses that ever the King made' (1582), in *The Poems of James VI of Scotland* (2 vols, Edinburgh: William Blackwood, 1955–8), vol. 2, p. 132; Jonson, op. cit. (note 46), vol. 4, p. 33.

144 Pierre Bourdieu, *The Field of Cultural Production*, trans. Richard Johnson (Cambridge: Cambridge University Press, 1993), p. 37.

145 'Her Egyptian revision': Eric Langley, *Narcissism and Suicide in Shakespeare and His Contemporaries* (Oxford: Oxford University Press, 2009), p. 183.

146 Park Honan, *William Shakespeare: A Life* (Oxford: Oxford University Press, 1998), p. 303

147 See Peter Bürger, *Theory of the Avant-Garde*, trans. Michael Shaw (Minneapolis: University of Minnesota Press, 1984), p. x.

148 Hugh Grady, *Shakespeare and Impure Aesthetics* (Cambridge: Cambridge University Press, 2009), p. 222.

149 For the dual message of the 'eastern star', and the belief at the time staged in the play both that a new star heralds the birth of the world ruler and that 'The heavens ... blaze forth the death of princes' [*Julius, 2,2,30*], see Geza Vermes, *The Nativity: History and Legend* (London: Penguin, 2006), pp. 100–9.

150 Michel Foucault, *The Order of Things: An Archaeology of the Human Sciences*, trans. anon. (London: Routledge, 1970), p. 16. That this chamberlain was also named Velazquez only compounds the force with which the painter separates his own artistic sovereignty in this picture from that of the sovereign himself: see Catherine Belsey, 'Making Space: Perspective Vision and the Lacanian Real', *Textual Practice*, 16 (2002), 31–55, here 52.

151 See John Margeson, 'Introduction' to George Chapman, *The Conspiracy and Tragedy of Byron* (Manchester: Manchester University Press, 1988), pp. 10–13.

8

Like an eagle in a dovecot

The intrusion of the time into the play

The sore itch of your opinion

'What's the matter, you dissentious rogues, / That, rubbing the sore itch of your opinion, / Make yourselves scabs?' [*1,1,153–5*]: the first words uttered by Coriolanus set the terms of the conflict between the protagonist and populace of Shakespeare's tragedy as a war over the matter of personal 'matter' itself, in a society like that of pre-revolutionary England, where 'dissentious opinion' has not yet evolved into the 'public opinion' that would be a foundation of the modern public sphere; defined by Jürgen Habermas as a 'sphere of private people come together as a public'. As the biopolitics of the *scab* metaphor imply when it is still applied to strike-breakers, and the philosopher explained in *The Structural Transformation of the Public Sphere*, 'opinion' still had the negative meaning in England and France during the Wars of Religion of the Latin *opinio*, in the sense of some symptomatic bodily irritation: 'terms like "common opinion," "general opinion" or "vulgar opinion" were completely lacking in Shakespeare, not to mention "public opinion"'. Within the lifetime of Shakespeare's audience, however, Habermas recounts, 'private opinion' would be validated by thinkers like Hobbes as the essential precondition of 'public opinion', when religion became a private matter of no concern to a state in which one opinion now mattered as much as another:[1]

> The space Hobbes left free for private religious scruples ... is turned inside out and extends itself into the bourgeois realm; thus bourgeois society renders itself valid as a rival political power, and ultimately topples Leviathan from his throne.[2]

For Habermas, freedom of conscience 'secured the first sphere of private autonomy'. Tellingly, for a play centred on the theatre metaphor that dramatizes the failure of a warrior to 'earn a dearer estimation' with the voters after 'He said he had wounds which he could show in private' [2,3,95; 165], the theorist finds a paradigm for this 'audience-oriented subjectivity' in Shakespeare's playhouse, where theatregoers included 'domestic servants, young clerks, and a *lumpenproletariat* always ready for a spectacle', and the pit became 'a place where the people congregated who were later counted among the cultured'.[3] For these groundlings were soon joined by skilled and educated artisans like shoemakers, tailors, printers and opticians, able 'to defend their vulgar wisdoms', as Coriolanus sneers, by 'their own choice' [1,1,204]. Habermas's neo-Kantian genealogy of the public sphere constituted by private individuals has been much criticized. But here it is corroborated by eye-witness reports of how London's amphitheatres were 'constructed so that everyone has a good view', and, as M.C. Bradbrook observed, '*everyone* becomes chief spectator'.[4] Thus for Habermas, the true revolution in the emergence of the public sphere, as a space where art first became 'an object of free choice and changing preference' for a public in which 'everyone was now entitled to judge', occurred in the theatre itself, with the overthrow that this tragedy appears to enact, when the nobles who had paraded in front of the action were dislodged from their stools on the side of the stage, and the audience which had previously applauded their display celebrated the unseating by throwing off its caps:[5]

> The people's enemy is gone, is gone!
> Our enemy is banished, he is gone! Hoo-oo!
> [*They all shout, and throw up their caps*]
>
> [3,3,136–7]

In Shakespeare's plays the actors are for ever being interrupted by hooray henrys 'who hoot and jeer from the side of the stage'; for Elizabethan and Jacobean theatregoing was always a public affair, Andrew Gurr reminds us, in which the visibility of the audience 'allowed them to play almost as large a part as the players'.[6] But nothing in the playhouse looks more distracting to modern eyes than the right of such aristocrats to sit on the stage itself, which Habermas reads as a dysfunctional relic of the feudal system of personal *presentation*, whereby publicity was the attribute of a monarch or manorial lord, who 'displayed himself as the embodiment of power'. In that premodern system, Habermas recounts, what *mattered* was the material body of the sovereign; for parliamentary representation, with representatives representing voters, had nothing to do with 'the publicity inseparable from a lord's concrete existence', which was *embodied* in his flesh and blood, like the livid battle scars that signify Coriolanus's valour. Shakespeare's Citizens do grasp the incarnational logic of this regime, when they admit that 'if he show us his wounds ... we are to put our tongues into those wounds' [2,3,5]. For a medieval parliament was not metaphorically representative of its electors, but, as the nobles in this play maintain, the metonymic *presence* of the entire country: 'as long as the estates of the realm *were* the country they represented their lordship not for but *before* the people'.[7]

Habermas's theatricalized account of the public sphere draws heavily but tacitly upon Carl Schmitt's Eucharistic concept of the *real presence* of representation: that 'To represent means to make an invisible being visible and present through a publicly present one'; and on his notion of the Shakespearean playhouse as a space that had not yet 'set up an opposition between the present of the play and the lived actuality of a contemporary present. Society too was on stage.'[8] But it is Schmitt's reactionary political theology, with its hankering after some commissarial dictator whose decision transcends economic or technological rationality, that helps us grasp how the representational revolution which Habermas celebrates – when the personal presence of the charismatic warlord was *excarnated* from the place of representation, and the sovereign Leviathan was 'toppled from his throne' – might be experienced, as it is in *Coriolanus*, as 'a sore upon us / You cannot tent' [3,1,234–5], the picked scab of what Eric Santner calls 'royal remains', exiguous relics of the strange substance of the king's sublime flesh that linger on the body politic like an unhealed wound scarring the traumatic scene of monarchy's dethronement:

> To represent in an eminent sense can only be done by a person, i.e., not simply by a 'deputy' but an authoritative person or an idea which, if represented, becomes personified ... But this is not true of production and consumption. Representation invests the representative person with a special dignity because the representative of a noble value cannot be without value.[9]

For Schmitt, the motto of the Globe – 'All the world's a stage' – reflected the fact that in this epoch when 'men of action saw themselves on centre stage' Shakespeare's theatre remained 'intensely integrated into its current reality, a part of the present in a society that conceived of its actions as theatre'. According to this fascist ideologue, therefore, it was the anachronistic yet abiding presence of the men-at-arms that thankfully prevented this 'barbaric' institution from achieving the representational transparency of the bourgeois liberal state, even as Shakespeare identified this bodily intrusion as the origin of the tragic.[10] Thus in *Coriolanus*, when the great man climbs on stage, 'All places yields to him ere he sits down' [*4,7,28*]. For as Ben Jonson complained, these exigent aristocrats simply did not grasp the logic of modern performance, since they never respected sightlines, nor 'made piece of their prospect the right way', but came to the playhouse as if still holding court: 'To see and to be seen. To make a general muster of themselves in their clothes of credit and possess the Stage against the Play. To dislike all but mark nothing.'[11] The theatre practitioner's objection to the toffs who treat the playhouse as 'a general muster' evokes the martial law of the Tudor state of emergency. The aptness of this Schmittian scenario to *Coriolanus* is thus well brought out by Rebecca Lemon, when she writes that, while Shakespeare 'heightens the play's decisionist dilemma' that 'a political solution cannot be located in an individual character's virtue', by making 'both the Tribunes and Coriolanus assert their right to decide the exception', it is the man of war who is shown to be liminal and anomalous: 'An oddity among his fellow citizens ... Coriolanus functions as both a sovereign and an exile, a figure who condenses the parallel attributes of sovereign power and bare life. [He] stands on the threshold.'[12]

In *Coriolanus* Shakespeare composed the great tragedy of representation when 'the nobility based in rights attached to land lost its power to represent' with the birth of the public sphere.[13] Such is the stark story as Rome emerges from a feudal economy – mystified in the myth of the Leviathan state, with its 'kingly crowned head' [*1,1,104*], when profiteers placate the starving workers with the fable that 'No public benefit which you receive / But it proceeds or comes from them to you' [*141–2*] – to an exchange economy in which the plebeians obtain 'corn at their own rates' by electing the Tribunes as deputies to be 'tongues o'th'common mouth' [*3,1,23*]. 'Sovereign is he who decides on the exception', Schmitt declared; but now it is the 'Triton of the minnows' who utters 'His absolute "shall"' [*92–3*].[14] Thus, as it moves from a warrior's wounds to the voters' voice, this play seems to prefigure the analysis of post-Schmittian thinkers such as Giorgio Agamben, Roberto Esposito and Santner himself, who identify the advent of modernity in 'the relocation of the dimension of the flesh from the body of the king to that of the people'.[15] In this narrative, because he 'inhabits the empty space of the exception' the wounded warrior becomes the itching scab, an anachronistic relic, as the body politic heals.[16] But what renders *Coriolanus* a tragedy is that this familiar mutation in the logic of sovereignty – from metonymy to metaphor – should be imagined, as it was by Schmitt, as *itself* a state of exception and breach of the constitutional norm:

> FIRST CITIZEN: For mine own part,
>   When I said 'banish him' I said 'twas pity.
> SECOND CITIZEN: And so did I.
> THIRD CITIZEN: And so did I.
>
> [*4,7,148–51*]

With nodding of their plumes

'They choose their magistrate', as Coriolanus incredulously expounds the new system of delegated representation, to be 'The horn and noise o'th'monster's', who 'puts his "popular shall" against a graver bench' [*3,1,98–108*]. For patricians who have dictated their own price this is a 'strange' innovation that 'will in time throw forth greater themes / For insurrection's arguing' [*1,1,208–10*]. And historians do interpret this Roman tragedy as a rehearsal for the English Revolution.[17] But when the Citizens celebrate their new parliamentary powers by throwing up their own 'caps / As they would hang them on the horns o'th'moon', the soldier's disgust at this 'rabble' [*210–16*] is so similar to Casca's report of how the 'rabblement ... threw up their sweaty nightcaps and uttered such a deal of stinking breath', in *Julius Caesar* – the play written, we think, to open the Globe in 1599 – that it seems as though Shakespeare's conflicted reaction to this crisis of representation must also be professional, because 'the tag-rag people clap and hiss ... as they use to do the players in the theatre' [*1,2,243–58*]. For all these Roman plays, each focused on the Forum, are propelled by a dawning realization, that, if the market is a theatre, the theatre is a market.[18] Thus Antony understands he is doomed when 'They cast their caps up, and carouse together' [*Antony, 4,13,12*] to celebrate his vanquishing. And in *Coriolanus* Shakespeare structured an entire drama around the implication that, as the playwright Thomas Dekker exclaimed, this meant that in an arena where the 'Gallant, Courtier, and Captain' had for long pranced and lorded over the scene, 'the garlic-mouth'd stinkards' could now 'cry out, "Away with the fool"':

> The theatre is your Poets' Royal Exchange [where] the Muses – that are now turned merchants – barter away that light commodity of words for a lighter ware than words – plaudits and the breath of the great beast ... Players are their factors who put away the stuff and make the best of it they possibly can ... Your Gallant, your Courtier, and your Captain had wont to be the soundest paymasters ... [But now] your Groundling and Gallery-Commoner buys his sport for a penny ... [since] the place is so free in entertainment, allowing a stool as well to the Farmer's son as to your Templar, that your Stinkard has the self-same liberty to be there in his Tobacco-fumes which your sweet Courtier hath; and your Carman and Tinker claim as strong a voice in their suffrage, and sit to give judgement on the play's life and death, as well as the proudest Momus among the tribe of Critic ...[19]

In an age of theatricalized politics, we see from Dekker's defence of the 'suffrage' of playgoers, theatrical representation becomes the medium through which a new representative politics is virtually configured, when by 'joining the two domains, as in a mirror', dramatic theory substitutes for a political theory which 'lags behind' a playhouse already reliant upon 'the illusion of the thing represented as the very condition of the representation'.[20] So, unlike the court masque, which arranged the seating and sightlines in the great hall so the monarch was not only the sole possessor of the perfect perspective but 'the observed of all observers' [*Hamlet, 3,1,154*], the playhouse provided the best available model for a future public sphere when it began to combine freedom and equality by promising every paying spectator a clear and unrestricted viewpoint.[21] As Habermas relates, the idea of the play on stage as a commodity everyone has equal claim to judge, of art as the object of choice, was thereby keyed to an optic that pitched opacity against transparency, the secret against the news.[22] Thus Shakespeare, who made this dichotomy central to *Coriolanus*, was precociously perceptive when he wrote about a nascent public sphere where 'Old men and beldames in the streets' speculate about state affairs, 'And he that speaks doth grip the hearer's wrist, / Whilst he that hears makes fearful action'. For as early as *King John* he had registered the interchange of public opinion as itself a form of mass consumption, when he had the blacksmith halt his work, his 'shears and measure in his hand' while 'his iron did on the anvil cool', with 'open mouth swallowing' the news relayed by the tailor, until 'Another lean, unwashed artificer cuts off his tale' [*John, 4,2,186–203*].

While Shakespeare's aristocrats, and even critics, denigrate 'the blunt monster with uncounted heads, / The still-discordant wav'ring multitude' [*2Henry IV, Ind. 18–19*], and compare the fluctuations of 'Rumour' to menstruation or the moon, it is precisely its changeability during upheavals like that when Bolingbroke upstages Richard, as 'Off goes his bonnet to oysterwench' [*Richard II, 2,1,30*], which defines this urban public as the sovereign of a consumer society. For when they 'sit by the fire ... making parties strong / And feebling such as stand not in their liking', as Coriolanus fumes, it is their very fickleness that invests consumers with the royal power to decide: 'With every minute you do change a mind / And call him noble that was now your hate' [*1,1,171–84*]. So again and again these Histories and Roman plays home in on the variability of consumer demand, when the same crowds who 'climbed up to walls and battlements, / To towers and windows' with 'greedy looks' to cheer their hero 'strew flowers in his way / That comes in triumph' over the fallen ruler's blood [*Julius Caesar, 1,1,37–50*]. Such is the 'Opinion' which initially 'sticks' on Coriolanus, when 'windows / Are smothered up, leads filled and ridges horsed / With variable complexions, all agreeing / In earnestness to see him' [*1,1,263; 2,1,196–9*]. But Eucharistic images of salivation and mastication already signal in this tragedy what Schmitt dreads and Habermas celebrates, that when the play becomes a commodity, like the 'cushions, leaden spoons ... doublets' [*1,6,5–6*] that Corolanus despises and the public craves, the devouring demos must dictate that 'the greatest taste / Most palates theirs' [*3,1,104–5*] as decisively in politics as art:

> The same process that converted culture into a commodity ... established [that] ... the issues discussed became 'general' not merely in their significance, but also in their accessibility: everyone had to *be able* to participate.[23]

'If you are learned', Coriolanus berates the nobles, 'Be not as common fools, if you are not, / Let them have cushions by you'

[*102–4*]; and this playhouse imagery confirms how for this proto-modern generation the dawn of the public sphere was experienced as a struggle literally over places for the best points of view. So *Coriolanus* stages the incompatibility of London's circus-like amphitheatres with the privileges of patronage, when the 'captain' who condemns 'stinkards' to drop off the body politic like exiguous 'scabs', discovers that if 'the greater part carries it' then he is the scab, and 'There's no more to be said, but he is banished. / An enemy to the people' [*2,3,34; 3,3,121–2*]. Yet if the mob Antony incites to 'Pluck down benches! / Pluck down forms' in *Julius Caesar* marks the dramatist's ambivalent reaction to the new Globe, when it murders the poet Cinna 'for his bad verses' [*3,2,246; 3,2,27*], critics note that by the time of *Coriolanus* Shakespeare's response to this metropolitan audience has crucially evolved, since the Citizens, as they are now pointedly termed, are not only 'allowed to speak for themselves' but to do so in a context which implies they 'do have a grievance'.[24] And it is the portrait of Coriolanus as a show-stealer, who refuses to play any part in the scene he nevertheless attempts to monopolize, and who is 'standing here' for election as Consul, he asserts, simply by his 'own desert' [*2,3,58–61*], which authorizes public impatience when this self-obsessed up-stager frustrates the progress of the representative process from metonymy to metaphor by professing to present nothing but himself: 'Not to be other than one thing' [*4,7,42*].

Willing neither to leave the stage nor be an actor on it, but waving 'his hat in scorn', Coriolanus installs himself, he taunts his onlookers, as one of the aristocratic hooligans who 'with nodding of their plumes, / Fan you into despair' [*2,3,156; 3,3,130–1*]. Like the infamous Bullingdon Club of wealthy thugs who asserted their archaic right to break glass at Oxford University into the late twentieth-century, this lordly wrecker exerts his sovereignty precisely by shattering the transparency of bourgeois illusion. In fact, his stance is expressly defined as that of the cavalier who will neither remove his plumed helmet nor settle in his seat: 'Not moving / From the casque to the cushion, but commanding peace / Even with the same ... garb / As he controlled the war' [*4,7,42–4*]. Considering therefore that it was only 'in the most perspicuous place of the two-penny galleries', according to Dekker, that the playgoer could 'with an open eye behold all parts' of the spectacle, it is significant that in *Coriolanus* the Citizens are zoned differentially by pricing into those paying for their places in 'irons of doit', in 'a cracked drachma', or in 'groats' [*1,6,5–6; 3,2,9*].[25] And as we keep being reminded how the penny-pinched are squeezed onto benches while their betters enjoy cushions [*1,6,5; 2,1,79; 3,1,104; 4,7,43; 5,3,53*], this battle for distinction over comfort and costume confirms Coriolanus's cultural affinity with the incorrigible stool-sitters who blocked the view of the London stage. As a type of *homo sacer*, this Roman general may well wear the werewolf hood of the Lupercalia; but the tensions of Shakespeare's Forum are precisely calibrated according to the internal contradictions of the seventeenth-century English playhouse, as reported by visitors like the German tourist Thomas Platter:

> The playhouses are so constructed that they play on a raised platform ... There are different galleries and places, however, where the seating is better and more comfortable and therefore more expensive. For whoever cares to stand below only pays one English penny, but if he wishes to sit he enters by another door, and pays another penny, while if he desires to sit in the most comfortable seats which are cushioned, where he not only sees well, but can also be seen, then he pays yet another penny at the door.[26]

Cavalierly, Coriolanus jeers that if 'their choice is rather to have my hat than my heart', he will doff his headwear 'most counterfeitly' [*2,3,85–91*] to the groundlings, like Bolingbroke. Loath to blame such an anachronism on the Bard, Pope annotated Coriolanus's hat as one of 'the many blunders and illiteracies of the first publishers of his works'; but, as Gurr explains, hats worn by playgoers had a powerful significance for Shakespeare: 'Sitting on stools to display fine clothes and smoking to show wealth were not the only marks that distinguished gallants. By no means the least obtrusive was their headgear and there is no reason to suppose a gallant would lower his feather for the multitude behind. Hats were worn in ascending order of social obtrusiveness and gallants wore hats with feathers as broad as ostrich plumes.'[27] 'Put your bonnet to his right use', Hamlet thus mocks Osric, ''Tis for the head' [*Hamlet, 5,2,92–3*]. So like the 'gloves, scarves and handkerchiefs' the 'Ladies and their maids' fling, or the shower of 'caps' the commons rain upon him [*2,1,249–53*], Coriolanus's obstructive headgear is metonymic of the invasion of the fictional time of the play by the real time of a Jacobean audience. Likewise at the start of *King Lear*, Gurr remarks, contemporary hierarchy was signified in the distinctions between the king's crown, ducal coronets and the bonnets of earls, for to flaunt a hat on stage was 'to focus social attention and tension on oneself in a situation full of ostentation'.[28]

As Jonson raged, stool-sitters in fancy helmets were deliberately occupying 'the Stage against the Play', and such 'fastidious impertinents' were no better than 'Stage-furniture or Arras-clothes', for faces painted 'in the hangings' had as much understanding of the show.[29] They were living embodiments of what Schmitt terms the intrusion of the political into the aesthetic space of the play, and Santner the representational deadlock in the transition from royal to popular sovereignty. Thus when Coriolanus imitates 'the bewitchment of some popular man', 'practising the insinuating nod' to his claque [91–3] with a suitably 'unbarbed sconce' [3,2,99], his provocation says as much about the conflicted 'beam of sight' [3,1,267] in a Jacobean theatre as about early modern elections. In particular, his non-cooperation in the rules of representation, when rather than 'debase the nature' of his 'seat' he interposes his own war-wounded body between the 'rabble' and what they 'hope to gain' [2,3,66; 3,1,138], parallels the distraction that played havoc with performances whenever provincial hotheads promenaded like strutting game-birds and imported the feathered crests and 'high temper of a warrior class' into the world of the play.[30] Thus, commenting on the play's zoomorphism, Andreas Höfele connects its protagonist to the rival form of theatre adjacent to the Globe, as a bear baited by a 'cry' of dogs [3,3,124; 4,6,156], and shows how Coriolanus personifies the violent affinity of the sovereign and the beast when he *stands* for Consul, and 'his "Standing" is to be taken quite literally'.[31] But what this animal imagery also suggests is how ruefully Shakespeare understood that the crowd that hoots him out will 'roar him in again', and 'As many coxcombs / As [they] threw up caps will he tumble down' [4,5,130–43], when the eagle-headed predator chooses to return:

> Let our Gallant advance himself up to the Throne of the Stage ... On the very rushes where the Comedy is to dance must our feathered *Estridge*, like a piece of Ordnance, be planted valiantly (because impudently) beating down the mews and hisses of the opposed rascality ... Present not yourself on the Stage until the quaking prologue is about to enter ... for if you should bestow your person upon the vulgar when the belly of the house is but half full, your apparel is quite eaten up, the fashion is lost, and the proportion of your body in more danger to be devoured than if it were served up on the

Counter amongst the Poultry ... It shall crown you ... to laugh aloud
in the middest of the most serious and saddest scene of the terriblest
Tragedy ... [or to] rise with a screwed and discontented face from
your stool to be gone ... and being on your feet, sneak not away like
a coward, but salute to all your gentle acquaintance that are spread
on stools about you ...[32]

With this bonnet in thy hand

In his topical Jacobean play about a veteran's failure to adapt
to peace Shakespeare registers 'the new way of looking ... and
awareness of people around one' inaugurated by the public amphitheatres, and predicts how freedom of consumer choice will revo-
lutionize patterns of theatrical obligation.[33] For with this economic
agency, *Coriolanus* records, the responsibility of the actor shifts
'from the *performing of* authority to *performing* authority', as the
audience 'ceases to fix on him as an employee of the authority for
whom he performs, and instead begin to identify him in a new way
with the character he personates'.[34] Yet Shakespeare nevertheless
inherited a theatre 'precariously poised between ritual and art', the
play also reminds us, where the elite could never 'forget themselves'
by entering into 'the idea of the play'.[35] So its sightlines could still be
blocked by some sociopath hogging the view, like the twenty-year-
old Earl of Ormond who, new in from Ireland, planted himself in
front of the box occupied by the Countess of Essex and her stepson,
who 'told his lordship that they had paid for their places as well
as he, and entreated him not to deprive them of the benefit of it.
Whereupon the lord stood up higher and hindered more their sight.
Then Captain Essex with his hand put him a little by, whereupon
the lord drew his sword and ran at him.'[36] Clearly, scenes like the
one when Coriolanus is 'apprehended' by the Tribune Sicinius,
whom he calls an 'old goat' he will shake out of his 'garments'
[*3,1,175–82*], would have been all too familiar to the dramatist and
his companions.

When Coriolanus 'draws his sword' rather than allowing the
magistrates to 'Lay hands upon him', daring the veterans in the
crowd to 'try upon yourselves what you have seen in me' [*221–4*],
the breach of decorum that causes his banishment evokes mêlées
like one at the Blackfriars theatre in 1603, when the Yorkshire
desperado Sir Richard Cholmley lost his stool to another hooray

after he got up to stretch his legs, whereupon 'he challenged him to a duel', and when this 'Lady's eldest son' protested he had no sword, gave him 'two or three good blows', before constables arrested them both.[37] The Catholic Cholmley had been a bravo in the Essex Revolt, and this fracas was one of the earl's sideshows that Shakespeare mimicked in *Twelfth Night*. But Gurr is surely right to regard such affrays as symptoms of a clash between the rival traditions which collided in Shakespeare's playhouse: that of the popular theatre of the marketplace, where the customer was now king, and that of the patronage theatre of the great hall, where servants had always been 'summoned to entertain their employer'.[38]

Although the practice of charging the bigwig a shilling to 'throne your self on stage' started with the boy-players in the 1570s, it seems most to have irritated the audience at the amphitheatres like the Globe, where 'the interference stool-sitters created for everyone else's vision would have been far worse, given the numbers occupying the galleries or standing at the sides'.[39] Webster therefore begins the Induction he added to *The Malcontent* warning the man-about-town played by actor William Sly that the 'gentlemen' will be angry if he sits on stage, and ends it with Sly and his cousin Sinklo led away to take tobacco in a private room.[40] More aggressively, Beaumont opens *The Knight of the Burning Pestle* with the rumpus of the Grocer and his wife clambering on stage, from where they disrupt the play with crude asides, sweets flung to the house and smokers' coughs. Shakespeare's Sly likewise snuggles beside his 'madam wife' to 'sit and mark' *The Taming of the Shrew* only to snore throughout the action. And in *The Taming of a Shrew* Sly is carried off to awaken outside the alehouse where he was asleep before he dreamed he watched the show [*Ind.2,136; SD.I,1,247*]. These crass stool-sitters are all commoner gate-crashers; but their uncouth interference between the players and the playgoers highlights the professional embarrassment to which Shakespeare's rudely disrupted plays-within-plays return over and again, of the inability of private patrons to play the representation game by entering into the aesthetic experience, in a medium of mass-entertainment that was now demanding not feathered panache but doffed plumage, and instead of selfish conspicuousness, social cosideration. All the frustration of these earlier episodes is paid back, however, when in *Coriolanus* the patron is made subservient to the playgoers:

Go to them with this bonnet in thy hand,
And thus far having stretched it – here be with them –
Thy knee bussing the stones ...

[3,2,73–5]

Coriolanus, who 'would rather be their servant' his way than sway
the voters in theirs [2,1,189–90], expects to be awarded the con-
sulship via the old boys' network: 'To gratify his noble service', as
his doting mentor Menenius asserts, 'that / Hath thus stood for his
country' [2,2,36]. So his mistake is that he thinks *value* and *valour*
still identical (as in French: *valeur*). But when he is 'Whoop'd out
of Rome' by slaves [4,5,74–7], it is possible to read in this reversal
not only an equivalent of the ejection of the privileged patron from
prime position on stage, and thus an assertion of the aesthetic,
but Shakespeare's warning to his colleagues to be careful what
they wish for when they agitate to make such theatrical 'angels'
less important than the play. For *Coriolanus* is one of a fraught
sequence of classical tragedies written in the late 1600s which the-
matize the rise of London's public amphitheatres as a time of ostra-
cism, when the great man is forced from the Forum, where he had
sat 'on Fortune's Hill ... beckoned from the rest below', and turns
his back on what Timon calls this 'detestable town' [*Timon, 1,1,75;
4,1,33*]. According to Jonathan Bate, Shakespeare was always 'a
provincial outsider' and countryman, a political 'idiot' who serenely
kept his 'distance from the cultural centre'.[41] But what these expul-
sions in fact register is the professional price to be paid on all sides
for banishment from 'the city of kites and crows' [4,5,41].

'He'll shake your Rome about your ears' [4,6,103], Coriolanus's
friends warn the Citizens as he departs the scene; and Dekker
indeed reprimanded the gallant about the consequences of sweep-
ing off stage in mid-performance: '[so] all eyes in the galleries will
leave walking after the Players and only follow you'. For the actors
came to dread the moment when, as Jonson protested, the lord was
'seen to rise, and go away, / To vex the Players, and to punish their
Poet – / Keep him in awe!' As George Chapman pleaded: 'if our
audience see / You on the stage depart before we end, / Our wits go
with you all, and we are fools'.[42] Stool-sitting was in fact quickly
banned at the Globe, where to improve general visibility the stage
was raised so high the practice became dangerous 'even without
the mews and hisses of penny-payers standing close against the

platform'.[43] Thus, from the instant in *Julius Caesar* when we learn that the conspirators 'are rid like madmen through the gates of Rome' [3,3,257], it is as if the violent extrusion of Brutus, Cassius, Timon, Antony and Coriolanus symbolically enacts the emancipation from its obsolete overlords for which the London audience had been striving all along:

> Here do we make his friends
> Blush that the world goes well, who rather had ...
> Dissentious numbers pest'ring the streets than see
> Our tradesmen singing ...
>
> [4,6,4–8]

That the demand to rid the public amphitheatre of redundant feudal patrons is shown to be irresistible in *Coriolanus* confirms how soon its author understood the new necessity for transparency of representation in this open 'marketplace', where 'the general louts' were now no longer 'woollen vassals, things created / To buy and sell with groats, to show bare heads in congregations, to yawn, be still, and wonder' [3,2,8–99], but paying customers. Yet the nausea expressed by Shakespeare's evicted noblemen at this 'mutable, rank-scented meinie', as some monstrous 'Hydra', a 'beast / With many heads' [3,1,70–96; 4,1,2], also betrays acute authorial unease at the unprecedented consumer pressure when 'Muses turn merchants', in an auditorium suddenly liberated from aristocratic supervision by the purchasing power of its accumulated 'groats'. If the psychology of Hamlet is so schizoid, as Robert Weimann proposes, that it as if it is composed out of the very split between elite and popular theatres his tragedy inscribes, the characterization of Coriolanus appears to be likewise constituted by the 'double worship' of Shakespeare's creative field, 'Where one part does disdain ... the other insult' [3,1,145–7], torn between the country and the city, or the patrimonial authority of the aristocratic patron and the proprietary authority of an emerging public that was ready to pay the price for its pleasure, and buy its 'sport for a penny':[44]

> ... my soul aches
> To know, when two authorities are up,
> Neither supreme, how soon confusion
> May enter 'twixt the gap of both and take
> The one by th'other.
>
> [3,1,111–15]

In staging the legitimacy crisis 'when two authorities are up' *Coriolanus* accurately reflects the representational confusion of a mixed monarchy, at a time when King James could still descend on Parliament and announce 'that I always sit in this place by representation, and therefore I conceive I may much more come personally when I will'.[45] But it is the Schmittian pathos of the man who lives Shakespeare's own professional nightmare of 'the reversal from king to beggar, like a reversal from hunted to hunter', when he switches roles from patron to player, or 'anti-theatrical ideologue to shape-shifting actor', that suggests why its response is so ambivalent when, as Santner puts it, 'The "mass" that is unleashed by way of the excarnation of sovereignty ... metastasizes within each individual'.[46] For this darling of the old patrimonial order is also, in Terry Eagleton's words, 'Shakespeare's most developed study of the bourgeois individualist', who presages a time 'not far off from Shakespeare's – when a whole society will fall prey to the ideology of self-authorship, when all individuals will be only begetters of themselves'.[47] So, far from being exalted, Coriolanus's self-creation is, as Catherine Belsey says, figured as 'pathetic rather than heroic'.[48] Yet if this great lord makes a 'proud beggar' when he is hooted 'out'o'th'city' by the 'clusters' [*4,6,130*], in his disdain for hired labour and vulgar profit he also expresses his creator's ambition to 'stand / As if a man were author of himself / And knew no other kin' [*5,3,35–7*].[49] Thus all the ravelled complexity of Shakespeare's multiple personality, as all at once a player, playwright, poet and proprietor, converges in Coriolanus's refusal to play anything but 'The man I am' [*3,2,14*], yet simultaneous discovery that 'the creature represents the flip side' of the political theology of absolute sovereignty that underpins his own claim to be a 'most absolute sir' [*4,5,135*]:[50]

> You are too absolute,
> Though therein you can never be too noble
> But when extremities speak.

> [*40–2*]

Shakespeare's ambivalent position between private servitude and professional service complicates our received narrative of the playhouse as evolving from patronage to commodity exchange, with 'players and audiences as producers and consumers, untrammelled by social considerations'.[51] For *Coriolanus* reveals instead how

Jacobean theatre remained bound to the master-slave dialectic and the 'royal remains' of the great house. Its anti-commercialism thus confirms recent accounts of the Shakespearean stage as a set up where power and commerce combined in 'an unsteady solution, at one moment one seeming to dominate' without either vanquishing the other.[52] But what it also exposes through the split personality of this cavalier turned comedian is the fragility of such co-existence. As Pierre Bourdieu explains, in words about the 'art-for-art's-sake' movement which apply equally to the early modern literary field, the first artists to assert creative freedom in any cultural system are caught in a double bind as 'dominated dominators'. They escape economic *demand* only to embrace political *command*. They are therefore 'fated to feel all the contradictions of "poor relations"'.[53] And by turning away from the pressing people to become a 'poor relation' of the powerful, the muffled yet now deferentially hatless Coriolanus who presents himself on the threshold of his enemy Aufidius's mansion does indeed seem to personify the creaturely and liminal condition of just such a 'dominated dominator' as the 'gentleman' Shakespeare himself:

CORIOLANUS:	Let me but stand. I will not hurt your hearth.
THIRD SERVINGMAN:	What are you?
CORIOLANUS:	A gentleman.
THIRD SERVINGMAN:	A marvellous poor one.
CORIOLANUS:	True, so I am.

[4,5,24–8]

The tartness of his face

In this play about 'standing' and '*understanding*', Coriolanus's emergence in Aufidius's courtyard as one of the 'companions' in 'mean apparel', the groundlings who dwell 'Under the canopy i'th'city' [4,4,SD; 4,5,37–41], could be thought to refer to Shakespeare's fugitive position as an insider / outsider, at once scavenging from the table of the great and subsisting below that 'most excellent canopy' [*Hamlet, 2,2,290*] of the Globe. Bourdieu identifies a symptom of this schizoid participation-exclusion among the pioneers of the literary field in Baudelaire's self-dramatization after 1848 as both 'torturer and victim, the wound and yet the knife', and proposes that the poet's concept of 'pure art' had its genesis in this double rupture with power and profit.[54] Likewise, the violent turnaround of *Coriolanus* from the capital to the courtyard can be read as an unflinching analysis of its author's own vagrancy as a 'strange one' who lives 'under the canopy' of the public playhouse yet cannot be got 'out of the house' of aristocratic power. So, while its protagonist's resolve to 'play the man I am' resounds like a fanfare for artistic freedom, comparable to Philip Sidney's determination to look in his 'heart and write'; or Rembrandt's to paint 'for liberty, not honour', the persistence of this tragedy is to go on to pose the question Bourdieu attributes to Flaubert: 'What if the power that the artist appropriates were only an imaginary version of powerlessness?'[55]

Suppose the flight into artistic freedom was *itself* prescribed? Bourdieu prompts us to ask. For what is at stake in *Coriolanus*, as it is in *Sentimental Education*, is the *interestedness of disinterestedness*, the social determination of 'a sovereign position that proclaims itself free of determination'.[56] Thus, while it had been the plebeians who tore the poet to pieces in *Julius Caesar*, here it will be Coriolanus's patrons who in the end 'tear him to pieces' [5,6,112] for pleasing the crowd. Shakespeare's text in fact betrays his vested interest in disinterest when its protagonist stockpiles grain during the famine, for records have the writer listed during the 1607 Midland riots hoarding brewers' malt.[57] So when Menenius admits a drinker will 'make a crooked face' if ale sold him touches his 'palate adversely' [2,1,50], the old lord's cynicism about consumer resistance strikes home. In the late 1600s, when the paying public clamoured for city comedy and 'corn at their own rates', the Stratford engrosser 'showed sourly' [5,3,13] and gave his customers *Coriolanus* and small beer. 'The tartness of his face sours ripe grapes' [5,4,14], complain the Citizens of Rome's grain hoarder. But such was also the unpalatable sharpness of the product when Shakespeare began to hoard his creative 'superfluity' [1,1,17], and to turn away from the public amphitheatre, 'As if a man were author of himself', into the managed scarcity of art. So what the backlash in this two-part drama reveals is the 'cracked heart' of divided loyalty caused by the rarefied refusal to supply what the city demands:

> This last old man,
> Whom with a cracked heart I have sent to Rome,
> Loved me above the measure of a father,
> Nay, godded me indeed.
>
> [5,3,8–11]

'I shall be loved when I am lacked' [*4,1,16*], calculates Shakespeare's protagonist; and there does seem to be a parallelism between that economic logic and the sourness of this play. For with its reflection that 'This is a happier and more comely time / Than when these fellows ran about the streets / Crying confusion' [*4,6,29–31*], the first half of *Coriolanus*, up to the turning-point when the patron is so 'disbenched' from the stage that his 'precipitation might down stretch / Below the beam of sight' [*2,2,67; 3,1,267*], reads like a declaration of creative independence for the Globe, of which Shakespeare was himself such a beneficiary that it was rumoured he spent at 'a rate of £1,000 a year'.[58] By the 1600s, theatre historians calculate, 24,000 Londoners packed the amphitheatres each week for nine months of the year; a figure of 'odds beyond arithmetic' to truly 'make a monster of the multitude' [*2,3,10; 3,1,244*], but one that raises an obvious question: Why, if the popular playhouses were so profitable, did Shakespeare's company, in less than a decade after 1600, abandon its popular methods?

'Why, by 1642 [when they were closed at the outbreak of the Civil War], were all the major theatres private ones?'[59] The key to this riddle is precisely the anti-commercial terms with which dramatists now began to stigmatize 'the shop's foreman, or some such brave spark', as Jonson railed, 'That may judge for his sixpence'.[60] A naive explanation for such hostility to the public sphere might be that 'Antagonism was one of the ways a playhouse ensured involvement ... Whenever a Shakespeare play insults the brutal nature of a lower-class crowd it seems to be partly to provoke a response.'[61] But this is to mistake the character for the play; and to ignore how, as Bourdieu relates, in the symbolic revolution by which artists free themselves from consumer demand and refuse 'to recognise any master but their art', the liberating illusion of 'making the market disappear' is sealed by 'indignation, contempt, and revolt': 'In the heroic phase of the conquest of autonomy,' an ethical rupture always validates the aesthetic break, as 'it is the distaste inspired in writers by the vulgar materialism of the new economic masters' which is constitutive of 'the world of art as a world apart'.[62] What we witness in this tragedy is more complex, therefore, than a mere provocation of the audience, for Coriolanus grasps that his aggression towards the public is a measure of *distinction*, when he insists he must 'go alone, / Like to a lonely dragon that his fen / Makes feared and talked of more than seen' [*4,1,30–2*]. The defector's antitheatrical prejudice in fact makes him look increasingly like Shakespeare's response to the rival who filled his plays with playgoing fools like Fabian Fitzdottrel, rushing to Blackfriars to strut in his new cloak, or Bartholomew Cokes, unable to tell puppets from people, Jonson himself:

> The very collecting of his plays into the 1616 Folio testifies to Jonson's impatience with the stage, and his desire to commit his 'Works' – significantly so named – to a more lasting medium ... For Jonson ... print offered an escape into a stabler medium. Lifting the play out of the turbulence of the public arena into the still silence of the page, enabled it to transcend the imperfections and vicissitudes of live performance.[63]

Jonas Barish has explained how Jonson's contempt for the 'loathèd stage' led him not merely to appeal to readers over the heads of audiences but to identify the new technology of print with the noble patron as ideal reader. Jonson's battle for literary autonomy was therefore waged backwards, by distancing his art from the public sphere as the creation of one who has 'lived twenty year, / Where I may handle silk as free, and near, / As any mercer', in the 'braveries' of upper class society.[64] For all his impatience with the 'monstrous and detested' sight of a 'fellow that has neither art, nor brain', perched upon the stage 'like an Aristarchus, or stark-ass, / Taking men's lines with a tobacco face, / In snuff, still spitting, using his wryed looks ... to turn / The good aspect of those that sit near him / From what they do behold', this bricklayer's son remained in thrall to his neoclassical prospectus of inducing some Maecenas to rescue him from the malodorous Globe and sponsor him to 'scorn the world'.[65] His 1611 dedication to William Herbert Earl of Pembroke of his Roman tragedy *Catiline*, the first play its author 'ever dedicated to any person', supplies a professional context, then, for Coriolanus's self-betraying defection, when it addresses the earl in similar antitheatrical terms to those with which Shakespeare's exile approaches his opponent:

> My lord, in so thick and dark an ignorance as now covers the age, I crave leave to stand by your light; and, by that, to be read. Posterity may pay your benefit the honor, and thanks, when it shall be known that you dare, in these jig-given times, to countenance a legitimate poem.[66]

The contrapuntal plot of *Coriolanus* seems to reflect how 'patronage intersects in the great house, the playhouse, and the printing house' in the Jacobean literary system.[67] Thus, like Jonson in his dreams, its protagonist will depend on his patron for publication of 'The book of his good acts, whence men have read his fame unparalleled happily amplified' [5,2,17–18]. In the second half of the play the theatre metaphor is therefore superseded by the Jonsonian idea that privileged readers of printed books will in 'th'interpretation of the time' [4,7,50] secure for the author a 'noble memory' [5,6,154], 'use him as the grace 'fore meat, / Their talk at table, and their thanks at end' [4,7,3–4]. This is the patrimonial concept of authorial identity Coriolanus's mother Volumnia upholds, when she reminds him her grandson is 'a poor epitome of yours, / Which by th'interpretation of full time / May show like all yourself' [5,3,67–9]. But when Shakespeare has these aristocrats also excoriate the Forum in the same Puritan discourse with which colleagues were now scorning the Globe – as 'a foul and pestilent congregation of vapours' [*Hamlet*, 2,2,293], where 'they made the air unwholesome' when they 'cast [their] stinking greasy caps' [4,6,138] – and contrasts this with the acuity of the Tribunes' analysis of the new representative process, the upshot is not simply to antagonize the garlic-eaters, but to problematize the old alliance of poetry and power against the breath of the great beast; to question the professional perversity of turning against 'this majestical roof fretted with golden fire' [*Hamlet*, 2,2,290], for the illusory emancipation of some 'world elsewhere':

> You common cry of curs, whose breath I hate
> As reek o'th'rotten fens, whose loves I prize
> As the dead carcasses of unburied men
> That do corrupt my air: I banish you ...
> > > > Despising
> For you the city, thus I turn by back.
> There is a world elsewhere.
>
> > > > > > [3,3,124–39]

A creeping thing

In a theatrical context, Coriolanus's disgust with the Forum resembles the alienation of those notables who, according to Jonson, were driven by the new rules of exchange to stand up 'between the Acts', and 'make affidavit to the whole house of their not understanding one Scene'.[68] Thus, with its repeated picture of the great man 'with his hat, thus raising it in scorn' [2,3,156], the play reads like a compulsive re-run of the representational impasse when some milord would 'rise with a screwed and discontented face from [his] stool to be gone'. But as Weimann notes, resistance to 'an elevated, purely imaginary, self-contained' theatrical space was waged by older performers as well, who still tended to believe that 'Players, representing something and someone else, also (re)presented themselves'.[69] So the question this poses is how far as a practitioner Shakespeare went along with the protest when he had the stool-sitter storm off the stage. For fifty years ago, in a pioneer study of the sociology of Shakespearean poetry, John Danby proposed that the Poet's picture in *Timon of Athens* of the literary system as 'the Hill of Fortune, and of writing bound to the patronage of either Great House or Public Theatre', complicates our picture of Shakespeare as the Bard of Bankside, by making the Elizabethan–Jacobean scene seem far less monolithic. And around 1605, when he was researching for *King Lear*, Danby suggested, the dramatist was himself reminded by Sidney's *Arcadia* of the alternative literary career he had rejected, grounded not in 'the unroofed commercial theatre' but within the sheltering aristocratic house.[70]

The great house dominated the representation of players 'even as it disappeared from their lives'; but what is revolutionary about the picture of this noble retreat in the literature of the 1600s, according to Danby, is that the writer now descends on the aristocratic mansion not as its creature, but 'as an outsider who feels himself the equal of any he might find inside'.[71] Such was the equality Jonson anticipated for himself in his poem *To Penshurst*, where he exulted how at 'the house of the literary "father" Sidney', the 'liberal board doth flow / With all that hospitality doth know ... Nor when I take my lodging need I pray / For fire, lights, or livery: all is there; As if thou then wert mine, or I reigned there'. With its library where 'the whole household' might imbibe 'the mysteries of manners, arms, and arts', the stately home of 'Kalendar' offered a jaded thespian an ivory tower remote from 'violent popular ignorance' [5,2,41], where none went 'empty-handed'; and during the next decades 'the "sons" of Ben would sentimentalize hock-carts and May-days in homage to such seigneurial establishments, 'where the same beer and bread / That is his Lordship's shall be mine'.[72] But the houses built by the

Sidneys and their Herbert in-laws at Penshurst and Wilton had in fact been founded on brute military might, and in Jonson's fantasy and the imaginary of *Coriolanus* this violence would be turned back by the poet against the playhouse, in a veritable *Kulturkampf*.

Jonson had been hooted off the London stage for his Roman epic *Sejanus*. So it is in line with the Jonsonian idyll that when Coriolanus abandons the open 'canopy' for the Volsce stronghold, the man who refused to please the crowd turns up at the mansion where his enemy 'feasts the nobles' disguised 'in mean apparel' like some strolling player; and that this feudal redoubt is defined in such nostalgic contrast to the marketplace, as 'a goodly house' where the 'feast smells well', and the exile is greeted with 'a thousand welcomes' as 'simply the rarest man i'th'world'. With its roistering lords, blazing hearth, tireless servants, festive music and bowls of 'Wine, wine, wine!', not to mention its potlatch of war, Aufidius's household is an epitome of the patriarchal economy as a world set apart from commerce, a wish-fulfilment of a weary poet's yearning for sanctuary from an 'ungrateful' and 'cankered' metropolis given over to 'increase tailors and breed ballad-makers' [*4,4,1–9; 4,5,1–41; 90; 160; 217*]. There is a throw-back here to scenes of Elizabethan drama, like that when Marlowe's destitute Aeneas lobbies Queen Dido while 'servitors pass through the hall / Bearing a banquet', which project touring as a precious relief for the 'tragedians of the city' [*Hamlet, 2,2,316*] and 'an economic world turned upside-down'.[73] Like Aeneas, or Jonson in his poem, Coriolanus will be seated at the banquet 'as if he were son and heir to Mars; set at upper end o'th'table' [*4,5,191*]. But what has now altered, the play suggests, is the degree of animus reflected back upon the city: 'He'll go, he says, and sowl the porter of Rome by th'ears. He will mow all down before him, and leave his passage polled' [*198–200*]. Thus, just as the great house was a strategic base in Jonson's fight-back, after his play 'suffered no less violence from the people' of London 'than the subject of it did from the rage of the people of Rome', so Aufidius's palace is the vantage from which to plot revenge in the specifically aesthetic form of the defeat of the theatre's egalitarian rules of representation and exchange:[74]

> But when they shall see, sir, his crest up again and the man in blood, they will out of their burrows like conies after rain, and revel all with him.
>
> [*4,6,207–9*]

'I tell you he does sit in gold, his eye / Red as 'twould burn Rome' [*5,1,63*]: like Nero, Coriolanus comes to stand for an art created to devastate the city that yet dreams of inflicting its 'intended fire' [*5,2,45*] on a captive public. Identification with the arsonist emperor, who would be taken up on the Stuart stage as a prototype artistic dictator, explains why Coriolanus sees no contradiction between 'preparing fire' [*5,3,69*], in Marlovian relish to watch 'Your temples burned' [*4,6,89*] and 'The fires i'th'lowest hell fold in the people' [*3,3,71*], and his intention to be 'loved' [*4,1,16*] by the city's residents for 'the brand / That should consume it' [*4,6,121*].[75] Such is the psychopathology of the artist as natural aristocrat, 'indifferent to honours and wholly focused on posterity': 'a kind of nothing, titleless, / Till he had forged himself a name o'th'fire / Of burning Rome' [*13–14*].[76] And when Coriolanus is described as 'the rock, the oak' [*5,2,105*], it is possible to glimpse in these metaphors a prehistory of the romantic ideology of the artist oblivious to society, whose art is autonomous to the extent that, as he says, 'Wife, mother, child, I know not' [*5,3,78*]. Thus the reification of Coriolanus as he 'moves like an engine' will negate all the social values of the Globe, as he 'sits in his state as a thing made for Alexander', and like Apelles 'What he bids be done is finished with his bidding. He wants nothing of a god but eternity and a heaven to throne in' [*5,4,15–20*]. This is the same discourse of consecration as will be lavished in *The Winter's Tale* on 'that rare Italian master' Giulio Romano [*5,2,87*]; but here Coriolanus's idolatrous canonization as *himself* an artificial 'thing / Made by some other deity than nature / That shapes men better', looks like the ultimate perversion of the Renaissance cult of artistic absolutism.[77]

'He is their god' [*4,6,94*], it is said; and 'Most absolute sir' [*4,5,135*] is how Aufidius greets his old enemy in a tribute that confirms what Roy Strong calls the 'profound alliance' between absolute art and absolute power.[78] So considering Coriolanus is banished from Rome for being 'too absolute' [*3,2,40*] in decrying Athens, because there 'people had more absolute power' [*3,1,119*], it is clear how his creator understands that the absolutism of art 'does not establish itself at the expense of political power, which, on the contrary, sustains it'. As Christian Jouhard comments, creative autonomy may be forged at this time by separation from the market, but it is power that decides its limit: 'it instigates, it suspends, it commands, it exploits'.[79] So fifty years ago, in what remains one of the finest essays on the play, D.J. Gordon concluded that its theme is indeed that 'The absoluteness of the self, the I, cannot be maintained'.[80] Coriolanus's masters will therefore allow just enough scope to his 'sovereignty' to let him triumph in the public arena on their behalf: 'he'll be to Rome, / As is the osprey to the fish, who takes it / By sovereignty of nature' [4,7,33–5]. Yet their recurring image for his genius is not a bird of prey but a butterfly: 'There is a differency between a grub and a butterfly, yet your butterfly was a grub' [5,4,9]. They follow him, we are therefore told, 'with no less confidence / Than boys pursuing summer butterflies' [4,6,97–8]; and the ambiguity about who is the pursuer here, and who the pursued, reminds us that in the world of these aristocratic vandals the prettiness of the aesthetic is truly no more than that of the 'gilded butterfly' Coriolanus becomes:[81]

> O' my word, the father's son! I'll swear 'tis a very pretty boy. O' my troth, I looked upon him o' Wednesday half an hour together. He's such a confirmed countenance! I saw him run after a gilded butterfly, and when he caught it he let it go again, and after it again, and over and over he comes, and up again, catched it again. Or whether his fall enraged him, or how 'twas, he did so set his teeth and tear it! O, I warrant, how he mammocked it!
>
> [1,3,54–9]

'So we'll live, / And pray, and sing, and tell old tales, and laugh / At gilded butterflies' [*King Lear, 5,3,11–13*]: instantly countermanded by Edmund, Lear's prospectus suggests how Shakespeare came to think of the aesthetic crushed by the pathos of the real. Throughout his career the dramatist had downplayed his real commercial strength and presented theatre as the fragile toy of a callous and capricious elite, like the 'worthless fancy' the Lord stages in *The Taming of the Shrew* when he inveigles the actors into his cruel prank on Sly [*Ind.1,40*]. Thus, valorizing 'disinterestedness against interest', 'largesse against prudence', as Bourdieu wrote, Shakespearean theatre prefigured the later mystification of art as 'a world elsewhere', through its pretence of being the petty plaything of some despot like Theseus or Hal.[82] In these plays the rule of art is that it succeeds to the extent it effaces its true economic value by offering itself as a trifle of the great.[83] Yet from the moment Sly is seated as such an obtuse auditor, Shakespeare also makes sure to invent a patron it would ultimately be possible to dislodge.[84] The shock reversal in the second half of this drama, however, is that what threatens whenever patrons interrupt the performers is played out to its bitter end, as the feast to which Coriolanus is welcomed like a wandering minstrel proves to be his doom.

From the 'fury of contradictions' in its 'wish for both dependence and independence', Stanley Cavell deduces that *Coriolanus* was written in direct response to Sidney's citation in *The Defence of Poetry* of the Fable of the Belly as a myth of *noblesse oblige*. Itself 'a play about food', with its audience as hungry 'starvers', *Coriolanus* is Shakespeare's defence of poetry, Cavell infers, as a theatrical communion in which the meat is in the words.[85] But if so, what is telling is how speechless its leading character becomes from the moment he allows his affairs to be 'servanted to others' [*5,2,79*]. Menenius supposes this means 'he had not dined' [*5,1,50*]; whereas it is because he *has* feasted with Aufidius that Coriolanus falls so short of words: '"Twas very faintly he said, "Rise", dismissed me ... with his speechless hand' [*5,1,66–7*]. Thus, halting 'to bite his lip / And "hmh"' [*5,1,48–9*], he 'talks like a knell, and his "hmh!" is a battery' [*5,4,17*]; and it is hard not to hear in this dull mechanization the dramatist's own strangled voice, bound in this metallic work 'to hold to his conditions' [*5,1,69*] like a hired hand. For Shakespeare seems here to perceive how it is the patron who 'sanctifies himself' in *reflected* glory by turning 'up the white o'th'eye to his discourse' [*4,5,194–5*], when the servant echoes his master's voice. And he further grasps the iron law of this 'entertainment', which, as Coriolanus demonstrates when he is seated beside his lord like a 'wedded mistress' [*4,5,116*], exacts as the price for protection the effeminization of the player into prostitution. Thus all the dramatist's apprehensions about the logic of service, with the actor as 'beggar in the great man's house', are shown to be justified by this ironic and chiasmic plot, where the fears rehearsed in the first half are played out in the second, and Coriolanus's terrified prediction of his travesty as a 'pretty boy' [*1,3,54*] in 'womanish toge' [*2,3,105*] provides the script for his subsequent emasculation as no 'more than a creeping thing' [*5,4,11*], humiliated, infantilized and speechless in Aufidius's court:[86]

> Away, my disposition; and possess me
> Some harlot's spirit! My throat of war be turned,
> Which choired with the drum, into a pipe
> Small as an eunuch or the virgin voice

That babies lull asleep! The smiles of knaves
Tent in my cheeks, and schoolboys' tears take up
The glasses of my sight! A beggar's tongue
Make motion through my lips, and my armed knees,
Who bowed but in my stirrup, bend like his
That hath received an alms!

[*3,2,110–20*]

Like a dull actor

Whether or not Philip Sidney's sister Mary dowager Countess of
Pembroke did write the letter attributed to her by a descendant,
commanding her son William to bring James I to see *As You Like It*
with the inducement that 'We have the man Shakespeare with us',
we know that at Christmas 1603 the King's Men were paid £30
for their 'pains and expenses' in travelling to Wilton, her Wiltshire
country house, 'and there presenting before His Majesty one play'.[87]
It is perhaps fanciful to read into Coriolanus's horror of effeminacy
some memory of the Wilton staging of the cross-dressed comedy.
But the court was at Winchester to escape the plague; so this
payment puts Shakespeare in exactly the double bind suffered by
Jonson, and represented in *Coriolanus*, of escaping a troubled city
only to bend the knee like one that 'hath received an alms'. Once
before he had supplied such a pseudo-classical tragedy to order,
when the 'Noble Roman History of *Titus Andronicus*' was 'played
by the Right Honourable the Earl of Derby, Earl of Pembroke, and
Earl of Sussex's servants' who acted at Wilton in 1593.[88] That play
begins and ends with a Roman election that gets abandoned in the
action; so perhaps *Coriolanus* arose from a commission that sent
Shakespeare back to this earliest text. For at Christmas 1609 the
King's Men were paid another £40 for 'private practice in the time
of infection' at Wilton.[89] Next year it would be the convoluted
Cymbeline, set partly in the Herbert's Welsh fiefdom, that they
brought to London from the country. Thus his resentment of the
salon culture of Wilton might well be the reason why Shakespeare
now denigrated his profession as a mere mouthing 'motion through
my lips' with a 'beggar's tongue'.

'The King's a beggar now the play is done' is how Shakespeare
closed *All's Well That Ends Well*, the Jacobean comedy about
another demanding widow and her headstrong heir he probably

wrote under instructions from the dowager Countess for the playboy earl. 'Delia, born of a race of poets', Marlowe cravenly called Lady Herbert, 'crowned with as many poems as Ariadne had stars'.[90] One of those poems, it has been suggested, was Shakespeare's gelid *The Rape of Lucrece*.[91] He could hardly have refused such commissions, for, as the actors Henry Condell and John Heminge recalled, William and his brother Philip, Earl of Montgomery, expected 'no man to come near but with a kind of religious address', and rewarded poets and players as they did the 'Country hands' who presented them with cream and fruit.[92] The self-centred, petulant William was, in particular, garlanded from boyhood in the adulation the play appears to parody, when Cominius extols Coriolanus as a boy-player, who 'At sixteen years ... with his Amazonian chin ... drove the bristled lips before him ... When he might act the woman in the scene' [2,2,83–92]. This characterization of the teenage Coriolanus as a crossed-dressed player was not in Shakespeare's source, and it undermines the very manliness it is supposedly intended to support. But the image of 'a boy impostor' mimicking the deeds of his heroic forebears to claim an identity that is not his own seems tailor-made for the swaggering nephew of Sir Philip Sidney.[93]

'A melancholy young man' who was 'too cold' to be popular, Pembroke none the less loved to prance at the annual musters, and cut a spectacular figure tilting as late as 1621 on horses dripping with 'oriental pearls'; but the 'note of flattery' in the exaggerations of the earl's 'wisdom, learning, virtue, poetical powers, and personal beauty' was detectable from the start, and in the 1600s the accolades in praise of this arrogant wastrel, who was in fact his mother's pawn, became so hyperbolic they can only have intended as 'sly mockery' of his self-importance.[94] Jonson had pictured 'the farmer and the clown' paying feudal dues to Mary Sidney and her family in 'Penshurst'; but by the time of *Coriolanus* it was her own son who was being satirised as a '*Rusticus*, or *Clown*'.[95] Thus, among more than a hundred works dedicated to William Herbert, Chapman's 1610 translation of Homer stands out for the obsequiousness with which the earl was praised there as 'past all others' for his 'form divine'; but Shakespeare may have picked up the hint of sarcasm in these encomia when in a play about the forced word and dumb mute he gives Cominius just such sycophantic lines:

I shall lack voice; the deeds of Coriolanus
Should not be uttered feebly. It is held
That valour is the chiefest virtue, and
Most dignifies the haver. If it be,
The man I speak of cannot in the world
Be singly counterpoised.

[2,2,78–83]

Tom May declared the Herberts' cult of Roman liberty the sign of nobility; but when May displeased him, the Earl of Montgomery broke his staff across the poet's back.[96] Such were the rites of service and magnanimity that made the Herbert brothers the most interfering artistic patrons in England, with careers as royal favourites that carried each to the office of Lord Chamberlain, which indeed made them protectors of the King's Men. Significantly, for Coriolanus's characterization as a patron turned player, both were avid theatregoers who acted from an early age in masques. But if Jonson rejoiced at the £20 Pembroke sent him each New Year to buy books, and Inigo Jones was ever grateful to the earl for funding his Italian tour, what perturbed Shakespeare, his play implies, was the stultifying aesthetic price the Herberts exacted for such benevolence, which was submission to the glacial classicism their uncle had dictated in his *Defence of Poetry*, and that their mother obeyed in her translation of Garnier's *Marc Antoine*, with its stilted didacticism and marmoreal verse. For if Leeds Barroll is right to link *Antony and Cleopatra* to the closet dramas dressed up in 'womanish toge' at Wilton, such as Samuel Daniel's *Cleopatra* and Thomas Kyd's version of Garnier's *Cornélie*, and to stress how as patrons the Herberts were distinguished by their 'interest in plays as plays', what is striking about *Coriolanus* is how methodically this Roman work reproduces the straitjacketed conditions of a coerced commission, as its protagonist enacts first the split between popular and private theatres, and then the theatrical calamity of a travesty which literally bends its knee to a haughty noblewoman's impossible contradictory demands.[97]

As Daniel's biographer Joan Rees concedes, given the Countess's imperious dictates and predisposition to regard drama as a form of feudal offering, 'It is remarkable … anything of any individuality got written' in her coterie at all.[98] So in the tragedy the climactic scene when Coriolanus weeps and kneels to his mother, just as she had 'corrected' him to do [5,3,57], his 'knee bussing the stones', reads like a mimetic working-out of 'our bending' author's [*Henry V, Epi.*2] professional double-bind and his ultimate scene of self-subjection, contorted by his patroness's incompatible directives to impress both the patricians and the paying public, and so reduced 'Like a dull actor' who has 'forgot [his] part', and is 'out / Even to a full disgrace' [*40–3*], to the dumbness of his own stage direction: '*He holds her by the hand silent*' [*182*].[99] Thus, required to produce a togas-and-sandals drama like that of the domineering lady of the house, while honouring his contract with the Globe, it is as if Shakespeare made his own 'womanish' subjection the subject of his tragedy and of its childlike entreaty: 'May I change these garments?' [*2,3,136*]. But as Martin Butler notes, the contradictions in the antitheatricalism of the neoclassical plays commanded by these Jacobean grandees could never be resolved.[100] And there is in fact no record of a single Stuart performance of this play. But we do know that when soon after Jonson dedicated *Catiline* to Pembroke, like *Sejanus* that other Roman ruin was catcalled off the boards. Thus Shakespeare's most studiedly antique production foretells the disastrous playhouse reception of all such 'unnatural scenes', when its protagonist returns to the public arena intent on artistic conquest, only to be laughed out of town:

> O mother, mother!
> What have you done? Behold, the heavens ope,
> The gods look down, and this unnatural scene
> They laugh at.
>
> [*5,3,183–5*]

'Lo here the work which she did impose, / Who only doth predominate by Muse', is how Daniel described his subordination to Lady Pembroke in the dedication of *Cleopatra*: 'She whose clear brightness … makes me what I am; Call'd up my spirits … To sing of state, and tragic notes to frame'. In a *risqué* allusion to James, the writer then said his task was 'To chase away the tyrant of the North / Gross Barbarism'.[101] As a response to Herbert patronage, such slavishness thus not only confirms how writers were expected to jump to the Countess's orders, but how much her 'predominance' was about imposing the neoclassical aesthetic of the 'Pembroke school': 'a shapely and complete artefact that could be admired for its skill and polish', like the Roman *gravitas* Hamlet would force upon the Players.[102] As David Bergeron exclaims, how many other literary figures of the 1600s 'self-consciously set out to shape the direction of dramatic form ... even if theatre history may see the effort as a failure?'[103] The question appertains directly to *Coriolanus*, for any account of this play must start with what it was that made this 'noble work' Shakespeare's least popular tragedy, as A.C. Bradley put it, while recognizing that for classicizing purists like T.S. Eliot the text is, 'with *Antony and Cleopatra*, Shakespeare's most assured artistic success'.[104] For with its pitching of a famous military family against the playhouse plebs, this unperformable play about unperformability does look like a back-handed compliment to the Herbert salon, where submission to impossible projects was the entry ticket to Wilton's ornamental gardens, riding-stables, picture galleries, and shelves of precious books.

Under the old earl the plays written for Pembroke's Men had enjoyed only chequered success. Yet Marlowe was desperate enough to hope that Herbert protection might 'keep him safe' from 'the blows of barbarism and ignorance'.[105] And in the dowager's time, John Aubrey recorded, Wilton did become 'like a College, an Arcadian place and a Paradise', modelled on Basilius's lodge in *Arcadia*.[106] Daniel had been a tutor there, and 'My best school' is how he obsequiously commemorated the house in the *Defence of Rhyme* he dedicated to William: 'having been first encourag'd or fram'd ... by your most Worthy and Honourable Mother'.[107] And in this palace of art and power, iron and butterflies, the two earls were tempted to 'think these trifles something', Heminge and Condell recalled, and extend to the living author 'so much favour' by their 'most noble patronage' as made 'our Shakespeare, by humble offer of his plays, a Fellow and a Friend'.[108] When Richard Burbage, the great tragedian who might have acted the part of Coriolanus at Wilton, died in 1619, Pembroke therefore declared how he mourned his 'old acquaintance' so much he could not watch another play.[109] As Barroll proposes, though it is seldom discussed, all the evidence thus puts Shakespeare in these last years back where he had started, within 'the interesting aura' of the Herberts, as 'aristocratic dispensers of largess'.[110] And that may be why Sir Fulke Greville, the wily old Menenius whose own tragedies conformed so faithfully to the Herberts' glyptic standards they were never staged, but whose *Monarchy* cued many of the patricians' speeches in *Coriolanus*, was pleased to count himself not only a servant to Queen Elizabeth and friend of Sir Philip Sidney but also the 'Master to Shakespeare.'[111]

Cut me to pieces

If *Coriolanus* was aimed at Wilton it may not be chance that it has a plot so similar to *Arcadia*, where Basilius also incites a revolt by refusing to rule, nor that its passive aggressor repeats Sidney's gambit of withdrawal from the town. Shakespeare's play foretells how in the years before the Civil War this Herbert clique would constitute 'not merely a collection of men and women linked by kinship' but the cast of what Gary Waller calls a psychodrama in which 'the contradictory forces of the broader conflicts of the age were enacted'. Waller traces 'the myths of patriarchy, political power, and lineage' which surrounded Mary Sidney, as the daughter of an upwardly mobile father, sister of the poet, 'whose influence and power over her increased after his death', and mother of 'one of the most brilliant, aggressive womanizers in the Jacobean court'. And he shows how the paradox of the Sidney inheritance was that with this indomitable dowager in command, the dynasty became a *matrix* for all the discourses of power, patronage and authorship that underwrote the masculine autonomy her brother had proclaimed, when his sisterly muse told him to despise the 'slave-born Muscovite' and look into his heart to write.[112] As Daniel testified when in 1611 he yet again asked her to 'Behold the work which thou didst impose', it was the Countess who had disclosed 'Unto our times, what noble powers there are / In women's hearts'.[113] Thus, if Shakespeare did cough up *Coriolanus* for Wilton, it cannot be chance that this staging of sovereign abjection, and of confusion of art with war, should foreground the contradictoriness of a martial performance *patronized by a woman*, nor that the incestuous and homoerotic dynamics of the Sidney family romance should be shadowed so darkly in its plot.

For feminists, Volumnia is Shakespeare's misogynistic caricature of the 'suffocating mother', whose murderous nurturing expresses 'the vulnerability inherent in feeding', yet also the compulsion 'to fend off that vulnerability by spitting out'.[114] In fact, Shakespeare might have taken this nexus of infantilism and food from the avidity with which supposed lackeys like Jonson 'consumed Penshurst'.[115] For if this belligerent virago whose idea of nourishment is so self-centred that she consoles herself that 'Anger's my meat: I sup upon myself / And so shall starve with feeding' [4,2,53], is a covert portrait of English literature's most smothering benefactress, what her

infanticidal nurturing surely figures is Shakespeare's own resistance
to Herbert tutelage, with its 'art made tongue-tied by authority'
[Sonnet 66], his *sotto voce* objection that to submit his text to
be 'corrected' by the light of *Astrophel and Stella* would be to let
'pebbles on the hungry beach / Fillip the stars ... Murd'ring impossibility to make / What cannot be slight work' [5,3,57–62]. The
sister of Philip Sidney embodied the self-subordination of a woman
as legitimating authority, Waller argues, being placed on a pedestal
merely to authorise the authorial agency of her idolized men: 'she
is autonomous only to the extent that she encourages and rewards
her (male) poets'.[116] But if we count Volumnia as Shakespeare's
arch contribution to the long gallery of literary likenesses of this
redoubtable matriarch, then what her status as guardian of the
sacred flame underscores is the crippling contradiction of his 'womanish' subjection to a dynasty who conducted their own careers
'as if a man were author of himself', while expecting their protégés
to continue to 'adhere to the ethic of the feudal contract' and to
execute 'what cannot be':[117]

> Behold our patroness, the life of Rome!
> Call all your tribes together, praise the gods,
> And make triumphant fires. Strew flowers before them.
> Unshout the noise that banished Martius,
> Repeal him with the welcome of his mother.
> Cry 'Welcome, ladies, welcome!'
>
> $\qquad\qquad\qquad\qquad\qquad\qquad\qquad\qquad$ [5,5,1–6]

With its perverse plan to 'unshout the noise' of the crowd celebrating the expulsion of the nobility from the stage, *Coriolanus* seems
to be Shakespeare's most intense meditation upon the incursion of
political power into the art of the stage. There is deep irony, therefore, when Volumnia is told 'you deserve / To have a temple built
you' [5,3,208], for the triumph of the patroness is here the death of
the performer befriended by the great. The 'man Shakespeare' has
revealed how well he understood the dangers of such a familiarity,
when he has his protagonist please the city to '*great shouts of the
people*' [SD, 5,6,48], while still insisting to his lord and master that
his public appearances have not undermined their 'great action',
since he is now 'no more infected' with love of the metropolis
'Than when I parted hence, but still subsisting / Under your great
command' [5,6,73]. As Bourdieu commented, the type of literary

salon pioneered at Wilton is a honey-trap for 'elitist refugees', who 'give themselves the illusion of reliving the aristocratic life' but then become compromised by the confused relations necessary to justify bad faith: through the false footing of the salon, 'those who hold power aim to impose their vision on artists' who all the while manoeuvre 'to assure themselves a mediating control'.[118]

At the heart of the Herbert programme was an irreconcilable contradiction, *Coriolanus* suggests, between the medieval concept of sovereignty and the modern royalty of the literary subject, a contradiction like that between personal presence and parliamentary representation. The play knows the *aporia* of the Philip Sidney tradition was its belief that art's 'sovereignty lies in its ability to serve and facilitate the power of the Sovereign' who calls it into being.[119] Nothing in this play about the meaning of 'standing' is therefore more laughable, by this light, than Coriolanus's plea to his patron to 'Stand to me' [*5,3,200*] in his professional decisions. For to the great lord Aufidius he will always remain the 'dominated dependant' that this great Maecenas 'took in' when he first came to his hearth: 'I raised him, and I pawned mine honour for his truth ... gave him way / In all his own desires; nay, let him choose / Out of my files, his projects to accomplish' [*5,6,20–33*].

'Shakespeare fulfilled his patronage contract in *Coriolanus*', Alvin Kernan has argued, by composing an 'elaborately wrought treatment of the crisis of the Stuart aristocracy'.[120] But if so, his greatest patron was unable to keep the bargain, because when the King's Men turned to Pembroke in 1619 to protect their rights in Shakespeare's texts, the then Lord Chamberlain could not halt publication of the pirate plays.[121] Aufidius's demystification of service exposes the brute reality, in any case, of a relationship that required the dependent to be seen to bow 'his nature, never known before / But to be rough, unswayable, and free', so as not to make the master appear a 'follower, not partner' [*5,6,24–5; 38*]. Thus it was 'stoutness', a Volscian quips, that accounted for Coriolanus's 'lack of stooping' [*26–8*] to either his patron or the public; and this joke may be at the expense of the corpulent Jonson, notorious for 'bearing it proudlier' than his social superiors.[122] But the violence in this scene must also mark some deep subjective trauma, when the lord who ends the play standing on the body of his servant reminds the actor he is nothing but a 'boy of tears' [*5,6,104*]: a 'squeaking' comedian, in Cleopatra's phrase, who can only ever 'boy' the great

[*Antony,* 5,2,212–16]. Such was the penalty for waiting on these 'lords and heads of the state' [5,6,93]: demotion of the 'free and unswayable' artist to hireling status among the labouring 'Men and lads' [112]. But far from submitting to the servility of a 'poor relation' with such crawling self-abasement, still less sentimentalizing the Herberts' 'more than usual attachment to theatricals and theater folk', the man these Welsh conquistadores liked to call their 'bard' terminated *Coriolanus* with his most insubordinate rejection of feudal livery as 'a twist of rotten silk' [5,6,98], and most confident assertion of freedom from the strangulating culture of the great house:[123]

> Cut me to pieces, Volsces. Men and lads,
> Stain all your edges on me. 'Boy!' False hound,
> If you have writ your annals true, 'tis there
> That, like an eagle in a dove-cot, I
> Fluttered your Volscians in Corioles.
> Alone I did it. 'Boy'!
>
> [5,6,112–17]

As much an 'eagle' in the 'dove-cot' of their toy theatre as these lords had been in the cockpit of the Globe, at the end Coriolanus challenges his overlords to cut him like a book. It may not be chance, therefore, that this circumcision image dates from the moment of publication of the Sonnets. For despite the author's old reluctance to publish, this Orphic dismemberment looks forward defiantly to the fate of his *Works* beside those family 'annals' on aristocratic library shelves. And the dedication of the 1623 Folio does indeed rehearse the servile feudal reasons why Shakespeare was at the mercy of the paperknives of 'the most Noble and Incomparable Pair of Brethren, William Earl of Pembroke, &c., Lord Chamberlain to the King's Most Excellent Majesty, and Philip Earl of Montgomery, &c., Gentleman of His Majesty's Bed-Chamber'. As the editors proffer obsequiously: 'For so much were Your Lordships' likings of the several parts, when they were acted', that 'the Volume ask'd to be yours'.[124]

In 1623 William Herbert was, in Barroll's phrase, 'lord of the London stage'; although the other dedicatee, his brother Philip, was either dyslexic or illiterate.[125] But on the next page of the Folio, a further dedication, 'To the great Variety of Readers', suggests why *Coriolanus* is such a divided text, when it impudently asserts that 'though you be a Magistrate of wit, and sit on the Stage of the Blackfriars, or Cockpit, to arraign Plays daily, know, these Plays have had their trial already, and stood out all appeals' on stage. These brazen words, in such cool contrast to the other parasitic dedication, are attributed to Jonson, who had dedicated *Catiline* to Pembroke 'with the same assurance that innocency would appeal before a magistrate' in the earl's provincial courts.[126] If so, they undermine the idea that Pembroke and the players adored each other, and read instead like sweet revenge for the years of condescension when consecration of 'your servant Shakespeare' had waited on the indulgence of those stool-sitters in feather-hats.[127] The awkwardness of *Coriolanus*, of course, is that, so far as we know, it never was 'put on trial' before a jury on a public stage. Ripped apart by the 'bifold authority' [*Troilus, 5,2,144*] of the city and the country, the time of history and the time of the play, its ferociously self-destructive ending testifies instead to the social violence encoded in a theatre that remained 'to double business bound' [*Hamlet, 3,3,41*].

When he wrote *Coriolanus* it seems that Shakespeare could see no way out of this double rupture with his public and patron except 'Kill, kill, kill, kill, kill ...' [*5,6,130*]. But the Folio editors identify a third possibility when they finally address the *Works* neither to princes nor playgoers but to the *understanding* of common readers, who will, in the election metaphor of *Coriolanus*, 'stand for your privileges, we know: to read, and censure'. This declaration echoes Jonson's doffing of his hat to his own common reader who, he says, he makes 'my Patron': entrusting 'my self and my Book rather to thy rustic candour than all the pomp of their pride and solemn ignorance to boot'.[128] But whatever his identity, for the writer of this second dedication there was only one way to free Will from those proud and pompous stool-sitters, which was for the reading public to 'Judge your sixpence-worth, your shilling's-worth, your five shillings-worth at a time, or higher ... But whatever you do, buy.'[129] Complete with Shakespeare's hitherto unpublished play about the impossibility of acting to order, the Folio would actually cost its 'great Variety of Readers' a pound. No wonder then that the last word of *Coriolanus* sounds as if it is addressed to its own imagined consumers, whom it summons to 'Assist'.[130] That final cry for help suggests how, despite all his misgivings about the age of mechanical reproduction, Shakespeare must have accepted in the end that, far away from both the palace and the playhouse, there was indeed to be 'a world elsewhere'.[131]

Notes

1 Jürgen Habermas, *The Structural Transformation of the Public Sphere*, originally *Strukturwandel der Öffenlichkeit* (Darmstadt and Neuwied: Hermann Luchterhand Verlag, 1962), trans. Thomas Burger and Frederick Lawrence (Cambridge: Polity Press, 1989), pp. 11, 27 and 89–90.

2 Jürgen Habermas, 'Sovereignty and the Führerdemokratie' (a commentary on Carl Schmitt), *Times Literary Supplement*, 26 September 1986, 1053.

3 Habermas, op. cit. (note 1), pp. 38–9 and 49.

4 'Constructed so that everyone': Thomas Platter, *Thomas Platter's Travel Diaries in England*, trans. Clare Williams (London: Jonathan Cape, 1937), p. 167; M.C. Bradbrook, *The Rise of the Common Player* (London: Chatto & Windus, 1962), p. 100. In an influential critique of *The Structural Transformation of the Public Sphere* David Norbrook claims the book 'makes no mention' of the English Revolution, and 'fails to acknowledge the religious motivations behind the emergence of the public sphere in England' ('*Areopagitica*, Censorship, and the Early Modern Public Sphere', in Richard Burt (ed.), *The Administration of Aesthetics: Censorship, Political Criticism, and the Public Sphere* (Minneapolis: University of Minnesota Press, 1994), pp. 5–6). In fact, Habermas specifically writes that a 'momentous step' in the emergence occurred as a result of he calls 'the religious civil war', when Hobbes 'projected a state independent of the views of the subjects ... The civil war came to an end under the dictate of a state authority neutralized in religious matters. One's religion was a private matter, a private conviction': op. cit. (note 1), p. 90. For a sharper critique of Habermas's 'idealist, ahistorical notions of "undistorted communication"' in the early modern public sphere, see Richard Burt, *Licensed By Authority: Ben Jonson and the Discourses of Censorship* (Ithaca: Cornell University Press, 1993), pp. 19–21, 32–4 and 181–2.

5 Habermas, op. cit. (note 1), pp. 38–40.

6 Alvin Kernan, *The Playwright as Magician: Shakespeare's Image of the Poet in the English Public Theater* (New Haven: Yale University Press, 1979), p. 71; Andrew Gurr, 'The Shakespearean Stage', in 'General Introduction', *The Norton Shakespeare: Tragedies*, ed. Stephen Greenblatt, Walter Cohen, Jean Howard and Katharine Eisaman Maus (New York: Norton, 2008), p. 84.

7 Habermas, op. cit. (note 1), pp. 7–9.

8 Carl Schmitt, *Constitutional Theory*, trans. and ed. Jeffrey Seitzer (Durham, NC: Duke University Press, 2008), p.243; *Hamlet or Hecuba: The Intrusion of the Time into the Play*, trans. David Pan and Jennifer Rust (New York: Telos Press, 2009), p.41. For Schmitt's influence on Habermas and the Frankfurt School, see Ellen Kennedy, 'Carl Schmitt and the Frankfurt School: A Rejoinder', *Telos*, 73 (1987), 101–16; and Jean-François Kervégan, *Que faire de Carl Schmitt?* (Paris: Gallimard, 2011), pp.65–70.

9 Eric Santner, *The Royal Remains: The People's Two Bodies and the Endgames of Sovereignty* (Chicago: University of Chicago Press, 2011); Carl Schmitt, *Roman Catholicism and Political Form* (orig. pub. 1923), trans. G.L. Ulmen (Westport: Greenwood Press, 1996), p.21. Schmitt's theory that in the Middle Ages the nobleman *embodied* the authority subsequently dispersed by parliamentary representation – as the priest 'stands for' rather than 'acts for' Christ – is most clearly set out on p.19. For a discussion of Habermas's indebtedness to Schmitt, see John P. McCormick, *Carl Schmitt's Critique of Liberalism: Against Politics as Technology* (Cambridge: Cambridge University Press, 1997), pp.164–70.

10 Schmitt, op. cit. (note 8), pp.41 and 65.

11 Ben Jonson, 'The Dedication to the Reader', *The New Inn*, in *Ben Jonson*, ed. C.H. Herford and P. and E. Simpson (11 vols, Oxford: Clarendon Press, 1925–52), vol. 6 (1938), p.397.

12 Rebecca Lemon, 'Arms and Laws in *Coriolanus*', in *The Law in Shakespeare*, ed. Constance Jordan and Karen Cunningham (Basingstoke: Palgrave, 2010), pp.241 and 243.

13 Habermas, op. cit. (note 1), pp.7–9.

14 Carl Schmitt, *Political Theology: Four Chapters on the Concept of Sovereignty* (Chicago: University of Chicago Press, 2005), p.5.

15 Santner, op. cit. (note 9), p.100. See also Giorgio Agamben, *Homo Sacer: Sovereign Power and Bare Life*, trans. Daniel Heller-Roazen (Stanford: Stanford University Press, 1998); and Roberto Esposito, *Bios: Biopolitics and Philosophy*, trans. Timothy Campbell (Minneapolis: University of Minnesota Press, 2008).

16 Maurizio Calbi, 'States of Exception: Auto-Immunity and the Body Politic in Shakespeare's *Coriolanus*', in Maria del Sapio Garbero Nancy Isenberg and Maddalena Pennacchia (eds), *Questioning Bodies in Shakespeare's Rome* (Göttingen: V & R unipress, 2010), 77–94, here 81.

17 See Richard Wilson, 'Against the Grain: Representing the Market in *Coriolanus*', in *Will Power: Essays on Shakespearean Authority* (Hemel Hempstead: Harvester, 1993), pp.83–117; Kathleen McLuskie, 'The Poet's Royal Exchange: Patronage and Commerce in

Early Modern Drama', in *Patronage, Politics and Literary Traditions in England, 1558–1658*, ed. Cedric Brown (Detroit: Wayne University Press, 1991), p.126; and Mark Kishlansky, *Parliamentary Selection: Social and Political Choice in Early Modern England* (Cambridge: Cambridge University Press, 1986), pp.3–9.

18 Jean-Christophe Agnew, *Worlds Apart: The Theater and the Market in Anglo-American Thought, 1550–1750* (Cambridge: Cambridge University Press, 1986), p.118. And see Douglas Bruster, *Drama and the Market in the Age of Shakespeare* (Cambridge: Cambridge University Press, 1992), p.70.

19 Thomas Dekker, *The Gull's Hornbook* (London, 1609), in *The Non-Dramatic Works*, ed. A.B. Grosart (4 vols, New York: Russell & Russell, 1963), vol. 2, pp.246–7.

20 Christian Jouhard, 'Power and Literature: The Terms of the Exchange 1624–42', in Burt, op. cit. (note 3), pp.70–1.

21 See Stephen Orgel, *The Illusion of Power: Political Theatre in the Renaissance* (Berkeley: University of California Press, 1975).

22 Habermas, op. cit. (note 1), pp.40 and 52. Cf. Jeremy Doty, 'Shakespeare's *Richard II*, "Popularity", and the Early Modern Public Sphere', *Shakespeare Quarterly*, 61:3 (2010), 183: 'Shakespeare makes private people paying attention to matters of state a topic of inquiry in itself'.

23 Ibid., p.37.

24 Annabel Patterson, *Shakespeare and the Popular Voice* (Oxford: Blackwell, 1989), p.129; Brents Stirling, *The Populace in Shakespeare* (New York: Columbia University Press, 1949), p.178. See also Thomas Betteridge, *Shakespearean Fantasy and Politics* (Hatfield: University of Hertfordshire Press, 2005), p.121: 'The Citizens are not a mob ... This becomes apparent above all in the responses of the Citizens who are happy to participate in the politics of the moment.'

25 Thomas Dekker, 'Raven's Almanac', in Dekker, op. cit. (note 19), vol. 4, p.184.

26 Platter, op. cit. (note 4), p.167. See Pierre Bourdieu, *Distinction: A Social Critique of the Judgement of Taste*, trans. Richard Nice (Cambridge, Mass.: Harvard University Press, 1984), originally *La distinction: Critique sociale du jugement* (Paris: Minuit, 1979).

27 Andrew Gurr, *Playgoing in Shakespeare's London* (3rd ed.; Cambridge: Cambridge University Press, 2004), p.46. On Coriolanus's obtrusive feathered headgear, see Marion Trousdale, '*Coriolanus* and the Playgoer in 1609', in *The Arts of Performance in Elizabethan and Early Stuart Drama: Essays for G.K.Hunter*, ed. Murray Biggs, Philip Edwards, Inga-Stina Ewbank and Eugene Waith (Edinburgh: Edinburgh University Press, 1991), p.132: 'Coriolanus, it would

appear, has a beard and wears a hat. This makes him not only a Roman but an Elizabethan Roman.'

28 Alexander Pope, 'Preface', *The Works of Shakespeare* (1725), in *Selected Works of Alexander Pope*, ed. Paul Hammond (Cambridge: Cambridge University Press, 1987), p.164; Andrew Gurr, 'Headgear as Paralinguistic Signifiers in *King Lear*', *Shakespeare Survey*, 55 (2002), 43–51; 'To sit on stage': Jonathan Haynes, *The Social Relations of Jonson's Theater* (Cambridge: Cambridge University Press, 1992), p.71. The anachronistic hat is discussed in Charles and Michelle Martindale, *Shakespeare and the Uses of Antiquity* (London: Routledge, 1990), pp.121–5.

29 Jonson, op. cit. (note 11). See also Michael Shapiro, *Children of the Revels* (New York: Columbia University Press, 1977), p.70.

30 Haynes (note 28), p.56.

31 Andreas Höfele, *Stage, Stake, and Scaffold* (Oxford: Oxford University Press, 2011), p.109.

32 Dekker, op. cit., (note 19).

33 Haynes, op. cit. (note 28), p.60.

34 Wilson, op. cit. (note 3), p.170.

35 Anne Barton, 'The Tyranny of the Audience', in *Shakespeare and the Idea of the Play* (London: Chatto & Windus, 1962), pp.41–2.

36 John Pory (1632), quoted Gurr, op. cit. (note 27), p.28; see Herbert Berry, 'The Stage and Boxes at Blackfriars', *Studies in Philology*, 63 (1966), 163–86.

37 Sir Hugh Cholmley, *Memoirs*, quoted in Gurr, op. cit. (note 27), pp.69–70 and 254.

38 Andrew Gurr, *The Shakespearean Stage, 1574–1642* (2nd ed., Cambridge: Cambridge University Press, 1980), p.24.

39 Ben Jonson, Induction to *Cynthia's Revels*, op. cit. (note 11), vol. 4, p.24; Gurr, op. cit. (note 27), p.30.

40 John Webster, 'The Induction', in John Marston, *The Malcontent*, ed. Bernard Harris (London: Ernest Benn, 1967), pp.9 and 14.

41 Jonathan Bate, *Soul of the Age: The Life, Mind, and World of William Shakespeare* (London: Penguin, 2009), p.39.

42 Dekker, op. cit. (note 19), p.246; Ben Jonson, *The Devil Is an Ass*, 3,5,43–4, in Jonson, op. cit. (note 11), vol. 6, p.224; George Chapman, *All Fools*, Pro, 30–2, in *The Plays of George Chapman: The Comedies*, ed. Allan Holaday (Chicago: Illinois University Press, 1970), p.236.

43 Gurr, op. cit. (note 27), p.30.

44 Robert Weimann, *Author's Pen and Actor's Voice: Playing and Writing in Shakespeare's Theatre* (Cambridge: Cambridge University Press, 2000), p.161.

45 James I, Speech to House of Lords, 10 March 1621, quoted in Paul

Christianson, 'The Ancient Constitution, c. 1604–1621', in Linda Levy Peck (ed.), *The Mental World of the Jacobean Court* (Cambridge: Cambridge University Press, 1991), p.89. For a conventional 'old historicist' reading of the play, see Andrew Hadfield, '*Coriolanus* and Politics', in *Lectures de 'Coriolan' de William Shakespeare*, ed. Guillaume Winter (Rennes; Presses Universitaires de Rennes, 2006), pp.13–25; originally pub. in *Shakespeare and Renaissance Politics* (London: Thomson, 2004), pp.170–7.

46 Meredith Anne Skura, *Shakespeare the Actor and the Purposes of Playing* (Chicago: Chicago University Press, 1993), p.145; Eve Rachele Sanders, 'The Body of the Actor in *Coriolanus*', *Shakespeare Quarterly*, 57 (2006), 391; Santner, op. cit. (note 9), p.96.

47 Terry Eagleton, *William Shakespeare* (Oxford: Basil Blackwell, 1986), pp.73–4.

48 Catherine Belsey, *The Subject of Tragedy: Identity and difference in Renaissance Drama* (London: Methuen, 1985), p.36.

49 Skura, op. cit. (note 46), p.195.

50 Julia Lupton, *Citizen-Saints: Shakespeare and Political Theology* (Chicago: University of Chicago Press, 2005), p.164.

51 Kathleen McLuskie and Felicity Dunsworth, 'Patronage and the Economics of Theatre', in *A New History of Early English Drama*, eds John Cox and David Scott Kastan (New York: Columbia University Press, 1997), p.426.

52 David Bergeron, *Textual Patronage in English Drama, 1570–1640* (Aldershot: Ashgate, 2006), p.14. Cf. Richard Dutton, review of *Shakespeare and Theatrical Patronage in Early Modern England*, ed. Paul Whitfield White and Susan Westfall (Cambridge: Cambridge University Press, 2002), *Shakespeare Quarterly*, 55 (2004), 220.

53 Pierre Bourdieu, *The Rules of Art: Genesis and Structure of the Literary Field*, trans. Susan Emmanuel (Cambridge: Polity Press, 1996), pp.77–80.

54 Ibid.

55 Philip Sidney, 'Astrophil and Stella', 1: l. 14; Rembrandt quoted in Svetlana Alpers, *Rembrandt's Enterprise: The Studio and the Market* (London: Thames and Hudson, 1988), p.114; Pierre Bourdieu, 'Field of Power, Literary Field, and Habitus', trans. Claud DuVerlie, in *The Field of Cultural Production*, ed. Randall Jonhson (Cambridge: Polity Press, 1993), p.174.

56 Ibid.

57 See Wilson, op. cit. (note 17), pp.83–90.

58 Quoted in John Maynard Keynes, *The Applied Theory of Money*, in *The Collected Writings of John Maynard Keynes* (30 vols, London: Macmillan/Cambridge University Press, 1971), vol. 6, p.137.

59 Alfred Harbage, *Shakespeare and the Rival Traditions* (Bloomington: Indiana University Press, 1952), pp.47–8. The figure of 24,000 advances Harbage's earlier estimate of an average attendance of '21,000 a week by 1605', in *Shakespeare's Audience* (New York: Columbia University Press, 1941), p.38.

60 Ben Jonson, Commendatory verses to John Fletcher's *The Faithful Shepherdess* (1608).

61 Tiffany Stern, *Making Shakespeare: From Stage to Page* (London: Routledge, 2004), p.28.

62 Bourdieu, op. cit. (note 53), pp.58–61 and 81.

63 Jonas Barish, *The Anti-theatrical Prejudice* (Berkeley: University of California Press, 1981), pp.138–9.

64 Ben Jonson, 'An Elegy', *Underwoods*, 42; discussed in Haynes, op. cit. (note 28), p.66, n. 65.

65 Ben Jonson, *Every Man Out of His Humour*, Induction, 178–83; John Manningham's diary, February 1602, quoted in Haynes, op. cit. (note 28), pp.85–6. But in *Ben Jonson, Authority, Criticism* (Basingtoke: Macmillan, 1996), Richard Dutton argues that, while Jonson was 'thoroughly engaged in the patronage system as a whole, and the old literary system that related to it, it is not clear if he sought through it specific advancement by attachment to a particular faction, or indeed … more sustained employment in an aristocratic household' (p.55).

66 Ben Jonson, 'Dedication to the Earl of Pembroke', *Catiline*, op. cit. (note 11), vol. 8 (1952), p.25.

67 Bergeron, op. cit. (note 52), p.12.

68 Jonson, op. cit. (note 11).

69 Weimann, op. cit. (note 44), p.196.

70 John F. Danby, *Poets on Fortune's Hill: Studies in Sidney, Shakespeare, Beaumont and Fletcher* (London: Faber & Faber, 1952), pp.16–17 et passim.

71 'Even as it disappeared': Skura, op. cit. (note 46), p.31; Danby, op. cit. (note 70), p.44.

72 'House of the literary "father" Sidney': Lynn Meskill, *Jonson and Envy* (Cambridge: Cambridge University Press, 2009), p.228; '"A school of tongues in this belly of mine"': Gluttony and Envy in Ben Jonson's "Penshurst"', *Enfers et Délices à la Renaissance*, ed. François Laroque (Paris: Presses Sorbonne Nouvelle, 2003), p.228; Ben Jonson, 'To Penshurst', *Underwoods*, 2, ll. 59–75,49–50, 53–4 and 96–8; Haynes, op cit. (note 28), p.134; and 'Festivity and the Dramatic Economy of Jonson's *Bartholomew Fair*', in *Ben Jonson*, ed. Richard Dutton (Harlow: Longman, 2000), p.182. For Jonson's relations with the Herberts, see Robert Evans, *Ben Jonson and the Poetics of Patronage* (Lewisburg: Bucknell University Press, 1989), pp.107–18;

David Riggs, *Ben Jonson* (Cambridge, Mass.: Harvard University Press, 1989), pp.179–80; and Brian O'Farrell, *Shakespeare's Patron: William Herbert, Third Earl of Pembroke, 1580–1630* (London: Continuum, 2011), pp.49–50 and 82–3. For Herbert patronage of poetry, see especially Dick Taylor, 'The Third Earl of Pembroke as a Patron of Poetry', *Tulane Studies in English*, 5 (1955), 41–67.

73 Christopher Marlowe, *Dido Queen of Carthage*, 2,1,70–1, in *Christopher Marlowe: The Complete Plays*, eds Frank Romany and Robert Lindsey (London: Penguin, 2003), p.17. For a commentary, see Richard Wilson, 'Tragedy, Patronage, and Power', in Patrick Cheney (ed.), *The Cambridge Companion to Christopher Marlowe* (Cambridge: Cambridge University Press, 2004), pp.208–12.

74 Ben Jonson, 'To the No Less Noble, By Virtue, Than Blood, Esmé, L. Aubigny' (dedication to *Sejanus* first printed in the 1616 folio), repr. in Dutton, op. cit. (note 65), p.192.

75 It was A.C. Bradley who first pointed out that the Neronian idea of burning Rome was Shakespeare's, not Plutarch's, introduced as a way to negotiate Coriolanus's change of plan when he turns from exile to revenge: 'When he bids farewell to his mother and wife and friends … he comforts them … they shall always hear from him, and never aught but what is like him formerly … When we see him next … he will burn Rome … and the key idea lies in that idea of *burning*'; '*Coriolanus*: The Second British Academy Shakespeare Lecture' (Oxford: Oxford University Press for the British Academy, 1912). See also the important and stimulating essay by Martin Butler, 'Romans in Britain: *The Roman Actor* and the Early Stuart Classical Play', in Douglas Howard (ed.), *Philip Massinger: A Critical Reassessment* (Cambridge: Cambridge University Press, 1985), pp.139–70.

76 Bourdieu, op. cit. (note 53), p.134.

77 For the Renaissance prehistory of the romantic ideology of art's detachment from society, see especially Peter Bürger, *Theory of the Avant-Garde*, trans. Michael Shaw (Minneapolis: Minnesota University Press, 1984), pp.35–41.

78 Roy Strong, *Splendour at Court: Renaissance Spectacle and the Theatre of Power* (London: Thames and Hudson, 1973), p.19. See also Jonathan Goldberg, *James I and the Politics of Literature: Jonson, Shakespeare, Donne, and Their Contemporaries* (Stanford: Stanford University Press, 1989), pp.189–90: 'In *Coriolanus*, Shakespeare invests the absolutist strategies … with tragic implications'.

79 Jouhard, op. cit. (note 20), p.73.

80 D.J. Gordon, 'Name and Fame: Shakespeare's Coriolanus', in *The Renaissance Imagination: Lectures and essays by D.J. Gordon* (Berkeley: California University Press, 1980), p.219.

81 Maurice Charney points out that it is Coriolanus who figuratively becomes the butterfly his son pursues, in *Shakespeare's Roman Plays: The Function of Imagery in the Drama* (Cambridge, Mass.: Harvard University Press, 1961), p.168.

82 Pierre Bourdieu, 'Champ intellectual et projet créateur', *Les temps modernes*, November 1966, 865–906; repr. as 'Intellectual Field and Creative Project', trans. Sian France, in *Knowledge and Social Control: New Directions for the Sociology of Education*, ed. Michael Young (London: Collier-Macmillan, 1971), 161–88, esp. pp.162–4.

83 See Richard Wilson, 'The Management of Mirth: Shakespeare *via* Bourdieu', in *Marxist Shakespeares*, ed. Jean Howard and Scott Shershow (London: Routledge, 2001), pp.159–77.

84 See Stephen Orgel, 'Shakespeare Imagines an Audience', in *Shakespeare: Man of the Theater: Proceedings of the Second International Shakespeare Association, 1981*, ed. Kenneth Muir, Jay L. Halio and D.J. Palmer (Newark: University of Delaware Press, 1983), pp.39–40: 'an audience is invented that is conceived to be invidious to the success of the play, and then the uncomprehending or hostile spectators are banished'.

85 Stanley Cavell, '"Who does the wolf love?' Reading *Coriolanus*', in *Representing the English Renaissance*, ed. Stephen Greenblatt (Berkeley: University of California Press, 1988), pp.205 and 211–12; originally in *Representations*, 3 (1983), 1–20.

86 'Player as beggar': Skura, op. cit. (note 46), p.85 et passim.

87 E.K. Chambers, *William Shakespeare* (2 vols, Oxford: Clarendon Press, 1930), vol. 2, p.329; Michael Brennan, '"We Have the Man Shakespeare With Us": Wilton House and *As You Like It*', *Wiltshire Archaeological and Natural History Magazine*, 80 (1986), 225–7; and Leeds Barroll, *Politics, Plague, and Shakespeare's Theater* (Ithaca: Cornell University Press, 1991), pp.106–11: 'The court itself moved through Winchester to Salisbury, specifically to Wilton, the young earl of Pembroke's great house several miles west of the city … A fact not generally realized is that, from October to December 1603, the government of England was situated far to the west of London' (p.106).

88 For performances by this amalgamated company at Bath and Winchester in December 1593–94, see Michael Brennan, *Literary Patronage in the English Renaissance: The Pembroke Family* (London: Routledge, 1988), pp.92–6; Andrew Gurr, *The Shakespeare Playing Companies* (Oxford: Clarendon Press, 1996), pp.267–77; and for the possible connection with *Titus Andronicus*, see Lawrence Manley, 'From Strange's Men to Pembroke's Men: *2 Henry VI* and *The First Part of the Contention*', *Shakespeare Quarterly*, 54 (2003), 253–87,

esp.286–7. See also David George, 'Shakespeare and Pembroke's Men', *Shakespeare Quarterly*, 32 (1981), 305–23; and Jonathan Bate, 'Introduction', *The Arden Shakespeare: Titus Andronicus* (London: Thomson, 1995), pp.74–5. At New Year 1596 *Titus Andronicus* was definitely performed at Burleigh-on-the-Hill in Rutland, the seat of Sir John Harington: see Gustav Ungerer, 'An Unrecorded Elizabethan Performance of *Titus Andronicus*', *Shakespeare Survey*, 14 (1961), 102–9; and 'Shakespeare in Rutland', *Rutland Record*, 7 (1987), 242–8.

89 Malone Society Collections, 6, p.47; Rosalyn Lander Knutson, *The Repertory of Shakespeare's Company, 1594–1613* (Fayetteville: University of Arkansas Press, 1991), chap.5.

90 Christopher Marlowe, 'Dedicatory Epistle to Mary Sidney Herbert', trans. Brian Striar, in *The Collected Poems of Christopher Marlowe*, ed. Patrick Cheney and Brian Striar (New York: Oxford University Press, 2006), p.292.

91 Rolf Soellner, 'Shakespeare's *Lucrece* and the Garnier-Pembroke Connection', *Shakespeare Studies*, XV (1982), 1–20. Katherine Duncan-Jones has argued that in *Measure for Measure* Shakespeare also based the Duke's speech 'Be absolute for death' (3,1,5–41) on Mary Herbert's translation of Philip de Morney's *A Discourse of Life and Death*: 'Stoicism in *Measure for Measure*: A New Source', *Review of English Studies*, 28 (1977), 441–6. For Herbert's influence on the English stage, see Russell Leavenworth, *Daniel's 'Cleopatra': A Critical Study* (Salzburg: University of Salzburg, 1970), pp.3–5 and 119–28. In *Love's Labour's Lost*, it has been suggested, Shakespeare was 'mocking the pretensions of those courtiers who constantly threatened to withdraw from Court into the countryside', specifically 'Sidney's withdrawal, voluntary or forced, to Wilton or Penshurst': Fritz Levy, 'The Theater and the Court in the 1590s', in *The reign of Elizabeth I: Court and Culture in the Last Decade*, ed John Guy (Cambridge: Cambridge University Press, 1995), p.283.

92 Henry Condell and John Heminge, 'The Epistle Dedicatory' to the Shakespeare First Folio, repr. Shakespeare, op. cit. (note 1), p.3349.

93 'A boy impostor': Sanders, op. cit. (note 46), 397.

94 'A melancholy young man … too cold', Roland Whyte (agent for Robert Sidney), quoted in Brennan, op. cit. (note 88), p.100; 'Oriental pearls': O'Farrell, op. cit. (note 72), p.47; Dick Taylor, 'The Third Earl of Pembroke as a Patron of Poetry', *Tulane Studies in English*, 5 (1955), 46 and 50.

95 Jonson, op. cit. (note 71), l.48.

96 Tom May, Dedication to *Lucan's Pharsalia*, quoted ibid., p.54. The earl afterwards pretended he had not recognized the poet.

97 Leeds Barroll, 'Shakespeare, Noble Patrons, and "Common" Playing', in White and Westfall, op. cit (note 50), pp.102–3; Dutton, op. cit. (note 52), 220. See also Butler, op. cit. (note 75), esp. pp.140–6.

98 Joan Rees, *Samuel Daniel: A Critical and Biographical Study* (Liverpool: Liverpool University Press, 1964), p.50. For the lingering feudal concept of drama as offering, see M.C. Bradbrook, *The Rise of the Common Player: A Study of the Actor and Society* (Cambridge: Cambridge University Press, 1962), pp.243–64.

99 On Coriolanus's silence here, see Jarrett Walker, 'Voiceless Bodies and Bodiless Voices: The Drama of Human Reception in *Coriolanus*', *Shakespeare Quarterly*, 43 (1992), 170–85, esp.180.

100 Butler, op. cit. (note 75), pp.158–61.

101 Samuel Daniel, *Cleopatra* (London: 1594), sig. H5, ll. 1–8.

102 Rees, op. cit. (note 98), p.48. See also Margaret Hannay, *Philip's Phoenix: Mary Sidney, Countess of Pembroke* (Oxford: Oxford University Press, 1990), p.110. Hannay infers that Daniel was actually instructed by Mary Herbert in poetic composition (p.117).

103 David Bergeron, *Textual Patronage in English Drama, 1570–1640* (Aldershot: Ashgate, 2006), p.87.

104 Bradley, op. cit. (note 75), p.1; T.S. Eliot, 'Hamlet', in *Selected Prose of T.S.Eliot*, ed. Frank Kermode (London: Faber & Faber, 1975), p.47.

105 Marlowe, op. cit. (note 90), p.292.

106 John Aubrey, *Brief Lives*, ed. Oliver Lawson Dick (London: Secker and Warburg, 1949), pp.138–9. Aubrey adds that Mary Herbert's second house, Houghton Conquest, Bedfordshire, was also faithfully built in 1615 'according to the Description of Basilius's house in the first book of *Arcadia*'. For Wilton, see David Evett, *Literature and the Visual Arts in Tudor England* (Atlanta: Georgia University Press, 1990), p.214

107 Samuel Daniel, *Poems and A Defence of Rhyme*, ed. A.C. Sprague (Cambridge, Mass.: Harvard University Press, 1930), p.129.

108 Condell and Heminge, op. cit. (note 1), pp.3348–9. Gary Schmidgall, the most extreme advocate of the idea of Shakespeare as a patronage poet, considers the dedication 'poised and touching', but has to admit 'one wishes Heminge and Condell could have avoided calling the plays "these trifles," not once but twice': *Shakespeare and the Poet's Life* (Lexington: University Press of Kentucky, 1990), p.79.

109 The Earl of Pembroke to Viscount Doncaster, 20 May 1619, quoted in Henry Brown, *Shakespeare's Patrons and Other Essays* (London: Dent, 1912), p.66: 'And even now all the company are at the play, which I being tender hearted could not endure to see so soon after the loss of my old acquaintance Burbage'.

110 Leeds Barroll, op. cit. (note 97), pp.119–20.

111 Sir Fulke Greville, quoted by David Lloyd in *Statesmen and Favourites of England since the Reformation* (London: 1665), cited in Samuel Schoenbaum, *Shakespeare's Lives* (Oxford: Oxford University Press, 1970), p.118. For the influence of Greville's political writings and career on the composition of *Coriolanus*, see Wilson, op. cit. (note 17).

112 Gary Waller, 'The Countess of Pembroke and Gendered Reading', in *The Renaissance Englishwoman in Print: Counterbalancing the Canon*, ed. Anne Haselkorn and Betty Travitsky (Amherst: University of Massachusetts Press, 1990), pp.336–7 and 343 et passim.

113 Samuel Daniel, *Certain Small Works* (London: 1611), sig. E.4.

114 Janet Adelman, *Suffocating Mothers: Fantasies of Maternal Origin in Shakespeare's Plays, 'Hamlet' to 'The Tempest'* (London: Routledge, 1992), pp.148–9.

115 Meskill, op. cit. (note 72), p.233.

116 Waller, op. cit. (note 112), pp.331–3.

117 David Riggs, *Ben Jonson: A Life* (Cambridge, Mass.: Harvard University Press, 1989), p.232.

118 Bourdieu, op. cit. (note 53), p.51.

119 Fred Botting and Scott Wilson, *Bataille* (Basingstoke: Palgrave, 2001), pp.67–8. For an exhaustive analysis of this 'sovereign abjection', see Don Wayne, *Penshurst: The Semiotics of Place and the Poetics of History* (London: Methuen, 1984).

120 Alvin Kernan, *Shakespeare, the King's Playwright* (New Haven: Yale University Press, 1995), p.148.

121 See Samuel Schoenbaum, *Shakespeare: A Documentary Life* (Oxford: Oxford University Press, 1977), pp.257–8: 'Jaggard [the pirate printer] got round the restraint by ante-dating editions'.

122 For Jonson's 'large girth and weight throughout his *corpus*' and their relation to his appetite for patronage, see Meskill, op. cit. (note 72), pp.228–31: 'The glutton sits at the table of Philip Sidney, not only ready, but willing and very much *able*, to partake of huge quantities of whatever "meat" is placed before him from Sidney's literary larder' (pp.230–1).

123 Richard Dutton, 'Patronage, Politics, and the Master of the Revels, 1622–1640: The Case of Sir John Astley', *English Literary Renaissance*, 20 (1990), 297.

124 Condell and Heminge, op. cit. (note 1), p.3349.

125 Leeds Barroll, op cit. (note 96), p.120; Nigel Wheale, *Writing and Society: Literacy, Print and Politics in Britain, 1590–1660* (London: Routledge, 1999), p.23. See also Dick Taylor, 'The Earl of Montgomery and the Dedicatory Epistle of Shakespeare's First Folio', *Shakespeare Quarterly*, 10 (1959), 121–3; and Bergeron, op. cit. (note 102), pp.141–54.

126 Henry Condell and John Heminge, 'To the Great Variety of Readers,' op. cit. (note 1), p.3350. For Jonson's possible authorship of both dedications, see W.W. Greg, *The Shakespeare First Folio* (Oxford: Clarendon Press, 1955), pp.17–18. Cf. Richard Dutton, op. cit. (note 64), p.54: 'it is too simplistic' to construe from Jonson's connections with 'a family famous for its high-minded identification with humanist scholarship' any 'personal affiliation'.

127 For the supposed 'mutual respect' between Pembroke and Jonson, see Dutton, op. cit. (note 121), 298, and O'Farrell, op. cit. (note 72), pp.82–3.

128 Jonson, op. cit. (note 11).

129 Condell and Heminge, op. cit. (note 1), p.3350.

130 Cf. Weimann, op. cit. (note 44), p.234: 'Whatever authority the script retains at the moment of its ending is used to stimulate cultural involvement in the nonfictional world at the gates of the theatre. First and foremost, the call to "Assist" ... in its conjunction with "a noble memory," may not be entirely unrelated to a call for an imaginary kind of audience participation.'

131 Walter Benjamin, 'The Work of Art in the Age of Its Technological Reproducibility', trans. Harry Zohn, in *Illuminations*, ed. Hannah Arendt (London: Fontana 1968), p.221. The significance of Benjamin's essay as a response to Schmitt's incarnational concept of representation is discussed in McCormick, op. cit. (note 9), pp.168–70.

Epilogue

No sovereignty

Shakespeare's voyage to Greece

To excel the Golden Age

'I would with such perfection govern, sir, / T'excel the Golden Age' [*Tempest, 2,1,167–8*]: Gonzalo's fantasy of his ideal commonwealth in which, he says, 'no kind of traffic / Would I admit, no name of magistrate; / Letters should not be known; riches, poverty / And use of service none' [*149–51*], is Shakespeare's most explicit allusion to any philosophical text. But its near perfect quotation of Florio's translation of Montaigne's essay 'Of the Cannibals' is interrupted so cruelly by Antonio and Sebastian, when they object that this perfect state will perfect the perfect power, that critics have long assumed the philosopher was being similarly ridiculed for idealizing the technologically innocent Indians of Brazil, who 'desire no more then what their natural necessities direct them ... enter-call one another brethren', and hold all 'goods in common'.[1] Gonzalo's prospectus for a community without sovereignty where 'all things in common nature should produce / Without sweat or endeavour', is so heartlessly crushed by these mafiosi that it has been easy to assume that when Shakespeare has this vision trashed 'it is Montaigne's utopia he is allowing them to vilify', and that, as Leslie Fiedler regretted, he is 'on their side in the debate' over human perfectibility and 'the question concerning technology', for events in the play 'prove them, not Gonzalo, right'.[2] Like Thomas More, Montaigne had extolled the primitive communism of the Amerindians as an ethnologically fantastic model for a European future that would excel even the Golden Age of Greece and Rome. But in *The Tempest*, according to John Gillies, this utopian vision is made to look 'old-hat and just plain wrong-headed'.[3]

Perhaps the utopian idea of a society without sovereignty was ripe for 'the ironization it receives in *The Tempest*', for Hobbes would perform the same operation on an epic scale by applying irony to Montaigne's dream.[4] Yet as Fredric Jameson points out in *Archaeologies of the Future*, 'the desire called utopia' has always been structurally ambivalent.[5] And since the fall of Communism there has been a paradigm-shift in responses to the Orwellian scene when the cynics expose the contradiction of the old noble's perfect state, in which some are more equal than others, with their ruthless totalizing logic: 'No sovereignty ... Yet he would be king on't. / The latter end of his commonwealth forgets the beginning' [*148–57*].

This reorientation was flagged when Walter Cohen asserted that, despite this *aporia*, Gonzalo's fantasy reminds us how Marxism always wagered that history would have the 'latter end' of such a romance, and that it is through its happy *endings* that romance may yet offer a vision of 'that authentic history that may someday succeed'.[6] Thus, David Norbrook likened Antonio's carping to Foucault's critique of the Enlightenment, and insisted that 'the play does not endorse his cynicism'.[7] Likewise, Simon Palfrey affirmed that hopes of human perfectibility in Shakespeare's romances 'don't sink dead in the sludge – indeed Gonzalo's has a resistant quality ensured by the sarcasm of his audience'; and Kiernan Ryan concluded his millennial *Shakespeare* by quoting Henry James's euphoria that *The Tempest* 'renders the poverties and obscurities of our world ... in the dazzling terms of a richer and better life'. 'Dreaming on things to come' [Sonnet 107], Shakespeare spoke to these Presentist critics, therefore, not only of 'The weight of this sad time' [*King Lear, 5,3,322*] but of what Jameson identifies as our anxiety since Marx *about losing the future*.[8]

'"Since Marx" ... I cannot hear "Since Marx," since Marx, without hearing, like Marx, "Since Shakespeare".'[9] It was no accident that a belief that Shakespeare 'paves the way for the impossible, granting us a foretaste of the future through its estranged vision of our past', should coincide with Derrida's reading of *Hamlet* as a play in which 'what seems to be out in front, the future, comes back', to presage the return of our repressed hope for a democracy to come.[10] In *Specters of Marx* Derrida set the scene for the messianic turn in Shakespeare studies when he decrypted the haunted vigil on the 'immense terrace of Elsinore' as a prefiguration of Europe's post-1989 nostalgia for the 'good ghost' of a Marx 'which must not be renounced', and vowed 'there is a spirit of Marxism ... I will never be ready to renounce', as 'what remains irreducible to deconstruction ... is a certain emancipatory promise ... an idea of democracy'.[11] Like Hamlet, the philosopher reflected, 'we are in mourning for what is called Marxism'; and he later claimed he wrote his book in grief for his old Marxist teacher Louis Althusser.[12] But he also reset the terms for the debate about sovereignty and freedom when he warned that, because 'Hamlet could never know the peace of a good ending', what the Prince greets as an 'honest ghost' must be separated or purged from the stinking relics or the 'damned ghost' of the old sovereignty we have seen return too often in an 'old Europe' where 'The time is out of joint' [*1,5,142; 189; 3,2,75*]. Thus the problem of distinguishing 'the king's two bodies' becomes ever more imperative, the play seems to tell us, once we grasp what Derrida never ceased reminding us, that sovereignty is the dirty secret of democracy, and understand what Giorgio Agamben calls 'the dark mystery of sovereign power', which is implied by the expression that far from being safely sublimated into symbolic forms, 'the king never dies'.[13]

Just as Marx had trouble telling a progressive spirit from regressive spooks, or healthy *Geist* from poison gas, so our own work of mourning is an ordeal of undecidability, Derrida warned, awaiting the return of what might be yet another 'totalitarian monstrosity', as Hamlet awaits the Ghost, unsure if it is 'a spirit of health or goblin damned', bringing 'airs from heaven or blasts from hell': 'Be thy intents wicked or charitable, / Thou com'st in such a questionable shape / That I will speak to thee' [*1,4,21–5*].[14] 'Thou art a scholar ... Question it' [*1,1,40–3*]: 'Shakespeare will often have inspired this Marxian theatricalization' of critical scholarship, Derrida noted, as he guards the gates of meaning with the same vigilance as that with which he signs himself a *spear-shaker*. This pun on Shakespeare's bellicose surname stationed him as a sentinel alongside the night-watchman at the opening of the *Oresteia*, who also asks 'Who's there?' [*1,1,1*] at that eastward-facing postern where in work after work of the Western canon, 'the master of the house waits anxiously', in Derrida's signature metaphor, for the light of 'a stranger he will see arriving as a liberator'.[15] But the alarming picture of the dramatist as an armed gatekeeper of a Fortress Europe also suggested that the question provoked by this unfinished project of enlightenment – 'How do things stand with sovereignty in this scenario?' – was one reason for our continuing critical vigil over these plays, in which it seems that, as Eric Santner puts it, the revelation is not that

Shakespeare 'helps us to see through the theatrical and rhetorical work' of sovereignty, but rather that he helps us to recognize how much of the old royal personage *remains* in our own lives:[16]

> From what could be called the other time, from the eve of the play, the witnesses of history hope for a return, then, 'again' and 'again,' a coming and going ... 'What, ha's this thing appear'd again tonight?' ... [1,1,19]. A question of repetition: a spectre is always a *revenant*. One cannot control its comings and goings because it *begins by coming back*. Think as well of Macbeth, and remember the specter of Caesar. After having expired, he returns. Brutus also says '*again* ...' 'Well than I shall see thee again?' *Ghost*: 'Ay, at Philippi' [*Julius, 4,3,336–7*].[17]

No sovereignty: 'The latter end of his commonwealth forgets the beginning': the ghostliness of the perfect state is inseparable, these scare quotes seem to say, from the ghastliness of a perfect power, for it is sovereignty, whether of the artist or the king, that 'begins by coming back' as a precondition of utopia. *Hamlet* thus had a key role in Derrida's thinking about the (im)possibility of a 'democracy to come', and his teasing of the conundrum that one cannot combat 'this thing' called sovereignty 'without threatening, beyond the nation-state figure' of the monarchic ruler, the very 'principles of freedom and self-determination' he took to be at democracy's heart.[18] In truth, however, the philosopher's citations of the plays could make him sound as muddled as the 'good old lord Gonzalo' [*Tempest, 5,1,15*], with his eclectic cocktail of 'libertarian, liberal, communist, cosmopolitan, and utopian' ideals, all in fidelity to a '*uniquely* European heritage' of a democracy that has to 'remain indefinitely perfectible, hence in each of its future times, to come'.[19] His 'incessant procrastination' and 'ghostly elusiveness' result, it is felt, from Derrida's failure to declare *his own interest*, even though the New International he hailed as precursor of the state without sovereignty turned out to be reliant in practice on a European Defence Force.[20] Gonzalo's confusion of equality with his own sovereignty also arises from the fact that his interest is so imperceptible that, as Antonio snaps, 'he can see himself as king of an egalitarian society'.[21] 'Democracy and sovereignty are at the same time inseparable and in contradiction': this was the double bind that drew Derrida to Carl Schmitt, and the Nazi ideologue's brutal axiom that sovereign is he who decides on the exception.[22] But Shakespeare was also invested, the theorist now helps us perceive, in an unconditionality *without sovereignty*, where 'nature should bring forth' of its own [*2,1,163–4*], and *teknē* or exploiting knowledge 'should not be known', which he too hypothesized by conjecturing projects for the impossible, such as forgiveness, freedom, friendship, hospitality, justice, mourning, pardon, rogues and gifts.

Nothing is impossible

Like Derrida's, Shakespeare's work is prompted by the question with which Antonio dashes Gonzalo's dreams: 'What impossible matter will he make easy next?' [*2,1,87*]. So, when *Love's Labour's Lost* turns on whether laughter in face of death 'cannot be, it is impossible' [*5,2,833*]; *The Merchant of Venice* whether law says 'it is impossible' to coexist [*3,2,316*]; *Julius Caesar* whether 'It is impossible that ever Rome / Should breed' liberators [*5,3,99*]; *Twelfth Night* whether lovers can trust 'impossible passages' [*3,2,60*]; *Troilus and Cressida* whether 'proof is called impossibility' [*5,5,29*]; *Timon of Athens* whether friendship or gold solders 'impossibilities' [*4,3,380*]; *King Lear* whether it is 'almost impossible' to be a faithful inheritor [*2,4,237*]; *Othello* whether 'It is impossible' a monster can be man [*4,2,138*]; *Antony and Cleopatra* whether 'O Isis, 'tis impossible!' for love to conquer [*3,3,15*]; and *Pericles* whether we credit 'points that seem impossible' [*21,112*], what Hélène Cixous says about Derrida comes to look equally applicable to the Elizabethan dramatist: 'the scenarios of all his travels, displacements, and returns are always marked by the seal of the impossible. He will have loved only the impossible, that name for the fiction within fiction'.[23] And as his plays approach 'the promised end' [*King Lear, 5,3,263*], Shakespeare's love of the impossible is fictionalised in a fiction within the fiction which recurs as though by a repetition compulsion, when 'the old and miserable king' [*5,3,47*] divests himself of sovereignty and prostrates himself to beg forgiveness for his own power:

> When thou dost ask me blessing, I'll kneel down,
> And ask of thee forgiveness. So we'll live,
> And pray, and sing, and tell old tales, and laugh
> At gilded butterflies, and hear poor rogues
> Talk of court news; and we'll talk with them too,
> Who loses and who wins; who's in, who's out;

And take upon's the mystery of things,
As if we were God's spies; and we'll wear out,
In a walled prison, packs and sects of great ones,
That ebb and flow by the moon.

[*King Lear, 5,3,10–19*]

'A begging prince, what beggar pities not?' [*Richard III, 1,4,250*]: the Ubu-esque *topos* of 'The Abasement of the Proud King', in which a king 'to whom all have bowed' discovers he must learn to kneel, was always central to Shakespeare's dramaturgy.[24] In a familiar Kantian account, by staging the pathos of 'proud majesty made a subject' [*Richard II, 4,1,252*] this theatre 'nourished the cultural conditions that eventually permitted the nation to bring its King to trial'.[25] But this is also, as Foucault and Santner both caution, the divestment scenario of the unending endgames of modernity, where a humbled sovereignty, as figured by Beckett or Bacon in a wheelchair-bound Hamm or screaming pope, simply gives 'expression to the unavoidability, the inevitability of power, which can function in its full vigour and at the extreme point of its rationality even when in the hands of someone effectively discredited'.[26] And its old validity as an enactment of the power of weakness starts to be tested in *King Lear*, with Edmund's crushing response: 'Take them away' [*20*]. The Hobbesian bastard is dictator for only a minute, but his command is perhaps the cruellest instance in literature of the sovereignty that 'begins by coming back' to obliterate the 'puerile utopia' of the aesthetic as a 'walled prison' insulated from the violence of 'packs and sects of great ones'.[27] In the late twentieth century the banality of this evil was viewed through the lens of Peter Brook's film of the play, where the old king's fairy tale was undercut by a nightmare vision of his daughter hauled across the killing field, while he raved about their happy-ever-after, in obedience to the Captain's quiet order for 'some retention and appointed guard' [*48*] to 'hang Cordelia in prison' [*252*]. In the grip of such sovereign violence, the bare life of the extermination camp did come to seem what Agamben calls it, after Hannah Arendt: the condition in which unconditional totalitarian power all too readily agrees that 'everything is possible'.[28]

After 2001 the self-styled Presentist Shakespeareans took a calculated risk in cleaving to the unconditional belief that nothing is impossible. Lear's mouldy 'old tales' indeed recall the impossible ends of the Comedies, where happiness is salvaged from emergency, despite a father's grief that 'I cannot bid you my daughter live – / That were impossible' [*Much Ado, 5,1,263*], when sovereignty is rescued from itself to accept its own humanity; as the princess in *As You Like It* plans her eventual emergence: 'it is not impossible to me to set her before your eyes tomorrow, human as she is, and without any danger' [*5,2,58*]. '*Human as she is*': for recent critics these good endings follow the aporetic logic that is laid down in *The Two Gentlemen of Verona*: that 'nothing is impossible' [*3,2,352*], providing we understand that, as Helena explains in *All's Well That End's Well*, the 'impossible' is simply a name for the strangeness of the human event: 'Impossible be strange attempts to those / That weigh their pains in sense and do suppose / What hath been cannot be' [*1,1,207*]. So, like Beckett's depersonalized and Giacometti-famished survivors in Santner's book, towards the end Shakespeare's similarly attenuated and denuded characters 'acquire their particular strangeness by being rendered *merely human*'.[29]

Written, then, as if to validate Slavoj Žižek's claim that '*miracles do happen*', since 'the resurrection of the dead is already here', Shakespeare's romances bring the good news to the Presentist critics gathered in the series 'Shakespeare Now' that, as the King avers in *All's Well*, 'what impossibility would slay / In common sense, sense saves another way' [*2,1,176*], by trusting to 'freedom from misery, injustice and oppression' as a proxy for redemption.[30] Thus 'the impossible happens' in this playhouse, Ewan Fernie is convinced, in keeping with Theseus's warranty for the poet to 'body forth the forms of things unknown' [*Dream, 5,1,15*]. And when Lear assures Cordelia 'You are a spirit, I know' [*Lear, 4,7,49*], Fernie echoes Ernst Bloch in regarding this as a 'divine comedy' attesting to the 'principle of hope'.[31] In face of Bloch's equal insistence on the always unrealized *not yet*, Shakespeare studies have lately become impatient for such Žižekian rashness. Yet if the sweet dream of perpetual peace is coming to be realized in these texts, it is never without sovereignty, which strikes back hard in Lear's line about the mortal moon with all the deadly specificity of post-Elizabethan history, when for Catholics judged 'god's spies' fantasies of singing in some golden cage were blasted by the Gunpowder Plot. So, if Shakespeare inspires hope, as Ryan affirms, that our dreams of release from the coercions of such a history might one day be realized, he never loses sight of the conditions that shape these unknown forms, nor the

European prison walls that make such Kantian dreaming possible.[32] And this is all the more telling when Edmund silences Lear, because the old tale he terminates, where a sovereign kneels to beg forgiveness, will come back again, perhaps too late, to supply the endings for all of Shakespeare's final plays:

> There might you have beheld one joy crown another ... Our king being ready to leap out of himself for joy at his found daughter, as if that joy were now become a loss, cries, 'O, thy mother, thy mother!', then asks Bohemia forgiveness, then embraces his son-in law, then again worries he his daughter with clipping her. Now he thanks the old shepherd, which stands by like a weather-beaten conduit of many kings' reigns. [*Winter's*, 5,2,39–50]

'What I dream ... as a forgiveness worthy of its name', wrote Derrida, 'would be forgiveness without power: *unconditional but without sovereignty*'.[33] No sovereignty: the utopian end of his commonwealth *deliberately* forgets its dystopian beginning, as Shakespeare returns, over and again in these romances, to the Derridean project of a perfect state in which sovereignty does come back, but only to offer contrition for tears shed in 'many kings' reigns'. 'The most difficult task, at once necessary and apparently impossible', the dying philosopher reflected, 'would be to dissociate *unconditonality* from *sovereignty*'. Yet this sheer 'madness' is the 'unpresentable task' of plays like *The Winter's Tale*, where 'scenes of repentance, confession, forgiveness, or apology' are arranged around the very 'theatrical space' described by Derrida, in which the repentance is played out, 'sincerely or not, in a grand convulsion [which] in its theatricality ... invites parasites to the ceremony'. Here, as in our own time, 'one sees entire communities ... sovereigns and heads of state "ask forgiveness"'.[34] Derrida asks what urgency compels these proliferating scenes of repentance. In the case of the plays a hint is offered by Jeffrey Knapp, who infers that Shakespeare conceives of players uniting audiences in 'shared examination of human frailty', so the mere act of 'drawing thousands together' would initiate a religion without religion by persuading congregations to prefer imperfection to perfection, meekness over power. Such a weak messianicity was the only religion Shakespeare espoused, Knapp concludes, in tying his art, as Prospero finally does, to the fallible humanity of bodies rather than the masterful sovereignty of authored books:[35]

> ARIEL: Him that you termed, sir, the good old lord Gonzalo;
>   His tears run down his beard like winter's drops
>   From eaves of reeds. Your charm so strongly works
>   'em
>   That if you now beheld them your affections
>   Would become tender.
> PROSPERO: Dost thou think so, spirit?
> ARIEL: Mine would, sir, were I human.
> PROSPERO: And mine shall.
>   [*Tempest, 5,1,15–20*]

Revising his 'project' [*Epi.12*] to be 'more confessional than venge-ful', Knapp asserts, Shakespeare's final sovereign aligns himself with a creaturely theology that refuses to disown the imperfections of 'flesh and blood' [*5,1,115*]. The project of such a human under-standing, which in her study of Shakespeare and 'the grammar of forgiveness' Sarah Beckwith boldly suggests amounts to a revival of the suppressed Catholic sacrament of penance, would already be the subtext, then, of Orsino's promise in *Twelfth Night* that when 'golden time convents / A solemn combination shall be made / Of our dear souls' [*5,1,369–71*], in the unlikely coexistence of *con-vents* with 'a kind of Puritan' [*2,3,140*] like Malvolio.[36] For Knapp, however, the turn came early in the reign of James with *All's Well That Ends Well*, a comedy set in the France of the wars of religion that laughs how 'young Charbonne the puritan and old Poisson the papist, howsome'er their hearts are severed in religion, their heads are both one, they may jowl horns together like any deer i'the'herd' [*1,3,45–8*]. Cued by the 1598 Edict of Nantes, the novelty of this coronation play about coercion and consent is therefore that it ends well not through power but *impotence*, when the king supposed to heal by touch is himself healed by the servant Helena, and in an Epilogue abdicates his prerogative: 'The King's a beggar now the play is done'. So with the poseur Paroles betraying theatre's com-plicity with power, and a minimal morality that 'There's place and means for every man alive' [*4,3,316*], *All's Well* marks a vital leap in Shakespeare's lifelong effort to beggar power with weakness. As Ryan avers, 'It redefines ending well as unending endeavour. It puts us on stage to make the fairy tale come true.'[37] Shakespeare has a theologically loaded word for this impossibility. Repeatedly he calls the dispensation 'grace' [*1,1,75; 1,3,206; 2,1,159; 4,5,15; 5,2,38*]; the redemptive state which Caliban seeks [*Tempest, 5,1,295*], and that Julia Lupton associates with the messianic impulse in liberalism that we might call 'the pursuit of happiness'.[38]

At one together

'What the devil should move me to undertake the recovery of this drum, being not ignorant of the impossibility' [*31*]: biographers view Paroles' humiliation, after the braggart admits the impossibility of his boast to retake his regimental drum, as a sign of his creator's self-disgust, as a 'man of words' demeaning himself to entertain the great.[39] This play-within-the-play is said to figure Shakespeare's own impossible theatrical undertakings as a beggar at the feast.[40] If so, the military farce would articulate its likely origin as a coronation commission by Philip Sidney's sister Mary Countess of Pembroke, and Paroles' ambush its author's inveiglement by this Herbert dynasty of British empire-builders, whose chatelaine is said to have urged her handsome son to bring the new king to enjoy *As You Like It* at their Wiltshire mansion, where 'we have the man Shakespeare'.[41] That was the 'balmy time' when the poet was tempted to declare that 'peace proclaims olives of endless age' [Sonnet 107]. And in his book about this stellar household, *Earls of Paradise: England and the Dream of Perfection*, Adam Nicolson makes a compelling case for a family story that Shakespeare did revise *As You Like It* for the first royal Christmas in 1603, classicizing the old comedy with Grecian pederasty to divert King James, and adding a masque of Hymen, the Greek god of marriage, to humour his hosts in their plan for an English Arcadia, a perfect state where sovereignty relaxes to 'fleet the time carelessly as they did in the golden world' [*1,1,102*]. Thus a play about the fraught politics of friendship now concluded with a return to ancient Greece in which 'unity and harmony bring happiness and increase ... Arcadia has triumphed. That, surely, was the countess's intention, a washing of Arcadian balm over the mind of a king inclined to absolutism and tyranny':[42]

> Then is there mirth in heaven
> When earthly things made even
> Atone together.

[As You, 5,4,97–9]

At one together: if it was inserted at Wilton, with its '*Still Music*' [*SD. 96*] this apotheosis of social harmony, which editors consider 'the most baffling moment in the play', would count as the original Stuart masque, predating Samuel Daniel's *Vision of the Twelve Goddesses*, and as a trial run for all those later epiphanies with which Shakespeare voyages back to the Greece of the pagan gods to evoke a primordial at-oneness, while disburdening his audience of any prescriptive faith.[43] His alienated pastoral of 'brothers in exile' [2,1,1], based on the class war that rives Sidney's *Arcadia*, would thus be tamed into 'the most convincing statement of Arcadia ever made', with its English forest re-enchanted by 'a Greek invocation to call fools into a circle' [2,5,59]. Legend even has it the dramatist now dutifully played the old retainer Adam, an Everyman who personifies the 'constant service' of this 'antique world' [2,3,58]. *Earls of Paradise* conjectures that Shakespeare's chores for the Herbert family dated indeed from the sonnets he commenced on orders of the countess to induce her son William to marry, before he fell in love himself not only with 'Mr. W.H.' but with idyllic Wilton, its 'summer's green all girded up with sheaves' [Sonnet 12].[44] This patrician fantasy is beguiling. But what Nicolson cannot deny is the elegiac theme of *Et in Arcadia Ego* which haunts Arden in the 'second childishness and mere oblivion' of failing Adam [2,7,164]; nor the undertow, as these poems consign the 'imperfect shade' [Sonnet 43] of youth to 'wastes of time' [Sonnet 12], that the only possible paradise is *language itself*.[45] The English Arcadia had been another 'dream of power', *Earls of Paradise* admits, 'because it relied on the imposition of authority'.[46] But the true story of the Sonnets is one of *disempowerment*, of art emancipated from sovereignty, and of the expulsion from the poem of its lord and master as an intruder himself:

> When I consider every thing that grows
> Holds in perfection but a little moment,
> That this huge stage presenteth naught but shows
> Whereon the stars in secret influence comment ...
> Then the conceit of this inconstant stay
> Sets you most rich in youth before my sight,
> Where wasteful time debateth with decay
> To change your day of youth to sullied night;
>   And all in war with time for love of you,
>   As he takes from you, I engraft you new.
>
> [Sonnet 15]

Shakespeare never wrote a country-house poem, but if his 1609 *Sonnets* were prompted by his access to a rich man's flowering lawns, his idealization of these utopian perspectives was as ambivalent as Jonson's reaction to his humiliating sojourn at the Sidneys' Penshurst, which was both 'an acknowledgement of dependency and servitude, and an assertion of freedom'.[47] That ambivalence lies behind his squirely deference towards the sovereign 'You' these texts address; as, in Sonnet 15, the 'yew' springing from 'Your youth' grafts the youth's perfection on the en*graved* leaf of the page. Divided, then, like all eulogies, between the liberation of language and obligation to the other, each of these sonnets is a similarly impossible work of mourning, in which the identity of the lord of light is eternally interred in 'sullied night'. No sovereignty: whatever its physical location, his 'inconstant stay' in that perfect place taught Shakespeare the 'conceit' of Sidney's 'Stella' sonnets and *Defence of Poesy*, that the sovereignty of the poem brooks no rival: 'Only the poet, disdaining to be tied to any such subjection ... doth grow in effect another nature ... the poets only deliver a golden'.[48] Perfection cannot be realized, Sidney himself ordained, except in a literary *performance*; or, as Stanley Cavell has it, in words that are allegorical of a perfect life.[49] But it was his *imperfect* life in the playhouse that freed a more socially integrated poet to turn this lesson back on Sidney's stellar world, with the reality check that 'this huge stage presenteth naught but shows' on which those 'real' stars, the 'unnumbered sparks' [*Julius, 3,1,63*] painted above the Globe, stare coldly down. As Wayne Koestenbaum arrestingly observes, 'Humiliation ends', in a Shakespearean sonnet, when 'words humiliate their absented meanings ... the missing flesh'.[50]

Shakespeare would not be allowed to forget the 'secret influence' his stellar patrons exercised with 'comments' on his 'huge stage' at the Globe. But it was his playhouse motto, 'All the world's a stage' [*As You, 2,7,138*], that attested how 'every thing that grows / Holds in perfection but a little moment'. So it is not simply that poetry is sovereign in Shakespeare's sonnets, the 'exception from any rule except the freedom to change'.[51] Richard Helgerson has shown how for Elizabethan poets this notion of being absolute sovereigns of the 'kingdom' of language usurped the authority of the monarch they ostensibly paged; and indeed, 'I cannot compare this *prerogative* to anything better' than the privilege of 'a great Princess', was how the rhetorician Richard Mulcaster defined poetic licence.[52] Yet in these sonnets it is not poetic sovereignty but the 'perfect love' [Sonnet 55] of the poet's creaturely persona, 'your sweet Will' [Sonnet 135], that exerts the royal right to pardon: 'Whilst I, my sovereign, watch the clock for you ... So true a fool is love that in your Will, / Though you do anything, he thinks no ill' [Sonnet 57]. Just as 'law itself is perfect wrong' [*John 3,1,189*] when mimed on stage, with 'princes to act, / And monarchs to behold the swelling scene' [*Henry V, Pro.3*], so these love poems about escaping Petrarchan servitude reverse the roles of the sovereign and creature until 'the guest becomes the host's host'.[53] In an act of authorial self-deposition, they free the sonneteer from all forms of sovereignty by abjecting him in the risible figure of poor 'Will', the humiliated and vagrant player, whose obligatory role as Arcadian poet is merely another ceremonial command:[54]

> As an unperfect actor on the stage
> Who with his fear is put besides his part,
> Or some fierce thing replete with too much rage
> Whose strength's abundance weakens his own heart,
> So I, for fear of trust, forget to say
> The perfect ceremony of love's rite ...
>
> > [Sonnet 23]

'My name is Will' [Sonnet 136], smiles the geeky incompetent in whom the all-conquering poet humanizes himself in his sonnets. For the pathos of 'Tongue-tied' Will [Sonnets 66, 80, 85 and 140] puts the same annihilating terror centre-stage in these poems as the 'speechless' hesitation [*Hamlet, 2,2,465*] that freezes the action of the plays. All through his dramatic work we have seen Shakespeare adopt the persona of the 'unlettered clerk' [Sonnet 85] silent in the textual world of his betters, an ironic self-deprecation in the style of Langland, self-portrayed as 'Long Will', a weed too weak for work, or Chaucer, staring at the ground lest his rhyming is 'not worth a turd'; and James Bednarz infers that the Ubu-esque tradition gave this 'Will in overplus' [Sonnet 135] the smirk of a poet smugly content to rest on the verdict of posterity 'to redress his self-imputed weakness'.[55] But by infantilizing himself as 'crying ... Will' [Sonnet 143], a dumbstruck 'motley to view' [Sonnet 110], in the royal progress of a sonnet sequence, and referring his text to the all-too-human fallibility of a player's memory, Shakespeare is surely using the actor's trepidation to sabotage the very possibility of poetic sovereignty. For once these poems mention his acting, the speaker never celebrates his talents as a poet again.[56] In *The King's Two Bodies* Kantorowicz traced 'the purely human model of man's perfection' to Dante's *Commedia*, where Virgil crowns the Poet, proclaiming 'I crown and mitre you over yourself'; and Helgerson and others identify this man-centred sovereignty with the investiture of *self*-crowned Elizabethan laureates.[57] But through the petty investiture crisis of a quivering 'Will', these sonnets that mingle clowns and kings with all the indecorum Sidney despised in the theatre, seem to envisage a yet further disrobing of monarchic power, and a far more radical humanizing of sovereignty, in the Orphic dismemberment of the regal sonneteer himself, into 'poetry in action, performed before the theatre audience'.[58]

In one of the few analyses to take 'the socially disgraced and abject' persona of 'Will' seriously, Elizabeth Heale has revealed how this 'ageing uncourtly' actor-figure is contrasted to Sidney's 'youthful idealizing Astrophil'.[59] By presenting a stammering 'Will' in the plight of the jester who earns his living by 'public means which public manners breeds' [Sonnet 111], yet whose conned words dry up on order to perform, as in his primal dramatic scene, the poems Shakespeare may have arranged and published under auspices of Sidney's heirs thus subordinate the Sidneian legacy of textual authority to verbal performance, and put literary sovereignty on hold. That 'fierce thing' or lion-hearted beast is breathless with palpitation in this crisis of attendance, when printed books are relegated to mere ushers, gasping harbingers of a plenitude that must go without saying: 'dumb presagers of my speaking breast, / Who ... look for recompense / More than that tongue that hath more expressed' [Sonnet 23]. So, though critics identify in these texts the 'invincible omnipotence' of a self-presence 'never compromised by its theatrical representation ... the imagined power of sole authorship, never capable of being wholly embodied or possessed', what is transcendent about them is how they subordinate the coming royalty of the phallogocentric poet to the uncrowned *attendant* 'Will', that 'poor player' [*Macbeth*, 5,5,23–4] waiting to be heard: 'O learn to read what silent love hath writ; / To hear with eyes' [Sonnet 23].[60] In place of the absolutist poetics and controlling ego of the self-consecrated Elizabethan penman promulgated by Sidney or Jonson, the distracted absent-mindedness of this 'poor player' augurs something far more modern: the potential that

Jacques Rancière finds in pensiveness to deconstruct the literary text 'in favour of an indeterminate expressive logic'; or which Judith Halberstam perceives in stuttering forgetfulness to dethrone the majestic ego in favour of 'a new version of selfhood'.[61]

'These pencilled figures are / Even such as they give out' [*Timon*, *1,1,163*]: Hugh Grady argues that scenes like the one with the Poet and the Painter in *Timon of Athens* reveal Shakespeare responding to Sidney's *Defence of Poesy* by asserting the supremacy of his text over a patronage system where 'Smoke and lukewarm water / Is your perfection' [*3,7,81–2*], and by outlining a creative autonomy 'closer to post-Kantian aesthetics' than to Aristotelian mimesis.[62] Yet in the sonnets about perfection he penned for the 'Lord of [his] love in vassalage' [Sonnet 26] the poet who signs himself 'your slave' [Sonnet 57] insists he enters as an *imperfect* player. Thus his only conceit is that, as practice makes perfect, perfection resides not so much in what Cavell calls the 'impossibility of the perfect text', as in its future *recital*: 'O let my books be then be the eloquence' [Sonnet 23].[63] For Shakespeare, a playwright who never produced an epic poem, and considered the sovereignty of *The Faerie Queene* to be a monument of 'wasted time' [Sonnet 106], 'perfection' can at best mean *word perfect*, his sonnets suggest, the perfect timing of the actor 'Creating every bad a perfect best' [Sonnet 114] by speaking on cue and in what Falstaff calls a 'true and perfect image of life' [*1Henry IV, 5,4,116*]. So when kingship becomes 'too perfect' in the lingo of imperfection, it is trumped by the game Hal rigs 'in the perfectness of time' [*2Henry IV, 4,4,74*], as when he tells Poins 'Thou art perfect' in the guise of power [*1Henry IV, 2,5,31; 3,1,198; 5,4,116*]. Like Shakespeare specializing in the palsied roles of Henry IV, Old Hamlet, or Caesar's Ghost, these King's Men may appear as 'perfect in the use of arms' [*2Henry IV, 4,1,153*] as kings themselves. But 'Such fellows are perfect' only in the parts that 'they con perfectly' [*Henry V, 3,6,65–70*]. For in this battle between the two competing monarchies of representation and presence, as the Chorus asserts in Shakespeare's most hyperbolic attempt to think of an art without sovereignty, there is no 'puissance' that is not 'imaginary', no power without the human imperfection of the actor's faltering pose:

> Suppose within the girdle of these walls
> Are now confined two mighty monarchies ...

Piece out our imperfections with your thoughts ...
And make imaginary puissance.

[*Henry V, Pro.23–5*]

The varying shore of the world

If these plays ask us to 'piece out imperfections' and make 'imaginary puissance', that is because their actor 'looks not only to his own role but to the audience to fill his emptiness'.[64] It is telling therefore that their aspiration to be 'at one' with the community is projected not onto English history, where the Land of Cockaigne in which 'Incertainties ... crown themselves assured' remains an ambiguous dream of 'things to come' [Sonnet 107], but on the pre-Christian or Mediterranean worlds that provide pretexts for almost everything Shakespeare produced for the Globe. Clifford Leech long ago noticed how Greek settings, in particular, 'gave Shakespeare special liberty', and that, if he was puzzled by Greece, 'he felt curiously free' when he sailed to 'these golden shores' [*Wives, 1,4,70*] in his imagination, as if he believed that in 'the constant service of the antique world' we 'should think ourselves for ever perfect' [*Timon, 1,2,82*], for all the imperfections of that most 'imperfect man', the Athenian 'who dreamt a dream of human brotherhood', when 'earthly things' might be 'made even' again, and so 'at one together'.[65] More specifically, this poet of the edge, obsessed by the liminality of borders, dawns, and crossings, turned to the horizon of the ancient world for 'a quite different attitude towards death' as self-transcendence.[66] Thus, as Grady remarks, the boundaries of the Greco-Roman Mediterranean held a defining place in Shakespeare's 'use of antiquity to signify emerging modernity'.[67]

The plays Shakespeare set 'upon the very hem of the sea' [*5,5,67*] in the mythopoeic landscape of Greece confront the 'Greeks and Merrygreeks', who in their contradictions and complexities are images of the fallen early modern men and women of London, or New Troy, with the 'rich conceit' [*5,4,82*] of a self-transcendence, 'Upon the beachèd verge of the salt flood' [*101*], which Grady is not alone in registering as an 'aesthetic shudder' or premonition of the sublime.[68] So, from *The Comedy of Errors* to *The Two Noble Kinsmen*, by this light, Shakespeare's voyage back to Greece was an uncanny homecoming, or return to source, to recall that perfect mutuality when 'We came into the world like brother and brother' for the time to come, when we again 'go hand in hand, not one before the other' [_Errors, 5,1,426_]. Yet if Shakespeare's Greece is a ruin, in the end, of 'fragments, scraps, the bits and greasy relics' [_Troilus, 5,2,159_] of broken promises, that is because of the way that the time of present power keeps intruding into this representational space of waiting. In _Antony and Cleopatra_, for instance, there is a lightning-flash of ghostly precognition at Alexandria, the perennial gateway between past and future, Europe and Asia, when Octavius proclaims that 'The time of universal peace is near' [_4,6,4_]. The future emperor Augustus will, however, shortly make this dream of perpetual peace identical with his own imperium, and so it turns out he is merely invoking 'the imperial theme' [_Macbeth, 1,3,128_] of Western hegemony, the occidental _translatio imperii_ or permanent state of exception that will for a while go by the name of the United Kingdom of Great Britain, and afterwards, even more briefly, the United States of America.[69]

Editors relate Caesar's forecast of the end of history in the _Pax Romana_ to Plutarch's statement that 'It was predestined the government of all the world should fall into Octavius Caesar's hands', to Virgil's ecstasy in his Fourth Eclogue that Augustus makes Time run back to fetch the Age of Gold, when 'Justice comes back to dwell with us, the rule of Saturn is restored', and to his euphoria that 'The Firstborn of the New Age is already on his way'.[70] So it is logical to connect this uncanny presentiment of the birth of Jesus Christ with King James's project to reunite Christendom as its _Rex Pacificus_, and to decode the prophecy as flattery of Britain's own would-be Augustus.[71] For some new world is surely coming in this play that mentions 'this great world' [_2,6,9_] twice as much as any other; in which flaming apocalyptic portents from the Book of Revelation fire expectancy; and in which the words 'becoming' and 'comely' keep recurring as pointers to the contingency of the future care of the self.[72] There is an incipient 'to-effect' in _Antony and Cleopatra_, as urgent as the 'odour of imminence' that for Cixous makes _Julius Caesar_, with its cries for 'peace, freedom, and liberty' [_3,1,111_], 'smell like time'.[73] But there is also the evil spirit of the old sovereign monstrosity, when the messianic prophecy is heralded by sinister music of oboes '_under the stage_', signifying that 'the god Hercules, whom Antony loved, / Now leaves him' [_4,3,13_]. In Plutarch it was Bacchus, god of wine and drama, who defected. But it seems Shakespeare altered a story that echoed the flight of the gods, and cry of Pan on the morning of Christ's Nativity, to one about the Globe's own guardian angel, as if to underscore the vulnerability of mere symbolic forms to the 'invisible presence of something unseen', like a strong-armed Hercules:[74]

2 SOLDIER:	Peace! What noise?
1 SOLDIER:	List, list!
2 SOLDIER:	Hark!
1 SOLDIER:	Music i'th'air.
3 SOLDIER:	Under the earth.
4 SOLDIER:	It signs well, does it not?
3 SOLDIER:	No.

[*Antony, 4,3,9–12*]

'Heard you of nothing strange about the streets?' [*3*]: on the starlit battlements where guards keep watch, a spectre is once more haunting Europe in *Antony and Cleopatra*, the spectre of a sovereignty that begins by coming back, and 'After the end of history, repeats itself, again and again'.[75] So, on the threshold of a New Age, this is the same ironic *contretemps* between pagan and Christian eschatologies as makes Brutus uncertain of a good end, when in the dark before dawn it is impossible to decide if the 'monstrous apparition' that makes his hair stand up is 'some god, some angel, or some devil' [*Julius, 4,2,230*]. Brutus's quandary returns him to that 'phantasma or hideous dream', 'Between the acting of a dreadful thing and the first motion' [*2,1,63–5*], which initiated the entire dramaturgy of suspenseful intermission in later Shakespeare, the world-historical 'interim' [*Hamlet, 5,2,74*] that Hamlet traces to the origins of the West, when he recounts how Pyrrhus' sword, 'Which was declining on the milky head / Of reverend Priam, seem'd i'th'air to stick' [*2,2,458–9*]. The Prince promises Horatio that in his case 'the issue of the business ... will be short' [*5,2,72–4*]; but, as *Free Will* has argued, it is precisely the temporal caesura Achilles' son offers the Renaissance avenger that dethrones the autonomous subject, here luridly associated with the hyperbolic authorship of the most classicizing of Elizabethan writers, the rival poet vying for Herbert patronage, the monstrous Marlowe, with his phallogocentric confidence that with the performative 'whiff and wind of his fell sword ... senseless Ilium, / Seeming to feel his blow, with flaming top / Stoops to his base' [*2,2,453–6*].[76]

    In *Dido, Queen of Carthage*, Marlowe's Homeric warrior 'stood

stone still' [2,1,263] *after* the massacre at Troy, contemplating geno-
cide with the pitilessness that excites Hamlet. But in Shakespeare,
'Pyrrhus' pause' [2,2,467] *precedes* the act, extending the 'interim'
of the player's attention into the eternal stasis of a picture, like the
painting by Rembrandt of Abraham with the sacrificial blade suspended over Isaac: 'So, as a painted tyrant, Pyrrhus stood, / And as
a neutral to his will and matter, / Did nothing' [460–2]. 'The play's
the thing', in this ethical turn away from sacrifice, to neutralize the
power of 'the king' [582]. Yet shortly after, the text will disclose the
compositional activity of the sovereign author, in the Prince's weird
post-hoc conceptualization of the play-within-the-play: 'About my
brain. Hum' [565].[77] As Julia Lupton remarks, the ordeal of undecidability Shakespeare stages in this messianic 'interim' will therefore continue to put the coming subject to the test: 'Is he a *principe*
in the Machiavellian sense of negotiating his own ascendancy? Or
does he institute a different kind of principality, becoming ... a
princeps in the sense of First Citizen, understood not as the imperial
terminator of representative rule but as the initiator of constitutionalism, an emperor in reverse?'[78] Will this paradoxical 'sovereign creature' [*Antony, 5,2,80*] that is emerging in Shakespearean
writing be 'some angel, or some devil': 'a spirit of health or goblin
damned', bringing 'airs from heaven or blasts from hell' [1,4,21–2]?
Will the advent of this monstrous *arrivant*, that is to say, be merely
the coming of yet another Caesar, or of a Christ?

As Foucault journeyed back to ancient Greece to excavate a
'care of the self' that was 'not an exercise in solitude, but a true
social practice', so Shakespeare would return many times to the
near coincidence of Jesus Christ and Julius Caesar, and an antiquity
when 'the work of oneself on oneself' was not yet self-fashioning,
but what one owed to the other.[79] Thus, 'My long sickness / Of
health and living now begins to mend', reflects Timon, 'And nothing
brings me all things' [*Timon, 5,2,71–3*]. Likewise, 'My desolation
does begin to make a better life' [*Antony, 5,2,1*], Cleopatra insists.
But a play that starts from Antony's apocalyptic vision of a 'new
heaven, new earth' [1,1,17] ends in a nativity so monstrous, with
its 'eastern star' [5,2,300] nursing her fatal asp, that the effect must
be to distance the messianic from any world order to which, in the
worst of all category mistakes, 'Herod of Jewry may do homage'
[1,2,24].[80] As Antony prophesied, 'mothers shall but smile when
they behold / Their infants quartered' [*Julius, 3,1,270*] in the

Massacre of Innocents that inaugurates the two thousand years of this supposed New Age of brotherhood. Yet it is to this same Mediterranean littoral and Hellenistic horizon, the 'marine verge' where 'darkling stand[s] / The varying shore o'th'world' [*Antony*, *4,16,10–11*], in the *agon* between two representations of the divine, that the romances keep returning, as, like Hölderlin, Shakespeare sets down scene after scene in the uncanny interstitial spaces of Alexandria, Antioch, Antium, Athens, Carthage, Corinth, Delphos, Syracuse, Tarsus, Troy or Tyre, the cosmopolitan thresholds of the early Church, and so returns to his own beginning, when he had situated the hopes of *The Comedy of Errors* in the haunted Ephesus of St Paul.[81]

Like Heidegger reading Hölderlin, Presentist criticism discovers in Shakespeare's later dramas an opening on 'a different history', which 'begins with the struggle over the decision about the coming or flight of the gods'.[82] What troubles this revaluation of the romances, of course, is precisely the inhospitality of their New Testament settings, the cold coming they prepare on the edge of the pagan world, in the twilight before the Christian dawn.[83] Yet critics have recently been struck by the aptness to these texts of Alain Badiou's post-Marxist reading of St Paul as a 'new figure of the militant', who helped us escape Schmitt's double bind when he affirmed that 'ye are not under the law, but under grace' [Romans, 6:14], for 'when I am weak, then am I strong. I am become a fool' [2 Corinthians, 12:10–11]. Paul, the only one of the Apostles not to know Jesus personally, 'challenged the Roman Empire and its "nomos of the earth"', in this light, by universalizing love.[84] And such is the humanizing project we can perhaps dimly recognize in these plays and poems. Lupton puts this memorably, when she introduces us to one 'Paul Shakespeare', a 'man without qualities', whose guardianship of the passages of Judaism into Christianity, Catholicism into Protestantism, and scripture into literature, makes him 'all things to all men' [1 Corinthians, 9:19].[85] Thus, if the etymology of 'romance' leads us back to Rome, it comes as no surprise that every one of Shakespeare's romances reverts to the same Pauline space of potentiality, where, as Jean-Luc Nancy writes, it was 'the inaugural *flight* of the Gods', and not their coming, that initiated the possibility of a self without sovereignty: 'This flight is not simply an absenting ... The flight of the gods traces or initiates an unprecedented meaning'. For as Milton put it in his *Nativity*

Ode, this was the pivotal instant and the given place where the 'kings sat still'.[86]

Stephen Greenblatt's claim that Shakespeare's stage is 'haunted by a sense of rituals and beliefs that ... have been *emptied out*', has more recently been countered by Gary Taylor's theologically sharper point that emptying out is 'the most fundamental religious experience', since the evidence of Christ's resurrection is precisely 'the disappearance of his body from the tomb'.[87] In the last plays, according to a negative political theology, it is therefore precisely the *disenchantment* of the world of sovereignty, and the evacuation of its royal remains, that creates the possibility to 'awake your faith'. 'Thou metst with things dying, I with things new-born' [*Winter's, 3,3,104; 5,3,95*]: to Nancy, this interregnal zone between birth and death is the setting for the defining dilemma of the West, the choice of either the technological *globalization* of which Caesar speaks or a veritable *mondialisation*, an *altermondialism*, through creation of a truly *human world* synonymous with the democracy and justice which are as yet nowhere, since 'injustice is unleashed everywhere: the earth trembles, viruses infect, men are criminals, executioners and liars'.[88] And such is indeed the world-historic choice between a wished-for perfection and the realized imperfection with which Shakespeare does seem to confront us in his own miracle play of earthquakes and epidemics, *Pericles*, when after all his restless wandering in the footsteps of Paul, as he approaches the liminal space of Ephesus, the king who has been reunited with the daughter he supposed dead, at long last *sits* stone-still

PERICLES:	But what music?
HELICANUS:	My lord, I hear none.
PERICLES:	None? The music of the spheres! List, my Marina.
LYSIMACHUS:	It is not good to cross him; give him way.
PERICLES:	Rarest sounds! Do ye not hear?
LYSIMACHUS:	Music, my lord?
	[*I hear.*]
PERICLES:	Most heavenly music!

[*Pericles, 5,1,222–31*]

Leave not a rack behind

No sovereignty: the king who comes back at the end of *Pericles* is as much a fool as the Lear who hoped to grasp 'the mystery of things', since 'This is the rarest dream, that e'er dull'd sleep / Did mock sad fools withal' [*161*]. But instead of the executioners having the last word, in this replay it is actors, audiences, and readers who must decide how the story is to end, by assigning to either the fool or politician the words '*I hear*'. Editors warn us that the text is so corrupt 'There is no solution to the problems of *Pericles*'.[89] But sailing towards Byzantium, this romance always promised a universal stillness, when 'the senate-house of planets all did sit / To knit ... their best perfections'. Its protagonist is a 'man on whom perfections wait'. He calls his story 'godlike perfect', and when he recites it to resurrect a dead queen the physician Cerimon prays to Apollo to 'perfect me in the characters' [*1,1,11; 80; 3,2,69; 5,1,206*]. So, like the song the Sirens sang to Odysseus, that Adorno and Horkheimer allegorized as a myth of the artistic *avant garde*, the onus is on interpreters to choose whether to join the old king in his 'wild beholding' of 'the music of the spheres', which we might hear as the song of the earth.[90] Unless the affirming words are assigned to the lecher Lysimachus, no one else can hear the heavenly harmony. Yet this has not stopped the editors inserting '*Celestial music*', when Pericles now has a vision of the goddess Diana ordering him to her Ephesian temple to kneel, not before the altar, but 'before the people all' [*241*].

As Shakespeare's 'Earls of Paradise' understood, the Neoplatonist ideology that 'the touches of sweet harmony' restore 'earthly things' to 'true perfection' [*Merchant, 5,1,56; 106; As You, 5,4,98*] is hard to resist. That was the illusion of power in the court masques, where technical marvels, 'the ability to overcome gravity, control the natural world, reveal the operations of the heavenly spheres, were supreme expressions of Renaissance kingship'.[91] But there is so much homely creatureliness in this salty tale of liars and criminals who rush out of the brothels to 'go hear the vestals sing' [*4,5,7*], that any angelic orchestra sounds precipitate. To impose such technological domination is to restore sovereignty, when the temple scene lets us piece out its imperfection for ourselves. For there Shakespeare recycles his oldest trick from *The Comedy of Errors*, when Pericles and his lost wife are reunited at the altar she serves in 'silver livery', after 'the nun' has fainted at his voice [*5,3,7–15*]. This might be enough for the king to offer his 'oblations' to the statue of Diana; but the stress on the ageing human bodies leaves us to decide 'who to thank – / Besides the gods – for this great miracle' [*80–9*], and so to determine whether this is 'natural causality rather than wondrous impossibility'.[92] And such uncertainty about the human potential for 'grace' is only heightened when Shakespeare restages the same tableau in *The Winter's Tale*, where 'all stand still' [5,3,95] for prayers led for the Syracusan tyrant Leontes by the aptly named Paulina, before the statue of the 'Lady' [44]:

> LEONTES: I am ashamed. Does not the stone rebuke me
> For being more stone than it? O royal piece!
> There's magic in thy majesty, which has
> My evils conjured to remembrance, and
> From thy admiring daughter took the spirits,
> Standing like stone with thee.
> [*The Winter's Tale*, 5,3,37–42]

'Here is a humanity which would claim to accuse itself all at once, publicly and spectacularly, of all the crimes committed in effect by itself against itself', comments Derrida of the culture of apology which Shakespeare's Sicilian ruler seems to initiate when he proclaims his 'shame perpetual' at his victims' graveside, where the 'tears' of humiliation are to be his 'recreation' [3,2,236–8].[93] And Paulina foreshadows deconstruction when she warns that 'A thousand knees, / Ten thousand years together, naked, fasting' [3,2,208–9], would not complete the mourning process, when it is the *impossibility* of affective withdrawal that thereby constitutes the subject: 'If one by one you wedded all the world / Or from the all that are took something good / To make a perfect woman, she you killed / Would be unparalleled' [5,1,13–16]. For the mastery and appropriation that have constituted human freedom are simply transferred from one form of sovereignty to another in such a scene of reparation, from technological control to 'the artistic mastery of symbols'.[94] So Hermione's statue is said to be by 'that rare Italian master Giulio Romano, who had he himself eternity and could put breath into his work, would beguile nature of her custom, so perfectly he is her ape' [5,2,87–90]. The eeriness of a fictive work attributed to an artist who died in 1546, the only Renaissance one mentioned by Shakespeare, intensifies the spectrality of an art that aspires to make such 'a perfect woman' [5,1,14]. Yet the saving grace is that even though this statue is the *chef d'oeuvre* of that 'rare master' William Shakespeare, this creaturely creation is 'now newly performed' by a boy-player. The Pygmalion myth haunts all these texts. But only in this 'chapel' [10] that doubles as a sculpture 'gallery' [86] does it cue such assurance that 'the resurrection of the dead is already here': in the anachronism of an art composed out of the impure colours of the carnation-tinted actor's blushing body, where 'our human actions' [3,2,27] are what *incarnate* the theatrical event.

As Lupton comments, religion is not so much evacuated in this playing with bodies as 'transported' into the afterlife of the stage.[95] So when the statue does 'move indeed' [5,3,88], this is a clinching moment for those critics who like to think these romances voyage back towards a homeland where 'wishes fall out as they're will'd' [*Pericles*, 5,2,16], that happens to be coded Christian.[96] And such seems to be the project of the one drama to deal directly with the uncanny coincidence of Caesar and Christ, or the transfer of sovereignty from one to the other, yet which still suspends in the ambivalence of its histrionics the shape of things to come. With *Cymbeline* Shakespeare devised a truly baroque 'archaeology of the future' prompted by the cosmic joke that the eponymous king reigned at the instant of the Nativity, without the good news about 'this gracious season' [5,6,401] ever being heard in Britain. This obliviousness propels a plot in which the ancient Britons refuse to surrender their sovereignty by paying up, and entering Christian history, when the adventitious decree goes 'out from Caesar Augustus, that all the world should be taxed' [Luke, 2:1]. Tortuously, Britain and Rome are reconciled; and editors suspect another nod to the *translatio imperii* of King James, Jonathan Goldberg viewing the play as a counterpart of Rubens's Banqueting House ceiling, where the Stuart patriarch joins Justice, Peace, Plenty and Unity in an apotheosis of empire.[97] But the Eternal City is now the Sodom of the Borgia popes, its 'smoky light' fuelled with the 'stinking tallow' [1,6,110] that defiles its painted heavens, a discolouration it shares with the ceiling at Whitehall. So the concluding piety that 'The fingers of the powers above do tune / The harmony of this peace' is occluded by all those 'crooked smokes' that 'climb to their nostrils / From our blest altars' [5,6,466–78]. No sovereignty: as we draw ever nearer to the 'event o'the'journey' [*Winter's Tale*, 3,1,31] in this landscape of Shakespearean antiquity, with each of these late works about lateness it seems that the state of human perfection remains 'the more delayed, delighted' [*Cymbeline*, 5,5,196], and for ever veiled in the faltering performance of its actors:

The climate's delicate, the air most sweet;
Fertile the isle, the temple much surpassing
The common praise it bears ... I shall report
For most it caught me, the celestial habits –
Methinks I so should term them – and the reverence
Of the grave wearers.

[*Winter's, 3,1,1–6*]

'In the morning the boat glided slowly on the calm water toward Delos, and at once ... a veiled great beginning was expressed ... Δῆλος, the manifest, the one that reveals and does not hide but, at the same time, the one that conceals': Heidegger's long-deferred luxury cruise to Greece supplied a climax to the philosopher's life of thinking about the disappearing gods that strangely reprised the same voyage in the romances, with its tragicomic mix of musing on 'the unconcealed' and grumpy discomfiture at the chattering tourists with their 'technological entanglement' of cameras and transistors. It is tempting to smile; but Heidegger's botheration at 'the tourist's zeal, in which one was, without being aware, included', is very similar to Gonzalo's amnesia about his own sovereignty on his imagined island of perfection, while the challenge it poses echoes Shakespeare's: 'How man sets himself free in relation to a power that is capable of warding off the violence in the essence of technology'.[98] Of course, the philosopher's real *faux pas* was the truly unforgivable category error at the hour of decision, his 1933 'Journey to Syracuse', compounded by his self-exonerating sophistry that 'Greater men have made mistakes: Hegel saw Napoleon as the World Spirit, and Hölderlin as a prince of the feast to which the gods and Christ had been invited'.[99] When Shakespeare dramatized the allure of Syracuse in *The Tempest*, however, and set his play on an island near the Sicily where Plato had envisaged the tyrant realizing the totalitarian dream of the City as a work of art 'T'excel the Golden Age', he presented the problem of sovereignty as the very same 'question concerning technology'.

Prospero's premonition that 'The cloud-capped towers, the gorgeous palaces, / The solemn temples, the great globe itself' – the entire panorama, in fact, of Shakespeare's own progress from the pavilion to the playhouse – 'Yea, all which it inherit', *shall dissolve*, has always seemed a peculiar reason to be as 'cheerful' as he commands [*4,1,147–54*]. But then the play has consistently exposed what he calls the 'vanity of mine art' [41] as no more than the reali-sation of 'a perfected male fantasy', as from the instant he directs his daughter to lift up 'the fringed curtains of thine eye ... And say what thou seest' [1,2,412], successive unveilings have revealed every perspective on this New World to be a mere *enframing* by the Old.[100] *The Tempest* is uniquely aware of the collusion between the mechanics of Renaissance theatre and the actual discovery scenes of colonialism, and so of its own complicity in the sovereignty that always begins by coming back in the idea that the essence of human freedom resides in mastery and appropriation. No artwork has ever been more alert to the inescapable imbrication of the documents of civilization with such barbarism than this tragicomedy that turns on an impresario's decision to deconstruct his own theatre, unmask its violence, and, in the sinister pun that implicates the cloud machinery of the Globe in the darkest arts of the Elizabethan torture chamber, 'leave not a rack behind' [4,1,156]. As Greenblatt comments, the most momentous ethical choice in all Shakespeare is therefore Prospero's last-minute resolution to give up his theatrical machinery, 'the romance equivalent of martial law'.[101]

'Be not afeared. The isle is full of noises, / Sounds and sweet airs': on Prospero's isle Shakespeare came near to solving the 'question concerning technology', by envisioning an art that will 'give delight but hurt not' [3,2,130–1]. *The Tempest* opens with Shakespeare's perennial question, 'Where's the Master?' [1,1,8]; but with its dis-mantling of 'the great globe', this final renunciation of sovereignty, in favour of the 'noise' and 'sounds' of a language beyond master-ing, anticipates Enlightenment hostility to theatrical 'scenes and machines' as an absolutist imposition upon the *disinterestedness* of the stage.[102] Prospero's foregoing of mastery through abandonment of his Faustian magic seems indeed almost to prefigure Heidegger's ultimate disavowal of the sovereignty of all decision-making, in his understanding that 'Freedom reveals itself as the "letting-be" of what is'; and to anticipate Arendt's corollary that 'If men wish to be free, it is precisely sovereignty they must renounce'.[103] For his deactivation does seem to open a door to that impossible freedom without sovereignty in which, as Agamben dreams, 'humanity will play with law as children play with disused objects, to free them from it for good'; for now even Shakespeare's own technological sphere, 'the great globe itself', is miniaturized into the 'fair play' [5,1,178] of a Beckettian *Endspiel*, as this whole 'world' is sacrificed to the other, and the rise and fall of kings and queens is transposed into a lovers' game of chess:[104]

MIRANDA: Sweet lord, you play me false.
FERDINAND: No, my dearest love,
              I would not for the world.

[*5,1,174–6*]

'Pardon's the word for all', Shakespeare's Ubu-like king decrees [*Cymbeline, 5,6,423*]; and in his late book *On Late Style* Edward Said responded that by so disabling sovereignty the last plays attain a serene perfection in 'holiness and resolution'.[105] We might prefer to see these peripatetic, multi-confessional dramas of art and power, in which the writer seems to struggle like Ariel for the 'liberty' of aesthetic space [*Tempest, 1,2,246*], while begging with Prospero to be released from the sovereignty of his own art, as closer to the restless spirit of Derrida, however, when he pondered the impossibility of such a reprieve, and the impasse that 'if we were to begin to accuse ourselves, in asking forgiveness, of all the crimes of the past against humanity, there would no longer be an innocent person on earth', considering that 'we are all heir to crimes against humanity.'[106] Such a tight knot of sovereignty and service, investiture and divestment, has long been the *agon* of critics who situate these plays in a 'tense dependence' upon patronage, and see Shakespeare's Machiavellian prince as victorious over his weak king.[107] The dismantling theme of *Free Will* has been, however, that our 'culture of anorexia' makes us alive to the *askesis* by which abdication, abjection, and apology define the subtractive power of weakness.[108] So, when at the very end the master tells us that his 'charms are all o'erthrown', and 'what strength' he has is his own, 'Which is most faint' [*Epi.1–3*], we recognise in that professed weakness not only the striptease scenario of modern art, but a final Shakespearean assertion of sovereign freedom: an *aporia* that literally cries out for endless deconstruction. So, 'Pray you, undo *this* button' [*King Lear, 5,3,308*]:

As you from crimes would pardoned be
Let your indulgence set me free.

[*Tempest, Epi.19–20*]

Notes

1 Michel de Montaigne, 'Of the Canniballes,' in *The Essayes*, trans. John Florio (London: 1603), repr. in William Shakespeare, *The Arden Shakespeare: The Tempest*, ed. Virginia Mason Vaughan and Alden T. Vaughan (London: Thomson Learning, 1999), p.309. As Howard Felperin emphasizes, Gonzalo projects a new world that 'actually excels the Golden Age': *Shakespearean Romance* (Princeton: Princeton University Press, 1972), p.259.

2 Leslie Fiedler, *The Stranger in Shakespeare* (London: Croom Helm, 1973), pp.193–4; 'The Question': Martin Heidegger, *The Question Concerning Technology and Other Essays*, trans. William Lovitt (New York: Harper Row, 1977).

3 John Gillies, 'The Figure of the New World in *The Tempest*,' in Peter Hulme and William Sherman (eds), *'The Tempest' and Its Travels* (London: Reaktion, 2000), p.192.

4 David Sedley, 'Nasty, Brutish, and Long: the Life of Montaigne's *Essais* in Hobbes's Theory of Contract', in *Montaigne After Theory: Theory After Montaigne*, ed. Zahi Zalloua (Seattle: University of Washington Press, 2009), p.173.

5 Fredric Jameson, *Archaeologies of the Future: The Desire Called Utopia and Other Science Fictions* (London: Verso, 2007), p.1.

6 Walter Cohen, *Drama of a Nation: Public Theater in Renaissance England and Spain* (Ithaca: Cornell University Press, 1988), p.391.

7 David Norbrook, 'What Cares These Roarers for the Name of King?' in Gordon McMullan and Jonathan Hope (eds), *The Politics of Tragicomedy: Shakespeare and After* (London: Routledge, 1992), p.34.

8 Simon Palfrey, *Late Shakespeare: A New World of Words* (Oxford: Oxford University Press, 1997), p.145; Kiernan Ryan, *Shakespeare* (London: Palgrave, 2002), p.176; Henry James, *Selected Literary Criticism*, ed. Morris Shapira (Cambridge: Cambridge University Press, 1981), p.302; Jameson, op. cit. (note 5). For the Late Plays as realizations of 'the improbable and unashamedly fictive', see also R.S. White, *Let Wonder Seem Familiar: Endings in Shakespeare's Romance Vision* (London: Athlone Press, 1985), p.2.

9 Jacques Derrida, *Specters of Marx: The State of the Debt, the Work of Mourning, and the New International*, trans. Peggy Kamuf (London: Routledge, 1994), p.17.

10 Ibid., p.10; Ryan, op. cit. (note 8), p.121.

11 Derrida, op. cit. (note 9), pp.59 and 88–9. 'The immense terrace of Elsinore' is a quotation (p.5) from Paul Valéry's famous 1919 essay, 'La Crise de l'esprit', in *Oeuvres* (Paris: Gallimard, Bibliothethèque

Pléïade, 1957), vol. 1, p.993, to which Derrida's meditation on *Hamlet* is in part a response: 'Now, on the immense terrace of Elisinore, which stretches from Basel to Cologne ... the European Hamlet looks at thousands of spectres ... Hamlet does not know what to do with all these skulls. But if he abandons them! ... Will he cease to be himself?'

12 Jacques Derrida and Elizabeth Roudinesco, *For What Tomorrow: A Dialogue*, trans. Jeff Fort (Stanford: Stanford University Press, 2004), p.103; op. cit. (note 9), p.54.

13 Giorgio Agamben, *Homo Sacer: Sovereign Power and Bare Life*, trans. Daniel Heller-Roazen (Stanford: Stanford University Press, 1998), p.93.

14 Ibid., pp.29, 75, 88 and 105. For commentaries on Marx's Shakespearean spectrality, see Marjorie Garber, *Shakespeare's Ghost Writers: Literature as Uncanny Causality* (London: Methuen, 1987), pp.56–60; Richard Halpern, 'An Impure History of Ghosts: Derrida, Marx, Shakespeare', in *Marxist Shakespeares*, ed. Jean Howard and Scott Cutler Shershow (London: Routledge, 2001), pp.31–52; Martin Harries, *Scare Quotes from Shakespeare: Marx, Keynes, and the Language of Reenchantment* (Stanford: Stanford University Press, 2000), pp.57–122; and Richard Wilson, *Shakespeare in French Theory: King of Shadows* (London: Routledge, 2007), pp.42–7 and 68–73.

15 Derrida, op. cit. (note 9), pp.5 and 18; Jacques Derrida, *Of Hospitality: Anne Dufourmantelle Invites Jacques Derrida to Respond*, trans. Rachel Bowlby (Stanford: Stanford University Press, 2000), p.121. For the Heideggerian interpretation of the watchman on the walls at the beginning of the *Agamemnon*, to which Derrida was responding, see in particular Martin Heidegger, *Sojourns: The Journey to Greece*, trans. John Panteleimon Manoussakis (New York: University of New York Press, 2005, pp.19–22 (originally published as *Aufenthalte* (Frankfurt: Victoria Klostermann, 1989).

16 'How do things stand with sovereignty': Vincent Leitch, 'Late Derrida: The Politics of Sovereignty', in *The Late Derrida*, eds W.J.T. Mitchell and Arnold Davidson (Chicago: University of Chicago Press, 2007), pp.25–6; Eric Santner, *The Royal Remains: The People's Two Bodies and the Endgames of Sovereignty* (Chicago: University of Chicago Press, 2011), p.46.

17 Derrida, op. cit. (note 9), pp.10–11.

18 Jacques Derrida, *Rogues: Two Essays on Reason*, trans. Pascale-Anne Brault (Stanford: Stanford University Press, 2005), p.158; Nicholas Royle, 'The Poet, *Julius Caesar*, and the Democracy to Come', *Angles on Derrida: Jacques Derrida and Anglophone Literature: Oxford Literary Review: 25* (2004), 41–2.

19 'Weird cocktail': Simon Critchley, 'Derrida: The Reader,' in Simon

Glendinning and Robert Eaglestone (eds), *Derrida's Legacies: Literature and philosophy* (London: Routledge, 2008), p.3; 'libertarian, liberal ...': Leitch, op. cit. (note 16), p.25. Leitch points out that Derrida's attempt to think a democratic sovereign state without sovereignty 'quietly presupposes ownership of private property' – as does Gonzalo's; 'uniquely *European*': Jacques Derrida, *The Other Heading: Reflections on Today's Europe*, trans. Pascale-Anne Brault and Michael Naas (Bloomington: Indiana University Press, 1992), p.78; 'indefinitely perfectible': *The Politics of Friendship*, trans. George Collins (London: Verso, 1997), p.306.

20 'Incessant procrastination': Savoj Žižek, *The Sublime Object of Ideology* (London: Verso, 1989), p.191; 'ghostly elusiveness': Halpern, 'An impure history of ghosts', in Jean, p.42; 'European Defence Force': Giovanna Borradori, *Philosophy in a Time of Terror: Dialogues with Jürgen Habermas and Jacques Derrida* (Chicago: University of Chicago Press, 2003), pp.116–17; Jacques Derrida, *Learning to Live: The Last Interview* (Basingstoke: Palgrave, 2007), p.42.

21 Norbrook, op. cit. (note 7), p.255.

22 'Democracy and sovereignty: Derrida, op. cit. (note 18), p.100; Derrida and Roudinesco, op. cit. (note 12), p.144; Carl Schmitt, *The Concept of the Political*, trans. George Schwab (Chicago: University of Chicago Press, 1996), originally pub. as *Der Begriff des Politschen* (Berlin: Duncker and Humboldt, 1932).

23 Hélène Cixous, 'This Stranjejew Body', in Bettina Bergo, Joseph Cohen and Raphael Zagury-Orly (eds), *Judeities: Questions for Jacques Derrida*, trans. Bettina Bergo and Michael B. Smith (New York: Fordham University Press, 2007), p.66.

24 'Abasement of the Proud King': Maynard Mack, *'King Lear' in Our Time* (Berkeley: California University Press, 1965), p.49; 'a king to whom everyone has bowed': Meredith Ann Skura, *Shakespeare the Actor and the Purposes of Playing* (Chicago: University of Chicago Press, 1993), pp.145 and 285, n. 94.

25 David Scott Kastan, 'Proud Majesty Made a Subject: Shakespeare and the Spectacle of Rule', *Shakespeare Quarterly*, 37 (1986), 459–75, here 460–1.

26 Michel Foucault, *Abnormal: Lectures at the Collège de France, 1974–1975*, trans. Graham Burchell (New York: Picador, 2003), p.13; Santner, op. cit. (note 16), pp.251–2.

27 'Puerile utopia': Charles Baudelaire, quoted in Michael Hamburger, *The Truth of Poetry: Tensions in Modern Poetry from Baudelaire to the 1960s* (Manchester: Carcanet Press, 1982), p.5.

28 Agamben, op. cit. (note 13), p.170.

29 Santner, op. cit. (note 16), p.251. For the 'strangeness' of the 'event' in

Shakespeare, see Nicholas Royle, 'Derrida's event', in Glendinning and Eaglestone, op. cit. (note 19), pp. 39–42.

30 'Miracles do happen': Slavoj Žižek, *The Ticklish Subject: The Absent Centre of Political Ontology* (London: Verso, 2000), p. 135; 'the resurrection is already here': *The Puppet and the Dwarf: The Perverse Core of Christianity* (Cambridge, Mass.: MIT Press, 2003), p. 87; 'a metaphor for freedom': Kiernan Ryan, 'Where Hope Is Coldest: *All's Well That Ends Well*', in Ewan Fernie (ed.), *Spiritual Shakespeares* (London: Routledge, 2005), p. 38. Edited by Ewan Fernie and Simon Palfrey, 'Shakespeare Now' is a series of critical studies published in London by Continuum.

31 Fernie, 'Introduction: Shakespeare, spirituality and contemporary criticism,' ibid., pp. 16–17. Cf. Ernst Bloch, *The Utopian Function of Art and Literature: Selected Essays*, trans. Jack Zipes and Frank Mecklenburg (Cambridge, Mass.: MIT Press, 1988).

32 Ryan, op. cit. (note 8), p. 121.

33 Jacques Derrida, *Cosmopolitanism and Forgiveness*, trans. Mark Dooley and Michael Hughes (London: Routledge, 2002), p. 59.

34 Ibid., pp. 69 and 26–7.

35 Jeffrey Knapp, *Shakespeare's Tribe: Church, Nation, and Theater in Renaissance England* (Chicago: University of Chicago Press, 2002, pp. 53–4.

36 Sarah Beckwith, *Shakespeare and the Grammar of Forgiveness* (New York: Cornell University Press, 2011).

37 Ryan, op. cit. (note 30), p. 49.

38 Julia Lupton, *Citizen-Saints: Shakespeare and Political Theology* (Chicago: University of Chicago Press, 2005), p. 179.

39 'Man of words': Charles Nicholl, *The Lodger: Shakespeare on Silver Street* (London: Allen Lane, 2007), p. 267.

40 Skura, op. cit. (note 24) p. 137.

41 Samuel Schoenbaum, *William Shakespeare: A Documentary Life* (Oxford: Oxford University Press, 1975), p. 126.

42 Adam Nicolson, *Earls of Paradise: England and the Dream of Perfection* (London: Harper Press, 2008), pp. 148–9. For *As You Like It* and the Herberts, see also Leeds Barroll, *Politics, Plague, and Shakespeare's Theater* (Ithaca: Cornell University Press, 1991), pp. 38–41 and 124.

43 'The most baffling moment': Stephen Orgel, *The Authentic Shakespeare and Other Problems of the Early Modern Stage* (London: Routledge, 2002), p. 17; 'relieve the audience': Gary Taylor, 'Divine [ ]sences', *Shakespeare Survey*, 54 (2002), 13–30, here 15. Taylor describes Hymen as 'a figure whose essence is the absence of essence' (15). For the masque and 'the power of wonder' associated with the Late Plays,

see Peter Platt, *Reason Diminished: Shakespeare and the Marvelous* (Lincoln: University of Nebraska Press, 1997), pp.129–30

44 Barroll, op. cit. (note 42), pp.132–3. For the play's connections with Sidney's *Arcadia*, see Brian Gibbons, 'Amorous Fictions in *As You Like It*', in *Shakespeare and Multiplicity* (Cambridge: Cambridge University Press, 1993), pp.153–81.

45 For *As You Like It* and the theme of 'Death in Arcadia' see Richard Cody, *The Landscape of the Mind: Pastoralism and Platonic Theory in Tasso's 'Aminta' and Shakespeare's Early Comedies* (Oxford: Clarendon Press, 1969), pp.69 and 161–2. The classic study remains Erwin Panofsky,'*Et in Arcadia Ego*: Poussin and the Elegiac Tradition', in *Meaning in the Visual Arts* (New York: Doubleday, 1955), pp.295–320.

46 Nicolson, op. cit. (note 42), p.268.

47 Don Wayne, *Penshurst: The Semiotics of Place and the Poetics of History* (London: Methuen, 1984), p.173.

48 Sir Philip Sidney, *A Defence of Poetry*, in *Miscellaneous Prose of Sir Philip Sidney*, ed. Katherine Duncan Jones (Oxford: Clarendon Press, 1973), p.78. Cf. David Mikics, *Who Was Jacques Derrida? An Intellectual Biography* (New Haven: Yale University Press, 2009), p.247: '[Derrida] embodied a contradiction that is still ours, between the liberation that we sense in an extended field of meaning and our ethical obligation to others'.

49 'A *literary* performance': Verena Olejniczak Lobsien, '"Transformed in show, but more transformed in mind": Sidney's *Old Arcadia* and the Performance of Perfection', in Susanne Rupp and Tobias Döring (eds), *Performances of the Sacred in Late Medieval and Early Modern England* (Amsterdam: Rodopi, 2005), p.117; Stanley Cavell, *Conditions Handsome and Unhandsome: The Constitution of Emersonian Perfectionism* (Chicago: Chicago University Press, 1990), p.34. For a discussion of Cavell's notion of poetry and perfection, see Ulrich Baer, 'The Perfection of Poetry: Rainer Maria Rilke and Paul Celan', *New German Critique*, 91 (2004), 171–89.

50 Wayne Koestenbaum, *Humiliation* (New York: Picador, 2011), pp.43–5.

51 Jonathan Goldberg, *Shakespeare's Hand* (Minneapolis: Minnesota University Press, 2003), p.37. Cf. Joel Fineman, *The Subjectivity Effect in Western Literary Tradition: Essays Toward the Release of Shakespeare's Will* (Cambridge, Mass.: MIT Press, 1991), pp.110–13, 169 and 193–4. Louis Marin saw the same 'subjectivity-effect' deconstructing the elegiac genre in Poussin's Arcadian paintings, in 'Panofsky and Poussin in Arcadia', *Sublime Poussin*, trans. Catherine Porter (Stanford: Stanford University Press, 1999), p.119: 'Who is …

ego, I, functioning like the three letters, EGO, that Poussin paints on the wall of the sarcophagous, assigning him to the place of painting himself when he paints ... Yes, to be sure, even in Death Arcadia can be ... I, the dead painter in the painted tomb; I, in the utopian happiness of painting, Arcadia.'

52 Richard Helgerson, *Forms of Nationhood: The Elizabethan Writing of England* (Chicago: University of Chicago Press, 1992), pp.1–3, quoting Edmund Spenser to Gabriel Harvey, in *The Works of Edmund Spenser: A Variorum Edition*, ed. Edwin Greenlaw et al, 11 vols,. (Batimore: Johns Hopkins University Press, 1932–57), vol. 10, p.16; Richard Mulcaster, *The First Part of the Elementary Which Treateth of Chiefly of the Right Writing of the English Tongue* (Menston: Scolar Pres, 1970), p.158.

53 'The guest becomes the host': Jacques Derrida and Anne Dufourmantelle, *Of Hospitality*, trans. Rachel Bowlby (Stanford: Stanford University Press, 2000), p.125. For the professional background to the Sonnets, see M.C. Bradbrook, *The Rise of the Common Player: A Study of Actor and Society in Shakespeare's England* (London, Chatto & Windus, 1962). Cf. Alvin Kernan, *Shakespeare, the King's Playwright: Theater in the Stuart Court, 1603–1613* (New Haven: Yale University Press, 1995), p.180: 'One way of describing the plot of the sonnets is to speak of a movement from the lyric to the dramatic mode ... both a love story and a description of a failed patronage relationship'.

54 See Patrick Cheney, '"O, Let My Books Be ... Dumb Presagers": Poetry and Theater in Shakespeare's Sonnets', *Shakespeare Quarterly*, 52 (2001), 222–54, here 234–5. Cheney's perception that 'Shakespeare does not use his poetry to erase his role in the theater but rather makes his shameful theatrical profession a part of his self-presentation' in the Sonnets qualifies his later argument for the dramatist's *invisible* poetic authorship.

55 William Langland, *The Vision of William Concerning Piers the Plowman*, ed. Walter Skeat (2 vols, Oxford: Oxford University Press, 1969), 1: B, Passus XV, 148 and C, Passus VI, 22–5; Geoffrey Chaucer, *The Canterbury Tales*, fragment VII, ll 697 and 930, in *The Works of Geoffrey Chaucer*, ed. F.N. Robinson (Boston: Houghton Mifflin, 1957), pp.164 and 167; James Bednarz, *Shakespeare and the Poet's War* (New York: Columbia University Press, 2001), pp.124–5.

56 Jeffrey Knapp, *Shakespeare Only* (Chicago: Chicago University Press, 2009), p.31.

57 Ernst Kantorowicz, *The King's Two Bodies: A Study in Medieval Political Theology* (Princeton: Princeton University Press, 1981), pp.492–4; Richard Helgerson, *Self-Crowned Laureates: Spenser,*

Jonson, Milton, and the Literary System (Berkeley: University of California Press, 1983).

58 Patrick Cheney, *Shakespeare's Literary Authorship* (Cambridge: Cambridge University Press, 2009), p. 183.

59 Elizabeth Heale, 'Will in the *Sonnets*', *Shakespeare*, 5 (2009), 218–33, here 221 and 225. Cf. Anne Ferry, *The 'Inward' Language: Wyatt, Sidney, Shakespeare, Donne* (Chicago: University of Chicago Press, 1983), chap. 4.

60 'Imagined omnipotence': Jonathan Crewe, *Trials of Authorship: Anterior Forms and Poetic Reconstruction from Wyatt to Shakespeare* (Berkeley: University of California Press, 1990), pp. 158–9.

61 Jacques Rancière, *The Emancipated Spectator*, trans. Gregory Elliott (London: Verso, 2009), pp 122–3; Judith Halberstam, *The Queer Art of Failure* (Durham, NC: Duke University Press, 2011), pp. 60, 80 et passim.

62 Hugh Grady, *Shakespeare and Impure Aesthetics* (Cambridge: Cambridge University Press, 2009), p. 101.

63 Stanley Cavell, 'The Interminable Shakespearean Text', in *Philosophy the Day After Tomorrow* (Cambridge Mass.: Harvard University Press, 2005), p. 36; 'I might put it as the wonder that these orders of words can have been found, that these things can be said at all … namely, that *anyone* can have been responsible for these texts, in however imperfect states'.

64 Skura, op. cit. (note 24), p. 29. For a provoking riff on the Chorus in *Henry V* as 'a spiralling upping of the ante' of undecidability, see Clare Connors, 'Derrida and the Fiction of Force,' *Angelaki*, 12:2 (2007), 12–15.

65 Clifford Leech, 'Shakespeare's Greeks', in B.W. Jackson (ed.), *Stratford Papers on Shakespeare* (Toronto: McMaster University Press, 1963), pp. 1–20, here pp. 18–19.

66 Lisa Hopkins, *Shakespeare on the Edge: Border Crossing in the Tragedies and the Henriad* (Aldershot: Ashgate, 2005), p. 8.

67 Grady, op. cit. (note 62), pp. 92 and 94.

68 Ibid., p. 126. Cf. G. Wilson Knight, *The Wheel of Fire: Interpretations of Shakespeare's Sombre Tragedies* (London: Methuen, 1949), p. 207. For the alienated modernity of Shakespeare's Greeks, see T.J.B. Spencer, '"Greeks" and "Merrygreeks": A Background to *Timon of Athens* and *Troilus and Cressida*', in Richard Hosley (ed.), *Essays on Shakespeare and Elizabethan Drama in Honor of Hardin Craig* (Columbia, Mo.: University of Missouri Press, 1962), pp. 223–33. And for Elizabethan aversion to Greek democratic politics, see Robert Miola, 'Timon in Shakespeare's Athens', *Shakespeare Quarterly*, 31 (1980), 21–30.

69 Cf. Peggy Kamuf, 'Introduction', in Jacques Derrida, *Without Alibi*, trans. Peggy Kamuf (Stanford: Stanford University Press, 2002), p. 14: America, 'the effective or practical name for the theological-political myth we call sovereignty'. For the Augustan imperium as a permanent state of emergency, with the sovereign as a 'living state of exception', see Giorgio Agamben, *State of Exception*, trans. Kevin Attell (Chicago: Chicago University Press, 2005), pp. 67–8 and 80–3.

70 T.J.B. Spencer (ed.), *Shakespeare's Plutarch* (Harmondsworth: Penguin, 1964), p. 245; Virgil, *The Pastoral Poems*, trans. E.V. Rieu (Harmondsworth: Penguin, 1954), IV, ll. 4–8, p. 53.

71 Emrys Jones (ed.), 'Introduction', *Antony and Cleopatra* (Harmondsworth: Penguin, 1977), p. 47. For James's reiterated call for a 'general Christian union' in the period 1603–6, see W.B. Patterson, *King James VI and I and the Reunion of Christendom* (Cambridge: Cambridge University Press, 1997), pp. 36–57 *et passim*.

72 'The world' is mentioned 44 times (twice as many times as in *Hamlet*); 'Comely' and 'becoming': see Janet Adelman, *The Common Liar: An Essay on 'Antony and Cleopatra'* (New Haven: Yale University Press, 1973), pp. 144–5; and Geoffrey Miles, *Shakespeare and the Constant Romans* (Oxford: Clarendon Press, 1996), pp. 178–81. For the 'grotesque' allusion to 'another "eastern star"' and another nativity,' see Andrew Fichter, '*Antony and Cleopatra*: "The Time of Universal Peace"', *Shakespeare Survey*, 33 (1980), 109. For Shakespeare's 'outstanding' use of the book of Revelation in *Antony and Cleopatra*, see Naseeb Shaheen, *Biblical References in Shakespeare's Plays* (Newark: University of Delaware Press, 1999), pp. 644–57.

73 Hélène Cixous, 'What Is It O'Clock? or The Door (We Never Enter)', trans. Catherine MacGillivray, in *Stigmata: Escaping Texts* (London: Routledge, 1998), p. 61; 'to-effect': Nicholas Royle, 'The Poet: *Julius Caesar* and the Democracy to Come', *Oxford Literary Review*, 25 (2003), 41.

74 'Invisible presence': Taylor, op. cit. (note 43), p. 29. For the lament of the old gods 'On the Morning of Christ's Nativity', see Sir James Frazer, *The Dying God* (London: Macmillan, 1911), pp. 6–8; C.A. Patrides, 'The Cessation of the Oracles: The History of a Legend', *Modern Language Review*, 60 (1965), 500–7; and John Boardman, *The Great God Pan: The Survival of an Image* (London: Thames and Hudson, 1997), pp. 42–3. And for a commentary on Milton's similar concept of immanence, see David Quint, 'Expectation and Prematurity in Milton's *Nativity Ode*', in J. Martin Evans (ed.), *John Milton: Twentieth-Century Perspectives: Milton Early Poems* (London: Routledge, 2003), pp. 81–105.

75 Derrida, op. cit. (note 9), p. 10.

76 Christopher Pye, *The Vanishing: Shakespeare, the Subject, and Early Modern Culture* (Durham, NC: Duke University Press, 2000), pp. 112 and 125.

77 The pensive 'Hum' appears only in the second quarto. For an acute analysis of this uncannily prospective retrospection, see Luke Wilson, *Theatres of Intention: Drama and the Law in Early Modern England* (Stanford: Stanford University Press, 2000), pp. 31–4.

78 Julia Lupton, *Thinking with Shakespeare: Essays on Politics and Life* (Chicago: University of Chicago Press, 2011), pp. 89–90.

79 Michel Foucault, *The Care of the Self (The History of Sexuality, Volume 3)*, trans. Robert Hurley (New York: Pantheon, 1986), p. 51. For Shakespeare's fascination with the ironic near coincidence of the 'two J.C.s', see Wilson, 'A Bleeding Head Where They Begun: *Julius Caesar* and the Mystical Foundation of Authority', op. cit. (note 14), pp. 194–200.

80 For Herod, see Shaheen, op. cit. (note 72), p. 649: 'Many in Shakespeare's audience, unacquainted with Plutarch, may have thought that this mention of Herod was a reference to the Biblical Herod the Great who slaughtered the babes at Jesus' birth'.

81 'Marine verge': Steve Mentz, *At the Bottom of Shakespeare's Ocean* (London: Continuum, 2009), p. 93. For a commentary on Hölderlin, tragedy and the caesura as the equilibrium between two representations of the divine, see Phillipe Lacoue-Labarthe, *Heidegger, Art and Politics*, trans. Chris Turner (Oxford: Basil Blackwell, 1990), pp. 41–6. Antium, where Coriolanus is exiled, perhaps confirms this Pauline itinerary, as the place of the 'Three Taverns', where St Paul was welcomed on his way to Rome.

82 Martin Heidegger, 'Hölderlins Hymnen "Germania" und "Der Rhein"' (1934–35), quoted in Emmanuel Faye, *Heidegger: The Introduction of Nazism into Philosophy*, trans. Michael Smith (New Haven: Yale University Press, 2009), p. 104.

83 See Constance Relihan, 'Liminal Geography: *Pericles* and the Politics of Place,' in Alison Thorne (ed.), *Shakespeare's Romances* (Basingstoke: Palgrave Macmillan, 2003), pp 71–90.

84 Alain Badiou, *Saint Paul: The Foundation of Universalism*, trans. Ray Brassier (Stanford: Stanford University Press, 2003), p. 2; Benjamin Lazier, 'On the Origins of "Political Theology": Judaism and Heresy between the Wars', *New German Critique*, 105 (2008), 143–64, here 162. For an insightful commentary, see Peter Hallward, *Badiou: A Subject to Truth* (Minneapolis: Minnesota University Press, 2003), pp. 108–16. And for the relevance to Shakespeare, see, in particular, Lowell Gallagher, 'Waiting for Gobbo', in Fernie, op. cit. (note 29), pp. 80–8.

85 Lupton, op. cit. (note 78), p.219; Badiou, op. cit. (note 82), p.2.

86 Jean-Luc Nancy, *The Creation of the World,* or *Globalization,* trans. François Raffoul and David Pettigrew (New York: State University of New York Press, 2007), p.85; John Milton, 'On the Morning of Christ's Nativity', IV, l. 59, in *John Milton: The Complete Shorter Poems,* ed. John Carey (London: Longman, 1997), p.106.

87 Stephen Greenblatt, *Shakespearean Negotiations: The Circulation of Social Energy in Renaissance England* (Oxford: Clarendon Press, 1988), p.119; Taylor, op. cit. (note 43), p.29.

88 Nancy, op. cit. (note 86), p.111.

89 Philip Edwards (ed.), 'Introduction', *Pericles* (Harmondsworth: Penguin, 1976), p.41.

90 Theodor Adorno and Max Horkheimer, *The Dialectic of Enlightenment* (London: Continuum, 1986), p.34. For commentaries, see Albrecht Wellmer, 'The Death of the Sirens and the Origin of the Work of Art', and Rebecca Comay, 'Adorno's Siren Song', *New German Critique,* 81 (2000), 5–20 and 21–48.

91 Stephen Orgel, *The Illusion of Power: Political Theater in the English Renaissance* (Berkeley: University of California Press, 1975), p.58.

92 Robert Miola, '"An Alien People Clutching their Gods"?: Shakespeare's Ancient Religions', *Shakespeare Survey,* 54 (2002), pp.31–45, here p.40.

93 Derrida, op. cit. (note 33), p.29.

94 'artistic mastery': Leslie Paul Thiele, *Timely Meditations: Martin Heidegger and Postmodern Politics* (Princeton: Princeton University Press, 1995), p.123.

95 Lupton, op. cit. (note 38), p.207; Julia Lupton, *Afterlives of the Saints: Hagiography, Typology, and Renaissance Literature* (Stanford: Stanford University Press, 1996).

96 Ryan, op. cit. (note 8), p.109. For the Marian overtones of the statue scene, see in particular Lupton, op. cit. (note 95), pp.176–8 and 206–18; and Richard Wilson, *Secret Shakespeare: Studies in Theatre, Religion, and Resistance* (Manchester: Manchester University Press, 2004), pp.257–66.

97 Jonathan Goldberg, *James I and the Politics of Literature* (Stanford: Stanford University Press, 1983), p.240. For the coincidence of the reign of Cymbeline, the *Pax Romana* and the birth of Christ, see Emrys Jones, 'Stuart *Cymbeline*', *Essays in Criticism,* 11 (1961), 88–92; Robin Moffet, '*Cymbeline* and the Nativity', *Shakespeare Quarterly,* 13 (1962), 207–18; Howard Felperin, *Shakespearean Romance* (Princeton: Princeton University Press, 1972), pp.180–8; Hugh Richmond, 'Shakespeare's Roman Trilogy: The Climax in *Cymbeline*', *Studies in the Literary Imagination,* 5 (1972), 129–39;

Glynne Wickham, 'From Tragedy to Tragi-Comedy: *King Lear* as Prologue', *Shakespeare Quarterly*, 26 (1973), 36; Marjorie Garber, '*Cymbeline* and the Languages of Myth', *Mosaic*, 10 (1977), 113–14; and David Bergeron, '*Cymbeline*: Shakespeare's Last Roman Play', *Shakespeare Quarterly*, 31 (1980), 31–41.

98 Heidegger, op. cit. (note 15), pp.26, 29–31 and 42,

99 Martin Heidegger, letter to Hans-Peter Hempel, 19 September 1960, quoted in Rüdiger Safranski, *Martin Heidegger*, trans. Ewald Osers (Cambridge, Mass.: Harvard University Press, 1998), p.229.

100 'Perfected male fantasy': Jeanne Addison Roberts, *The Shakespearean Wild: Geography, Genus, and Gender* (Lincoln: Nebraska University Press, 1991), p.51.

101 Stephen Greenblatt, 'Shakespeare and the Uses of Power', *New York Review of Books*, 12 April 2007, 76–7.

102 'Scenes and machines': Joseph Addison, *The Spectator*, I: 180, quoted in Sean Gaston, *Derrida and Disinterest* (London: Continuum, 2005), p.44.

103 Martin Heidegger, *Existence and Being* (Washington, DC: Gateway, 1949), p.305; Hannah Arendt, 'What Is Freedom?' in *Between Past and Future* (Harmondsworth: Penguin, 1968), p.165.

104 Agamben, op. cit. (note 69), p.64.

105 Edward Said, *On Late Style* (London: Bloomsbury, 2007), p.6. For the persistence of this complacent reading, see Martin Butler (ed.), 'Introduction', *William Shakesppeare: 'Cymbeline'* (Cambridge: Cambridge University Press, 2005), p.6: 'Shakespeare's life ended in a mood of philosophical calm and otherwordliness'.

106 Derrida, op. cit. (note 33), p.29–30.

107 Joseph Lowenstein, 'Plays Agonistic and Competitive: The Textual Approach to Elsinore', *Renaissance Drama*, 19 (1988), 63–96, here 82. See Michael Manheim, *The Weak King Dilemma in the Shakespearean History Play* (New York: Syracuse University Press, 1973).

108 René Girard, *Anorexie et désir mimétique* (Paris: Editions L'Herne, 2008), pp.81.

Index